C000264667

STREE

Lincolnshire

Boston, Grantham, Grimsby, Lincoln, Peterborough, Scunthorpe

First published in 2003 by

Philip's, a division of
Octopus Publishing Group Ltd
2-4 Heron Quays, London E14 4JP

Second edition 2007
First impression 2007
LINBA

ISBN-10   0-540-09083-2 (pocket)
ISBN-13   978-0-540-09083-9 (pocket)

© Philip's 2007

o|s Ordnance Survey®

This product includes mapping data licensed from
Ordnance Survey® with the permission of the
Controller of Her Majesty's Stationery Office.
© Crown copyright 2007. All rights reserved.
Licence number 100011710.

No part of this publication may be reproduced,
stored in a retrieval system or transmitted in any
form or by any means, electronic, mechanical,
photocopying, recording or otherwise, without the
permission of the Publishers and the copyright
owner.

To the best of the Publishers' knowledge, the
information in this atlas was correct at the time of
going to press. No responsibility can be accepted
for any errors or their consequences.

The representation in this atlas of a road, track
or path is no evidence of the existence of a right
of way.

Data for the speed cameras provided by
PocketGPSWorld.com Ltd.

Ordnance Survey and the OS Symbol are
registered trademarks of Ordnance Survey, the
national mapping agency of Great Britain.

Post Office is a trade mark of Post Office Ltd in
the UK and other countries.

Printed by Toppan, China

Contents

II **List of mobile speed cameras**

III **Key to map symbols**

IV **Key to map pages**

VI **Route Planning**

X **Administrative and Postcode boundaries**

1 **Street maps** at 1⅓ inches to 1 mile

178 **Street maps** at 2⅔ inches to 1 mile

234 **Street map of Lincoln city centre**
at 5⅓ inches to 1 mile

235 **Index** of towns, villages, streets, hospitals, industrial
estates, railway stations, schools, shopping centres,
universities and places of interest

Digital Data

The exceptionally high-quality mapping found in this atlas is available as digital data in TIFF
format, which is easily convertible to other bitmapped (raster) image formats.

The index is also available in digital form as a standard database table. It contains all the details
found in the printed index together with the National Grid reference for the map square in which
each entry is named.

For further information and to discuss your requirements, please contact james.mann@philips-
maps.co.uk

Mobile speed cameras

The vast majority of speed cameras used on Britain's roads are operated by safety camera partnerships. These comprise local authorities, the police, Her Majesty's Court Service (HMCS) and the Highways Agency.

This table lists the sites where each safety camera partnership may enforce speed limits through the use of mobile cameras or detectors. These are usually set up on the roadside or a bridge spanning the road and operated by a police or civilian enforcement officer. The speed limit at each site (if available) is shown in red type, followed by the approximate location in black type.

A15
60 Ashby de la Launde & Bloxholm, Ashby Lodge

60 Aswarby S/B

A15–B1191
60 Dunsby Hollow

A16
40 Burwell

50/60 Deeping Bypass

60 Ludborough, North Thoresby

60 Stickney Fenside

60 Wyberton, Boston Tytton Lane

A17
60 Fleet Hargate

60 Moulton Common

60 Wigtoft, Hoffleet Stow

A52
60 Horbling and Swaton

60 Horbling, Bridge End

60 Ropsley

A153
40 Billinghay

50 Tattershall

A158
40/50 Scremby to Candlesby

A631
60 Dale Bridge

50/60 Hemswell

B1188
30 Branston

60 Canwick (Highfield House)

60 Potterhanworth

B1191
60 Martin Dales

III

22a	**Motorway** with junction number
	Primary route – dual/single carriageway
	A road – dual/single carriageway
	B road – dual/single carriageway
	Minor road – dual/single carriageway
	Other minor road – dual/single carriageway
	Road under construction
	Tunnel, covered road
30 30	**Speed cameras - single, multiple**
	Rural track, private road or narrow road in urban area
	Gate or obstruction to traffic (restrictions may not apply at all times or to all vehicles)
	Path, bridleway, byway open to all traffic, road used as a public path
	Pedestrianised area
DY7	**Postcode boundaries**
	County and unitary authority boundaries
	Railway, tunnel, railway under construction
	Tramway, tramway under construction
	Miniature railway
Walsall	**Railway station**
	Private railway station
South Shields	**Metro station**
	Tram stop, tram stop under construction
	Bus, coach station

◆	**Ambulance station**
◆	**Coastguard station**
◆	**Fire station**
◆	**Police station**
+	**Accident and Emergency entrance to hospital**
H	**Hospital**
+	**Place of worship**
i	**Information Centre** (open all year)
	Shopping Centre
P P&R	**Parking, Park and Ride**
PO	**Post Office**
Å 🚐	**Camping site, caravan site**
► ✕	**Golf course, picnic site**
Prim Sch	**Important buildings, schools, colleges, universities and hospitals**
	Built up area
	Woods
River Ouse	**Tidal water, water name**
	Non-tidal water – lake, river, canal or stream
	Lock, weir, tunnel
Church	**Non-Roman antiquity**
ROMAN FORT	**Roman antiquity**
87	**Adjoining page indicators and overlap bands** The colour of the arrow and the band indicates the scale of the adjoining or overlapping page (see scales below)
237	

Enlarged mapping only

	Railway or bus station building
	Place of interest
	Parkland

■ The small numbers around the edges of the maps identify the 1 kilometre National Grid lines ■ The dark grey border on the inside edge of some pages indicates that the mapping does not continue onto the adjacent page

Acad	**Academy**	Inst	**Institute**	Recn Gd	**Recreation**
Allot Gdns	**Allotments**	Ct	**Law Court**		**Ground**
Cemy	**Cemetery**	L Ctr	**Leisure Centre**	Resr	**Reservoir**
C Ctr	**Civic Centre**	LC	**Level Crossing**	Ret Pk	**Retail Park**
CH	**Club House**	Liby	**Library**	Sch	**School**
Coll	**College**	Mkt	**Market**	Sh Ctr	**Shopping Centre**
Crem	**Crematorium**	Meml	**Memorial**	TH	**Town Hall/House**
Ent	**Enterprise**	Mon	**Monument**	Trad Est	**Trading Estate**
Ex H	**Exhibition Hall**	Mus	**Museum**	Univ	**University**
Ind Est	**Industrial Estate**	Obsy	**Observatory**	W Twr	**Water Tower**
IRB Sta	**Inshore Rescue**	Pal	**Royal Palace**	Wks	**Works**
	Boat Station	PH	**Public House**	YH	**Youth Hostel**

The scale of the maps on the pages numbered in blue is 4.2 cm to 1 km • 2⅔ inches to 1 mile • 1: 23810

0	¼		½		¾		1 mile
0	250m	500m	750m	1 kilometre			

The scale of the maps on pages numbered in green is 2.1 cm to 1 km • 1⅓ inches to 1 mile • 1: 47620

0	¼	½	¾	1 mile
0	250m 500m 750m	1kilometre		

The scale of the maps on pages numbered in red is 8.4 cm to 1 km • 5⅓ inches to 1 mile • 1: 11900

0	220 yards		440 yards		660 yards	½ mile
0	125m	250m	375m	½ kilometre		

Key to map pages

Map pages at 1⅓ inches to 1 mile — 138

Map pages at 5⅓ inches to 1 mile — 234

Map pages at 2⅓ inches to 1 mile — 180

East Yorkshire and Northern Lincolnshire STREET ATLAS

North Yorkshire STREET ATLAS

South Yorkshire STREET ATLAS

Nottinghamshire STREET ATLAS

Hunstanton Heacham Snettisham Dersingham

King's Lynn

Norfolk STREET ATLAS

Downham Market Littleport

March

Cambridgeshire STREET ATLAS

Ramsey

Chatteris

Wisbech

Leverington Foul Anchor West Walton

116

Stickford **114** New Leake **115** Wainfleet St Mary Wainfleet All Saints
Wrangle
Midville **113** Sibsey
112 Stickney Frithville Hurn's End
127 Leverton **126** Butterwick Fishtoft Scrane End
160 Sutton Bridge **161** Terrington St Clement
159 Long Sutton **148** Holbeach St Matthew **149** Gedney Drove End Gedney Dyke
216 Holbeach **170**
125 Cowbridge **208 209** Boston
124 Langrick Hubbert's Bridge
Coningsby Tattershall Bridge **111** Gipsey Bridge
110 Chapel Hill
123 Swineshead Bridge
South Kyme **122** Heckington Anwick
Kirton **136** Sutterton Fosdyke Holbeach St Marks **146** Moulton Seas End Surfleet
137 Wyberton **135** Bicker **134** Swineshead Donington **145** Gosberton **144** Gosberton Clough
133 Horbling Pointon **143** Dowsby Rippingale
Helpringham **132** Billingborough
Osbournby Pinchbeck **214** Spalding Whaplode **158** Whaplode St Catherine **168** Whaplode Drove **169** Gorefield
215 Holbeach **216**
Tydd St Giles **177** Guyhirn
176 Parson Drove Thorney
175 Eye Newborough
174 Crowland **166** Deeping St Nicholas **167** Shepeau Stow
156 Moulton Chapel **157**
155 Twenty **165** Baston
154 Bourne **213** Thurlby **164** Market Deeping **217** Maxey
Morton Edenham Eastgate Uffington **172** **173** Glinton Barnack
153 Swinstead Castle Bytham **162** Clipsham Essendine Ryhall **171** Stamford **218–219**
152 Corby Glen Ingoldsby Irnham
141 Great Ponton Ingoldsby
140 Swayfield
151 Colsterworth South Witham
150 Sproxton Wymondham

Whittlesey Farcet
Newark **227** Peterborough Yaxley Morborne
226 **225** **231** **230** **233** Haddon **232**
224 **223** **222** Castor **229** **228** Water Newton
221 **220** Glinton
173 **172**

Newark-on-Trent **104** Stapleford **105** Beckingham Fenton Fulbeck Cranwell Leasingham **120** Sleaford **121** Ruskington
107 Wellingore **106** Navenby **108** Digby **109** Billinghay Timberland
128 **129** Great Gonerby Grantham **210 211** Denton Harlaxton **139** Croxton Kerrial
130 Barkston **131** Londonthorpe Ropsley
138 Muston Saltby
117 Claypole Balderton **118** Hough-on-the-Hill **119** Honington Marston Long Bennington Bottesford
150 Wymondham Melton Mowbray

Leicestershire and Rutland STREET ATLAS

Northamptonshire STREET ATLAS

Oakham Empingham Easton on the Hill Water Newton Oundle Corby Desborough

Bingham Cotgrave Southwell Lowdham Calverton
Nottingham West Bridgford Keyworth Sileby Syston Leicester Loughborough Mountsorrel East Leake Market Harborough Lutterworth
Hucknall Ravenshead Blidworth Rainworth

Scale

15 miles 20 km 10 5 0

A1(M) Sawtry

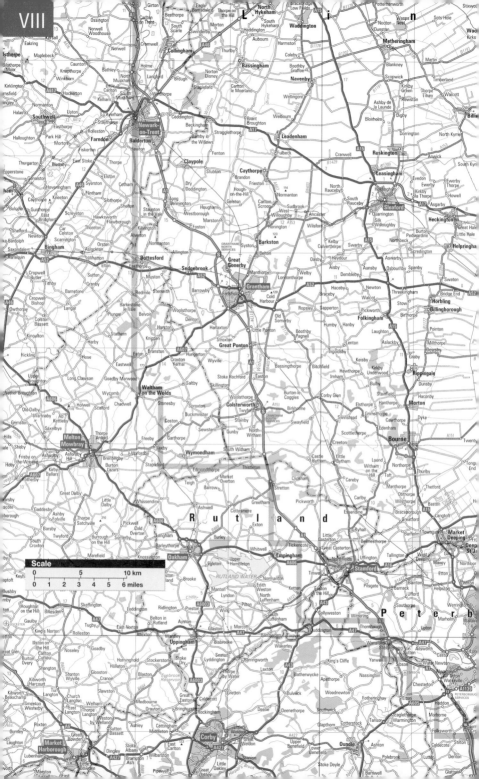

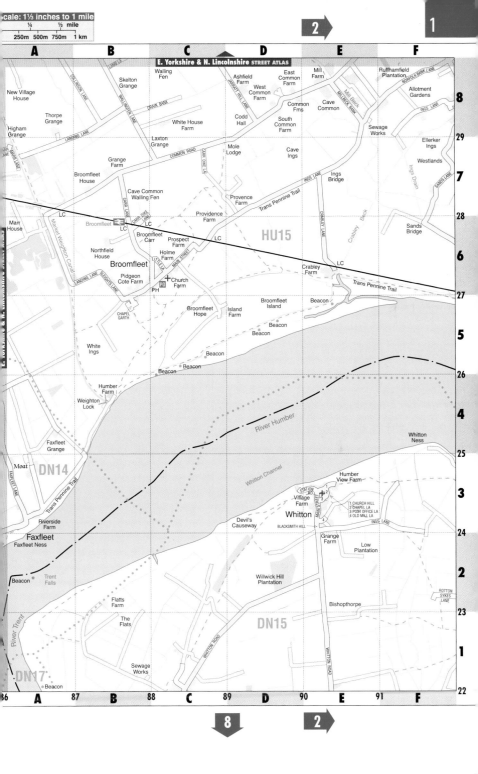

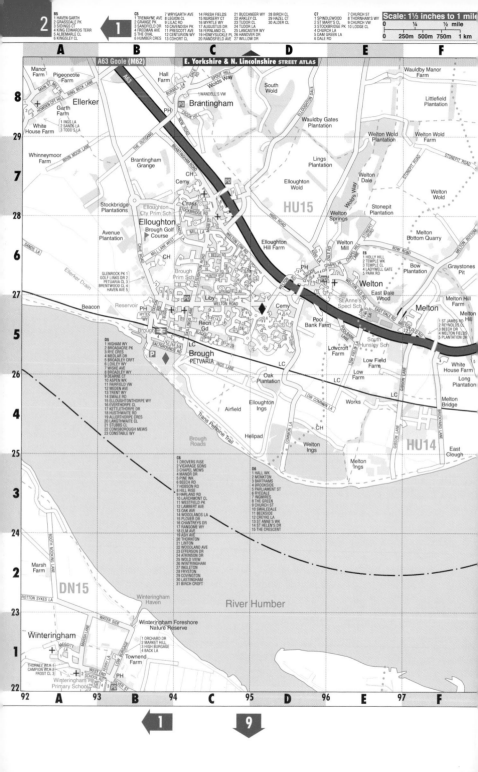

B5
1 HAVEN GARTH
2 GRASSDALE PK
3 SIDINGS CT
4 KING EDWARDS TERR
5 ALBEMARLE CL
6 KINGSLEY CL

C5
1 TREMAYNE AVE
2 GRANGE PK
3 SANDFIELD DR
4 FREEMAN AVE
5 THE OVAL
6 HUMBER CRES

7 WRYGARTH AVE
8 LEGION CL
9 LILAC RD
10 CAVENDISH PK
11 PRESCOTT AVE
12 CENTURION WY
13 COHORT CL

14 FRESH FIELDS
15 NURSERY CT
16 MYRTLE WY
17 AUGUSTUS DR
18 FERNLAND CL
19 HONEYSUCKLE PL
20 RANDSFIELD AVE

21 BUCCANEER WY
22 ARKLEY CL
23 TUDOR CL
24 TUDOR LA
25 LANCASTER WY
26 HANOVER DR
27 WILLOW DR

28 BIRCH CL
29 HAZEL CT
30 ALDER CL

C7
1 SPINDLEWOOD
2 ST MARY'S CL
3 STOCKBRIDGE RD
4 CHURCH LA
5 DAM GREEN LA
6 DALE RD

7 CHURCH ST
8 THORNHAM'S WY
9 CHURCH VW
10 LODGE CL

A63 Goole (M62)

E. Yorkshire & N. Lincolnshire STREET ATLAS

A   B   C   D   E   F

Manor Farm
Pigeoncote Farm
Ellerker
Garth Farm
White House Farm
Whinneymoor Farm

Hall Farm
Brantingham

South Wold

Wauldby Manor Farm
Littlefield Plantation

Welton Wold Plantation
Welton Wold Farm

Brantingham Grange

Stockbridge Plantations

Avenue Plantation

Elloughton City Prim Sch
Elloughton
Brough Golf Course

Cross

Wauldby Gates Plantation

Lings Plantation

Elloughton Wold

HU15

Welton Dale

Welton Wold

Welton Springs
Stonepit Plantation

Welton Mill

Melton Bottom Quarry

Bow Plantation

Graystones Pit

E6
1 HOLLY HILL
2 TEMPLE WK
3 TEMPLE CL
4 LADYWELL GATE
5 PARK RD

Welton

East Dale Wood

Melton Hill Farm
Melton Hill

Melton

E5
1 ST JAMES RD
2 REYNOLDS CL
3 BEECH DR
4 MELTON FIELDS
5 PLANTATION CL

White House Farm

Long Plantation

Melton Bridge

HU14

East Clough

D5
1 HIGHAM WY
2 BROADACRE PK
3 RYE CRES
4 MEDLAR DR
5 BROADLEY CRFT
6 LOXLEY WY
7 WISKE AVE
8 BROADLEY WY
9 DEARNE CT
10 ASPEN WK
11 FAIRFIELD VW
12 MEDEN AVE
13 TRENT WY
14 SWALE RD
15 ELLOUGHTONTHORPE WY
16 EVERTHORPE CL
17 KETTLETHORPE DR
18 HUSTHWAITE RD
19 ALLERTHORPE CRES
20 LANGTHWAITE CL
21 STUBBS CL
22 CONISBOROUGH MEWS
23 CONSTABLE WY

Brough
PETVARIA

C6
1 DROVERS RISE
2 VICARAGE GDNS
3 CHAPEL MEWS
4 MANOR DR
5 PINE WK
6 BEECH RD
7 HOBSON RD
8 HILL RISE
9 HARLAND RD
10 LARCHMONT CL
11 WESTFIELD PK
12 LAMBERT AVE
13 OAK AVE
14 WOODLANDS LA
15 PLOVER DR
16 CHANTREYS DR
17 RANSOME WY
18 ELM AVE
19 ASH AVE
20 THORNTON
21 LINTON
22 WOODLAND AVE
23 EFFERSON DR
24 ATKINSON DR
25 WOLD VIEW
26 WINTRINGHAM
27 INGLETON
28 FRYSTON
29 COVINGTON
30 LASTINGHAM
31 BIRCH CROFT

D6
1 HALL WK
2 MONKTON
3 BARTRAMS
4 BROOKSIDE
5 PARLIAMENT ST
6 RYEDALE
7 INGMIRES
8 THE GREEN
9 CHURCH ST
10 SWALEDALE
11 BECKSIDE
12 CREYKE LA
13 ST ANNE'S WK
14 ST HELEN'S DR
15 THE CRESCENT

Oak Plantation

Elloughton Ings

Airfield

Helipad

Lowcroft Farm

Low Field Farm

Low Farm

Works

Welton Ings

Melton Ings

Marsh Farm

DN15

Winteringham
Winteringham Haven

Winteringham Foreshore Nature Reserve

River Humber

Townend Farm

Winteringham Primary School

92   93   94   95   96   97
A   B   C   D   E   F

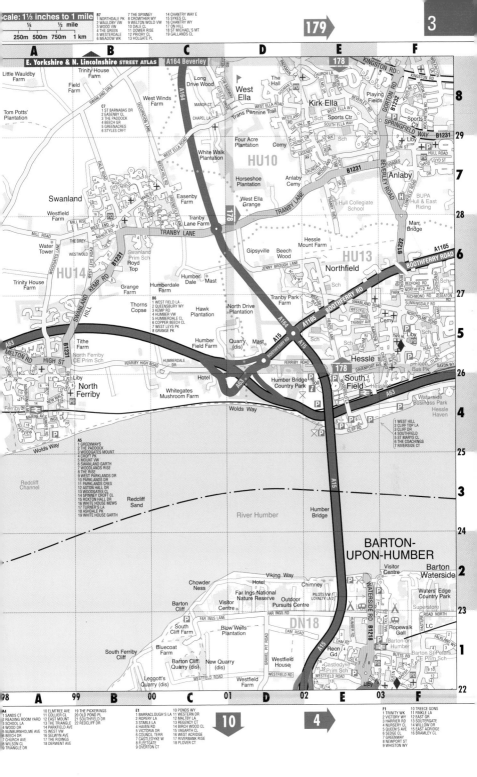

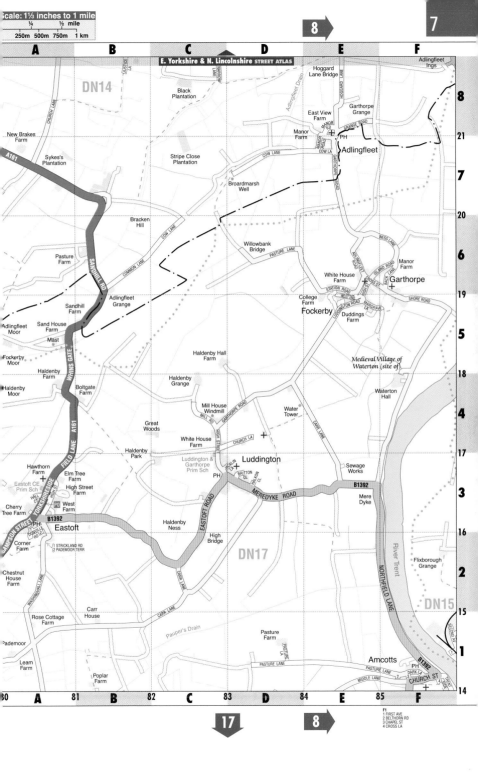

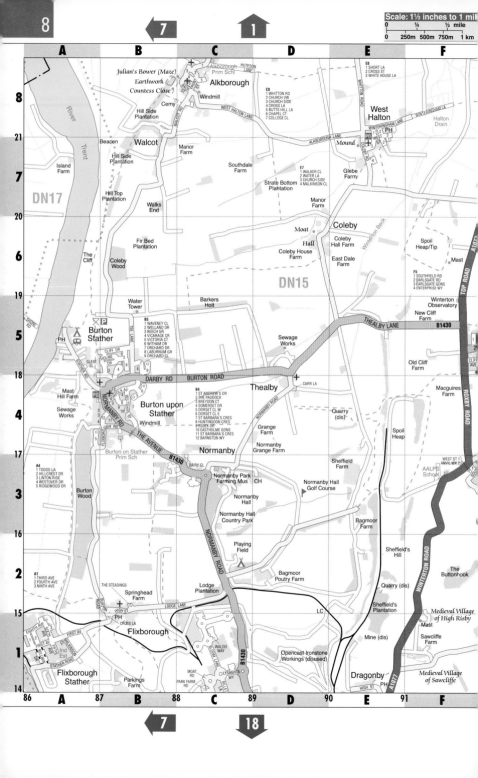

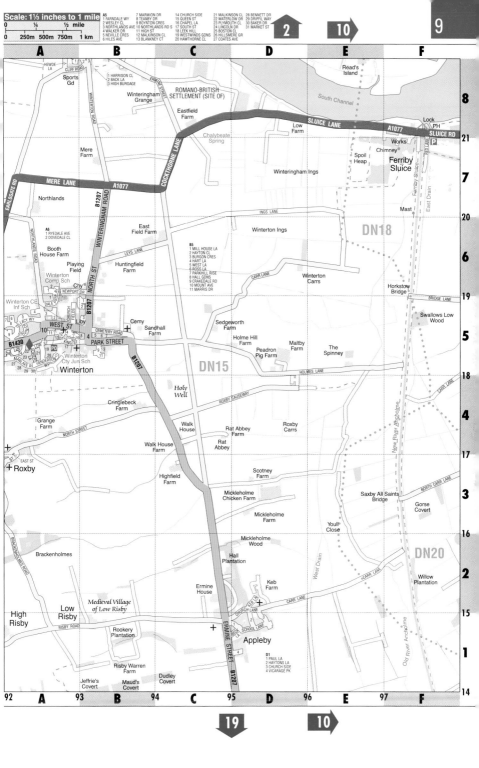

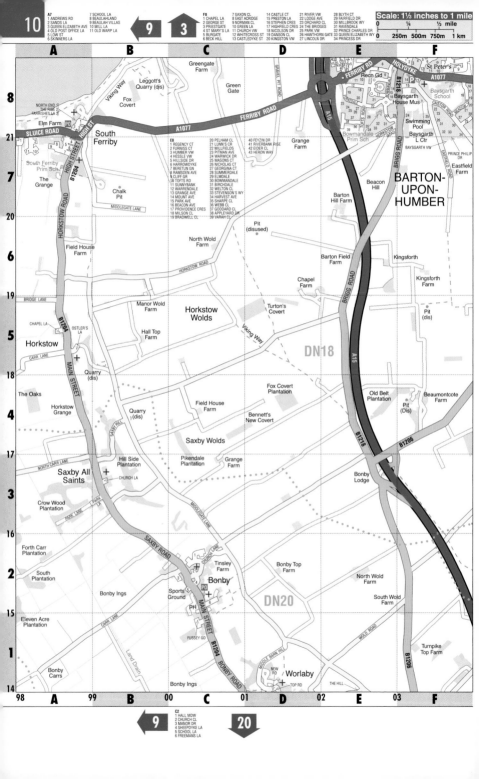

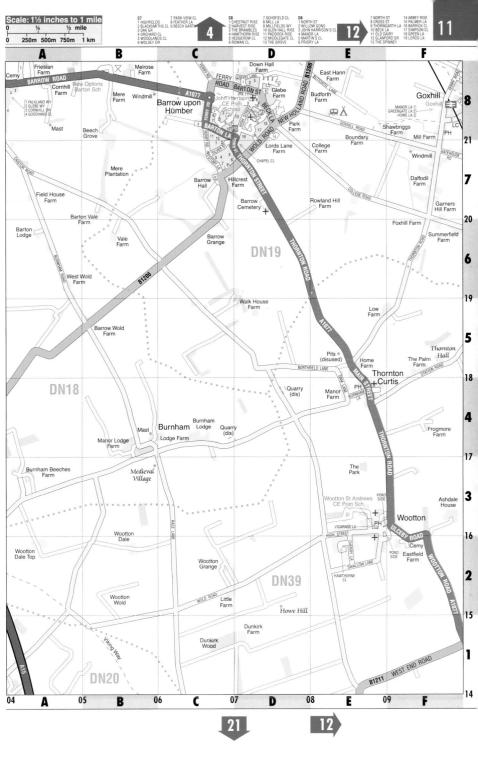

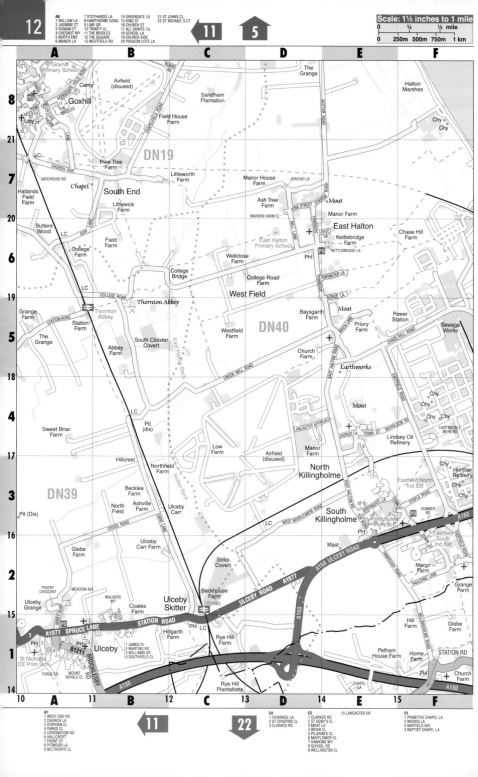

Scale: 1⅓ inches to 1 mile

¼ ½ mile
250m 500m 750m 1 km

E. Yorkshire & N. Lincolnshire STREET ATLAS

Foulholme Sands

Cherry Cobb Sands

Oil Terminal

HAVEN RD

LC

Killingholme Haven Pits Nature Reserve

Killingholme Marshes

Mast

Sewage Works

Killingholme High Lighthouse

STATION ROAD

LC

Burkinshaw's Covert

EAST MIDDLE MERE ROAD

ROPER ROAD

MARSH LANE

Oil Refineries

LC

DN40

HUMBER RD

South Killingholme Haven

186

LC

A160

HUMBER ROAD

A1173

HUMBER ROAD

WEST HAVEN

LC

SOUTHERN WY

Water Tower

WEST RIVERSIDE

SOUTHERN ROAD

SEVEN QUAY RD

Immingham Dock

187

Chy

HUMBER ROAD

Houlton's Covert

MANBY ROAD

186

East End Farm

Immingham Golf Course

ROBINSON ROAD

LC

MANBY ROAD BY PASS

DRESLEY WAY

Chimney

LC

Cemy

CH

STANSFIELD GDNS

CHURCH LANE

WASHDYKE LANE

Football Gd

WOODLANDS

MANBY RD

BATTERY ST

P

Sports Ground

Chimney

MILL LANE

PILGRIMS WY

Recn Gd

ROYAL DR

Sch

P

Liby

Sch

Immingham

KINGS RD

KINGS RD

A1173

QUEENS RD

LAPORTE ROAD

Chimney

Humber Bank Factories

DN41

Luxmore Farm

B1210

PH

PELHAM RD

P

PO

MARGARET ST

PILGRIM AVENUE

PO

TALBOT RD

HADLEIGH RD

CORFE WALK

A1173

Spoil Heap

NETHERLANDS WY

Kiln Lane Ind Est

EUROPA WY

KILN LANE

LC

HOBSON WY

HABROUGH RD

HUME BRAE

For full street detail of the highlighted area see pages 186 & 187.

186   23   187   187

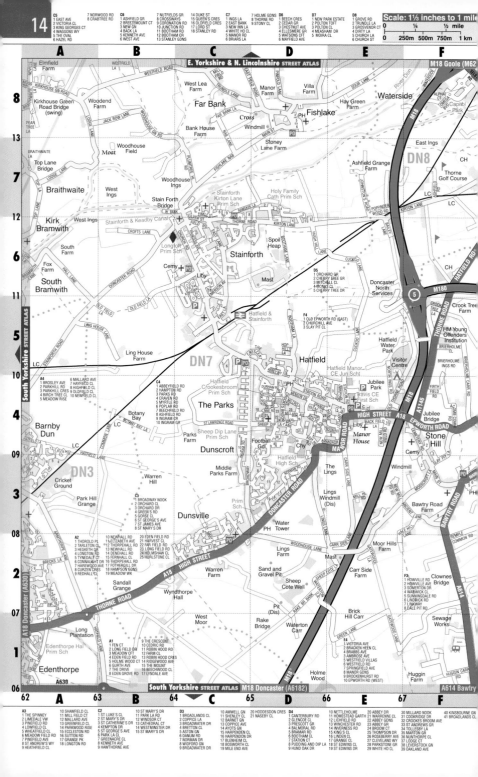

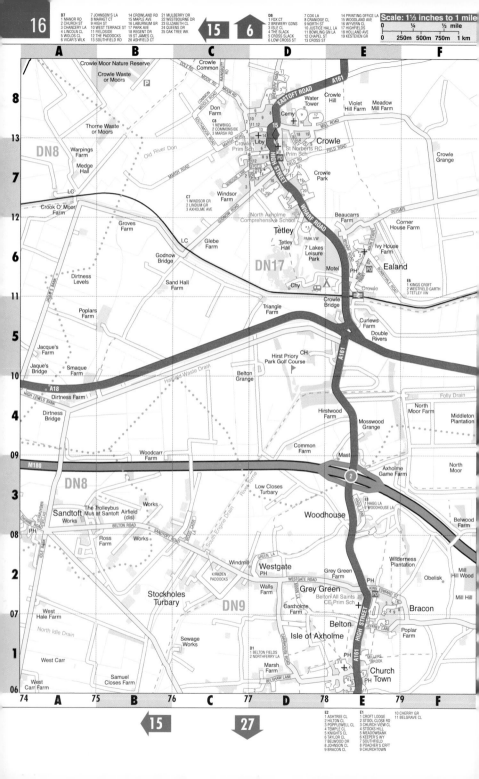

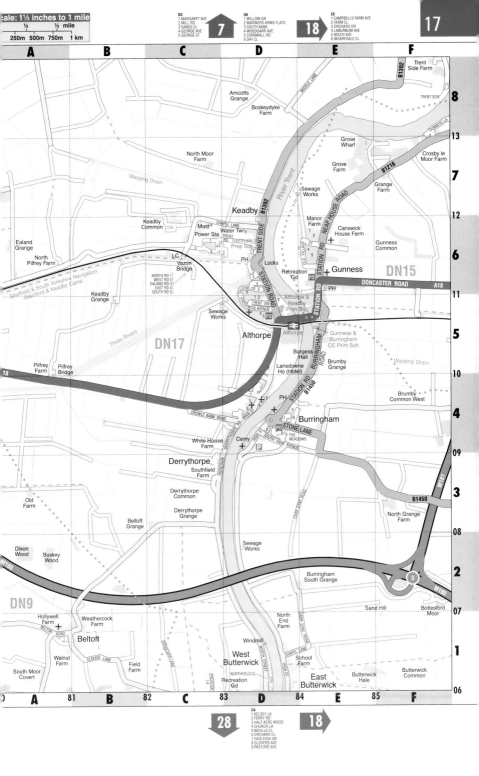

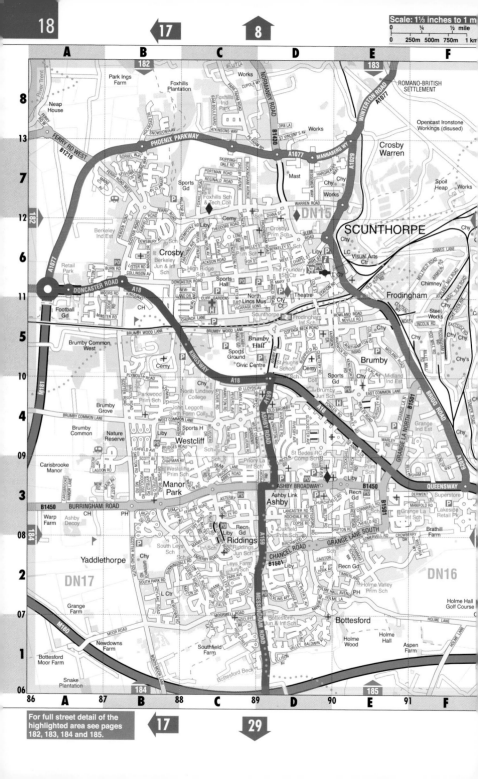

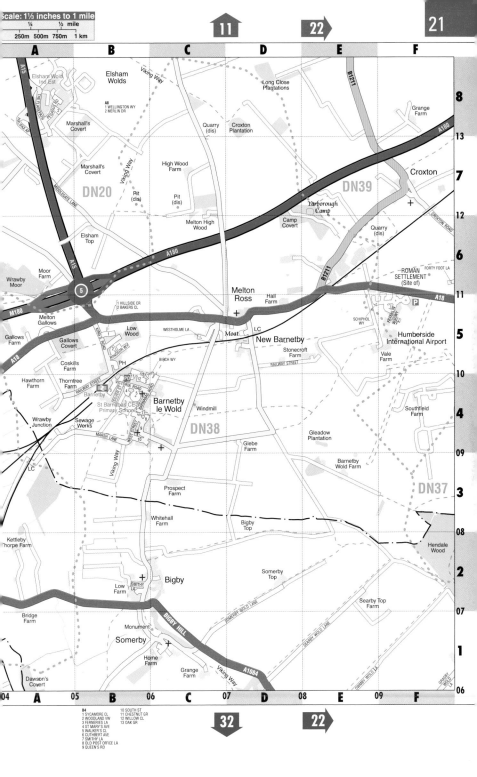

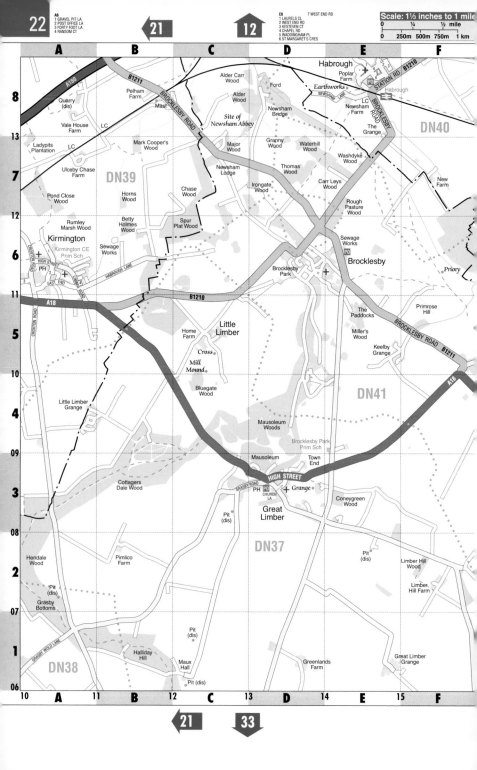

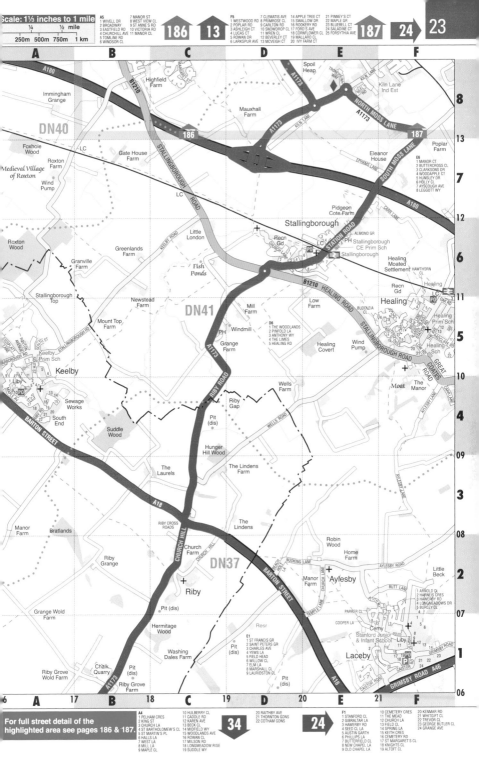

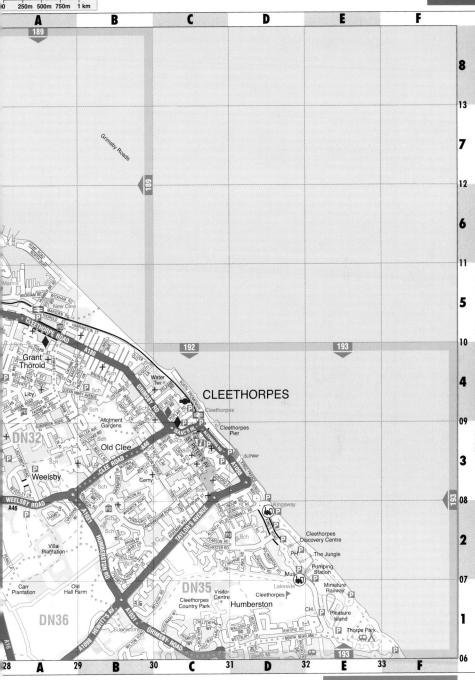

195　　36

For full street detail of the highlighted areas see pages 189, 192 & 193.

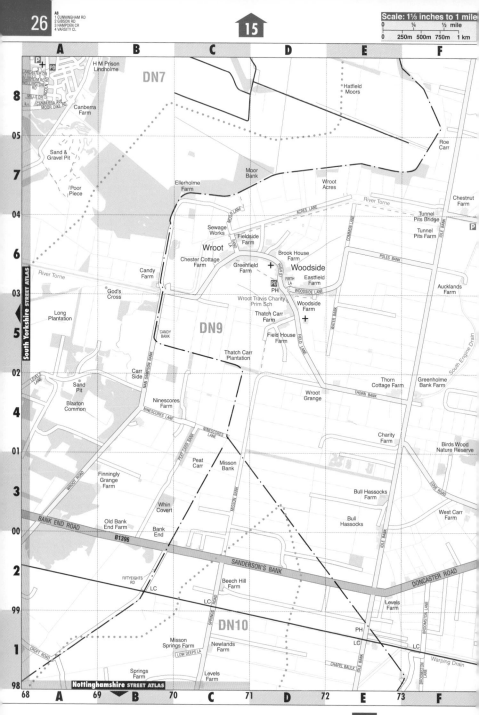

26

AR
1 CUNNINGHAM RD
2 GIBSON RD
3 HAMPDEN CR
4 VARSITY CL

15

Scale: 1⅓ inches to 1 mile
0   ¼   ½   mile
0   250m 500m 750m   1 km

South Yorkshire STREET ATLAS

DN7

H M Prison
Lindholme

Hatfield
Moors

Roe
Carr

Sand &
Gravel Pit

Canberra
Farm

Poor
Piece

Moor
Bank

Ellerholme
Farm

Wroot
Acres

River Torne

Chestnut
Farm

Tunnel
Pits Bridge

Tunnel
Pits Farm

Sewage
Works

Fieldside
Farm

Wroot

Chester Cottage
Farm

Greenfield
Farm

Brook House
Farm

Woodside

River Torne

Candy
Farm

Eastfield
Farm

Poles Bank

Aucklands
Farm

God's
Cross

Wroot Travis Charity
Prim Sch

Woodside
Farm

Long
Plantation

DN9

Thatch Carr
Farm

Field House
Farm

Thatch Carr
Plantation

Carr
Side

Thorn
Cottage Farm

Greenholme
Bank Farm

Sand
Pit

Ninescores
Farm

Wroot
Grange

South Engine Drain

Blaxton
Common

Thorn Bank

Charity
Farm

Ninescores Lane

Birds Wood
Nature Reserve

Peat
Carr

Misson
Bank

Bull Hassocks
Farm

West Carr
Farm

Finningley
Grange
Farm

Whin
Covert

Bull
Hassocks

Bank End Road

Old Bank
End Farm

Bank
End

B1396

Sanderson's Bank

Doncaster Road

FIFTYEIGHTS
RD

LC

Beech Hill
Farm

Levels
Farm

DN10

Misson
Springs Farm

Newlands
Farm

PH

Springs
Farm

LOW DEEPS LA

Levels
Farm

Warping Drain

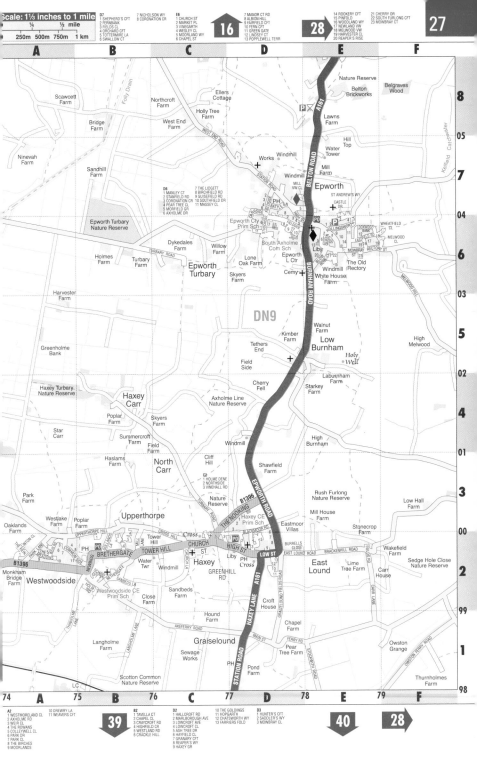

Scale: 1⅓ inches to 1 mile

¼ ½ mile

250m 500m 750m 1 km

D7
1 SHEPHERD'S CFT
2 FERNBANK
3 FIELDS CL
4 ORCHARD CFT
5 TOTTERMIRE LA
6 SWALLOW CT

E6
1 CHURCH ST
2 MARKET PL
3 VINEGARTH
4 WESLEY CL
5 MOORLAND WY
6 CHAPEL ST

7 MANOR CT RD
8 ALBION HILL
9 FAIRFIELD CFT
10 FERN CFT
11 GREEN GATE
12 LINDSEY CT
13 POPPLEWELL TERR

14 ROOKERY CFT
15 PINFOLD
16 WOODLAND WY
17 NEWLAND VW
18 MELWOOD VW
19 HARVESTER CL
20 REAPER'S RISE

21 CHERRY OR
22 SOUTH FURLONG CFT
23 MOWBRAY CT

16   28   27

DN9

Epworth

Low Burnham

High Burnham

Haxey Carr

North Carr

Upperthorpe

Haxey

Westwoodside

Graiselound

East Lound

A2
1 WESTMORELAND CL
2 AXHOLME RD
3 WEIR CL
4 THE ROWANS
5 COLLEYWELL CL
6 PARK DR
7 PARK CL
8 THE BIRCHES
9 MOORLANDS
10 DREWRY LA
11 WEAVERS CFT

B2
1 TAVELLA CT
2 CHAPEL CL
3 CRAYCROFT RD
4 HIGHFIELD CR
5 WESTLAND RD
6 CRACKLE HILL

D2
1 HALLCROFT RD
2 MARLBOROUGH AVE
3 LOWCROFT AVE
4 LOWCROFT CL
5 ASH TREE DR
6 HAYFIELD CL
7 GRANARY CFT
8 REAPER'S WY
9 HAXEY GR

10 THE GOLDINGS
11 HOPGARTH
12 CHATSWORTH WY
13 FARRIERS FOLD

D3
1 HUNTER'S CFT
2 SADDLER'S WY
3 MOWBRAY CL

39   40   28

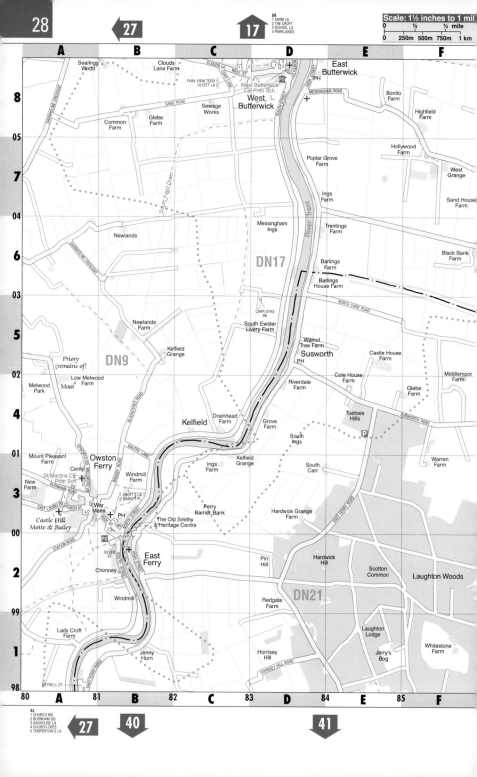

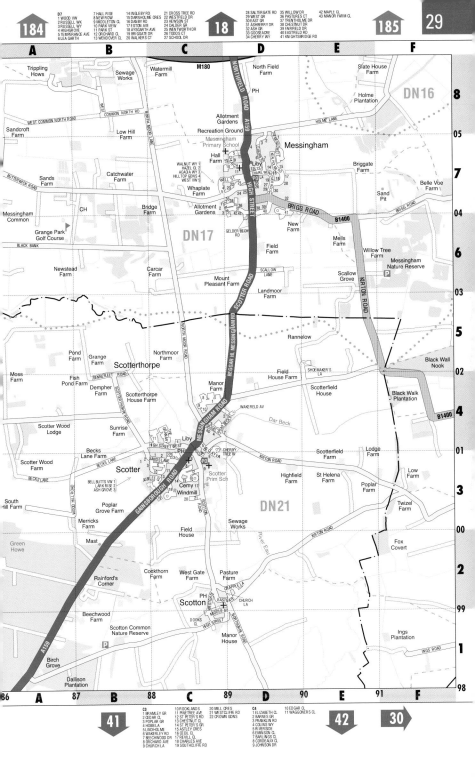

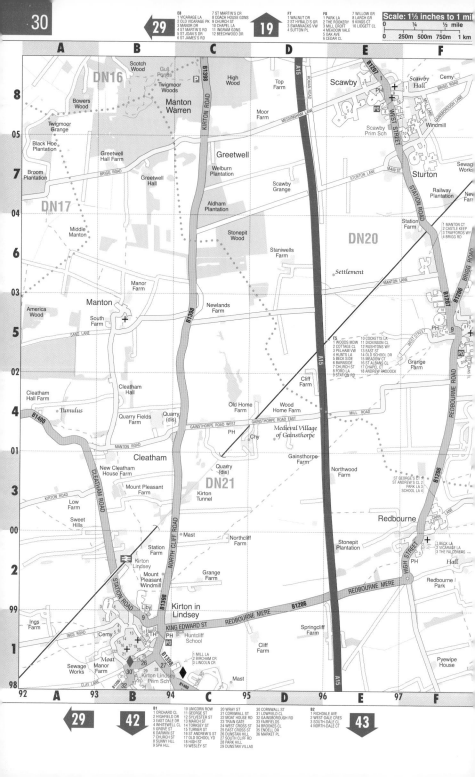

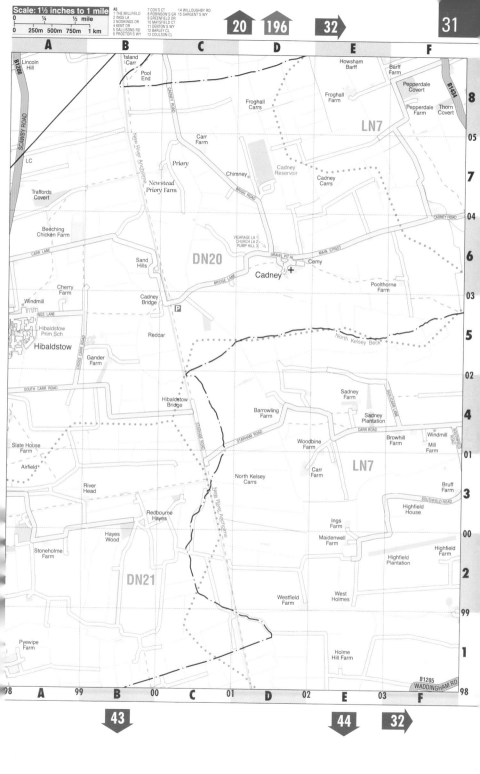

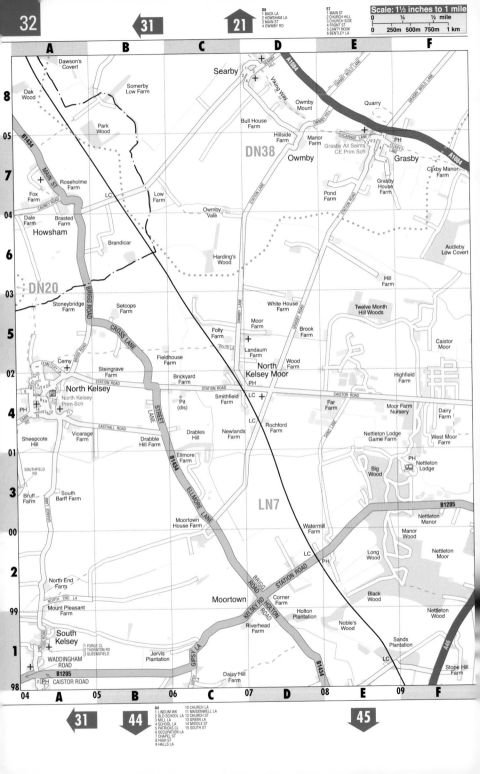

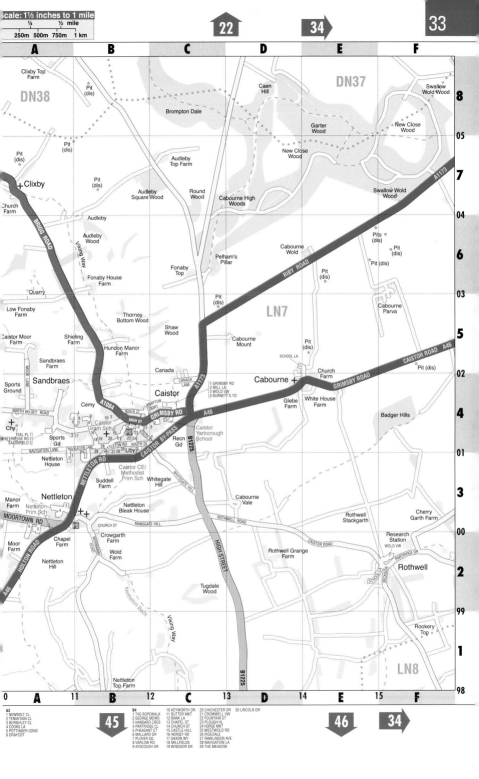

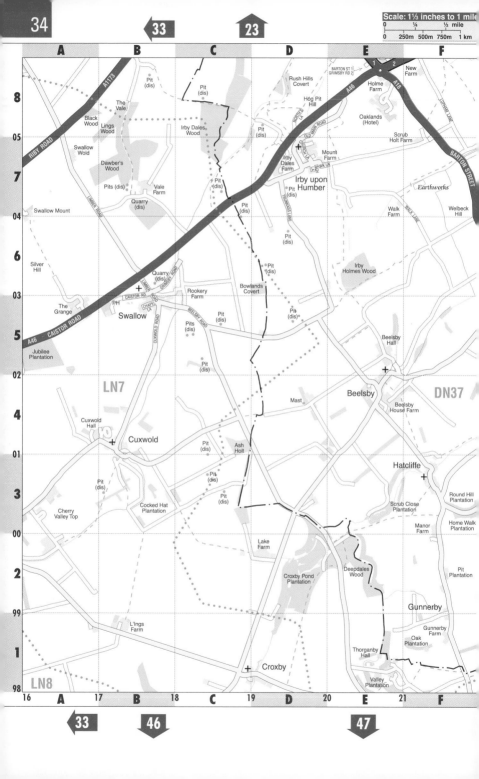

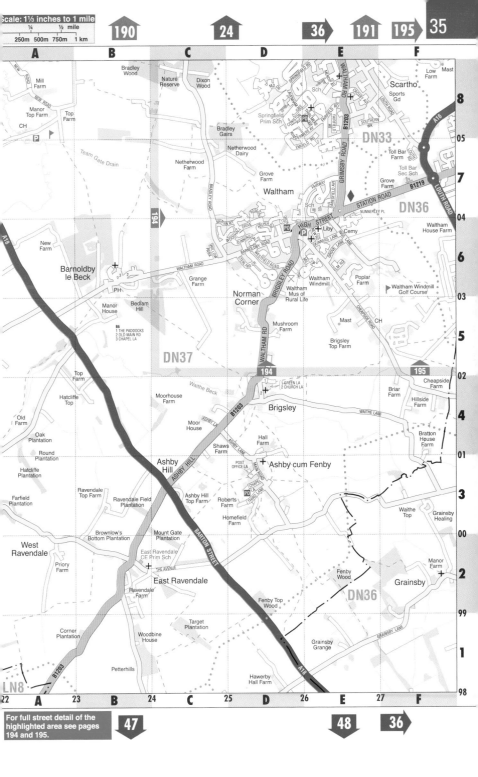

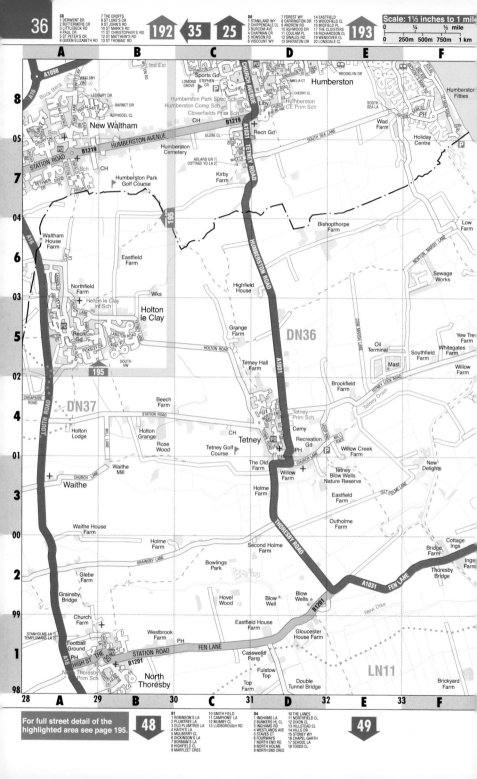

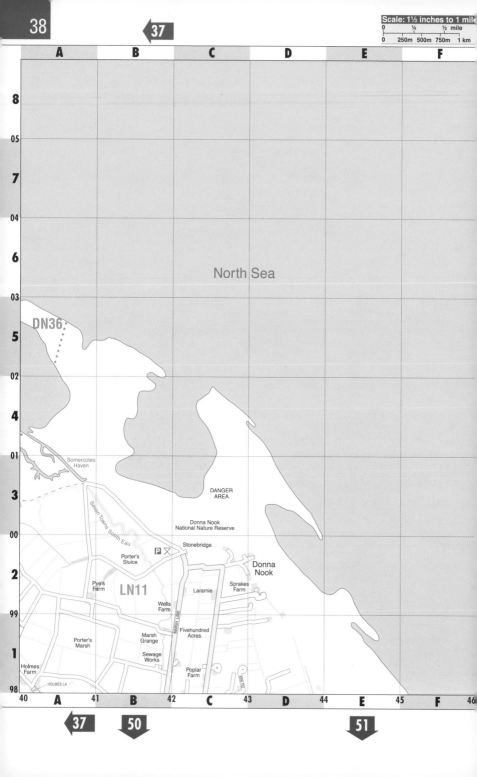

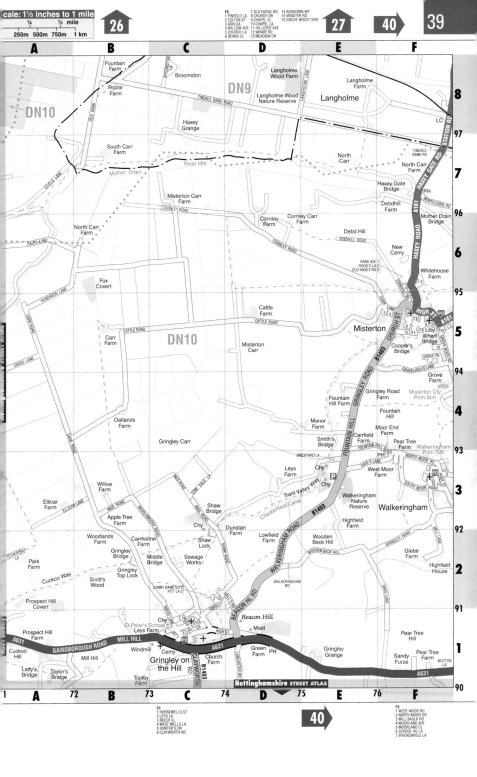

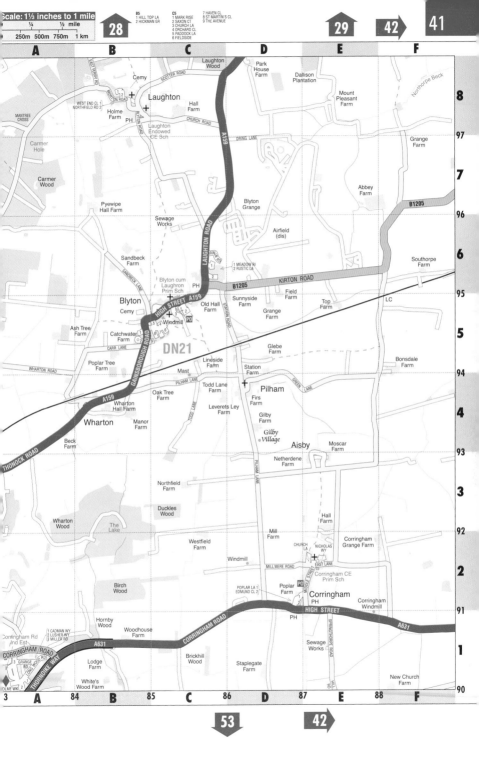

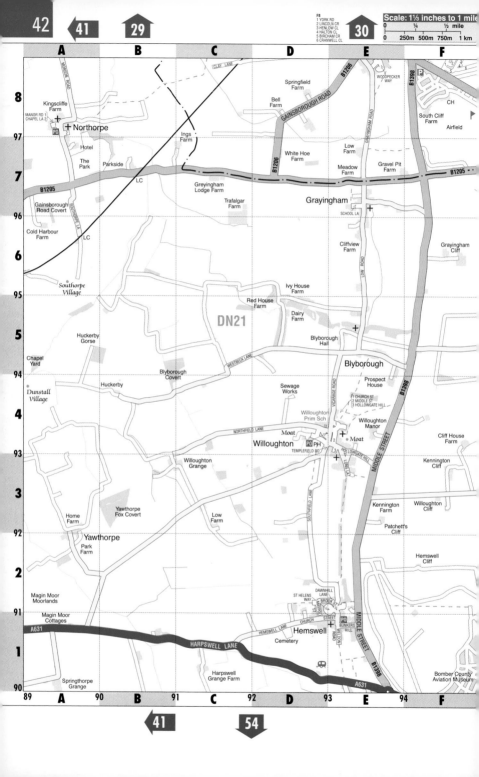

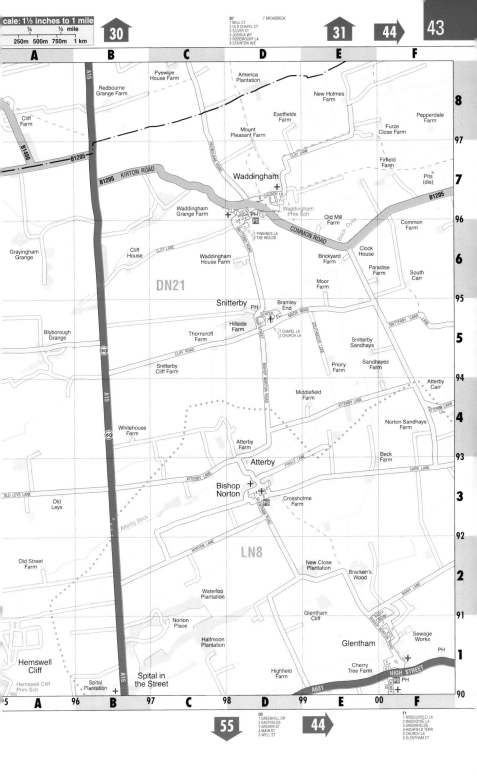

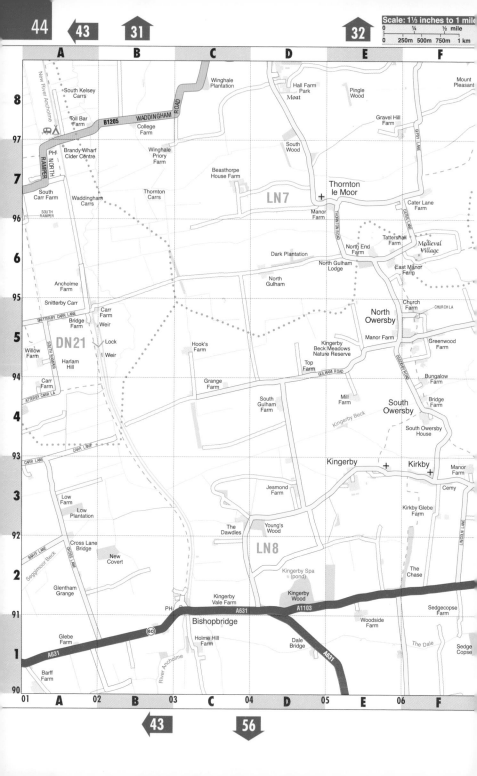

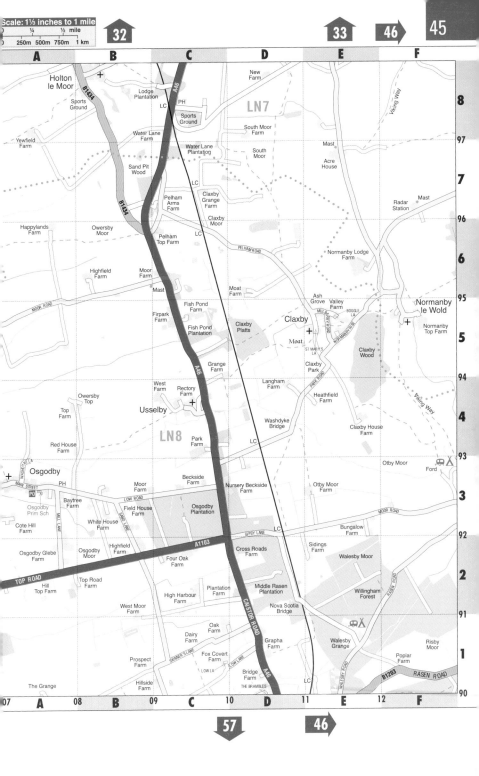

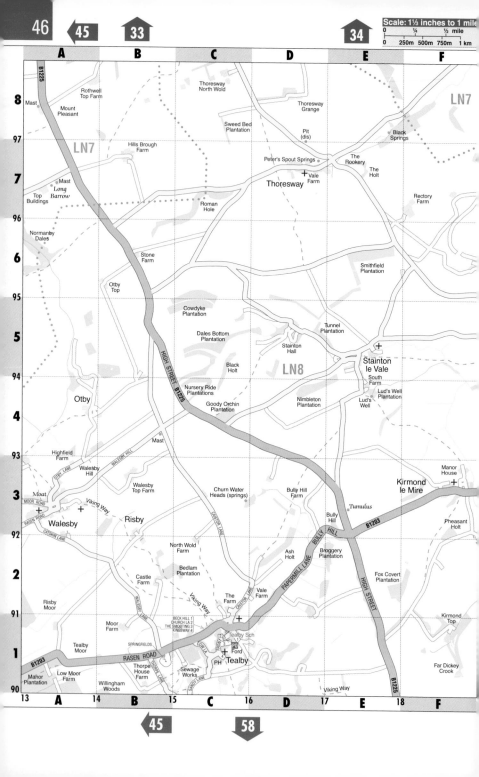

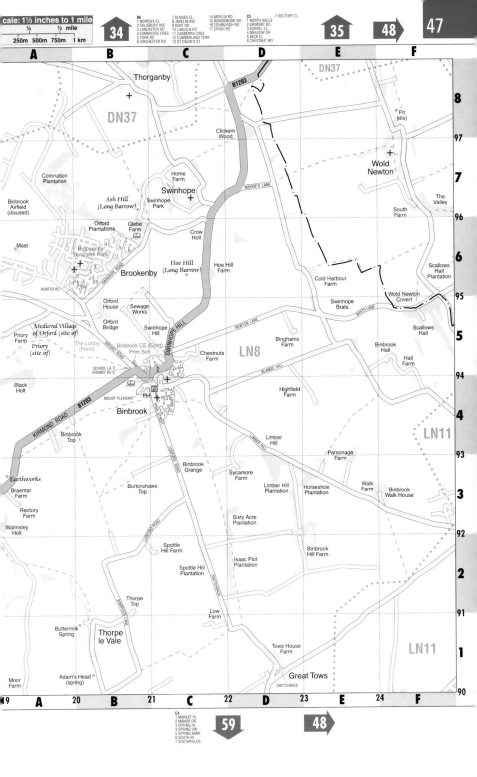

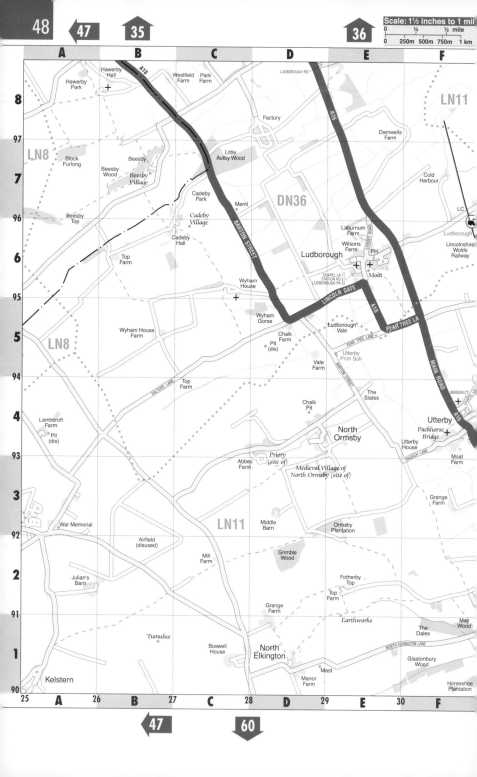

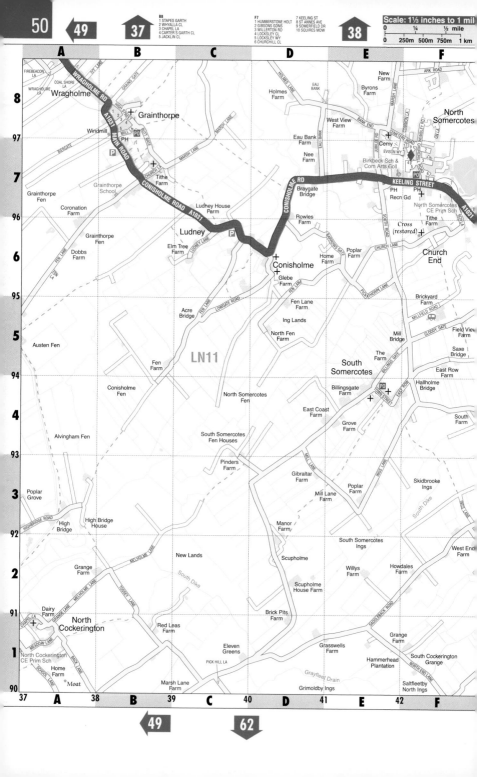

38

Scale: 1⅓ inches to 1 mile
¼ ½ mile
250m 500m 750m 1 km

A B C D E F

DANGER AREA

New East Marsh

Sand Haile Flats

North Somercotes Warren

Jarvis's Farm

Samphire Bed

Warren Farm

Donna Nook National Nature Reserve

WARREN ROAD

Salt Box Farm

P

Dunes

Skidbrooke Farm

Michaels Farm

Owes Lane Farm

Skidbrooke North End

P

OWES LANE

Salt Marsh

Toby's Hill Nature Reserve

Buttons Farm

LN11

Saltfleet

Grange Farm

PINK HILL LANE

MARSH LA

SEA LANE

A1031

MAIN ROAD

PH

CHURCH LANE

LOUTH ROAD

MILL LA

Saltfleet Haven

SUNDERFLEET LANE

Gowts Farm

Bridge Farm

Weldon House

White House Farm

JELLY GATE

Dunes

Skidbrooke Ings

Skidbrooke

SADDLEBACK ROAD

Sea View Farm

SEA VIEW

Stone Bridge

Saltfleetby - Theddlethorpe Dunes National Nature Reserve

West View Farm

Ivy Farm

Laburnum Farm

Queen's Bridge

Willow Farm

WEST LANE

Viewpoint

P

Great Eau

Lands End Farm

SWALLOW GATE ROAD

Elm House Farm

B1200

Rimac

Rimac Farm

RIMAC ROAD

Saltfleetby St Clement

Poplar Farm

PH

Dunes

INGS LA

LONE GATES

FISKNEY GATE ROAD

MAIN ROAD

SALTER GATE

Sturdys Farm

Beulah Farm

Saltfleetby CE Prim Sch

B1200

White House Farm

Sphinx Farm

MILL LANE

BACK STREET

A1031

CRABTREE LANE

Cloves Bridge

LN12

SALTFLEET RD

Saltfleetby All Saints

CHURCHILL LA

P

Saltfleetby - Theddlethorpe Dunes National Nature Reserve

43 A 44 B 45 C 46 D 47 E 48 F

8 97 7 96 6 95 5 94 4 93 3 92 2 91 1 90

C4
1 BOTOLPH'S VW
2 HOLMES CL
3 JACKLIN DR
4 THE HILL
5 PUMP LA
6 HAVEN BANK
7 GREYFLEET BANK

63

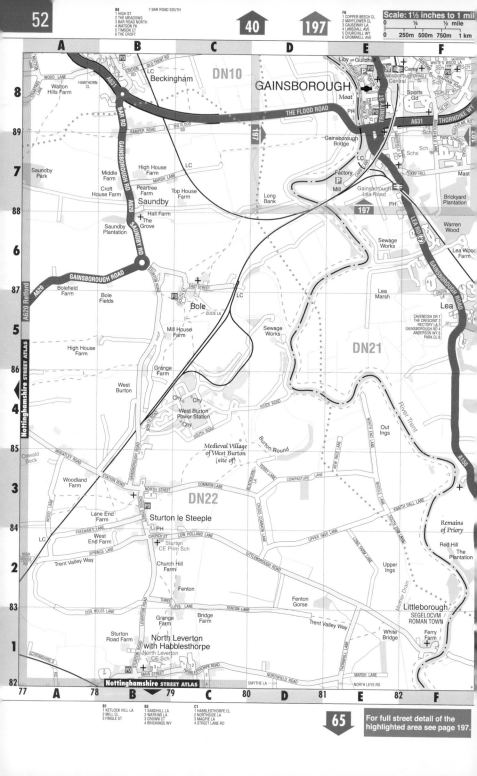

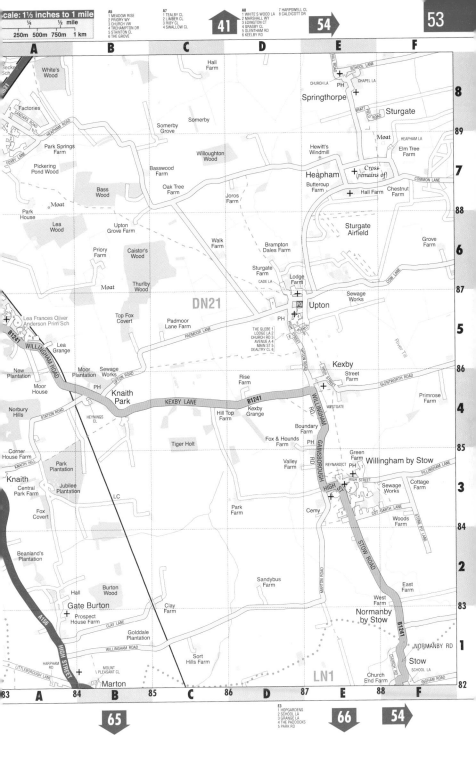

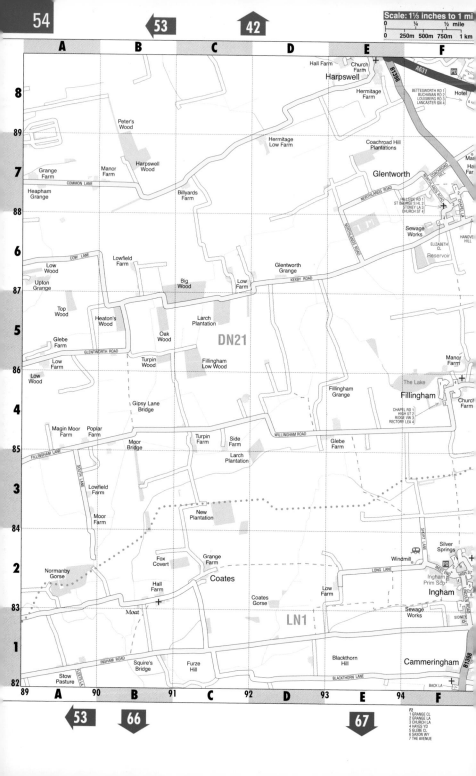

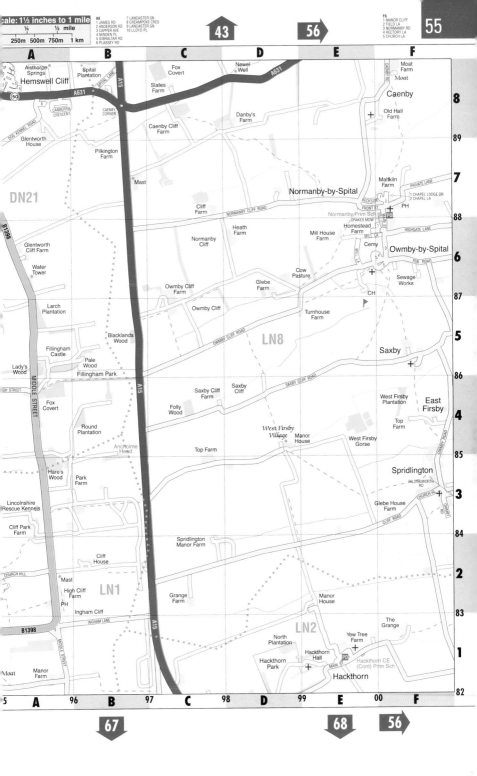

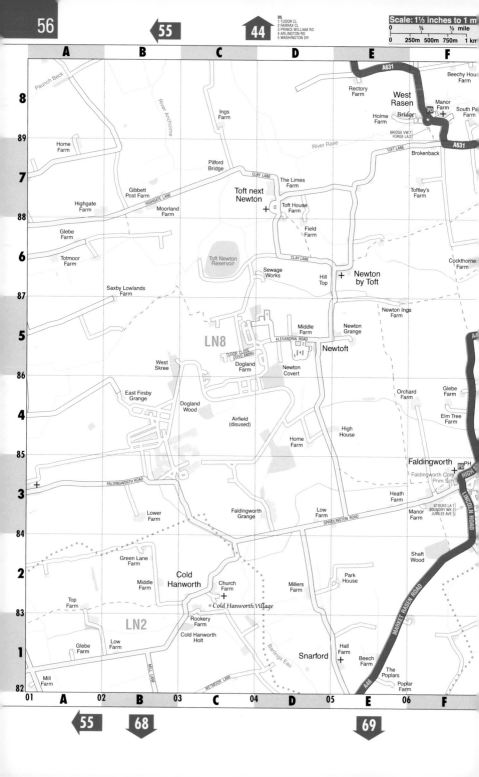

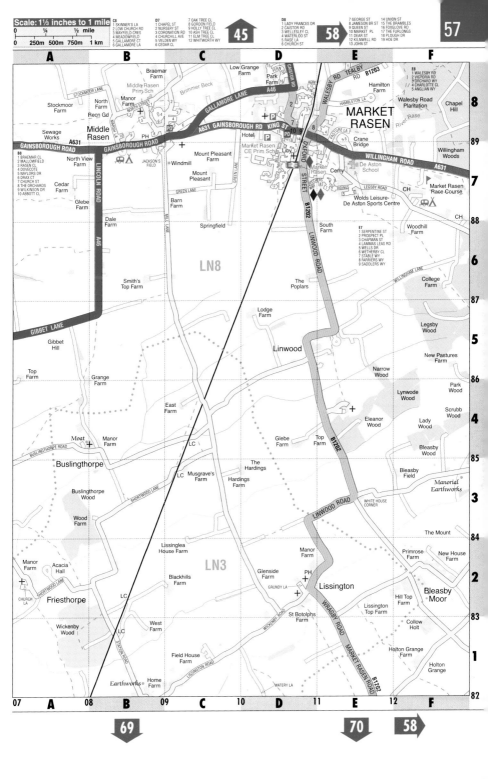

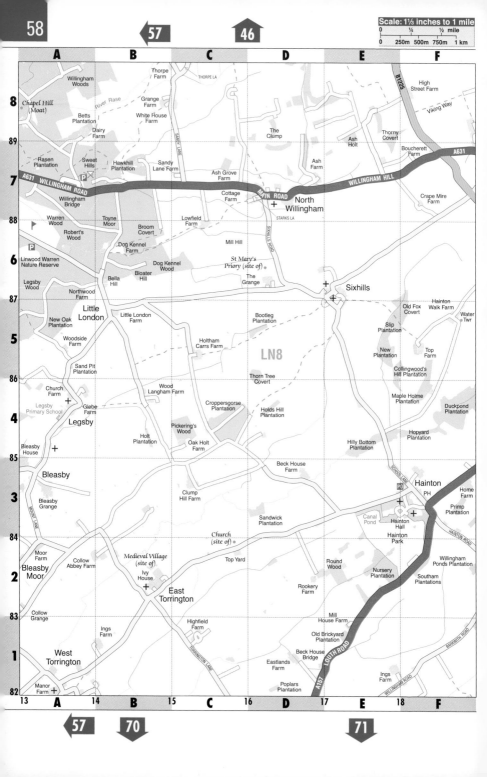

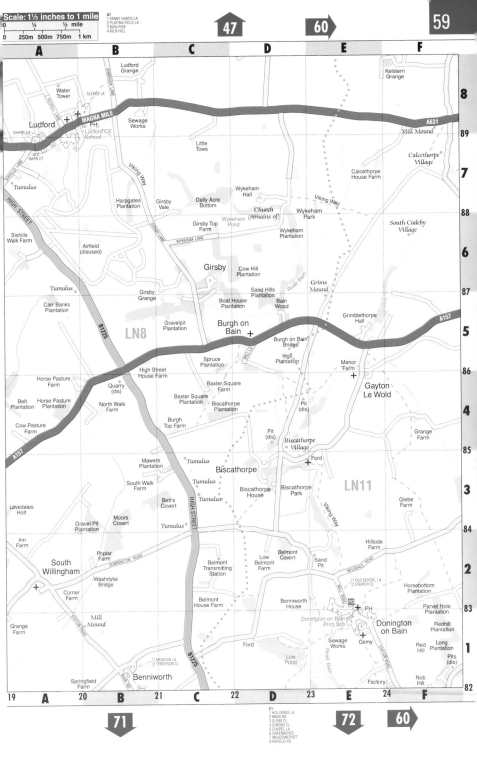

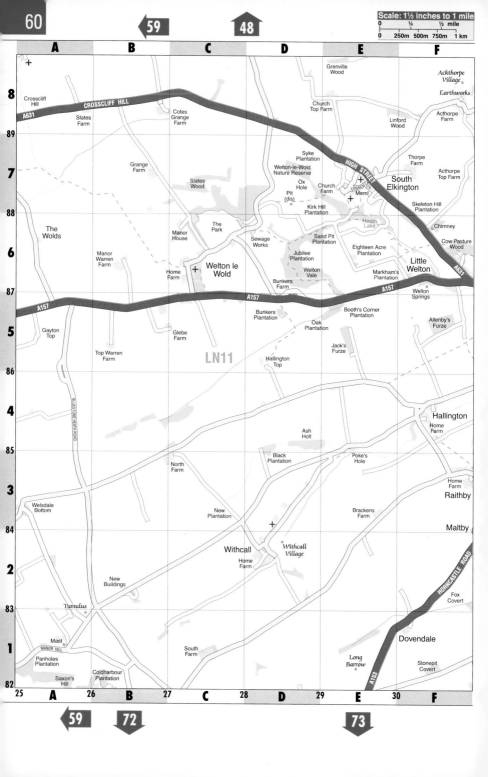

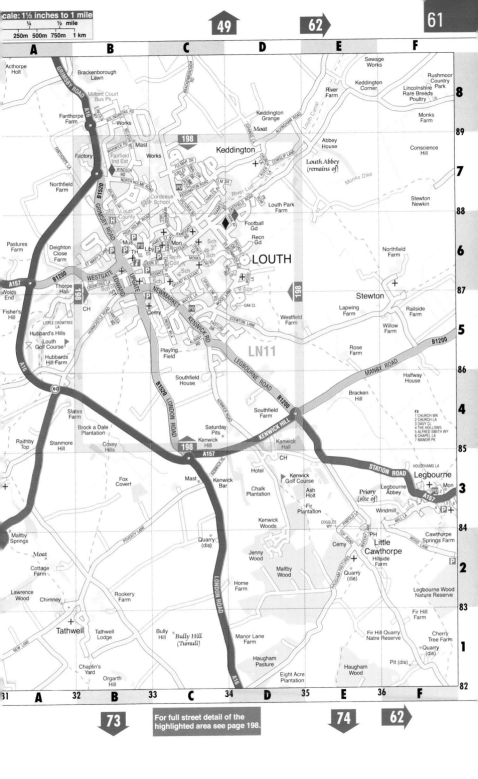

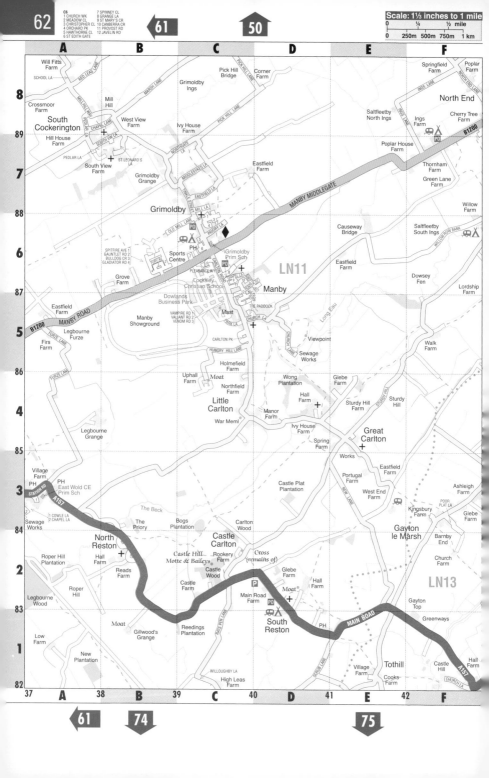

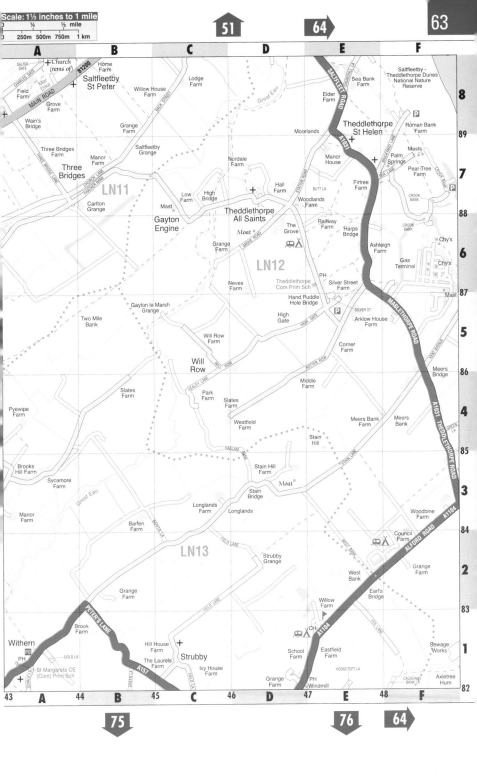

B5
1 CAMBRIDGE RD N
2 LINKS AVE
3 CAMBRIDGE RD S
4 IVEL GR
5 WHITEHEAD CL
6 IVEL CL

63

Scale: 1½ inches to 1 mile

A4
1 THE FAIRWAY
2 THE DRIVE
3 FALDOS WY
4 GOLF RD
5 LYLE CL
6 THE GREEN
7 EAGLE CL

C3
1 QUEENS PK CL
2 NEWSTEAD RD
3 DYMOKE CL
4 BROOKE DR
5 DYMOKE RD
6 ARDEN CL

C2
1 MILL FIELD
2 CAMPLING WY
3 BARTON CL
4 AUBREY PARKER CL
5 PARKINSON'S WY
6 JAMES AVE
7 ST PETER'S LA
8 BRAY AVE
9 ETON RD

1 PARK RD E
2 CROMER AVE
3 HIGH ST
4 PROMENADE
5 YORK RD

MABLETHORPE
LN12
Trusthorpe
Thorpe

A3
1 ORCHARD WY
2 ORCHARD CL
3 CHURCH CL
4 MALBOROUGH DR
5 OAKHAM AVE
6 WINCHESTER DR
7 CHELTENHAM WY

63

76

B3
1 HAWTHORN DR
2 MAYFLOWER WY
3 TRENCHARD RD
4 NELSON RD
5 STANLEY AVE
6 MAXWELL DR
7 KENSINGTON GDNS
8 STRAND CL
9 TOWER CL
10 HARLEQUIN DR
11 MARIAN AVE
12 HARRIS BOULEVARD
13 ELM AVE
14 KING ST
15 MARINA RD
16 ANCASTER RD
17 RIPON PL
18 VYNER CL
19 FOXE END

B4
20 KNOWLE ST
21 PARK AVE
22 PARRY RD
23 THE BOULEVARD

B4
1 LONG ACRE
2 ST ANDREWS RD
3 SHERWOOD RD
4 RUGBY RD
5 MALVERN RD
6 HARROW RD
7 REPTON RD
8 QUEENSWAY
9 SOMERSBY AVE

10 FITZWILLIAM ST
11 WELLINGTON AVE
12 CHAUCER AVE
13 RUSKIN RD
14 KINGSLEY RD
15 CHARLES WRIGHT CL
16 TENNYSON AVE
17 TENNYSON RD
18 HIGH ST
19 ADMIRALTY RD

20 STATION RD
21 ALEXANDRA RD
22 ALEXANDRA PK

77

C1
1 HALL LEAS DR
2 TRUSTHORPE RD
3 HIGHGATE
4 HIGHFIELD AVE
5 OUNDLE RD
6 UPPINGHAM RD
7 WILLOUGHBY RD
8 MARINE AVE
9 HARDING CL

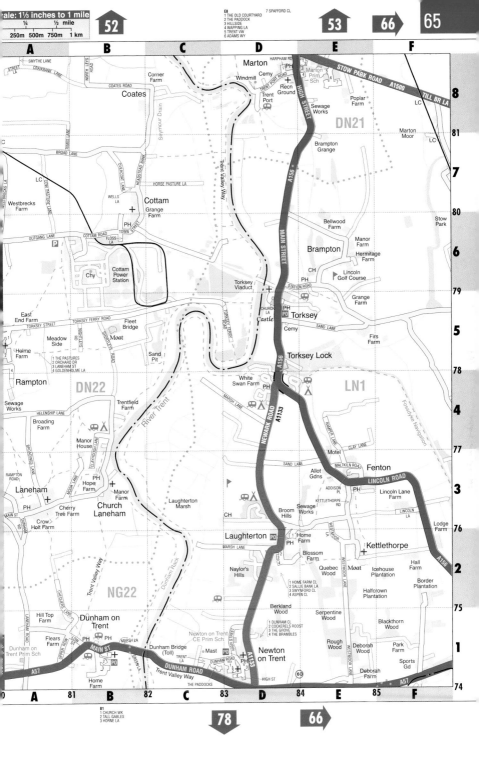

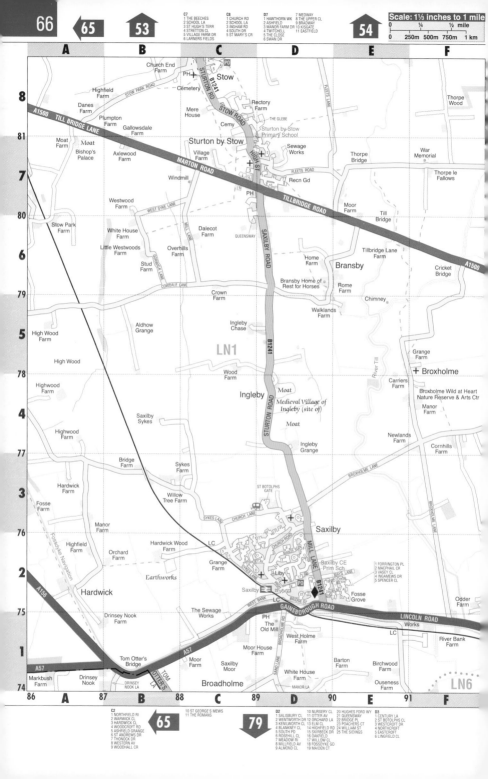

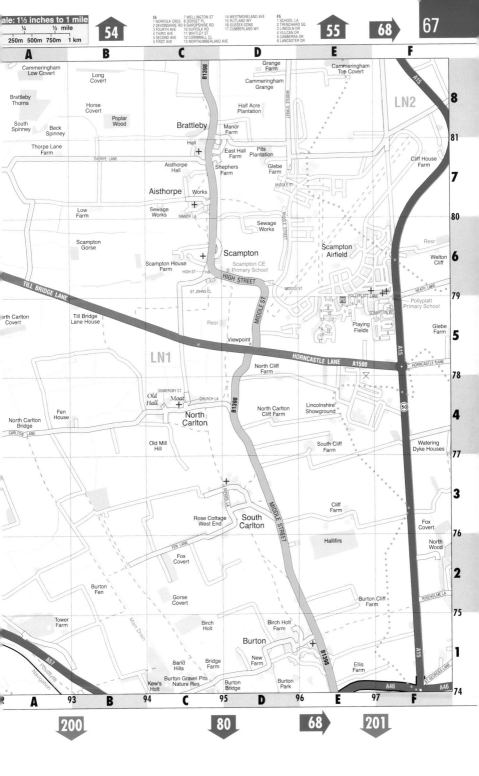

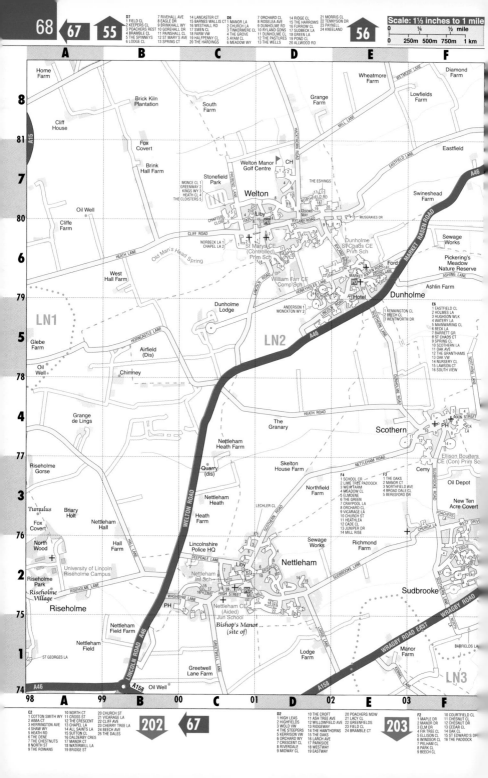

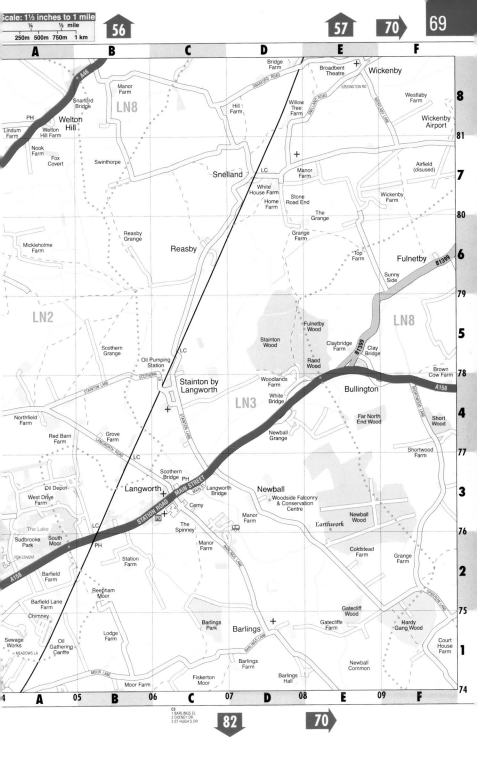

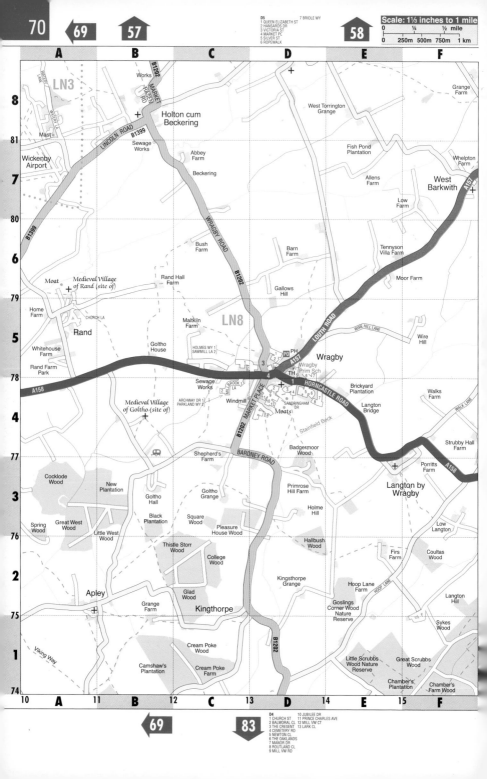

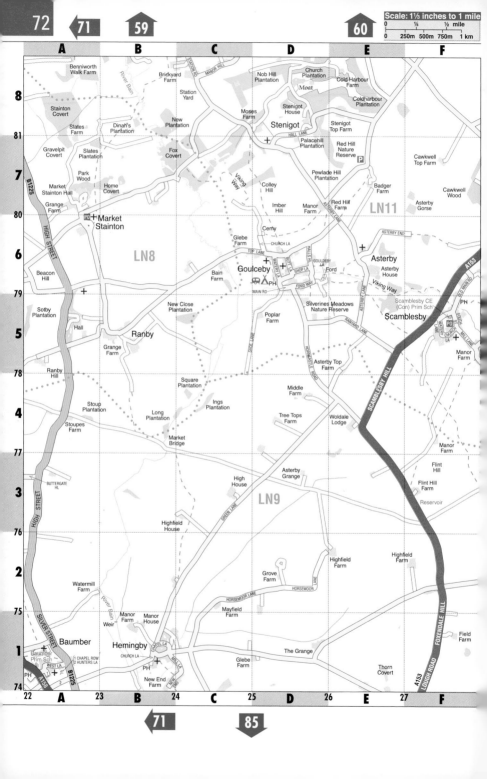

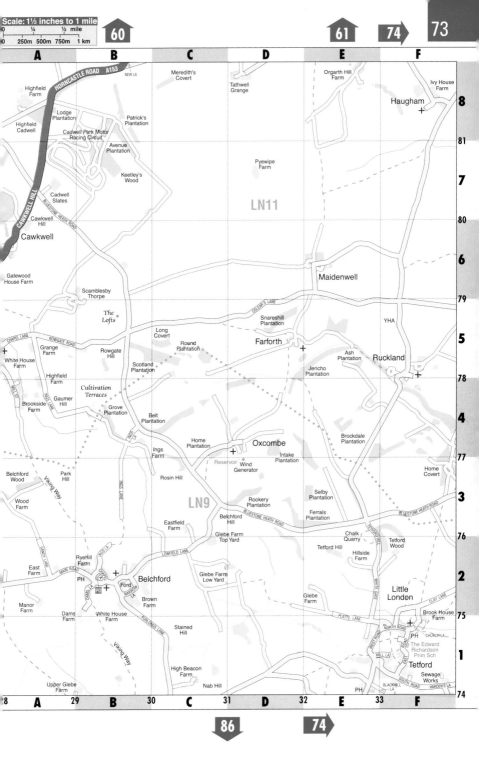

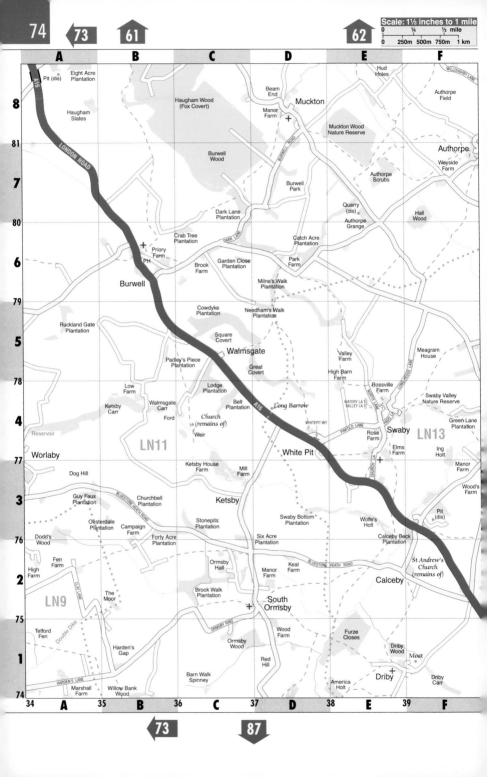

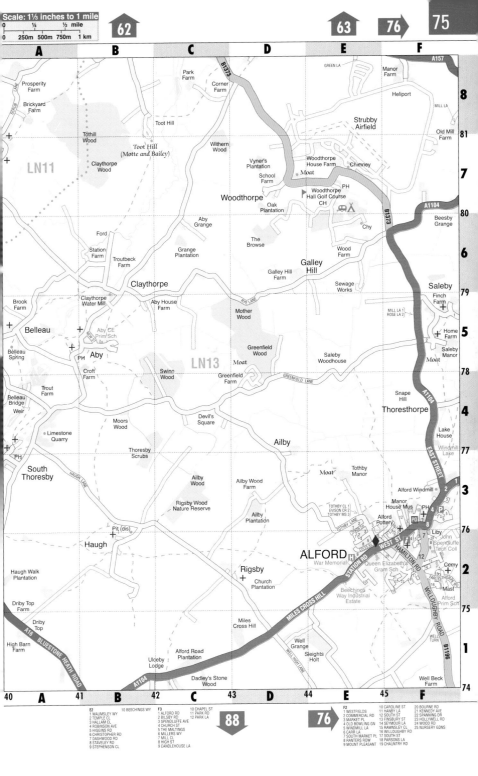

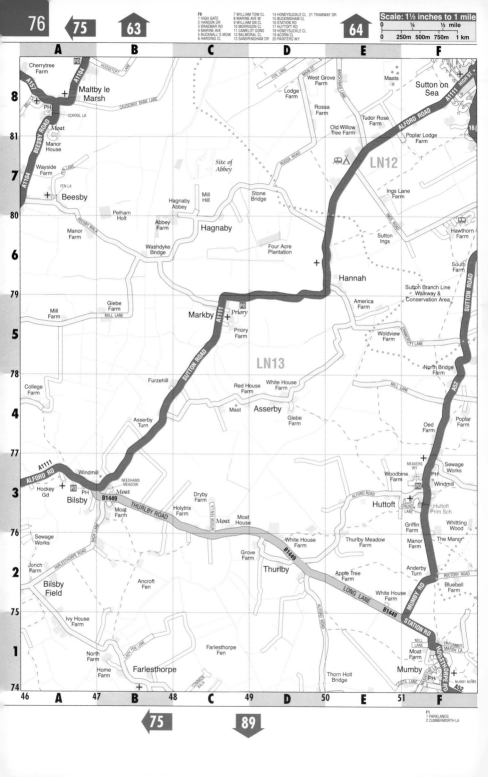

cale: 1⅓ inches to 1 mile

¼   ½   mile

250m 500m 750m 1 km

64

Scale: 1⅓ inches to 1 mile
0   ¼   ½ mile
0 250m 500m 750m 1 km

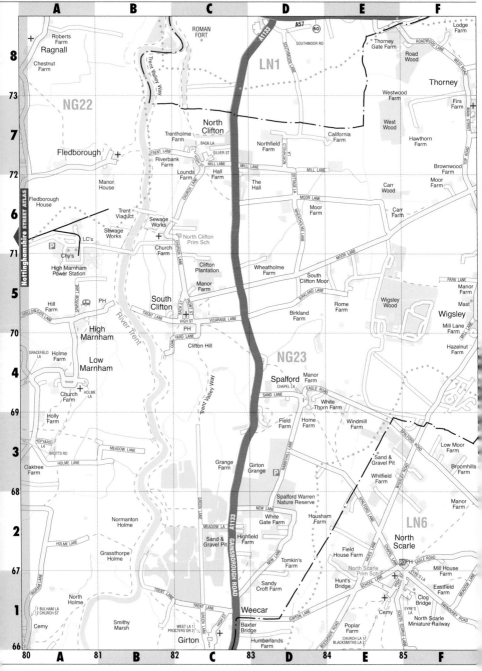

A57

A1133

LN1

Roberts Farm

Ragnall

Chestnut Farm

NG22

Trent Valley Way

ROMAN FORT

SOUTHMOOR RD

Thorney Gate Farm

Road Wood

Lodge Farm

ROADWOOD LANE

WEST LA

Thorney

Fledborough

North Clifton

Trentholme Farm

BACK LA

SILVER ST

Riverbank Farm

Lounds Farm

Hall Farm

MILL LANE

Northfield Farm

The Hall

California Farm

Westwood Farm

West Wood

Hawthorn Farm

Firs Farm

Brownwood Farm

MAIN STREET

Manor House

Fledborough House

Trent Viaduct

Sewage Works

Sewage Works

CHURCH LANE

North Clifton Prim Sch

MILL LANE

COTTAGE LA

CLIFTON RD

MOOR LANE

Moor Farm

WHEATING ML LANE

Carr Wood

Carr Farm

Moor Farm

Chy's

LC's

High Marnham Power Station

Church Farm

Clifton Plantation

Manor Farm

South Clifton

Wheatholme Farm

South Clifton Moor

BIRKLAND LANE

MOOR LANE

PARK LANE

Manor Farm

Mast

Wigsley

River Trent

SPARROW LANE

Hill Farm

PH

High Marnham

HIGH ST

BACK ST

PINFOLD LA

TRENT LANE

VICARAGE LANE

PH

Birkland Farm

Rome Farm

Wigsley Wood

Mill Lane Farm

Hazelnut Farm

HOLLOW GATE LANE

GRACEFIELD LA

Holme Farm

Low Marnham

QUAD LANE

Clifton Hill

NG23

Spalford

CHAPEL LA

Manor Farm

EAGLE ROAD

White Thorn Farm

SPALFORD ROAD

Holme Farm

Church Farm

HOLME LA

Holly Farm

Trent Valley Way

MEADOW LANE

SAND LANE

Field Farm

Home Farm

Windmill Farm

Low Moor Farm

Broomhills Farm

HUPYARD LA

BROTTS RD

HOLME LANE

Oaktree Farm

Grange Farm

Girton Grange

RABBITHILL LANE

Spalford Warren Nature Reserve

NEW LANE

Housham Farm

Sand & Gravel Pit

Whitfield Farm

WIGSLEY LANE

Manor Farm

LN6

Normanton Holme

GREEN LANE

MEADOW LANE

A1133 GAINSBOROUGH ROAD

White Gate Farm

Highfield Farm

Field House Farm

SPALFORD LANE

EYRES LA

North Scarle

Grasshorpe Holme

HOLME LANE

NEW LANE

Tomkin's Farm

CHAPEL LA

Hunt's Bridge

North Scarle Prim Sch

SCHOOL LANE

PH

EAGLE ROAD

Mill House Farm

EYRE'S LA

Eastfield Farm

MEADOW LANE

INGRAM LANE

North Holme

TRENT LANE

GREEN LANE

Sandy Croft Farm

GIRTON LANE

Clog Bridge

Cemy

Poplar Farm

SHINNINGS ROAD

North Scarle Miniature Railway

Cemy

1 BULHAM LA
2 CHURCH ST

Smithy Marsh

Girton

WEST LA 1
PROCTERS DR 2

Weecar

Baxter Bridge

Humberlands Farm

EYRE'S LA

BESTTHORPE ROAD

CHURCH LA 1
BLACKSMITHS LA 2

Nottinghamshire STREET ATLAS

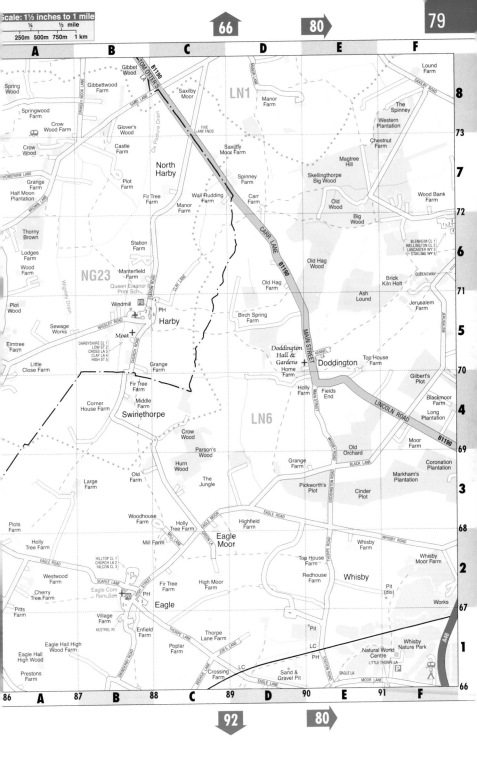

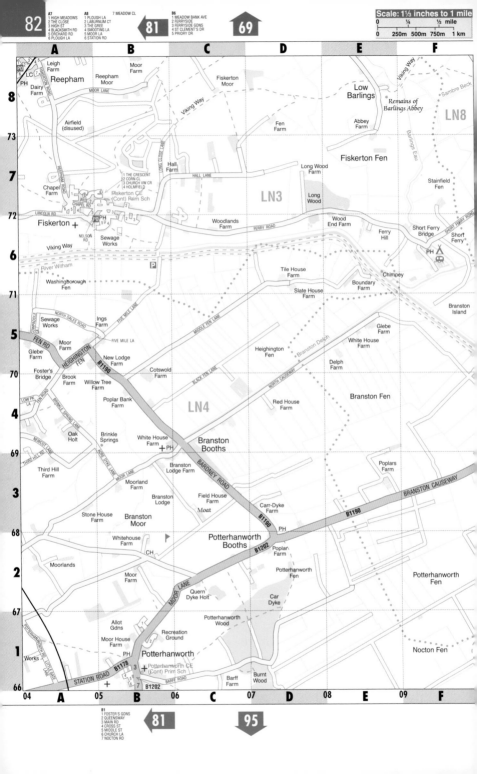

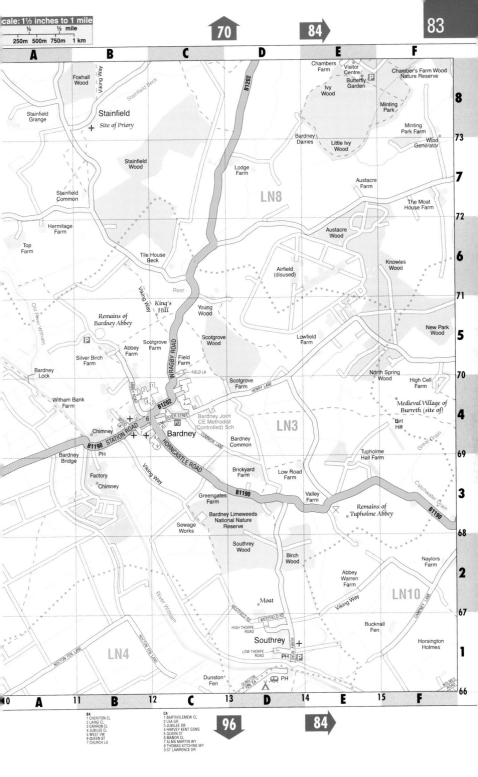

A   B   C   D   E   F

8
73
7
72
6
71
5
70
4
69
3
68
2
67
1
66

Foxhall Wood
Stainfield Grange
Stainfield
Site of Priory
Stainfield Wood
Stainfield Common
Hermitage Farm
Top Farm
Tile House Beck
Viking Way
Stainfield Beck
Viking Way
King's Hill
Resr
Remains of Bardney Abbey
Scotgrove Farm
Abbey Farm
Silver Birch Farm
Bardney Lock
Witham Bank Farm
Chimney
WRAGBY ROAD
Field Farm
FIELD LA
Scotgrove Wood
Young Wood
Scotgrove Farm
HENRY LANE
Bardney
STATION ROAD
FERRY ROAD
B1202
SILVER STREET
HORNCASTLE ROAD
COMMON LANE
B1190
Bardney Bridge
PH
Factory
Chimney
Viking Way
Greengates Farm
B1190
Bardney Limeweeds National Nature Reserve
Sewage Works
Southrey Wood
Brickyard Farm
Bardney Common
Bardney Joint CE Methodist (Controlled) Sch
LN3
Low Road Farm
Valley Farm
Birch Wood
Moat
River Witham
WESTFIELD RD
HIGH THORPE ROAD
LOW THORPE ROAD
Southrey
WESTFIELD RD
FERRY ROAD
PH
Dunston Fen
DUNSTON FEN EA
PH
NOCTON FEN LANE
NOCTON FEN LANE
LN4

B1202
Chambers Farm
Visitor Centre
Butterfly Garden
Chamber's Farm Wood Nature Reserve
Ivy Wood
Minting Park
Bardney Dairies
Little Ivy Wood
Minting Park Farm
Wind Generator
Lodge Farm
LN8
Austacre Farm
The Moat House Farm
Austacre Wood
Airfield (disused)
Knowles Wood
Lowfield Farm
New Park Wood
North Spring Wood
High Cell Farm
Medieval Village of Burreth (site of)
Birt Hill
Great Drain
Tupholme Hall Farm
Remains of Tupholme Abbey
Catchwater Drain
B1190
Naylors Farm
Abbey Warren Farm
LN10
Viking Way
Bucknall Fen
CAMBERS LANE
Horsington Holmes
HOLMES ROAD

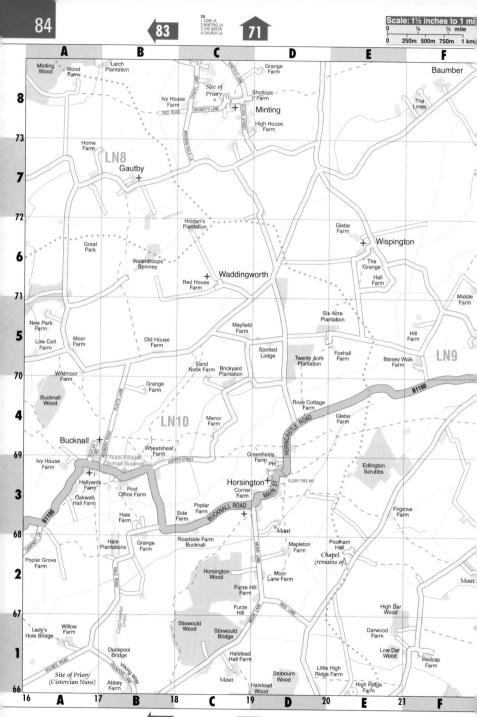

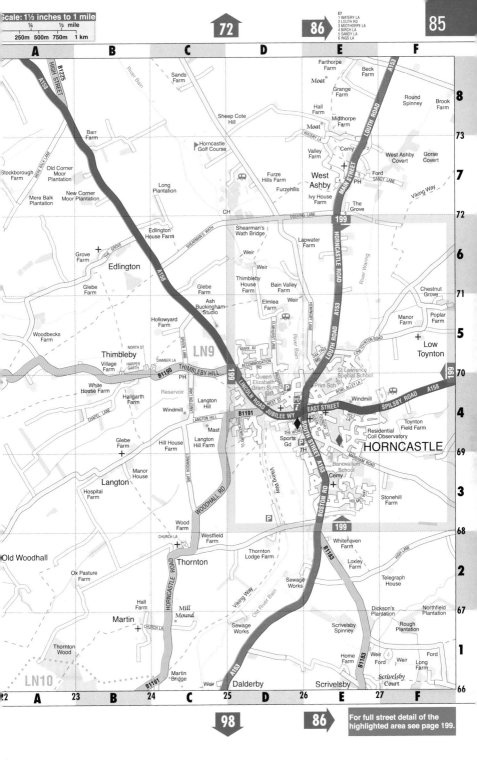

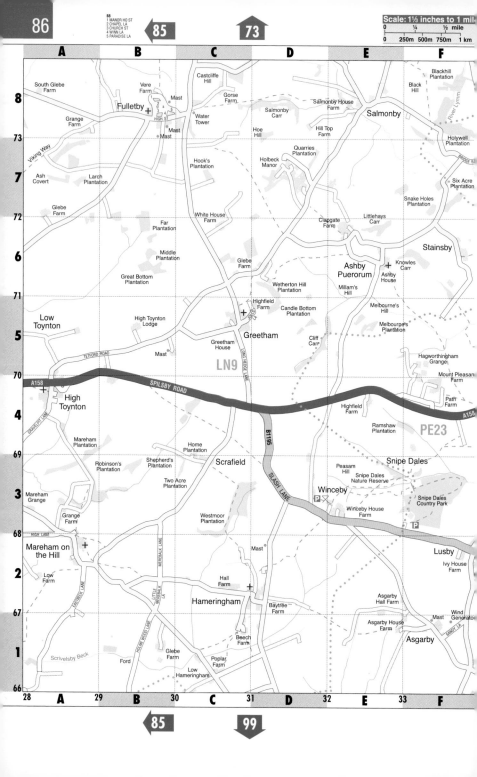

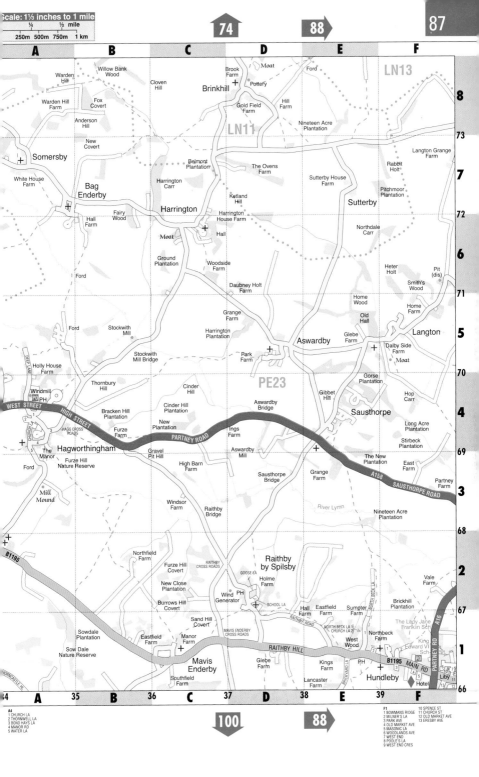

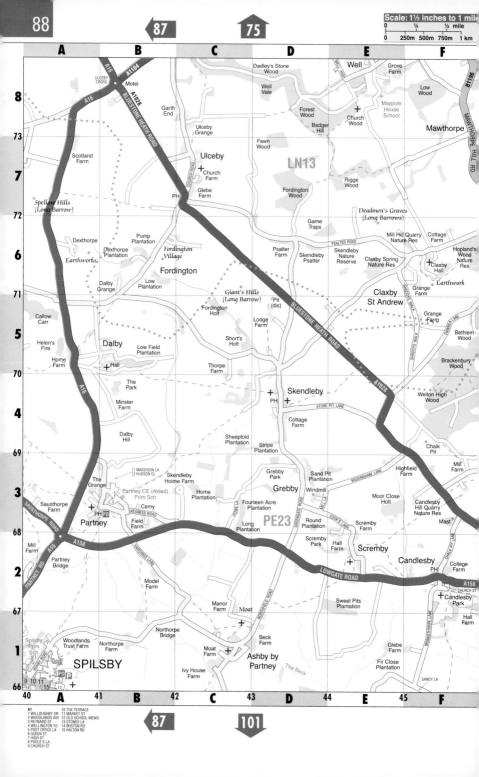

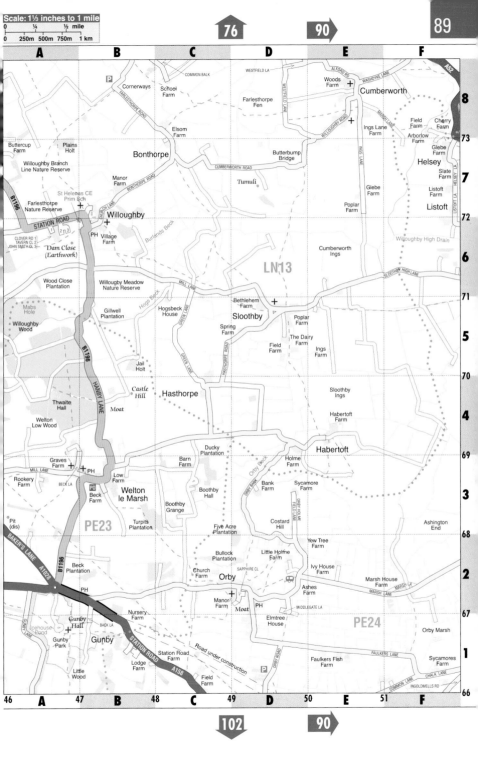

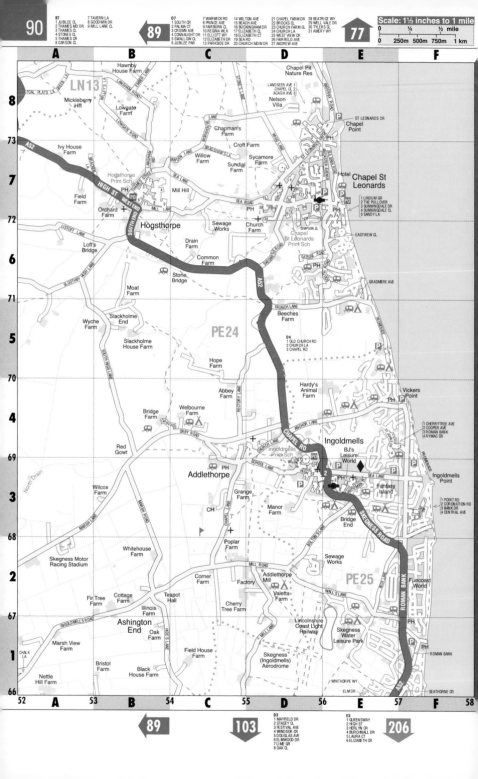

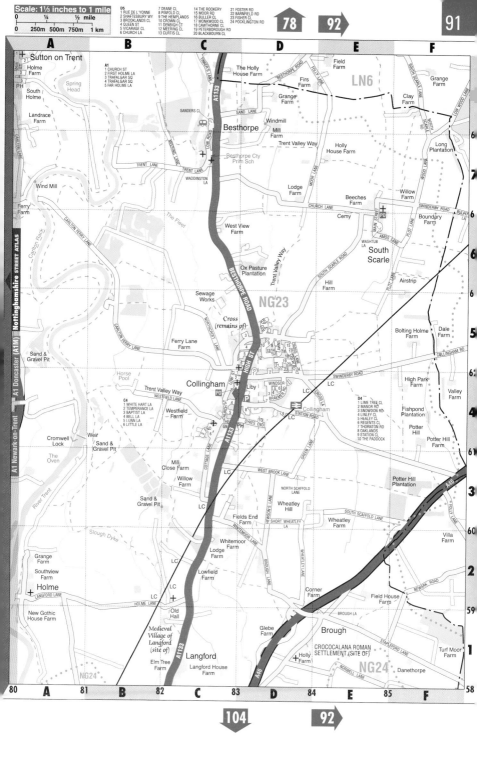

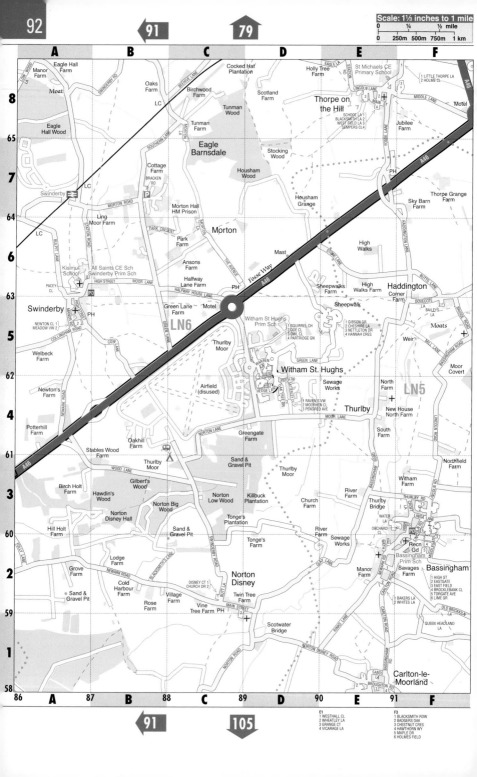

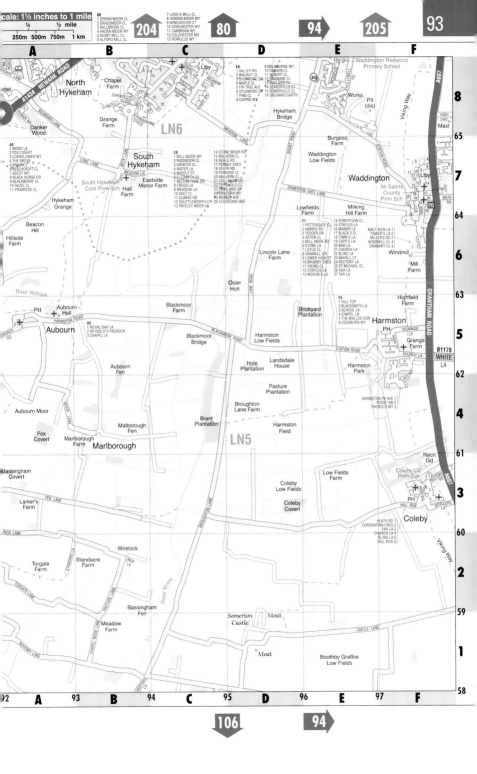

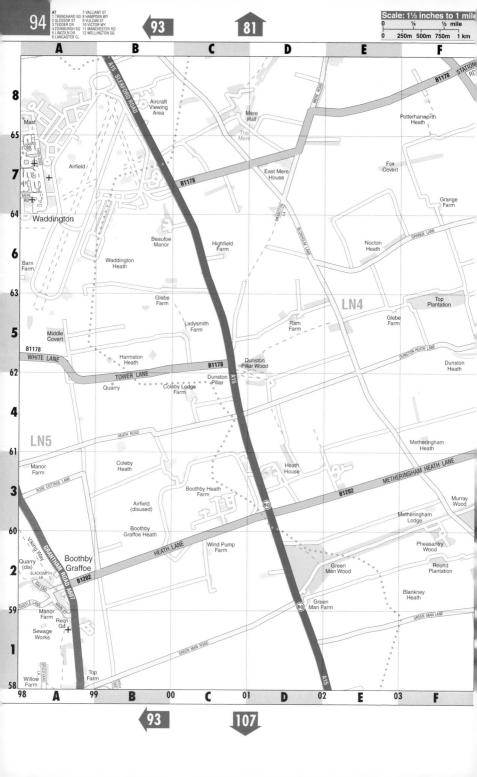

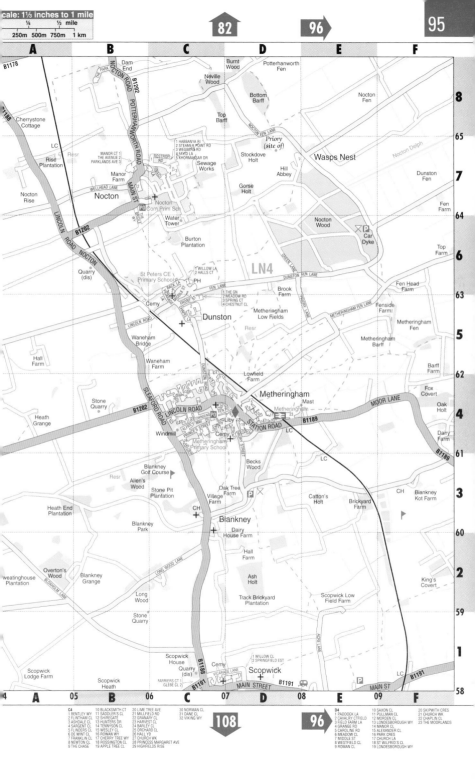

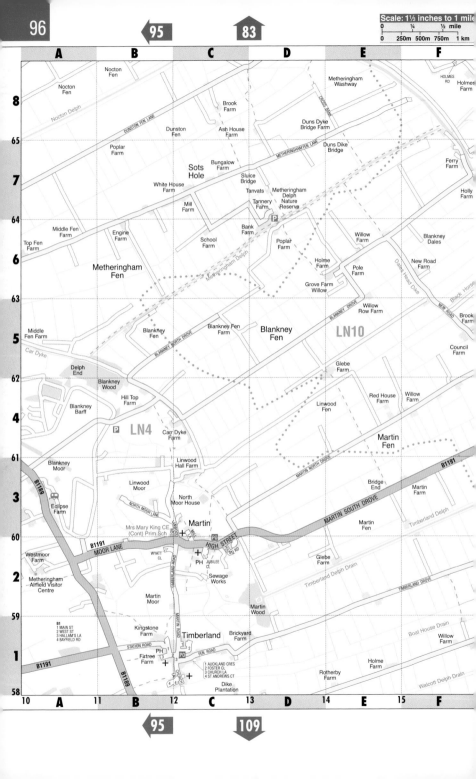

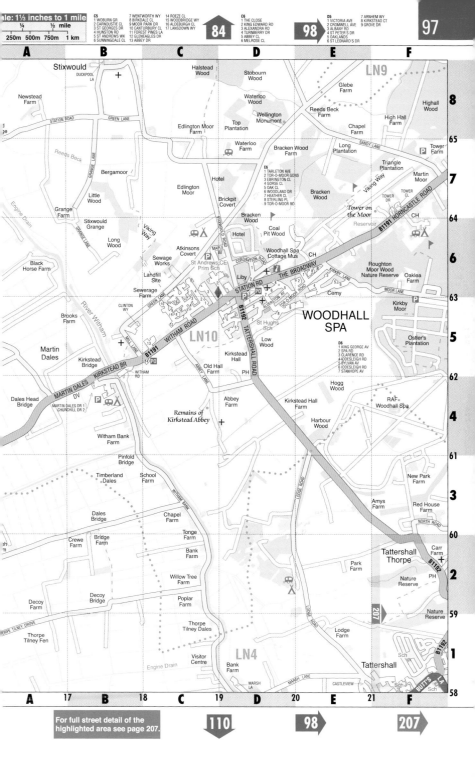

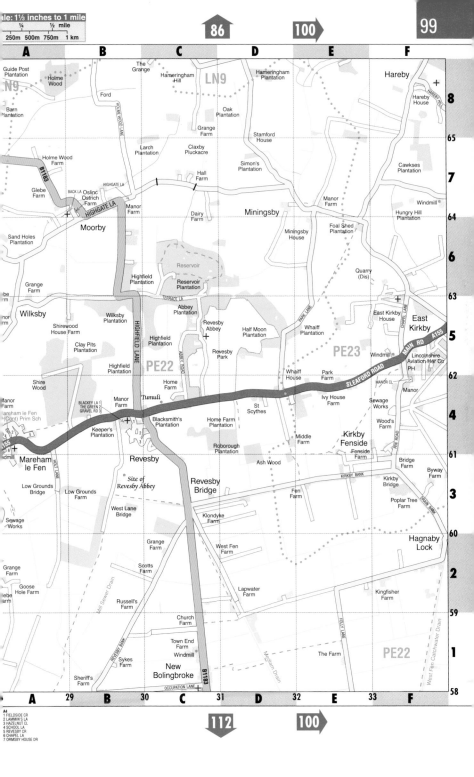

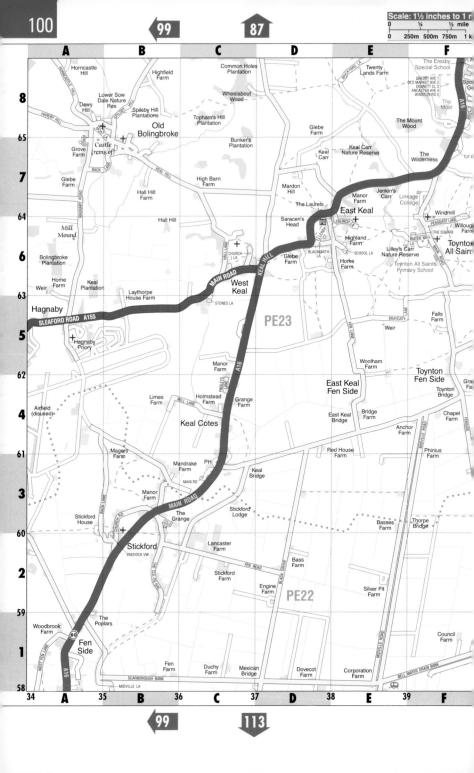

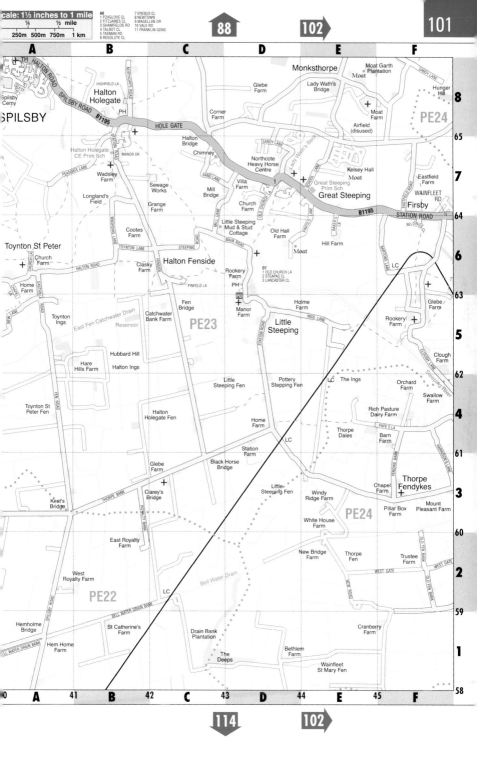

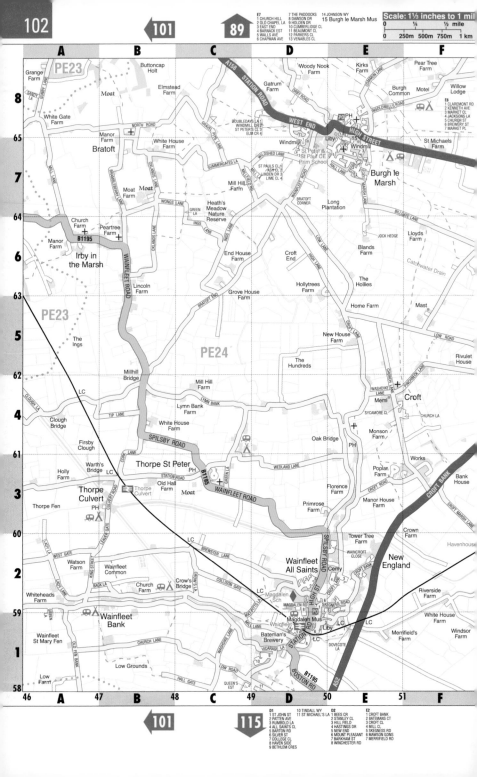

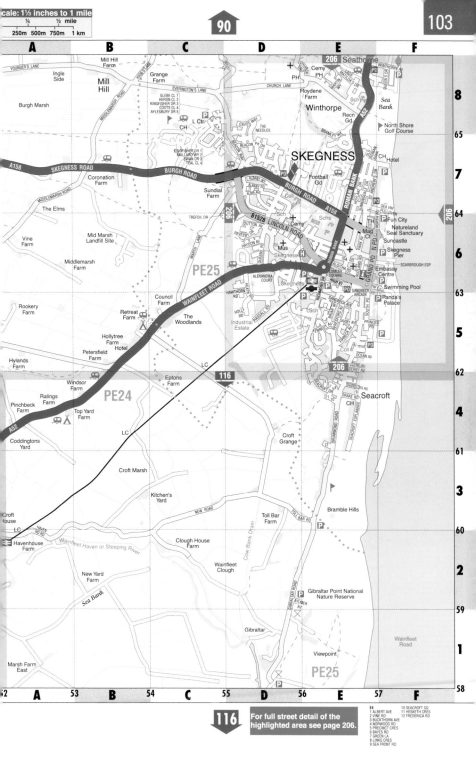

A B C D E F

8

Younger's Lane
Mill Hill Farm
Ingle Side
Mill Hill
Grange Farm
EVERINGTON'S LANE
Burgh Marsh
GLEBE CL 1
HERON CL 2
KINGFISHER DR 3
COOTS CL 4
AYLESBURY DR 5
CHURCH LANE
Cemy
PH
Roydene Farm
Winthorpe
Sch
Sea Bank
65
L Ctr
CH
DAVID'S WAY
THE NEEDLES
BEACON WY
Recn Gd
North Shore Golf Course

7
A158 SKEGNESS ROAD
Coronation Farm
BURGH ROAD
KINGFISHER DR 1
MALLARD WY 2
SWAN DR 3
TEAL CL 4
Sundial Farm
ALBANY AV
ALBANY RD
BLAKE RD
SKEGNESS
Football Gd
BURGH ROAD A158
ROMAN BANK
Hotel
MIDDLEMARSH ROAD
The Elms
TREFOIL DR
206
B1528
Coll
Sch
LINCOLN ROAD
Cemy
Schs
Fun City
Natureland Seal Sanctuary
Suncastle
64

6
Vine Farm
Mid Marsh Landfill Site
WARTH LANE
QUEENS RD
HAYDON RD
REVESBY AV
DUTTON AV
Mus
Skegness
Skegness Pier
SCARBROUGH ESP
Middlemarsh Farm
PE25
H
Embassy Centre
Swimming Pool

63
WAINFLEET ROAD
Council Farm
ALEXANDRA COURT
HAWTHORN RD
HEATH RD
HOLLY RD
PASCALL RD
Skegness
Panda's Palace
Rookery Farm
Retreat Farm
The Woodlands
Sch
KENNEDY AV
SAXBY AVE
PRINCES
5
Hollytree Farm Hotel
Petersfield Farm
Industrial Estate
Coll
OCEAN AV
Hylands Farm
LC
62
PE24
Windsor Farm
Eptons Farm
116
Seacroft
DRUMMOND ROAD
DRAKE RD
CH
4
Pinchbeck Farm
Ralings Farm
Top Yard Farm
A52
LC
Croft Grange
61

Coddingtons Yard
Croft Marsh
Kitchen's Yard
NEW ROAD
Bramble Hills
3
Croft House
LC
HAVEN RD
Havenhouse Farm
Wainfleet Haven or Steeping River
Clough House Farm
Toll Bar Farm
TOLL BAR RD
60

New Yard Farm
Wainfleet Clough
Cow Bank Drain
Gibraltar Point National Nature Reserve
2
Sea Bank
GIBRALTAR
AYLMER AV
59

Marsh Farm East
Gibraltar
Viewpoint
PE25
Wainfleet Road
1
58

52 A 53 B 54 C 55 D 56 E 57 F

116

For full street detail of the
highlighted area see page 206.

E4
1 ALBERT AVE
2 VINE RD
3 BUCKTHORN AVE
4 NORWOOD RD
5 PRECINCT CRES
6 BAYES RD
7 GREEN LA
8 LINKS CRES
9 SEA FRONT RD
10 SEACROFT SQ
11 HESKETH CRES
12 FREDERICA RD

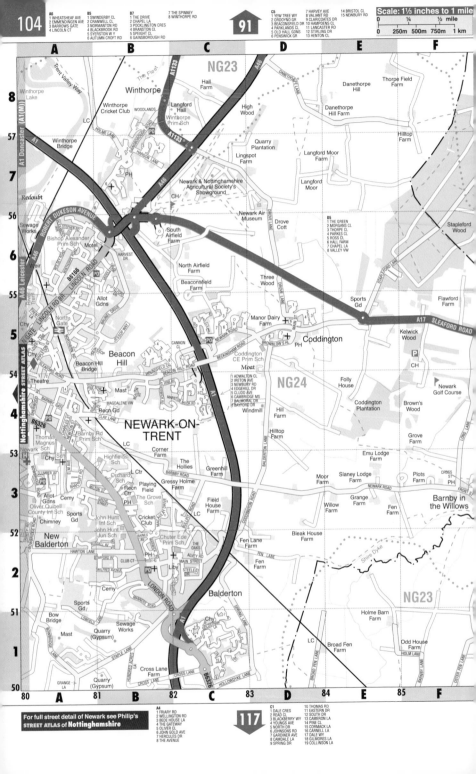

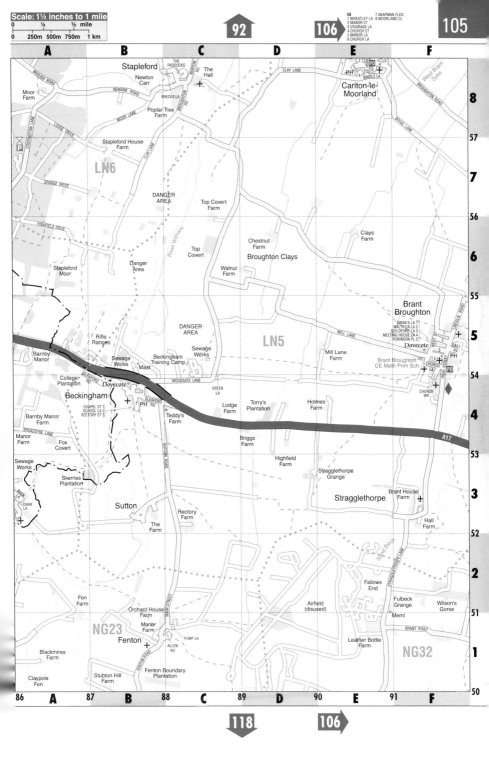

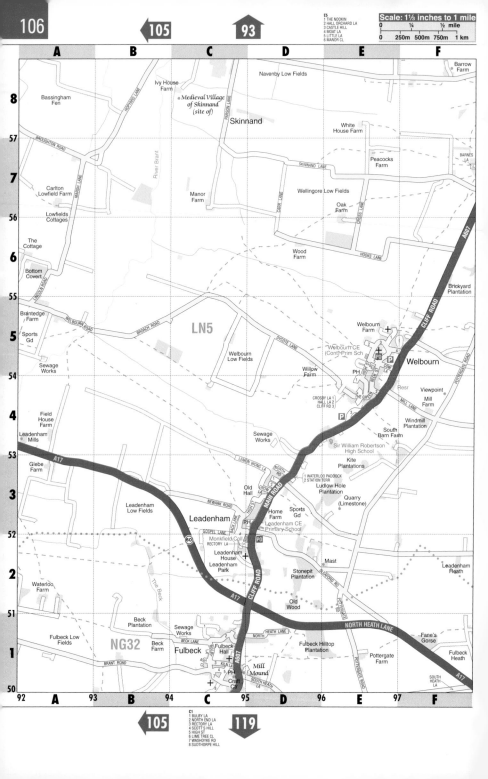

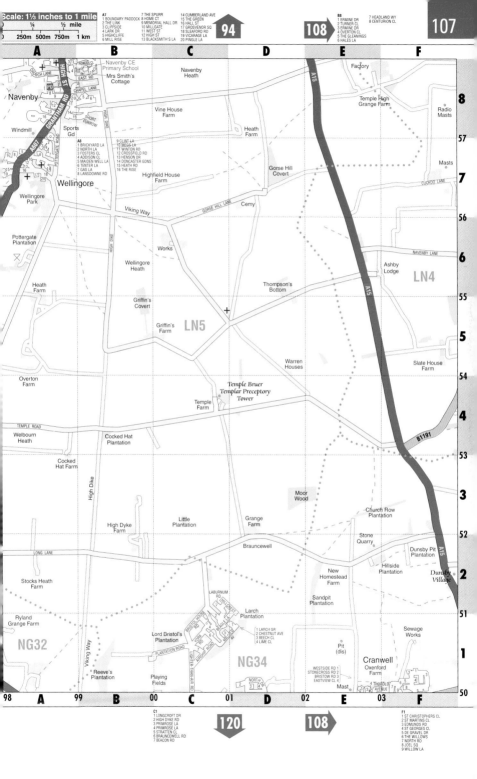

A7
1 BOUNDARY PADDOCK
2 THE LINK
3 CLIFFSIDE
4 LARK DR
5 HIGHCLIFFE
6 MILL RISE

7 THE SPURR
8 HOME CT
9 MEMORIAL HALL DR
10 MILLGATE
11 WEST ST
12 HIGH ST
13 BLACKSMITH'S LA

14 CUMBERLAND AVE
15 THE GREEN
16 HALL ST
17 GROSVENOR SQ
18 SLEAFORD RD
19 VICARAGE RD
20 PINGLE LA

94

B8
1 ERMINE DR
2 TURNER CL
3 ERMINE DR
4 OVERTON CL
5 THE GLEANINGS
6 HALES LA

7 HEADLAND WY
8 CENTURION CL

108

107

A   B   C   D   E   F

Navenby

Navenby CE Primary School

Mrs Smith's Cottage

Navenby Heath

Factory

Temple High Grange Farm

Radio Masts

8

Windmill

Vine House Farm

Heath Farm

Masts

57

Wellingore

A8
1 BRICKYARD LA
2 NORTH LA
3 FOSTERS CL
4 ADDISON CL
5 MAIDEN WELL LA
6 TENTER LA
7 GAS LA
8 LANSDOWNE RD

9 CLINT LA
10 MEGS LA
11 WINTON RD
12 CROSSFIELD RD
13 HENSON DR
14 DONCASTER GDNS
15 HEATH RD
16 THE RISE

Highfield House Farm

Gorse Hill Covert

Masts

7

Wellingore Park

Viking Way

GORSE HILL LANE

Cemy

CUCKOO LANE

56

Pottergate Plantation

Works

NAVENBY LANE

6

Heath Farm

Wellingore Heath

Thompson's Bottom

Ashby Lodge

LN4

55

Griffin's Covert

Griffin's Farm

LN5

5

Overton Farm

Warren Houses

Slate House Farm

54

Temple Bruer Templar Preceptory Tower

Temple Farm

4

Welbourn Heath

TEMPLE ROAD

Cocked Hat Plantation

B1191

53

Cocked Hat Farm

High Dike

Moor Wood

3

High Dyke Farm

Little Plantation

Grange Farm

Church Row Plantation

52

Long Lane

Braucewell

Stone Quarry

Dunsby Pit Plantation

Hillside Plantation

2

Stocks Heath Farm

New Homestead Farm

Dunsby Village

Ryland Grange Farm

NG32

Viking Way

Sandpit Plantation

51

Lord Bristol's Plantation

LABURNUM RD

Larch Plantation

1 LARCH GR
2 CHESTNUT AVE
3 BEECH CL
4 LIME CL

Sewage Works

Pit (dis)

Cranwell Oxenford Farm

1

Reeve's Plantation

PLANTATION ROAD

Playing Fields

NG34

WESTSIDE RD 1
STONECROSS RD 2
BRISTOW RD 3
EASTVIEW CL 4

Mast

THOROLD AVENUE

50

98   A   **99**   B   **00**   C   **01**   D   **02**   E   **03**   F

C1
1 LONGCROFT DR
2 HIGH DYKE RD
3 PRIMROSE LA
4 PRIMROSE LA
5 STRATTEN CL
6 BRAUNCEWELL RD
7 BEACON RD

F1
1 ST CHRISTOPHERS CL
2 ST MARTINS CL
3 EDMUNDS RD
4 ST GEORGES CL
5 DE GRAVEL DR
6 THE WILLOWS
7 NORTH RD
8 JOEL SQ
9 WILLOW LA

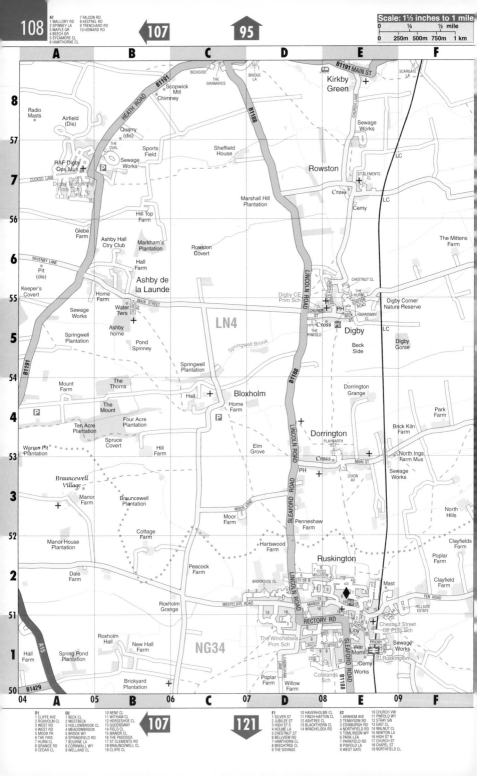

108

A7
1 MALLORY RD
2 SPINNEY LA
3 MAPLE GR
4 BEECH GR
5 SYCAMORE CL
6 HAWTHORNE CL

7 FALCON RD
8 KESTREL RD
9 TRENCHARD RD
10 HOWARD RD

107

95

Scale: 1⅓ inches to 1 mile
0   ¼   ½ mile
0 250m 500m 750m 1 km

8

57

7

56

6

55

5

54

4

53

3

52

2

51

1

50

A   B   C   D   E   F

B1191 MAIN ST
SCARGATE
LA

Kirkby
Green

BECKSIDE
THE
GRANARIES
BRIDGE
LA

Scopwick
Mill
Chimney

HEATH ROAD
B1191

Radio
Masts

Airfield
(Dis)

Quarry
(dis)

THE
OVAL

Sports
Field

Sheffield
House

Sewage
Works

Rowston

LC

RAF Digby
Ops Mus

P

Digby Tedder
Prim Sch

CUCKOO LANE

St Clements
Cl

Cross

Cemy

LC

Hill Top
Farm

Marshall Hill
Plantation

Glebe
Farm

Ashby Hall
Ctry Club

Markham's
Plantation

Rowston
Covert

The Mittens
Farm

NAVENBY LANE

Pit
(dis)

Hall
Farm

Ashby de
la Launde

LINCOLN ROAD

CHESTNUT CL

STATION
ROAD

NORTH CL

THE
HURN

HARROWBY
BECK
ST

Digby Corner
Nature Reserve

Keeper's
Covert

Home
Farm

MAIN STREET

Water
Twrs

Sewage
Works

Digby CE
Prim Sch

CHURCH
ST

PH

Cross

Digby

LC

B1191

Springwell
Plantation

Ashby
horne

Pond
Spinney

Springwell Brook

THE
PINFOLD

Beck
Side

Digby
Gorse

Springwell
Plantation

Dorrington
Grange

Mount
Farm

The
Thorns

Hall

Home
Farm

Bloxholm

Dorrington

Brick Kiln
Farm

Park
Farm

P

The
Mount

Four Acre
Plantation

Spruce
Covert

Hill
Farm

P

LINCOLN ROAD

Elm
Grove

PLAYGARTH
EST

Cross

MAIN ST

North Ings
Farm Mus

Sewage
Works

Warren Pit
Plantation

Brauncewell
Village

Manor
Farm

Brauncewell
Plantation

PH

DIXON
AV

North
Hills

Clayfields
Farm

Cottage
Farm

MOOR LANE

Moor
Farm

SLEAFORD ROAD

Penneshaw
Farm

Poplar
Farm

Manor House
Plantation

Hartswood
Farm

Ruskington

Clayfield
Farm

Dale
Farm

Peacock
Farm

BROOKSIDE CL

MILLVIEW

Mast

FEN ROAD

LINCOLN ROAD

HILLSIDE
ESTATE

Roxholm
Grange

WESTCLIFFE ROAD

MANOR
RD

RECTORY RD

Chestnut Street
CE Prim Sch

A15

Roxholm
Hall

New Hall
Farm

NG34

The Winchelsea
Prim Sch

LEASINGHAM
LANE

War
Mem

Priory

Sewage
Works

Ruskington

Hall
Farm

Spring Pond
Plantation

SLEAFORD ROAD

Cemy

Brickyard
Plantation

B1429

Poplar
Farm

Willow
Farm

Cotlands
Sch

B1188

LN4

04   A   05   B   06   C   07   D   08   E   09   F

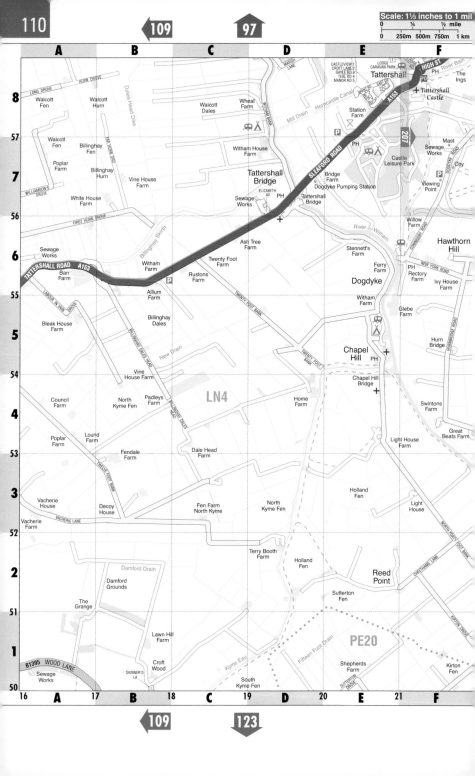

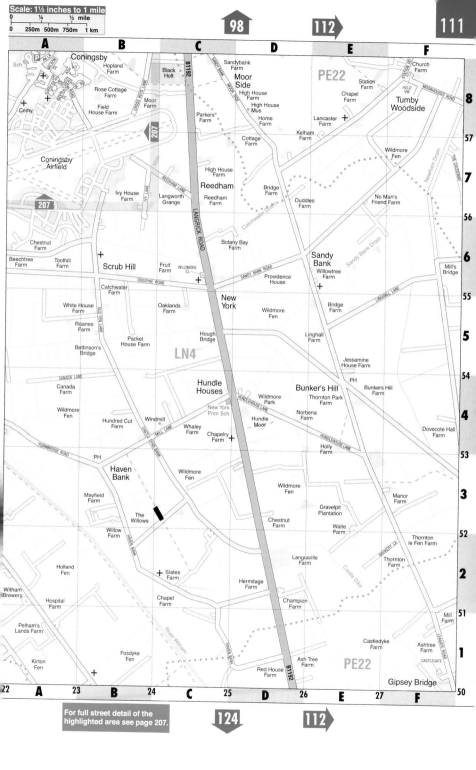

111
99

Scale: 1½ inches to 1 mile

0   ¼   ½   mile
0   250m 500m 750m 1 km

A   **B**   **C**   **D**   **E**   **F**

Wildmore Fen

Moorhouses Bridge

8

Moorhouses

Mill Farm

MOORHOUSES ROAD

Church Farm

57

Slate House Farm

Watkinson's Bridge

Chapel Farm

REVESBY BANK

Gaunt House

Glebe Farm

CHAPEL ROAD

Wheatsheaf Farm

Station Farm

PH

New Bolingbroke

B1183

KINGS

Medlam Bridge

Bowsers Farm

Hill's Folly

Coronation Farm

Musgrave's Farm

Musgrave's Bridge

Stickney Farm Park

FOLLY LANE

WEST FEN LANE

HALL LANE

Medlam House

Medlam Manor

STICKNEY LANE

Boston Farm

Stickney Bridge

Whyte Acre

7

Fen Farm

MAIN ROAD

MEDLAM LANE

Medlam

Sewage Works

MEDLAM CL

Medlam Farm

Glebe Farm

Stickney Grange

56

COLD HARBOUR LANE

MEDLAM LANE

Rainbow End

West Fen Farm

6

Royalty Farm

Carrington Park

War Meml

Chase House Farm

Carrington

55

Bramley Farm

Carrington House Farm

The Beeches

Skirbeck Farm

Chapel Farm

5

BEECHES LANE

Carrington Grange

West Houses

WESTHOUSES

Arkendale

Barkers Yard

54

LN4

Green Lane Farm

Westville Farm

Henley House

Sycamore Farm

War Memorial

4

B1183

PE22

Caudwell Farm

Tennant's Bridge

53

Mayfield Farm

Westville Farm

Short's Corner

SHORT'S CORNER

Harvestman Farm

Hakerley Bridge

Bishop's Farm

3

Bridge Farm

Wildmore Fen

West Fen Drain

WESTVILLE ROAD

Home Farm

White House Farm

CARRINGTON ROAD

Medlam Farm

Medlam Drain

52

2

Set Aside Farm

Primrose Hill Farm

Riggalls Farm

THACKER'S ROAD

Bradleys Farm

STAINT ROAD

Home Farm

51

Newham Farm

Grange Farm

Slate House Farm

Meml

Frithville

Works

Black House Farm

B1184

1

NEWHAM LANE

Newham

PH

Newham Drain

PEACOCK'S RD

Canister Bridge

CANISTER LANE

B1184

Black House Farm

Frithville Prim Sch

WESTVILLE ROAD

WEST FEN DRAIN BANK

HALE LANE

B1183 BOSTON ROAD

50

28   **A**   29   **B**   30   **C**   31   **D**   32   **E**   33   **F**

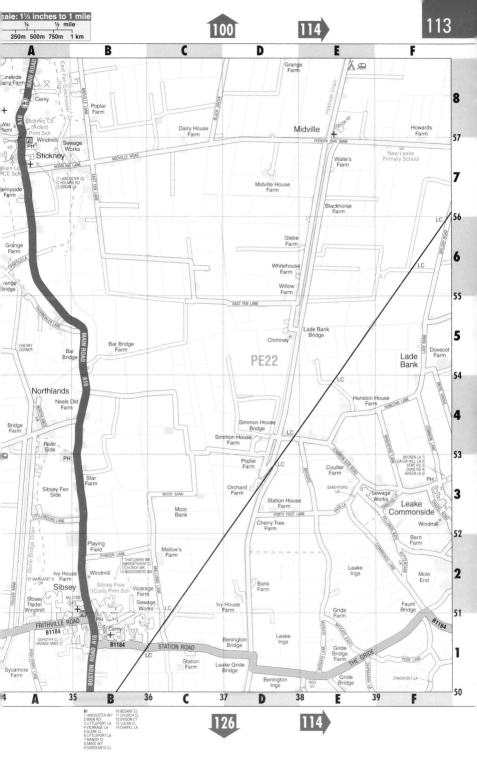

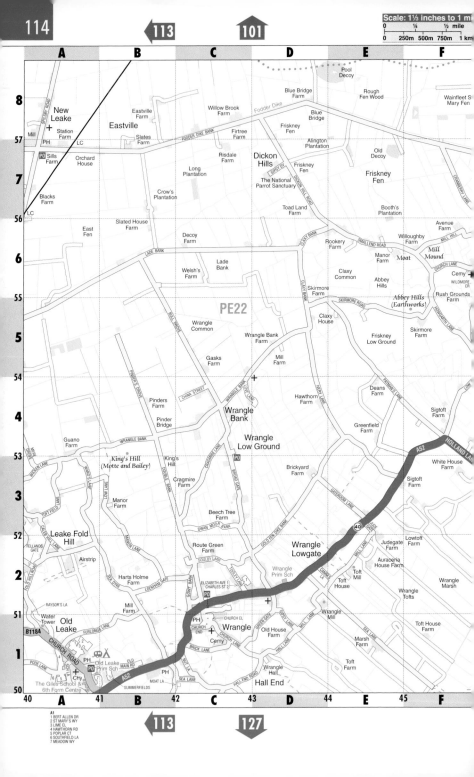

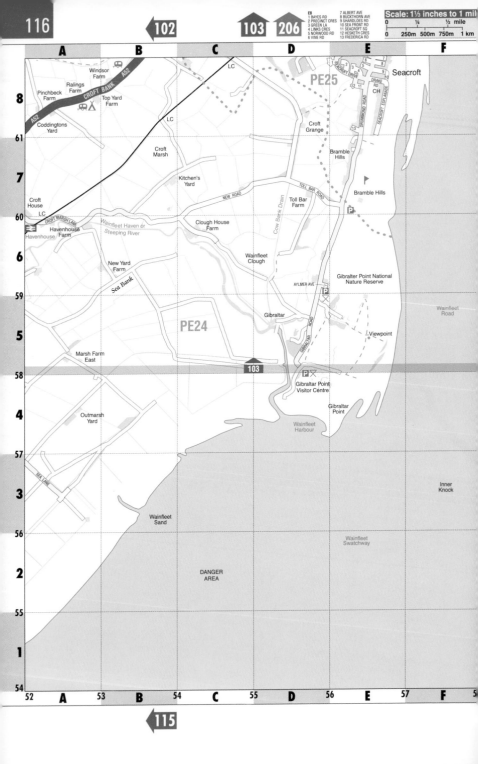

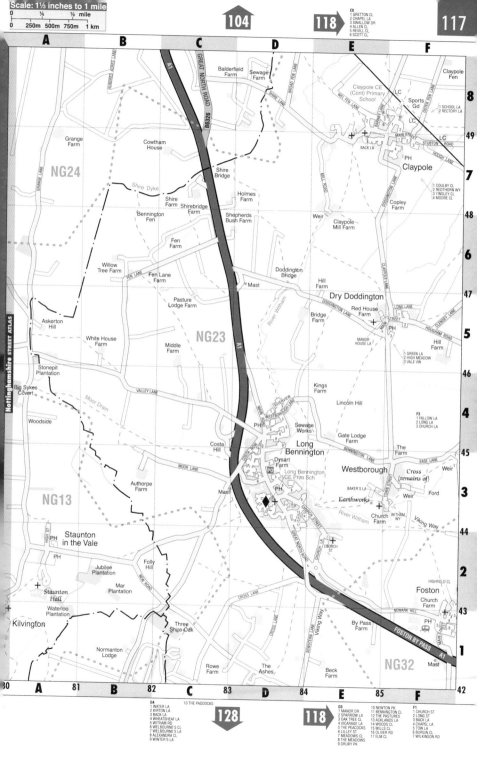

E8
1 GRETTON CL
2 CHAPEL LA
3 SWALLOW DR
4 ALLEN CL
5 REVILL CL
6 SCOTT CL

Scale: 1⅓ inches to 1 mile

0   ¼   ½ mile
0 250m 500m 750m 1 km

Nottinghamshire STREET ATLAS

Balderfield Farm
Sewage Farm
Claypole CE (Cont) Primary School
Claypole Fen
Sports Gd
LC
1 SCHOOL LA
2 RECTORY LA
LC
49
BACK LA
PH
Claypole
LC
STUBTON ROAD
HOUGH LANE
7
8

Grange Farm
NG24
Cowtham House
Shire Bridge
Shire Dyke
SHIRE LANE
BROAD FEN LANE
WEST FEN LANE
MAIN STREET
MAIN STREET
DODDINGTON LANE
1 COULBY CL
2 REDTHORN WY
3 TINSLEY CL
4 MOORE CL
Copley Farm

Shire Farm
Shirebridge Farm
Holmes Farm
Bennington Fen
Shepherds Bush Farm
Weir
Claypole Mill Farm
48

Fen Farm
WILLOW Tree Farm
Fen Lane Farm
Doddington Bridge
Hill Farm
Dry Doddington
LONG LANE
Hill Farm
6
47

Pasture Lodge Farm
Mast
MILL ROAD
River Witham
Bridge Farm
Red House Farm
MAIN STREET
PH
CLENBY LANE
HOUGHAM ROAD
5

Askerton Hill
NG23
White House Farm
Middle Farm
DODDINGTON LANE
MANOR HOUSE LA
1 GREEN LA
2 HIGH MEADOW
3 VALE VW
46

Stonepit Plantation
VALLEY LANE
Kings Farm
Lincoln Hill
F3
1 FALLOW LA
2 LONG LA
3 CHURCH LA
4

Big Sykes Covert
Moor Drain
RIVERVIEW
WESTBOROUGH LA
Sewage Works
Gate Lodge Farm
The Farm
45

Woodside
A1
Costa Hill
PH
Long Bennington
Dysart Farm
Long Bennington CE Prim Sch
BENNINGTON LANE
Westborough
Cross (remains of)
Weir
EASE LANE

MOOR LANE
Authorpe Farm
NG13
Mast
PH
BAKER'S LA
Earthworks
JOHN STREET
Weir
Ford
3

Staunton in the Vale
HIGH ST
PH
Jubilee Plantation
NEW ROAD
Folly Hill
CHURCH STREET
GREAT NORTH ROAD
Church Farm
River Witham
WITHAM WY
Viking Way
44

Staunton Hall
Mar Plantation
CHURCH ST
CHURCH LA
Foston
Church Farm
PH
NEWARK HILL
HIGHFIELD CL
2
43

Waterloo Plantation
Three Shire Oak
CROSS LANE
FOSTON BY PASS
A1
Mast
1

Kilvington
Normanton Lodge
Rowe Farm
The Ashes
VIKING WAY
Beck Farm
MAIN ST
NG32
42

A   81   B   82   C   83   D   84   E   85   F   42

D4
1 WATER LA
2 KIRTON LA
3 BACK LA
4 WHEATSHEAF LA
5 WITHAM RD
6 WELBOURNE'S CL
7 WELBOURNE'S LA
8 ALEXANDRA CL
9 WINTER'S LA

10 THE PADDOCKS

D3
1 MANOR DR
2 SPARROW LA
3 OAK TREE CL
4 VICARAGE LA
5 THE PEACOCKS
6 LILLEY ST
7 MEADOWS CL
8 THE MEADOWS
9 DRURY PK
10 NEWTON PK
11 BENNINGTON CL
12 THE PASTURES
13 ACKLANDS LA
14 WOODS CL
15 MILLS CL
16 OLIVER RD
17 ELM CL

F1
1 CHURCH ST
2 LONG ST
3 BACK LA
4 CHAPEL LA
5 TOW LA
6 BURGIN CL
7 WILKINSON RD

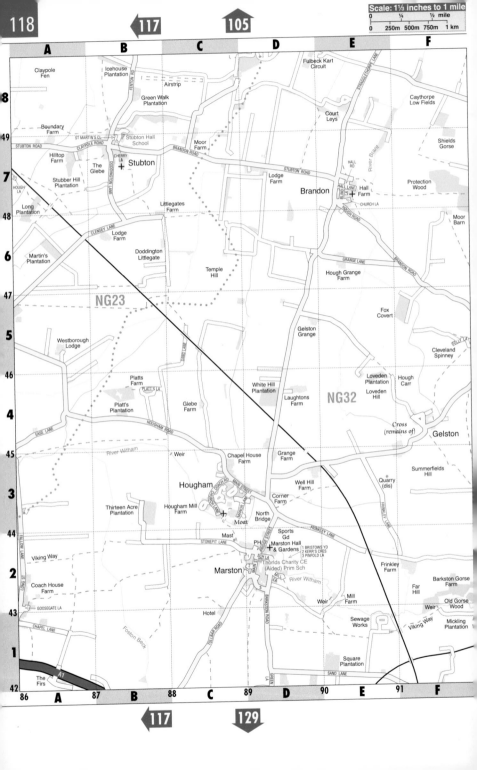

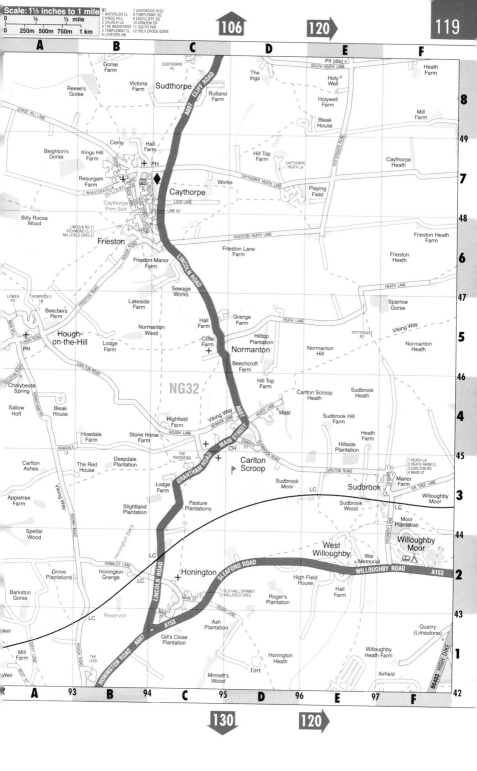

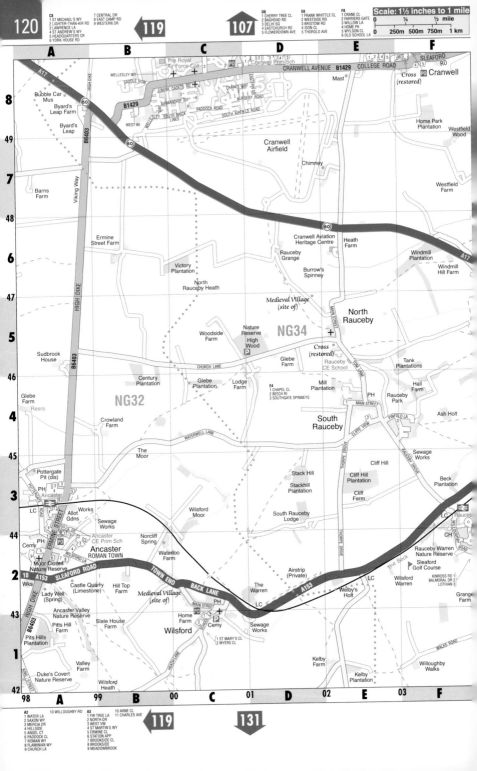

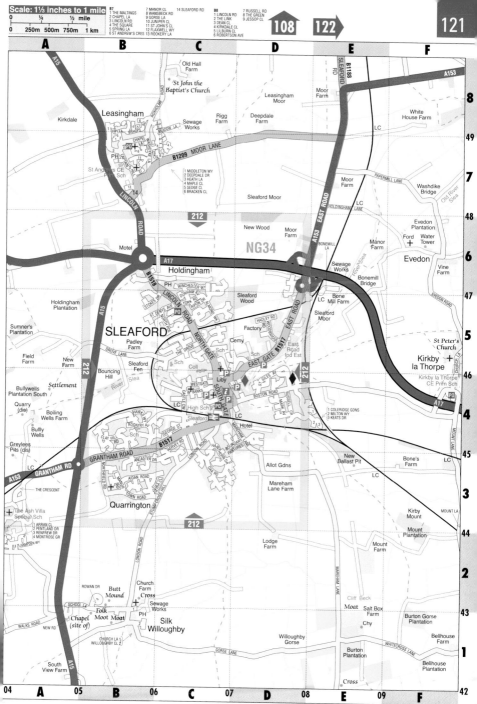

B7
1 THE MALTINGS
2 CHAPEL LA
3 LINCOLN RD
4 THE SQUARE
5 SPRING LA
6 ST ANDREW'S CRES

7 MANOR CL
8 WANGBECK RD
9 GORSE LA
10 JUNIPER CL
11 ST JOHN'S CL
12 FLAXWELL WY
13 ROOKERY LA

14 SLEAFORD RD

B8
1 LINCOLN RD
2 THE LINK
3 DEAN CL
4 KIRKDALE CL
5 LILBURN CL
6 ROBERTSON AVE

7 RUSSELL RD
8 THE GREEN
9 JESSOP CL

Old Hall Farm

St John the Baptist's Church

Leasingham Moor

Moor Farm

A153

B1188

White House Farm

Kirkdale

Leasingham

Rigg Farm

Deepdale Farm

Sewage Works

PAPERMILL LANE

Washdike Bridge

Old River Slea

St Andrew's CE Prim Sch

B1209 MOOR LANE

Moor Farm

LC LANE

LC

Evedon Plantation

1 MIDDLETON WY
2 DEEPDALE DR
3 HEATH LA
4 MAPLE CL
5 SEDGE CL
6 BRACKEN CL

Sleaford Moor

212

New Wood

Moor Farm

NG34

Motel

A17

Holdingham

B1518

LINCOLN ROAD

A15

Holdingham Plantation

Sumner's Plantation

Field Farm

New Farm

212

Bouncing Hill

Bullywells Plantation South

Quarry (dis)

Boiling Wells Farm

Bully Wells

Greylees Pits (dis)

A153 GRANTHAM RD

THE CRESCENT

The Ash Villa Special Sch

1 ARRAN CL
2 PENTLAND DR
3 RENFREW DR
4 MONTROSE GR

5 HAMPDEN WY

Padley Farm

SLEAFORD

Sleaford Fen

The DRIVE

DROVE LANE

River Slea

Sch

Coll

WESTGATE

Sch

Sleaford High Sch

LC

Settlement

NORTH GATE

PO

Cemy

Sch

Sch

Factory

HADLEY RD

Sleaford Wood

Sleaford Moor

EAST ROAD

A153

Bonemill LA

Sewage Works

River Slea

Bonemill Bridge

Bone Mill Farm

LC

Manor Farm

Ford

Water Tower

Evedon

Vine Farm

St Peter's Church

Kirkby la Thorpe

Kirkby la Thorpe CE Prim Sch

East Road Ind Est

EAST GATE B1517

212

A17

PO

Libby

P

SOUTH GATE

Hotel

BESSELS WY

BOSTON ROAD

RUSSELL DR

1 COLERIDGE GDNS
2 MILTON WY
3 KEATS DR

New Ballast Pit

Bone's Farm

LC

MOUNT LANE

1 2 3

Sch

HAWKS WY

CLAY HILL

ROOKERY AV

B1517 KIRKBY RD

B1518 HARVEY RD

LONDON RD

Allot Gdns

Mareham Lane Farm

Kirby Mount

Mount Plantation

GRANTHAM ROAD

NORTHFIELD RD

ANCASTER DR

AIDAN ROAD

TOWN ROAD

Quarrington

212

Lodge Farm

MAREHAM LANE

Mount Farm

Mount Plantation

MOUNT LA

ROWAN DR

SCHOOL LA

Butt Mound

Church Farm Cross

Chapel (site of)

Folk Moot Moat

PH

Silk Willoughby

Sewage Works

Cliff Beck

Moat

Salt Box Farm

Chy

Burton Gorse Plantation

Bellhouse Farm

WALKS ROAD

NEW RD

A15

South View Farm

CHURCH LA 1
WILLOUGHBY CL 2

GORSE LANE

Willoughby Gorse

WHITECROSS LANE

Burton Plantation

Cross

Bellhouse Plantation

132 122

For full street detail of the highlighted area see page 212.

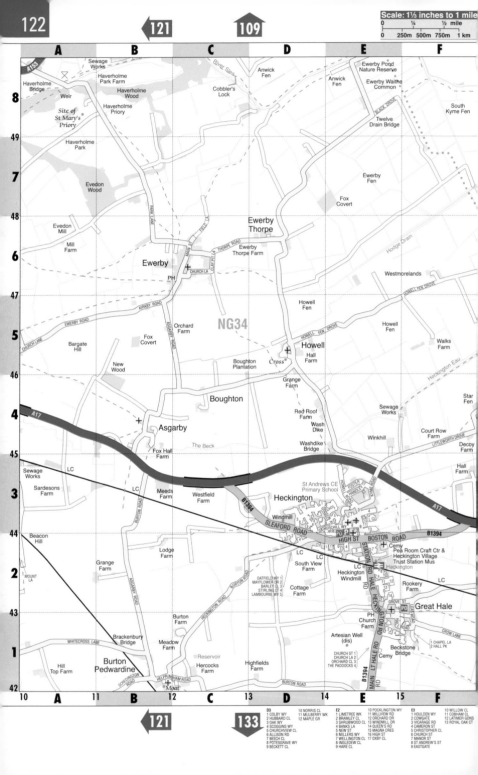

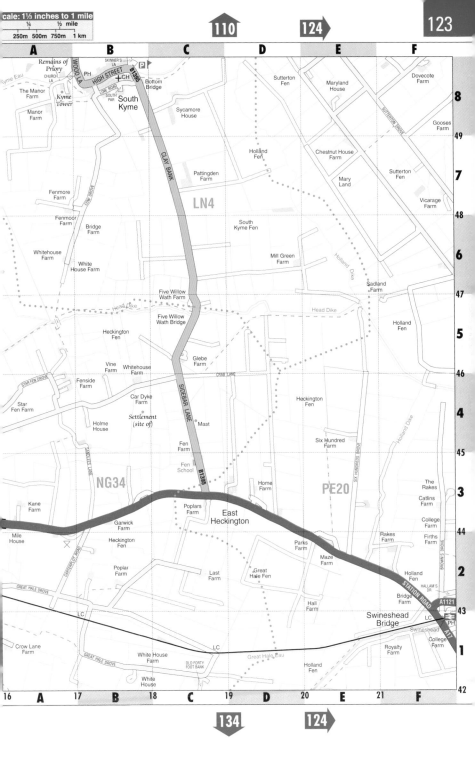

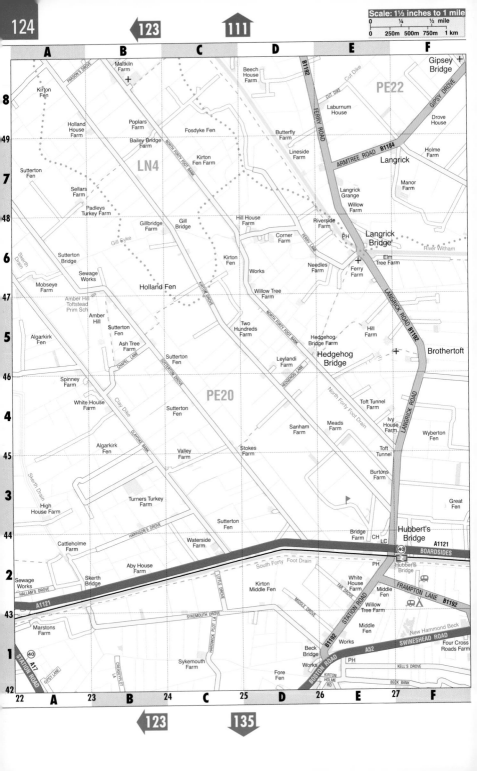

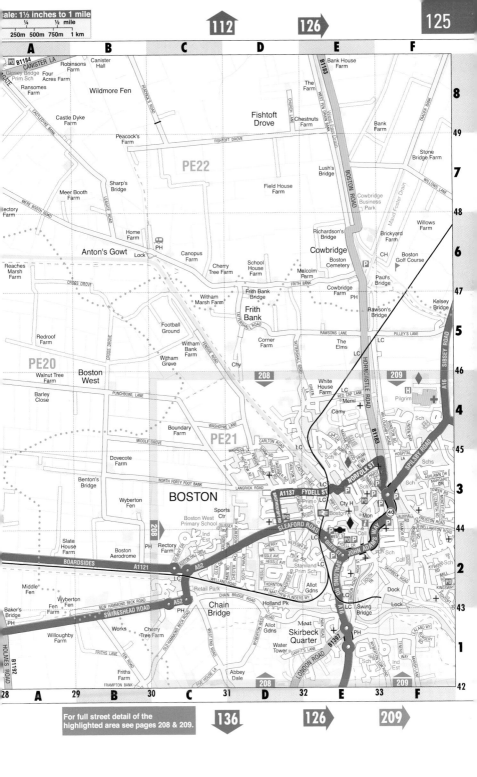

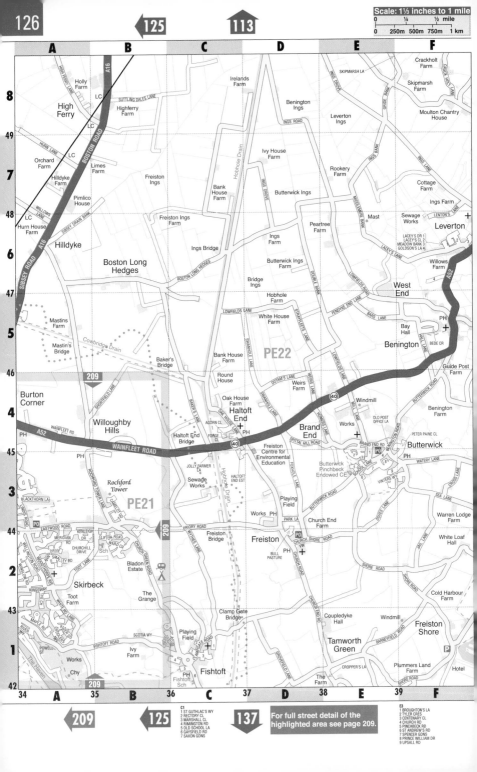

Scale: 1⅓ inches to 1 mile

| 0 | ¼ | ½ | mile |

| 0 | 250m | 500m | 750m | 1 km |

A B C D E F

8

Sewage
Works

Whitehouse
Farm

Sea
Bank

Toft
Marsh

Shaw Lane

Sunnyville

Home
Farm

Moat
House

Leake
Hurn's
End

Green
Farm

Sailor's
Home

49

Heronshaw
Hall

Sports
Ctr

Hampton House
Farm

Bowsers
Farm

Moat

HAMPTON LANE

PH

Works

Leverton
L ctr

7

War
Memorial

Beech Tree
Farm

Leverton
Outgate

Old Lodge
Farm

Lodge
Farm

48

Leverton
Highgate

Sycamore
Farm

Burton
Farm

40

The
Grange

Hall
Farm

6

Leverton
Lucasgate

47

PE22

5

Churchway

Benington
Sea End

46

Glebe
Farm

4

Old House
Farm

Maltbys
Farm

CROWHALL LANE

45

3

THE   WASH

44

P

Butterwick
Low

2

Freiston Shore
Nature Reserve

43

1

40 A 41 B 42 C 43 D 44 E 45 F 42

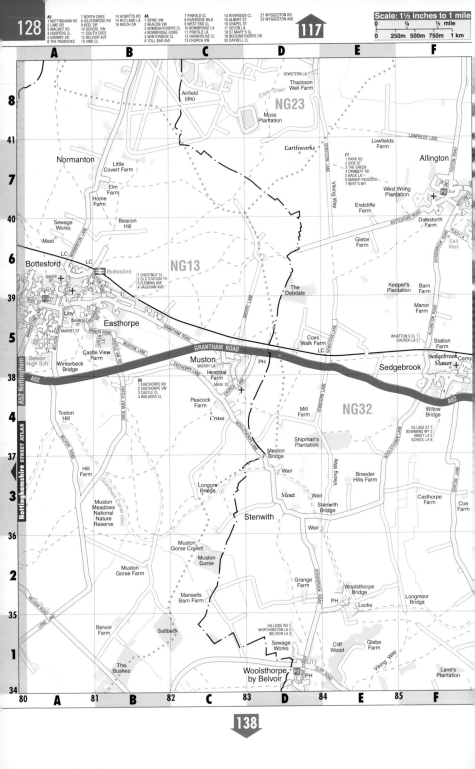

Scale: 1⅓ inches to 1 mile

0   ¼   ½   mile
0   250m 500m 750m 1 km

A5
1 NOTTINGHAM RD
2 LIME GR
3 WALNUT RD
4 HOOPERS CL
5 GRANBY DR
6 THE PADDOCKS

7 NORTH CRES
8 SILVERWOOD RD
9 KEEL DR
10 SCHOOL VW
11 SOUTH CRES
12 BELVOIR AVE
13 VINE CL

14 HOWITTS RD
15 RUTLAND LA
16 BEECH DR

A6
1 SPIRE VW
2 BEACON VW
3 WIMBISHTHORPE CL
4 BOWBRIDGE GDNS
5 WINTERBECK CL
6 TOLL BAR AVE

7 PINFOLD CL
8 RIVERSIDE WLK
9 WEST END CL
10 BOWBRIDGE FARM
11 PINFOLD LA
12 FARMHOUSE CL
13 CHURCH VW

14 RIVERSIDE CL
15 ALBERT ST
16 CHAPEL ST
17 DEVON LA
18 ST MARY'S CL
19 BECKINGTHORPE DR
20 DAYBELL CL

21 WYGGESTON RD
22 WYGGESTON AVE

NG23

SEWSTERN LA

Thackson Well Farm

Ease Drain

Airfield (dis)

Moss Plantation

Normanton

Little Covert Farm

Elm Farm

Home Farm

Beacon Hill

Sewage Works

Mast

LC

LC

Bottesford

Bottesford

NG13

1 CHESTNUT CL
2 OLD STATION YD
3 FLEMING AVE
4 VAUGHAN AVE

Queen

PO

Liby

High St

Market St

Eastthorpe

Castle View Farm

Winterbeck Bridge

Belvoir High Sch

A52 Nottingham

Toston Hill

Hill Farm

Grantham Canal (dis)

Muston Meadows National Nature Reserve

Muston Gorse Farm

Belvoir Farm

Saltbeck

The Bushes

Earthworks

Lowfields Farm

Allington

F7
1 PARK RD
2 SIDE ST
3 THE GREEN
4 TAMBERT RD
5 BACK LA
6 MANOR PADDOCK
7 BERT'S WY

West Wong Plantation

Endcliffe Farm

Glebe Farm

The Debdale

Keeper's Plantation

Dalesorth Farm

Salt Well

Manor Farm

Barn Farm

WHATTON'S CL 1
CHURCH LA 2

Coxs Walk Farm

LC

GRANTHAM ROAD

Muston

SKERRY LA

Hospital Farm

MAIN ST

Peacock Farm

Cross

B5
1 EASTTHORPE RD
2 EASTTHORPE VW
3 CASTLE CL
4 WALKERS CL

PH

Sedgebrook

Station Farm

Sedgebrook Manor

Cemy

A52

Willow Bridge

NG32

Mill Farm

Shipman's Plantation

Muston Bridge

Weir

Longore Bridge

Moat

Weir

Stenwith Bridge

Stenwith

Weir

Viking Way

Breeder Hills Farm

VILLAGE ST 1
BOWMANS WY 2
ABBEY LA 3
SCHOOL LA 4

Casthorpe Farm

Coe Farm

Muston Gorse Covert

Muston Gorse

Mansells Barn Farm

Grange Farm

Woolsthorpe Bridge

PH

Locks

Longmoor Bridge

HILLSIDE RD 1
WORTHINGTON LA 2
BELVOIR LA 3

Sewage Works

Woolsthorpe by Belvoir

PO

PH

Cliff Wood

Glebe Farm

Viking Way

Lane's Plantation

Nottinghamshire STREET ATLAS

A52 Nottingham

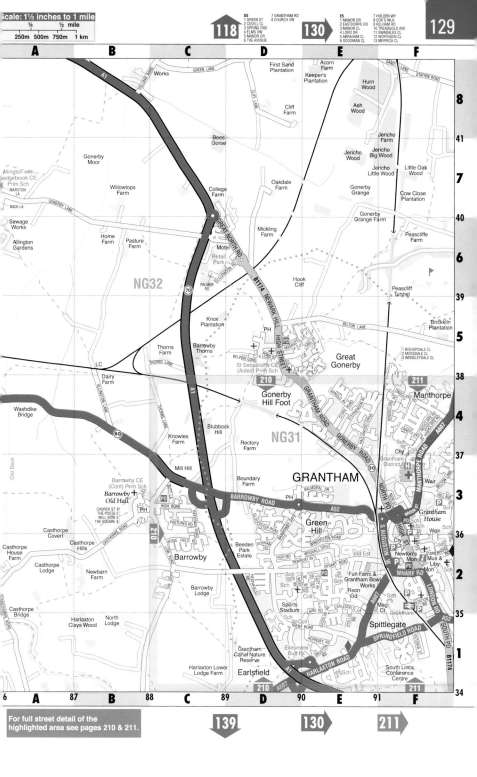

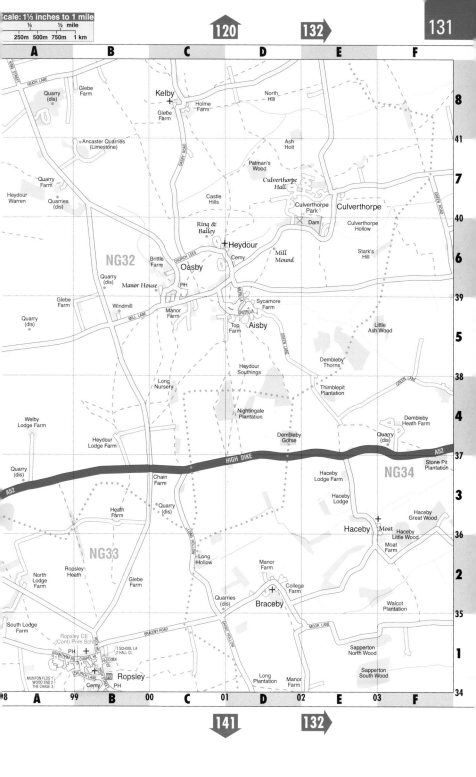

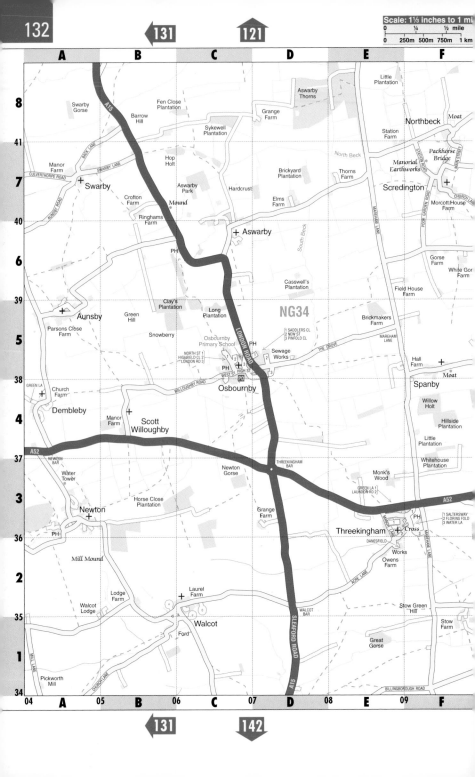

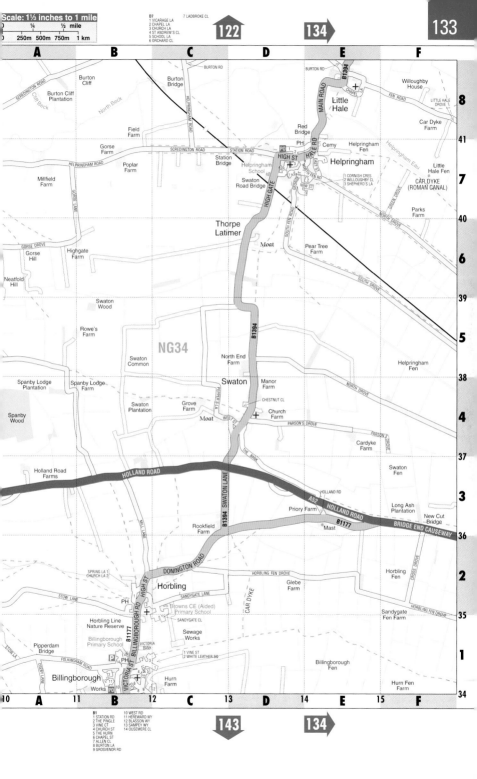

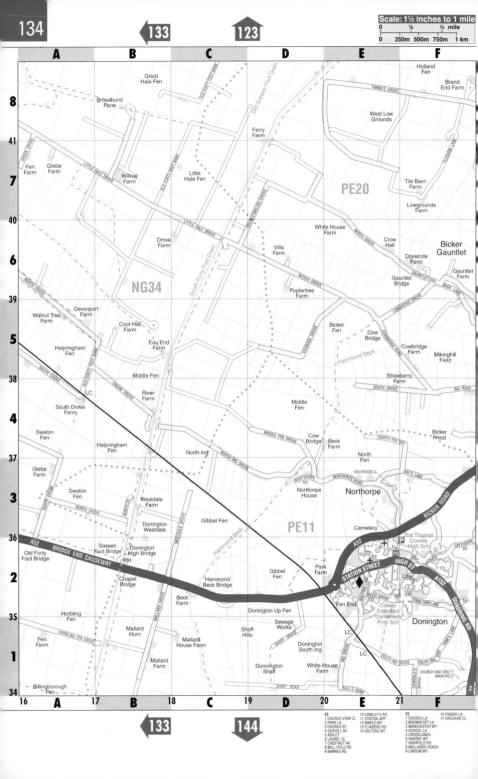

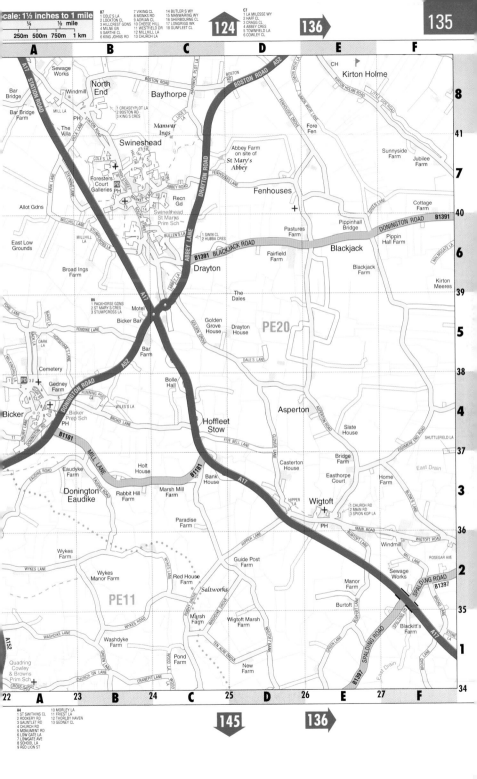

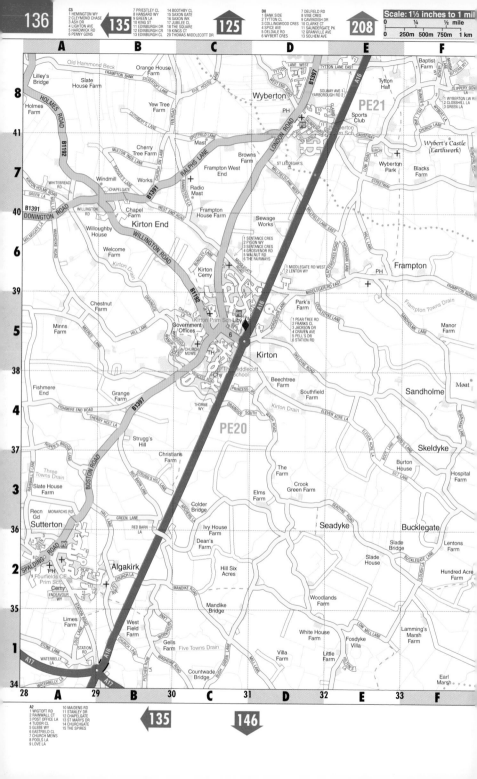

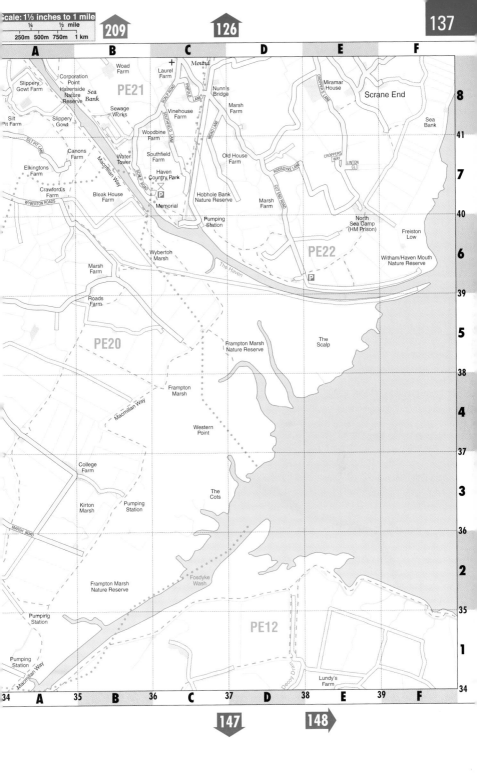

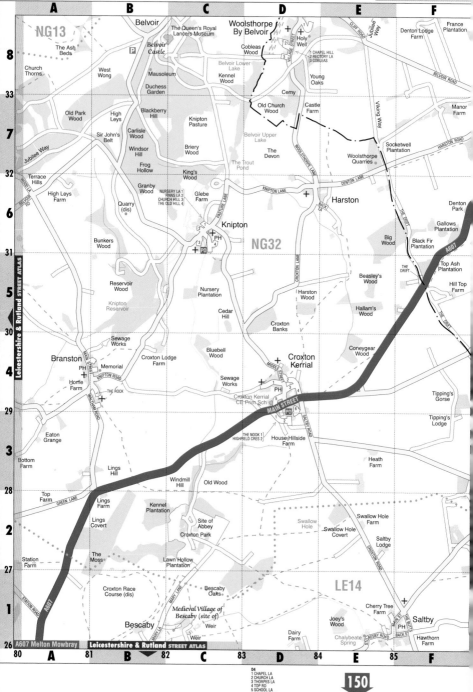

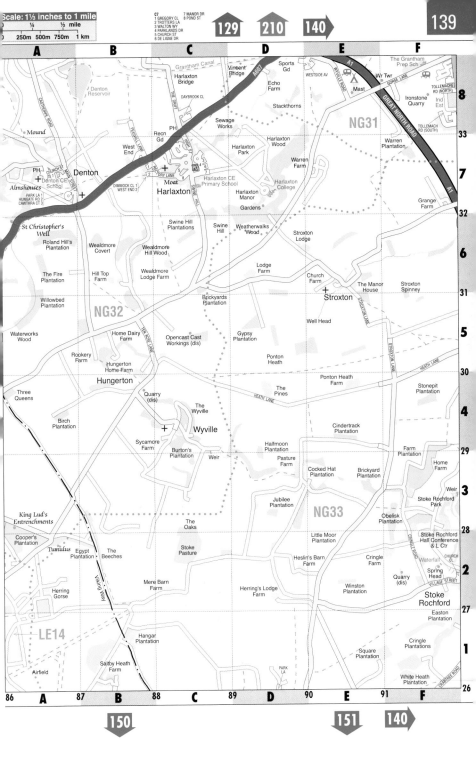

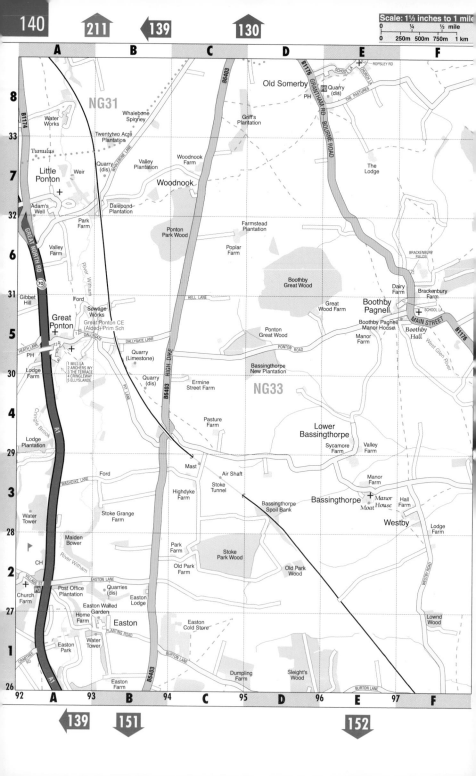

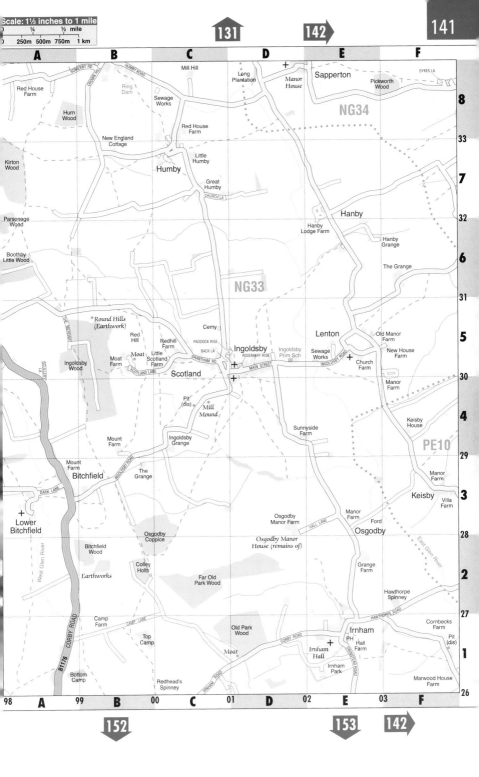

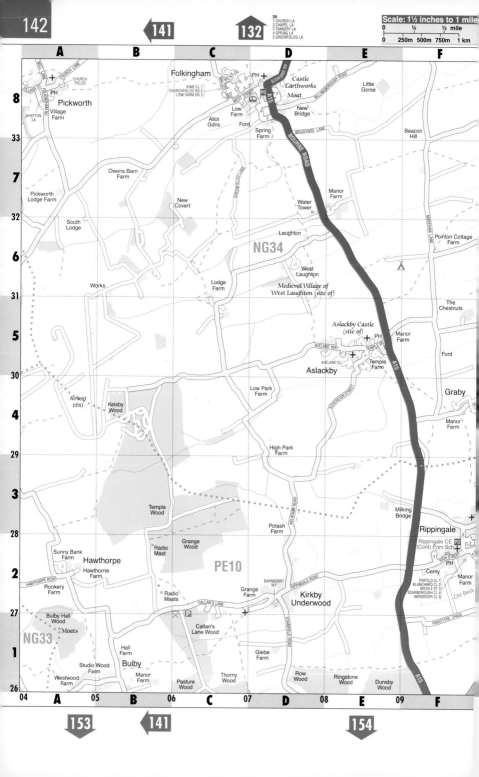

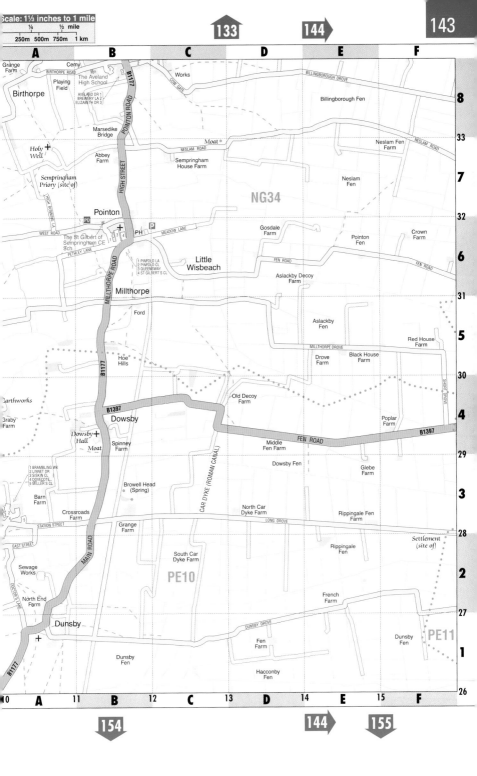

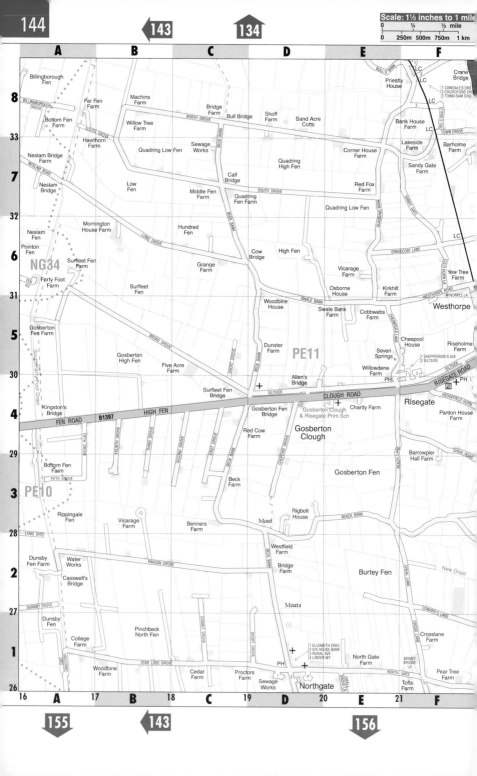

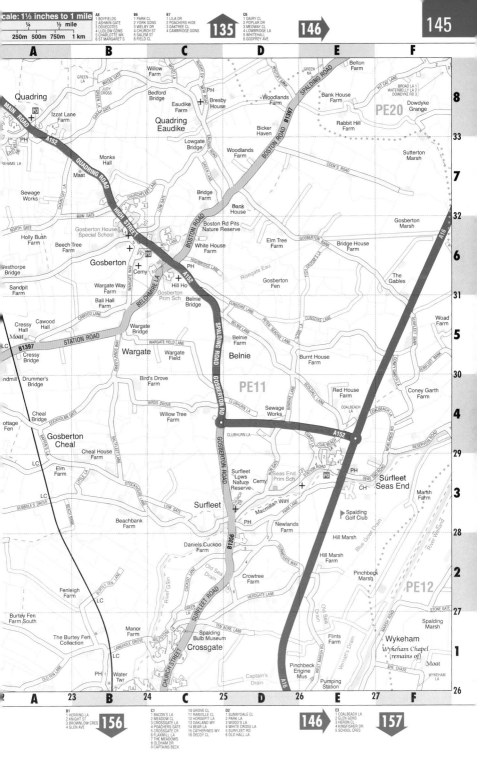

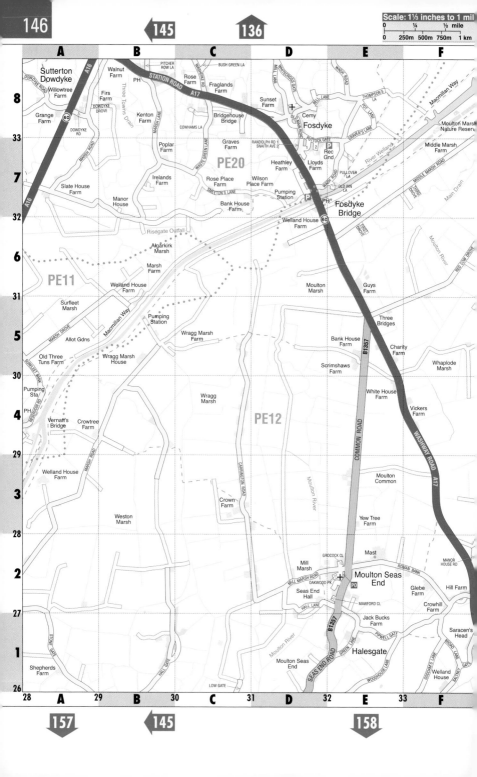

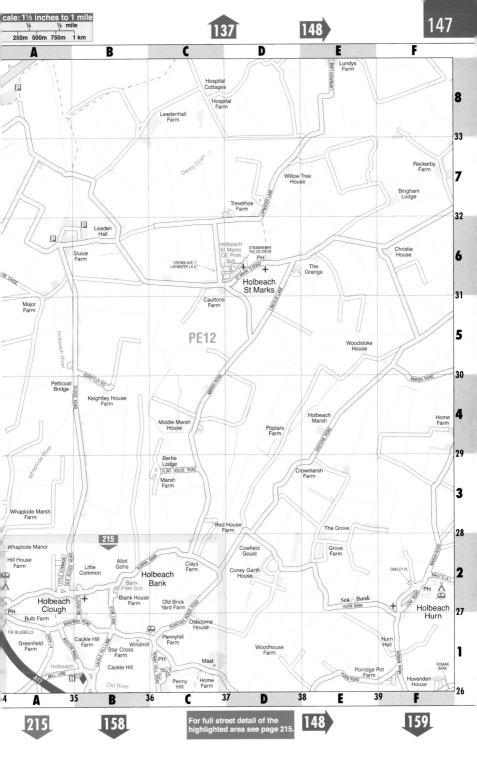

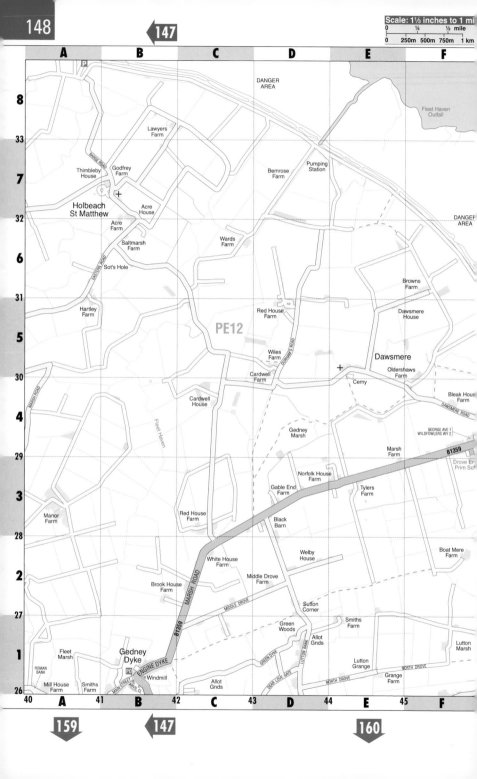

Scale: 1½ inches to 1 mi

DANGER
AREA

Fleet Haven
Outfall

Lawyers
Farm

Bemrose
Farm

Pumping
Station

Thimbleby
House

Godfrey
Farm

Holbeach
St Matthew

Acre
House

Acre
Farm

DANGER
AREA

Saltmarsh
Farm

Wards
Farm

Sot's Hole

Browns
Farm

Hartley
Farm

Dawsmere
House

Red House
Farm

PE12

Wiles
Farm

Dawsmere

Cardwell
Farm

Oldershaws
Farm

Cemy

Cardwell
House

Bleak House
Farm

Fleet Haven

DAWSMERE ROAD

Gedney
Marsh

GEORGE AVE 1
WILDFOWLERS WY 2

Marsh
Farm

B1359

Drove End
Prim Sch

Norfolk House
Farm

Manor
Farm

Gable End
Farm

Tylers
Farm

Red House
Farm

Black
Barn

Boat Mere
Farm

Welby
House

White House
Farm

MARSH ROAD

Middle Drove
Farm

Brook House
Farm

MIDDLE DROVE

Sutton
Corner

Smiths
Farm

Lutton
Marsh

B1359

GREEN DYKE

Green
Woods

Allot
Gnds

LUTTON BANK

Fleet
Marsh

Gedney
Dyke

ENGINE DYKE

Lutton
Grange

Lutton
Grange

NORTH DROVE

ROMAN
BANK

PO

Windmill

MAIN STREET

Allot
Gnds

BEAR DYKE GATE

NORTH DROVE

Grange
Farm

Mill House
Farm

Smiths
Farm

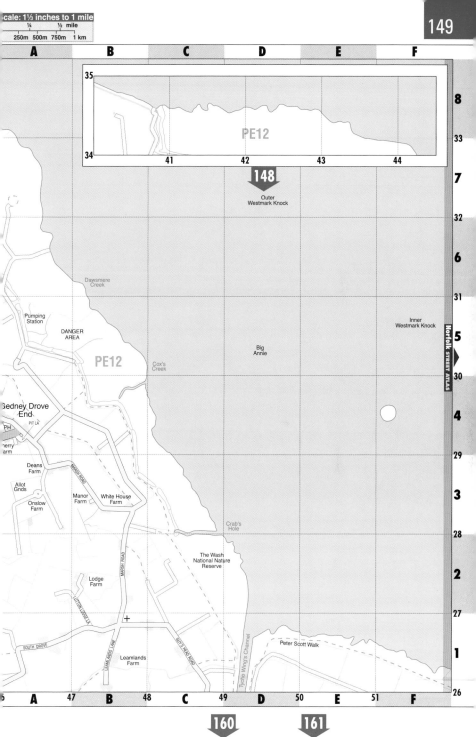

scale: 1⅓ inches to 1 mile

¼   ½ mile

250m   500m   750m   1 km

A   B   C   D   E   F

35

PE12

34

41   42   43   44

148

8

33

7

Outer
Westmark Knock

32

6

Dawsmere
Creek

31

Inner
Westmark Knock

Pumping
Station

DANGER
AREA

PE12

Big
Annie

Cox's
Creek

5

30

Gedney Drove
End

PH

PIT LA

4

29

herry
arm

Deans
Farm

Allot
Gnds

Onslow
Farm

MARSH ROAD

Manor
Farm

White House
Farm

Crab's
Hole

3

28

The Wash
National Nature
Reserve

MARSH ROAD

Lodge
Farm

2

27

LUTTON LODGE LA

SOUTH DROVE

LEAM ABBS LANE

BULL'S HEAD ROAD

Tycho Wing's Channel

Peter Scott Walk

Leamlands
Farm

1

26

A   47   B   48   C   49   D   50   E   51   F

Norfolk STREET ATLAS

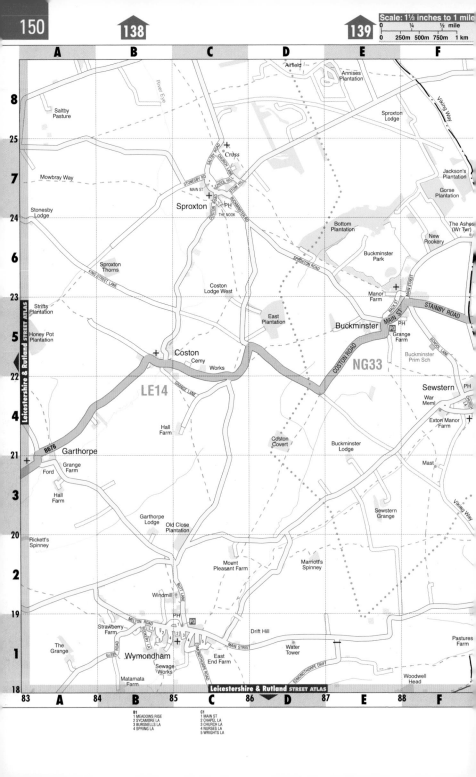

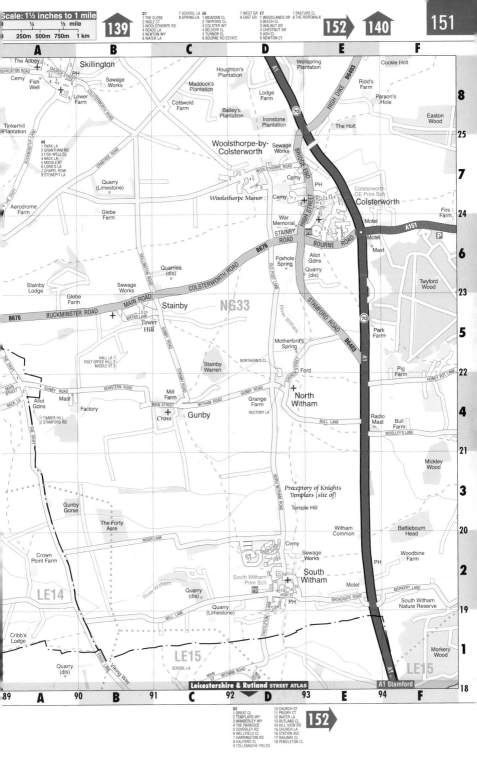

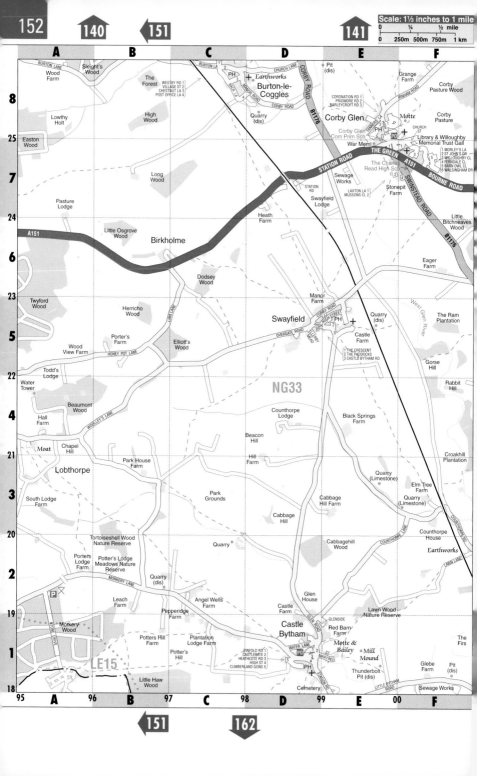

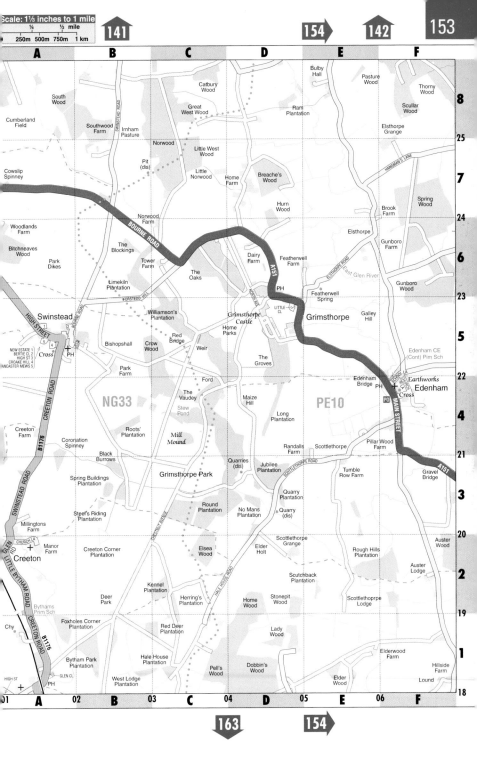

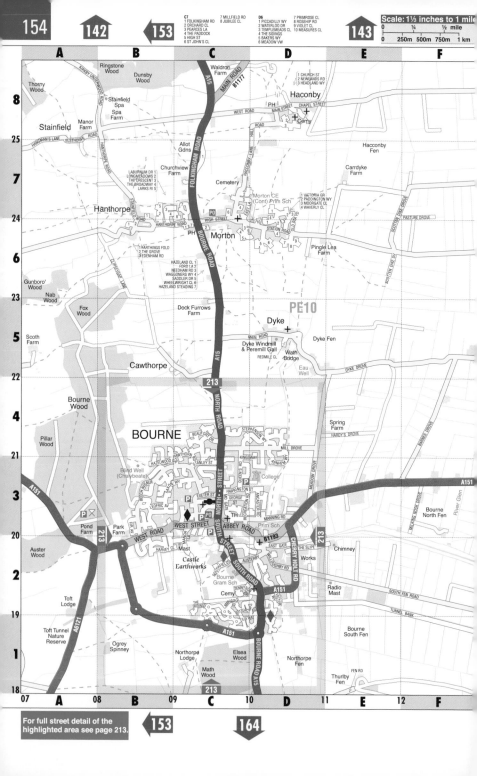

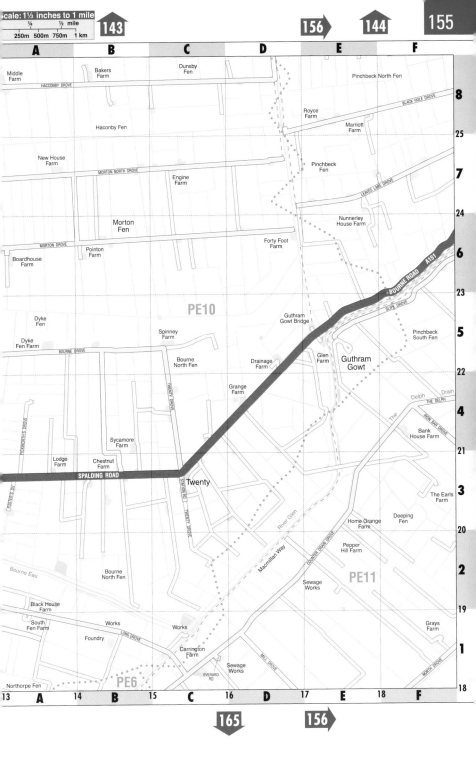

A **B** **C** **D** **E** **F**

Middle Farm

Bakers Farm

Dunsby Fen

Pinchbeck North Fen

HACONBY DROVE

8

Royce Farm

Haconby Fen

Marriott Farm

25

New House Farm

MORTON NORTH DROVE

Engine Farm

Pinchbeck Fen

7

LEAVES LAKE DROVE

Morton Fen

Nunnerley House Farm

24

MORTON DROVE

Pointon Farm

Forty Foot Farm

A151

BOURNE ROAD

6

Boardhouse Farm

23

SLIPE DROVE

PE10

Dyke Fen

Spinney Farm

Guthram Gowt Bridge

Pinchbeck South Fen

5

Dyke Fen Farm

BOURNE DROVE

Bourne North Fen

Drainage Farm

Glen Farm

Guthram Gowt

22

Delph Drain

THE DELPH

Grange Farm

The

IRON BAR DROVE

4

PICKWORTH'S DRIVE

Sycamore Farm

Bank House Farm

21

Lodge Farm

Chestnut Farm

SPALDING ROAD

STATION RD

Twenty

River Glen

The Earls Farm

3

FOSTER'S DV.

Home Grange Farm

Deeping Fen

20

Bourne Eau

Bourne North Fen

Macmillan Way

COUNTER DRAIN DROVE

Pepper Hill Farm

PE11

2

Black House Farm

Sewage Works

19

South Fen Farm

Works

LONG DROVE

Works

Grays Farm

1

Foundry

Carrington Farm

MILL DROVE

NORTH DROVE

EVERARD RD

Sewage Works

Northorpe Fen

PE6

18

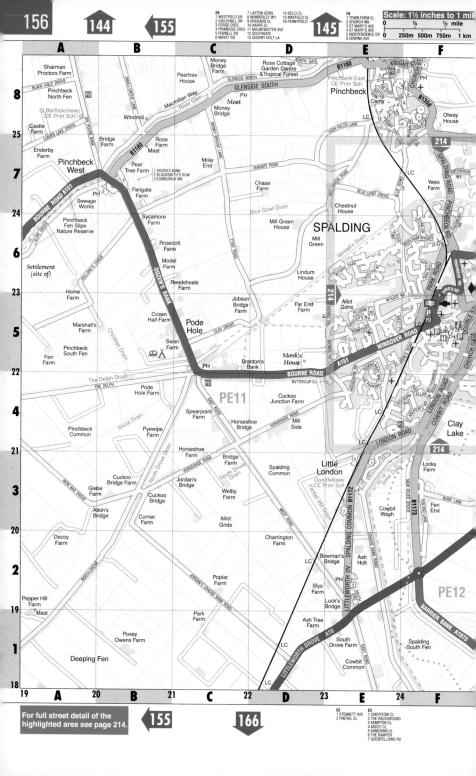

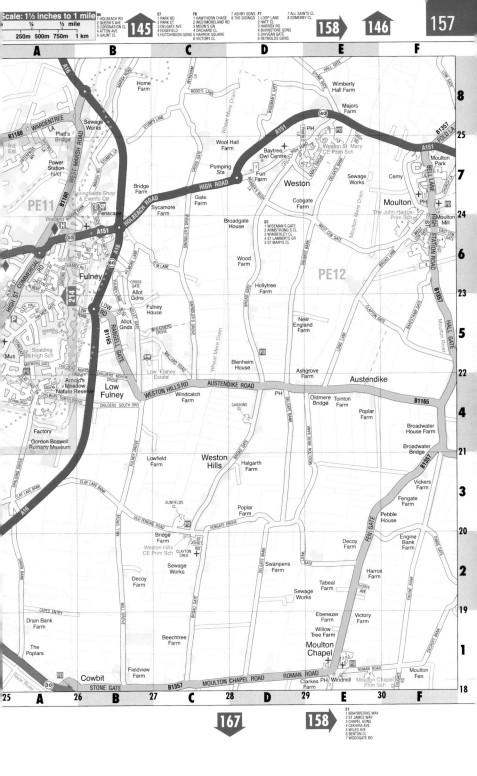

160

148

159

149

Scale: 1⅛ inches to 1 mile

0   ¼   ½ mile
0   250m 500m 750m 1 km

A8
1 DEAR LOVE GATE
2 ROPER'S GATE
3 CONGREVES CL
4 BACK LA
5 SCHOOL LA
6 MARRIOT'S GATE

7 BARHOLME AVE
8 PUDDINGPOKE LA
9 COLLEYSGATE
10 ST NICHOLAS WY
11 VICARAGE LA
12 OLD VICARAGE LA
13 CRISPIN CL

14 RICHARD BUSBY WY
15 CHURCH GDNS

Lutton

Cemy

St Nicholas
Prim Sch

**Lutton
Gowts**

216

Hill
Top
Windmill

Monmouth
House

Monmouth Lane

Maze
Farm

South Drove

Old Leam
Farm

Lutton Leam

King's Creek

Rookery Road

Guy's Head Road

Guy's Head
RD

Guys Hea
Farm

Curlew Lodge
Farm

Curlew Lodge Lane

The Peele
School

Eagle
Plantation

Butterfly and
Falconry Park

**Little
London**

Allot
Gdns

Woad Lane

Avenue
Farm

King John
Farm

New House
Farm

Westmere House
Farm

Avenue Farm Road

Guys Head Road

Windmill

Common
Farm

Hospital Drove

Sewage
Works

Westmere
Farm

Westmere Creek

Bridge
Farm

Petts Lane

Nene Outfall Cut

East Bank

PE12

Liby

Cemy

PH

Chimney

Bridge Road

**Little
Sutton**

Grove
Farm

The Beeches

Allot
Gdns

**Port Sutton
Bridge**

Long
Sutton

Windmill

Chimney

A17

Mast

Hundreds Lane

Bridge Road

A17

Westmere
Prim Sch

Sewage
Works

CH

Sutton Bridge
Golf Course

East Bank
Farm

Carnoustie
CT

Seagate
Farm

Vicarage Lane

A1101

Crosby Row 1
Granville Terr 2

Prince's St

PO

Cross Keys
Bridge

**Sutton
Crosses**

216

Winter's Lane

Woodward's Lane

Hundreds Lane

Piccaver
Farm

Home
Farm

Hospital Drove

Fields
Farm

Allot
Gdns

Railway Lane

PH

Gimmel's
Gate

Allot
Gdns

Cross
Gate

Willow Tree
Farm

Markillie Lane

Shaws Lane

Peterspoint

Peterspoint
Farm

Petts Lane

Chalk Lane

Grange
Farm

Spendla's Lane

Allot Gdns

North Road

South Holland
Lodge

South Holland Main Drain

South Holland
Bridge

Sewage
Works

Centenary Wy

Sharpe's
Bridge

Gipsy Lane

Cross
Rd

Tydd St Mary's
Marsh

Gibbons
Farm

New
Marsh

Woodmill
Bank

Strawberry
Hall

Cross Gate

Greenside Lane

Allot Gdns

River Nene

Nene Way

Nene Outfall Cut

**Tydd
St Mary**

Tydd St Mary CE
(Aided) Prim Sch

PH

Common Way

Grange
Farm

Marsh Road

Long Road

Gunthorpe
Farm

Holme
Farm

Draw Dike

Willows
Cl

Church Way

Rectory Rd

PE13

A1101 Main Road

Middle Road

Long House
Farm

Front Rd

Gunthorpe Road

PE14

Marsh
Farm

World's
End Rd

Hix's La

Church La

Allot
Gdns

For full street detail of the
highlighted area see page 216.

159

170

E4
1 WITHINGTON ST
2 CHESTNUT TERR
3 KENT CL
4 PEBBLE CL
5 HARRIET CL
6 LONGDON CL
7 DARWIN CL
8 TWO SISTERS CL
9 MOUNT TUMBLEDOWN CL

10 GOOSE GN
11 ANNE RD
12 CHARLES RD
13 ST MATTHEW'S DR
14 ALLENBY'S CHASE
15 ROYAL CL
16 GAS HO LA
17 QUEEN ST
18 KING ST
19 MILL LA

20 WHARF ST
21 CHURCH ST
22 CHURCH GATE
23 FLINT GATE

F4
1 NENE MDWS
2 CUSTOMHOUSE ST
3 LIME ST
4 BRIDGE RD
5 HIGH ST
6 BRIDGE RD
7 TOOKILL'S LA
8 NENELANDS

A B C D E F

Norfolk STREET ATLAS

Peter Scott Walk

Head Lighthouse (Dis)
East Lighthouse (Dis)

P

River Nene
WEST BANK RD

8

25

Lighthouse Farm

Walkers Marsh

7

Kamarad Farm

Wingland Marsh

Nene Lodge Farm

Terrington Marsh

24

Nene Way

New Intake Farm

Bankside Farm

Sharpes Bank Farm

Burman Farm

6

Clarks Farm

New Marsh Common

Fern House Farm

PE12

SLUICE ROAD

23

Grange Farm

Grove Farm

Myrobella Farm

5

Weatherall Farm

Creek Farm

HOSPITAL ROAD

Grange Farm

COCKHOLE ROAD

Wingland Grange

Sycamore Farm

PE34

Bungalow Farm

White House Farm

ANCHOR ROAD

Middle Crown Farm

Home Farm

Tommyshop Farm

22

Red House Farm

Bellmount

Sewage Works

Eversfield Farm

Bleak House Farm

GARNER'S LANE

Middle Crown Farm

MIDDLE ROAD

Old Common Marsh

NEW ROMAN BANK

4

Allot Gdns

ORANGE ROAD

OLD ROMAN BANK

21

Crown Farm

New Inland Marsh

Orange Row

A17

White House Farm

NEW ROMAN BANK

Poplar Tree Farm

BRUSH MEADOW LANE

Emorsgate

BEACON HILL RD

Emorsgate Farm

CHURCH BANK

CHAPEL ROAD

3

GRANGE ROAD

Walpole Cross Keys

PH

Sea Newland Field

ORANGE LANE

EMORSGATE

LOW LANE

Terrington St Clement

PH

SUTTON ROAD

Whitehouse Farm

Spencer Farm

Plumbs Farm

MARKET LANE

Dovecote Farm

POPE'S LANE

20

KING JOHN BANK

Walpole House

LITTLE HOLME RD

Poplar Farm

STATION ROAD

GRANGE LANE

South Green

LOVELL WY 1
HOWARD CL 2
SPRING GR 3
SUTTON RD 4

Lovell's Hall

2

EASTLANDS BANK

Bonnetts Farm

Cockles Farm

A17 King's Lynn

Allot Gdns

Crown Farm

Norfolk Cycle Way

MARKET LANE

A17

19

PE14

Old Inclosed Marsh

EASTLANDS BANK

Station Farm

HAY GREEN RD (SOUTH)

Experimental Husbandry Farm

1

WINDSOR ROAD

Long Four Farm

MARKET LANE

Hankinson's Est

Tuxhill Farm

TUXHILL ROAD

HAY GN RD

HAY GREEN ROAD

BULLOCK ROAD

Hay Green

JANKIN LA

Cherry Farm

Highenden House

EDGE BANK

Feale Abbey

18

A 49 50 B 51 C 52 D 53 E 54 F

Norfolk STREET ATLAS

F3
1 ORANGE ROW RD
2 CHURCH BANK
3 ORANGE ROW
4 KING WILLIAM CL
5 WESLEY AVE
6 THE SALTINGS
7 BRELLOWS HILL
8 CAVE'S CL
9 WESLEY RD
10 MARSHLAND ST
11 WESLEY CL
12 FFOLKES DR
13 COBBS HILL

Norfolk STREET ATLAS

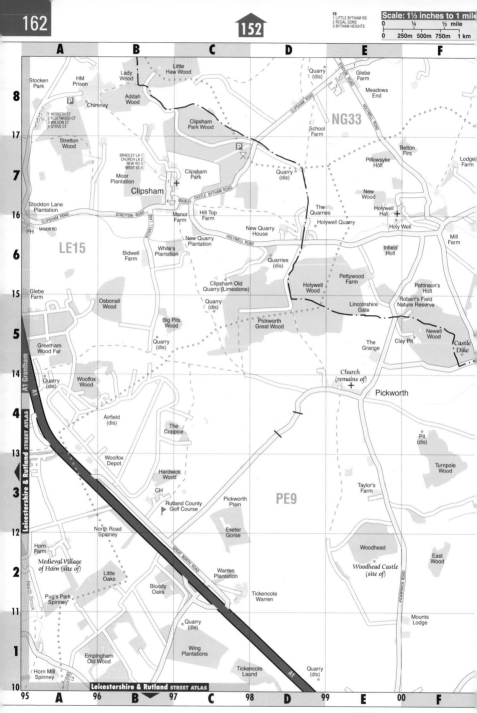

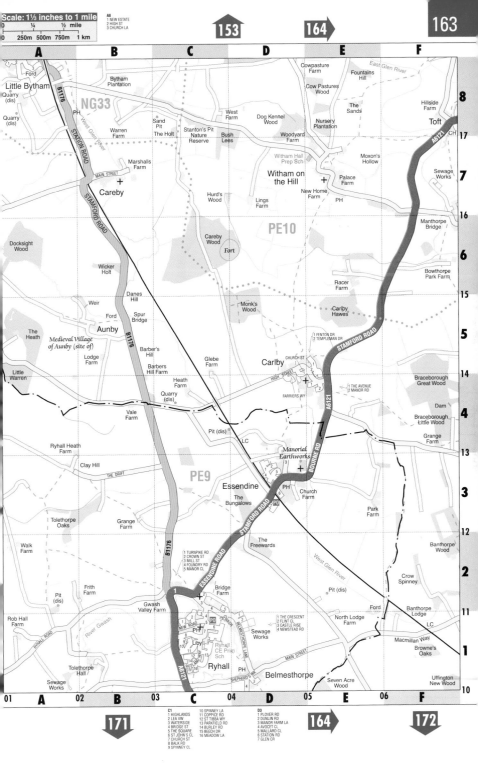

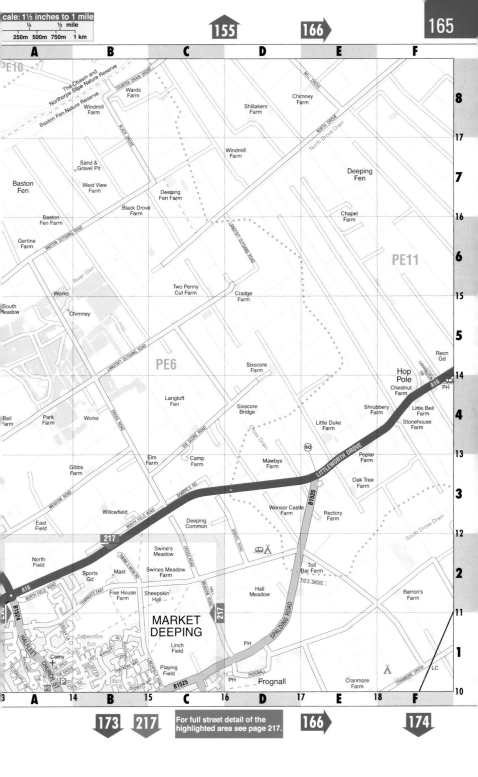

cale: 1⅓ inches to 1 mile

¼   ½ mile
250m 500m 750m 1 km

155

166

165

A   B   C   D   E   F

PE10

The Chasm and Slipe Nature Reserve

Northorpe Fen Nature Reserve

Baston Fen Nature Reserve

Wards Farm

COUNTER DRAIN DRIVE

MILL DROVE

8

Windmill Farm

Shillakers Farm

Chimney Farm

NORTH DROVE

North Drove Drain

17

BLACK DROVE

Sand & Gravel Pit

Windmill Farm

Deeping Fen

7

Baston Fen

West View Farm

Deeping Fen Farm

Chapel Farm

16

Black Drove Farm

Baston Fen Farm

LANGTOFT OUTGANG ROAD

PE11

6

Gertine Farm

BASTON OUTGANG ROAD

River Glen

Two Penny Cut Farm

Cradge Farm

15

South Meadow

Works

Chimney

5

PE6

Recn Gd

Bell Farm

Park Farm

LANGTOFT OUTGANG ROAD

Works

Langtoft Fen

Sixscore Farm

Hop Pole

CARDYKE DROVE

A16

14

Chestnut Farm

Shrubbery Farm

Little Bell Farm

PH

CROSS ROAD

SIX SCORE ROAD

Sixscore Bridge

Cross Drain

Little Duke Farm

LITTLEWORTH DROVE

Stonehouse Farm

4

Gibbs Farm

Elm Farm

Camp Farm

Mawbys Farm

Poplar Farm

13

MEADOW ROAD

SHARPE'S RD

Oak Tree Farm

Willowfield

Deeping Common

Wensor Castle Farm

B1525

Rectory Farm

3

East Field

NORTH FIELD ROAD

GRAVEL ROAD

South Drove Drain

12

217

Swine's Meadow

CROSS ROAD

Toll Bar Farm

2

North Field

Sports Gd

Mast

Swines Meadow Farm

HALL MEADOW ROAD

TYE S DROVE

Barron's Farm

A16

NORTH FIELD ROAD

Five House Farm

TOWNGATE EAST

Sheepskin Hall

Hall Meadow

SPALDING ROAD

11

B1524

MARKET DEEPING

217

PH

1

HALL FIELD ROAD

CHURCH ST

Superstore

Sch

Cemy

Linch Field

PH

CRANMORE DROVE

LC

B1525

Playing Field

FROGNALL

Cranmore Farm

10

PH

Frognall

3   A   14   B   15   C   16   D   17   E   18   F   10

173   217

For full street detail of the highlighted area see page 217.

166

174

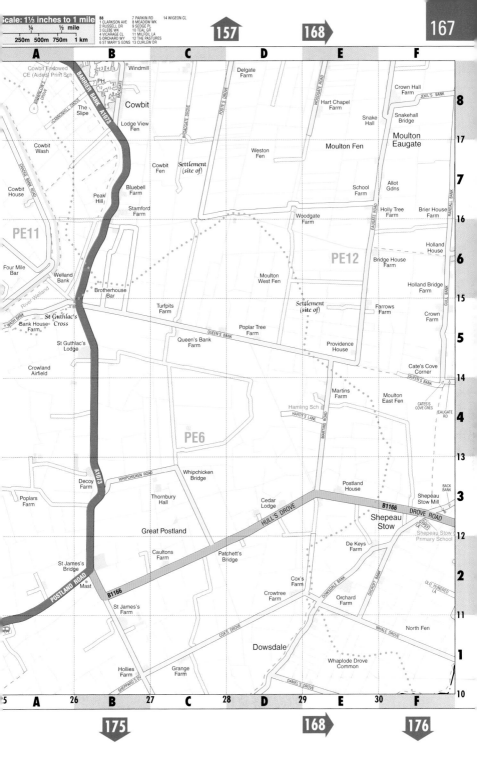

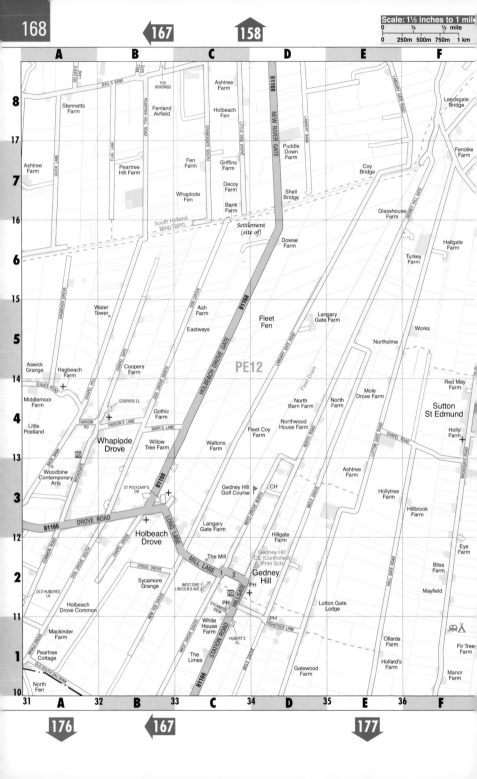

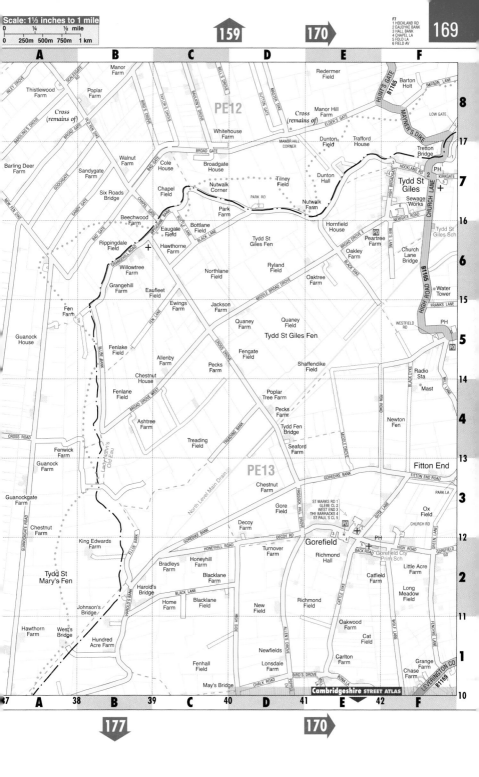

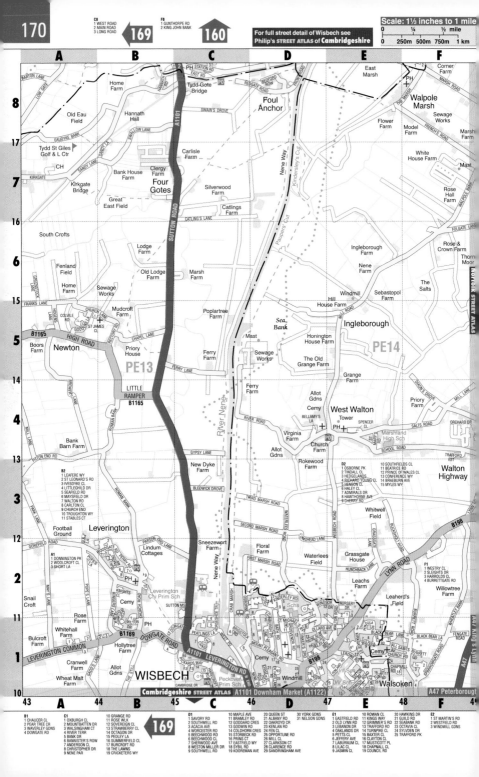

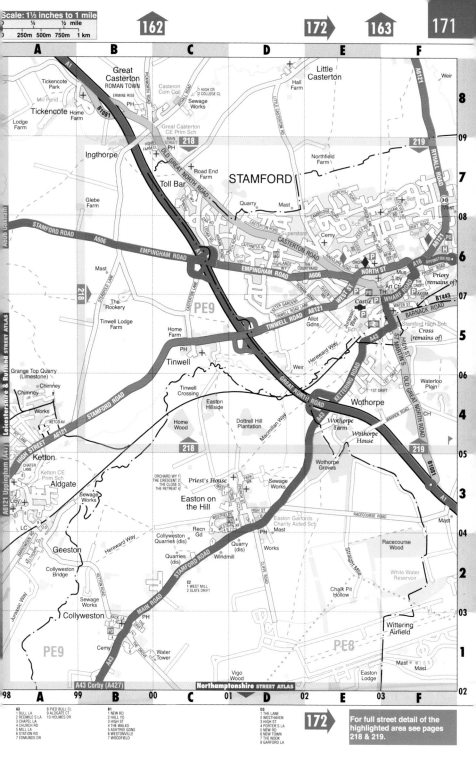

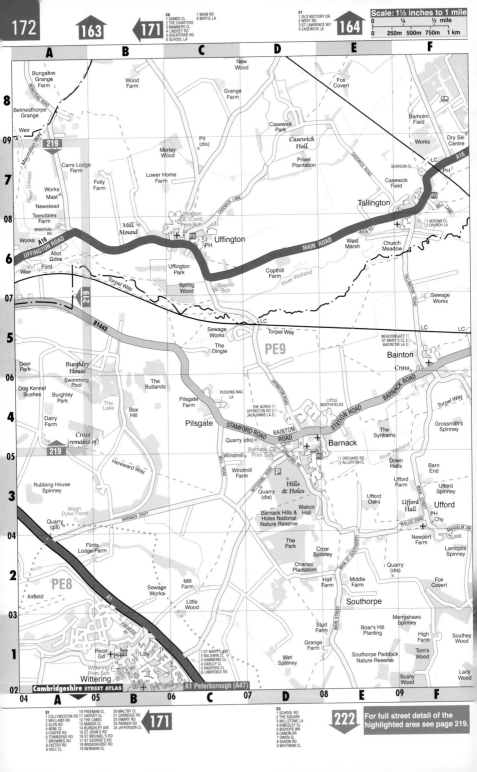

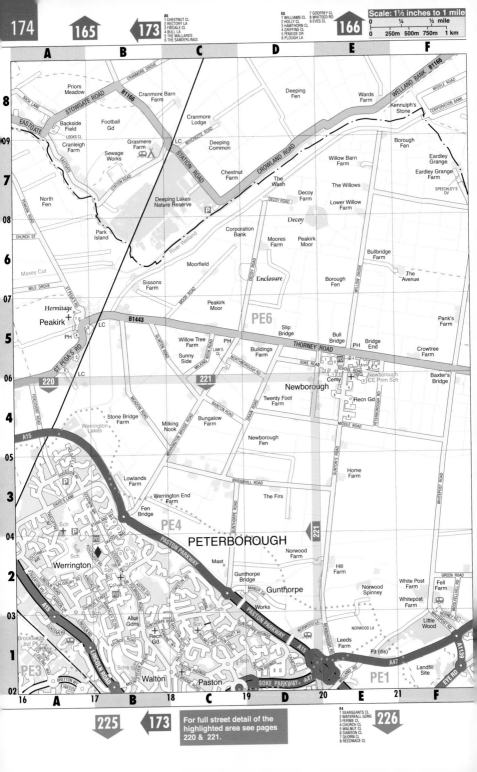

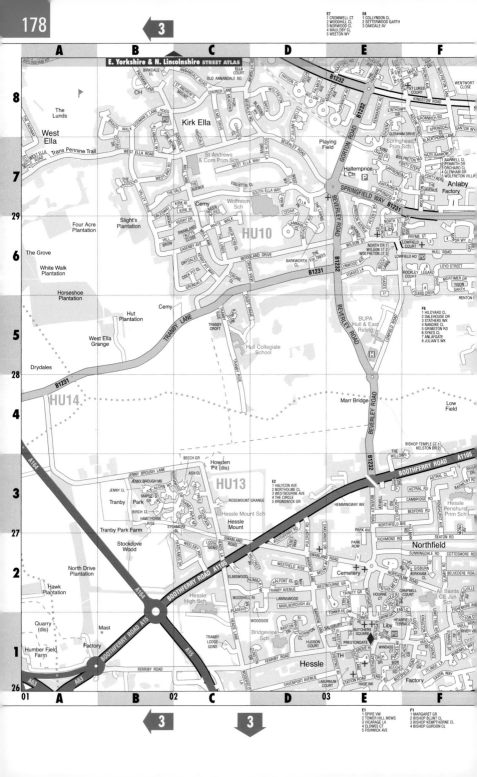

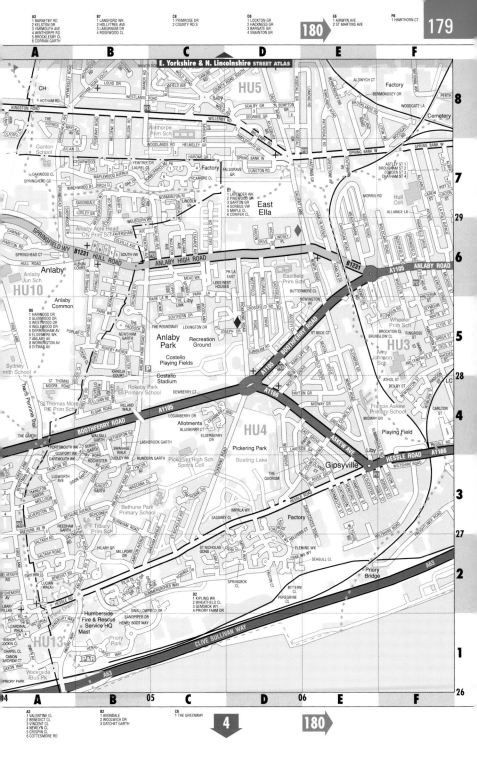

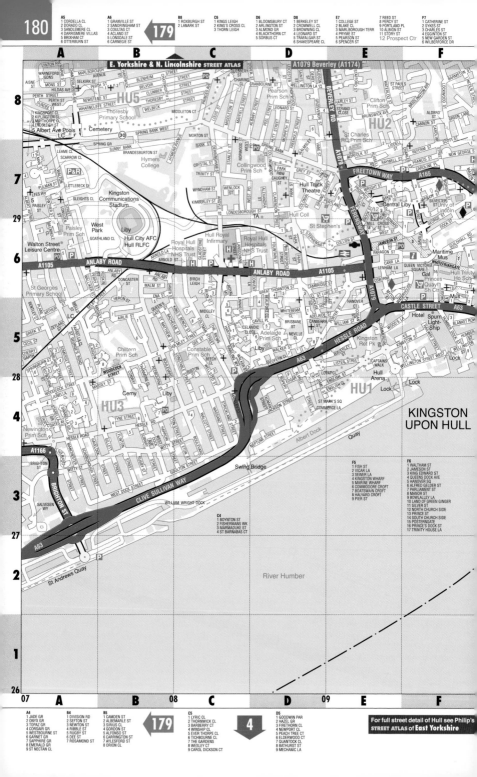

E. Yorkshire & N. Lincolnshire STREET ATLAS

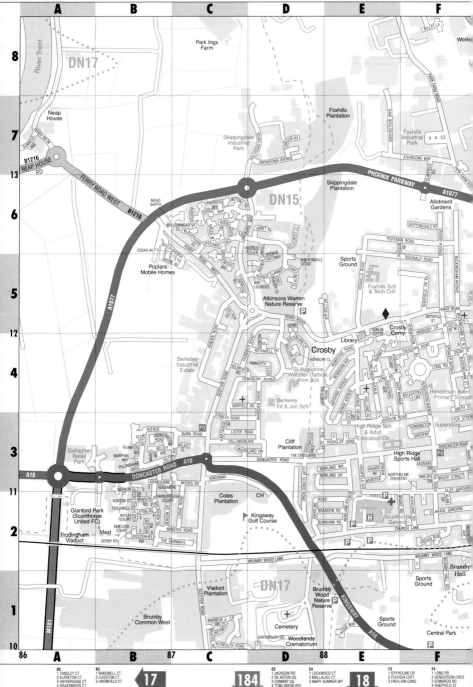

17

8

C5
1 ACACIA AVE
2 MAPLE AVE
3 PIPPIN CT
4 RUSSET CL

C6
1 POPPY CL
2 WOODALE CL
3 FLETCHER CL
4 COLTSFOOT CL
5 ST MARY'S CT
6 HERON CL

B2
1 TANSLEY CT
2 ALFRETON CT
3 HATHERSAGE CT
4 GRASSMOOR CT
5 EASTWOOD CT
6 BELPER CT

B3
1 BAKEWELL CT
2 ILKESTON CT
3 DROMFIELD CT

17

184

E3
1 JACKSON RD
2 DE ASTON SQ
3 CONWAY SQ
4 TOMLINSON AVE
5 ASHDOWN AVE

E4
1 LOCKWOOD CT
2 MALLALIEU CT
3 MARY SUMNER WY

18

F2
1 ERYHOLME CR
2 FUCHSIA CRFT
3 PAVILION GDNS

F4
1 LONG RD
2 HENDERSON CRES
3 EDWARDS RD
4 SHEFFIELD ST
5 BUCKINGHAM ST
6 Comm Ctr

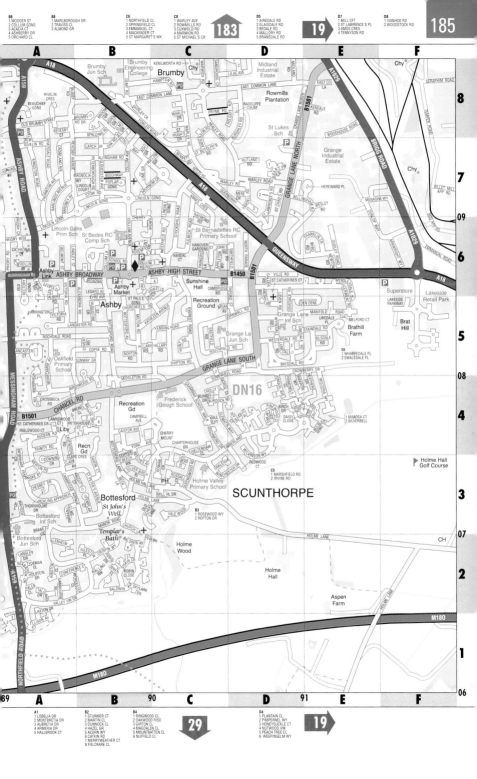

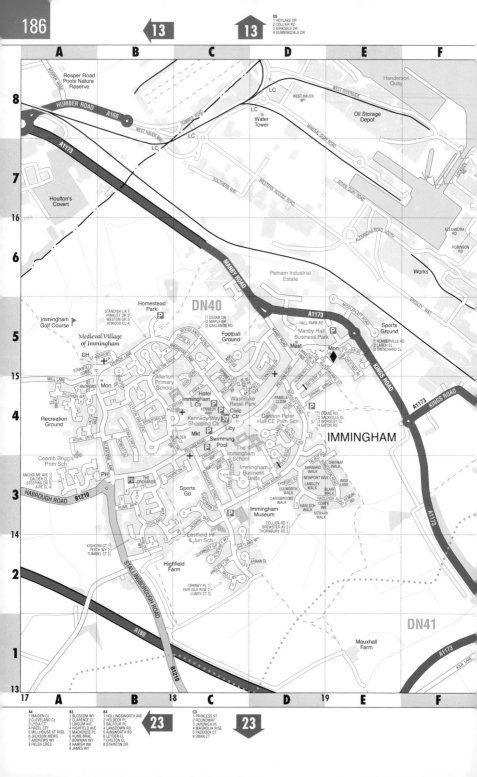

13

A B C D E F

8

7

16

6

Immingham
Dock

EAST RIVERSIDE

Oil
Storage
Depot

EAST DOCK ROAD

LC

Oil
Storage
Depot

Chy

QUEENS RD

LC

East
Gate

DN40

A1173

QUEENS ROAD

LAPORTE ROAD

Chimney

Works

Humber Bank
Factories

Chimney

5

15

4

3

EUROPA WAY

SCANDINAVIAN WAY

NETHERLANDS WAY

EUROPA WAY

Spoil Heap

Kiln Lane
Ind Est

KILN LANE

LAPORTE WAY

MONKLOWNS W

LC

Kiln Lane
Trading Est

14

2

TRONDHEIM WAY

BELL'S RD

OSBORNE RD

Kiln Lane
Ind Est

DN41

HESSON WAY

South
Marsh Road
Ind Est

SOUTH MARSH ROAD

Power
Station

NORTH MOSS LANE

SOUTH MARSH ROAD

LC

Chimney

1

Poplar
Farm

20 A B 21 C D 22 E F 13

23 24 24

24

A1
1 FERNDOWN
2 SERVICE RD 12
3 SERVICE RD 14
4 SERVICE RD 13
5 RAVENSCAR RD
6 SERVICE RD 10
7 SERVICE RD 9
8 SERVICE RD 8
9 SERVICE RD 26

190

A3
1 ATHENIAN WY
2 FISKERTON WY
3 SARGON WY

24

24

D1
1 BRIDGE GDNS
2 CLEVELAND GDNS
3 CLEVELAND ST
4 CLAYDEN ST
5 STANSTED ST
6 CLAVERING ST
7 STORTFORD ST
8 SANDFORD ST

E1
1 CORPORATION RD
2 ARMSTRONG PL W
3 ARMSTRONG PL E
4 AYSCOUGH ST

191

F1
1 ANNESLEY ST
2 WATKIN ST STH

GRIMSBY

River Humber

The Dock Tower
Mast
Piers
Locks
Locks
Royal Dock
Brown St
Fish Docks
WHARNCLIFFE RD
KEMP ROAD
NORTH QUAY

DN31

Grimsby Marina

FARINGDON RD

Works

WICKHAM ROAD

Works

D1
1 CASSWELL CL
2 RUTLAND ST
3 MANSEL ST
4 SIDNEY ST

MURRAY STREET

WICKHAM RD

ROBINSON ST

RIBY STREET

New Clee

MARSDEN ROAD

DN35

CLEETHORPE ROAD

Grimsby Docks

The Caxton Theatre & Arts Ctr

Strand
Jun Sch

Strand
Inf Sch

BATH ST

BELPER

THOROLD STREET

STIRLING ST

HARRINGTON STREET

DN32

A180

High Point Ret Pk

Victoria Retail Pk

PRINCE ALBERT GARD

NELSON STREET

DUNCOMBE GDNS

InShops

COMBER PL

Ice House

East Marsh

ALBERT PLACE

SUFFOLK CT

SUSSEX CT

GUILDFORD ST

GRIMSBY ROAD

A180

HAMILTON STREET

GRAFTON ST

MONTAGUE ST

SPENCER

TAYLOR ST

BLUNDELL AVE

A16 VICTORIA ST N

B1213 FREEMAN STREET

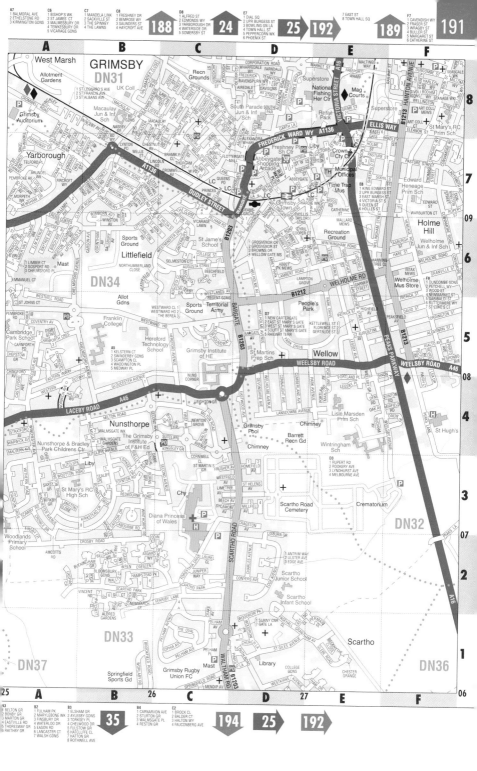

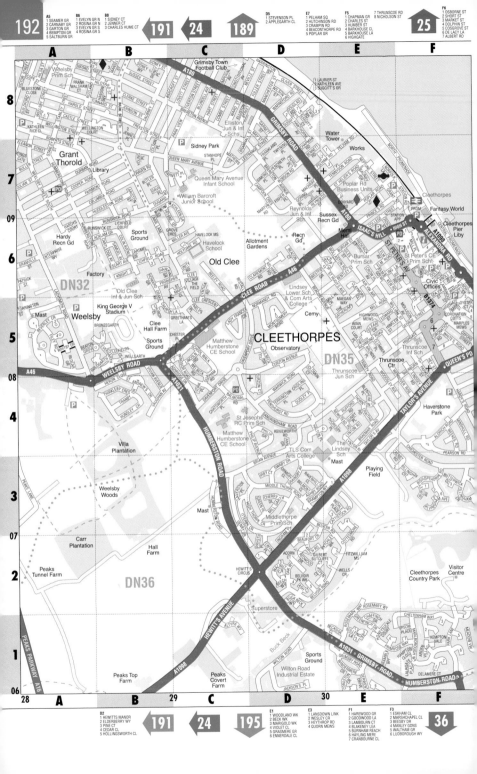

A **B** **C** **D** **E** **F**

8
7
09
6
5
08
4
3
07
2
07
1
06

IRB Station
SLIPWAY

KINGSWAY
A1098
MIDDLANDS AVE
FIRST PARADE

Hotel!

Cleethorpes Leisure Ctr
Ringsway
Paddling Pool
Fishing Lake

CROMWELL ROAD
SIGNHILLS AVE
BRADFORD AVE
LINDUM RD

Signhills
Infant & Junior
School

Cleethorpes Coast
Light Railway
Sand Pit

CHICHESTER ROAD

Meridian
Point
Retail Pk

Cleethorpes
Discovery Centre
Playtowers

PH
The Jungle Zoo
Showground

Cleethorpes Coast
Light Railway
& Museum
Lakeside

Cleethorpes
Nature Reserve

DN35
Cleethorpes

Miniature
Railway

Humberston

CARLYLE CLOSE
ROCHESTER

CH
Pleasure Island
Theme Park

WALDORF RD
MAYFAIR CT
WESTBURY RD
WHITEHALL 'N SEA LA
CTRY COTTS
NORTH SEA LA
SOUTH SEA LA
HOLDAN CLOSE

CAVENDISH CL
CARLTON CL
SEAFORD ROAD
BERNERS RD
NORTH SEA LANE

HILTON
FAIR PLACE
KING ST

Thorpe Park

DN36

Epperstone
Residential
Caravan Park

Beachcomber
Holiday
Centre

ANTHONY'S BANK ROAD

A1
1 WESTPORT RD
2 WESTBURY PK
3 FAIRFIELD CT
4 WEYFORD RD
5 GROVENOR CT
6 WHITEHALL RD
7 KINGSTON CL

36

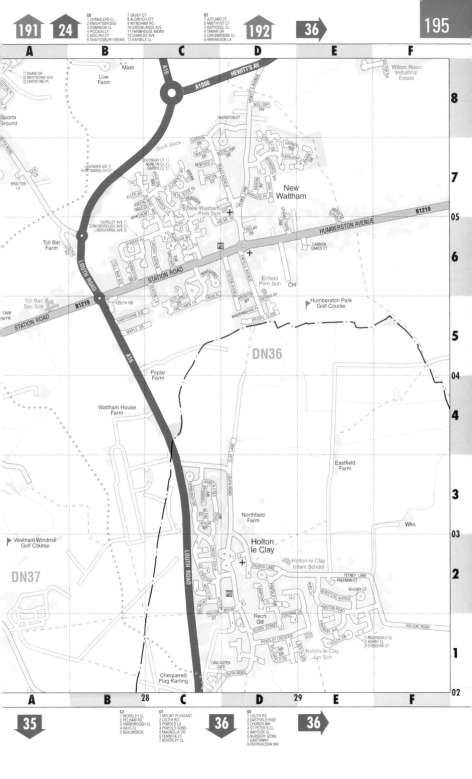

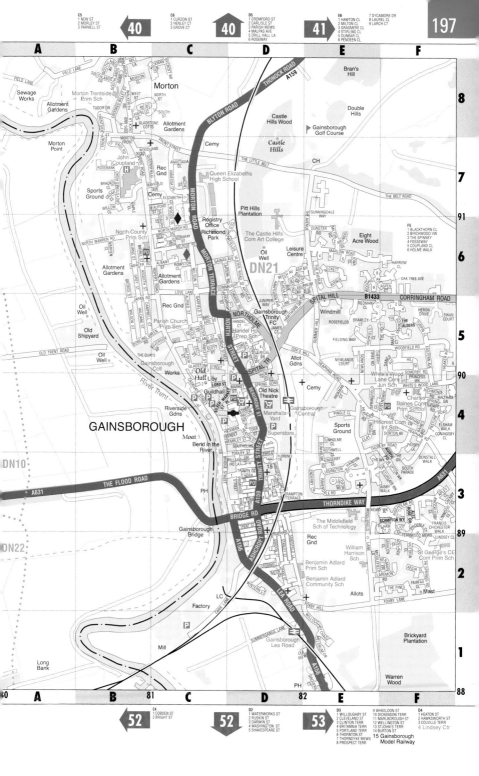

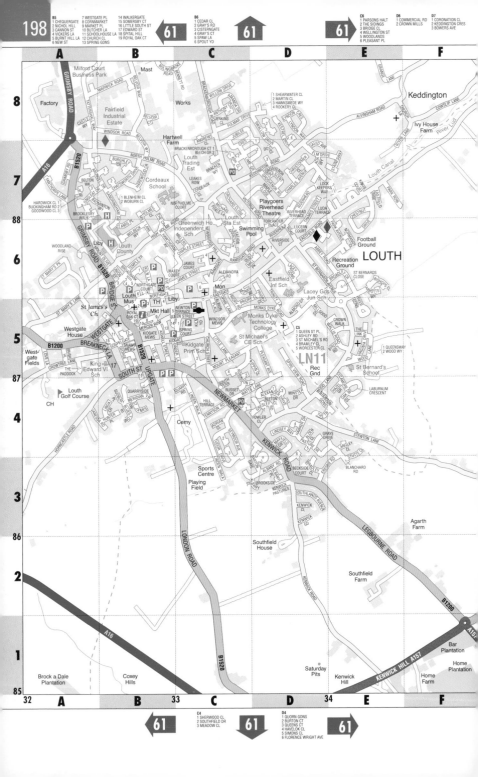

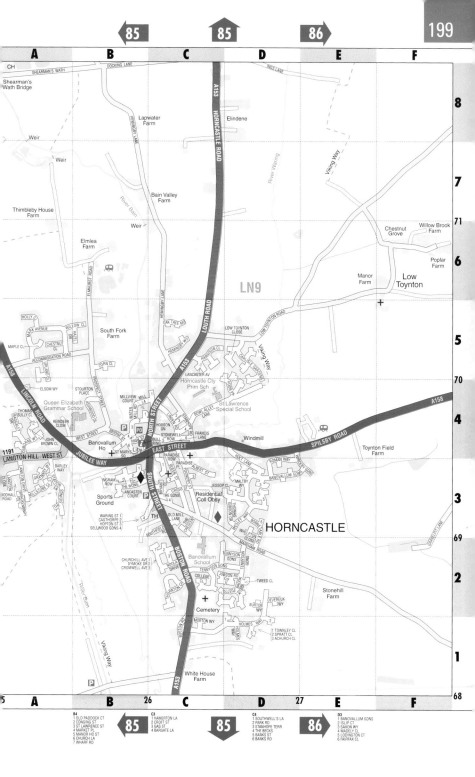

A4
1 HAMPDEN CL
2 LANCASTER WY
3 HALIFAX CL
4 STIRLING WY
5 WHITLEY CL
6 SUNDERLAND GR
7 MITCHELL CL

B1
1 LUTON CL
2 PRESTWICK CL
3 CHIVENOR CL

C1
1 OLD WOOD
2 WASDALE CL
3 BURNMOOR CL
4 BAYWOOD CL
5 HICKORY RD
6 BRIAR CL
7 WHITETHORN GR
8 DELLFIELD CT
9 WOODFIELD CL
10 SATINWOOD CL
11 TULIPWOOD AVE

D1
1 THIRLMERE WY
2 BUTTERMERE CL
3 ENNERDALE CL
4 RINGWOOD CL
5 PEARTREE CL
6 ELMWOOD CL
7 OLD POND CL

E1
1 STONES LA
2 GOLDCREST CL
3 SHEARWATER CL

A5
1 BEAVER CL
2 BROOKFIELD CL

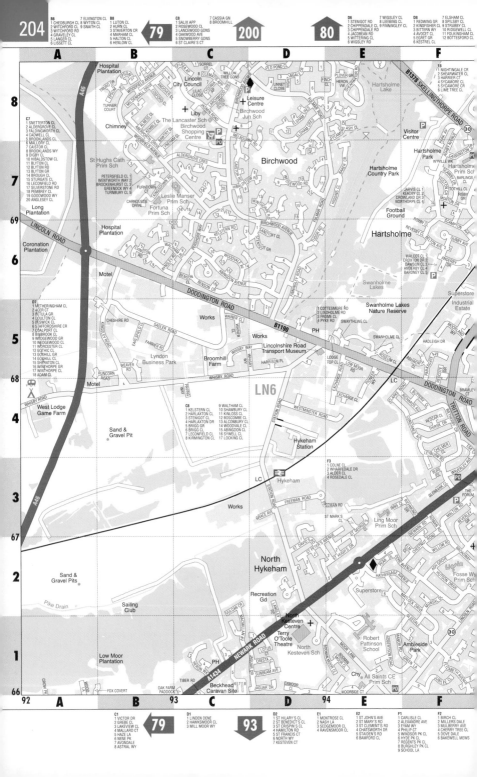

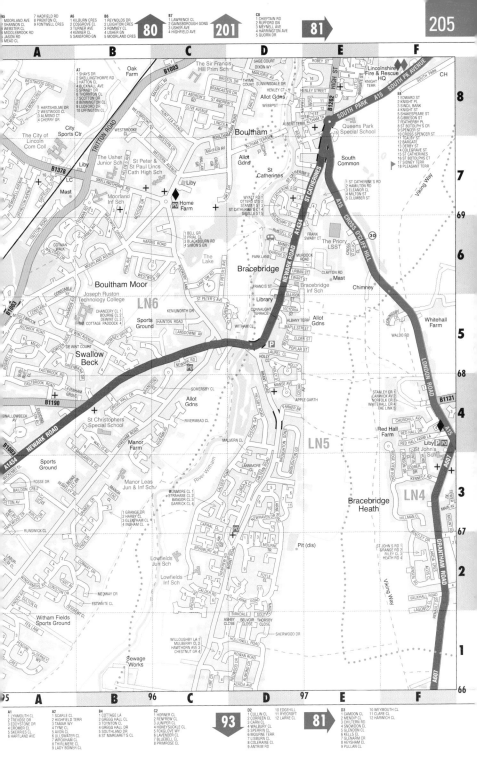

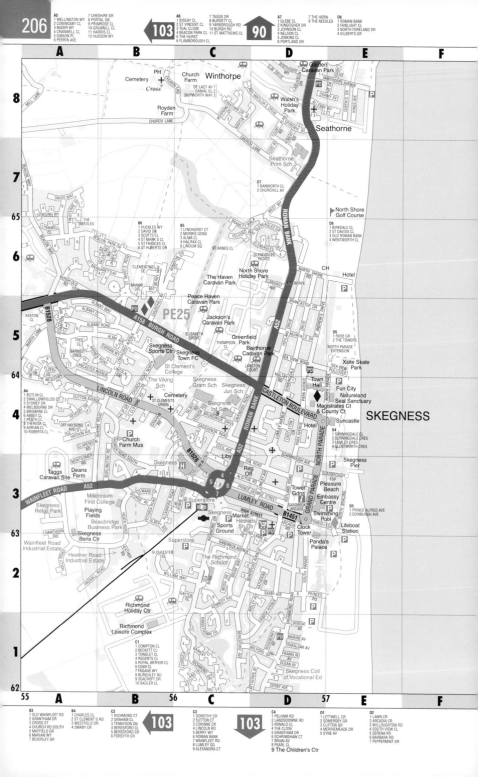

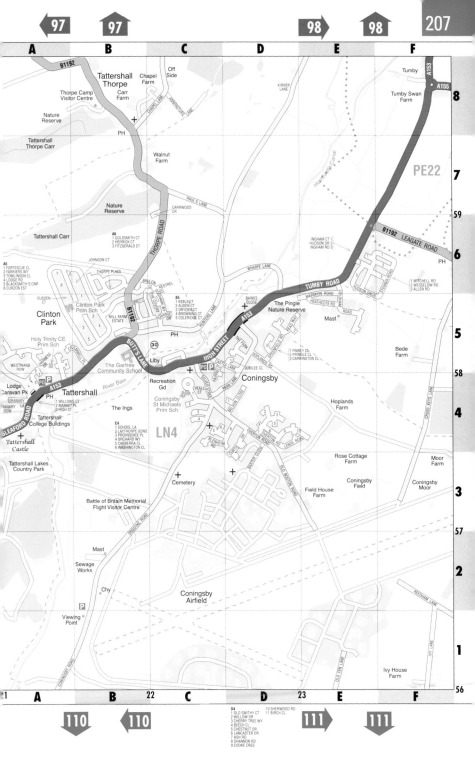

A B C D E F

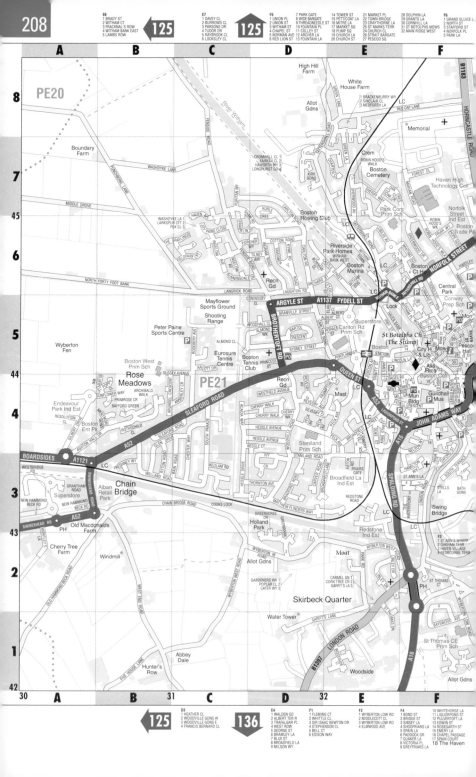

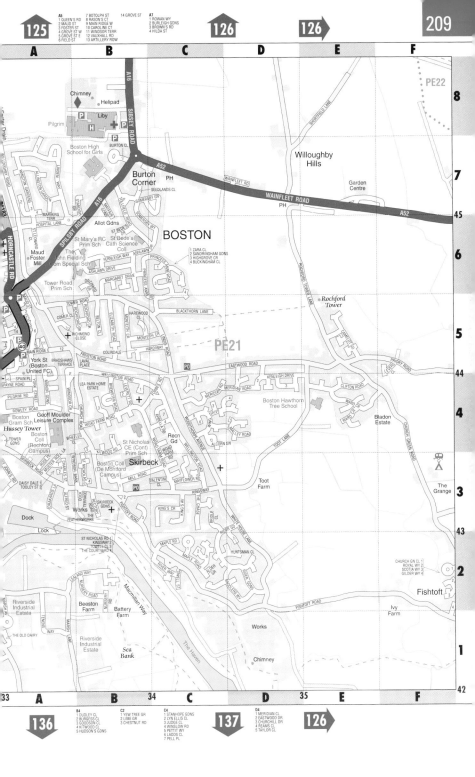

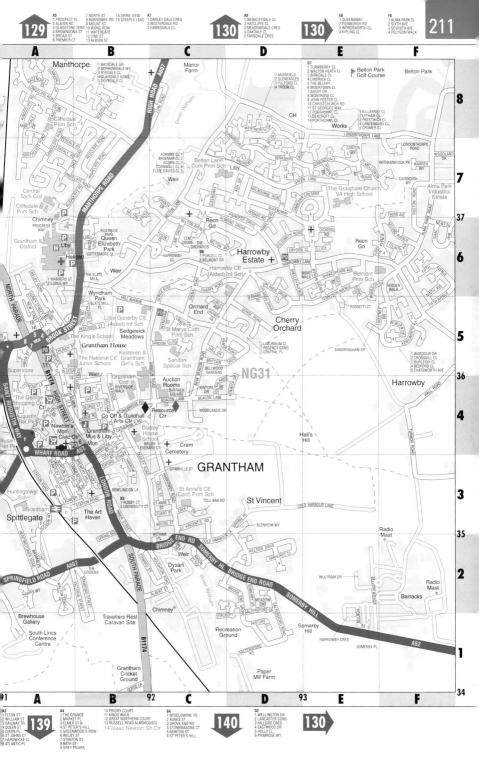

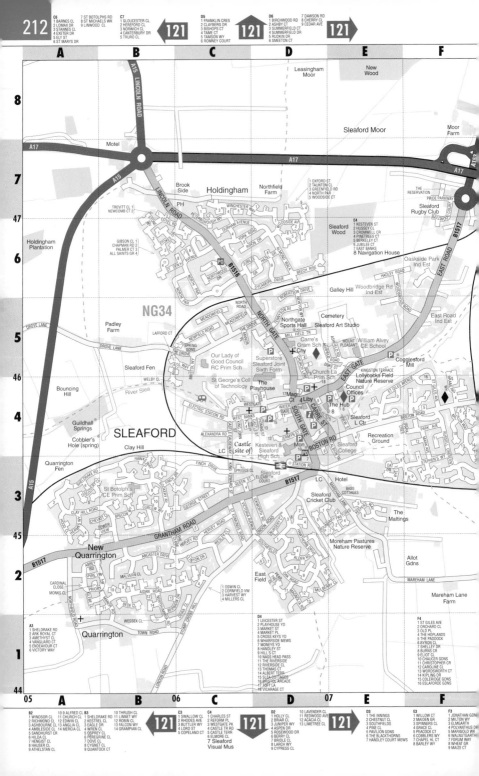

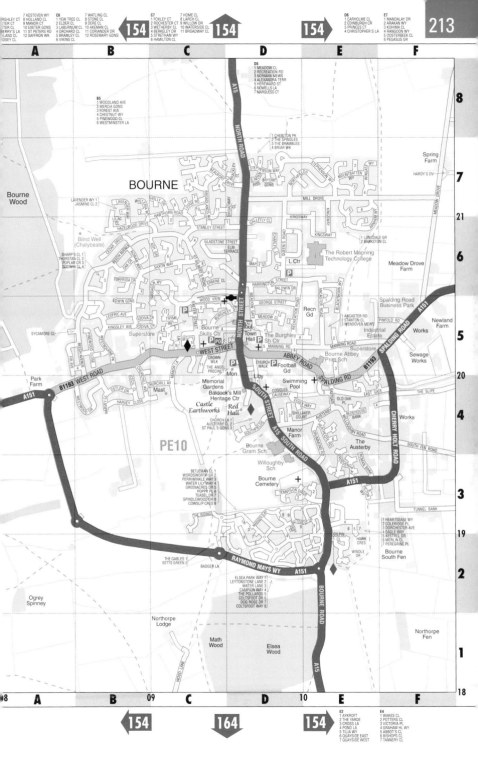

154   154   154

BOURNE

Bourne Wood

Park Farm

PE10

Ogrey Spinney

Spring Farm

Meadow Drove Farm

Newland Farm

Spalding Road Business Park

Sewage Works

Works

Bourne South Fen

Northorpe Fen

Math Wood

Elsea Wood

Northorpe Lodge

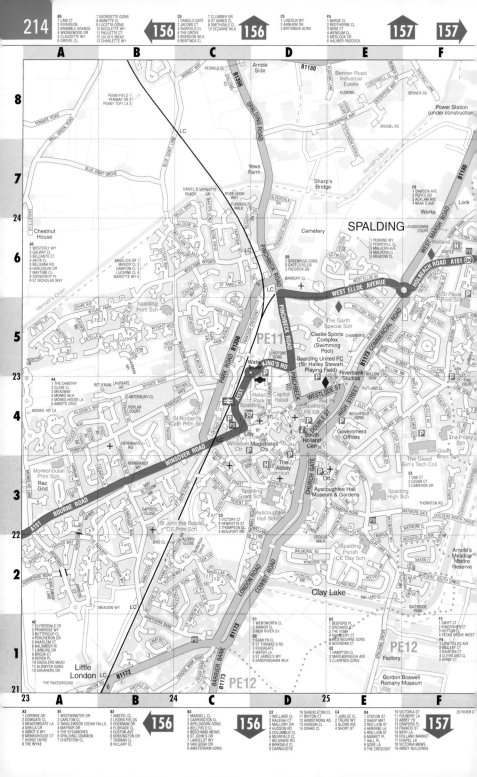

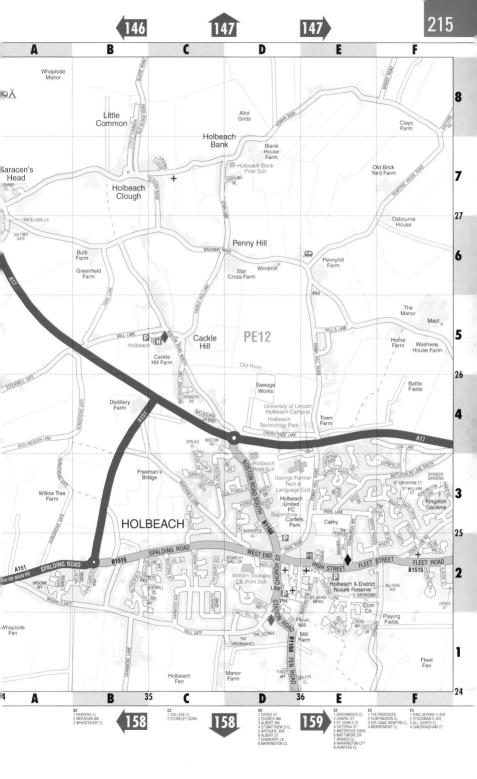

B2
1 REAPERS CL
2 MERIDIAN WK
3 WHEATSHEAF CL

C2
1 COLLEGE CL
2 STUKELEY GDNS

D2
1 CROSS ST
2 CHURCH WK
3 ALBERT WK
4 ST MATTHEW'S CL
5 ARTHURS AVE
6 ALBERT ST
7 CHANCERY LA
8 BARRINGTON CL

E2
1 GREENWOOD CL
2 CHAPEL ST
3 ST JOHN'S ST
4 VICTORIA ST
5 WATERSIDE GDNS
6 MATTIMORE DR
7 DRAKES CL
8 HARRINGTON CFT
9 HUNTERS CL

E3
1 THE PADDOCKS
2 HUNTINGDON CL
3 SIR ISAAC NEWTON CL
4 MONDEMONT CL

F3
1 KING GEORGE V AVE
2 STOCKMAN S AVE
3 ALL SAINTS CL
4 SANDRINGHAM CT

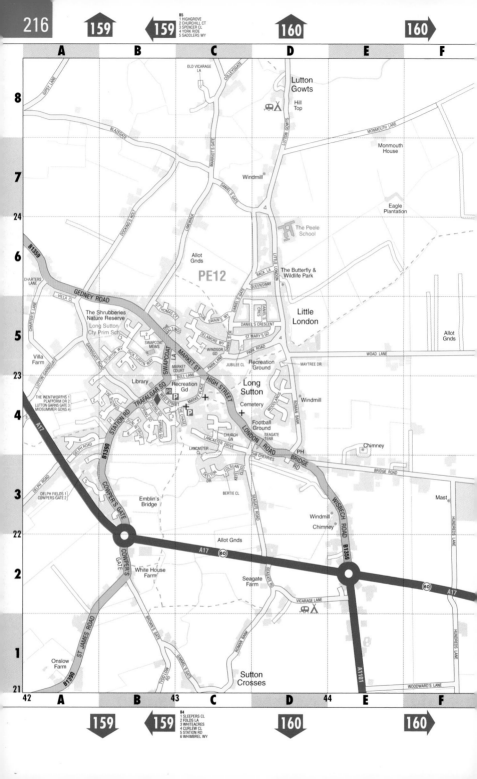

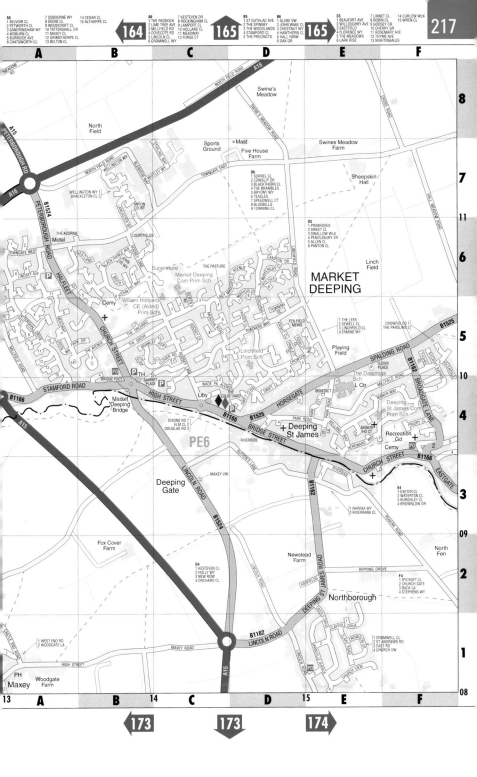

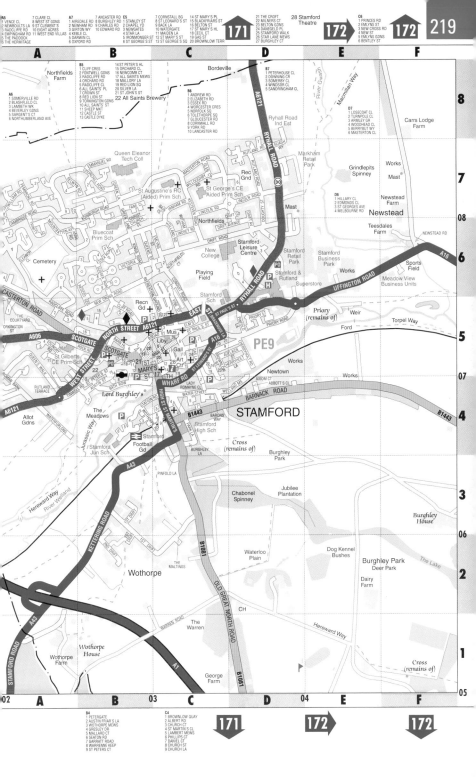

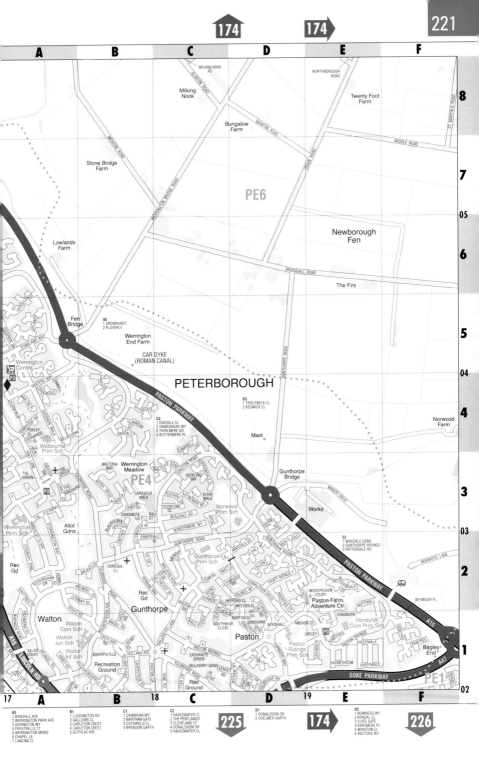

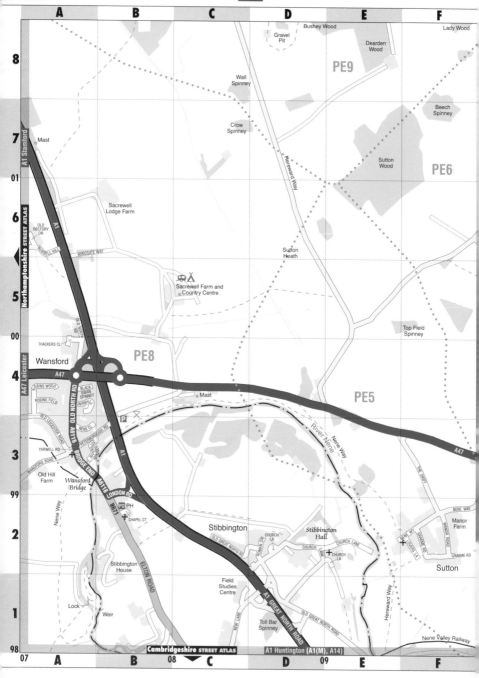

A B C D E F

8

7

01

6

5

00

4

99

3

2

1

98

07 A B 08 C D 09 E F

Northamptonshire STREET ATLAS

A1 Stamford

A47 Leicester

Mast

Sacrewell
Lodge Farm

OLD
RECTORY
DR

RUSSELL HILL

WINDGATE WAY

Sacrewell Farm and
Country Centre

THACKERS CL

PE8

Wansford

A47

ROBINS WOOD

ROBINS FIELD

OLD LEICESTER ROAD

YARWELL RD

WANSFORD ROAD

Old Hill
Farm

Wansford
Bridge

Nene Way

OLD NORTH RD

A6118

BRIDGE END

A6118

LONDON RD

B671

PO PH

CHAPEL CT

BLACK
SWAN
SPINNEY

NENE CL

PETERBOROUGH RD

A1

Mast

P

Stibbington
House

ELTON ROAD

NEW LANE

Lock

Weir

Stibbington

Field
Studies
Centre

Toll Bar
Spinney

A1 GREAT NORTH ROAD

OLD GREAT NORTH RD

ROMAN DR

CHURCH
LA

CHURCH

Stibbington
Hall

CHURCH LANE

CHURCH LA

Gravel
Pit

Bushey Wood

Wall
Spinney

Crow
Spinney

Dearden
Wood

Hereward Way

Sutton
Heath

PE9

Lady Wood

Beech
Spinney

Sutton
Wood

PE6

Top Field
Spinney

PE5

River Nene

Nene Way

A47

THE DRIFT

NENE WAY

GRAEME LA

MANOR ROAD

Manor
Farm

NENE WAY

GRAEME RD

Sutton

Hereward Way

Nene Valley Railway

A1 Huntington (A1(M), A14)

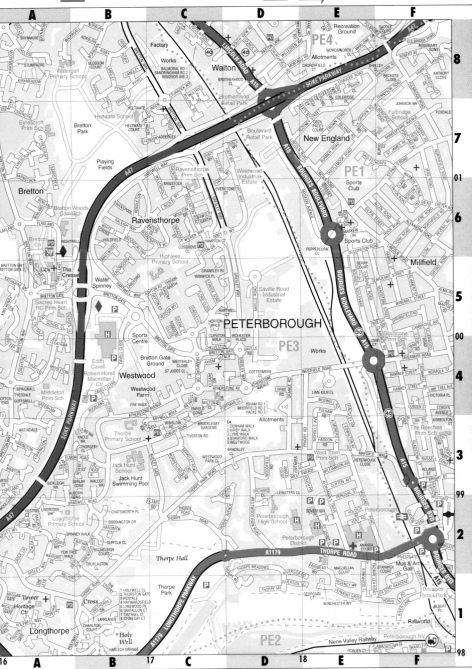

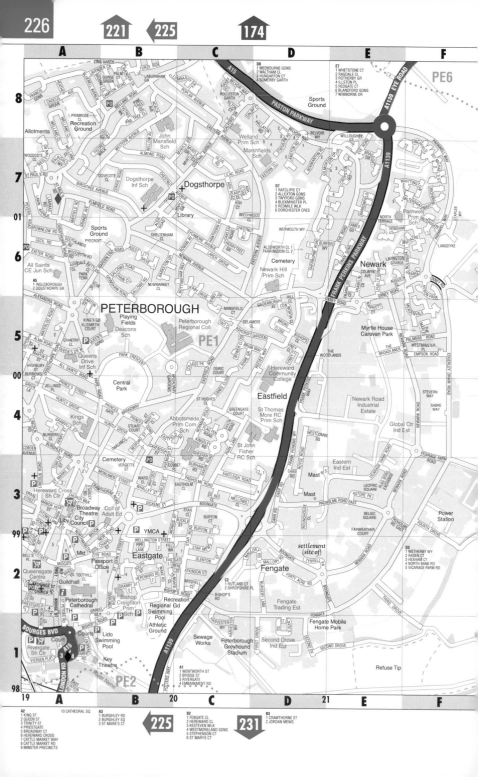

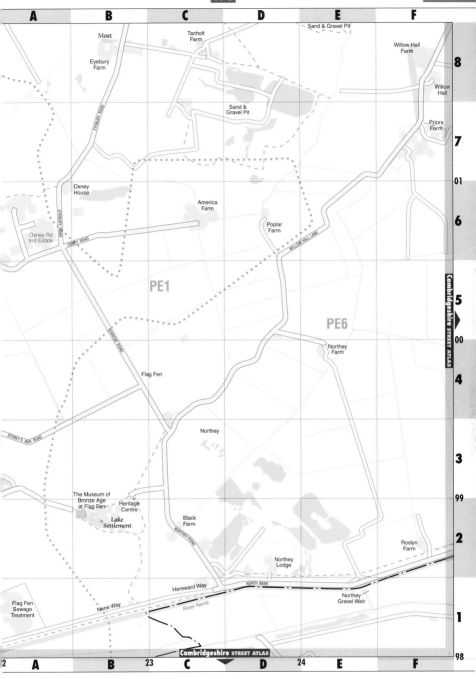

223

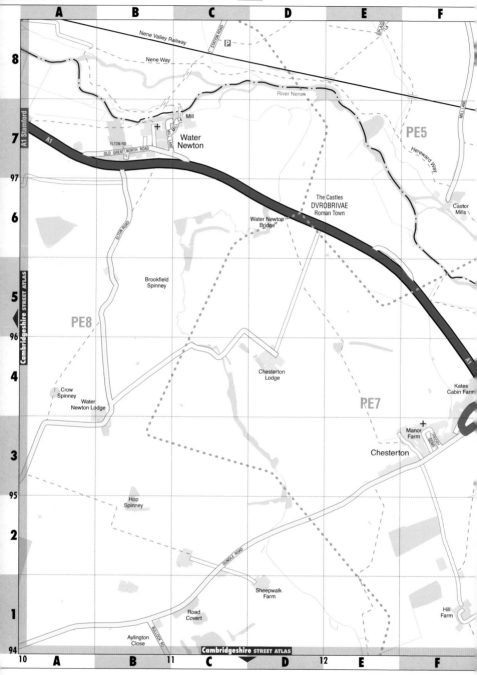

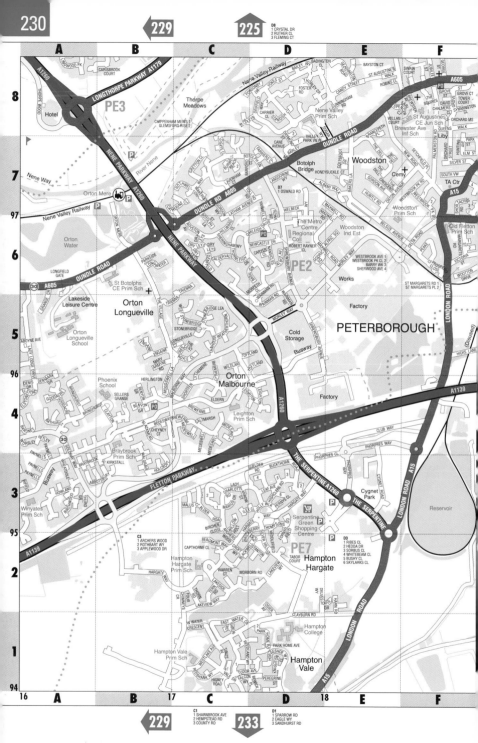

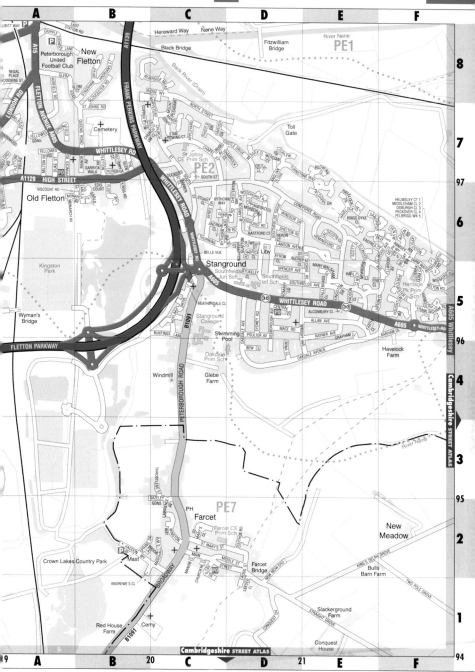

229

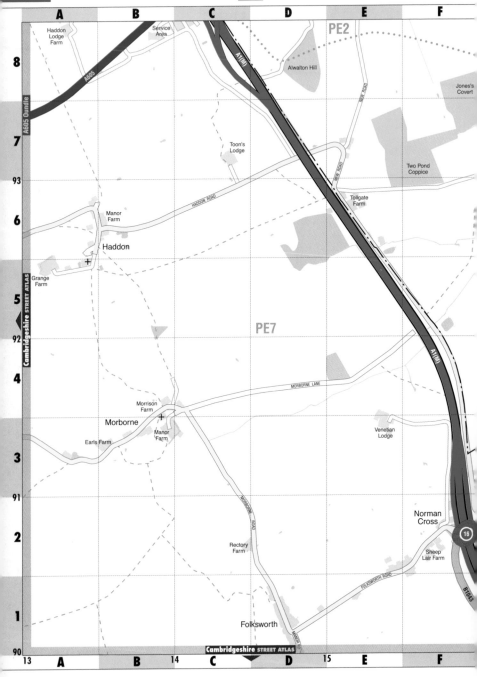

PE2

8

7

93

6

Yaxley

B1091

5

92

4

3

91

2

1

90

Orton Brick Works

Pit
(dis)

Madam
White's
Covert

LONDON ROAD

1 STEPHENSON CL
2 PARTRIDGE CL
3 NIGHTINGALE DR
4 FARADAY CL

GAVEL ST 1
MAGISTRATES RD 2
EAGLE WY 3
BEWICK PL 4
HORSESHOE WY 5
HIGH CT WY 6

Spendelows
Farm

Yaxley
Lodge Farm

PE7

Cemy

BROADWAY

Yaxley
Jun Sch

Liby

MALTING
SQUARE

A15

Heye's Farm

Yards End Dyke

Hod
Fen

Fourfields
Prim Sch

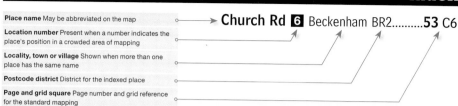

Place name May be abbreviated on the map

Location number Present when a number indicates the place's position in a crowded area of mapping

Locality, town or village Shown when more than one place has the same name

Postcode district District for the indexed place

Page and grid square Page number and grid reference for the standard mapping

Church Rd [6] Beckenham BR2..........**53** C6

Cities, towns and villages are listed in CAPITAL LETTERS Public and commercial buildings are highlighted in magenta
Places of interest are highlighted in blue with a star★

Abbreviations used in the index

Acad	Academy	Comm	Common	Gd	Ground	L	Leisure	Prom	Promenade
App	Approach	Cott	Cottage	Gdn	Garden	La	Lane	Rd	Road
Arc	Arcade	Cres	Crescent	Gn	Green	Liby	Library	Recn	Recreation
Ave	Avenue	Cswy	Causeway	Gr	Grove	Mdw	Meadow	Ret	Retail
Bglw	Bungalow	Ct	Court	H	Hall	Meml	Memorial	Sh	Shopping
Bldg	Building	Ctr	Centre	Ho	House	Mkt	Market	Sq	Square
Bsns, Bus	Business	Ctry	Country	Hospl	Hospital	Mus	Museum	St	Street
Bvd	Boulevard	Cty	County	HQ	Headquarters	Orch	Orchard	Sta	Station
Cath	Cathedral	Dr	Drive	Hts	Heights	Pal	Palace	Terr	Terrace
Cir	Circus	Dro	Drove	Ind	Industrial	Par	Parade	TH	Town Hall
Cl	Close	Ed	Education	Inst	Institute	Pas	Passage	Univ	University
Cnr	Corner	Emb	Embankment	Int	International	Pk	Park	Wk, Wlk	Walk
Coll	College	Est	Estate	Intc	Interchange	Pl	Place	Wr	Water
Com	Community	Ex	Exhibition	Junc	Junction	Prec	Precinct	Yd	Yard

Index of towns, villages, streets, hospitals, industrial estates, railway stations, schools, shopping centres, universities and places of interest

1st Drift PE9 ....219 B2
1st Main Rd DN36 .....36 F8
2nd Ave DN36 ....36 F8
2nd Drift PE9.........219 B2
4th Ave DN36.........36 F8
12th Ave DN36.........36 F8

A

ALPS Coll DN15 ....8 F3
Aalsmeer Rise [6] PE11.. 214 A2
Abbey Bldgs [19] PE11.... 214 D4
Abbey Cl
  Coningsby LN4..........207 B5
  [6] Skegness PE25.......206 A4
  [5] Woodhall Spa LN10 ...97 C6
Abbey Cres [4] PE20......135 C7
Abbeydale Cres NG31... 211 A8
Abbey Dr
  [20] Hatfield DN7 ....14 D4
  [5] Woodhall Spa LN10 ...97 C5
Abbey Dr E DN32..........191 D6
Abbey Dr W DN32........191 D6
Abbeyfield Rd [1] DN7....14 C4
Abbeygate DN31...........191 D7
Abbey Gdns [22] DN7.....14 D4
Abbey Gr [22] DN7.........14 D4
Abbey La
  Sedgebrook NG32........128 F4
  Swineshead PE20 ......135 C6
  Woodhall Spa LN10 .....97 C5
Abbey Mews [1] PE6......166 F1
Abbey Pk Mews DN32...191 D6
Abbey Pk Rd DN32......191 D6
Abbey Pl
  [2] Lincoln LN2..........234 C2
  Thorney PE6............176 A3
Abbey Rd
  Alvingham LN11..........49 F2
  Bardney LN3............83 B4
  Bourne PE10 ....213 D5
  Grimsby DN32...........191 D6
  Hatfield DN7 ....14 D4
  Louth LN11 ....198 D6
  Peterborough PE4.......221 A1
  Revesby PE22 ....99 C5
  Scunthorpe DN17 ....194 F6
  Sleaford NG34..........212 A2
  Swineshead PE20 ......135 C7
  Ulceby DN39 ....12 A1
Abbey Rise [14] DN19....11 D8

Abbey St
  Kingston upon Hull
    HU9....................181 C7
  Lincoln LN2 ....234 C2
Abbey Way DN7 ....14 D5
Abbey Wlk
  [10] Crowland PE6.......166 F1
  Grimsby DN31...........191 D7
Abbey Yd [12] PE11......214 D4
Abbotsbury PE2 ....230 A3
Abbot's Cl [5] PE10......213 E4
Abbots Cres [8] PE11.... 214 A4
Abbots Dr [1] PE6........175 B8
Abbots Gdns [1] PE12 ...158 B6
Abbotsmede Prim Com Sch
  PE1....................226 C4
Abbots Rd DN17 ....184 F6
Abbot St LN11 ....201 E1
Abbotsway DN32........191 D6
Abbot's Way [5] PE11.... 214 A3
Abbott Cl [10] LN8 ....57 B8
Abbott's Cl PE9..........219 D4
Abbotts Gr PE4...........220 F6
Abbotts Grange DN36....195 E7
Abbotts Way LN11 ......198 E6
Abbot Way PE7 ....233 D4
Abercorn St DN16 ....183 A2
Aberdeen Cl PE9 ....218 D6
Aberporth Dr LN6........204 B8
Abingdon Ave LN6.......204 C6
Abingdon Cl [11] LN6....204 C6
Aboyne Ave PE2 ....229 F5
Abraham Cl [5] NG31....129 E5
ABY LN13...............75 B5
Aby CE Prim Sch LN13...75 B5
Acacia Ave
  Chapel St Leonard PE24 ...90 D8
  Gainsborough DN21 .....197 D6
  Peterborough PE1.......226 B8
  Scunthorpe DN15 ....182 C5
  Spalding PE11 ....214 F5
  Waddington LN5 ....205 D1
  [3] Wisbech PE13.......170 D1
Acacia Cl [2] NG32......210 B4
Acacia Ct [3] DN16 ......185 B6
Acacia Way
  Boston PE21 ....208 C4
  Messingham DN17.......29 C7
Acadia Gr HU3 ....178 F1
Accommodation Rd
  LN9....................199 A5
Acer Cl LN6.............204 D7
Acer Ct [2] LN6 ....204 D7

Acer Gr [3] DN17........184 C5
Acer Rd PE1............226 B6
Achille Rd DN34 ....190 D5
Achurch Cl LN9..........199 D1
Acklam Ave [3] PE11....214 F6
Acklam Gr DN32.........192 B6
Acklands La [18] NG23...117 D3
Acland St
  Gainsborough DN21 .....197 C5
  [4] Kingston upon Hull
    HU3....................180 A6
  Peterborough PE1.......225 F3
Acomb Comm Rd DN7 ...14 F4
Acorn Cl
  Freiston PE22 ....126 C4
  Grantham NG31.........211 C7
  Lincoln LN5 ....205 D7
  [19] Sutton on Sea LN12...76 F8
Acorn Ct DN35..........192 D2
Acorns The PE6.........217 A6
Acorn Way
  [5] Bottesford DN16.....185 B2
  Hessle HU13 ....178 B3
Acre Cl LN8 ....57 D8
Acre Dyke La LN4........82 B4
Acre La
  Scopwick LN4 ....95 E1
  Threekingham NG34 .....132 E2
Acres La DN9............26 D7
Acres The [1] PE9 ....172 D4
Acton Cl [2] DN32........189 C1
Acton Gr LN6............204 D7
Adam Smith St DN31.....188 F1
Adamstiles [2] NG32.....210 B4
Adams Way [6] DN21....65 E8
Ada Way LN11 ....198 D7
Adderley St HU3 ....180 B5
Addington Way [3] PE4...221 A3
Addison Cl [1] LN5 ......107 A8
Addison Dr LN2..........202 B6
Addison Pl LN1..........65 E3
ADDLETHORPE PE24 ....90 C3
Adelaide Cl
  Gainsborough DN21 .....197 F2
  [19] Waddington LN5 ....93 E8
Adelaide Prim Sch
  HU3....................180 D5
Adelaide St
  Kingston upon Hull
    HU3....................180 D5
  Stamford PE9...........219 D5
Adelphi Cl [5] DN36.....195 C6
Adelphi Dr DN33.........194 E7

Adlard Gr DN36..........36 C7
ADLINGFLEET DN14 .....7 E7
Adlingfleet Rd DN17 .....7 E6
Admirals Dr [7] PE13....170 D2
Admiralty Rd [13] LN12...64 B4
Adrian Cl
  Louth LN11 ....198 C5
  [5] Skegness PE25......206 A4
  [9] Swineshead PE20....135 B7
Advent Cl [2] DN39......12 A1
Adwalton Cl NG24 ....104 C4
Aegir Cl DN21...........197 F2
Africa Cl DN34..........190 D4
Agard Ave DN15 ....182 E3
Agnes St [2] NG31.......211 B4
Aidan Rd NG34 ....212 B2
AILBY LN13.............75 D4
AILSWORTH PE5 ....223 D3
Aima Ct [2] LN2..........68 C2
Ainsdale Dr PE4.........220 F3
Ainslie St DN32..........191 E6
Ainsworth Rd [8] DN40...186 B4
Ainthorpe Gr HU5 ....179 C7
Ainthorpe Prim Sch
  HU5....................179 C8
Aintree Dr PE11 ....214 B1
Aire Cl DN40............186 A3
Airedale Cl
  [12] Broughton DN20 ....19 E4
  Peterborough PE3.......226 A6
Airedale Rd
  [1] Scunthorpe DN16....185 D5
  [1] Stamford PE9........219 A2
Airedale Way DN31......191 D8
Aire Rd NG31...........210 E3
Airlie St HU3............180 B5
Airmanship Rd NG34.....120 B8
Airmyn Ave [1] HU3......179 E6
Airship Rd NG34.........107 C1
AISBY
  Heydour NG32..........131 D5
  Pilham DN21............41 D4
Aisby Wlk DN21..........197 F3
Aisne Cl LN1............201 E7
Aisne St HU5............180 A8
AISTHORPE LN1 ....67 C7
Ajax Cl DN34...........190 D4
Ajax Ct DN31...........182 F5
Akeferry Rd DN9.........27 C1
Akeman Ct [10] PE10....213 C6
Akeman St LN4..........81 A1
Akita Cl [4] PE11........204 A5
Alabala Cl LN4..........203 C1

1st–Alb

Alabala La LN4 ....81 F4
Alan Cres DN15..........182 F2
Alba Cl DN17 ....184 D5
Alban Ret Pk PE21.......208 B3
Albany Cl
  Louth LN11 ....198 D3
  Skegness PE25.........206 A5
Albany Pl LN11 ....198 D3
Albany Rd
  Louth LN11 ....198 D3
  Skegness PE25.........206 A5
  [21] Wisbech PE13......170 D1
Albany St
  Gainsborough DN21 .....197 C6
  Kingston upon Hull HU3 ...180 A4
  Lincoln LN1 ....234 A4
Albany Terr LN5..........205 D5
Albany Way PE25 ....206 A5
Albany Wlk PE2..........230 D7
Albatross Dr DN37.......190 B7
Albemarle Cl [5] HU15....2 B5
Albemarle St [2] HU3.....180 B5
Alberta Cres DN17.......184 E3
Albert Ave
  Kingston upon Hull
    HU3....................180 A7
  Long Sutton PE12 ......159 A4
  [1] Skegness PE25......206 A3
Albert Ave Pools HU3....180 A7
Albert Cl [7] DN32.......189 B1
Albert Cres LN1..........201 D4
Albert Ct PE21...........208 E5
Albertine Ct [4] DN37....194 C5
Albert Marson Ct [6]
  DN16..................183 B2
Albert Pl
  Grimsby DN32...........189 B1
  Peterborough PE3.......225 F1
Albert Rd
  [7] Cleethorpes DN35 ...192 F6
  Scunthorpe DN16 ....185 A5
  Skegness PE25.........206 B3
  [2] Stamford PE9........219 C4
Albert St [7] DN32.......189 B1
Albert St W [5] DN32.....189 B1
Albert St
  Boston PE21 ....208 A5
  [15] Bottesford NG13....128 A6
  Brigg DN20 ....196 C3

Albert St *continued*
Grantham NG31 . . . . 211 C2
6 Holbeach PE12 . . . . 215 D2
Horncastle LN9 . . . . 199 C3
7 New Holland DN19 . . . . . . 4 E2
Spalding PE11 . . . . 214 E5
Thorne/Moorends DN8 . . . . 15 B8
Albert Terr
2 Boston PE21 . . . . 208 E4
Boultham LN5 . . . . 205 D8
14 Sleaford NG34 . . . . 212 D4
Albert Wlk 8 PE12 . . . . . 215 D2
Albery Way LN6 . . . . 195 C7
Albion Cl LN1 . . . . 201 C6
Albion Cres LN1 . . . . 201 C6
Albion Ct HU4 . . . . 179 B6
Albion Hill 8 DN9 . . . . . . 27 E6
Albion Pl LN11 . . . . 198 C5
Albion Rd 2 NG31 . . . . . . 211 A5
Albion St
6 Crowland PE6 . . . . 166 E1
18 Grantham NG31 . . . . . . 211 A5
Grimsby DN32 . . . . 189 B1
Holbeach PE12 . . . . 215 F2
10 Kingston upon Hull
HU1 . . . . 180 E7
Spalding PE11 . . . . 214 E5
Albion Terr
4 Misterton DN10 . . . . . . 40 A5
Sleaford NG34 . . . . 212 D4
Albourne Ave DN15 . . . . . 183 A2
Alconbury Cl
13 Birchwood LN6 . . . . . . 204 C6
Peterborough PE2 . . . . . . 231 E5
Alcorn Gn PE21 . . . . 209 C4
Aldbro' St HU2 . . . . 180 F8
Aldburgh Cl 18 LN10 . . . . 97 C5
Aldenham Cl DN40 . . . . . . 186 C4
Alder Cl
30 Brough HU15 . . . . 2 C5
3 Lincoln LN6 . . . . 204 F3
Louth LN11 . . . . 198 D4
Alder Gr PE21 . . . . 209 C2
Aldergrove Cl LN6 . . . . . 204 C7
Aldergrove Cres LN6 . . . . 204 C7
Alderlands Cl 8 PE25 . . . 175 B8
Alderley Edge DN37 . . . . . 194 C4
Alderman's Dr PE3 . . . . . . 225 E3
Alderney Way
Immingham DN40 . . . . . . 186 C2
Lincoln LN6 . . . . 205 A1
Alder Rd
Peterborough PE7 . . . . . . 230 C3
Sleaford NG34 . . . . 212 D2
Alderson Mews 5
HU9 . . . . 181 C7
Alders The DN21 . . . . 197 F5
Alder View DN33 . . . . 190 F3
ALDGATE PE9 . . . . 171 A3
Aldgate Ct 9 PE9 . . . . . 171 A3
Aldred Gdns DN33 . . . . . . 191 B1
Aldrich Rd DN35 . . . . 192 F4
Aldrin Cl PE11 . . . . 214 C2
Aldsworth Cl 1 PE1 . . . . 226 D6
Aldwych Croft 8
DN36 . . . . 195 C6
Aldwych Ct HU5 . . . . 179 E8
Aldwych Gdns 11 PE11 . . 214 A2
Alec Rose Gr DN21 . . . . . . 197 F3
Alexander Ave NG24 . . . . 104 A6
Alexander Cl 18 LN4 . . . . 95 D4
Alexander Ct LN1 . . . . 198 D4
Alexander Rd DN16 . . . . . . 183 C3
Alexandra Cl 8 NG23 . . . . 117 D4
Alexandra Ct 9 PE25 . . . 206 C3
Alexandra Dock N
DN31 . . . . 188 F2
Alexandra Pk 22 LN12 . . . . 64 B4
Alexandra Rd
Cleethorpes DN35 . . . . 192 F6
Grantham NG31 . . . . 210 F3
Grimsby DN31 . . . . 188 F1
Immingham DN40 . . . . . . 186 F6
Louth LN11 . . . . 198 C6
21 Mablethorpe/Sutton on Sea
LN12 . . . . 64 B4
Peterborough PE1 . . . . . . 225 F6
Scunthorpe DN16 . . . . 185 B6
Skegness PE25 . . . . 206 B3
Sleaford NG34 . . . . 212 C4
Spalding PE11 . . . . 214 E3
3 Woodhall Spa LN10 . . . . 97 C6
Alexandra Rd S DN40 . . . 186 E6
Alexandra Ret Pk
DN31 . . . . 188 F1
Alexandra St HU3 . . . . 180 D7
Alexandra Terr LN1 . . . . 234 A3
Alexandra Terraces 4
PE10 . . . . 213 D5
Alexandra Wharf DN31 . . 191 D7
Alexandre Ave 2 LN6 . . . 204 F1
Alexandria Rd LN8 . . . . . . 56 C5
Alfonso St 5 HU3 . . . . 180 B5
ALFORD LN13 . . . . 75 E2
Alford Mill Cl 6 LN6 . . . . 93 B8
Alford Pottery* LN13 . . . 75 F2
Alford Prim Sch LN13 . . . 75 F2
Alford Rd
1 Alford LN13 . . . . 75 F3
Bilsby LN13 . . . . 76 A3
Mablethorpe/Sutton on Sea
LN12 . . . . 64 A3
Alford St NG31 . . . . 211 B5
Alford War Meml Hospl
LN13 . . . . 75 E2

Alford Windmill* LN13 . . . 75 F3
Alfred Ave LN4 . . . . 95 C4
Alfred Cl 10 NG34 . . . . . . 212 B2
Alfred Gelder St 6
HU1 . . . . 180 F6
Alfred Smith Way 5
LN11 . . . . 61 F3
Alfred St
Boston PE21 . . . . 209 A3
Gainsborough DN21 . . . . . 197 C5
Grimsby DN31 . . . . 191 D8
Kingston upon Hull HU3 . 180 D5
Lincoln LN5 . . . . 201 C1
Alfreton Ct 2 DN15 . . . . 182 B2
Alfric Sq PE2 . . . . 230 D6
ALGAKIRK PE20 . . . . 136 B2
Algernon St DN32 . . . . 191 F5
Algitha Rd PE25 . . . . 206 C3
Allan Rd PE7 . . . . 233 D6
Allenby Ave DN34 . . . . . . 191 A6
Allenby Cres LN11 . . . . . 49 A2
Allenby Ind Est LN2 . . . . 202 D4
Allenby Rd LN2 . . . . 202 D4
Allenby's Chase 14
PE12 . . . . 160 E4
Allenby Way PE25 . . . . . . 206 D8
Allen Cl
7 Billingborough
NG34 . . . . 133 B1
4 Claypole NG23 . . . . . . 117 E8
6 Market Deeping PE6 . . . 217 D5
Allen Rd
Coningsby LN4 . . . . 207 F6
Fenton NG23 . . . . 105 C1
Peterborough PE1 . . . . . . 225 E6
Allen's Dro PE13 . . . . 169 D1
Allerthorpe Cres 19
HU15 . . . . 169 D1
Allerton Cl PE9 . . . . 172 D3
Allerton Ct DN34 . . . . . . 186 B4
Allerton Garth PE7 . . . . . 229 A4
Allerton Prim Sch
DN40 . . . . 186 B4
Allestree Dr DN33 . . . . . . 194 E7
Allexton Gdns 2 PE1 . . . 226 D7
Alliance Ave HU3 . . . . 179 F7
Alliance La HU3 . . . . 179 F7
ALLINGTON NG32 . . . . 128 F7
Allington Dr DN37 . . . . . . 188 A2
Allington Gdn PE21 . . . . 209 A7
Allington La NG32 . . . . . . 129 B4
Allington Rd NG32 . . . . . . 128 F6
Allington with Sedgebrook
CE Prim Sch NG32 . . . . 129 A7
Allison Ave PE12 . . . . 215 E2
Allison Cl DN34 . . . . 29 D7
Allison Pl 8 LN1 . . . . 201 D4
Allison Rd 6 NG34 . . . . . . 122 D3
Allison St LN1 . . . . 201 D4
Allotment La PE5 . . . . 223 E2
All Saints Ave 8 LN13 . . 170 C1
All Saints Brewery* 22
PE9 . . . . 219 B5
All Saints CE (Aided) Prim
Sch PE22 . . . . 115 A6
All Saints CE Jun Sch
Kingston upon Hull
HU3 . . . . 178 F2
Peterborough PE1 . . . . . . 226 A6
All Saints CE Prim Sch
LN6 . . . . 204 C1
All Saints CE Sch
Swinderby Prim Sch
LN6 . . . . 92 B6
All Saints Cl
8 Holbeach PE12 . . . . 215 F3
7 Moulton PE12 . . . . 157 F7
4 Wainfleet All Saints
PE24 . . . . 114 F6
All Saints' Cl 17 DN19 . . . 12 A8
All Saints Cty Prim Sch
LN5 . . . . 93 F7
All Saints Gr 4 NG34 . . . 212 B6
All Saints La 14 NG34 . . . 68 C2
All Saints Mews 17
PE9 . . . . 219 B5
All Saints' Pl 6 PE9 . . . 219 B5
All Saints' Rd 1 PE24 . . . 226 A5
All Saints' St
Kingston upon Hull
HU3 . . . . 180 D8
10 Stamford PE9 . . . . 219 B5
Allwood Rd 20 LN6 . . . . . . 68 D6
Alma Ave PE25 . . . . 206 B5
Alma Cl
Kingston upon Hull
HU10 . . . . 178 D7
3 Skegness PE25 . . . . 206 D7
Alma Martin Way 7
LN3 . . . . 83 C4
Alma Pk Cl 1 NG31 . . . . 211 F6
Alma Pk Ind Est
Grantham NG31 . . . . 211 F7
Londonthorpe & Harrowby
without NG31 . . . . 130 C4
Alma Pk Rd NG31 . . . . . . 211 F6
Alma Rd PE13 . . . . 225 C3
Alma St 6 HU9 . . . . 181 B7

Almond Ave
Heighington LN4 . . . . . . 81 F4
Lincoln LN6 . . . . 205 A8
Almond Cl
Boston PE21 . . . . 208 C5
5 Saxilby LN1 . . . . 66 D2
Almond Cres
Lincoln LN6 . . . . 205 A8
Louth LN11 . . . . 198 D5
Waddington LN5 . . . . 205 D1
Almond Ct LN6 . . . . 205 A8
Almond Gr
Brigg DN20 . . . . 196 B4
Grantham NG31 . . . . 211 C6
3 Kingston upon Hull
HU3 . . . . 180 D6
3 Scunthorpe DN16 . . . . . . 185 B8
Skellingthorpe LN6 . . . . . 200 A4
Stallingborough DN41 . . . . 23 E6
Almond Rd PE1 . . . . 226 B7
Almond Wlk
Boston PE21 . . . . 208 D5
3 Sleaford NG34 . . . . 212 D6
Almoners La PE3 . . . . 225 E3
Alness Cl LN1 . . . . 204 B8
Alnwick PE2 . . . . 229 F3
Altham Terr LN5 . . . . 205 D7
ALTHORPE DN17 . . . . 17 D5
Althorpe Cl 18 PE6 . . . . . . 184 E1
Althorpe & Keadby Prim
Sch DN17 . . . . 17 D5
Althorpe Sta DN17 . . . . . 17 D5
Altoft Cl 10 DN37 . . . . 23 F1
Altyre Way DN36 . . . . 192 C1
Alverston Ave LN10 . . . . 97 C5
Alveston Rd DN17 . . . . . . 184 D8
Alvey Rd NG24 . . . . 104 C2
ALVINGHAM LN11 . . . . 49 E2
Alvingham Ave DN35 . . . . 192 F3
Alvingham Rd
Keddington LN11 . . . . . . 198 E8
Scunthorpe DN16 . . . . . . 185 B7
Alvis Cl LN4 . . . . 205 F2
Alvis Dr PE7 . . . . 233 D6
ALWALTON PE2 . . . . 229 A4
Alwyn Rd 10 DN8 . . . . 15 B8
Amanda Ct PE3 . . . . 225 E2
Amanda Dr
Hatfield DN7 . . . . 14 D4
Louth LN11 . . . . 198 C8
Ambergate Specl Sch
Ambergate Wlk NG31 . . . 210 E3
Amber High Toftstead Prim
Sch PE20 . . . . 124 A5
Amberley Cres PE21 . . . . 208 C4
Amberley Slope PE21 . . . 208 C4
Amble Cl LN1 . . . . 201 E8
Ambleside Cl 4 LN4 . . . . 212 B2
Ambleside Dr PE11 . . . . 214 B2
Ambleside Pk LN6 . . . . . . 204 F1
Ambrose Ave 2 DN7 . . . . 14 E4
Ambury Gdns 9 PE6 . . . . 166 F1
Amcott Ave DN10 . . . . 40 A4
AMCOTTS DN17 . . . . 36 D8
Amcotts Rd DN33 . . . . 191 A2
Amelia Ct DN36 . . . . 36 D8
Amery Way 31 PE24 . . . . 90 D7
Amesbury Ave DN33 . . . 194 D7
Amethyst Cl 3 NG34 . . . . 212 A3
Amethyst Ct 2 DN35 . . . 195 D7
Amman Sq 1 NG34 . . . . . 120 D8
Amos Cl DN31 . . . . 194 D7
Amos Cres 8 DN16 . . . . . . 185 D7
Amos La NG23 . . . . 91 E6
Amos Way 8 PE22 . . . . . . 113 B1
Ampleforth Ave DN32 . . . 190 F8
Ampleforth Gr HU5 . . . . . 179 D8
Amstel Cl 1 PE11 . . . . . . 214 B2
Amsterdam Gdns 9
PE11 . . . . 214 B3
Amwell Gn 10 DN7 . . . . . . 14 D3
Amy Johnson Sch HU3 . . 179 F5
Anastasia Cl DN21 . . . . . . 197 C7
ANCASTER NG32 . . . . 120 B2
Ancaster Ave
Chapel St Leonard PE24 . . . 90 D7
Grimsby DN33 . . . . 194 D8
Lincoln LN2 . . . . 202 B5
Spilsby PE23 . . . . 100 F8
Ancaster CE Prim Sch
NG32 . . . . 120 A3
Ancaster Cl LN1 . . . . 203 E6
Ancaster Ct
Horncastle LN9 . . . . 199 B3
Scunthorpe DN16 . . . . . . 185 A5
Ancaster Dr NG34 . . . . . . 212 B2
Ancaster Rd
Bourne PE10 . . . . 213 E5
14 Mablethorpe/Sutton on Sea
LN12 . . . . 64 B3
2 Stamford PE9 . . . . 219 A7
Ancaster Sta NG32 . . . . . 120 A3
Ancholme Ave DN40 . . . . 186 A3
Ancholme Bsns Pk
DN20 . . . . 196 A4
Ancholme Cl LN4 . . . . 201 D8
Ancholme Gdns 8
DN20 . . . . 196 C3
Ancholme Leisure Ctr
DN20 . . . . 196 A3
Ancholme Rd DN16 . . . . . . 185 D6
Ancholme Way DN20 . . . . 196 B3
Anchorage St 4 DN20 . . . 18 E8
Anchor Cl DN8 . . . . 15 A8

Anchor Ct PE4 . . . . 221 D1
Anchor La PE25 . . . . 90 D4
Anchor Rd
Scunthorpe DN16 . . . . 19 B4
Sutton Bridge PE34 . . . . 161 C4
Anchor St LN5 . . . . 234 A1
Anchors Way 7 DN20 . . . 196 A3
Ancient La DN7 . . . . 14 E3
ANDERBY PE24 . . . . 77 A2
Anderby Cl LN6 . . . . 204 F6
ANDERBY CREEK PE24 . . . 77 C3
Anderby Dr
Grimsby DN37 . . . . 190 D7
Lincoln LN6 . . . . 204 F6
Anderby Drainage Mus*
PE24 . . . . 77 C2
Anderby Rd 6 PE6 . . . . . . 77 D1
Anderson LN2 . . . . 68 D5
Anderson Way DN21 . . . . 52 F5
Andover Cl LN6 . . . . 204 B8
Andrea Cl PE2 . . . . 231 C6
Andrew Ave 27 PE24 . . . . 90 D7
Andrew Cl PE25 . . . . 223 D2
Andrewe's Cl PE7 . . . . . . 231 B1
Andrew Paddock 18
DN20 . . . . 30 F5
Andrew Rd
9 Humberston DN36 . . . . 36 D8
1 Stamford PE9 . . . . 219 B6
Andrews Cl LN11 . . . . . . 198 C7
Andrews Cres PE4 . . . . . . 221 D2
Andrews Rd 8 LN11 . . . . . 10 A7
Andrews Way 8 DN40 . . . 186 A4
Angel Ct 5 NG22 . . . . 120 A7
Angelica Dr PE11 . . . . . . 214 B6
Angell La PE12 . . . . 215 E1
Angel Prec The PE10 . . . . 213 C5
Angerstein Rd DN17 . . . 184 F5
Anglesey Cl 20 LN6 . . . . 204 C7
Anglesey Dr DN40 . . . . . . 186 C2
Anglia Cl 18 NG34 . . . . . . 212 B2
Anglia Ct PE2 . . . . 231 D6
Anglian Way 5 LN8 . . . . . 57 E8
Angus Cl 8 PE9 . . . . 218 D6
Angus Ct PE3 . . . . 225 D3
ANLABY HU10 . . . . 179 A6
Anlaby Acre Head Cty Prim
Sch HU4 . . . . 179 B7
Anlaby Ave 7 HU4 . . . . . . 179 B7
Anlaby High Rd HU4 . . . . 179 C5
Anlaby Jun Sch HU4 . . . . 179 A6
ANLABY PARK HU4 . . . . . . 179 C5
Anlaby Pk Rd N HU4 . . . . 179 B5
Anlaby Pk Rd S HU4 . . . . 179 B2
Anlaby Rd HU3 . . . . 179 F6
Annadale Rd HU10 . . . . . . 178 F6
Anne Rd
Stamford PE9 . . . . 219 A6
5 Sutton Bridge PE12 . . . 160 E4
Annes Cres DN16 . . . . 185 C7
Annesley St 1 LN1 . . . . . . 188 F1
Annette Cl 8 PE11 . . . . . . 214 B5
Ann Gr DN35 . . . . 192 D4
Anningson La 6 DN36 . . . 195 D7
Annpasture La LN4 . . . . . 207 C8
Anson Cl
Grantham NG31 . . . . 211 C2
Skellingthorpe LN6 . . . . . 200 A4
Anson Ct PE6 . . . . 217 B7
Antelope Rd DN18 . . . . . . 4 A1
Anthony Cl PE1 . . . . 225 F8
Anthony Cres LN11 . . . . 198 C8
Anthony's Bank Rd
DN36 . . . . 193 D1
Anthony Way 8 DN41 . . . 23 D6
ANTON'S GOWT PE22 . . . 125 B6
Antrim Rd 8 LN5 . . . . 205 D2
Antrim Way 3 LN1 . . . . . . 191 D2
Anvil Cl PE12 . . . . 148 B1
Anvil Wlk 2 DN15 . . . . . . 8 F3
ANWICK NG34 . . . . 109 B1
Anzio Cres LN1 . . . . 201 E7
Anzio Terr LN1 . . . . 201 E7
Anzio Wlk LN1 . . . . 201 E7
Apeldoorn Gdns 3
PE11 . . . . 214 B3
APLEY LN8 . . . . 70 A2
Apley Cl
Gainsborough DN21 . . . . . 197 F3
Lincoln LN2 . . . . 202 A8
Appian Way
8 Baston PE6 . . . . 164 E5
11 Bracebridge Heath
LN4 . . . . 81 A1
West Marsh DN31 . . . . . . 188 C2
APPLEBY DN15 . . . . 9 D1
Appleby Cl DN17 . . . . 184 F5
Appleby Ct 17 DN32 . . . . 189 C1
Appleby Gdns DN20 . . . . 19 D4
Appleby La DN20 . . . . 9 D4
Appleby Rd DN16 . . . . . . 183 E3
Apple Cl LN4 . . . . 81 F4
Appledore Cl HU9 . . . . . . 181 C6
Apple Garth LN5 . . . . 205 D4
Appletree Gr PE10 . . . . . . 213 D6
Applegarth Rd 8 HU8 . . . 181 A7
Appleton Gate NG24 . . . . 104 A5
Appleton Gdns LN6 . . . . . 185 C6
Apple Tree Cl 19 LN4 . . . . 95 C4
Apple Tree 14 DN41 . . . . . 23 F5

Applewood Dr
5 Gonerby Hill Foot
NG31 . . . . 210 F8
3 Hampton Hargate
PE7 . . . . 230 C3
Appleyard PE2 . . . . 231 C7
Appleyard Dr 8 DN18 . . . 10 E8
Apsley Way PE3 . . . . 225 A2
Aqua Dr LN12 . . . . 46 B2
Aquila Way PE6 . . . . 164 E2
Arabis Cl 3 LN2 . . . . 202 C8
Arakan Way 2 PE10 . . . . 213 E7
Arbella Rd PE21 . . . . 209 C4
Arboretum Ave LN2 . . . . . 234 C2
Arboretum The* LN2 . . . 234 C3
Arboretum View LN2 . . . 234 C2
Arborfield Cl 6 PE6 . . . . 173 C4
Arbroath Gdns PE2 . . . . 229 C4
Arbury Cl PE3 . . . . 225 A3
Arcadia Cres 2 PE25 . . . 206 D2
Arcadia Rd PE25 . . . . 206 D3
Archer La 12 PE21 . . . . . . 208 F5
Archer Rd
Branston LN4 . . . . 81 E2
Waltham DN37 . . . . 194 D4
Archers Dro PE6 . . . . 176 D6
Archers La PE20 . . . . 136 C3
Archer St
3 Bishop Norton LN8 . . . . 43 D3
Lincoln LN5 . . . . 234 B1
Archers Wood 1 PE7 . . . 230 C3
Archibald Wlk PE21 . . . . 208 B4
Archway Dr LN8 . . . . 70 C4
Arcon Dr HU4 . . . . 179 D6
Arcott Dr PE2 . . . . 208 C5
Arden Cl 6 LN12 . . . . 64 C3
Arden Moor Way 4
LN6 . . . . 93 B8
Ardent Rd DN18 . . . . 4 A1
Arden Village DN35 . . . . 192 F1
Argyle Ct 8 DN15 . . . . . . 183 B3
Argyle St
Boston PE21 . . . . 208 D5
Kingston upon Hull HU3 . . 180 C7
Argyll Way 2 PE25 . . . . . 218 F5
Ariston St DN32 . . . . 192 B7
Arkley Cl 22 HU15 . . . . 2 C5
Ark Cl LN11 . . . . 50 F8
Ark Royal Ct 8 NG34 . . . 212 A3
Arkwright St DN21 . . . . . . 197 C5
Arkwright Way DN16 . . . 185 F6
Arlington Rd 4 LN8 . . . . . 56 D5
Arlington St 2 HU3 . . . . . 180 C6
Armeria Dr 4 DN17 . . . . . 185 A1
Armley Gr 3 PE9 . . . . 219 D7
Armstrong Pl E 3
DN31 . . . . 188 E1
Armstrong Pl W 2
DN31 . . . . 188 E1
Armstrong Rd 12 PE11 . . 214 C2
Armstrong's Cl 2
PE12 . . . . 157 D7
Armstrong's La PE22 . . . 115 B7
Armstrong St LN1 . . . . . . 188 F1
Armthorpe La DN3 . . . . . . 14 A3
Armtree Rd PE22 . . . . 124 E7
Arne Cl 10 NG32 . . . . 120 A3
Arnhem Ave 1 NG34 . . . . 108 B8
Arnhem Cl LN1 . . . . 201 E2
Arnhem Dr
16 Caythorpe NG32 . . . . 119 B7
2 Spalding PE11 . . . . . . 214 C5
Arnhem Way
Bourne PE10 . . . . 213 E6
7 Woodhall Spa LN10 . . . 97 D5
Arnold Ave NG31 . . . . 210 E8
Arnold Cl DN37 . . . . 23 F2
Arnold Ct DN37 . . . . 189 C3
Arnold La HU3 . . . . 180 B6
Arnold's Meadow Nature
Reserve* PE12 . . . . 114 A2
Arnold St HU3 . . . . 180 B6
Arran Cl
Immingham DN40 . . . . . . 186 D2
New Waltham DN36 . . . . . 195 C7
Sleaford NG34 . . . . 121 A1
Arran Rd PE9 . . . . 218 D7
Arras Cl LN1 . . . . 201 E6
Arrow Ct PE7 . . . . 230 C3
Art Coll Ct DN32 . . . . 191 F7
Art Coll News DN32 . . . . 189 F8
Art Haven The* NG31 . . . 211 B6
Arthur Mellows Village Coll
PE6 . . . . 220 B7
Arthur Rd DN21 . . . . 197 D6
Arthurs' Ave 5 PE21 . . . 215 D7
Arthur St
Grimsby DN31 . . . . 191 C7
Kingston upon Hull HU3 . . 180 A5
6 Lincoln LN5 . . . . 201 F7
Arthur Taylor St 1
LN1 . . . . 201 F7
Artillery Row 13 PE21 . . 209 A4
Artindale PE3 . . . . 225 A1
Artis Ct PE3 . . . . 225 A1
Arundel Cl
Gainsborough DN21 . . . . . 197 E3
Kingston upon Hull HU10 . . 181 C8
Arundel Cres PE21 . . . . 208 B6
Arundel Dr LN11 . . . . 198 A4
Arundel Pl DN35 . . . . 192 E6
Arundel Rd 4 NG34 . . . . 212 B2
Arundel St 3 HU3 . . . . . . 180 B6
Arundel Wlk DN34 . . . . . . 191 A1
Ascendale PE6 . . . . 217 F5
Ascot Cl 4 PE11 . . . . 156 C1

scot Dr
7 Grantham NG31 . . . . . . 211 D7
Peterborough PE1 . . . . . . 226 B6
scot Rd DN37 . . . . 194 D4
scott Cl HU4 . . . . 179 D5
scot Way 7 LN6. . . . . . .93 A8
SGARBY
Asgarby and Howell
NG34. . . . . 122 B4
Lusby with Winceby LN9 . . .86 F1
sgarby Rd NG34 . . . . . . 122 B2
sgard Way DN33. . . . . . .191 B2
sh Ave 19 HU15. . . . . . . .2 C6
Ashberry Dr
31 Messingham DN17. . . . . .29 D7
4 Scunthorpe DN16. . . . . 185 B6
shbourne 6 DN37. . . . . 194 C4
shbourne 5 DN34. . . . . 212 B2
shbourne Cl DN15. . . . . 182 B3
sh Buckingham Studio*
LN9 . . . . .85 C5
shburn Cl 1 PF6. . . . . . 220 D7
shburnham Rd 20 DN16. . .15 A8
SHBY DN16. . . . . 185 B5
shby Ave LN6. . . . . 204 F7
shby Broadway DN16. . . 185 A6
shby Cl 2 NG34 . . . . . . 212 D6
SHBY BY PARTNEY
PE23. . . . . .88 D1
shby Cl
Bracebridge LN5 . . . . . . 205 D1
Grimsby DN37 . . . . 190 D8
Holton le Clay DN36 . . . . 195 E1
Kingston upon Hull HU4 . . 179 B7
shby Ct 2 NG34 . . . . . . 212 D6
DN37 . . . . .35 D3
SHBY CUM FENBY
DN37. . . . . .35 D3
SHBY DE LA LAUNDE
LN4. . . . . 108 B6
Cleethorpes DN35 . . . . . 192 D3
Kingston upon Hull HU4 . . 179 B4
Scunthorpe DN16 . . . . . 183 A1
Spilsby PE23 . . . . .88 A1
sh Cl
Burgh le Marsh PE24. . . . 102 D7
6 Colsterworth NG33 . . . 151 E7
Hessle HU13 . . . . 178 C3
Holbeach PE12 . . . . 215 C3
Langtoft PE6 . . . . 164 E2
Lincoln LN6 . . . . 204 E8
Louth LN11 . . . . 198 C7
Peterborough PE1 . . . . . 226 C7
Spalding PE11 . . . . 214 F5
1 Thorney PE6 . . . . 175 F3
shcroft Gdns PE1. . . . . . 226 C5
shcroft Rd DN21. . . . . . 197 D2
sh Ct
Cleethorpes DN35 . . . . . 192 D2
5 Donington PE11 . . . . . 134 E2
Peterborough PE1 . . . . . 226 C7
Spalding PE11 . . . . 214 F6
shdale Cl 8 LN4 . . . . . . .95 C4
shdale Pk 18 HU14 . . . . . .3 A5
shdene Cl HU10 . . . . . . 178 E7
shdown Ave 5 DN15 . . . 182 E3
shdown Cl 3 DN20. . . . . 196 E3
shdown Way 14 DN10 . . . .39 F5
sh Dr
Kingston upon Hull
HU10. . . . . 178 F8
3 Kirton PE20 . . . . 136 C5
sheridge LN4. . . . . .81 E2
shfield 4 LN1. . . . . .66 D7
shfield Ave 2 DN8. . . . . .15 A7
shfield Ct 20 DN17. . . . . .16 D7
shfield Gr 1 DN17. . . . . .16 D7
shfield Grange 5 LN1 . . . 66 C2
shfield Pk DN17 . . . . . . 184 C5
shfield Rd
3 Hatfield DN7 . . . . .14 C4
Sleaford NG34. . . . . . . 212 D5
Thorne DN8. . . . . 14 F7
shfield St 3 LN2. . . . . . 202 B3
sh Gr
Bourne PE10 . . . . 213 C6
Brigg DN20 . . . . 196 B4
Cherry Willingham/Reepham
LN3 . . . . 203 D5
Gainsborough DN21 . . . . 197 D6
Grantham NG31. . . . . . . 211 D7
Lincoln LN6 . . . . 204 F2
32 Messingham DN17. . . . .29 D7
Scunthorpe DN16. . . . . . 185 B7
sh Hill Cres DN7. . . . . . . 14 D4
sh Hill Rd DN7 . . . . .14 D4
Ashing La LN2. . . . . .68 F6
ASHINGTON END PE24 . . .90 B1
Ash La 28 LN5 . . . . .93 F6
shlawn Dr PE21. . . . . . . 209 B6
Ashlea 3 DN10. . . . . .39 F5
shleigh PE2 . . . . 229 C6
shleigh Ct 3 DN41 . . . . . 23 F5
Ashley Cl LN12 . . . . .64 C1
Ashley Dr NG31. . . . . . . 210 E8
Ashley Pool La 5 PE6 . . . 176 A2
Ashley Rd 2 LN11 . . . . . 198 C5
Ashlin Gr LN1 . . . . 234 A3
Ash Pk PE4. . . . . 220 F6
Ash Pl 6 PE9 . . . . 218 D6

Ash Rd
7 Coningsby LN4. . . . . . 207 D4
Peterborough PE1 . . . . . 226 C7
Ashridge Dr DN32 . . . . . 192 C5
ASHTON PE9. . . . . 173 A4
Ashton Hall Dr PE21 . . . 208 A1
Ashton Rd PE3 . . . . 225 B5
Ashtons Ct LN5. . . . . . . 201 E1
Ash Tree Ave DN34. . . . . 191 A6
Ash Tree Ave 11 LN2 . . . .68 D2
Ashtree Cl
1 Belton DN9. . . . . .16 E2
12 Ruskington NG34 . . . . 108 E1
Ash Tree Cl
Immingham DN40 . . . . . 186 C5
10 Market Rasen LN8 . . . 57 D7
Ash Tree Dr 5 DN9 . . . . .27 D2
Ashtree Gdns 5 PE9 . . . . 171 B1
Ash Tree Rd 7 DN8. . . . . .15 B7
Ash Villa Specl Sch The
NG34 . . . . 121 A3
Ashwell Ave 2 HU9. . . . . . 5 E8
Ashwin Gate 2 PE11 . . . 145 A8
Ashwood Cl LN9. . . . . . . 199 B4
Ashwood Dr 10 DN36. . . . .36 D8
Ashworth Cl LN6. . . . . . 204 F5
Askew Ave 6 LN6. . . . . . 204 E8
Askew's Dro PE4. . . . . . 166 D2
Askew's La PE7. . . . . . . 233 E4
ASLACKBY NG34 . . . . . . 142 D5
Aslackby Rd NG34 . . . . . 142 D3
Aspen Cl LN2 . . . . .65 D2
Aspen Ct
Cleethorpes DN35 . . . . . 192 D2
Gainsborough DN21 . . . . 197 F6
Aspen Dr 4 NG34 . . . . . 212 D2
Aspen Gr DN16 . . . . 185 B8
Aspen Wlk 10 HU15 . . . . . 2 D5
ASPERTON PE20 . . . . . . 135 D4
Asperton Rd PE20 . . . . . 135 E4
Asphodel Cl 3 DN36. . . . 195 D2
Asquith St DN21 . . . . . . 197 B6
ASSERBY LN13. . . . . . . .76 D4
ASTERBY LN11. . . . . . . .72 E6
Asterby Cl LN2 . . . . 202 A7
Asterby La LN11. . . . . . . .72 E6
Asterby Rd DN17. . . . . . 184 F5
Aster Cl LN2. . . . . 202 A5
Aster Dr PE4 . . . . 221 B3
Astley Cres 18 DN7. . . . . .29 C3
Astley La LN6. . . . . 179 F7
Aston Cl
4 Waddington LN5. . . . . .93 F7
Yaxley PE7. . . . . 233 E6
Aston Gn 5 DN7 . . . . . . .14 D3
Aston Hall Dr 12 HU14 . . . 3 A5
Astore Pk PE1 . . . . 226 E3
Astral Cl HU13 . . . . 178 F3
Astral Rd HU13 . . . . 178 F3
Astral Way 8 LN6. . . . . . 204 C1
Astwick Rd LN6. . . . . . . 205 A5
ASWARBY NG34. . . . . . 132 D6
Aswell St LN11 . . . . 198 B5
Athelstan St 9 NG34 . . . 212 B2
Athena Dr DN31 . . . . . . 188 C2
Athenian Way 1 DN11 . . 188 A3
Atherstone Ave PE3. . . . 225 B4
Atherton Way DN20. . . . 196 B4
Atholl Ave HU13 . . . . . . 178 A3
Athol St HU3 . . . . 179 F4
Atkinson Ave DN20. . . . . 196 C5
Atkinson Dr 24 HU1 . . . . .2 C6
Atkinson La DN37. . . . . . 194 E4
Atkinsons Warren Nature
Reserve* DN15 . . . . . 182 D5
Atkinsons Way 15 DN15 . 182 F7
Atlantic Pl 8 NG31. . . . . 211 A3
Atlas Rd DN17 . . . . 184 F8
ATTERBY LN8. . . . . .43 D3
Atterby Carr La DN21 . . . .43 F4
Atterby La LN8 . . . . .43 C3
Atterby Rd DN21 . . . . . . .43 D3
Atwater Cl LN2 . . . . 202 D7
Atwater Ct 2 LN2. . . . . . 202 D7
Atwater Gr LN2. . . . . . . 202 D7
Atwood Dr DN40. . . . . . 186 B5
Auborn Gdns PE21 . . . . . 209 B4
AUBOURN LN5. . . . . . . .93 A5
Aubourn Ave LN6. . . . . . 201 F7
Aubourn Hall* LN5 . . . . .93 A5
Aubretia Ave PE4. . . . . . 221 A3
Aubretia Dr 3 DN17. . . . 185 A1
Aubrey Parker Cl 4
LN12. . . . . .64 C2
Auckland Cres 1 LN4. . . . 96 C1
Auckland Rd
Grimsby DN31. . . . . 189 B2
Scunthorpe DN15. . . . . . 182 F2
Auden Cl LN2 . . . . 234 C4
Auden Ct 2 LN4. . . . . . . 207 B5
Audern Rd DN15. . . . . . 185 A4
Audley Gate PE13. . . . . . 225 C3
Augusta Cl
Grimsby DN34 . . . . 191 C5
Peterborough PE1 . . . . . 226 E6
Augusta Oaks DN34. . . . 191 C6
Augusta St DN34. . . . . . 191 C6
Augustin Ret Pk NG31. . . 211 A4
Augustus Dr 17 HU15 . . . . 2 C5
AUNBY PE9 . . . . 163 A8
AUNSBY NG34. . . . . . . 132 A5
Aunsby Rd NG34 . . . . . . 132 A5
AUSTENDIKE PE12 . . . . 157 C4
Austendike Rd PE12. . . . 157 C4

AUSTEN FEN LN11. . . . . .49 F5
Austen Wlk LN2 . . . . . . 202 C6
Austerby PE10 . . . . 213 E4
Austerby Cl PE10 . . . . . 213 D4
Austerby The PE10 . . . . 213 E4
Austin Cres 3 DN17. . . . 184 F3
Austin Garth 5 DN37 . . . .23 F1
Austin Friar's La 2
PE9. . . . . 219 B4
Austin Garth 5 DN37 . . . .23 F1
Austin St PE9. . . . . 219 B4
AUTHORPE LN11 . . . . . . .74 F7
Autumn Croft Rd 6
NG24 . . . . 104 B5
Autumn Pk Ind Est
NG31 . . . . 210 F4
Avebury Gdns PE11 . . . . 214 F4
Avend Cl
Aslackby & Laughton
NG34. . . . . 142 C5
5 Bourne PE10 . . . . 213 C5
Aveland Dr NG34 . . . . . . 143 B8
Aveland High Sch The
NG34 . . . . 143 B8
Aveland Way
Aslackby & Laughton
NG34. . . . . 142 C5
3 Baston PE6. . . . . 164 E4
Avensword La DN15 . . . . 182 D5
Avenue A DN21 . . . . .53 D5
Avenue B DN21 . . . . .53 D5
Avenue Cannes DN15 . . . 182 D5
Avenue Clamart DN15 . . . 182 D5
Avenue Farm Rd PE12 . . . 160 D6
Avenue Fontenay
DN15 . . . . 182 D5
Avenue Lourdes DN15 . . . 182 D5
Avenue Nozay 2 DN20. . . .19 E4
Avenue Rd NG31. . . . . . 211 B4
Avenue Rouen DN15 . . . . 182 D5
Avenue Terr LN1 . . . . . . 234 A3
Avenue The
8 Blyton DN21. . . . . . . .41 C5
Burton upon Stather DN15 . .8 B7
Carlby PE9. . . . . 163 E4
Deeping St Nicholas
PE11. . . . . 166 C7
East Ravendale DN37 . . . .35 C2
Friskney PE22 . . . . 115 A6
Gainsborough DN21 . . . . 197 E6
Grantham NG31. . . . . . . 210 E4
6 Great Gonerby NG31 . . 129 D5
Grimsby DN37 . . . . 190 E8
Healing DN41. . . . . .23 F5
7 Ingham LN1. . . . . .54 F2
Kingston upon Hull
HU10. . . . . 178 C7
Lincoln LN1 . . . . 234 A3
Market Deeping PE6 . . . . 217 B5
6 Newark-on-Trent
NG24. . . . . 104 A4
Nocton LN4 . . . . .95 B7
Swinderby LN6. . . . . . . .92 C6
Avenue Vivian DN15 . . . . 182 E4
Aviary Cl LN2 . . . . 211 C5
Avignon Rd PE11 . . . . . . 214 A5
Avocet Cl
4 Birchwood LN6. . . . . . 204 D8
4 Essendine PE9 . . . . . . 163 D3
Avon Cl
Grantham NG31. . . . . . . 210 E3
6 Lincoln LN6. . . . . 205 A4
Avon Ct PE4 . . . . 221 C2
Avondale
1 Kingston upon Hull
HU4. . . . . 179 B2
6 Lincoln LN6. . . . . 204 C1
Avondale St LN2 . . . . . . 234 C2
Avon Rd DN16 . . . . 183 C2
Axholme Ave LN7. . . . . . .16 C7
Axholme Cl HU9 . . . . . . 181 B5
Axholme Dr DN9 . . . . . . .27 D6
Axholme Rd 19 DN8. . . . .15 B7
Axholme Line Nature
Reserve* DN9 . . . . . . .27 C4
Axholme Rd
Scunthorpe DN15 . . . . . 182 D2
2 Westwoodside DN9 . . . .27 A2
Axiom Ave PE3 . . . . 225 C4
Axiom Ct PE9. . . . . 219 D4
Ayam Cl 5 LN2. . . . . . . .68 C6
Aydon Rd PE7 . . . . 231 F6
Aylesbury Gr HU5. . . . . . 179 D8
Aylesby Gdns 2 LN1. . . . 201 E8
Aylesby Rd
Aylesby DN37 . . . . 190 B6
Scunthorpe DN17. . . . . . 184 F5
Aylesford St 7 HU3. . . . . 180 B5
Aynsley Rd LN6. . . . . . . 204 B6
Ayots Gn 14 DN7 . . . . . . .14 D3
Ayr Ct DN16 . . . . 218 E6
Ayscough Ave
Spalding PE11 . . . . 214 D3
7 Stallingborough DN41 . . 23 E6
Ayscoughfee Hall Mus &
Gdns* PE11. . . . . 214 D3
Ayscoughfee Hall Sch
PE11. . . . . 214 D3
Ayscough Gr LN4 . . . . . . .33 B4
Ayscough St 4 DN31 . . . 188 E1
Aysgarth Ave 18 DN37 . . 188 F7
Azalea Cl PE3 . . . . 225 A2

Azalea Rd LN2. . . . . 202 C8

B

Babington Row HU9 . . . . 181 C8
Bacheler St HU3 . . . . . . 180 B5
Back Bank
Crowland PE12 . . . . 167 F3
Whaplode PE12 . . . . 168 A3
Back Field La DN7 . . . . . . 14 E4
Backgate PE12. . . . . 167 B8
Back La
5 Allington NG32 . . . . . . 128 F7
Aswarby & Swarby
NG34. . . . . 132 A7
Barnby in the Willows
NG24. . . . . 105 A3
Belvoir NG32 . . . . 138 D6
Bicker PE20. . . . . 134 F6
Bilsby LN13. . . . . .76 A2
Bolingbroke PE23 . . . . . 100 A7
Buckminster NG33. . . . . 151 A4
Burton Coggles NG33 . . . 152 C8
Cammeringham LN1 . . . . .54 F1
Candlesby with Gunby
PE23. . . . . .89 B1
Caythorpe NG32 . . . . . . 119 B7
Claxby with Moorby PE22 . .99 B7
Claypole NG23 . . . . 117 E2
Collyweston PE9 . . . . . . 171 B1
Colsterworth NG33 . . . . 151 E7
3 Deeping St James
PE6. . . . . 217 F4
Dunston LN4 . . . . .95 C6
Eye PE6 . . . . 175 A1
3 Foston NG32 . . . . 117 F1
Garthorpe & Fockerby
DN17. . . . . 7 F6
Heighington/Washingborough
LN4 . . . . .81 F4
Holbeach PE12 . . . . 215 D2
Ingoldsby NG33. . . . . . . 141 C5
Leadenham LN5. . . . . . . 106 C3
Long Bennington NG23 . . 128 D8
Long Sutton PE12 . . . . . 216 D6
4 Lutton PE12 . . . . 160 A8
North Clifton NG23. . . . . .78 C7
North Cockerington LN11 . .50 A1
Scothern LN2 . . . . .68 F4
3 Scarby cum Owmby
DN58. . . . . .32 D8
4 Skillington NG33 . . . . 151 A8
4 Stainforth DN7 . . . . . . 14 C6
2 Stamford PE9 . . . . . . 219 C5
South Clifton NG23 . . . . .78 C7
Wainfleet All Saints
PE24 . . . . 102 A2
Wilsford NG32. . . . . 120 C2
Winteringham DN15 . . . . . 2 B1
Wood Enderby PE22 . . . . .98 F6
Yaxley PE7 . . . . 233 E1
Back Rd
Gorefield PE13. . . . . 169 E2
Murrow PE13. . . . . 177 E6
Back St
Alkborough DN15 . . . . . . .8 C8
Buckminster NG33. . . . . 150 E5
East Stockwith DN21. . . . .40 B5
Saltfleetby LN11 . . . . . . .51 C1
South Clifton NG23 . . . . .78 C5
Sproxton LE14 . . . . 138 F1
Bacon's La 1 PE11 . . . . . 145 C1
Bacon St DN21 . . . . 197 D2
Bader Cl
2 Lincoln LN6. . . . . 205 B6
The Wildoons DN37 . . . . 190 E8
Bader Way 3 PE25 . . . . . 206 A5
Badge Cl PE10 . . . . 213 F7
Badgate PE12. . . . . 167 B8
Bad Gate PE12 . . . . 169 B6
Badger Cl PE10 . . . . 213 C2
Badger La PE10 . . . . 136 B7
Badger's La PE12. . . . . . .24 E6
Badgers Oak 2 LN5 . . . . .92 F3
Badger Way 1 DN20. . . . . 19 E4
Badinton La PE7 . . . . . . 233 D8
Badminton Way LN11 . . . 198 A2
Baffen's La 2 PE11 . . . . . 145 A4
BAG ENDERBY PE23. . . . .87 B7
Baggaley Dr LN9 . . . . . . 199 A4
Baggholme Rd LN2 . . . . 234 C2
Baghdad Rd NG34. . . . . 120 D8
Bagsby Rd DN9 . . . . .28 B3
Baildon Cres DN15 . . . . . .8 E8
Baildon Rd DN15 . . . . . . 182 D4
Bailey Cl DN21 . . . . .14 E6
Baileys Cl LN2 . . . . 68 D5
Bailey La DN21 . . . . 92 F5
Bailey Way 8 DN20. . . . . 19 E4
Bailgate 3 LN1. . . . . . . 234 B3
Bailgate LN1 . . . . 234 B3
Bail La PE23 . . . . 87 F1
Bain Cl PE9 . . . . 219 C7
Baines Ave 2 LN6. . . . . . 205 A5
Baines La LN4 . . . . 207 D5
Baines Rd DN21. . . . . . . 197 F4
Bain Rd PE21 . . . . 208 C3
Bain Rise 3 LN8 . . . . 59 A7
Bain St LN1 . . . . 201 D8
BAINTON CY. 172 F5
Bainton Rd
Barnack PE9 . . . . 172 D4
Newborough PE6. . . . . . 221 D8

Bakersfield DN20 . . . . . . 196 F7
Bakers La
Bassingham LN5 . . . . . . .92 E2
Peterborough PE2 . . . . . 230 E7
Baker's La
Candleby with Gunby
PE23. . . . . .89 A2
Fishtoft PE21 . . . . 126 C4
Great Steeping PE23 . . . . 101 E6
Westborough & Dry
Doddington NG23 . . . . . 117 E3
Baker St HU2 . . . . 180 E3
Bakers Way 5 PE10 . . . . 154 D6
Bakestraw Gate PE12 . . . 157 F5
Bakewell Cl 3 DN15 . . . . 182 B3
Bakewell Mews 4 LN6. . . 204 F2
Bakewell Rd PE4 . . . . . . 229 C2
Bala Ct PE4 . . . . 221 B3
Balder Ct 2 DN33 . . . . . 191 C2
BALDERTON NG24. . . . . 104 C2
Balderton La NG24. . . . . 104 D3
Baldock's Mill Heritage
Ctr* PE10 . . . . 213 D4
Baldwin Ave LN6. . . . . . 185 B2
Baldwin Cl PE8 . . . . 172 C1
Baldwin Gr PE10. . . . . . 213 D6
Balfour Pl 3 DN40. . . . . 186 B4
Balfour St
Gainsborough DN21 . . . . 197 C5
2 Kingston upon Hull
HU9. . . . . 181 C8
Balintore Rise PE2 . . . . . 229 D4
Balk Rd 8 PE9 . . . . 163 C1
Balliol Dr DN16. . . . . . . 185 B4
Ball's La PE12 . . . . 159 A4
Balmoral Ave
1 Grimsby DN34 . . . . . . 191 A7
Spalding PE11 . . . . 214 D2
Balmoral Cl
6 Mablethorpe/Sutton on
Sea LN12 . . . . .76 F8
2 Wragby LN8 . . . . 70 D4
Balmoral Ct DN17. . . . . 184 F4
Balmoral Dr
Beacon Hill NG24. . . . . . 104 C4
Grantham NG31. . . . . . . 210 E6
Sleaford NG34. . . . . . . 212 C2
Balmoral Rd
Cleethorpes DN35 . . . . . 192 C4
3 Hatfield DN7. . . . . 14 D4
1 Peterborough PE4 . . . . 225 D8
Balmoral Way PE12 . . . . 159 A8
Bamber St PE1 . . . . 225 F4
Bamford Ave 1 HU9 . . . . . 5 F8
Bamford Cl 6 LN6. . . . . . 204 E2
Banbury Cl PE11. . . . . . . 214 E3
Banbury Cl 6 DN33 . . . . 189 C1
Banbury Rd DN16 . . . . . 183 D2
Bancroft Rd NG24 . . . . . 104 C3
Bangor Cl LN5 . . . . 205 C3
Bank Dr
Ingoldmells PE25. . . . . . . 90 F3
5 Wisbech PE13. . . . . . . 170 C1
Bank End LN11 . . . . 50 E8
Bank End Rd DN9. . . . . . . 26 A7
Bank La 12 HU7 . . . . .33 B4
Bank's Ave 4 PE11 . . . . . 214 A6
Bank Side 1 HU13 . . . . . 178 C3
Banks La 1 NG34. . . . . . 122 C2
Banks Rd 5 LN9. . . . . . . 199 C4
Bank St
Boston PE21 . . . . 208 F5
4 Lincoln LN6. . . . . 234 B2
Lincoln LN2 . . . . 234 B2
Bank The
Parson Drove PE13. . . . . 177 C7
Swaton NG34. . . . . 133 D4
Bannister Dr 11 HU9. . . . 181 C7
Bannister's La PE20. . . . 136 C7
Bannister's Row 6
PE13. . . . . 170 C1
Banovallum Sch LN9 . . . 199 D3
Banovallum Sch La LN9 . . 199 C3
Baptist Chapel La 4
DN40. . . . . .12 F2
Baptist La 3 NG23. . . . . 191 C4
Barbara Ct 3 DN34. . . . . 194 F2
Barbara Rd 8 PE25. . . . . 206 D2
Barberry Cl 8 DN18 . . . . .10 E8
Barberry Cl 1 HU3. . . . . 180 C5
Barbers Dro PE6. . . . . . 176 C4
Barbers Hill PE4 . . . . . . 220 F7
Barbican Way DN34 . . . . 191 C1
Barcroft St DN35. . . . . . 189 C1
Bardney CE/
Methodist (Controlled)
Sch LN3 . . . . .83 C4
Bardney Linewood National
Nature Reserve* LN3 . . .83 C1
Bardney Rd
Branston & Mere LN4 . . . .82 C3
Wragby LN8 . . . . .70 C4
Bardots Leisure Ctr
LN5. . . . . 205 C5
Barehams La PE11 . . . . . 145 A3
Barfen La LN13. . . . . . . .63 B3
Barff La LN8. . . . . .43 F2

Barff Mdw LN8 . . . . .43 E1
Barff Rd LN4 . . . . .82 B1
Barfields La LN3 . . . . .68 F1
Barford Cl PE2 . . . . .230 C7
Bargate
 Grimsby DN24 . . . . .191 C5
 12 Lincoln LN5 . . . . .205 E8
Bargate Ave DN32 . . . . .191 D5
Bargate Gr **3** HU5 . . . . .179 D8
Bargate La **4** LN9 . . . . .199 C3
Barge Cl **1** PE11 . . . . .214 F5
Barge Rd PE2 . . . . .148 A7
Barham Cl PE2 . . . . .231 F5
BARHOLM PE9 . . . . .164 C1
Barholme Ave **7** PE2 . . . . . .160 A8
Barkestone La NG13 . . . . . . .128 A5
Barkham St **2** LN2 . . . . . . .102 D2
Barkhouse Cl **3** DN35 . . . . .192 F5
Barkhouse La **6** DN35 . . . . .192 F5
Bark St DN35 . . . . .192 F5
BARKSTON NG32 . . . . .130 B8
Barkston Cl PE10 . . . . .213 E6
Barkston Dr PE1 . . . . .226 B6
Barkston Gdns LN2 . . . . .202 B7
Barkston Rd NG32 . . . . .118 D2
Barkston & Syston CE
 (Aided) Prim Sch
 NG32 . . . . .130 B8
Barkwith Rd LN8 . . . . .58 F1
Barkworth Cl HU10 . . . . .178 D6
Barkworth St **3** DN37 . . . . .194 C4
Bar La **20** LN5 . . . . .93 F7
Barley Cl
 Heckington NG34 . . . . .122 D2
 12 Hibaldstow DN20 . . . . . .31 A5
 20 Metheringham LN4 . . . . . .95 C4
Barleycroft Rd NG13 . . . . . . .152 E8
Barleyfield PE6 . . . . .164 E2
Barley Gr **4** PE11 . . . . .166 C6
Barley Mews PE2 . . . . .230 D7
Barley Way LN9 . . . . .199 A3
BARLINGS LN3 . . . . .69 D1
Barlings Ave DN16 . . . . .185 A7
Barlings Cl
 1 Barlings LN3 . . . . .69 C3
 Hartsholme LN6 . . . . .204 F7
 7 Scotter DN21 . . . . .29 C4
Barlings La LN3 . . . . .69 C2
Barmouth Dr DN37 . . . . .190 E8
Barmston St HU2 . . . . .180 F8
BARNACK PE9 . . . . .172 E4
Barnack CE Prim Sch
 PE9 . . . . .172 D4
Barnack Dr PE9 . . . . .172 B3
Barnack Est **4** PE24 . . . . . .102 E7
Barnack Hill & Holes
 National Nature
 Reserve* PE9 . . . . .172 D3
Barnack Rd
 Bainton PE9 . . . . .172 E4
 St Martin's without PE9 . . . .219 D4
Barnard Ave DN20 . . . . .196 B3
Barnard Way **9** PE3 . . . . . .224 F3
Barnard Wlk DN40 . . . . .186 D3
Barnberry Way HU10 . . . . . . .142 D2
BARNBY DUN DN3 . . . . .14 A4
Barnby Gate NG24 . . . . .104 F3
Barnby La NG13 . . . . .104 F1
Barnby Rd NG24 . . . . .104 C3
Barnby Rd Prim Sch
 NG24 . . . . .104 A4
Barn Cl
 2 Maxey PE6 . . . . .173 C2
 Peterborough PE4 . . . . .220 F3
Barnes Cl **1** NG34 . . . . .212 C6
Barnes Cres
 Scunthorpe DN15 . . . . .182 E4
 Skegness DN25 . . . . .206 A5
Barnes Dro PE10 . . . . .154 F4
Barnes La LN5 . . . . .106 F7
Barnes Rd
 9 Donington PE11 . . . . . . .134 E2
 Skegness PE25 . . . . .206 A5
Barnes Way PE4 . . . . .220 F3
Barnetby La DN20 . . . . .20 F7
BARNETBY LE WOLD
 DN38 . . . . .21 C4
Barnetby Rd
 1 Kingston upon Hull
 HU13 . . . . .179 A3
 Scunthorpe DN17 . . . . .184 F5
Barnetby Sta DN38 . . . . .21 B4
Barnet Dr DN36 . . . . .195 E7
Barnet Gn **2** DN7 . . . . .14 D3
Barnfield Rd PE22 . . . . .126 E6
Barneyfield Rd PE22 . . . . . . .126 E6
Barn Hill PE9 . . . . .219 B5
BARNOLDBY LE BECK
 DN37 . . . . .35 B6
Barnoldby Rd DN37 . . . . .194 C4
Barn Owl Cl
 Corby Glen NG33 . . . . .152 F7
 1 Langtoft PE6 . . . . .164 F3
Barnside **6** DN20 . . . . .30 F5
Barnstaple Rd **8**
 DN17 . . . . .184 D8
Barnstock PE3 . . . . .225 A7
Barnston Way **12** DN16 . . . . .8 B4
Barnswallace Ct **18** LN2 . . . .68 C2
Barnwell Rd **8** PE2 . . . . . . .218 E6
Barnwell Terr **2** NG31 . . . . .210 F3

Baron Ave DN36 . . . . .195 D7
Baron Ct PE4 . . . . .221 B4
Baroness Rd DN34 . . . . .190 F6
Barons Way PE9 . . . . .219 C4
Barrack Sq NG31 . . . . .211 C4
Barracks The PE13 . . . . .169 E2
Barraclough's La **1**
 . . . . .3 E1
Barratt's Cl LN2 . . . . .234 C4
Bar Rd DN10 . . . . .52 B8
Bar Rd N **8** DN10 . . . . .52 B8
Bar Rd S **8** DN10 . . . . .52 B8
Barrett Gr **7** LN2 . . . . .68 E6
Barrett's Cl PE12 . . . . .215 D3
Barrick Cl **16** DN19 . . . . .11 D8
Barrier Bank
 Cowbit PE12 . . . . .156 F2
 Spalding PE12 . . . . .214 C1
Barrington Cl **6** PE12 . . . . . .215 D2
Barrington Gate PE12 . . . . . .215 E1
Barrow Blow Wells Nature
 Reserve* DN19 . . . . .4 D1
BARROWBY NG32 . . . . .210 A5
Barrowby CE (Controlled)
 Prim Sch NG32 . . . . .129 B3
Barrowby Gate NG31 . . . . . . .210 D4
Barrowby Rd **6** NG31 . . . . . .211 A5
Barrowby Rd PE9 . . . . .171 A2
Barrowfield PE12 . . . . .215 E1
BARROW HANN DN19 . . . . . . .4 E1
Barrow Haven Reedbed
 Nature Reserve* DN19 . . . .4 B2
Barrow Haven Sta DN19 . . . . .4 C2
Barrow La HU13 . . . . .178 D2
Barrow Rd
 Barton-upon-Humber
 DN18 . . . . .11 A8
 New Holland DN19 . . . . .4 E1
Barrows Gate
 3 Barrow Hill NG24 . . . . . .104 A6
 North Somercotes LN11 . . . .50 D6
BARROW UPON HUMBER
 DN19 . . . . .11 C8
Barr's La PE12 . . . . .168 B4
Barry Ave DN34 . . . . .190 F3
Barry Wlk **3** PE22 . . . . .230 F7
Bars La
 Benington PE22 . . . . .126 E5
 Bicker PE20 . . . . .135 A5
Bartholemew Cl **1** LN3 . . . . .83 C4
Bartol Cres PE21 . . . . .208 D5
Barton Cl
 3 Mablethorpe LN12 . . . . . .64 C2
 Paston PE4 . . . . .221 D1
Barton Dr HU13 . . . . .178 D1
Barton Gate LN11 . . . . .198 D4
Barton La
 Barrow upon Humber
 DN19 . . . . .11 C8
 Tydd St Mary PE13 . . . . . . .169 F8
Barton-on-Humber Sta
 DN18 . . . . .3 D2
Barton Outdoor Pursuits
 Ctr* DN18 . . . . .3 D2
Barton Rd
 5 Wainfleet All Saints
 PE24 . . . . .102 D1
 Wrawby DN20 . . . . .196 F6
Barton St Peters CE Prim
 Sch DN18 . . . . .3 F1
Bartons La PE23 . . . . .101 F6
Barton St
 Aylesby DN37 . . . . .23 D2
 Barrow upon Humber
 DN19 . . . . .11 C8
 Fotherby LN11 . . . . .49 A2
 Irby DN37 . . . . .34 F7
 Keelby DN41 . . . . .23 A4
 Ludborough DN36 . . . . .48 C6
BARTON-UPON-HUMBER
 DN18 . . . . .10 F7
BARTON WATERSIDE
 DN18 . . . . .3 F2
Bartram Gate **2** PE4 . . . . . .221 C1
Bartrams **3** HU15 . . . . .2 D6
Basic Slag Rd DN16 . . . . . . .183 E2
Basil Gn PE2 . . . . .230 D6
Baslow Rd DN15 . . . . .182 B2
Bass Cotts NG34 . . . . .212 E3
Bassett Cl **2** DN20 . . . . .19 E3
Bassett Rd DN35 . . . . .193 A4
BASSINGHAM LN5 . . . . .92 F2
Bassingham Cres **2** LN1 . . .201 F7
Bassingham La PE23 . . . . .88 C3
Bassingham Prim Sch
 LN5 . . . . .92 F2
Bassingham Rd LN5 . . . . .92 F5
BASSINGTHORPE
 NG33 . . . . .140 E3
BASTON PE6 . . . . .164 E4
Baston CE Prim Sch
 PE6 . . . . .164 E5
Baston Edge Dro PE10 . . . . .164 E7
Baston Fen Nature
 Reserve* PE6 . . . . .165 A8
Baston Outgang Rd
 PE6 . . . . .165 A6
Bateman's Cl **3** PE12 . . . . . .159 D7
Batemans Ct PE24 . . . . .102 E2
Bath Gdns PE21 . . . . .208 F3
Bath La **15** PE11 . . . . .214 D4
Bath Rd
 Bracebridge Heath LN4 . . . . .81 A2
 Wisbech PE13 . . . . .170 D1
Bath Row PE9 . . . . .219 B4
Bath St
 8 Grantham NG31 . . . . . . .211 A4

Bath St continued
 Grimsby DN32 . . . . .189 C1
Bathurst PE2 . . . . .230 A4
Bathurst St
 8 Kingston upon Hull
 HU3 . . . . .180 D5
 Lincoln LN2 . . . . .202 D3
Battery St DN40 . . . . .186 D4
Battlefields La N PE12 . . . . . .159 A8
Battlefields La S PE12 . . . . . .215 F3
Battle of Britain Meml
 Flight Visitor Ctr*
 LN4 . . . . .207 B3
Baulkin's Dro PE12 . . . . .159 C1
BAUMBER LN9 . . . . .72 A1
Baumber Prim Sch LN9 . . . . . .72 A1
Bawtry Cl LN6 . . . . .204 C8
Bawtry Rd DN7 . . . . .14 F3
Baxter Cl
 Coningsby LN4 . . . . .207 D3
 18 Wisbech PE13 . . . . .170 E1
Baxter Gdns PE11 . . . . .214 F7
Bayard St DN21 . . . . .197 C5
Bayes Rd **6** PE25 . . . . .103 E4
Bayford La **9** NG24 . . . . . . .104 A4
Bayford Gn PE21 . . . . .208 B3
Bayons Ave DN33 . . . . .194 D8
Baysdale Gr NG31 . . . . .211 B8
Baysdale Rd DN16 . . . . .185 D5
Baysgarth House Mus*
 DN18 . . . . .10 F8
Baysgarth Leisure Ctr
 DN18 . . . . .10 F8
Baysgarth Sch DN18 . . . . . . .10 F8
Baysgarth View DN18 . . . . . .10 F7
Bayston Ct PE2 . . . . .230 E8
Bayswater Pl **1** DN21 . . . . . .194 D8
Bayswood Ave PE21 . . . . . . .208 F1
BAYTHORPE PE20 . . . . .135 C8
Baytree Ave DN34 . . . . .191 A6
Baytree Owl Ctr*
 PE12 . . . . .157 D7
Baywood Cl LN6 . . . . .200 C1
Beach Ave **15** PE24 . . . . .90 D7
Beach Bank
 Pinchbeck PE11 . . . . .144 E3
 Surfleet PE11 . . . . .145 A3
Beach Holt La DN37 . . . . .23 D2
Beach La PE11 . . . . .144 F3
Beachside **10** LN4 . . . . .77 A8
Beacon Ave
 6 Barton-upon-Humber
 DN18 . . . . .10 E8
 Cleethorpes DN35 . . . . . . .192 D6
Beacon Ct DN35 . . . . .192 D6
BEACON HILL NG24 . . . . . . .104 B5
Beacon Hill La PE34 . . . . . . .161 E3
Beacon Hill Rd
 Gringley-on-the-Hill
 DN10 . . . . .39 D1
 Newark-on-Trent NG24 . . . .104 B4
Beacon Hts NG24 . . . . .104 B4
Beacon La NG31 . . . . .211 C4
Beacon Pk Cl **4** PE25 . . . . . .206 A6
Beacon Pk Dr PE25 . . . . .206 A6
Beacon Rd NG24 . . . . .104 C1
Beaconsfield Dr **3**
 NG24 . . . . .104 C5
Beaconthorpe Rd **4**
 DN35 . . . . .192 E7
Beacon View **2** NG13 . . . . . .128 A6
Beacon Way PE25 . . . . .206 A6
Beaford Ct DN17 . . . . .184 C8
Beagle Cl **16** DN20 . . . . .19 E4
Beagle La NG34 . . . . .107 C1
Bean St HU3 . . . . .180 C6
Beatrice Rd **1** PE13 . . . . . . .170 D2
Beatrice Way **12** PE24 . . . . . .90 D7
Beatty Ave DN33 . . . . .194 F7
Beaubridge Bsns Pk
 PE25 . . . . .206 B3
Beauchamp St **3**
 DN16 . . . . .183 B1
Beauchamp Wlk **7**
 DN16 . . . . .183 B2
Beauchief Gdns DN16 . . . . . .185 A8
Beaufort Ave **1** PE6 . . . . . . .217 C5
Beaufort Cl
 Kingston upon Hull
 HU3 . . . . .180 D6
 Lincoln LN2 . . . . .202 D8
 Scunthorpe DN15 . . . . .182 B6
 Spalding PE11 . . . . .214 F5
Beaufort Dr
 Bourne PE10 . . . . .213 C7
 4 Spalding PE11 . . . . .214 C3
Beaufort Rd LN2 . . . . .202 D8
Beaufort St DN21 . . . . .197 B7
Beaulahland **8** DN18 . . . . . . .10 A7
Beaulah Villas **9** DN18 . . . . .10 A7
Beaulieu Ct **6** PE6 . . . . .175 A1
Beaumonde Cl DN36 . . . . . . .195 C2
Beaumont Cl **III** PE2 . . . . . . .231 D7
Beaumont Cl **13** HU9 . . . . . . .181 D7
Beaumont Dr **2** NG31 . . . . . .210 F8
Beaumont Fee LN1 . . . . .234 A2
Beaumont St DN21 . . . . .197 D4
Beaumont Way PE7 . . . . .230 C2
Beauvale Gdns PE4 . . . . .221 C3
Beauvoir Pl PE7 . . . . .233 E5
Beaver Cl **1** LN6 . . . . .200 A5
Beccelm Dr **9** NG31 . . . . . . .211 D8
Beck Bank
 Gosberton PE11 . . . . .144 C3
 Kirton PE20 . . . . .124 E1

Beck Cl
 5 Binbrook LN8 . . . . .47 C5
 6 Keelby DN41 . . . . .23 A4
 1 Ruskington NG34 . . . . . .108 D2
Becke Cl LN3 . . . . .203 E5
Beckets Cl PE1 . . . . .225 F8
Beckett Ave DN21 . . . . .197 E6
Beckett Cl
 6 Heckington NG34 . . . . . .122 D3
 3 Skegness PE25 . . . . . . .206 C1
Beckett Dr PE11 . . . . .214 C6
Beckett Sch DN21 . . . . .53 A8
Beckhall LN7 . . . . .68 D6
Beckhead Cvn Site
 LN6 . . . . .204 C1
Beck Hill
 6 Barton-upon-Humber
 DN18 . . . . .10 F8
 Tealby LN8 . . . . .46 C1
Beckhole Cl HU3 . . . . .180 A6
Beckhythe Cl DN33 . . . . .191 E1
BECKINGHAM
 Barnby in the Willows
 NG24 . . . . .105 A4
Beckingham DN10 . . . . .40 B1
Beckingham Rd PE2 . . . . .229 F3
Beckingham Rd
 Coddington NG34 . . . . .104 C5
 Walkeringham DN10 . . . . . . .40 A2
Beckingthorpe Dr **19**
 NG13 . . . . .128 A6
Beck La
 Appleby DN15 . . . . .9 D1
 3 Barton-upon-Humber
 DN18 . . . . .10 F8
 Auborn Haddington & South
 Hykeham LN6 . . . . .93 B7
 18 Barrow upon Humber
 DN19 . . . . .11 D8
 7 Broughton DN20 . . . . . . .19 E3
 Fulbeck NG32 . . . . .106 C1
 Heighington/Washingborough
 LN4 . . . . .81 F4
 Ingoldmells PE25 . . . . .90 E2
 Redbourne LN7 . . . . .30 F2
 4 Scunthorpe DN16 . . . . . .185 B3
 Welton le Marsh PE23 . . . . .89 A3
Beckside
 11 Brough HU15 . . . . .2 D6
 Normanby by Spital LN8 . . . .55 E7
 Rothwell LN7 . . . . .33 F2
 Scopwick LN4 . . . . .108 C8
Beck Side **5** DN20 . . . . .30 F5
Beckside Cl DN36 . . . . .192 E1
Beckside Ct LN11 . . . . .198 D3
Becks La DN21 . . . . .29 A3
Beck St
 Digby LN4 . . . . .108 E5
 Welbourn LN5 . . . . .106 E4
Becks The **4** LN9 . . . . .199 C4
Beck Way NG31 . . . . .164 C8
Beck Wlk **8** DN35 . . . . .192 E3
Bedale PE21 . . . . .208 B3
Bedale Rd **8** DN16 . . . . .185 D5
Bede Cres PE21 . . . . .208 D5
Bedehouse Bank PE10 . . . . . .213 E4
Bede House La **3**
 NG24 . . . . .104 A4
Bede Rd PE1 . . . . .226 A6
Bede Rd **8** PE6 . . . . .164 E5
Bedford Cl NG32 . . . . .211 F5
Bedford Ct **16** PE6 . . . . .176 A3
Bedford Pl **1** PE11 . . . . . . .214 D3
Bedford Rd
 Humberston DN35 . . . . . . .193 A1
 Kingston upon Hull HU13 . . .178 F3
 RAF Cranwell NG34 . . . . . .107 D1
 5 Sudbrooke LN2 . . . . . . .68 F2
 2 Thorney PE6 . . . . .176 A3
Beech Cres **1** NG34 . . . . . . .108 E2
Beechcroft Rd DN33 . . . . . . .210 C3
Beech Dr
 18 Bottesford NG13 . . . . . .128 A5
 North Ferriby HU14 . . . . .3 A4
 12 Ryhall PE9 . . . . .163 C1
 Welton HU14 . . . . .2 F5

Beechers Way LN8 . . . . .57 D7
Beeches Ave DN16 . . . . .185 B8
Beeches La PE22 . . . . .112 C1
Beeches Prim Sch The
 PE1 . . . . .225 F7
Beeches The **1** LN1 . . . . . . .66 C5
Beechfield Ct DN34 . . . . .191 C6
Beechfield Rd **7** DN7 . . . . . .14 C
Beech Garth **9** DN19 . . . . . . .11 C
Beech Gr
 Allanby with Anlaby Common
 HU13 . . . . .178 C
 3 Burton upon Stather
 DN15 . . . . .8 B
 Donington PE11 . . . . .134 E1
 Holton le Clay DN36 . . . . . .195 E1
 Louth LN11 . . . . .198 C
 4 Scopwick Heath LN4 . . .108 A2
 Stamford PE9 . . . . .218 D
Beech Hill Rd LN3 . . . . .75 C
Beechings Way **10** LN13 . . . .75 E
Beechings Way Ind Est
 LN13 . . . . .75 E
Beech La **12** PE6 . . . . .175 A
Beech Lawn HU10 . . . . .178 E
Beech Rd
 Branston LN4 . . . . .81 D
 6 Brough HU15 . . . . .2 D
 Glinton PE6 . . . . .220 B
Beech Rise
 Sleaford NG34 . . . . .212 D6
 2 South Rauceby NG34 . . .120 E4
 Welton LN5 . . . . .205 D
Beech Tree Ave **17** DN8 . . . . .15 A
Beechtree Cl **3** NG34 . . . . . .108 E
Beechway DN16 . . . . .185 B
Beech Way DN35 . . . . .192 D
Beechwood Ave
 Grimsby DN33 . . . . .190 F1
 Immingham DN40 . . . . .186 C
Beechwood Cl
 DN20 . . . . .19 E
Beechwood Dr
 12 Scawby DN20 . . . . .30 F
 7 Scotter DN21 . . . . .29 C
Beechwood Rd **5**
 DN15 . . . . .170 D
Beeden Pk Est NG31 . . . . . . .210 C4
Bee Field The LN2 . . . . .202 F
Beehive La LN6 . . . . .79 C
Beeley Rd DN32 . . . . .192 C
BEELSBY DN37 . . . . .34 E4
Beelsby Rd LN4 . . . . .34 C5
Beel's Rd DN41 . . . . .187 B2
BEESBY LN13 . . . . .76 A
Beesby Dr **3** DN35 . . . . .192 F3
Beesby Rd
 Maltby le Marsh LN13 . . . . . .76 A
 Scunthorpe DN17 . . . . .184 E5
Beesby Wlk LN13 . . . . .76 A
Bees Cnr **1** PE24 . . . . .102 D2
Bee's La PE13 . . . . .169 F
Beeson St DN31 . . . . .188 E1
Beeson St DN31 . . . . .188 E1
Beeston Dr PE7 . . . . .231 F5
Beeton Cl LN11 . . . . .198 D4
Beeton Cres PE7 . . . . .233 E5
Beevor St LN6 . . . . .201 C2
Beggar Hill Messingham
 Rd DN21 . . . . .29 D4
Beggar's La PE22 . . . . .98 F3
Begger's Bush La PE12 . . . . .157 D7
Beilby St HU3 . . . . .179 F4
Belcanto Ct **3** PE11 . . . . . . .214 A5
BELCHFORD LN9 . . . . .73 B2
Belchmire La LN6 . . . . .145 B5
Beldings Cl PE23 . . . . .101 F6
Belfry The **5** NG31 . . . . .211 D7
Belgic Sq PE1 . . . . .226 E3
Belgrave Cl **11** DN9 . . . . .16 E1
Belgrave Dr HU4 . . . . .179 D5
Belgrave Rd
 7 Spalding PE11 . . . . .214 C2
Belgrave Sq **1** DN15 . . . . . .183 B3
Belgravia Cl LN6 . . . . .200 E1
Belham Rd PE1 . . . . .225 E7
Belisana Rd **5** PE11 . . . . . . .214 A5
Bellamy Ct HU9 . . . . .181 C
Bellamy's La PE14 . . . . .170 D4
Bellbutts View DN21 . . . . .29 B3
Bell Cl NG31 . . . . .210 E7
Bell Cl **5** PE21 . . . . .208 F3
BELLEAU LN13 . . . . .75 A5
Belleisle Rd DN34 . . . . .190 D4
Belle Vue Rd LN1 . . . . .234 A3
Belle Vue Rd LN1 . . . . .234 A3
Belle Vue Terr
 Lincoln LN1 . . . . .234 A3
 7 Horne/Moorends
 DN8 . . . . .15 A8
Bellfield Cl **4** DN21 . . . . . . .214 B3
Bellflower Cl **2** LN12 . . . . . . .202 C6
Bell Gr LN6 . . . . .205 C6
Bellingham Rd DN16 . . . . . . .185 D7
Bellingham's Dro PE13 . . . . . .166 F7
Bell La
 4 Collingham NG23 . . . . . .91 C4
 Fosdyke PE20 . . . . .146 D8
 Market Deeping PE6 . . . . . .217 E4
 Moulton PE12 . . . . .157 F7
 Scunthorpe DN15 . . . . .183 A4

ELLMOUNT PE34 161 E4
ell's Dro PE12 159 C1
ell's Pl PE1 226 A2
ellview Rd 6 NG34 108 E1
ellwin Dr DN15 8 A1
ellwood Cres 5 DN8 15 A8
ellwood Gdns NG31 211 C5
ellwood Grange 1 LN3 203 E7
ell Wr Drain Bank
Eastville PE22 101 B1
New Leake PE22 100 E1
ELMESTHORPE PE9 163 D1
elmesthorpe La PE9 163 D1
elmont DN36 195 C1
elmont Cl DN35 192 D3
elmont Gr 2 NG31 211 D6
elmont Prim Sch NG31 211 E6
elmont St
Kingston upon Hull HU9 181 D8
Lincoln LN2 202 B3
Scunthorpe DN16 185 A6
ELNIE PE11 145 D5
elnie La PE11 145 D5
elper Ct
6 Crosby DN15 182 B2
Grimsby DN32 189 C1
elsay Dr PE2 231 F5
elshaw La DN9 16 D1
elsize Ave PE2 230 E6
elthorn Rd 2 DN17 7 F1
ELTOFT DN9 17 B1
ELTON
Belton and Manthorpe NG32 130 B6
Belton DN9 16 E1
elton All Saints CE Prim Sch DN9 16 E2
elton Ave
Grantham NG31 211 C6
Lincoln LN6 204 F6
elton Cl
Boston PE21 209 B5
13 Market Deeping PE6 217 A5
elton Fields 1 DN9 16 D1
elton Gdns 23 PE9 219 C5
elton Gr
Grantham NG31 211 B7
1 Grimsby DN33 191 A3
elton House* NG32 130 B6
elton La
Grantham NG31 211 C6
Great Gonerby NG31 129 E5
elton La Com Prim Sch NG31 211 D7
elton Pk* NG32 211 F8
elton Pk Dr 7 LN6 93 C8
elton Rd
Belton DN9 17 A1
Epworth DN9 27 E7
Peterborough PE7 231 F5
Sandtoft DN9 16 B3
elton St 16 PE9 219 C5
elton Wlk LN11 198 A7
elt Rd The DN21 197 F7
elvedere Cl PE11 214 B2
elvedere Dr DN17 184 E7
elvedere Rd HU13 178 F2
ELVOIR NG32 138 B8
elvoir Ave
12 Bottesford NG13 128 A5
Grantham NG31 210 F1
Spitalgate NG31 211 E2
elvoir Castle* NG32 138 B8
elvoir Cl
Bracebridge LN5 205 D1
4 Colsterworth NG33 151 E6
1 Market Deeping PE6 217 A5
1 Stamford PE9 218 E6
elvoir Ct LN11 198 B8
elvoir Gdns NG31 129 D5
elvoir High Sch NG13 128 A5
elvoir La NG32 128 D1
elvoir Pk Wlk DN35 192 D2
elvoir Rd
Bottesford NG13 128 A4
Cleethorpes DN35 192 D2
Croxton Kerrial NG32 138 A6
elvoir St HU5 180 C8
elvoir Way
Eye PE1 226 D8
Louth LN11 198 B8
Peterborough PE1 226 C8
elwood Dr 7 DN9 16 E2
empton Gr
4 Grimsby DN32 192 A5
Kingston upon Hull HU5 179 D8
emrose Way 2 DN31 191 C8
enams Cl PE5 223 E2
enbow Way LN1 201 C6
endersough Dro PE12 159 C3
endike La PE11 145 D4
enedict Cl 2 HU4 179 A2
enedict Ct PE6 217 E5
enedict Rd HU4 179 A2
enedict Sq PE4 220 E2
ENINGTON PE22 126 F5
enington Rd PE22 126 E3
enjamin Adlard Com Sch DN21 197 E2
enjamin Adlard Prim Sch DN21 197 E2
enland PE3 225 A6
enner Rd PE11 214 E8
Benner Rd Ind Est PE11 214 E8
Bennett Dr 28 DN15 9 A5
Bennett Rd
Cleethorpes DN35 192 D7
Louth LN11 198 C8
Scunthorpe DN16 185 C7
Bennington Cl
8 Lincoln LN6 205 A7
11 Long Bennington NG23 117 D3
Bennington La NG23 117 E4
BENNIWORTH LN8 59 B1
Ben's Gate PE12 159 B5
Benson Cl LN6 204 C6
Benson Cres LN6 204 C6
Benson Ct LN11 48 F4
Bentinck Cl 6 PE11 214 C6
Bentinck Sq 2 LN2 202 B3
Bentinck St 4 LN2 202 B3
Bentley Ave PE7 233 E6
Bentley Ct HU3 180 A5
Bentley Dr LN4 205 F3
Bentley La 6 DN38 32 E7
Bentley St
Cleethorpes DN35 192 E6
6 Stamford PE9 219 C6
Bentley Way 1 LN4 95 C4
Benton Cl 6 PE12 157 E1
Benyon Gr PE2 230 B4
Berberis Cl 2 PE6 175 F3
Berea The DN34 191 C5
Beresford Ave PE25 206 C2
Beresford Cl 4 PE25 206 C2
Beresford Cres 5 PE25 206 C2
Beresford Dr 5 LN2 68 F3
Beretun Gn 7 DN18 10 E8
Berilldon Dr LN1 201 C7
Berkeley Ave
Green Hill NG31 210 E6
Lincoln LN6 205 A3
Berkeley Ct 5 NG34 212 E4
Berkeley Dr
4 Bourne PE10 213 C7
Lincoln LN6 205 A3
Berkeley Ind Est DN15 182 C4
Berkeley Inf & Jun Sch DN15 182 D4
Berkeley Rd
Humberston DN35 193 A2
Peterborough PE3 225 C3
Berkeley St
1 Kingston upon Hull HU3 180 D8
Scunthorpe DN15 183 A4
Berkshire Dr NG31 211 D7
Bermondsey Dr HU5 179 E8
Bernadette Ave HU4 179 B5
Bernard St LN2 202 B4
Berners Rd DN35 193 B1
Bernicia Dr NG34 212 B2
Berrybut Way 5 PE9 219 D7
Berry Cl 6 NG34 212 D2
Berry Ct PE1 225 E5
Berryfield End 7 NG32 210 A5
Berryman Way HU13 179 A3
Berry Way 5 PE25 206 C3
Bert Allen Dr 1 PE22 114 A1
Bertie Cl
Long Sutton PE12 216 C3
Swinstead NG33 153 A5
Bertie La 8 PE9 172 C6
Bert's Way 7 NG32 128 F7
Berwick Ct DN40 186 C4
Besant Cl 10 PE22 113 B1
BESCABY LE14 138 B1
Bessemer Way DN15 183 B6
Bestall Rd DN32 192 C6
BESTHORPE NG23 91 C7
Besthorpe Cty Prim Sch NG23 91 C7
Besthorpe Rd
Besthorpe NG23 91 C6
North Scarle NG23 78 D1
Beswick Cl 5 LN6 204 D7
Bethlehem St DN32 191 D7
Bethlem Cres 9 PE24 102 D1
Bethune Ave HU4 179 A3
Bethune Ave W HU13 179 A3
Bethune Pk Prim Sch HU4 179 B3
Betjeman Cl
Bourne PE10 213 D3
Spalding PE11 214 B4
Betony Cl DN15 182 C6
Bettesworth Rd DN21 54 F8
Bettles Cl PE1 226 A6
Betula Gr 3 LN6 204 D7
Betula Way 1 DN17 184 C5
Beverley Cl 7 DN36 195 D1
Beverley Cres DN32 192 A5
Beverley Ct
12 Healing DN41 23 F5
Westcliffe DN17 184 D7
Beverley Gdns 4 PE9 219 A6
Beverley Gr
Lincoln LN6 204 F3
7 Skegness PE25 206 B3
Beverley Rd HU3 180 D8
Beverstone PE2 229 D5
Bevishall PE4 221 D1
Bew Cl PE2 231 D4
Bewholme Gr 3 HU9 5 D8
Bewick Pl PE7 233 D8
Bexley Ct 10 DN32 189 C1
BICKER PE20 135 A4
Bicker Dro PE20 134 D6
BICKER GAUNTLET PE20 134 F6
Bicker Prep Sch PE30 135 A4
Bicker Rd PE11 134 F3
Bickleigh Wlk PE3 225 A3
Bidwell La LE15 162 B6
Biergate LN11 49 F7
Bifield PE2 229 F3
BIGBY DN38 21 C2
Bigby Gr DN17 184 F4
Bigby High Rd DN20 196 D2
Bigby Hill DN38 21 C1
Bigby Rd 6 DN20 196 C3
Bigby St DN20 196 C3
Billet La DN15 182 F8
Billet Mill App Rd DN16 19 A4
Billet Mill Rd DN16 183 E1
Billgate La PE24 102 E7
BILLINGBOROUGH NG34 133 A1
Billingborough Dro NG34 143 E8
Billingborough Prim Sch NG34 133 B1
Billingborough Rd
Billingborough NG34 133 B1
Folkingham NG34 132 E1
BILLINGHAY LN4 109 F5
Billinghay CE Prim Sch LN4 109 F6
Billinghay Cottage* 9 LN4 109 F5
Billinghay Ct DN35 192 F3
Billinghay Dales Head LN4 110 B4
Billings Gate LN11 50 E5
BILSBY LN13 76 A3
Bilsby Cl LN2 202 A7
BILSBY FIELD LN13 76 A2
Bilsby Rd 2 LN13 75 F3
Bilsdale Gr HU9 181 F8
Bilsdale Rd DN16 185 E5
BINBROOK LN8 47 B4
Binbrook Cl 8 LN6 204 D7
Binbrook (Controlled) Prim Sch LN8 47 B5
Binbrook La LN8 47 B2
Binbrook Way DN37 190 E8
Bircham Cres DN21 30 C1
Birch Ave
Brigg DN20 196 B4
Grimsby DN34 191 A6
Birch Cl
28 Brough HU15 2 C5
11 Coningsby LN4 207 D4
Hessle HU13 178 B3
Kingston upon Hull HU5 179 B7
1 Lincoln LN6 204 F2
Wyberton PE21 136 E7
Birch Croft 31 HU15 2 C6
Birchdale 31 DN18 10 E8
Birch Dr DN17 185 D4
Birchen Cl PE7 230 C3
Birches The 8 DN9 27 A2
Birchfield Rd 8 DN9 27 D6
Birch Gr
Gainsborough DN21 197 D6
Spalding PE11 214 F3
Birchin Way DN31 188 D1
Birch La 4 LN9 85 E7
Birch Leigh HU3 180 C6
Birch Rd
Louth LN11 198 E5
6 Stamford PE9 218 D7
Birchtree Ave PE1 226 A7
Birch Tree Cl 4 DN3 14 A4
Birch Way DN38 21 C5
Birch Way Ind Est DN31 188 D1
BIRCHWOOD LN6 204 D7
Birchwood PE2 230 A3
Birchwood Ave
Birchwood LN6 200 D1
Kingston upon Hull HU5 179 A7
Birchwood Cl 4 NG31 210 F7
Birch Wood Cl 14 DN18 3 E1
Birchwood Jun Sch LN6 204 C8
Birchwood Rd
Scunthorpe DN16 185 A4
1 Sleaford NG34 212 D6
Birchwood Sh Ctr LN6 204 C8
Birchwood View 2 DN21 197 F5
Birdcroft La DN10 40 A3
Birds Dro PE11 145 C4
Bird's Dro
Gorefield PE13 169 D1
Sutton St James PE12 169 B8
Birds Holt Cl LN6 200 A3
Birds Wood Nature Reserve* DN9 26 F4
Birkbeck Sch & Com Arts Coll LN11 50 E7
Birkdale
Lincoln LN5 205 D1
9 Waltham DN37 194 C4
Birkdale Ave 1 PE4 221 A3
Birkdale Cl
3 Grantham NG31 211 D7
Heighington/Washingborough LN4 203 E1
Kingston upon Hull HU10 178 B8
1 Skegness PE25 206 D6
3 Spalding PE11 214 C2
8 Woodhall Spa LN10 97 C5
Birkdale Dr 3 DN40 186 D5
Birkdale Rd DN17 184 D3
Birkdale Way HU9 181 D8
Birketts La LN11 49 D5
BIRKHOLME NG33 152 B6
Birkland La NG23 78 D5
Birkwood PE22 98 E2
Birkwood La PE22 98 E3
Birmingham Cl 5 NG31 210 E5
Birrel St DN21 197 B6
BIRTHORPE NG34 143 A8
Birthorpe Rd NG34 143 A8
BISCATHORPE LN11 59 D3
Biscay Cl 1 PE25 206 A6
Bishop Alexander Prim Sch NG24 104 A6
Bishop Blunt Cl 2 HU13 178 F1
BISHOPBRIDGE LN8 44 C1
Bishop Burton Coll DN20 19 E3
Bishop Cockin Cl HU13 179 A1
Bishop Creighton Prim Sch PE1 226 B2
Bishopdale Cl NG31 129 F5
Bishop Grosseteste Coll LN1 201 F6
Bishop Gurdon Cl 4 HU13 178 F1
Bishop Kempthorne Cl 3 HU13 178 F1
Bishop King CE (Aided) Prim Sch LN5 201 F1
Bishop King Ct 7 LN5 201 F1
Bishop La HU1 181 A6
Bishop La Staithe HU2 181 A6
BISHOP NORTON LN8 43 D3
Bishop Norton Rd LN8 43 E1
Bishops Cl
6 Bourne PE10 213 E4
Louth LN11 198 E6
Peterborough PE1 226 D5
Bishops Ct 3 NG34 212 D5
Bishopsfield PE4 221 B1
Bishop's La LN8 47 D7
Bishop's Pal The* LN2 234 B3
Bishop's Pl 5 LN2 68 C6
Bishops Rd
Leasingham NG34 121 B7
Lincoln LN2 202 C5
Bishop's Rd PE1 226 A1
Bishops Wlk 5 PE9 172 D3
Bishop's Wlk 1 DN34 191 C6
Bishop Temple Ct HU13 178 F3
Bishopthorpe Rd DN35 192 F3
BITCHFIELD NG33 141 B3
Bittern Cl HU4 179 D2
Bittern Way
3 Birchwood LN6 204 D8
Wyberton PE21 136 F8
BJ's Leisure Ctr PE25 90 E3
Black Bank DN17 29 A6
Black Bear La PE13 170 F1
Blackberry Cl 9 LN6 93 A8
Blackberry Way 3 NG24 104 C1
Blackbourn Cl 20 NG23 91 D5
Blackbourn Rd LN6 205 C6
Blackbrook Rd 4 NG24 104 B5
Blackburn Ave HU15 2 C5
Blackburn Cl 2 NG31 210 D5
Blackburn La DN22 52 D3
Black Dike PE13 169 E6
Blackdown Garth PE4 221 B3
Black Dro
Anwick LN4 109 D2
Baston PE6 165 B8
Ewerby & Evedon NG34 122 E8
Midville PE22 100 D2
Thorney PE6 175 F5
Wisbech St Mary PE13 177 B4
Black Dyke PE13 169 F4
Blackdykes Rd DN9 28 B4
Blackey La PE22 99 B4
Black Fen La LN4 82 C4
Blackfiars Ct LN2 202 E6
Blackfriargate HU1 181 A5
Blackfriars Rd LN2 202 E6
Blackfriars St 15 PE9 219 C5
Blackfriars Wlk LN2 202 E6
Blackhill La LN9 73 F1
Black Hole Dro PE11 155 F8
Black Horse Dr 8 LN6 93 A8
BLACKJACK PE20 135 E6
Blackjack Rd PE20 135 C6
Black La
Doddington & Whisby LN6 79 E3
Gorefield PE13 169 C2
Blackmead PE2 230 B4
Blackmoor Rd
Aubourn Haddington & South Hykeham LN5 93 C5
Haxey DN9 27 D2
Black Prince Ave PE6 217 B6
Black's Cl 17 LN5 93 F7
Blacksmith Hill DN15 1 E3
Blacksmith La
Boothby Graffoe LN5 94 A2
East Keal PE23 100 D6
2 Harmston LN5 93 F5
Thorpe on the Hill LN6 92 E8
Blacksmith Rd 4 LN3 82 A7
Blacksmith Row 1 LN5 92 F3
Blacksmiths Cl 2 DN19 11 C7
Blacksmith's Cnr 5 LN4 207 A5
Blacksmiths Ct 10 LN4 95 C4
Blacksmiths La
North Scarle LN6 78 E1
Welby NG32 130 F5
Blacksmith's La
13 Navenby/Wellingore LN5 107 A7
Norton Disney LN6 92 B2
Blacksmith's Row PE11 156 B7
Black Swan Spinney PE8 222 A4
Blackthorn 5 PE9 218 C7
Blackthorn Cl
1 Gainsborough DN21 197 F5
1 Lincoln LN2 202 C8
3 Market Deeping PE6 217 D6
13 Ruskington NG34 108 E1
Scunthorpe DN15 182 C6
Blackthorn Ct 4 HU3 180 D6
Blackthorn La
Boston PE21 209 C5
Cammeringham LN1 54 E1
Kingston upon Hull HU10 178 F7
Blackthorns The
4 Broughton DN20 19 D4
6 Sleaford NG34 212 D3
Blackthorn Way PE10 213 E5
Blackwell Rd PE7 230 C2
Bladon Est PE21 209 F4
Bladons Wlk HU10 178 D8
Blaides Staithe 1 HU1 181 A6
Blair Wlk DN40 186 E3
Blake Ave DN17 184 E7
Blake Cl 2 HU2 180 E7
Blakeney Lea 4 DN35 192 F1
Blanchard Cl PE10 142 F2
Blanchard Rd LN11 198 E3
Blandford Gdns 6 PE1 226 E7
Blands Hill LN8 47 D5
Blanket Row HU1 180 F5
BLANKNEY LN4 95 D3
Blankney Cl 4 LN1 66 D2
Blankney Cres LN2 201 F8
Blankney Ct 13 DN15 9 A5
Blankney Dro LN10 96 E5
Blankney N Dro LN4 96 B5
Blashfield Cl 2 PE9 219 A6
Blasson Way 12 NG34 133 B1
Blatherwick Rd NG24 104 B4
Blaydon Gr 1 DN34 190 E4
Blazegate PE12 216 B8
BLEASBY LN8 58 A3
BLEASBY MOOR LN3 57 F2
Bledwick Dro PE13 170 C3
Blenheim Cl
17 Hatfield DN7 14 D3
Louth LN11 198 B7
Skellingthorpe LN6 79 F6
Blenheim Ct DN16 185 A2
Blenheim Pl DN35 192 E4
Blenheim Rd
Coningsby LN4 207 C4
Lincoln LN1 201 D4
Moorland Prison DN7 26 A8
Blenheim St HU5 180 B8
Blenheim Way
Londonthorpe & Harrowby without NG31 211 D3
Market Deeping PE6 217 B7
Yaxley PE7 233 E5
Blenkin St HU9 181 B7
Blind La
Coleby LN5 93 F3
Hough-on-the-Hill NG32 118 E7
4 Maxey PE6 173 C7
22 Waddington LN5 93 F7
Bloomfield Ave HU5 179 C8
Bloom La DN15 8 C1
Bloomsbury Ct 1 HU3 180 D6
Bloomsbury Gdns DN33 191 B2
Blossom Ct PE3 225 B8
Blossom Way 1 DN40 186 B3
Blow Row DN9 27 E6
Blow's La PE20 135 F3
BLOXHOLM LN4 108 C4
Bloxholm La
Blankney LN4 95 A2
Bracebridge Heath LN4 81 B1
Nocton LN4 94 D6
Bluebell Ave PE1 226 A8
Bluebell Cl
7 Lincoln LN5 205 C2
Scunthorpe DN15 183 C3
Bluebell Ct 23 DN41 23 F5
Bluebell Gr 1 DN20 196 B4
Bluebell Rd 2 PE9 218 D7
Bluebells 8 PE6 217 D6
Bluebells The PE12 215 A6
Bluebell Wlk PE21 208 B4
Blueberry Ct HU4 179 C4
Bluecoat Prim Sch PE9 219 B6
Bluegate NG31 211 A5
Blue Gowt Dro PE11 214 A7
Blue Gowt La PE11 214 B7
Blue St 7 PE21 208 E4
Bluestone Cl DN32 192 A8

Bluestone Heath Rd
Scamblesby LN11 .... 73 A7
Skendleby PE23 .... 88 D5
South Ormsby cum Ketsby LN11 .... 74 B3
South Thoresby LN13 .... 75 A1
Tetford LN11 .... 73 F3
Ulceby with Fordington LN13 .... 88 B8
Welton le Wold LN11 .... 60 A4
Bluestone La DN40 .... 186 B4
Bluestone Rise LN11 .... 198 B4
Bluestone Way 24 LN12 .... 77 A7
Blundell Ave DN35 .... 189 E1
Blundell Pk (Grimsby Town FC) DN35 .... 192 C8
BLYBOROUGH DN21 .... 42 E5
Blyth Ct 28 DN18 .... 10 F8
Blyth St 2 HU9 .... 181 B7
Blyth Way DN37 .... 23 E2
BLYTON DN21 .... 41 C5
Blyton Cl 11 LN6 .... 204 C7
Blyton cum Laughron Prim Sch DN21 .... 41 C6
Blyton Gr 13 LN6 .... 204 C7
Blyton Rd
12 Birchwood LN6 .... 204 C7
Laughton DN21 .... 41 B8
Thonock DN21 .... 197 C8
Boardsides
Frampton PE20 .... 124 F2
Wyberton PE21 .... 208 A3
Boating Dyke Way 19 DN8 .... 15 A8
Boatswain Croft 7 HU1 .... 180 F5
Bobbin La LN2 .... 202 E6
Bodiam Way DN32 .... 191 F8
Bodmin Cl DN17 .... 184 D8
Bodmin Moor Cl LN6 .... 204 D1
Boggle La LN8 .... 45 E5
BOLE DN22 .... 52 C5
Boleyn Ave PE2 .... 230 C8
Bolingbroke Castle (remains of)* PE23 .... 100 A7
Bolingbroke Rd
Cleethorpes DN35 .... 193 A3
Louth LN11 .... 198 B8
Scunthorpe DN17 .... 184 E4
Bolsover Rd DN15 .... 182 B2
Bolton Ave LN6 .... 205 A3
Bolton's La PE25 .... 90 D2
Bomber Cty Aviation Mus* DN21 .... 42 F1
Bon Accord Rd HU13 .... 178 E1
Bona La PE13 .... 169 E1
BONBY DN20 .... 10 C2
Bonby Gr
2 Grimsby DN33 .... 191 A3
Scunthorpe DN17 .... 184 F5
Bonby Rd DN20 .... 10 C1
Bond Hays La 3 PE23 .... 87 A4
Bond St
1 Boston PE21 .... 208 F4
Kingston upon Hull HU1 .... 180 F7
Bonemill La NG34 .... 121 E6
Bonnetable Rd LN9 .... 199 D3
Bonnyhale Rd DN17 .... 16 E6
BONTHORPE LN13 .... 89 B7
Bonthorpe Rd LN13 .... 89 B7
Boongate PE1 .... 226 C3
Boonground La PE22 .... 115 A3
Bootham Cl 6 DN7 .... 14 D4
Bootham Cres 12 DN7 .... 14 C6
Bootham La DN7 .... 14 D5
Bootham Rd 11 DN7 .... 14 C6
Boothby Cl 14 PE20 .... 136 C5
BOOTHBY GRAFFOE LN5 .... 94 A2
BOOTHBY PAGNELL NG33 .... 140 E5
Boothby Pagnell Manor House* NG33 .... 140 E5
Boothferry Rd HU13 .... 178 B2
Booth Nooking La DN15 .... 2 A2
Boot La PE20 .... 136 E3
Borman's La 7 DN36 .... 36 B1
Borrowdale Cl PE4 .... 221 C3
Borrowdale Way NG31 .... 211 B8
Borthwick Pl PE2 .... 229 D6
Bos App Rd DN16 .... 185 F7
Boscombe Cl 12 LN6 .... 204 C6
BOSTON PE21 .... 209 C6
Boston Aerodrome PE21 .... 125 B2
Boston Carlton Rd Prim Sch PE21 .... 208 E5
Boston Coll (De Montfort Campus) PE21 .... 209 B3
Boston Coll (Rochford Campus) PE21 .... 209 A4
Boston Coll (Sam Newson Centre) PE21 .... 208 F4
Boston Ent Pk PE21 .... 208 A4
Boston Gram Sch PE21 .... 209 A4
Boston Hawthorn Tree Sch PE21 .... 209 D4
Boston High Sch for Girls PE21 .... 209 B7
BOSTON LONG HEDGES PE22 .... 126 B6
Boston Long Hedges PE22 .... 126 C6
Boston Rd
Algarkirk PE20 .... 136 A3
Frithville PE22 .... 125 E7
Gosberton PE11 .... 145 C6
Heckington NG34 .... 122 E2
Holbeach PE12 .... 215 C4
Horncastle LN9 .... 199 C1
Sleaford NG34 .... 212 D4
14 Spilsby PE23 .... 88 A1
Swineshead PE20 .... 124 D1
Wainfleet St Mary PE24 .... 102 D1
Boston Rd N PE12 .... 215 C5
Boston Rd Pits Nature Reserve* PE11 .... 145 C6
Boston Rd S PE12 .... 215 D3
Boston Sta PE21 .... 208 E5
Boston Stump (St Botolph's Ch)* PE21 .... 208 F5
Boston Trade Pk PE21 .... 208 F6
BOSTON WEST PE20 .... 125 B4
Boston W Prim Sch PE21 .... 208 B5
Boswell Cl PE1 .... 225 E8
Boswell Dr LN6 .... 205 A5
Bosworth Cl 18 DN7 .... 14 D3
Botany Bay La DN3 .... 14 B4
Bothwell Gr 3 HU9 .... 5 E8
Botolph Gn PE2 .... 230 C7
Botolph St 7 PE21 .... 209 A5
Botolph's View 1 LN11 .... 51 C4
Botteford Jun & Inf Schools DN16 .... 185 A2
BOTTESFORD
Bottesford NG13 .... 128 A6
Scunthorpe DN16 .... 185 B3
Bottesford Ave DN16 .... 185 B5
Bottesford Cl 12 LN6 .... 204 D8
Bottesford La DN16 .... 185 B4
Bottesford Rd
Allington NG32 .... 128 E6
Scunthorpe DN16 .... 185 B5
Bottesford Sports Ctr DN17 .... 184 C3
Bottesford Sta NG13 .... 128 B6
Bottle La PE13 .... 169 C7
Bottlings The 8 DN20 .... 196 C3
Bottom St NG32 .... 128 F7
BOUGHTON NG34 .... 122 C4
Boughton Ave DN15 .... 182 F4
Boulevard HU3 .... 180 B5
Boulevard Ave DN31 .... 188 E1
Boulevard Gdns DN31 .... 191 B8
Boulevard Ret Pk PE1 .... 225 D7
Boulevard The 23 LN12 .... 64 B3
Boulevard Way DN31 .... 191 B7
Boulevard Wlk DN31 .... 191 B8
BOULTHAM LN5 .... 205 D8
Boultham Ave LN5 .... 201 D1
Boultham Mere Nature Reserve* LN6 .... 201 B3
BOULTHAM MOOR LN6 .... 205 B6
Boultham Pk Rd LN6 .... 201 D1
Boundaries The PE12 .... 215 D1
Boundary La LN6 .... 93 A8
Boundary Paddock 1 LN5 .... 107 A7
Boundary Pastures NG34 .... 212 D3
Boundary Rd DN33 .... 194 E6
Boundary St LN5 .... 205 D7
Boundry Wlk LN8 .... 56 F3
Bourges Bvd PE1 .... 225 D7
Bourgess Ret Pk PE3 .... 225 F1
BOURNE PE10 .... 213 C7
Bourne Abbey Prim Sch PE10 .... 213 E5
Bourne Cl LN6 .... 205 B5
Bourne Dro PE10 .... 155 A5
Bourne Gram Sch PE10 .... 213 D4
Bourne La 7 NG34 .... 108 D2
Bourne Outdoor Swimming Pool PE10 .... 213 D4
Bourne Rd
20 Alford LN13 .... 75 F2
Baston PE6 .... 164 E3
Bourne PE10 .... 213 E2
Colsterworth NG33 .... 151 E6
Essendine PE9 .... 163 E3
Folkingham NG34 .... 142 D8
Morton PE10 .... 154 C6
Old Somerby NG33 .... 140 D8
Pinchbeck PE11 .... 155 F5
Spalding PE11 .... 214 A3
Swinstead NG33 .... 153 A5
Thurlby PE10 .... 164 D8
Bourne Rd Est 6 NG33 .... 151 E6
Bourne Skills Ctr PE10 .... 213 D5
Bourne St HU2 .... 181 A7
Bourne Westfield Prim Sch PE10 .... 213 B5
Bovill Cl DN31 .... 191 C7
Bowbridge Gdns 4 NG13 .... 128 A6
Bowbridge La
10 Bottesford NG13 .... 128 A6
Hawton NG24 .... 104 A1
Bowbridge Rd NG24 .... 104 A2
Bowden Dr LN6 .... 205 A5
Bowditch Rd PE11 .... 214 E3
Bower Cl PE1 .... 226 C5
Bowers Ave
Grimsby DN31 .... 191 B7
3 Louth LN11 .... 198 D7
Bowfield Cl DN37 .... 190 D8
Bow Gate PE11 .... 145 B6
Bowlalley La 9 HU1 .... 180 F6
Bowl Alley La LN9 .... 199 C4
Bowling Gn La
11 Crowle DN17 .... 16 D8
Grantham NG31 .... 211 B3
3 Grimsby DN32 .... 191 E7
Bowling Gn Rd DN21 .... 197 B5
Bowling La DN35 .... 192 E6
Bowman Ave PE22 .... 115 A6
Bowman Cl PE21 .... 208 D6
Bowmandale 30 DN18 .... 10 E8
Bowmandale Prim Sch DN18 .... 10 E8
Bowmans Ridge 1 PE23 .... 87 F1
Bowmans Way NG32 .... 128 F4
Bowman Way 7 DN40 .... 186 B3
Bowness Way 1 PE4 .... 221 D2
Bow Rd HU15 .... 2 E6
Boxer Rd PE8 .... 172 B1
Boxgrove Cl 8 PE6 .... 175 A1
Boyfields 1 PE11 .... 145 A8
Boynton Cres 9 DN15 .... 9 A5
Boynton St 1 HU3 .... 180 C4
Bozeat Way PE3 .... 225 C6
Brabbs Ave 4 DN7 .... 14 E4
BRACEBOROUGH PE9 .... 164 B4
BRACEBRIDGE LN5 .... 205 D6
BRACEBRIDGE HEATH LN4 .... 205 E3
Bracebridge Inf Sch LN5 .... 205 E6
BRACEBY NG34 .... 131 D2
Braceby Rd NG33 .... 131 B1
Brackenborough Ct LN11 .... 198 C7
Brackenborough Rd
Brackenborough with Little Grimsby LN11 .... 49 C1
Keddington LN11 .... 61 C8
Louth LN11 .... 198 C8
Brackenbury Way PE21 .... 208 E8
Brackenbury Cl LN9 .... 199 A3
Brackenbury Fields NG33 .... 140 F6
Bracken Cl
Gainsborough DN21 .... 197 B7
Leasingham NG34 .... 121 C7
Bracken Heen Cl 2 DN7 .... 14 E4
Brackenhill Rd DN9 .... 27 E2
Brackenholmes Rd DN15 .... 9 A2
Bracken La PE24 .... 90 A7
Bracken Pk DN33 .... 194 E8
Bracken Pl DN37 .... 190 C6
Bracken Rd LN6 .... 92 B7
Bracken Way LN11 .... 198 C7
Brackley Cl
Bourne PE10 .... 213 D7
Peterborough PE3 .... 225 D3
Brackwood PE2 .... 229 D6
BRACON DN9 .... 16 F2
Bracon Cl 9 DN9 .... 16 E2
Bradbury Ave LN5 .... 205 C2
Bradden St PE3 .... 225 C6
Bradegate Dr PE1 .... 226 E7
Bradford Ave DN35 .... 193 A5
Bradford Cl 10 NG31 .... 210 D5
Bradford Rd
Boston PE21 .... 208 D3
Immingham DN40 .... 186 B4
Brading Ave NG31 .... 210 E4
BRADLEY DN37 .... 190 E2
Bradley Cl LN11 .... 198 D3
Bradley & Dixon Woods Nature Reserve* DN37 .... 194 A8
Bradley La LE15 .... 162 B7
Bradley Rd
Bradley DN37 .... 194 B6
Grimsby DN37 .... 190 E2
Bradley St DN32 .... 191 F7
Bradman Ct 17 DN32 .... 189 C1
Bradshaw's La PE24 .... 90 C7
Bradshaws Terr PE21 .... 209 A5
Bradway 9 LN1 .... 66 D7
Bradwell Cl 19 DN18 .... 10 E8
Bradwell Rd PE3 .... 225 A2
Brady St 1 PE21 .... 208 E6
Braeburn Ave 14 PE13 .... 170 D2
Braemar Cl
Grantham NG31 .... 211 C7
1 Middle Rasen LN8 .... 57 B8
Stamford PE9 .... 218 E6
Braemar Rd
Cleethorpes DN35 .... 192 E4
3 Mablethorpe/Sutton on Sea LN12 .... 76 F8
Braemer Rd NG23 .... 91 D4
Braeton La DN33 .... 195 A7
Braids Wlk HU10 .... 178 B8
Brailsford Cl 3 PE3 .... 225 A4
BRAITHWAITE DN7 .... 14 A7
Braithwaite La DN7 .... 14 A8
Bramar Rd 5 DN7 .... 14 D4
Brambleberry La PE24 .... 102 B7
Bramble Cl
Grimsby DN31 .... 191 C7
4 Welton/Dunholme LN2 .... 68 D7
Bramble Ct 24 LN2 .... 68 D2
Bramble Gr 2 PE9 .... 218 D6
Bramble Grange 3 PE11 .... 214 B5
Bramble Hills PE25 .... 103 E3
Brambles The
3 Barrow upon Humber DN19 .... 11 C8
Bourne PE10 .... 213 D7
Grantham NG31 .... 211 A2
Holbeach PE12 .... 215 F2
4 Market Deeping PE6 .... 217 D6
15 Market Rasen LN8 .... 57 D8
Newton on Trent LN1 .... 65 D1
Bramble Way
2 Brigg DN20 .... 196 B4
Humberston DN36 .... 192 E1
Bramblewood Cl 6 NG31 .... 210 F8
Brambling Wlk PE10 .... 143 A3
Bramhall St DN35 .... 192 C7
Bramley Cl
1 Barton-upon-Humber DN18 .... 3 F1
5 Bourne PE10 .... 213 C6
8 Fleet PE12 .... 159 C7
2 Heckington NG34 .... 122 E2
4 Louth LN11 .... 198 C5
Bramley Cres DN16 .... 185 A3
Bramley Ct
Gainsborough DN21 .... 197 F5
Lincoln LN6 .... 204 F4
Bramley Gr 1 DN21 .... 29 C3
Bramley La 6 PE21 .... 208 E4
Bramley Mdws 7 PE12 .... 159 D7
Bramley Rd
Market Deeping PE6 .... 217 B5
11 Wisbech PE13 .... 170 D1
Bramley Wlk PE25 .... 206 C6
Bramling Way NG34 .... 212 F4
BRAMPTON LN1 .... 65 E6
Brampton Ct PE2 .... 231 D6
Brampton Way DN35 .... 192 D3
Bramwith La DN7 .... 14 A6
Brancaster Dr
Lincoln LN6 .... 205 C8
Skegness PE25 .... 206 D5
Brancepeth Pl PE2 .... 230 E7
Branches La PE12 .... 159 A7
BRAND END PE22 .... 126 D4
Brand End Rd PE22 .... 126 E4
Brandesburton St HU3 .... 180 B7
BRANDON NG32 .... 118 D7
Brandon Rd
Hough-on-the-Hill NG32 .... 118 E6
Scunthorpe DN15 .... 182 D2
Stubton NG23 .... 118 C7
Brandy Wharf Cider Ctr* DN21 .... 44 A7
Brankwell Cres DN17 .... 184 E3
BRANSBY LN1 .... 66 E6
Bransby Home of Rest for Horses* LN1 .... 66 D6
Bransdale Gr HU9 .... 181 F8
Bransdale Rd 5 DN16 .... 185 D5
Bransdale Way DN37 .... 190 E8
BRANSTON
Branston and Mere LN4 .... 81 E2
Croxton Kerrial NG32 .... 138 A4
BRANSTON BOOTHS LN4 .... 82 C4
Branston Causeway LN3 .... 82 F3
Branston CE Inf Sch LN4 .... 81 D2
Branston Cl
Lincoln LN6 .... 205 B4
4 Winthorpe NG24 .... 104 B7
Branston Com Coll LN4 .... 81 E2
Branston Jun Sch LN4 .... 81 E2
Branston La LN4 .... 94 D7
Branston Rd LN4 .... 81 E3
BRANT BROUGHTON LN5 .... 105 F5
Brant Broughton CE Methodist Prim Sch LN5 .... 105 F5
BRANTINGHAM HU15 .... 2 C8
Brantingham Rd HU15 .... 2 B7
Brant Rd
Fulbeck NG32 .... 105 F1
Lincoln LN5 .... 205 D2
Scunthorpe DN15 .... 182 E2
Waddington LN5 .... 93 D7
Brassey Cl PE1 .... 225 E6
BRATOFT PE24 .... 102 B7
Bratoft Cnr PE24 .... 102 D7
Bratoft End PE24 .... 102 C5
Brats La LN8 .... 47 E5
Bratt Field Rd DN21 .... 53 F8
BRATTLEBY LN1 .... 67 C8
Brattleby Cres LN2 .... 201 F7
Brauncewell Cl 18 NG34 .... 108 D2
Brauncewell Rd 6 NG34 .... 107 C1
Bray Ave 8 LN12 .... 64 C2
Braybrook PE2 .... 230 A3
Braybrook Prim Sch PE2 .... 230 B4
Braybrooks Way 1 PE12 .... 157 E1
Bray Cl DN33 .... 191 B2
Brayfields 3 PE11 .... 156 F8
Brayford St LN5 .... 234 A2
Brayford Waterfront LN1 .... 234 A2
Brayford Way 1 LN1 .... 234 A2
Brayford Wharf E LN5 .... 234 A1
Brayford Wharf N LN1 .... 234 A2
Braygate La PE23 .... 100 E5
Brazenose La PE9 .... 219 C5
Brazil St HU9 .... 181 C
Breakneck La LN11 .... 198 A
Brecks La
Kirk Sandall DN3 .... 14 A
Stapleford LN6 .... 105 C
Brecon Cl NG31 .... 210 D
Brecon Way NG34 .... 212 E
Breda Ct 8 PE11 .... 214 A
Breedon Dr LN1 .... 201 D
Breezemount Ct 2 DN7 .... 14 C
Brellows Hill 7 PE34 .... 161 F
Bremerhaven Way DN33 190
Brendon Cl NG31 .... 210 C
Brendon Garth 4 PE4 .... 221 C
Brendon Wlk 5 PE11 .... 214 C
Brent Rd LN4 110
Brentwood Cl HU15 2
Brereton Ave DN35 .... 192 C
Brethergate DN9 27
BRETTON PE3 225
Bretton Cl 4 DN7 .... 14 C
Bretton Ctr PE3 .... 225 A
Bretton Gate 2 PE3 .... 225 A
Bretton Gn 1 PE3 .... 225 A
Bretton Way
Bretton PE3 .... 225 A
3 Peterborough PE3 220
Bretton Woods Com Sch PE3 .... 225 A
Brewerne PE2 .... 230 F
Brewers La PE13 .... 170 A
Brewery Gdns 2 DN17 .... 16 D
Brewery Hill NG31 .... 211 B
Brewery La NG34 .... 143 B
Brewery Rd DN17 .... 16 D
Brewery St 6 PE24 .... 102 B
Brewhouse Gall* NG31 .... 211 A
Brewster Ave
Immingham DN40 .... 186 D
Peterborough PE2 .... 230 F
Brewster Ave Inf Sch PE2 230
Brewster La PE24 .... 102 C
Brewster Rd PE21 .... 209 B
Breydon Ct 3 DN15 .... 8 B
Brian Ave
Cleethorpes DN35 .... 192 C
Scunthorpe DN16 .... 185 C
7 Skegness PE25 .... 206 C
Waltham DN37 .... 194 D
Briar Cl
6 Birchwood LN6 .... 200 C
5 Lincoln LN6 .... 93 A
Skegness PE25 .... 206 C
2 Sleaford NG34 .... 212 D
4 South Killingholme DN40 .... 12 E
Briar La
Grimsby DN33 .... 194 D
Healing DN41 .... 23 F
Briars La 6 DN7 .... 14 C
Briars The HU13 .... 178 E
Briar Way
Peterborough PE1 .... 226 C
Scunthorpe DN15 .... 182 C
Skegness PE25 .... 206 C
Briar Wlk PE10 .... 213 D
Briarwood Cl 6 NG31 .... 210 F
Brickberry Cl PE7 .... 230 C
Bricken Field La LN9 .... 84 C
Brickenhole La 7 DN10 .... 39 F
Brickings Way 4 DN22 .... 52 B
Brick La
North Killingholme DN40 .... 12 E
Wrangle PE22 .... 114 C
Brickyard La
Folkingham NG34 .... 142 D
Hundleby PE23 .... 87 E
Mablethorpe & Sutton LN12 .... 76 E
Melton HU14 .... 2 F
Navenby LN5 .... 94 A
Theddlethorpe St Helen LN12 .... 63 F
Walkeringham DN10 .... 39 E
Bridge Cl
Kingston upon Hull HU9 .... 181 D
3 Louth LN11 .... 198 C
Bridge Dro PE13 .... 177 B
Bridge End
Colsterworth NG33 .... 151 D
Wansford PE8 .... 222 A
Bridge End Causeway NG34 .... 133 F
Bridge End Gr NG31 .... 211 D
Bridge End Rd NG31 .... 211 C
Bridge Foot PE6 .... 217 B
Bridgegate Dr HU9 .... 181 C
Bridge Gdns 1 DN31 .... 188 D
Bridgehill Rd PE6 .... 221 D
Bridge La
Cadney DN20 .... 31 C
Horkstow DN18 .... 9 F
Scopwick LN4 .... 108 D
Bridge Pl 22 LN1 .... 66 D
Bridge Rd
Aubourn Haddington & South Hykeham LN5 .... 92 F
Gainsborough DN21 .... 197 D
Greetham with Somersby LN9 .... 86 F
Long Sutton PE12 .... 216 D
4 Sutton Bridge PE12 .... 160 F
Bridge St N 1 DN32 .... 189 B

Bridges Rd DN17 . . . . 184 E7
Bridge St
1 Billinghay LN4 . . . . 109 F5
2 Boston PE21. . . . . .208 F4
Brigg DN20 . . . . 196 A3
Gainsborough DN21 . . . .197 C3
Grantham NG31. . . . . . . 211 C3
Horncastle LN9 . . . . .199 B4
Louth LN11 . . . . .193 B6
Market Deeping PE6 . . . .217 D4
Marston NG32 . . . . 118 D2
10 Nettleham LN2 . . . . . . .68 C2
2 Peterborough PE1 . . . . 226 A1
4 Ryhall PE9 . . . . 163 C1
Saxilby LN1 . . . . .66 D2
27 Thorne/Moorends
DN8. . . . . .15 A8
Bridges The **24** DN18. . 10 F8
Bridge View LN8 . . . . . . .56 F8
Bridgeview Sch HU13 . . 178 D1
Bridgewater Rd DN17 . . 184 D8
Bridle Cl
Fishtoft PE21. . . . . 209 C3
7 Sleaford NG34 . . . . . . 212 D2
Bridle La LN5. . . . . .105 E8
Bridles The **11** DN19 . . . 12 A8
Bridle Way **4** LN8 . . . . . .70 D5
Bridle Way The LN4 . . . . .95 B7
Bridlington Ave HU2 . . . .180 F8
Bridport HU3 . . . . 184 C8
Brierholme Carr Rd
DN7. . . . . 14 F5
Brierholme Cl DN7. . . . . 14 F5
Brierholme Ings Rd
DN7. . . . . 14 F5
BRIGG DN20 . . . . .196 E4
Briggate Dr **10** DN17 . . .29 D7
Brigg Cl **6** LN6. . . . . 204 C6
Brigg Dr HU13. . . . . .178 F3
Brigg Gr **5** LN6 . . . . 204 C6
Brigg La LN5 . . . . 105 F8
Brigg Prep Sch DN20 . . . 196 C3
Brigg Prim Sch DN20 . . . 196 C4
Brigg Rd
Barton-upon-Humber
DN18. . . . . 10 E5
Broughton DN20 . . . . . . .19 E3
Cadney DN20 . . . . 31 D7
Grasby LN7 . . . . .33 A6
Hibaldstow DN20 . . . . . . 30 F6
North Kelsey LN7. . . . . . .32 A5
Scawby DN20. . . . . 30 F8
Scunthorpe DN16 . . . . . .183 D2
South Kelsey LN7. . . . . . .32 A1
Wrawby DN20 . . . . 196 F5
Brigg Sta DN20 . . . . 196 C2
Brighowgate DN32. . . . . 191 D6
Brighton St
2 Cleethorpes DN35 . . . . 193 A5
Kingston upon Hull HU3 . . 180 A3
Bright St
5 Gainsborough
DN21. . . . . .197 C4
Kingston upon Hull HU8 . .181 B8
Peterborough PE1 . . . . . .225 F3
BRIGSLEY DN37 . . . . . . .35 D4
Brigsley Rd DN37 . . . . . . 194 D2
Brigstock Ct PE3 . . . . . . 225 C6
Brigstock Rd PE13 . . . . . 170 C1
Brimbles Way PE2 . . . . . 229 E5
Brimhurst PE2 . . . . 230 A4
Brinkhall Way **3** LN2 . . . .68 D7
BRINKHILL LN11 . . . . . . .87 E8
Brinkhill Pottery * LN11. .87 E8
Brinkle Spring La LN4 . . .82 A4
Brisbane Cl
5 Skegness PE25. . . . . . 206 A4
15 Waddington LN5 . . . . . 93 E8
Brisbane St HU3 . . . . . . .180 D5
Bristol Arc **16** LN2 . . . . . 234 C2
Bristol Ave PE4 . . . . .220 F3
Bristol Cl
14 Beacon Hill NG24. . . . 104 C5
Grantham NG31. . . . . . . 210 E4
Bristol Dr LN6 . . . . 205 C8
Bristol House Rd NG34. . 107 C1
Bristol Rd
Kingston upon Hull
HU5. . . . . .179 C8
Scunthorpe DN17 . . . . . .182 C1
Bristol Way NG34 . . . . . .212 B5
Bristow Rd
3 Cranwell & Byard's Leap
NG34. . . . . .120 C5
Cranwell NG34. . . . . 107 C1
Bristows Yd NG32 . . . . . .113 D2
Britannia Cres DN34 . . . .190 D5
Britannia Gdns 3
PE11. . . . . .214 C5
Britannia Terr 4
DN21. . . . . 197 C3
Briton Cl **11** PE21 . . . . . 214 C2
Brittain Dr NG31. . . . . . . 211 C5
Britton Cl DN17. . . . . .7 D3
Brixham Cl
Grimsby DN33 . . . . .194 E6
7 Kingston upon Hull
HU3. . . . . .180 A5
Broach Rd LN5 . . . . .106 B5
Broadacre Pk **2** HU15 . . . .2 D5
Broadbank LN11. . . . . . . .198 B6
Broadbeck **7** DN21. . . . . .43 D7
Broadbent Theatre *
LN3 . . . . .69 E8
Broad Cl PE1 . . . . 226 D5
Broad Dale Cl LN2 . . . . . .68 F3
Broad Dro PE11. . . . . . . .144 B5
Broad Dro E PE13. . . . . . 169 E6

Broad Dro W PE13. . . . . 169 B4
Broad Fen La NG23 . . . . 104 D1
Broadfield La **2** PE21 . . .208 E4
Broadfield La Ind Est
PE21. . . . . .208 E3
Broadfield St PE21. . . . . .208 E4
Broadgate
Gedney PE12. . . . . 159 D6
Lincoln LN2 . . . . .234 B2
Whaplode PE12 . . . . 168 A3
Broad Gate
Sutton St James PE12. . . 169 A8
Weston PE12 . . . . 157 C1
Wrangle PE22 . . . . 114 C3
Broadgate Dro PE12 . . . 167 C8
Broadgate Pk PE6 . . . . . .217 F4
Broadgate Rd
South Witham NG33 . . . 151 E2
Sutton St Edmund PE12. .168 F3
BROADHOLME LN1. . . . . .66 C1
Broadholme La LN1 . . . . . .66 D1
Broadhurst Rd **18** PE8. . .172 B1
Broadings La DN22 . . . . . .65 A4
Broad La
Bicker PE20 . . . . .135 B4
Moulton PE12 . . . . 157 F6
South Leverton DN22 . . . .65 A7
Sutterton PE20 . . . . .135 F1
Whaplode PE12 . . . . 146 F1
Broadlands Ave PE10 . . . 213 C7
Broadlands Cl **1** DN7. . . .14 D3
Broadlands The PE11. . . .226 E5
Broadley Ave HU10. . . . . 178 D6
Broadley Cl **6** HU9. . . . . 181 C7
Broadley Cres LN11 . . . . .198 E6
Broadley Croft **6** HU15 . . .2 D5
Broadley Way **6** HU15 . . . .2 D5
Broad St
5 Grantham NG31 . . . . . 211 A5
Spalding PE11 . . . . 214 D4
Stamford PE9. . . . . .219 B5
Broadsyke La NG24 . . . . 105 A4
Broadwater Dr **3** DN7. . . .14 D3
Broadwater La PE12. . . . 158 A4
Broadway
Ashby DN16. . . . . .185 B6
Crowland PE6 . . . . 175 B8
Farcet PE7. . . . . .231 C1
3 Grimsby DN34 . . . . . . 190 D4
Hatfield DN7 . . . . .14 C3
2 Keelby DN41. . . . . .23 A5
Lincoln LN2 . . . . .234 C3
Mablethorpe/Sutton on Sea
LN12. . . . . .77 A8
Peterborough PE1 . . . . . .226 A3
Spalding PE11 . . . . 214 A2
Yaxley PE7 . . . . 233 E5
Broadway Cl
11 Bourne PE10 . . . . 213 C7
4 Lincoln LN2 . . . . 201 F6
Broadway Ct **5** PE1 . . . . .226 A2
Broadway Gdns PE1 . . . .226 B5
Broadway Nook **1** DN7 . .14 C3
Broadway The
Morton LN6 . . . . .154 B7
Woodhall Spa LN10 . . . . . .97 D6
Broadway Theatre *
PE1. . . . . .226 A3
Broad Wheel Rd PE6. . . .173 B3
Brock Cl **1** DN33 . . . . . . 191 C2
Brockenhurst Cl LN6. . . .204 B7
Brockenhurst Rd 9
DN7 . . . . .14 E4
Brocklebank Cl LN5. . . . . .92 F2
BROCKLESBY DN41 . . . . . 22 E6
Brocklesby Cl
Gainsborough DN21 . . . .197 F3
9 Kingston upon Hull
HU13. . . . . .179 A3
Brocklesby Gdns PE3 . . .225 C3
Brocklesby Pk Prim Sch
DN37. . . . . .22 D4
Brocklesby Pl DN34 . . . . 190 E4
Brocklesby Rd
Brocklesby DN41. . . . . . .22 E5
Grimsby DN34 . . . . .190 E4
Habrough DN40. . . . . . . .22 E8
Scunthorpe DN17 . . . . . .184 F4
Ulceby DN39 . . . . .12 A1
Brocklesby Wlk LN11 . . . 198 A7
Brocks Cl **22** PE24 . . . . . .90 D7
Brockton Cl HU3 . . . . 179 F5
Brodsworth Rd PE7 . . . . .231 F5
Bromwich Rd HU10 . . . . .178 F8
Bronzegarth DN32 . . . . . 192 B5
Brookdale Rd DN17 . . . . .184 D6
Brook Dr **4** LN12. . . . . . . .64 C3
Brooke Ave PE9. . . . . . . .218 E4
BROOKENBY LN8 . . . . . . .47 B6
Brookenby Bsns Pk LN8. .47 B6
Brookes Cl **34** DN20. . . . .30 B1
Brooke St DN16. . . . . .15 A8
Brookfield Ave LN2 . . . . . .68 D2
Brookfield Cl
3 Skellingthorpe LN6. . . 200 A5
4 Thorne/Moorends
DN8. . . . . .15 A8
Brookfield Home Pk
PE4. . . . . .220 E2
Brookfield Rd DN33 . . . . .191 B1
Brookfields Ind Pk
PE6. . . . . .220 F2
Brookfurlong PE3. . . . . . .225 B6
Brook La
Farcet PE7. . . . . .231 B2
Scawby DN20. . . . . .20 A1
Brooklands **1** DN20 . . . . .19 E3

Brooklands Ave
Broughton DN20 . . . . .19 D4
Cleethorpes DN35 . . . . . 193 A5
Brooklands Cl
5 Birchwood LN6. . . . . . 204 C7
3 Collingham NG23 . . . . .91 D5
Brooklands Rd HU5. . . . . 179 E8
Brooklands Way 8
LN6. . . . . .204 C7
Brooklyn Dr DN36. . . . . .193 B1
Brook Rd LN9 . . . . 199 D2
Brookside
8 Ancaster NG32. . . . . . 120 A3
4 Brough HU15 . . . . .2 D6
Louth LN11 . . . . .198 D3
Peterborough PE4 . . . . . .221 B2
Brookside Cl
7 Ancaster NG32. . . . . . 120 A3
Ruskington NG34. . . . . . 108 D2
Brook St
Grantham NG31. . . . . . . 211 A5
Hemswell DN21. . . . . . . .42 D2
Kingston upon Hull HU2 . .180 E7
Lincoln LN2 . . . . .234 B2
Peterborough PE1 . . . . . .226 A2
Brook Way **5** NG34. . . . . 108 D2
Broom Cl **7** PE1 . . . . 226 A8
Broom Gr LN6 . . . . .14 D4
Broome Way PE12 . . . . . .215 A2
BROOMFLEET HU15 . . . . . 1 B6
Broomfleet Sta HU15 . . . . 1 B6
Broom Gr DN16 . . . . .185 B8
Broomhill **8** LN6 . . . . . . .204 C8
Broomston La DN9. . . . . . 26 F1
Broomwood Cl 2
NG31. . . . . .210 F7
Brosley Ave **1** DN3 . . . . . .14 A4
Brotherhood Cl PE4. . . . .225 D8
Brotherhood Ret Pk
PE4. . . . . .225 D8
BROTHERTOFT PE20. . . . .124 F5
Brothertoft Rd PE21 . . . .208 D5
Brotts Rd NG23 . . . . .78 A3
BROUGH
Brough HU15 . . . . .2 C5
Collingham NG23 . . . . . . .91 E1
Brougham St HU3 . . . . . .179 F7
Brough Cl **14** LN6 . . . . . .204 C7
Brough La NG23 . . . . .91 D2
Brough Prim Sch HU15 . . .2 C6
Brough Rd LN6 . . . . .105 A4
2 Brough HU15 . . . . .2 B5
BROUGHTON DN20 . . . . . .19 D3
BROUGHTON COMMON
DN20 . . . . .19 F5
Broughton Gdns LN5. . . .205 D3
Broughton Inf Sch
DN20 . . . . .19 E3
Broughton La LN5 . . . . . . .93 C3
Broughton Rd
Carlton-le-Moorland
LN5. . . . . .92 C1
Stapleford LN6. . . . . 105 C8
Broughton's La 1
PE22. . . . . .126 E3
Browndons St 4
NG31. . . . . .211 A5
Brownes Rd **7** PE8. . . . . .172 B1
Browning Cl
3 Kingston upon Hull
HU3. . . . . .179 B1
1 Scunthorpe DN17. . . . .184 E6
Browning Ct **4** LN4. . . . . 207 B5
Browning Dr LN2 . . . . . . .202 B7
Brown La NG23 . . . . .79 A7
Brownlow Cres 3
PE11. . . . . .145 B1
Brownlow Dr **4** PE6. . . . .217 E4
Brownlow Quay 1
PE9. . . . . .219 C4
Brownlow Rd PE11 . . . . . 226 A6
Brownlow's Dro PE12 . . .167 A8
Brownlow's Hill NG24 . . .104 D5
Brownlow Terr **20** PE9 . . 219 C5
Browns CE (Aided) Prim
Sch NG34 . . . . 133 C2
Brown's Gate
Long Sutton PE12 . . . . . .216 B1
Spalding PE11 . . . . 214 C4
Browns La **13** DN8 . . . . . .15 A8
Browns Orch DN20 . . . . . 191 D6
Brown's Rd **3** PE21. . . . . 209 A7
Brown St DN31 . . . . 189 C3
BROXHOLME LN1 . . . . . . .66 F5
Broxholme Gdns 2
LN2. . . . . .201 F8
Broxholme La LN1 . . . . . . .66 F5
Broxholme Wild at Heart
Nature Reserve & Arts
Ctr* LN1 . . . . .67 F4
Bruce Cl
7 Broughton DN20 . . . . . .19 D3
Lincoln LN2 . . . . .234 C4
Bruce St DN15. . . . . .182 F3
Brudenell **7** PE3 . . . . . . .229 E2
Brudenell Cl **1** PE6. . . . . 164 E5
Brulon Cl LN4 . . . . .207 B6
Brumby DN16 . . . . 185 C8
Brumby Comm La LN2 . . .184 B7
Brumby Comm Nature
Reserve* DN17 . . . . . . 184 C7
Brumby Cres **10** LN5 . . . . .93 F7
Brumby Engineering Coll
DN16 . . . . .185 B8

Brumby Hall Gdns
DN17 . . . . .182 F2
Brumby House Dr
DN16 . . . . .185 A8
Brumby Jun Sch DN16 . . .185 B8
Brumby's Terr **4** HU9. . . 181 D7
Brumby Wood La
DN15 . . . . .182 C2
Brumby Wood Nature
Reserve* DN17 . . . . . . 182 E2
Brunel Cl DN16. . . . . 185 B4
Brunel Dr
Newark NG24 . . . . 104 B5
Yaxley PE7 . . . . 233 D6
Brunel Rd PE11. . . . . 214 E8
Brunslow Cl HU3 . . . . . . .179 E5
Brunswick Ave HU2 . . . . .180 E8
Brunswick Cres **5** PE6 . . 206 C4
Brunswick Gr **6** HU13 . . .178 E2
Brunswick Sq LN4 . . . . . 109 F6
Brunton Way DN36 . . . . .195 D5
Brush Meadow La
PE34. . . . . 161 E3
Brushtrokes Ceramics*
DN37 . . . . .194 E3
Bryant Cl LN9 . . . . 199 D7
Brynmore PE3 . . . . .225 A8
Bryony Gdns PE10 . . . . . .213 D7
Bryony Way **5** PE6 . . . . . 217 D6
Bubble Car Mus*
NG34 . . . . .120 A8
Buccaneer Way **21** HU15 . . 2 C5
Buchanan Cl 201 D8
Buchanan Rd DN21 . . . . . .54 F8
Buchanan St LN1 . . . . . . 201 D8
Buck Beck Way DN36 . . . 192 D2
Buck Cl LN2 . . . . 202 D6
Buckfast Cl DN37 . . . . . . 188 A1
Buckfast Cl DN17 . . . . . . 184 D8
Buckfast Rd **4** LN11 . . . . 201 E6
Buckingham Ave DN15 . .182 F5
Buckingham Cl
Fishtoft PE21. . . . . 209 C6
13 Mablethorpe & Sutton
LN12. . . . . .76 F8
Buckingham Dr **18** PE24. . 90 D7
Buckingham Gr DN33 . . .191 B2
Buckingham Rd LN11 . . . 198 A7
Buckingham St N
DN15 . . . . .182 F5
Buckingham St S DN15 . .182 F4
Buckingham St 5
DN15 . . . . .182 F4
Buckland Ct **3** PE4. . . . . 225 B4
Buckland Way **5** DN15 . . 182 F5
BUCKLEGATE PE20. . . . . .136 F3
Bucklegate La PE20. . . . .136 F2
Buckle St **2** LN1 . . . . 234 C3
BUCKMINSTER NG33 . . . .150 E5
Buckminster Gdns
NG31. . . . . .210 F2
Buckminster La NG33 . . . 151 A7
Buckminster Pl 4
PE1. . . . . .226 D7
Buckminster Prim Sch
NG33 . . . . .150 F5
Buckminster Rd
Gunby & Stainby NG33 . . . 151 A3
Sproxton LE14. . . . . .150 C7
BUCKNALL LN10 . . . . .84 A4
Bucknall Ave LN6 . . . . . .205 A7
Bucknall Rd LN10 . . . . . . .84 C3
Bucknall's Mdw LN12. . . .76 F8
Buckshoft Rd PE14. . . . . .170 E3
Buckthorn Ave
3 Skegness PE25. . . . . . 103 E4
Skegness PE25. . . . . 103 E4
Buckthorn Rd PE7 . . . . . .230 D3
Buddleia Cl DN41 . . . . . . .23 A1
Buddleia Dr LN4 . . . . .81 D3
Bude Cl DN36. . . . . 195 C7
Bukehorn Rd PE6 . . . . . . 175 D4
BULBY PE10 . . . . 142 B1
Bulby La **5** NG32 . . . . . . 106 C1
Bulham La NG23 . . . . .78 A1
Bull Bank LN11. . . . . .49 D7
Bulldog Cres LN11 . . . . . .62 B6
Bull Dro PE22 . . . . 114 B5
Bullen's La PE20 . . . . 135 C6
Buller Cl **18** NG23 . . . . . . .91 D5
Buller St **4** DN32. . . . . . . 191 F7
Bullfinch La DN35. . . . . . .192 E1
Bullingham Rd LN2 . . . . .202 D6
BULLINGTON LN8 . . . . . . .69 E4
Bullivant Rd DN7 . . . . . . .14 E4
Bull La
1 Ketton PE9. . . . . 171 A3
Long Sutton PE12 . . . . . .216 C4
North Witham NG33 . . . . 151 E4
4 Peakirk PE6 . . . . 174 A5
Bull Moor Rd DN7 . . . . . . .15 A4
Bullock Rd
Terrington St Clement
PE34 . . . . .161 F1
Thorney PE8 . . . . 228 B1
Bullock's Short Gate
PE12. . . . . .159 C4
Bull Pasture PE22. . . . . . 126 D2
Bullpit Rd NG24 . . . . 104 C3
Bull Ring LN9. . . . . .199 B4
Bull's Bank PE11. . . . . . . 144 E8
Bully Hill LN8. . . . . .46 D2
Bulpit La LN11. . . . . .91 F7
Bulwick Ave DN33 . . . . . .194 E7
Bungley La PE20 . . . . 136 C6
Bunkers Hill
Hemswell DN21. . . . . . . .42 E1
Lincoln LN2 . . . . .202 D6
BUNKER'S HILL LN4. . . . . 111 E4

Bunkers Hill Cl **2** DN36. . .36 D4
Bunker's Hill La PE21 . . . 136 F8
BUPA Hull & E Riding
Hospl HU10 . . . . 178 E5
Burchnall Cl PE6. . . . . . . 217 D6
Burchnall Dr **4** PE25 . . . . .90 E3
Burcom Ave **8** DN36. . . . .36 D8
Burcott Garth HU4. . . . . .179 B3
Burcroft Rd **17** PE13 . . . .170 C1
Burdett **8** PE25. . . . . 206 A6
Burdock Rd DN16. . . . . . .185 C4
Bure Cl LN6 . . . . 204 F3
Burford Way PE1 . . . . . . .226 D6
Burgar Rd **11** DN8. . . . . . .15 A7
Burgate **6** DN18. . . . . 10 F8
Burgess Cl **2** PE21 . . . . . 209 B4
Burgess Dr PE12 . . . . 159 C7
Burgess Rd DN20 . . . . . . 196 E3
BURGH LE MARSH
PE24. . . . . .102 E7
Burgh le Marsh Mus* **15**
PE24 . . . . .102 E7
Burghley Av **14** PE8 . . . . .172 B1
Burghley Cl
Birchwood LN6 . . . . 200 E1
22 Crowland PE6. . . . . . . 166 F1
3 Market Deeping PE6 . . 217 E4
3 Nettleton LN7. . . . . . . .33 A3
Burghley Cres LN11 . . . . .198 B7
Burghley Ct
1 Bourne PE10 . . . . 213 C5
12 Stamford PE9. . . . . . . 219 C5
Burghley House* PE9. . . 219 F3
Burghley La **8** PE9 . . . . . 219 C4
Burghley Pk Cl **8** LN6. . . 204 F1
Burghley Rd
Birchwood LN6 . . . . 200 E1
1 Peterborough PE1 . . . . 226 A3
Scunthorpe DN16 . . . . . .185 D7
8 Skegness PE25. . . . . . 206 C1
12 Stamford PE9. . . . . . . 219 A4
Burghley Sh Ctr The
PE10. . . . . .213 D5
1 Peterborough PE1 . . . . 226 A3
Burghley St PE10 . . . . . . 213 C5
BURGH ON BAIN LN8. . . . .59 D5
Burgh Rd
Friskney PE22 . . . . 115 A7
Skegness PE25 . . . . 103 C2
Burgin Cl **13** NG32 . . . . . 117 F1
Burgon Cres **3** DN15 . . . . .9 B5
Burke St (North) 7
DN15 . . . . .183 A4
Burke St DN15. . . . . 183 A4
Burland Ct **3** LN4 . . . . . .203 B2
Burleigh Ct NG31 . . . . . . 211 F5
Burleigh Gdns **3** PE21. . .209 A7
Burleigh St HU8 . . . . 181 C8
Burley Ave DN15. . . . . . . 192 F3
Burley Cl DN37 . . . . .23 F2
Burley Rd **14** PE9 . . . . . . 163 C1
Burlies' Gate PE12 . . . . . 159 E4
Burlington Rd PE25 . . . . . 206 B3
Burma Rd DN16 . . . . .5 D8
Burmer Rd PE1. . . . . 225 F2
Burneside Cl LN2 . . . . . . 202 B8
Burnet Dr DN16. . . . . 185 C4
Burnett's Yd LN7 . . . . .33 C4
BURNHAM DN18 . . . . .11 C4
Burnham La
Kirton PE20 . . . . .136 F4
Thornton Curtis DN39 . . . .11 E4
Burnham Rd
Barton-upon-Humber
DN18. . . . . 11 A6
Epworth DN9. . . . . .27 E6
Kingston upon Hull HU4 . .179 B3
Owston Ferry DN9. . . . . . .28 A3
Scunthorpe DN16 . . . . . .182 D2
Burnham Reach 5
DN35 . . . . .192 F1
Burnham Sq **2** DN9 . . . . . .28 A3
Burnmoor Cl **3** LN6 . . . . 200 C1
Burn Rd DN15. . . . . 182 C3
Burns Cl
Grantham NG31. . . . . . . 211 E6
Peterborough PE1 . . . . . .225 F7
Burns Cres **8** NG34 . . . . . 212 F4
Burns Gdns **2** LN5 . . . . . 205 D3
Burns Gr DN33 . . . . .191 D3
Burnside Dr PE6. . . . . . . 175 B5
Burnside Rd **6** PE25. . . . .217 A5
Burns St **6** DN21. . . . . . . .218 F6
Burns St DN21 . . . . .197 B6
Burnstone Gdns 4
PE12. . . . . .157 F7
Burnt Hill La **5** LN11 . . . .198 B5
Burrells Cl DN9. . . . . .27 D2
Burrettgate Rd 4
PE13. . . . . .170 F1
Burrett Gdns **2** PE13 . . . .170 F1
Burrett Rd PE13 . . . . 170 F2
Burrill La HU15 . . . . .2 B8
BURRINGHAM DN17 . . . . .17 E4
Burringham Rd
Burringham DN17 . . . . . .17 E5
Scunthorpe DN17 . . . . . .184 D5
Burrow La PE12 . . . . .156 F3
Burrows Ct **2** PE21 . . . . .208 E7
Burrows Ct PE1 . . . . .226 A5
Burrs The HU15 . . . . .2 B8
Bursar Prim Sch DN35 . . .192 E6
Bursar St DN35 . . . . 192 E6

Bursnells La 3 LE14.....150 B1
Burswood PE2.........229 F2
Burtey Fen Collection
The* PE11.............145 B1
Burtey Fen La PE11......145 B2
Burtoft La PE20..........135 E2
BURTON LN1 ....67 D1
Burton Cl PE21 ....209 B7
BURTON CORNER
PE21...................209 B7
Burton Ct
2 Louth LN11.......... 198 D4
Peterborough PE1........ 226 C3
Burtonfield Cl 1 LN3 ....203 E6
Burton Gravel Pits Nature
Reserve* LN1...........67 C1
Burton La
8 Billingborough
NG34...................133 B1
Burton Coggles NG33 .....140 E1
Burton La End LN1...... 200 C8
BURTON-LE-COGGLES
NG33 .... 152 D8
Burton Mews LN4....... 203 D1
Burton on Stather Prim
Sch DN15 ....8 B4
BURTON PEDWARDINE
NG34 ....122 B1
Burton Rd
Burton upon Stather
DN15...................8 C4
Heckington NG34........ 122 C2
Lincoln LN1 .... 234 A4
Spalding PE11 ....214 B2
Burton Ridge 2 LN1.... 201 D7
Burton St
14 Gainsborough
DN21................ 197 D3
Peterborough PE1........ 226 C3
BURTON STATHER DN15 ....8 B5
BURTON UPON STATHER
DN15 ....8 B4
Burton Way LN9 .... 199 D2
BURWELL LN11 ....74 B6
Burwell Cl LN2 .... 202 A8
Burwell Dr DN33..........191 B3
Burwell Rd LN11..........74 D7
Burwell Reach PE2 ..... 230 C7
Burystead PE2...........231 B8
Bush Cl HU4............ 179 D3
Bushfield PE2 ....229 E3
Bushfield Com Coll
PE2....................229 E3
Bushfield Ct PE2.........229 E3
Bushfield Rd DN16.......183 B1
Bushfield Rd Inf Sch
DN16 .... 183 A1
Bushfield Sports Ctr
PE2....................229 E4
Bush Gn La
Algarkirk PE20.......... 146 C8
Fosdyke PE20 .... 136 C1
Bush Meadow La PE12.. 215 A4
Bushy Cl 5 PE7 .... 230 D3
BUSLINGTHORPE LN8 .....57 A4
Buslingthorpe Rd LN8.....57 A4
Bustards' La PE14....... 161 C1
Butcher La 10 LN11 ......198 B5
Butchers Sq HU13 ....178 E1
Butchery Ct 3 LN2 ....234 B2
Butforth La DN19 ....11 E8
Butler Pl DN35..........192 B7
Butler's Way 14 PE20 ....135 B7
Butlin Cl 1 PE25 .... 206 A4
Buttercake La PE22 ....113 F2
Buttercross Cl 2 DN41....23 E6
Buttercup Cl
1 Kingston upon Hull
HU9................. 181 D7
3 Spalding PE11 .... 214 A2
3 Stamford PE9........ 218 D7
Buttercup Ct PE6 .... 217 D6
Buttercup Dr PE10 ...... 213 D3
Buttercup Paddock 4
PE12...................158 B6
Butterfield Cl 7 DN37 ....23 F1
Butterfly & Wildlife Pk
The* PE12............ 216 D6
Buttergate Hill LN9 ....71 F3
Buttermere Cl
2 Birchwood LN6....... 200 D1
East Ella HU4...........179 E6
Buttermere Cres 2
DN36 ....36 C8
Buttermere Pl 4 PE4 ... 221 C3
Buttermere Way 6
DN32 ....191 F8
Butter Mkt 11 LN7 ....33 B4
BUTTERWICK PE22.......126 F4
Butterwick Cl DN35......192 F3
Butterwick Pinchbeck
Endowed CE Sch
PE22...................126 E3
Butterwick Rd
Benington PE22..........126 F4
Messingham DN17.........29 A7
Buttery Cl LN6...........204 F4
Buttfield Rd HU13 ....178 E1
Butt Gate LN11 ....50 B8
Butt La
Barrowby NG32......... 210 A6
Goulceby LN11............72 D6
Laceby DN37 ....23 F2
Norton Disney LN6 ....92 C2
Butt La *continued*
Theddlethorpe All Saints
LN12...................63 E7
Walcott LN4............ 109 C7
Wymondham LE14........ 150 C2
Buttler Way 3 NG34.... 212 C3
Butts Hill La 5 DN15 ......8 C8
Butts La LN5 ....92 F6
Butt's La LN4............207 B5
Butts Rd DN18.............3 F1
Butts The LE14...........138 F1
Buxton Ct DN15..........182 B2
Bycroft Rd DN21........ 197 C8
Byfield Rd DN17 .... 184 D6
Byland Cl LN2 ....202 E6
Byland Ct 4 HU9.........181 E8
Byland Gr DN37......... 188 A1
Byrd Rd DN16 ....185 E6
Byron Ave
Grantham NG31.........211 E6
Lincoln LN2 .... 202 A6
Byron Cl
Peterborough PE2....... 231 D6
Scunthorpe DN17 ....184 E6
6 Sleaford NG34 ....212 F4
Byron Gr DN33.......... 191 C4
Byron Rd LN12............64 B4
Byron Way PE9 ....218 E5
Bytham Hts 3 NG33 .....162 E8
Bythams Prim Sch The
NG33 .... 153 A2
Bythorne Bank PE13 .....169 B6
Bythorn Rd PE2......... 231 C6
Bythorn Way PE2 .... 231 C6
Bywood Pl DN37........ 190 C6

C

CABOURNE LN7...........33 D4
Cabourne Ave LN2.......202 B7
Cabourne Ct LN2 ....202 B7
Cabourne Rd DN33 ....191 B3
CACKLE HILL PE12 ...... 215 C5
Cackle Hill La PE12..... 215 C5
Caddle Rd 11 DN41 ....23 A4
Cade Cl 12 LN2 ....68 F4
Cade Dro PE12 .... 159 D4
Cade La DN21 ....53 D6
Cades Field Rd 24 LN12 ...77 A8
Cadman Way DN21........41 A1
CADNEY DN20 ....31 D6
Cadney Rd DN20........ 196 C1
Cadwell Cl 4 LN6 ...... 204 C7
Cadwell Pk Motor Racing
Circuit* LN11...........73 B8
CAENBY LN8..............55 F8
Caenby Cl DN21 ....197 F3
Caenby Cnr LN8 ....55 B8
Caenby Rd
Caenby LN8 ....43 F1
Cleethorpes DN35........192 E4
Scunthorpe DN17 ....184 E5
Caesar Cl 7 PE6 ....164 E5
Cagthorpe LN9 ....199 B3
Cairns Way 8 LN5.........93 E8
CAISTOR LN7 ....33 B4
Caistor Ave DN16 ....185 B4
Caistor By-pass LN7 ......33 B3
Caistor CE/Methodist Prim
Sch LN7 ....33 B3
Caistor Cl 7 LN6 .... 204 C7
Caistor Dr
Bracebridge Heath LN4.....81 A2
Grimsby DN33 ....191 B3
Caistor Gram Sch LN7 ....33 B4
Caistor La LN8............46 C3
Caistor Rd
Barton-upon-Humber
DN18...................11 A7
Birchwood LN6 .... 204 C7
Cabourne LN7 ....33 F5
Caistor LN7 ....32 E4
Laceby DN37 ....23 E1
2 Market Rasen LN8 ......57 D8
Middle Rasen LN8 ....45 D2
Rothwell LN7 ....33 E2
South Kelsey LN7..........32 A1
Swallow LN7 ....34 A5
Caistor Yarborough Sch
LN7.....................33 C4
Caithness Rd PE9........218 E6
CALCEBY LN13............74 E2
Caldbeck Cl PE4........ 221 D2
Caldecote Cl PE2 ....231 E6
Calder Cl
Grantham NG31..........210 E3
Immingham DN40 .... 186 A3
Calderdale Dr PE11 ..... 214 D7
Calder Gn 24 DN17........29 D7
Calder Rd
Lincoln LN5 .... 205 C2
Scunthorpe DN16 .... 185 D6
Caldervale PE2 .... 230 C6
Caldicott Dr 8 DN21......53 A8
Caleb Hill La
Leake Commonside
PE22...................113 F3
Old Leake PE22 .... 114 A3
Caledonian Rd 4 PE9 ...218 F6
Caledonia Pk HU9 ....181 B5
Callan's La PE10........ 142 C2
Calver Cres DN37....... 190 D7
Calvert La HU4 .... 179 D7
Calvert Rd HU5 .... 179 D8
Camargue Ave DN37 .....194 F4
Camarthen Cl 4 NG31....210 E5
Cambrai Cl LN1..........201 E7
Cambrian Cl NG31 ....210 E7
Cambrian Way
Holton le Clay DN36 ..... 195 C3
11 North Hykeham LN6.....93 B8
1 Peterborough PE4 .... 221 C1
Cambridge Ave
Lincoln LN1 .... 201 D4
Peterborough PE1........225 F5
Scunthorpe DN16 .... 185 A3
Cambridge Cres 4 LN8 ...47 B6
Cambridge Dr
Heighington/
Washingborough LN4 ... 203 D1
Wisbech PE13 .... 170 C1
Cambridge Gdns 4
PE11...................145 B7
Cambridge Mdws
NG24 .... 104 C4
Cambridge Pk Sch
DN34 .... 191 A5
Cambridge Rd
Grimsby DN34...........190 F5
Kingston upon Hull HU13 ..178 F3
Scunthorpe DN16 .... 185 C6
Stamford PE9........... 219 A6
Cambridge Rd N 1
LN12....................64 B5
Cambridge Rd S 3
LN12....................64 B5
Cambridge St
Cleethorpes DN35........192 F6
Grantham NG31...........211 B3
Kingston upon Hull HU3 .. 180 D6
Camdale La 8 NG24.... 104 C1
Camden St 1 HU3........180 B5
Camdon Cl 1 LN5 ...... 205 D3
Camel Gate PE12 ....157 B7
Camelia Cl PE4..........221 B3
Camelot Gdns
Boston PE21 ....209 E5
11 Mablethorpe/Sutton on Sea
LN12 ....76 F8
Cameron Dr 3 PE11 ....214 E3
Cameron La 13 NG24.... 104 C1
Cameron St 4 NG34.....122 E3
Camilla Cl HU9 .... 181 A5
CAMMERINGHAM LN1.....54 F1
Camm's La PE22........ 114 D2
Campain's La PE11 ..... 166 C7
Campbell Ave DN16......185 B4
Campbell Cl 4 NG31 ....210 F5
Campbell Ct HU13 ....178 E2
Campbell Dr PE4 .... 221 C4
Campbell Gr DN37.......190 E8
Campbells Cl PE11.......214 B1
Campbells Farm Ave 1
DN15 ....17 E6
Campbell St DN21 ....197 B5
Campden Cres DN35.... 192 D7
Campion Ave HU4 ....179 B2
Campion Cl PE11 ....214 B6
Campion Dr PE6........ 217 D6
Campion Gr 4 PE9 ..... 218 D7
Campion Rd PE1.........226 B8
Campions Cl DN36...... 195 D2
Campions' La 11 DN36 ....36 B1
Campion Way PE10 ..... 213 D2
Camp La NG33...........141 B1
Campling Pl PE12....... 215 D7
Campling Way 2 LN12....64 C2
Campney La LN10.........83 F1
Campus Way LN6....... 201 D3
Camwood Cres LN6..... 200 C1
Canada La
Caistor LN7 ....33 C4
Wildmore LN4 .... 111 A4
Canal La DN10............40 B5
CANAL SIDE DN8..........15 A7
Canal View 12 DN8........15 A7
Canberra Ave DN7 ....26 A8
Canberra Cl 5 LN4 ..... 207 C4
Canberra Cres
11 Binbrook Tech Pk
LN8.....................47 B6
Grantham NG31......... 211 D7
10 Manby LN11............62 C6
Canberra Dr 5 LN1.......67 F5
Canberra St HU3 .... 180 D5
Canberra Way LN6...... 200 A4
Candidus Ct 6 PE4......220 F5
Candlehouse La 9
LN13....................75 F3
CANDLESBY PE23.........88 F2
Candlesby Hill Quarry
Nature Reserve* PE23...88 F2
Candlesby Rd DN37..... 190 C7
Candy Bank DN9..........26 B5
Candy St PE2............230 E8
Cane Ave PE2 .... 230 D7
Canister La
Frithville PE22.......... 112 C1
Langriville PE22..........124 F8
Cannon Cl NG24 .... 104 C5
Cannonhill Dro PE12.... 167 A8
Cannon Oakes Ct
DN36 ....195 E6
Cannon Peter Hall CE Prim
Sch DN40 .... 186 D4
Cannon St
Kingston upon Hull
HU2....................180 F8
1 Lincoln LN2...........202 B3
3 Louth LN11...........198 B5
Canon Dr 6 PE9 .... 172 D3
Canon Peter Hall CE Prim
Sch The DN40 .... 186 D4
Canonsfield PE4 ....220 E4
Canon Tardrew Ct
HU13 .... 179 A1
Canterbury Cl
Grantham NG31..........211 E7
1 Scunthorpe DN17...... 184 D7
Spalding PE11 ....214 B4
Canterbury Dr
Grimsby DN34.......... 191 C6
Heighington/Washingborough
LN4 .... 203 D1
4 Sleaford NG34 .... 212 C7
Canterbury Rd
1 Hatfield DN7 ....14 D4
Peterborough PE4 ....220 F3
Cant's Dro PE13 .... 177 C4
Canturbury Cl 10 LN10 ....97 C5
Canty Nook 5 DN38 ......32 E7
Canwell PE4............ 221 A4
CANWICK LN4 ....81 B4
Canwick Ave LN4 ....205 F4
Canwick Hill LN4 ....81 A4
Canwick Rd
Canwick LN5 ....81 A4
Lincoln LN5 ....234 B1
Washingborough LN4 ......81 D4
Capes Entry PE12....... 157 A2
Capitol Pk DN8 ....14 F8
Capper Ave 3 DN21 ......55 A8
Cappitt Dr 2 PE10...... 164 C8
Capp's La 19 LN5 ....93 F7
Capstan Way 17 DN8......15 A8
Captains Beck 9 PE11.. 145 C1
Captain's Hill NG34 .....121 B7
Captains Wlk HU1 ....180 E5
Capthorne Cl PE7....... 230 C2
Caravan Pk LN6 .... 204 C1
Carbis Cl DN36 .... 195 C7
Cardiff Ave DN36 .... 195 C6
Cardigan Rd HU3 ....179 E6
Cardinal Cl
Lincoln LN2 .... 202 D5
New Quarrington NG34... 212 A2
Cardinal Ct 3 DN37 ..... 194 C5
Cardinals Gate PE4 ......220 E4
Cardinal Wlk HU13...... 179 A1
Cardyke Dr 13 PE6.......164 E5
CAREBY PE9.............163 B7
Carew St HU3 ....179 F7
Carholme Cl 1 PE10.... 213 D6
Carholme Rd LN1....... 201 C4
Carisbrook Ct PE3 ....230 B8
Carisbrooke Cl
2 Lincoln LN1...........201 E6
5 New Waltham DN36... 195 D7
Carisbrooke Gr PE9......218 E5
Carisbrooke Manor La
DN17 .... 184 A5
Carisbrooke Wlk DN40 .. 186 D3
CARLBY PE9............ 163 D5
Carleton Crest 3 PE4....221 B1
Carline Rd LN1 .... 234 A3
Carlisle Cl
6 Grantham NG31...... 210 D5
1 Lincoln LN6...........204 F1
Carlisle Gdns LN9...... 199 D5
Carlisle St 2 DN21 ..... 197 D5
Carlisle Way 9 LN4.......81 A2
Carlton Ave DN41..........23 F5
Carlton Bvd LN2 .... 202 D5
Carlton Cl
Humberston DN35........193 B1
8 Leverington PE13......170 B2
2 Spalding PE11 ....214 B1
Carlton Ctr Ret Pk
LN2................... 202 D6
Carlton Ferry La NG23 ....91 A6
Carlton Gr LN2 ....201 F7
Carlton La
Broxholme LN1 ....67 A4
Sutton-on-Trent NG23 ......91 A7
CARLTON-LE-MOORLAND
LN5...................105 E8
Carlton Mews 9 LN4 ... 203 D1
Carlton Pk LN11 ....62 C5
Carlton Rd
Ancaster NG32 ....119 E3
Bassingham LN5 ....92 E2
Boston PE21 .... 208 D5
Grimsby DN34...........191 B6
9 Healing DN41 ....23 F5
Hough-on-the-Hill NG32 ...119 B5
Manby LN11...............62 C6
CARLTON SCROOP
NG32 .... 119 D3
Carlton St
Kingston upon Hull
HU3...................179 F4
Lincoln LN1 .... 234 A4
12 Scunthorpe DN15......183 B3
Carlton Wlk LN2........ 202 A7
Carlyle Cl DN35......... 193 A2
Carlyle Wlk LN2 ....202 B6
Carmel Gn PE21 ....208 E2
Carmen Cres DN36...... 195 C3
Carnaby Gr 2 DN32 .... 192 A5
Carnarvon Ave 1
DN34 ....191 B4
Carn Cl 3 LN5 .... 205 D2
Carnegie Rd 21 PE8......172 B1
Carnegie St 6 HU3 ..... 180 A6
Carnell La 16 NG24 ..... 104 C1
Carnforth Cres DN34.... 191 A5
Carnforth Parade
DN34 .... 191 A5
Carnoustie
9 Spalding PE11 .... 214 C2
7 Waltham DN37 .... 194 C4
Carnoustie Cl 2 LN10 ....97 C5
Carnoustie Ct PE12 ......160 F4
Carnoustie Dr LN6.......204 B7
Carol Dickson Ct 9
HU3 .... 180 C5
Caroline Cl 12 NG34 .....212 F4
Caroline Ct 10 PE21..... 209 A5
Caroline Pl HU2 ....180 F7
Caroline Rd 5 LN4 ....95 D4
Caroline St
10 Alford LN13 ....75 F2
Kingston upon Hull HU2 ...180 F8
Carradale PE2.......... 229 D5
Carral Cl LN5........... 205 C3
Carram Way LN1........ 201 C7
Carr Dike La HU15 ....1 C7
Carr Dyke Bank DN17 .....28 D5
Carr Dyke Rd DN17 ....17 D3
Carre's Gram Sch
NG34 .... 212 D5
Carre's Sq LN4 ....109 E6
Carre St NG34 .... 212 D4
Carr Gate LN4 ....109 F6
Carrhouse Rd DN9.........16 D1
Carrier Cl PE3 .... 230 D8
CARRINGTON PE22...... 112 D6
Carrington Cl
Coningsby LN4.......... 207 D5
2 Spalding PE11 ....214 B3
Carrington Dr
Deeping St Nicholas
PE11...................165 F5
8 Humberston DN36 ......36 D8
Lincoln LN6 ....204 F7
Carrington Rd
Carrington PE22 .... 112 D3
Moulton PE12 .... 146 C3
Spalding PE11 ....214 B4
Carrington's Dro PE6 ... 175 C7
Carrington St 6 HU3 ....180 B5
Carr La
6 Alford LN13 ....75 F2
Appleby DN15 ....9 D2
Bishop Norton LN8 ....43 F3
Blyton DN21..............41 B5
Bonby DN20..............10 B1
Broomfleet HU15...........1 B7
Broughton DN20 .... 196 A6
Burton upon Stather DN15 ...8 D4
Doddington & Whisby LN6...79 D6
Gainsborough DN21 ..... 197 C1
Garthorpe & Fockerby
DN17.....................7 E4
Grimsby DN32...........192 B7
Haxey DN9...............27 E2
Healing DN41 ....23 F4
Hibaldstow DN20..........31 A6
Horkstow DN18.............9 F4
Kingston upon Hull HU1 ...180 E6
Luddington & Haldenby
DN17.....................7 C1
Misterton DN10...........39 F5
Redbourne DN21..........30 F3
Skinnard LN5........... 106 D7
Stallingborough DN41......23 F7
Ulceby DN39 ....12 B3
West Butterwick DN17 .....28 C8
Wildsworth DN21 ....40 F8
Winterton DN15............9 D6
Worlaby DN20.............20 B7
Carroll Pl 4 HU1 .... 181 A7
Carron Cl 3 LN3 ....83 B4
Carron Dr PE4...........220 E3
Carr Rd
Gringley on the Hill
DN10....................39 A4
North Kelsey LN7..........31 E4
Peterborough PE1....... 226 D3
Carrside DN9.............27 D6
Carr Side La DN7 ....14 E2
Carr St LN1............. 201 D4
Carrwood Cres LN4 ..... 207 C7
Carson Ave DN34 ....191 B6
Carson Cl 6 PE24 ....90 B7
Carson Rd DN21 .... 197 C6
Cartergate DN32........ 191 C7
Carterplot Rd NG34..... 123 A2
Carters Cl 6 PE3........224 F3
Carter's Garth Cl 4
LN11....................50 B8
Cartledge Ave DN32......192 B6
Cartmel Gr DN32 ....192 B6
Cartmel Way 14 PE6 .... 175 A1
Carver Rd
Boston PE21 .... 208 D3
Immingham DN40 .... 186 D3
Caryer Cl PE2 .... 230 D6
Cary La 3 DN20 ....196 B3
Carysfort Cl PE7........ 233 D4
Casewick La 4 PE9......172 F7
Casewick Rd PE9 ....172 E7
Caskgate St DN21....... 197 C4
Caspian Cres DN33 ..... 191 A2
Cassbrook Dr 2 LN11.....49 B8
Cassia Gn 7 LN6 .... 204 C8
Cassons Cl PE12........ 157 D4
Casson's Rd 1 DN8........15 A8
Casswell Cl 1 DN32 .... 189 D1
Casswell Cres 4 LN11 ....49 B8
Casswell Dr PE11 .... 145 A7
Castella Dr DN16 .... 183 D3
Casterton Com Coll
PE9.................... 171 C8
Casterton La PE9 .... 218 C4
Casterton Rd PE9........218 E6
Casthorpe Rd
3 Barrowby NG32 ...... 210 A5
Denton NG32........... 139 A8

ASTLE BYTHAM
NG33........................152 D1
astle Bytham Rd
Clipsham LE15...............162 C7
Swayfield NG33..............152 E5
ASTLE CARLTON LN11....62 C2
astle Causeway NG34...212 C4
astle Cl
3 Bottesford NG13.........128 B5
Spalding PE11..............214 F6
astle Ct 10 DN18..........10 F8
astle Dr
Epworth DN9.................27 E7
Holbeach PE12..............215 E1
Northborough PE6..........217 E2
astle Dyke 18 PE9........219 B5
astledyke Bank PE22...125 A8
astledyke Prim Sch
DN18...........................3 E1
astledyke S 3 DN18.....10 F8
astledyke W 7 DN18......3 E1
astle End Rd PE21........217 A1
astlefields 2 PE11.......214 D5
astleford Ave DN34......191 A4
astlegate
Castle Bytham NG33......152 D1
Grantham NG31.............211 B4
Thornton le Fen PE22....111 F1
astle Hill
16 Caistor LN7..............33 B4
4 Lincoln LN1...............234 B3
1 Welburn LN5.............106 E5
astle Hills Com Art Coll
DN21..........................197 D7
astle Keep DN20...........30 F6
astle La
Boothby Graffoe LN5........93 E1
Coningsby LN4..............207 C5
Lincoln LN1..................234 A4
astle Rise PE9..............163 D1
astle Sports Complex
PE11..........................214 E5
astle St
Boston PE21.................208 D6
Grimsby DN32...............192 A8
Kingston upon Hull HU1..180 E5
Lincoln LN1..................234 A4
Sleaford NG34..............212 D4
12 Stamford PE9...........219 B5
astle Terr 5 NG34........212 C4
astle Terr Rd 4
NG34..........................212 C4
ASTLETHORPE DN20.....20 A1
astleton Cres PE25.......206 D4
astleton Rd DN15.........182 B2
astleview
Coningsby LN4..............110 E8
Tattershall LN4...............97 E1
astle View Rd LN11.......109 D7
astle View Rd NG13.....128 B4
astle Way LN11............198 A8
ASTOR PE5....................223 D1
astor CE Sch PE5..........223 E2
astor Mythams National
Nature Reserve*
PE6...........................223 D7
astor Rd
Marholm PE6................220 B1
Peterborough PE6.........224 C6
asworth Way PE5.........223 D2
ater La LN7....................44 F7
ater Way PE21.............208 D2
ates's Cove Cnr PE6...167 F4
athedral Ct
13 Hatfield DN7.............14 C2
Scunthorpe DN17..........185 A6
athedral Dr PE11.........214 C5
athedral Sq 16 PE21...226 A2
athedral St LN2............234 B2
atherine Ct PE2............230 B7
atherine Gr 8 DN20......19 E3
atherine St
6 Grimsby DN32...........191 F7
1 Kingston upon Hull
HU2...........................180 F7
atherines Way 18
PE11..........................145 C1
athwaite PE4................221 E1
atkin Rd 6 DN16..........185 B2
atley PE4.....................221 E1
atling's La PE13...........170 C7
atskin La LN8.................46 A3
attistock Rd DN35........192 E3
atle Dike PE13............169 D7
atle Mkt Rd 17 PE21...226 A2
atle Mkt Way 7 PE21...226 A1
atle Rd DN10................89 B5
aughey St HU3.............180 D7
auseway
Burgh le Marsh PE24.....102 E7
Wyberton PE21.............136 E2
auseway Bank La LN13...63 F1
auseway La 3 DN21.......52 F6
auseway La LN4...........109 E5
auseway The
6 Northorpe PE10.........164 C8
Revesby PE22...............111 F7
Thorney PE6.................175 E2
avalry Ct 2 LN4.............95 D4
avell Ct PE3................225 B4
avendish Ct DN35.........193 B1
avendish Dr
6 Boston PE21..............136 D8
Gainsborough DN21........52 F5
avendish Mews 6
LN4...........................203 D1

Cavendish Pk 10 HU15.....2 C5
Cavendish Rd
Scunthorpe DN16..........185 A4
Skegness PE25.............206 C4
Cavendish St PE11.......226 B3
Cavendish Way
1 Grimsby DN32...........191 F7
Harrowby Est NG31.......211 F7
Spalding PE11..............214 C6
Cave Rd HU15.................2 B6
Caverstede Rd PE4......221 B1
Cave's Cl 8 PE34..........161 F8
Cave's La DN10..............39 E3
Cavill Pl HU3................180 D5
CAWKWELL LN11...........73 A5
Cawkwell Cl 28 LN12....77 A7
Cawkwell Hill LN11........73 A6
Cawood La PE11..........145 B5
Cawthorne St 11 NG23...91 D5
Cawthorne Dr HU4........179 C3
CAWTHORPE PE10........154 B5
Cawthra Ct NG32..........139 A7
Caxton Theatre & Arts Ctr
The* DN32...................189 B1
Cayley Rd LN8...............178 F6
CAYTHORPE NG32........119 C7
Caythorpe Heath La
NG32..........................119 D7
Caythorpe Prim Sch
NG32..........................119 B7
Caythorpe Rd PE11......134 F2
Cecil Ave PE25.............206 C4
Cecil Cl
Bourne PE10................213 B4
16 Scotter DN21............29 C3
Cecil Ct 11 PE9............219 C5
Cecile Cres LN15..........182 E3
Cecil Pacey Ct PE3......225 E7
Cecil Pywell Ave PE12..215 C7
Cecil Rd PE11...............226 A6
Cecil St
Gainsborough DN21.......197 C5
Grantham NG31............211 C3
Kingston upon Hull
HU1...........................179 F5
Lincoln LN1..................234 A4
Cedar Ave
4 Cleethorpes DN35.....192 D2
Gainsborough DN21........197 B7
Kingston upon Hull
HU10...........................178 D7
1 Louth LN11................198 B6
14 Market Deeping PE6..217 A5
6 Market Rasen LN8.......57 D7
9 Ruskington NG34......108 D1
9 Scawby DN20..............30 F8
9 Scotter DN21..............29 C3
13 Sudbrooke LN2..........68 F2
Cedar Ct
2 Spalding PE11...........214 E3
The Willows DN37.........190 E8
Cedar Dr
Bourne PE10................213 B6
Holbeach PE12............215 C4
Immingham DN40.........186 C5
Cedar Gr PE1...............226 B8
Cedar Rd PE11............218 D6
Cedarwood Cl 1 NG31..210 F7
Cedarwood Dr HU5......179 B7
Cedric Rd 10 DN3...........14 A1
Cekhira Ave 4 PE12.....157 E1
Celta Rd PE2................231 F6
Celtic Cl PE2................231 D7
Cemetery Cres DN37.....23 F1
Cemetery La LN7...........32 A5
Cemetery Rd
Hatfield DN7..................14 F4
16 Laceby DN37.............23 F1
North Somercotes LN11...50 E8
Scunthorpe DN16.........185 B8
Winterton DN15..............9 B5
14 Wragby LN8..............70 D4
Centaur Rd LN6...........201 D2
Centenary Cl 3 PE22...126 E3
Centenary Way PE12...160 F2
Central Ave
Ingoldmells PE25...........90 F3
Peterborough PE1.........226 C2
Central Dr 7 NG34.......120 C8
Central Parade DN34....191 F1
Central PI HU13.............211 D5
Central Prom DN35.......192 F6
Central Sq
Brigg DN20..................196 C4
Peterborough PE2.........231 D5
Central Tech Coll
NG31..........................211 A7
Central Way DN16........183 D2
Centurion Cl 8 LN5.......107 B8
Centurion Way 12 HU15...2 C5
Century La 1 LN1...........66 D3
Cerris Rd PE1...............226 B3
Ceylon St 9 HU9............5 D8
Chadburn PE4...............221 E1
Chadwell Springs
DN37..........................194 B4
Chaffinch Cl DN15........182 D5
Chaffinch Dr DN35.......192 E1
CHAIN BRIDGE PE21....208 B3
Chain Bridge Rd PE21...208 B3
Chain Cl PE1................226 B6
Chaintoft La PE11.........145 A7

Chaldean Way PE11.......214 B6
Chalfont Ave LN12..........64 A5
Chalfont Cl HU13...........178 D2
Chalfonts The LN4...........81 E2
Chalgrove Way LN6.......200 E2
Chalk La
Burgh le Marsh PE24......89 F1
Sutton Bridge PE12.......160 F3
Withern with Stain LN13...63 A1
Chalk Pit La PE23............88 F2
Chalk Rd PE13..............169 D1
Chamber's Ct PE11......214 E5
Chamber's Farm Wood
Nature Reserve* LN8....83 F8
Chambers St NG31.......211 A5
Chamomile Cl DN16......185 D5
Champion Way LN12......64 B2
Chancel Rd DN16..........185 A4
Chancel Wlk LN12..........19 E3
Chancery Cl LN6...........205 B5
Chancery Ct 4 PE11.....214 D3
Chancery La
3 Crowle DN17..............16 D7
4 Eye PE6....................175 A1
1 Holbeach PE12..........215 D2
Chanctonbury Cl 20
LN12............................77 A8
Chanctonbury Way 19
LN12............................77 A8
Chandlers PE2..............229 E5
Chandlers Cl 1 DN36....195 C6
Chandlers Ct HU9..........181 C6
Chandos Rd DN17........184 F7
Chanterlands Ave HU5..180 A8
Chandlers Dr 18 HU15...2 C6
Chantry Cl
Grimsby DN31...............191 C7
Peterborough PE1.........226 A5
Chantry La DN31...........191 C7
Chantry The 1 PE11.....214 A4
Chantry Way 14 HU14.....3 B7
Chantry Way E 14 HU14...3 B7
Chapel Baulk DN9..........26 E1
Chapel Cl
Barrow upon Humber
DN19...........................11 D7
Chapel St Leonard PE24..90 D8
Cherry Willingham/Reepham
LN3............................203 F8
9 Misterton DN10...........39 F5
Northfield HU13............179 A1
11 South Rauceby NG34..120 E4
9 Westwoodside DN9.....27 B2
Chapel Ct
4 Alkborough DN15..........8 C8
Brigg DN20..................196 C3
17 Hibaldstow DN20........30 F5
Scunthorpe DN15.........183 B4
Wansford PE8..............222 B2
Chapel Dro PE12..........168 B2
Chapel Farm Dr PE2....
PE24..........................214 A4
Chapelfield Rd DN19.......5 C1
Chapel Garth
Broomfleet HU15............1 B5
16 Messingham DN17......36 D4
Chapelgate PE12..........159 D7
CHAPELGATE PE12.......159 D7
Chapelgate
Kirton End PE20............136 B7
14 Sutton PE20.............136 A2
Chapel Gate
Sutton St James PE12...159 B1
Whaplode PE12.............168 B5
Chapel Gdns
3 Moulton PE12.............157 E1
12 Whaplode PE12.........158 B7
Chapel Hill HU15.............2 D6
CHAPEL HILL LN4.........110 E5
Chapel Hill
Ropsley NG33..............131 B1
Whaplode PE12.............168 A4
Woolsthorpe by Belvoir
NG32..........................138 D8
Chapel Hill Ct 7 NG34..212 E8
Chapel Hill La HU15........2 C6
Chapel La
Addlethorpe PE24..........90 C3
Amber Hill PE20............124 B5
Anwick NG34................109 B1
Ashby cum Fenby DN37...35 D3
4 Aubourn Haddington &
South Hykeham LN5......93 A5
3 Barnetby le Beck DN37..35 B6
4 Barrowby NG32.........210 A5
Barton-upon-Humber
DN18...........................10 B2
Belchford LN9................73 B2
Branston & Mere LN4.....81 E2
1 Claypole NG23..........117 E8
1 Croxton Kerrial
NG32..........................138 D4
5 Donington on Bain
LN11............................59 E1
Dunston LN4..................95 C5
East Kirkby PE23...........99 F5
11 Elsham DN20............20 F7
2 Folkingham NG34......142 D8
4 Foston NG23.............117 F1
Friskney Eaudike PE22...115 A6
1 Fulletby LN9...............86 B8
Gainsborough DN21......197 B8
Glentworth LN2...............54 F7
3 Grainthorpe LN11........51 A5
Habrough DN40..............22 E8
4 Harmston LN5.............93 F5
Heckington NG34.........122 F1

Chapel La continued
Heighington/Washingborough
LN4............................81 E4
2 Helpringham NG34.....133 D7
Hemingby LN9................72 B1
Horkstow DN18...............10 A5
Keadby with Althorpe
DN17...........................17 C6
Kingston upon Hull HU1..181 A6
2 Leasingham NG34.....121 B7
6 Legbourne LN11..........61 F3
Lincoln LN1..................234 A4
Little Hale NG34...........133 E8
Ludborough DN36..........48 E6
Ludford LN8...................59 A8
Manby LN11...................62 C6
6 Mareham le Fen PE22...99 A4
Messingham DN17..........29 D7
Minting LN9....................84 C8
15 Misterton DN10..........39 F5
Navenby/Wellingore
LN5............................107 A8
13 Nettleham LN2..........68 C2
7 Newark-on-Trent
NG24..........................104 D5
Newton PE13................170 B5
Normanby by Spital LN8...55 F7
North Cockerington LN11..49 F1
North Kelsey LN7...........33 A4
North Scarle LN6.............78 E2
6 Peterborough PE4......221 A3
Scambleby LN13............73 A5
10 Scawby DN20.............30 E8
12 Sibsey PE22.............113 B1
17 Spalding PE11.........214 D4
Spalford NG23................78 D4
Springthorpe DN21.........53 E8
Swallow LN7...................34 B5
Tattershall Thorpe LN4...207 C8
Thimbleby LN9................85 B4
14 Thorne/Moorends
DN8.............................15 A8
Toynton St Peter PE23...101 A6
4 Tydd St Giles PE13.....169 F7
Utterby LN11...................48 F4
Welton/Dunholme LN2.....68 C6
West/East Butterwick
DN17...........................17 D1
Whitton DN15..................1 E3
12 Winterton DN15..........9 A5
2 Winthorpe PE25.........104 B7
Wrawby DN20.................20 E4
4 Wymondham LE14.....150 C1
Chapel Lodge Dr LN8....55 F7
Chapel Mews 3 HU15.....2 C6
Chapel Nook La LN5......93 B1
Chapel Pas 18 PE21.....208 F4
Chapel Pit Nature
Reserve* PE24..............90 D8
Chapel Rd
Branston LN4.................81 E2
4 Broughton DN20..........19 E3
Carrington PE22...........112 B8
Fillingham DN21.............54 F4
Fiskerton LN3.................82 A6
4 Habrough DN40...........22 E8
Ingoldmells PE25............90 D4
Leake Commonside PE22..113 F3
Sutton St Edmund PE12..168 E4
Terrington St Clement
PE34..........................161 F3
Chapel Row
Baumber LN9..................72 A1
7 Skillington NG33........151 A8
Chapel St
Alford LN13.....................75 F3
3 Amcotts DN17...............7 F1
Beckingham LN5...........105 B4
6 Billingborough NG34..133 B1
4 Boston PE21..............208 F5
10 Bottesford NG13......128 A6
Caistor LN7....................33 B4
4 Crowland PE6............175 B8
6 Epworth DN9...............27 C6
Goxhill DN19..................12 A8
Haconby PE10..............154 D8
2 Holbeach PE12..........215 E2
1 Market Rasen LN8.......57 D7
7 North Kelsey LN7........32 A4
16 Ruskington NG34.....108 E2
Scunthorpe DN15..........183 A3
Yaxley PE7...................233 D5
Chapel Way 2 DN10......39 F5
Chapel Yd 2 PE9...........219 C5
Chaplin Cl 22 LN4..........95 D4
Chaplin St LN5..............234 A1
Chapman Dr
Cleethorpes DN35.........192 D7
2 Sleaford NG34..........212 B6

Chapman St
Kingston upon Hull
HU8...........................181 A8
3 Market Rasen LN8......57 E7
Chapnall Cl 1 PE13.......170 E1
Chapnall Rd PE13.........170 E1
Chappell Rd 3 PE13.....166 C6
Chapter Cl LN2..............68 C7
Chapter Wk 12 DN20...119 E3
Charing Cl HU3.............180 C3
Chariots Way 6 PE6......164 E5
Charity St NG32............119 D4
Charles Ave
11 Ancaster NG32.........120 A2
2 Grimsby DN33...........191 D2
3 Laceby DN37..............23 E1
Louth LN11..................198 D7
12 New Waltham DN36...195 C6
8 Scotter DN21..............29 C3
Charles Baines Com Prim
Sch DN21....................197 F4
Charles Cl
Bourne PE10................213 D6
1 Skegness PE25.........206 B4
Charles Cope Rd PE2...229 F5
Charles Gate LN11..........63 A8
Charles Hume Ct 3
DN32..........................192 B8
Charles Lovell Way
DN17..........................184 D8
Charles Rd
8 Fleet Hargate PE12....159 C7
9 Stamford PE9............219 A7
12 Sutton Bridge PE12...160 E4
Charles Read High Sch The
NG33..........................152 F7
Charles St W LN1..........201 D4
Charles St
Boston PE21.................209 A3
2 Cleethorpes DN35......192 F5
3 Kingston upon Hull
HU2...........................180 F5
4 Louth LN11................234 B1
Louth LN11..................198 C6
Newark-on-Trent NG24..104 A4
Peterborough PE1.........226 B3
1 Sleaford NG34...........212 C4
Wrange PE22................114 C2
Charlestown Way HU9...181 B6
Charlesworth St 2
LN1...........................201 D3
Charles Wright Cl 16
LN12............................64 B4
Charlette Way 13 PE11...214 B5
Charlock Dr LN11..........218 D6
Charlotte Cl 4 LN8..........57 E7
Charlotte Ct 14 LN8......181 A7
Charlotte Wlk 5 LN11...145 A8
Charlton Ct PE21..........225 B1
Charlton St DN31..........188 D1
Charnwood Cl PE22......231 A7
Charter Cl PE11............208 E2
Charterhouse Dr DN21..185 C4
Charterhouse La 1
LN2............................181 A7
Charters La PE12..........216 A6
Charter's La PE12.........216 A5
Charters The 2 PE9......172 C6
Chase Hill Rd DN40.......22 E5
Chase St PE13..............170 E3
Chase The
Boston PE21.................209 C3
Crowland PE6...............166 F1
Holbeach PE12............215 E2
Long Sutton PE12.........216 C4
8 Metheringham LN4.....95 C4
Pinchbeck PE11...........156 E8
Weston PE12................145 F1
Whaplode PE12............147 A6
Wisbech PE13..............170 C1
Chasm & Northorpe Slipe
Nature Reserve The*
PE10..........................165 B8
Chater La PE9...............171 A3
Chater Rd 5 PE8..........172 C6
Chatham St HU3...........179 F7
Chatsfield PE2..............230 E6
Chatsworth Ave NG31...211 F5
Chatsworth Cl
4 Lincoln LN6...............202 C8
3 Market Deeping PE6...217 A5
Chatsworth Dr
4 Lincoln LN6...............204 C3
Louth LN11..................198 B7
Chatsworth Pl
Cleethorpes DN35.........192 C4
Peterborough PE2.........225 B2
Chatsworth Rd PE9......218 E6
Chatsworth St HU5......180 B8
Chatsworth Way 12
DN9............................27 D2
Chatterton Ave LN1.......201 E8
Chatterton Cres DN15..183 A5
Chaucer Ave
12 Mablethorpe/Sutton on
Sea LN12.....................64 B4
Scunthorpe DN17.........184 D7
Chaucer Cl 1 PE13.......170 B1
Chaucer Dr LN2............202 C6
Chaucer Gdns 10 NG24..104 A3
Chaucer Rd PE1............225 E8
Chaucer's Way PE11....214 A4
Chauntry Rd 10 LN13....75 F2
Cheal La PE11...............144 F2

Cheal Rd PE11 . . . . .144 F4
Cheapside
 Kingston upon Hull
  HU8 . . . . .181 A8
 Waltham DN37 . . . . .194 F2
Cheapside Rd DN36 . . . . . .36 A4
Chedburgh Cl **1** LN6 . . . .204 B6
Chedworth Cl **1** LN2 . . . .202 D7
Chedworth Rd LN2 . . . . . .202 D7
Cheese Hill **10** PE20 . . . .135 B7
Cheesemans Cl **4**
 DN37 . . . . .194 E4
Cheesemans La LN4 . . . . .194 E4
Cheethams La LN4 . . . . . .110 F2
Chelmer Cl LN6 . . . . .204 F4
Chelmer Garth **2** PE4 . . .221 D1
Chelmsford Ave DN34 . . . .191 A5
Chelmsford Dr LN3 . . . . . .210 F4
Chelmsford Pl DN34 . . . . .191 A6
Chelmsford St LN5 . . . . . .234 B1
Chelsea Cl LN6 . . . . .200 D2
Chelsea Wlk DN35 . . . . . .193 A1
Cheltenham Cl
 Peterborough PE1 . . . . . .226 B6
 Scunthorpe DN16 . . . . . .185 C4
Cheltenham Way
 Humberston DN35 . . . . . .192 F1
 7 Mablethorpe/Sutton on Sea
  LN12 . . . . .64 A3
Chelveston Way PE3 . . . . .225 C4
Chelwood Dr **2** DN33 . . .191 B3
Chelwood Rd DN17 . . . . . .184 F7
Chepstow Cl **6** PE11 . . . .156 E3
Chepstow Gr DN34 . . . . . .191 A5
Chequered Flag Karting*
 DN36 . . . . .195 C1
Chequergate **1** LN11 . . .198 B5
Chequers La DN22 . . . . . . .65 A2
Chequers The DN15 . . . . .182 D3
Cheriton Cl **11** LN3 . . . . .203 E5
Cheriton Pk PE10 . . . . . . .213 D7
Cherries The PE12 . . . . . .216 D4
Cherry Ave LN4 . . . . .81 D2
Cherry Cl
 Humberston DN36 . . . . . . .36 D8
 8 Sleaford NG34 . . . . . .212 D6
Cherry Cnr PE22 . . . . .113 A5
Cherry Cobb Sands Rd
 HU12 . . . . .13 F8
Cherry Dale DN35 . . . . . . .192 D3
Cherryfields PE2 . . . . .229 E6
Cherry Garth HU3 . . . . . . .180 A5
Cherry Gr
 10 Belton DN9 . . . . .16 E1
 Lincoln LN6 . . . . .205 A8
 16 Market Deeping PE6 . .217 C5
 Scunthorpe DN16 . . . . . . .185 B6
Cherry Holt **1** LN3 . . . . .203 E5
Cherryholt La PE9 . . . . . . .219 D5
Cherry Holt La
 13 Pinchbeck PE11 . . . .156 E8
 Sutterton PE20 . . . . .136 A4
Cherryholt Rd PE9 . . . . . . .219 D5
Cherry Holt Rd PE10 . . . . .213 F4
Cherry La
 Barrow upon Humber
  DN19 . . . . .11 D8
 7 Fleet PE12 . . . . .159 C7
 Stubton NG23 . . . . .118 B7
 Wootton DN39 . . . . .11 E2
Cherry Mount DN16 . . . . . .185 C4
Cherry Orch
 21 Epworth DN9 . . . . . .27 E6
 Grantham NG31 . . . . .211 D5
Cherry Orton Rd PE2 . . . . .229 F5
Cherry Rd **8** DN13 . . . . .170 D2
Cherrytree Ave PE25 . . . . .90 E4
Cherry Tree Ave **4**
 DN20 . . . . .196 B4
Cherry Tree Cl **4** LN6 . . .204 F2
Cherry Tree Cres DN34 . . .190 F6
Cherry Tree Dr **5** DN7 . . .14 D5
Cherrytree Gr PE1 . . . . . . .226 C6
Cherry Tree Gr
 2 Hatfield DN7 . . . . .14 D5
 Spalding PE11 . . . . .214 F5
Cherry Tree La
 Holbeach PE12 . . . . .215 D4
 23 Nettleham LN2 . . . . .68 C2
Cherry Tree Rd DN21 . . . . .197 E5
Cherry Tree Rise DN21 . . .29 C4
 Pinchbeck's Bsns Pk
  DN31 . . . . .188 C2
Cherry Tree Way
 5 Coningsby LN4 . . . . . .207 D4
 17 Metheringham LN4 . . .95 C4
Cherry Way **34** DN17 . . . .29 D7
CHERRY WILLINGHAM
 LN3 . . . . .203 E5
Cherry Willingham Com
 Sch LN3 . . . . .203 D7
Cherry Willingham Prim
 Sch LN3 . . . . .203 D5
Cherry Wlk PE1 . . . . .208 D4
Cherrywood Dr NG31 . . . . .210 F8
Chesboule La PE11 . . . . . .144 E5
Chesham Dr **7** PE6 . . . . .164 E4
Cheshire Gr **7** PE25 . . . .206 A5
Cheshire La LN6 . . . . .92 E5
Cheshire Rd LN6 . . . . .200 D2
Cheshire Wlk DN37 . . . . . .190 E8
Chesney Ct DN16 . . . . .185 A3
Chesney Rd LN2 . . . . .202 D7
Chesnut Cl **11** LN2 . . . . . .68 F2
Chesnut Dr **12** LN2 . . . . . .68 F2

Chesnut Way **4** DN19 . . . .12 A8
Chesswick Ave DN17 . . . . .17 D5
Chester Cl LN4 . . . . .203 D1
Chesterfield Rd DN15 . . . .182 B2
Chester Gdns **8** NG31 . . .210 D5
Chester Grange DN33 . . . .191 E1
Chester Pl DN32 . . . . .192 C5
Chester Rd PE1 . . . . .226 C3
CHESTERTON PE7 . . . . . .228 F3
Chesterton Gr PE22 . . . . .231 D6
Chester Way PE21 . . . . . .208 C3
Chestnut Ave
 7 Donington PE11 . . . . .134 E2
 Edenham PE10 . . . . .153 C2
 Gainsborough DN21 . . . . .197 D6
 Grimsby DN31 . . . . .191 B7
 Holbeach PE12 . . . . .215 C3
 Immingham DN40 . . . . . . .186 E5
 Kingston upon Hull
  HU3 . . . . .178 E1
 Peterborough PE1 . . . . . .226 B7
 RAF Cranwell NG34 . . . . .107 D1
 Spalding PE11 . . . . .214 E5
 3 Stainforth DN7 . . . . . .14 D6
 6 Thorne/Moorends
  DN8 . . . . .15 B7
Chestnut Cl
 Bottesford NG13 . . . . .128 B6
 Digby LN4 . . . . .108 E6
 Glinton PE6 . . . . .220 B8
 Horncastle LN9 . . . . .199 A5
 4 Metheringham LN4 . . . .95 C4
 1 Peakirk PE6 . . . . .174 A5
 13 Scotter DN21 . . . . . .29 C3
 2 Sleaford NG34 . . . . . .212 D3
 Swaton NG34 . . . . .133 D4
 18 Waltham DN37 . . . . .194 C4
Chestnut Cres **3** LN5 . . . .92 F3
Chestnut Dr
 5 Coningsby LN4 . . . . . .207 D4
 Louth LN11 . . . . .198 E6
 38 Messingham DN17 . . .29 D7
 8 Thorney PE6 . . . . .176 A3
Chestnut Gdns PE6 . . . . . .218 D5
Chestnut Gr
 11 Barnetby le Wold
  DN38 . . . . .21 B4
 4 Broughton DN20 . . . . .19 E4
 4 Colsterworth NG33 . . .151 E7
 1 Grantham NG31 . . . . .210 D2
 Waddington LN5 . . . . .205 C1
Chestnut La NG33 . . . . . . .152 C8
Chestnut Rd
 3 Boston PE21 . . . . . . .209 C2
 Lincoln LN6 . . . . .204 F2
 Waltham DN37 . . . . .194 C4
Chestnut Rise **10** DN11 . .11 C8
Chestnut St CE Prim Sch
 NG34 . . . . .108 F1
Chestnut St
 Lincoln LN11 . . . . .234 A4
 5 Ruskington NG34 . . . .108 E6
Chestnuts The **7** LN2 . . . .68 C2
Chestnut Terr **2** PE12 . . .160 E4
Chestnut Way
 6 Binbrook LN8 . . . . . . .47 C5
 4 Bourne PE10 . . . . . . .213 B5
 3 Market Deeping PE6 . .217 B4
 Scunthorpe DN16 . . . . . . .185 B8
Chestnut Wlk **5** DN41 . . .24 A5
Cheviot Ave PE4 . . . . .221 C2
Cheviot Cl
 Gonerby Hill Foot
  NG31 . . . . .210 E7
 Sleaford NG34 . . . . .212 A3
 6 Thorne/Moorends
  DN8 . . . . .15 A7
Cheviot St LN2 . . . . .234 C2
Chichester Cl **6** NG31 . . .210 E5
Chichester Dr **20** LN7 . . .33 B4
Chichester Rd
 6 Binbrook Tech Pk
  LN8 . . . . .47 B6
 4 Bracebridge Heath
  LN4 . . . . .81 A4
 Cleethorpes DN35 . . . . . .192 F4
Chieftain Rd **1** LN6 . . . . .205 C8
Chieftain Way **1** LN6 . . . .205 C8
Childergate La PE12 . . . . .159 D2
Childers' N Dro
 Cowbit PE12 . . . . .157 B5
 Spalding PE11 . . . . .214 F3
Childers' S Dro
 Cowbit PE12 . . . . .157 B4
 Spalding PE11 . . . . .214 F2
Chiltern Cl NG31 . . . . .210 E7
Chiltern Cres DN17 . . . . . .184 D8
Chiltern Dr
 Spalding PE11 . . . . .214 E6
 Waltham DN37 . . . . .194 C2
Chiltern Prim Sch HU3 . . .180 B5
Chiltern Rd **8** DN15 . . . . .205 D3
Chiltern Rise PE4 . . . . . . .221 B2
Chiltern Way
 3 Grimsby DN33 . . . . . .194 E8
 62 North Hykeham LN6 . .93 C8
Chilton Cl **7** DN40 . . . . . .186 B4
China St PE22 . . . . .114 C4
Chingford Ave DN34 . . . . .191 A4
Chippendale Cl
 2 Birchwood LN6 . . . . .204 D6
 2 Humberston DN36 . . .36 D8
Chippendale Rd **3**
 LN6 . . . . .204 D6
Chippenham Mews **1**
 PE2 . . . . .230 C2
Chisenhale PE2 . . . . .229 E6
Chivenor Cl **3** LN6 . . . . .200 B1

Cholmley St HU3 . . . . .180 B5
Chopdike Dro PE11 . . . . . .144 D3
Christ Church CE PE9 . . . .219 B7
Christchurch Rd **10**
 NG31 . . . . .211 D7
Christine Pl DN33 . . . . . . .195 A8
Christopher Cl
 6 Heckington NG34 . . . .122 E3
 Louth LN11 . . . . .198 D7
 3 Manby LN11 . . . . .62 C6
 Peterborough PE1 . . . . . .225 F8
Christopher Cres **11**
 NG34 . . . . .212 F4
Christopher Dr **8**
 PE13 . . . . .170 C1
Christopher Rd **6** LN13 . .75 E2
Christopher's La **4**
 PE10 . . . . .213 D6
Church Ave
 Ashby de la Launde &
  Bloxholm LN4 . . . . .108 B5
 Humberston DN36 . . . . . . .36 C8
 7 North Ferriby HU14 . . .3 A4
Church Balk DN8 . . . . .15 B8
Church Bank **2** PE34 . . . .161 F3
Church Cl
 2 Bonby DN20 . . . . .10 C2
 24 Boston PE21 . . . . . .208 F5
 Donington on Bain LN11 . .59 E2
 Grimsby DN32 . . . . .192 B5
 12 Louth LN11 . . . . . . .198 B5
 16 Mablethorpe/Sutton on Sea
  LN12 . . . . .77 A8
 4 Newborough PE6 . . . .174 E4
 14 Sibsey PE22 . . . . . .113 B1
 11 Sleaford NG34 . . . . .212 B2
 Stoke Rochford NG33 . . . .139 F2
 3 Thorne/Moorends
  DN8 . . . . .15 B8
 Wrangle PE22 . . . . .114 C1
Church Cres **4** DN9 . . . . .28 A3
Church Ct
 Scunthorpe DN15 . . . . . . .183 B4
 3 Stamford PE9 . . . . . .219 C4
Church Dr
 Lincoln LN6 . . . . .201 D1
 8 Misterton DN10 . . . . .39 F5
 Norton Disney LN6 . . . . . .92 C1
 Peterborough PE2 . . . . . .229 F4
 Surfleet PE11 . . . . .145 D3
Church End
 Gedney PE12 . . . . .159 D7
 3 Leverington PE13 . . . .170 B2
CHURCH END LN11 . . . . .50 F6
Church End
 Skegness PE25 . . . . .206 B8
 Wrangle PE22 . . . . .114 C1
Church End Dro PE11 . . . .134 F1
Church Farm Cl **23**
 PE24 . . . . .90 D7
Churchfield Ct PE4 . . . . . .225 E8
Churchfield Rd
 Peterborough PE4 . . . . . .221 B1
 Scunthorpe DN16 . . . . . . .185 B5
Church Fields
 Pickworth NG34 . . . . .142 A8
 Winterton DN15 . . . . .9 A5
Churchfields Rd NG34 . . . .142 C8
Churchfleet La PE11 . . . . .145 B7
Churchgate
 Gedney PE12 . . . . .159 D7
 14 Sutterton PE20 . . . .136 A2
Church Gate
 Fleet PE12 . . . . .159 B6
 2 Market Deeping PE6 . .217 F4
 Spalding PE11 . . . . .214 D3
 22 Sutton Bridge PE12 .160 E4
 Whaplode PE12 . . . . .158 B6
Churchgate Mews **6**
 PE12 . . . . .159 D7
Church Gdns **15** PE12 . . .160 A8
Church Gn PE12 . . . . .216 C4
Church Gn Cl PE21 . . . . . .209 F2
Church Gn La
 Frampton PE20 . . . . .136 B7
 Quadring PE11 . . . . .135 A1
Church Gn Rd PE21 . . . . . .209 F4
Church Hill
 Belvoir NG32 . . . . .138 C6
 1 Burgh le Marsh PE24 .102 E7
 Castor PE5 . . . . .223 E2
 2 Grasby DN38 . . . . . . .32 E7
 Heighington/Washingborough
  LN4 . . . . .203 B2
 Ingham LN1 . . . . .55 A2
 Riby DN37 . . . . .23 C2
 Spridlington LN8 . . . . .55 F3
 Whitton DN15 . . . . .1 E3
Church Hill Cl PE7 . . . . . . .231 C1
Churchill Ave
 Bourne PE10 . . . . .213 B4
 Bracebridge Heath LN4 . . .205 F4
 Brigg DN20 . . . . .196 D4
 2 Hatfield DN7 . . . . .14 F4
 Horncastle LN9 . . . . .199 C2
 4 Keelby DN41 . . . . . . .23 A5
 4 Market Rasen LN8 . . .57 D7
 2 Skegness PE25 . . . . .206 D7
Churchill Cl **6** LN11 . . . . .50 F7
Churchill Ct **2** PE12 . . . .216 B5
Churchill Dr
 3 Boston PE21 . . . . . . .209 D4
 2 Martin LN10 . . . . .97 B4
 Spalding PE11 . . . . .214 D2

Churchill La LN12 . . . . .63 E8
Churchill Rd
 Gorefield PE13 . . . . .169 F3
 North Somercotes LN11 . . .50 F7
 Stamford PE9 . . . . .219 B7
Churchill St HU9 . . . . .181 D7
Churchill Way
 Grimsby DN32 . . . . .191 F7
 Heckington NG34 . . . . . . .122 D3
 5 Lea DN21 . . . . .122 F6
Church La
 Addlethorpe PE24 . . . . . . .90 D4
 Algarkirk PE20 . . . . .136 B2
 Alvingham LN11 . . . . .49 F2
 9 Ancaster NG32 . . . . .120 A2
 Appleby DN15 . . . . .9 D1
 Aylesby DN37 . . . . .23 E2
 Balderton NG24 . . . . .104 C2
 7 Bardney LN3 . . . . . . .83 B4
 Baumber LN9 . . . . .72 B1
 Benniworth LN8 . . . . .71 E8
 Besthorpe NG23 . . . . .91 D7
 4 Billinghay LN4 . . . . . .109 F5
 Blyton DN21 . . . . .41 C5
 Bonby DN20 . . . . .10 C2
 19 Boston PE21 . . . . . .208 F5
 Bottesford NG13 . . . . .128 C4
 Bourne PE10 . . . . .213 D4
 Brant Broughton LN5 . . . .105 F5
 Brigsley DN37 . . . . .35 D4
 4 Brough HU15 . . . . . . .2 C7
 15 Broughton DN20 . . . .19 E3
 Buckminster NG33 . . . . . .150 F4
 Burton Coggles NG33 . . . .152 D8
 Cadney DN20 . . . . .31 D6
 Carlton-le-Moorland
  LN5 . . . . .105 E8
 3 Carlton NG32 . . . . . . .119 B7
 24 Chapel St Leonard
  PE24 . . . . .90 D7
 Cherry Willingham/Reepham
  LN3 . . . . .203 E5
 Clipsham LE15 . . . . .162 B7
 Coleby LN5 . . . . .93 F3
 8 Collingham NG23 . . . .91 D5
 Corringham DN21 . . . . . . .41 E2
 Counthorpe & Creeton
  NG33 . . . . .153 A2
 Croft PE24 . . . . .102 E5
 2 Crowland PE6 . . . . . .166 F1
 2 Croxton Kerrial
  NG32 . . . . .138 D4
 1 Donington PE11 . . . . .134 F2
 Eagle & Swinethorpe LN6 . .79 B2
 East Keal PE23 . . . . .100 E6
 Edenham PE10 . . . . .153 F4
 Elkington LN11 . . . . .60 E7
 Ewerby & Evedon NG34 . . .122 C6
 5 Fishlake DN7 . . . . . . .14 D8
 1 Folkingham NG34 . . . .142 D8
 Fotherby LN11 . . . . .49 A2
 Friesthorpe LN3 . . . . .57 A2
 Friskney PE22 . . . . .114 F6
 Frithville PE22 . . . . .125 D8
 5 Glentham LN8 . . . . . .43 F1
 Goulceby LN11 . . . . .72 D6
 Grainthorpe LN11 . . . . . . .50 B7
 Great Gonerby NG31 . . . . .210 C8
 Great Limber DN37 . . . . . .22 D3
 Grimsby DN37 . . . . .190 E2
 1 Hagworthingham PE23 . .87 A4
 Harmston LN5 . . . . .93 F5
 Haxey DN9 . . . . .27 C2
 Heckington NG34 . . . . . . .122 E1
 3 Helpringham LN4 . . . .133 D7
 4 Helpston PE6 . . . . . . .173 C4
 Holton le Clay DN36 . . . . .195 D2
 Horbling NG34 . . . . .133 B2
 6 Horncastle LN9 . . . . .199 B4
 Hougham NG32 . . . . .118 C3
 Humberston DN36 . . . . . . .36 D8
 Huttoft LN13 . . . . .76 E3
 Immingham DN40 . . . . . . .186 B5
 3 Ingham LN1 . . . . .54 F2
 Ingoldmells PE25 . . . . . . .206 C8
 4 Keadby with Althorpe
  DN17 . . . . .17 D4
 Keddington LN11 . . . . . . .198 E8
 4 Keelby DN41 . . . . . . .23 A4
 Kingston upon Hull
  HU10 . . . . .178 C8
 Kirkby la Thorpe NG34 . . .121 F4
 Kirkby on Bain LN10 . . . . .98 C5
 Kirton PE20 . . . . .136 C5
 12 Laceby DN37 . . . . . .23 F1
 2 Legbourne LN11 . . . .61 F3
 Lincoln LN2 . . . . .234 B4
 8 Little Bytham NG33 . .163 A8
 Londonthorpe & Harrowby
  without NG31 . . . . .130 D5
 Long Bennington NG23 . . .117 E2
 Luddington & Haldenby
  DN17 . . . . .7 D4
 Lutton PE12 . . . . .160 A8
 12 Mablethorpe/Sutton on Sea
  LN12 . . . . .77 A8
 3 Mareham le Fen PE22 . .98 F4
 Marshchapel DN36 . . . . . .37 B1
 12 Metheringham LN4 . .95 D4
 Minting LN9 . . . . .84 C8
 5 Misterton DN10 . . . . .39 F5
 Misterton LN13 . . . . .89 B6
 Moulton PE12 . . . . .157 F7
 Navenby LN5 . . . . .107 A8
 Newton PE13 . . . . .170 A5
 North Carlton LN1 . . . . . . .67 C4
 10 North Kelsey LN7 . . .32 A4
 North Kyme LN4 . . . . .109 F3

Church La _continued_
 North Rauceby NG32 120
 North Scarle LN6 78
 North Somercotes LN11 . .50
 Old Somerby NG33 44
 Owersby LN8 44
 5 Owmby LN8 55
 Peterborough PE2 229
 Pickworth NG34 132
 6 Potterhanworth LN4 . .82
 Rand LN8 70
 Ropsley & Humby NG33 . .131
 Roughton LN9 85
 Saltfleetby LN12 63
 Saxby All Saints DN20 . . .10
 Saxilby with Ingleby LN1 . .66
 Scamblesby LN11 72
 Scawby DN20 20
 Scopwick LN4 108
 9 Scotter DN21 29
 Scredington NG34 132
 Scunthorpe DN15 182
 Sedgebrook NG32 128
 Silk Willoughby NG34 121
 Skegness PE25 206
 Skidbrooke with Saltfleet
  Haven LN11 51
 Sleaford NG34 212
 Snitterby DN21 43
 South Clifton NG23 78
 South Kyme LN4 123
 15 South Witham NG33 . .151
 Spilsby PE23 87
 Springthorpe DN21 53
 Sproxton LE14 150
 Stallingborough DN41 23
 9 Stamford PE9 219
 Sudbrooke LN2 68
 Swaby LN13 74
 15 Swineshead PE20 . . .135
 Tallington PE9 172
 Tealby LN8 46
 Tetford LN9 73
 Tetney DN36 36
 3 Timberland LN4 96
 Torksey LN1 65
 Toynton St Peter PE23 . . .101
 Twin Rivers DN14 7
 Tydd St Giles PE13 169
 Tydd St Mary PE13 160
 2 Ulceby DN39 12
 Utterby LN11 48
 Waddingham DN21 43
 21 Waddington LN5 93
 Wainfleet St Mary PE24 . .102
 Wainthorpe DN36 36
 Waltham DN37 194
 Wansford PE8 222
 Welby NG32 91
 2 Welton/Dunholme
  LN2 68
 3 Westborough & Dry
  Doddington NG23 117
 West Keal PE23 100
 Withern with Stain LN13 . .62
 Wood Enderby LN9 98
 Wrangle PE22 114
 Wyberton PE21 114
 3 Wymondham LE14 . . .150
CHURCH LANEHAM
 DN22 65
Church La Prim Sch
 NG34 212
Church Lees NG32 131
Church Mdws PE20 136
Church Meadow Dr **20**
 PE24 90
Church Mews **7** PE22 . . .136
Church Pk **17** LN12 77
Church Rd
 Auborn Haddington & South
  Hykeham LN5 92
 4 Bicker PE20 135
 2 Boston PE21 209
 4 Butterwick PE22 126
 Friskney PE22 79
 Harby NG23 79
 4 Ketton PE9 171
 Laughton DN21 41
 3 Mablethorpe/Sutton on Sea
  LN12 64
 North Ferriby HU14 3
 Old Leake PE22 114
 Saxilby LN1 66
 Skellingthorpe LN6 200
 Stainforth DN7 14
 Stickford PE22 100
 1 Stow LN1 66
 Ulceby with Fordington
  LN13 88
 Upton DN21 53
 Wigtoft PE20 135
 Wisbech PE13 170
 Wittering PE8 172
Church Rd N PE25 206
Church Rd S **8** PE25 206
Church Rise **8** PE22 98
Church Row HU8 181
Church Side
 3 Alkborough DN15 8
 3 Appleby DN15 9
 19 Goxhill DN19 12
 3 Grasby DN38 32
 3 West Halton DN15 . . .8
 4 Winterton DN15 9
Church Sq DN15 183

hurch St
4 Alford LN13 . . . . .75 F3
Amcotts DN17 . . . . .7 F1
Barkston Heath LN32 . . . . .130 B8
2 Barrowby NG32 . . . . .210 A5
3 Baston PE6 . . . . .164 E4
Beckingham DN10 . . . . .40 A1
1 Billingborough NG34 . . . . . . .133 B1
2 Billinghay LN4 . . . . .109 F5
20 Boston PE21 . . . . .208 F5
Bottesford NG13 . . . . .128 A5
3 Brough HU15 . . . . .2 C7
8 Burgh le Marsh PE24 . . . .102 E8
2 Caistor LN7 . . . . .33 B4
Candlesby PE23 . . . . .88 F2
Carlby PE9 . . . . .163 D5
4 Carlton-le-Moorland
LN5 . . . . .105 E8
Collingham NG23 . . . . .91 C4
Corby Glen NG33 . . . . .152 F8
2 Crowle DN17 . . . . .16 D7
Denton NG32 . . . . .139 A7
Digby LN4 . . . . .108 D5
3 Donington PE11 . . . . .134 E2
Easton on the Hill PE9 . . . . .171 D3
Elsham DN20 . . . . .20 F7
1 Epworth DN9 . . . . .27 E6
6 Fishlake DN7 . . . . .14 A8
1 Foston NG32 . . . . .117 F1
7 Fulletby LN9 . . . . .86 B8
Gainsborough DN21 . . . . .197 C5
Glentworth DN21 . . . . .54 F6
4 Gosberton PE11 . . . . .145 B6
13 Goxhill DN19 . . . . .12 A8
Grantham NG31 . . . . .211 A5
Grimsby DN32 . . . . .189 B1
1 Haconby PE10 . . . . .154 D8
3 Harlaxton NG32 . . . . .139 C7
Haxey DN9 . . . . .27 C2
8 Heckington NG34 . . . . .122 E3
Hemswell DN21 . . . . .42 D1
3 Hibaldstow DN20 . . . . .30 F5
Holbeach PE12 . . . . .215 D2
Kingston upon Hull
HU10 .178 E6
7 Kirton in Lindsey DN21 . . . .30 B1
Long Bennington NG23 . . . . . . .117 D3
Louth LN11 . . . . .198 C5
Market Deeping PE6 . . . . .217 B5
6 Market Rasen LN8 . . . . .57 D8
Messingham DN17 . . . . .29 D7
7 Middle Rasen LN8 . . . . .57 B8
Misterton DN10 . . . . .39 F5
20 Nettleham LN2 . . . . .68 C2
Nettleton LN7 . . . . .33 B3
Northborough PE6 . . . . .173 F6
12 North Kelsey LN7 . . . . .32 A4
North Witham NG33 . . . . .151 D4
Owston Ferry DN9 . . . . .28 A3
Peterborough PE2 . . . . .231 C7
Peterborough PE7 . . . . .220 F3
Peterborough PE7 . . . . .229 A4
Pinchbeck PE11 . . . . .156 B8
1 Ropsley NG34 . . . . .108 E2
1 Ryhall PE9 . . . . .163 C1
9 Scawby DN20 . . . . .30 E8
6 Scothern LN2 . . . . .68 F4
Skillington NG33 . . . . .151 A8
12 South Witham NG33 . . . . . .151 D2
Spalding PE11 . . . . .214 D4
1 Spilsby PE23 . . . . .87 B7
8 Stamford PE9 . . . . .219 C4
Sturton le Steeple DN22 . . . . . . .52 B2
1 Sutton Bridge PE12 . . . . . . .160 E4
1 Sutton on Trent NG23 . . . . .91 A8
28 Thorne/Moorends
DN8 . . . . .15 A8
8 Thorney PE6 . . . . .176 A3
Thurlby PE10 . . . . .164 D7
Willoughton DN21 . . . . .42 E4
1 Wragby LN8 . . . . .70 D4
Yaxley PE7 . . . . .233 D4
hurchthorpe 1 LN11 . . . . .49 B8
hurchtown 3 DN20 . . . . .16 E1
hurch View
2 Alkborough DN15 . . . . .8 C8
1 Barton-upon-Humber
DN18 . . . . .10 F8
1 Beckingham DN10 . . . . .40 A1
1 Bottesford NG13 . . . . .128 A6
2 Brough HU15 . . . . .2 C7
Freiston PE22 . . . . .126 D2
3 Gainsborough DN21 . . . . .53 A5
3 Great Gonerby NG31 . . . . .129 D5
Grimsby DN34 . . . . .190 E7
Northborough PE6 . . . . .173 F6
12 Ruskington NG34 . . . . .108 E2
4 Waltham DN37 . . . . .194 E4
hurchview Cl 5
NG34 . . . . .122 D3
hurch View Cl
5 Belton DN9 . . . . .16 E1
1 Donington PE11 . . . . .134 E2
Peterborough PE2 . . . . .231 B7
hurch View Cres LN3 . . . . .82 B7
hurchway PE7 . . . . .127 A5
hurch Way PE13 . . . . .160 A1
hurch Wlk
Bourne PE10 . . . . .213 D5
Brant Broughton &
Stragglethorpe LN5 . . . . .105 F4
1 Dunham-on-Trent
NG22 . . . . .65 B1
2 Holbeach PE12 . . . . .215 D2
6 Holton le Clay DN36 . . . . . .195 D2
1 Legbourne LN11 . . . . .61 F3
1 Manby LN11 . . . . .62 C6

Church Wlk _continued_
21 Metheringham LN4 . . . . .95 D4
1 Owston Ferry DN9 . . . . .28 A3
1 Peterborough PE1 . . . . .226 A3
2 Pinchbeck PE11 . . . . .156 F8
Sibsey PE22 . . . . .113 B3
Upton PE6 . . . . .223 B5
Yaxley PE7 . . . . .233 D4
Chuter Ede Prim Sch
NG24 . . . . .104 C2
Cinder La LN1 . . . . .198 B5
Circle The 4 HU13 . . . . .178 E2
Cirencester Cl LN6 . . . . .93 B8
Cissbury Cl 12 LN12 . . . . .77 A8
Cissbury Ring PE4 . . . . .221 A2
Cissplatt La DN41 . . . . .186 E4
Cisterngate 3 LN11 . . . . .198 B6
Citadel Way HU9 . . . . .181 A6
City of Lincoln Com Coll
The LN6 .205 A8
City Rd PE1 . . . . .226 A2
City Sports Ctr LN6 . . . . .205 A8
City Sq Ctr LN1 . . . . .234 B2
Claires Wlk DN17 . . . . .184 C7
Clampgate Rd PE21 . . . . .126 C1
Clapgate Pits Nature
Reserve* DN15 . . . . .19 E5
Clapgate Gate PE12 . . . . .157 E5
Clara Terr LN1 . . . . .234 A3
Clare Ave DN17 . . . . .184 D7
Clare Cl
11 Lincoln LN6 . . . . .205 D3
7 Stamford PE9 . . . . .219 A5
Clare Cres DN34 . . . . .185 A3
Clare Ct
4 Baston PE6 . . . . .164 E4
2 Grimsby DN34 . . . . .191 A5
Claremont Rd
1 Burgh le Marsh
PE24 . . . . .102 E8
Gainsborough DN21 . . . . .197 E2
Grimsby DN32 . . . . .192 D6
Claremont St LN2 . . . . .234 C2
Clarence Cl 2 DN40 . . . . .186 B3
Clarence Gdns 3
PE11 . . . . .214 E2
Clarence Rd
Peterborough PE1 . . . . .225 E5
28 Wisbech PE13 . . . . .170 C1
3 Woodhall Spa LN10 . . . . . . .97 D6
Clarence St
Kingston upon Hull
HU1 . . . . .181 A6
1 Lincoln LN5 . . . . .68 C2
Clarendon Gdns 1
LN1 . . . . .201 E8
Clarendon Rd
Grimsby DN34 . . . . .190 E4
Scunthorpe DN17 . . . . .184 F7
Skegness PE25 . . . . .206 A4
Clarendon St HU3 . . . . .180 D7
Clarendon View LN1 . . . . .201 E8
Clarendon Way PE6 . . . . .220 D8
Clare Rd
Northborough PE6 . . . . .217 E1
Peterborough PE1 . . . . .225 F6
Claricoates Dr 9
NG24 . . . . .104 C8
Clarina St LN2 . . . . .202 B4
Clark Ave DN31 . . . . .191 A7
Clarke Cl 10 PE21 . . . . .136 D8
Clarke Rd 11 LN6 . . . . .93 C8
Clarkes Rd 3 DN40 . . . . .12 E4
Clarke St 2 DN15 . . . . .183 A3
CLARK'S HILL PE12 . . . . .159 B3
Clarkson Ave 1 PE12 . . . . . . .167 B8
Clarkson Ct 27 PE13 . . . . .170 C1
Clarkson Infants Sch The
PE13 . . . . .170 C1
Clarksons Dr 3 DN41 . . . . . . .23 E6
Clasketgate LN2 . . . . .234 B2
Clatterdykes Rd PE20 . . . . . . .136 E6
Claudette Ave LN1 . . . . .214 B5
Claudette Way 5
PE11 . . . . .214 B5
Claudius Rd LN6 . . . . .93 B8
Clavering St 6 DN31 . . . . .188 D1
CLAXBY LN8 . . . . .45 D5
Claxby Rd DN17 . . . . .184 F5
CLAXBY ST ANDREW
LN13 . . . . .88 E6
Claxby Springs Nature
Reserve* LN13 . . . . .88 E6
Claxy Bank PE22 . . . . .114 D6
Clay Bank LN4 . . . . .123 C7
Clay Bank Rd DN8 . . . . .15 C6
Clayberg Dr 2 NG34 . . . . .212 D5
Clayburn Rd PE7 . . . . .230 D1
Clayden St 4 DN31 . . . . .188 D1
Claydike Bank PE20 . . . . .124 B4
Clay Dro PE11 . . . . .156 C5
Clayfield Rd DN15 . . . . .182 F6
Clay Hill Rd NG34 . . . . .212 D4
Clayhough La DN22 . . . . .65 F5
Clay La
Carlton-le-Moorland
LN5 . . . . .105 D8
Castor PE5 . . . . .223 D4
Fenton LN1 . . . . .79 C5
Gate Burton DN21 . . . . .53 B1
Harby NG23 . . . . .79 C5
Holton le Clay DN36 . . . . .195 D3
Kirton in Lindsey DN21 . . . . .30 A1
Newark NG24 . . . . .104 B4
Norton Disney LN6 . . . . .92 D2
Scotter DN21 . . . . .37 F5
Stapleford LN6 . . . . .105 D3
Tetford LN9 . . . . .73 F2

Clay La _continued_
Toft Newton LN8 . . . . .56 C7
Waddingham DN21 . . . . .43 D7
CLAY LAKE PE11 . . . . .214 E2
Clay Lake Bank PE12 . . . . . . .157 A3
Clay Lake La PE11 . . . . .214 E2
Claymore CI DN35 . . . . .192 E6
Clay Pit La NG34 . . . . .122 C6
CLAYPOLE NG23 . . . . .117 F7
Claypole CE (Controlled)
Prim Sch NG23 . . . . .117 F8
Claypole Dr PE6 . . . . .217 E1
Claypole La NG23 . . . . .117 E6
Claypole Rd NG23 . . . . .118 A7
Claythorne Dr DN21 . . . . .197 E4
CLAYTHORPE LN13 . . . . .75 B6
Claythorpe Wr Mill
LN13 . . . . .75 B5
Clayton Pl 2 . . . . .230 B4
Clayton Cl 12 PE13 . . . . .170 E1
Clayton Cres PE12 . . . . .157 C2
Clayton Rd LN5 . . . . .205 E6
Clayworth Rd 6 DN10 . . . . . . .39 C1
CLEATHAM 30 B3
Cleatham PE3 . . . . .225 A4
Cleatham Rd DN21 . . . . .30 B3
Clee Cres DN32 . . . . .192 C6
Cleefields Cl DN32 . . . . .192 B5
Clee Ness Dr DN36 . . . . .193 A1
Clee Rd DN35 . . . . .192 C5
Cleethorpe Rd DN32 . . . . .189 B1
CLEETHORPES DN35 . . . . .192 D5
Cleethorpes Coast Light Rly
& Mus* DN35 . . . . .193 B3
Cleethorpes Ctry Pk*
DN35 . . . . .192 F2
Cleethorpes Discovery
Ctr* DN35 . . . . .193 B3
Cleethorpes Leisure Ctr
DN35 . . . . .193 A4
Cleethorpes Nature
Reserve* DN35 . . . . .193 A3
Cleethorpes Showground*
DN35 . . . . .193 C3
Cleethorpes Sta DN35 . . . . . . .192 F7
Clee Village DN32 . . . . .192 C6
Clematis App LN6 . . . . .204 C8
Clematis Ave 7 DN41 . . . . .23 F5
Clematis Cl LN4 . . . . .81 D2
Clematis Way DN16 . . . . .185 C4
Clementine Ct PE25 . . . . .206 B6
Clensey La NG23 . . . . .117 F5
Clevedon St 5 DN35 . . . . .192 B8
Clevedon Rd DN17 . . . . .184 D8
Cleveland Ave 28 LN6 . . . . . . .93 C8
Cleveland Gdns 2
DN31 . . . . .188 D1
Cleveland Cl
2 Immingham DN40 . . . . .186 A4
2 Scunthorpe DN17 . . . . .184 D8
2 Spalding PE11 . . . . .214 F4
Cleveland Ct 3 PE4 . . . . .221 C2
Cleveland St
2 Gainsborough
DN21 . . . . .197 D3
3 Grimsby DN31 . . . . .188 D1
Kingston upon Hull HU8 . . . . . . .181 A8
Cleveland Way 27 DN7 . . . . . . .14 D4
Cleve Pl 8 PE6 . . . . .175 A1
Cley Hall Gdns PE11 . . . . .214 E4
Cleymond Chase 2
PE20 . . . . .136 C5
Cliff Ave
22 Nettleham LN2 . . . . .68 C2
Winterton DN15 . . . . .9 A5
Cliff Closes Rd DN15 . . . . .182 D3
Cliff Cres 1 PE25 . . . . .219 B5
Cliff Dr
Burton upon Stather
DN15 . . . . .8 B5
3 Kingston upon Hull
HU3 . . . . .3 E4
Cliffedale Prim Sch
NG31 . . . . .211 A8
Cliffe Rd
Easton on the Hill PE9 . . . . .171 D2
Gonerby Hill Foot NG31 . . . . .210 F7
Cliffe View NG34 . . . . .120 E4
Cliffe View Rd DN15 . . . . .182 F2
Cliff Gdns DN15 . . . . .182 D3
Cliff Gr 9 DN18 . . . . .10 E3
Cliff La
Marston NG32 . . . . .129 D8
Waddingham LN4 . . . . .43 C6
Washingborough LN4 . . . . .81 D4
Clifford Rd PE25 . . . . .206 B4
Cliff Rd
Fulbeck NG32 . . . . .119 C8
Hessle HU13 . . . . .3 F4
Leadenham LN5 . . . . .106 D2
Snitterby DN21 . . . . .43 C5
Spridlington LN8 . . . . .55 B4
Stamford PE9 . . . . .219 B5
Welbourn LN5 . . . . .106 E4
Welton LN2 . . . . .68 C5
Winteringham DN15 . . . . .9 A8
Woolsthorpe by Belvoir
NG32 . . . . .128 D1
Cliffside 3 LN5 . . . . .107 A7
Cliff St DN16 . . . . .183 C2
Cliff The DN15 . . . . .182 D3
Cliff Top La 2 HU13 . . . . .3 E4
Clifton Ave PE3 . . . . .225 E3
Clifton Ct 2 DN8 . . . . .15 A8
Clifton Rd 3 PE25 . . . . .206 D1
Clifton Prim Sch HU2 . . . . .180 E8

Clifton Rd
Boston PE21 . . . . .209 E4
Grimsby DN34 . . . . .191 A6
Clifton St LN5 . . . . .234 B1
Clint La 9 LN5 . . . . .107 A8
Clinton Dr NG34 . . . . .212 C2
CLINTON PARK LN4 . . . . .207 A5
Clinton Pk Prim Sch
LN4 . . . . .207 A5
Clinton Terr 3 DN21 . . . . .197 D3
Clinton Way LN10 . . . . .97 B5
Clipseygap La PE10 . . . . .154 B6
CLIPSHAM LE15 . . . . .162 B7
Clipsham Rd PE9 . . . . .162 D8
Clipston Wlk PE3 . . . . .225 C5
Clive Ave LN6 . . . . .205 C8
Clive Sullivan Way
Barton-upon-Humber
DN19 . . . . .4 A4
Kingston upon Hull HU4 . . . . . . .179 C1
CLIXBY DN38 . . . . .33 A7
Clixby Cl DN35 . . . . .193 A3
Clixby La DN38 . . . . .32 E7
Cloddy Gate LN17 . . . . .50 F5
Cloister Cl DN17 . . . . .184 E6
Cloisters The
Grimsby DN37 . . . . .190 D7
3 Humberston DN36 . . . . .36 D8
Welton LN2 . . . . .68 C7
Cloister Wk 14 LN20 . . . . .19 E3
Cloot Dro PE6 . . . . .166 F2
Close The
Barkston DN32 . . . . .130 A8
1 Colsterworth NG33 . . . . . . .151 D7
Easton on the Hill PE9 . . . . .171 C3
2 Fiskerton LN3 . . . . .82 A7
3 Goxhill DN19 . . . . .5 A1
Scunthorpe DN16 . . . . .183 B2
4 Skegness PE25 . . . . .206 C4
5 Sturton by Stow LN1 . . . . . . .66 D7
Closshill La PE21 . . . . .136 F8
Clouds La
Belton DN9 . . . . .17 B1
West Butterwick DN17 . . . . .28 C8
Clough La
Firsby PE23 . . . . .101 F5
Kirton PE20 . . . . .136 F2
Clough Rd
Gosberton PE11 . . . . .144 D4
Holbeach PE12 . . . . .215 B7
Cloven Ends 4 PE6 . . . . .164 F3
Clover Ct DN20 . . . . .196 B4
Cloverfields Prim Sch
DN36 . . . . .36 C8
Clover Gdns 6 PE9 . . . . .218 C2
Clover La PE20 . . . . .135 D4
Clover Rd
8 Bracebridge Heath
DN31 . . . . .81 A1
Market Deeping PE6 . . . . .217 C5
Misterton LN13 . . . . .89 A6
Clover Way PE11 . . . . .214 B6
Clowes Ct 4 HU13 . . . . .178 E1
Club Ct NG24 . . . . .104 B2
Clubhurn La PE11 . . . . .145 D6
Club Way PE7 . . . . .230 E4
Clumber Ave NG24 . . . . .104 C4
Clumber Ave NG24 . . . . .104 A3
Clumber Dr 7 PE11 . . . . .214 C6
Clumber Pl DN35 . . . . .192 E5
Clumber St
Kingston upon Hull
HU5 . . . . .180 C8
Lincoln LN5 . . . . .205 E2
Clutton's Cl PE6 . . . . .166 E1
Clyde Cl 1 NG31 . . . . .210 E2
Clydesdale Cres 1
PE11 . . . . .214 A2
Clyde St HU3 . . . . .179 F5
Clyfton Cres DN40 . . . . .186 B4
Coach House Gdns 8
DN20 . . . . .30 E8
Coachings The HU13 . . . . .3 E4
Coach Rd NG32 . . . . .118 C3
Coachroad Hill DN21 . . . . .54 F7
Coalbeach La PE11 . . . . .145 E3
Coalbeach La S PE11 . . . . . . .145 E4
Coalport Cl 7 LN6 . . . . .204 D7
Coal Shore La LN11 . . . . .37 D5
Coal Yd La NG23 . . . . .78 C4
COATES
North Leverton with
Habblesthorpe DN22 . . . . .65 B8
Stow LN1 . . . . .54 C2
Coates Ave DN15 . . . . .9 A5
Coates Rd DN22 . . . . .65 B8
Cobbet Pl PE1 . . . . .226 B3
Cobblers Way 6 NG34 . . . . . . .212 E3
Cobbs Hill 13 PE34 . . . . .161 F3
Coben Ave PE1 . . . . .225 F4
Cobden St
1 Gainsborough
DN21 . . . . .197 C4
Kingston upon Hull HU3 . . . . . . .179 F7
Peterborough PE1 . . . . .225 F4
Cob Gate PE12 . . . . .158 A6
Cobgate Cl 2 PE12 . . . . .158 B6
Cobham Cl 11 NG34 . . . . .122 C3
Cobhas NG32 . . . . .138 D8
Cochran Cl 3 NG31 . . . . .210 F8
Cockburn Fen Dike
PE12 . . . . .159 B2
Cockburn Way 6 DN15 . . . . .93 F5
Cockerels Roost LN1 . . . . .65 D1
Cocketts La 10 DN20 . . . . .30 F5

Cocklehole Rd PE34 . . . . .161 B5
Cock Pit CI HU10 . . . . .178 C6
Cockthorne La DN15 . . . . .9 C7
CODDINGTON NG24 . . . . .104 D5
Coddington CE Prim Sch
NG24 . . . . .104 D5
Coddington La LN6 . . . . .105 A7
Coddington Rd NG24 . . . . .104 C3
Coelus St HU9 . . . . .181 A7
Cogan St HU1 . . . . .180 E5
Coggles Causeway
PE10 . . . . .213 D4
Cogglesford Mill*
NG34 . . . . .212 F5
Coggles Way LN11 . . . . .61 E3
Cohort Cl 13 HU15 . . . . .2 C5
Coke Oven Ave DN16 . . . . .183 F2
Colchester Mews 12
LN6 . . . . .93 B8
Coldham Rd LN4 . . . . .207 E6
COLD HANWORTH LN2 . . . . . . .56 C2
COLD HARBOUR NG33 . . . . . . .130 D1
Cold Harbour La
Carrington PE22 . . . . .112 B6
Covenham St Mary LN11 . . . . . . .49 D5
Grantham NG31 . . . . .211 C2
Coldhorn Cres 14
PE13 . . . . .170 D1
Cold Hurn La PE11 . . . . .144 F6
COLEBY
Lincoln LN5 . . . . .93 F3
West Halton DN15 . . . . .8 E6
Coleby CE Prim Sch
LN5 . . . . .93 F3
Coleby Rd DN15 . . . . .8 E7
Coleby St LN2 . . . . .202 B3
Colegrave St 14 LN5 . . . . .205 E8
Cole La PE22 . . . . .100 B3
Colenso Terr 3 LN1 . . . . .201 D4
Coleraine Cl 13 LN5 . . . . .205 D2
Coleridge Ave DN17 . . . . .184 D7
Coleridge Ct 5 LN4 . . . . .207 B5
Coleridge Gdns
Lincoln LN2 . . . . .202 B7
15 Sleaford NG34 . . . . .212 F4
Coleridge Gn 3 LN2 . . . . .202 C7
Coleridge Pl
Bourne PE10 . . . . .213 E3
Peterborough PE1 . . . . .225 E8
Coles Ave LN13 . . . . .75 C2
Coles Cl PE12 . . . . .215 E3
Cole's La 1 LE20 . . . . .135 B7
Cole St DN15 . . . . .183 B3
Colin Ave DN32 . . . . .192 B6
Colindale PE9 . . . . .209 B5
Colin Rd DN16 . . . . .183 C2
Colins Wy 8 DN21 . . . . .29 C4
College Ave DN33 . . . . .194 F8
College Cl
7 Alkborough DN15 . . . . .8 C8
1 Holbeach PE12 . . . . .215 C2
Horncastle LN9 . . . . .199 C5
Lincoln LN1 . . . . .201 F6
Stamford PE9 . . . . .171 C8
7 Wainfleet All Saints
PE24 . . . . .102 D1
College Gdns 3 DN33 . . . . . . .194 F8
College Pk
Horncastle LN9 . . . . .199 C5
Peterborough PE1 . . . . .226 C3
College Rd
Barrow upon Humber
DN19 . . . . .11 E7
Cranwell & Byard's Leap
NG34 . . . . .120 E8
Thornton Curtis DN39 . . . . .12 B6
College St
Cleethorpes DN35 . . . . .192 E6
Grantham NG31 . . . . .211 B3
Grimsby DN34 . . . . .191 C6
1 Kingston upon Hull
HU2 . . . . .180 E7
College Yd DN20 . . . . .196 B3
Colleysgate Rd PE12 . . . . .216 C8
Colley St 11 PE21 . . . . .208 F5
Collelywell Cl 5 DN9 . . . . .27 A2
Collier Cl 11 HU14 . . . . .3 A4
Collier Rd 2 DN40 . . . . .186 D5
Collier St HU1 . . . . .180 E6
COLLINGHAM NG23 . . . . .91 C4
Collingham Rd PE3 . . . . .229 F3
Collingham La NG23 . . . . .91 F5
Collingham 31 LN6 . . . . .93 C8
Collingwood Cres
3 Boston PE21 . . . . .136 D8
Grimsby DN34 . . . . .190 D4
Collingwood Prim Sch
HU3 . . . . .180 C7
Collingwood St 1 DN33 . . . . . .180 D3
Collinson Ave 1 DN33 . . . . . . .182 C3
Collinson La
19 Balderton NG24 . . . . .104 C1
Newport HU15 . . . . .1 A8
Collison Gate PE12 . . . . .102 C2
Collum Ave DN16 . . . . .185 B6
Collum Gdns 2 DN16 . . . . .185 B5
Collum House Rd
DN16 . . . . .185 B6
Collum La DN16 . . . . .185 B6
Collynson Cl 1 HU10 . . . . .178 B8
COLLYWESTON PE9 . . . . .171 B1
Collyweston Rd 1 PE8 . . . . . . .172 B1
Colne Cl 1 LN6 . . . . .204 F3
Colne Ct 6 NG31 . . . . .210 E2

Colne Valley Visitor Ctr *
PE6 . . . . .227 B2
Colonial St HU2 . . . . .180 D7
Colonsay Ct DN36. . . . . . .195 C7
Colson Pl DN35 . . . . .192 B7
Colster Way 3 NG33. . . . .151 E6
COLSTERWORTH NG33. . .151 E7
Colsterworth CE Prim Sch
  NG33 . . . . .151 E7
Colsterworth Rd NG33. . .151 C6
Colsuan Gdns PE22 . . . . .216 C3
Coltman St HU3 . . . . .180 C5
Colton Cl 6 PE6. . . . . . . .164 E4
Colton St
  Brigg DN20 . . . . .196 B4
  2 Hatfield DN7 . . . . .39 F5
Coltsfoot Cl 4 DN15. . . . .182 C6
Coltsfoot Dr
  Bourne PE10 . . . . .213 D2
  Bradley DN37 . . . . .194 B5
  Peterborough PE2 . . . . .230 E7
Coltsfoot Way PE10 . . . . .213 D2
Columbia Rd DN32. . . . . .192 A7
Columbus Cl 6 PE11. . . . .214 C2
Columbus Way DN33. . . . .190 F3
Colvile Rd PE13. . . . . . . .170 A5
Colville Ave HU4. . . . . . . .179 B6
Colville Terr 3 DN21. . . . .197 D4
Colwyn Ave PE1 . . . . .226 E6
Comber Pl DN32. . . . . . . .189 B1
Combe St DN35. . . . . .192 C8
Comber Cl PE21 . . . . .209 A5
Comforts Ave DN15 . . . . .183 A2
Commerce La HU1. . . . . . .180 D4
Commerce Rd PE2 . . . . . .229 C5
Commercial Rd
  2 Alford LN13 . . . . .75 F2
  Grantham NG31. . . . . . .211 A3
  Kingston upon Hull HU1. .180 E5
  1 Louth LN11. . . . . .198 D6
  Scunthorpe DN16 . . . . .183 D3
  Spalding PE11. . . . . . . .214 E5
Commodore Croft 6
  HU1. . . . . .180 F5
Common Balk LN13 . . . . .76 C1
Common Dro PE6. . . . . . .166 C3
Common La
  Bardney LN3 . . . . .83 C4
  Barnby Dun with Kirk Sandall
  DN3. . . . . .14 B4
  Burgh le Marsh PE24. . . .89 F1
  Heapham DN21 . . . . . . .53 F7
  North Somercotes LN11 . .50 F8
  Old Leake PE22 . . . . . . .113 F4
  Sturton le Steeple DN22 .52 C3
  Twin Rivers DN14 . . . . . .7 B6
  Welton HU15 . . . . .2 D4
  Woodside DN9. . . . . . . .26 E6
Common Mid Rd DN17. . .16 C8
Common Rd
  Broughton DN20 . . . . . .19 E4
  Gedney Hill PE12. . . . . .176 F8
  Moulton PE12 . . . . .146 E3
  Parson Drove PE12 . . . .176 F6
  South Cave HU15 . . . . . .1 C7
  Waddingham DN21 . . . . .43 D6
  Whaplode PE12 . . . . . . .168 A2
  Wrangle PE22 . . . . .114 B4
Commonside
  2 Crowle DN17 . . . . . . .16 C8
  Westwoodside DN9 . . . . .27 A2
Common Side Rd PE22. . .113 E4
Common Way PE13 . . . . .160 B3
Comper Swift Cl 1
  PE2. . . . . .77 A7
Compton Cl 1 PE25. . . . .206 C1
Compton Dr DN34 . . . . . .191 C2
Concast Rd DN16 . . . . . . .19 A3
Conduit La NL11. . . . . . . .211 A4
Conduit Rd PE9. . . . . .219 C6
Coney Garth La PE11. . . . .145 F5
Coneygree Rd PE2 . . . . . .231 D6
Conference Ct DN6 . . . . . .185 A2
Conference Way 13
  PE13. . . . . .170 D2
Conging St 3 LN9. . . . . . .199 B4
Congreves Cl 3 PE12. . . .160 A8
Conifer Cl
  6 Kingston upon Hull
  HU5. . . . . .179 C7
  2 Scunthorpe DN17 . . . .184 C5
Conifers The PE2 . . . . . . .229 F6
CONINGSBY LN4 . . . . . . .207 D4
Coningsby Airfield
  LN4. . . . . .207 C2
Coningsby Cl
  Boston PE21 . . . . .208 D5
  Gainsborough DN21 . . . .197 F4
  2 Skegness PE25 . . . . . .206 A5
Coningsby Cres LN4 . . . . .205 F5
Coningsby Dr DN34 . . . . .191 A5
Coningsby Rd
  Coningsby LN4. . . . . . . .207 A1
  Peterborough PE3. . . . . .220 E1
  Scunthorpe DN17 . . . . .184 D5
Coningsby St Michaels
  Prim Sch LN4. . . . . .207 C4
Coningsby St LN12 . . . . . .234 C2
Conisborough Ave
  HU15. . . . . .195 B6
Conisborough Mews 22
  HU15. . . . . .2 D5
CONISHOLME LN11. . . . . .50 D6
Conisholme Rd LN11. . . . .50 B7
Coniston Ave 1 DN33. . . .194 E7

Coniston Cres DN36. . . . . .192 E1
Coniston Dr LN6. . . . . . . .205 A2
Coniston Rd PE4. . . . . . . .221 C3
Connaught Ave DN32 . . . .191 D4
Connaught Dr
  2 Chapel St Leonard
  PE24. . . . . .90 D7
  6 Kirk Sandall DN3 . . . .14 A2
Connaught Rd DN21 . . . . .197 C6
Connaught Terr LN5. . . . . .205 D5
Conquest Dro PE7 . . . . . . .231 D1
Consort Ct HU9 . . . . .181 B5
Constable Ave LN6. . . . . . .205 A6
Constable Cl LN6. . . . . . . .205 A5
Constable Prim Sch
  HU3. . . . . .180 C5
Constable St HU3. . . . . . . .180 C5
Constable Way 2 HU15. . .2 D5
Constance Ave LN6 . . . . . .204 F4
Constitutional Ave
  DN35. . . . . .192 C8
Convamore Rd DN32 . . . . .191 F6
Convent La HU3 . . . . .180 D6
Conway Ave
  Grimsby DN34 . . . . .191 A7
  Peterborough PE4. . . . . .221 A2
Conway Cl HU3. . . . . .180 B5
Conway Dr LN6. . . . . .205 B2
Conway Prep Sch
  PE21. . . . . .208 F5
Conway Sq 3 DN15. . . . . .182 E3
Conworth Cl PE1 . . . . .226 D5
Conyard Rd DN35 . . . . . . .192 E7
Conyers Ave DN33 . . . . . .191 D2
Cook Cl Rd PE7. . . . . .233 D6
Cook Dr PE11. . . . . .214 C2
Cooke Cres 6 LN4. . . . . . .207 D4
Cookridge Dr 31 DN7 . . . .14 C4
Cooks La
  Grimsby DN37 . . . . .24 B5
  4 Nettleton LN7. . . . . . .33 A3
Coomb Brigg's Prim Sch
  DN40. . . . . .186 A3
Cooper Ave PE25 . . . . .90 E4
Cooper La DN37 . . . . .23 E1
Cooper Rd DN32. . . . . . . .192 A7
Coopers Cl PE12. . . . . . . .168 B4
Coopers Holt Cl LN6. . . . .200 A3
Coots Cl PE25 . . . . .103 C8
Coots La LN13. . . . . .76 E1
Copeland PE3 . . . . .225 A3
Copeland Ct 5 NG34. . . . .212 C3
Cope St DN32 . . . . .192 A8
Copper Beech Cl
  1 Gainsborough DN21. . .52 F6
  6 Swanland HU14 . . . . .3 C7
Copper Beech Way
  PE2. . . . . .231 B7
Copper Beech Wlk
  DN16. . . . . .185 B3
Copper St LN10. . . . . .84 B3
Coppice Ave 13 DN7 . . . . .14 D3
Coppice La 2 DN7 . . . . . . .14 D3
Coppice Rd 11 PE9 . . . . . .163 C1
Coppice Side HU14 . . . . . .179 C6
Coppingford Cl PE2. . . . . .231 D6
Copse Cl DN40. . . . . .186 C5
Copse The
  Brigg DN20 . . . . .196 E2
  Grimsby DN33 . . . . .194 F8
  18 Mablethorpe/Sutton on Sea
  LN12. . . . . .77 A7
Copsewood PE4 . . . . .221 A4
Copthill Sch PE9 . . . . .172 C6
Coral Dr 1 DN37 . . . . .194 C5
CORBY GLEN NG33 . . . . .152 E8
Corby Glen Com Prim Sch
  NG33. . . . . .152 E8
Corby Pk HU14 . . . . .3 A5
Corby Rd
  Burton Coggles NG33 . . .141 A1
  Scunthorpe DN16 . . . . .183 C2
  Swayfield NG33. . . . . . .152 D5
Cordage Ct LN1. . . . . .234 A3
Cordeaux Cl
  Louth LN11. . . . . .198 C7
  8 Scotter DN21. . . . . . .29 C4
Cordeaux Sch LN11. . . . . .198 B7
Cordella Cl 1 HU3 . . . . . .180 A5
Cordon Rd DN35. . . . . . . .206 C1
Corfe Ave PE4 . . . . .221 A2
Corfe Cl 1 NG31. . . . . . . .210 E5
Corfe Wlk DN40 . . . . .186 D3
Coriander Dr 11 PE10 . . . .213 C6
Corinne Cres 3 DN35. . . . .206 C3
Corinne Gr 1 PE11 . . . . . .214 A3
Corinthian Ave DN34. . . . .191 B6
Corinthian Way HU9. . . . . .181 D6
Cork La PE24 . . . . .102 C7
Cork Tree Cres PE21 . . . . .208 E2
Cormack La 16 NG24 . . . .104 C1
Cormorant Dr DN37. . . . . .190 C8
Corn Cl
  Fiskerton LN3 . . . . .82 B7
  Horncastle LN9 . . . . . . .199 B5
Cornfield Cl 4 DN21. . . . . .194 D8
Cornfield Rd PE12. . . . . . .215 F3
Cornfield View 2
  NG34. . . . . .212 C2
Cornflower Cl
  3 Healing DN41. . . . . . .23 F5
  Stamford PE9. . . . . .218 C6

Cornflower Way 3 LN6 . .93 A8
Cornhill LN5. . . . . .234 B2
Cornhill Dr DN36. . . . . . . .11 A8
Cornhill La PE21. . . . . . . .208 E5
Cornish Cres NG34. . . . . .133 E7
Corley Rd DN10 . . . . .39 C7
Cornmarket 8 PE9 . . . . . .219 C5
Cornstall Bldgs 7 PE9 . . .219 C5
Cornwall Cl
  Grantham NG31. . . . . . .211 C7
  1 Scampton LN1. . . . . . .67 E5
Cornwallis Rd LN2. . . . . . .202 D4
Cornwall Rd
  9 Keadby DN17 . . . . . . .17 D6
  Scunthorpe DN16 . . . . .185 C5
  8 Stamford PE9. . . . . . .219 B6
Cornwall St 21 DN21. . . . .30 B1
Cornwall Way 8 NG34 . . .108 D2
Cornwell Cl DN33 . . . . . . .191 C3
Corona Dr 3 DN8 . . . . . . .15 A8
Coronation Ave
  3 Crowland PE6. . . . . . .175 B8
  4 Deeping St Nicholas
  PE11. . . . . .166 C6
  Parson Drove PE12 . . . .177 A7
Coronation Cl
  17 Louth LN11. . . . . . . .198 D7
  8 Spalding PE11 . . . . . .157 B6
Coronation Cotts DN35. . .192 F5
Coronation Cres
  Coleby LN5. . . . . .93 F3
  8 Epworth DN9 . . . . . . .27 D6
Coronation Rd
  Cleethorpes DN35 . . . . .192 F5
  Corby Glen NG33 . . . . .152 E8
  Ingoldmells PE25 . . . . . .90 F3
  8 Market Rasen LN8 . . .57 D7
  8 Stainforth DN7 . . . . . .14 C6
  8 Ulceby DN39. . . . . . . .12 A1
  Woodhall Spa LN10 . . . .97 D6
Corporation Bank 12
  PE6. . . . . .166 E1
Corporation Rd
  1 Grimsby DN31. . . . . . .188 E1
  Grimsby DN31 . . . . .191 D8
  8 Kingston upon Hull HU9 .5 D8
  4 Scunthorpe DN15. . . .183 A3
Corran Garth 8 HU4 . . . . .179 A3
Correen Cl 2 LN5. . . . . . .205 D2
CORRINGHAM DN21. . . . .41 E2
Corringham CE Prim Sch
  DN21. . . . . .41 E2
Corringham Rd DN21. . . . .197 F5
Corringham Rd Ind Est
  DN21. . . . . .41 A1
Corsair Gr 4 HU4 . . . . . . .180 A4
Corwood Cl LN2 . . . . .202 E7
Cosford Cl LN6 . . . . .204 B8
Cosgrove Cl
  2 Lincoln LN6. . . . . . . .205 A6
  Peterborough PE3 . . . . .225 C6
Cosgrove St 8 DN35. . . . .192 F6
Costa Row NG23 . . . . .117 D3
Costello Stadium *
  HU4. . . . . .179 C4
COSTON LE14. . . . . .150 C5
Coston Rd NG33 . . . . .150 E5
Cotelands Sch NG34 . . . . .108 E1
Cot Garth La DN21. . . . . . .53 E3
Cotham Gdns 2 DN41. . . .23 A4
Cotham Rd LN6. . . . . .205 B6
Cotman Wlk LN6. . . . . . . .205 A6
Cotswold Cl
  22 Lincoln LN6. . . . . . .93 C8
  3 Peterborough PE4. . . .221 C1
Cotswold Dr
  Great Gonerby NG31. . . .210 E2
  Waltham DN37. . . . . . . .194 D4
Cotswold Rd
  Birchwood LN6 . . . . . . .204 D5
  Cleethorpes DN35 . . . . .192 E2
  Kingston upon Hull HU5 . .179 A8
  8 Stamford PE9. . . . . . .218 E5
Cottingham Ct DN15. . . . .183 A4
Cottingham Dr LN2. . . . . .202 B7
Cotton End PE3. . . . . .225 A4
Cotton Rd PE21. . . . . .208 D6
Cotton Smith Way 1
  LN2. . . . . .68 C2
Coulam Pl 11 DN36. . . . . .36 D8
Coulbeck Dr DN35. . . . . . .192 D5
Coulby Cl NG23. . . . . .117 F7
Coulman Rd DN16 . . . . . . .15 B8
Coulman St DN8. . . . . .15 B8
Coulson Cl 13 DN20 . . . . .31 A5
Coulson Dr HU13 . . . . . . .178 F2
Coulson Rd PE10 . . . . . . .201 D1
Coultas St 3 HU3 . . . . . . .180 A6
Coult Ave LN6 . . . . .93 F5
Council Ave HU4. . . . . . . .179 E3
Council Rd PE4. . . . . .170 E1
Council St PE25 . . . . .205 D8
Council Terr 6 DN18. . . . .3 E1

Count Alan Rd PE25 . . . . .206 D8
Counter Drain Dro
  PE11. . . . . .155 E2
Counthorpe La NG33. . . . .152 E2
Counthorpe Rd NG33 . . . .152 F3
County Rd
  3 Hampton Vale PE7 . . .230 C1
  Yaxley PE7. . . . . .233 C8
County Rd S 2 HU5 . . . . .179 C8
Coupland Cl 5 DN21 . . . .197 F5
Coupledyke La PE20 . . . . .136 D5
Courtfield Cl HU2. . . . . . . .68 F2
Courtfields PE6. . . . . .217 B6
Courtney St HU8. . . . . . . .181 B8
Court The PE24 . . . . .77 C3
Courtyard The
  Boston PE21 . . . . .209 B3
  Market Deeping PE6 . . .217 C4
  Stamford PE9. . . . . .219 A5
Covel Rd NG34 . . . . .212 B6
COVENHAM ST
  BARTHOLOMEW LN11. .49 C5
COVENHAM ST MARY
  LN11. . . . . .49 C5
Coventry Ave DN34 . . . . . .191 A5
Coventry Cl
  7 Grantham NG31. . . . .210 D5
  Peterborough PE4. . . . . .220 F3
Coventry Rd 7 DN8 . . . . . .15 B8
Cove Rd DN9 . . . . .26 F3
Coverley Rd 5 NG33. . . . .152 E7
Covert Rd DN16. . . . . .185 B5
Covert The
  Clinton Park LN4 . . . . . .207 C5
  Peterborough PE3 . . . . .225 B1
Covill Cl 2 NG31. . . . . . . .129 D5
Covington Cl HU15 . . . . . . .2 C6
Cowan's La HU11. . . . . . . .49 C8
Coward's La PE11. . . . . . . .144 F2
COWBIT PE12. . . . . .157 B1
Cowbit Dro PE11. . . . . . . .144 C1
Cowbit Rd PE12. . . . . .214 D2
COWBRIDGE PE22. . . . . .125 E6
Cowbridge Bsns Pk
  PE22. . . . . .125 E7
Cowbridge Rd DN20. . . . .134 E5
Cowbroads La PE22. . . . . .113 C2
Cowdale La LN1. . . . . .66 B6
Cowdale's Dro PE11. . . . . .134 F1
Cow Dro LN4 . . . . .123 B7
Cowes Rd NG34 . . . . .210 E4
Cowgate
  2 Heckington NG34. . . .122 E3
  Peterborough PE3 . . . . .225 F2
Cow Gate NG34 . . . . .143 C8
Cowhams La PE20 . . . . . . .146 C8
Cow La
  Minting LN8. . . . . .71 B1
  Swinderby LN6. . . . . . . .92 B5
  Tealby LN8 . . . . .46 C1
  Twin Rivers DN17 . . . . .7 C6
  Upton DN21. . . . . .52 F6
  Welbourn LN5 . . . . .106 C5
Cowle La LN11 . . . . .62 A3
Cowley Cl 6 PE20 . . . . . . .135 C2
Cowley Endowed
  (Combined) Prim Sch
  PE11. . . . . .134 E2
Cowley's Rd 10 PE11. . . . .134 E2
Cow Marsh La DN36 . . . . .36 E5
Cowpaddle La LN4 . . . . . . .84 A5
Cowpasture La DN22. . . . .52 D3
Cow Pasture La PE22 . . . . .65 A7
Cowper Ave DN17. . . . . . .184 D7
Cowper Dr LN2 . . . . .202 C7
Cowper Rd PE1 . . . . .226 C5
Cowpers Gate PE12 . . . . .216 A3
Cowslip Cres PE10 . . . . . .213 D3
Cowslip Dr 2 PE6 . . . . . . .217 D6
Cowslip La LN11 . . . . .198 F8
Cox La 7 DN17 . . . . .16 D8
Cox's Cl 7 DN20 . . . . .31 A5
Cox's Dro PE6 . . . . .167 C1
Cox's Hill DN21. . . . . .197 D5
Cox's Wlk 8 NG31. . . . . . .129 E5
Coxwold Gr HU4 . . . . .179 E5
Crabapple Gn PE2 . . . . . . .229 D6
Crab La PE20 . . . . .123 C4
Crabley La HU15 . . . . .1 E7
Crab Marsh PE13 . . . . . . .170 C2
Crabtree PE4 . . . . .221 F1
Crabtree La
  Beckingham DN10 . . . . .52 A8
  Mablethorpe & Sutton
  LN12. . . . . .77 A7
  Saltfleetby LN12. . . . . . .51 D1
Crabtree Rd
  Colsterworth NG33 . . . .151 B7
  Easton NG33 . . . . .140 A1
  8 Hatfield DN7 . . . . . . .14 C5
  Skillington NG33 . . . . . .139 F1
Crack Holt La PE22 . . . . . .126 F8
Crackle Hill Cl DN9 . . . . . .27 B2
Cradge Bank Rd
  Deeping St Nicholas
  PE11. . . . . .167 A7
  Spalding PE11 . . . . .214 C1
Cragg Cl 3 PE20 . . . . .135 C2
Cragmire La PE22. . . . . . . .87 A4
Cragstan Ave DN33 . . . . . .191 D3
Craig Cl 3 DN20 . . . . .31 D3
Craig St PE1 . . . . .225 F3

Craikbank La DN22 . . . . . .65 A4
Craikhill Ave DN40 . . . . . .186 A6
Craithie Rd DN35 . . . . . . .192 E1
Crake Ave DN33 . . . . .191 C5
Crakedale Rd 2 DN15. . . .191 C5
Crampin Rd 3 DN35. . . . .192 B7
Cranberry La PE22 . . . . . .114 A2
Cranberry Way HU4. 179
Cranbourne Chase LN6 . . .93 B3
Cranbourne Cl 7
  DN35. 192
Cranbourne Mews 6
  LN6. 203
Cranbourne St HU3 180
Crane Ave PE7. 233
Crane Cl 1 NG34 120
Crane Gr LN6. 205
Cranemore PE4 220
Cranepit La PE11 135
Crane Rd HU9 181
Crane's Gate PE12 158
Cranesgate S PE12. 168
Cranford Dr PE3 225
Cranidge Cl 8 DN17. 16
Cranmore Dro PE6 165
Cranmore La PE12. 215
CRANWELL NG34 120
Cranwell Airfield
  NG34 120
Cranwell Ave NG34 120
Cranwell Aviation Heritage
  Cantre * NG34. 120
Cranwell Cl
  2 Beacon Hill NG24. . . .104
  8 Kirton in Lindsey DN21 . .42
  4 Skegness PE25 206
Cranwell Dr DN37. 190
Cranwell Prim Sch
  NG34. 120
Cranwell St LN5 201
Crapple La DN21. 29
Craske La PE34 161
Craven Ave 4 PE20 136
Craven St HU9 181
Craven Rd
  Cleethorpes DN35 192
  8 Hatfield DN7. 14
Craven St N HU9 181
Craven St S HU9 181
Craven's La PE22 146
Craven St LN5 205
Crawcroft La LN13 76
Crawford Gdns 3 PE6 . . .175
Crawthorne Rd PE1. 226
Crawthorne St 1 PE1. 226
Craycroft Rd 8 DN7 14
Craypool La 7 LN2. 68
Craythorne La 22 PE21. . .208
Creampoke Cres 8
  DN21. 55
Crease Dro PE6. 175
Creaseyplot La PE20. 124
CREETON NG33 153
Creeton Rd NG33 153
Crescent Cl 7 LN2 68
Crescent Mews LN5. 93
Crescent St DN31 191
Crescent The
  Beckingham DN10 40
  Bracebridge Heath LN4. . .81
  8 Brough HU15. 2
  Easton on the Hill PE9 . .171
  10 Eye PE6. 175
  Fiskerton LN3 82
  Gainsborough DN21 197
  Hatfield DN7 14
  Holton le Clay DN36 . . .195
  Horncastle LN9 199
  9 Kirk Sandall DN3 14
  Louth LN11 198
  13 Mablethorpe/Sutton on Sea
  LN12. . . . . .64 A4
  Morton PE10 154
  12 Nettleham LN2 68
  Peterborough PE2 230
  Ryhall PE9. 163
  Sleaford NG34. 121
  9 Spalding PE11 214
  Swayfield NG33. 152
Cresent The 8 LN6. 70
Cresset The * PE3 225
Cressey St 8 DN31 189
Cresswell Cl PE11. 214
Cresta Cl LN6. 204
Cresta Dr DN17. 184
Cresta The DN31 191
Crester Dr PE4 221
Crew Rd NG23. 91
Cricketers Way 12
  PE13. 170
Cridling Pl DN35. 192
Cringle Rd PE4 139
Cringleway NG33 140
Cripple Sidings La
  PE2. 231
Crispin Cl
  5 Kingston upon Hull
  HU4. 179
  13 Lutton PE12 160
Crispin Way DN16. 185
Croake Hill NG33 153
Crocus Cl PE7. 233
Crocus Gr PE1 226
Crocus Wlk PE11 214
CROFT PE24 102
Croft Bank 1 PE24 102
Croft Cl 8 PE24. 102

roft Dr
Grantham NG31. . . . . . . 211 C3
Kingston upon Hull
HU10. . . . . 178 C6
roft La
Bassingham LN5. . . . . . . .92 F3
Cherry Willingham LN3 . . 203 E7
Coningsby LN4. . . . . 110 E8
Croft PE24. . . . . 102 E2
Scunthorpe DN17 . . . . . 184 E2
Croft Lodge **1** DN9. . . . . .16 E1
roft Marsh La PE24. . . . 102 F3
rofton Cl LN2 . . . . 202 D4
rofton Dr LN2 . . . . 202 D4
rofton Rd LN2. . . . . 202 D4
Croft Pk **4** HU14 . . . . .3 A5
roft Rd
Croft PE25. . . . . 102 E3
Finningley DN10. . . . . . . .26 A1
rofts La DN9. . . . . .14 B6
roft's La DN9. . . . . .28 B3
roft St
Horncastle LN9 . . . . 199 C3
Lincoln LN2 . . . . 234 B2
rofts The
Humberston DN36. . . . . . .36 C8
Scunthorpe DN16. . . . . . 183 B2
roft The
Beckingham DN10 . . . . . . .52 B8
Nettleham LN2. . . . . .68 D2
Stamford PE9 . . . . 219 C5
Thorne/Moorends
DN8. . . . . .15 B7
West/East Butterwick
DN17. . . . . .28 D8
roft View HU10 . . . . 178 C6
roft Way PE7. . . . . 230 C2
romarty Rd **8** PE9 . . . . . 218 E6
romer Ave
Grimsby DN34 . . . . 191 A5
Mablethorpe/Sutton on Sea
LN12. . . . . .64 D1
romer Ct
Harrowby Est NG31. . . . . 211 E7
Lincoln LN6. . . . . 205 A1
romford St **1** DN21 . . . 197 D5
romwell Ave
Gainsborough DN21. . . . . .52 F6
Grimsby DN31. . . . . 191 C7
Horncastle LN9 . . . . 199 C2
Woodhall Spa LN10 . . . . . .97 D5
romwell Cl
Boston PE21 . . . . 208 D7
Heighington/
Washingborough LN4 . . . 203 A2
Kingston upon Hull
HU3. . . . . 180 D8
Northborough PE6 . . . . . 217 E1
romwell Cres **8**
NG34. . . . . 212 E4
romwell Ct **1** HU10 . . . . 178 E7
romwell Mews
PE6. . . . . 173 C4
romwell Pl LN4. . . . . . . 207 A5
romwell Rd
Cleethorpes DN35. . . . . . 193 A4
Grimsby DN37. . . . . 188 A1
Peterborough PE1. . . . . . 225 F4
romwell St
Gainsborough DN21. . . . . 197 D2
Lincoln LN2 . . . . 202 B3
romwell View **2** LN7 . . . .33 B4
romwell Way **6** PE6 . . . 217 A6
rook Bank LN12 . . . . .63 F6
rooked Billet St
DN21. . . . . 197 B8
rookes Broom Ave **32**
DN7. . . . . .14 D4
rookes Broom La DN7 . . .14 D4
rook Hill HU15 . . . . .2 C8
rook Hill Rd DN10. . . . . . .12 C4
rook Tree La DN7 . . . . . . .14 E4
ropper's La PE22 . . . . . . 126 E1
roppers Way PE7 . . . . . . 137 E7
ropston Rd PE1. . . . . . . 226 E7
ROSBY DN15 . . . . 182 D4
rosby DN15 . . . . 182 F6
rosby House Flats
DN15. . . . . 183 B4
rosby La **1** LN5 . . . . . . 106 E4
rosby Prim Sch DN15 . . 183 A4
rosby Rd
Grimsby DN33 . . . . 191 B2
Scunthorpe DN15. . . . . . 183 B4
rosby Row PE12 . . . . . . 160 D4
ROSBY WARREN
DN15. . . . . 183 D6
rosland Rd DN37. . . . . . 190 D8
rosss Bank LN4. . . . . .96 D8
rossbeck Rd DN34 . . . . . 185 A4
rossberry Way **1**
PE6. . . . . 173 B4
ross Carr Rd DN20. . . . . .31 B5
rosscliff Hill LN11 . . . . . .60 A8
ross Coates Rd DN34 . . . 191 A6
ross Comm La DN22 . . . . .52 D3
ross Dro
Fleet PE12. . . . . 168 B2
Holland Fen with Brothertoft
PE20. . . . . 125 B5
Horbling NG34. . . . . 133 F2
Tydd St Giles PE13 . . . . . 169 C5
rossfield Rd
Kingston upon Hull
HU13. . . . . 178 E3
Navenby/Wellingore
LN5. . . . . 107 A8
ROSSGATE PE11. . . . . . . 145 C1

Cross Gate
Long Sutton PE12 . . . . . . 159 F3
Quadring PE11. . . . . 135 A1
Spalding PE12 . . . . 157 B6
Tydd St Mary PE13 . . . . . 160 A2
Weston PE12. . . . . 157 C7
Crossgate Cres **5**
PE11. . . . . 145 C1
Crossgate La **3** PE11 . . 145 C1
Crossgill Cl NG31. . . . . . 211 F5
Cross Hill
Gringley on the Hill
DN10. . . . . .39 C1
Haxey DN9. . . . . .27 C3
Cross Keys La LN4 . . . . . 207 F4
Cross Keys Yd **5**
NG34 . . . . 212 D4
Cross La
Alkborough DN15. . . . . . . .8 C8
Amcotts DN17 . . . . .7 F1
Balderton NG24. . . . . . . 104 B1
Bourne PE10 . . . . 213 E2
Butterwick PE22 . . . . . . 126 F3
Collingham NG23. . . . . . . .91 D5
Flixborough DN15 . . . . . . .8 B1
Glentham LN8 . . . . .44 A4
Gringley on the Hill DN10 . .39 A5
Harby NG23. . . . . .79 B5
Lincoln LN6. . . . . .93 C8
Long Bennington NG23 . . 117 D1
North Kelsey LN7. . . . . . . .32 B5
Pinchbeck PE11 . . . . 144 F1
Wellingore LN5. . . . . 106 E6
Crosslands **5** PE11. . . . 134 F2
Crossmoor Bank DN14 . . . .6 C5
Cross O'Cliff Cl LN5 . . . . 205 E6
Cross O'Cliff Hill LN5 . . . 205 E6
Cross Rd
Hatfield DN7 . . . . .15 B4
Langtoft PE6 . . . . 165 B4
Market Deeping PE6 . . . . 217 F8
Sutton St Edmund PE12. . 169 A4
Tydd St Mary PE13 . . . . . 160 B2
Ulceby DN39. . . . . .12 B3
Cross Slack **5** DN17. . . .16 D8
Cross Spencer St **10**
LN5. . . . . 205 E8
Cross St
Barnby in the Willows
NG24. . . . . 104 F3
Barrow upon Humber
DN19. . . . . .11 D8
Brigg DN20. . . . . 196 C5
Cleethorpes DN35. . . . . . 192 E6
Crowle DN17. . . . . .16 D7
Gainsborough DN21 . . . . 197 B8
Garthorpe & Fockerby
DN17. . . . . .7 E6
Grimsby DN31. . . . . 189 B2
Holbeach PE12. . . . . 215 D8
Horncastle LN9 . . . . 199 C3
Kingston upon Hull HU1 . 180 C6
Lincoln LN5. . . . . 234 B1
Nettleham LN2. . . . . .68 C2
Peterborough PE1. . . . . . 226 A2
Potter Hanworth LN4. . . . .82 B1
Scunthorpe DN15 . . . . . . 183 B4
Skegness PE25. . . . . 206 B3
Spalding PE11 . . . . 214 C3
Sturton le Steeple DN22 . . .52 B3
Waltham DN37. . . . . 194 E4
West Halton DN15 . . . . . . .8 B7
Whaplode PE12 . . . . 158 B7
Cross Tree Rd **21** DN17 . .29 C7
Crossways **8** DN7 . . . . . .14 C6
Crossway The DN34 . . . . 190 E3
Crowberry Dr DN31 . . . . 188 D5
Crowdyke Gate PE12 . . . . 158 A5
Crowfields PE12. . . . . . . 217 F5
Crowhall La PE22 . . . . . . 127 A4
Crow Hill Ave DN35 . . . . 192 E6
Crowhurst **1** PE4. . . . . 221 A5
Crow La
Gedney PE12. . . . . 159 D6
Great Hale NG34. . . . . . . 122 F3
Leadenham LN5. . . . . . . 106 D3
CROWLAND PE6. . . . . . . 166 E1
Crowland Ave
Grimsby DN34 . . . . 190 F4
Lincoln LN6. . . . . 185 A4
Crowland Dr LN6 . . . . . . 204 F7
**Crowland Ponds Nature
Reserve** * PE6. . . . . . . 166 D2
Crowland Rd
Crowle DN17. . . . . .16 D7
Deeping St James PE6 . . . 174 D7
Eye PE6 . . . . 175 A3
CROWLE DN17 . . . . .16 C7
Crowle Bank Rd DN17. . . .17 C4
Crowle Dr DN15 . . . . 191 A3
**Crowle Moor Nature
Reserve** * DN17. . . . . . . .6 B1
Crowle Prim Sch DN17. . . .16 C7
Crowle Rd DN17. . . . . . . .6 F2
Crowle St HU9. . . . . 181 D7
Crowle Sta DN17. . . . . . . .16 C5
Crown Ave
Chapel St Leonard
PE24. . . . . .90 D7
Holbeach PE12. . . . . 147 C6
Crown Cl **10** NG23 . . . . . .91 D5
Crown Ct **3** DN22. . . . . . .52 B3
Crown Dr DN21 . . . . 214 F6
Crown Gdns **22** DN21. . . .29 C3
Crown Hill NG34 . . . . . . 141 B8
Crown La **14** PE10. . . . . 164 C8
Crown Lakes Ctry Pk *
PE7. . . . . 231 B2

Crown Lodge PE12. . . . . 215 C7
Crown Mills **2** LN11 . . . 198 D6
Crown St
Peterborough PE1. . . . . . 225 E7
Ryhall PE9 . . . . 163 C2
Stamford PE9. . . . . 219 B5
Crown Wlk
Bourne PE10 . . . . 213 C5
Louth LN11 . . . . 198 E5
Crow Pk LN6 . . . . 204 A1
Crow's La PE24 . . . . 102 C2
Crowson Cres PE6 . . . . . 217 E1
Crowson Way PE6 . . . . . . 217 D5
Crowston Wlk **7** DN15. . 183 B3
Crowther Way **8** HU14. . . .3 B7
Crow Tree Bank DN8 . . . . .15 D4
Crowtree La LN11. . . . . . 198 A5
CROXBY DN37. . . . . .34 D1
Croxby Ave DN33 . . . . . . 194 F8
Croxby Gr DN33. . . . . . . 194 F7
CROXTON DN39. . . . . .21 F7
Croxton Dr LN6. . . . . . . 204 F6
CROXTON KERRIAL
NG32. . . . . 138 D4
Croxton Kerrial CE Prim
Sch NG32 . . . . 138 D4
Croxton La NG32. . . . . . . 138 D5
Croxton Rd
Croxton DN39 . . . . .21 F7
Croxton DN39 . . . . .22 A5
Sproxton LE14. . . . . 138 E2
Croyland Rd PE4. . . . . . . 221 B1
Croyland Way **15** PE6 . . 166 F1
Crusader Rd LN4 . . . . . . 201 C1
Crystal Dr **1** PE2 . . . . . 230 D8
Crystal St HU3. . . . . 180 C7
Cubitt Way PE2 . . . . 231 A8
Cuckoo La
Ashby de la Launde &
Bloxholm LN4. . . . . 107 F7
Hatfield DN7 . . . . .14 E6
Pinchbeck PE11 . . . . 145 C2
Cul-de-sac The PE22 . . . 100 B2
Cullin Cl **1** LN5 . . . . . . 205 D2
Culpins Cl PE11. . . . . . . 214 F5
CULVERTHORPE NG32 . 131 E7
Culverthorpe Hall *
NG32 . . . . 131 D7
Culverthorpe Rd NG34 . . 132 A7
Culvert Rd PE24 . . . . 102 B3
Cumberland Ave
Grimsby DN32 . . . . 191 D5
Navenby/Wellingore
LN5. . . . . 107 A7
Cumberland Gdns
NG33. . . . . 152 D1
Cumberland Rd DN35 . . . 193 A2
Cumberland St HU2. . . . . 181 A8
Cumberland Terr **12**
LN8. . . . . .47 B6
Cumberland Way **17**
LN1. . . . . .67 E5
Cumberlidge Cl **10**
PE24. . . . . 102 A7
CUMBERWORTH LN13. . .89 F8
Cumberworth La **2**
LN13. . . . . .76 F1
Cumberworth Rd LN13 . . .89 C7
Cunningham Rd
1 Moorland Prison
DN7. . . . . .26 A8
Woodston PE2 . . . . 230 E8
Cunsdike La PE11 . . . . . . 145 D5
Cupola Way DN15. . . . . . 183 A8
Curle Ave LN4. . . . . 234 C4
Curlew Cl **4** PE12 . . . . . 216 B4
Curlew Dr **1** DN18 . . . . 167 B8
Curlew Gr PE2. . . . . 231 D7
Curlew Lodge La PE12 . . 160 F8
Curlew Wlk **10** NG34. . . 212 B3
Curry Rd DN14 . . . . 190 F7
Curtis Cl **13** NG23. . . . . .91 D5
Curtis Dr
Coningsby LN4. . . . . 207 D4
Heighington LN4 . . . . .81 E4
Curzon Cres **8** DN3 . . . . .14 A2
Curzon Ave DN15 . . . . . . 192 D5
Curzon Ct DN35 . . . . 192 D5
Curzon Est **8** LN4 . . . . . 207 A4
Curzon Mews **3** LN4 . . . 203 D1
Curzon St
1 Gainsborough
DN21. . . . . 197 D5
Kingston upon Hull HU3 . 179 F7
Cushman Cres DN40 . . . . 186 C3
Customhouse St **2**
PE1. . . . . 160 F4
Cut Dike PE12 . . . . 124 D8
Cut End Rd PE22 . . . . . . 114 B7
Cuthbert Ave **6** DN38. . . .21 B4
Cuthbert's La PE20 . . . . . 136 B8
CUXWOLD LN7. . . . . .34 B4
Cuxwold Rd
3 Scunthorpe DN16. . . 185 C8
Swallow LN7 . . . . .34 B5
Cydonia App LN6. . . . . . 204 C8
Cygnet Cl **3** NG34. . . . . 212 B3
Cygnet Pk PE7 . . . . 230 E3
Cygnet Rd PE7. . . . . 230 E3
Cynthia Rd DN32. . . . . . 192 C5
Cypress Cl
2 Peterborough PE3 . . 225 A2
Sleaford NG34 . . . . 212 D2
Cypress St **2** LN5. . . . . . .9 D8
Cyrano Way DN37. . . . . . 190 C7
Cyril Cooper Ct DN32 . . . 191 D6

D

Daffodil Cl PE11. . . . . . . 214 B3
Daffodil Gr PE2 . . . . 231 C7
Dagger La HU1 . . . . 180 F6
Daggett Rd DN35 . . . . . . 193 A4
Daimler Ave PE7. . . . . . . 233 E6
D'aincourt Pk LN4 . . . . . .81 D2
Dairy Cl
1 Gosberton PE11. . . . . 145 C6
Normanby DN15. . . . . .8 C3
Dairycoates Ave HU3. . . . 180 A4
Dairycoates Rd HU4 . . . . 179 E3
Dairy Dr PE6 . . . . 176 E2
Daisy Cl DN16 . . . . 185 D4
Daisy Ct PE10 . . . . 213 D3
Daisy Dale PE21 . . . . 209 A3
DALBY PE23 . . . . .88 B5
Dalby Cl PE1 . . . . 226 C8
DALDERBY LN9 . . . . .85 D1
Dalderby Cres **10** LN2 . . .68 C2
Dale Cl
Peterborough PE2 . . . . . 229 F5
10 Swanland HU14. . . . . .3 B7
Dale Cres **11** NG24. . . . . 104 C1
Dalehouse Dr **2** HU10 . . 178 F6
Dale Pit Rd **8** DN7 . . . . . .14 F3
Dale Rd
6 Brough HU15 . . . . .2 C7
Grantham NG31. . . . . . . 211 A7
3 Swanland HU14 . . . . . .3 B7
Welton HU15 . . . . .2 E6
Dale St N DN15. . . . . 182 F5
Dale's La PE20. . . . . 135 D5
Dale St
Lincoln LN2 . . . . 202 B2
Scunthorpe DN15 . . . . . . 182 F4
Dales The
25 Nettleham LN2. . . . . .68 C2
Scunthorpe DN17 . . . . . . 184 E3
Dalesway HU10 . . . . 178 B6
Dale View DN33. . . . . . . 190 F3
Dale Way **3** NG24 . . . . . 104 C1
Dallisons Rd **5** DN20 . . . .31 A5
Dallygate NG33 . . . . 140 A5
Dallygate La NG33 . . . . . 140 A5
Dalmatian Way **14** DN20 . .19 E4
Dame Kendal Gr DN33 . . 191 B3
Damgate PE2 . . . . 215 E1
Dam Gn La **5** HU15 . . . . . .2 C7
Dam La **3** DN19 . . . . .11 E5
Dam Rd DN18 . . . . .3 D1
Danby Rd **18** DN32. . . . . .29 D7
Dane Cl
13 Broughton DN20 . . . . .19 E4
31 Metheringham LN4 . . .95 C4
Danegeld Pl **24** PE9 . . . 219 C5
Danes Cl LN5. . . . . 234 B3
Danes Cotts **8** LN2 . . . . 234 B3
Danes Ctyd **11** LN2. . . . 234 B3
Danesfield Ave DN37 . . . 194 E5
Danesgate
Lincoln LN2 . . . . 234 B3
11 New Holland DN19. . . .4 E2
Danes Rd DN21 . . . . 197 F5
Danes Terr LN2 . . . . 234 B3
Danethorpe La NG24 . . . 104 D8
Danial Cl PE25 . . . . 206 C8
Daniel Cres **10** LN4 . . . 203 D1
Daniel Ct **7** PE25 . . . . . 219 C4
Daniel's Cres PE12. . . . . 216 C5
Daniel's Dro PE12 . . . . . 167 D1
Daniels Gate **1** PE11 . . . 214 C6
Daniel's Gate PE12. . . . . 216 C7
Daniel's Reach PE11 . . . . 214 C7
Danish Ct PE4. . . . . 220 E4
Dansom La S HU8 . . . . . 181 B8
Danson Cl **9** DN18 . . . . . .10 F8
Danube Rd HU5 . . . . 179 C8
Danum Cl **1** DN8. . . . . . .15 B8
Danum Rd
6 Hatfield DN7 . . . . .14 D3
5 Stamford PE9. . . . . . . 184 F8
Dar Beck Rd DN21. . . . . . .29 C4
Darby Rd DN15 . . . . .8 B4
Darbyshire Cl NG23 . . . . .79 B5
Dark La
Amcotts DN17 . . . . .7 F1
Barnby in the Willows
NG24. . . . . 105 A3
Bicker PE20 . . . . 135 A5
Bitchfield & Bassingthorpe
NG33. . . . . 141 A3
Burwell LN11. . . . . .74 C6
Holbeach PE12 . . . . 215 B5
Darley Cl PE8. . . . . 172 C1
Darley Dale Cres **1**
NG31. . . . . 211 A7
Darley's La PE11. . . . . . . 214 A6
Darnholm Ct DN37. . . . . 190 E8
Darnholme Cres
Epworth DN9 . . . . .28 A8
18 Messingham DN17 . . . .29 D7
Darrismere Villas **4**
HU3. . . . . 180 A5
Dart Ave LN6 . . . . 205 A2
Dartmouth Rd DN17 . . . 182 D1
Dartmouth Wlk HU4 . . . 179 A3
Darwin Cl
3 Stamford PE9 . . . . . . 219 A7
5 Sutton Bridge PE12 . . 160 E4
10 Waddington LN5. . . . . .93 E8

Darwin Ct
Lincoln LN6 . . . . 202 B5
Little Coates DN34 . . . . . 190 F6
Darwin St
3 Gainsborough
DN21. . . . . 197 D2
5 Kirton in Lindsey DN21 . .30 B1
Dashwood Rd **2** LN13 . . .75 E2
Datchet Garth **8** HU4. . . 179 B2
Daubeney Ave LN11. . . . . .66 D2
Daubney St DN35 . . . . . . 189 E1
Davenport Ave HU13 . . . 178 D1
Davenport Dr DN35 . . . . 192 C4
Davey Cl **1** PE21 . . . . . . 208 E7
David Ave
Lincoln LN6 . . . . 201 D8
Louth LN11 . . . . 198 D7
David Chalmers Cl PE2 . 230 F8
David Dr PE25 . . . . 206 B6
David Rd DN36 . . . . 195 C5
David's Cl PE4. . . . . 220 C4
David's La
Benington PE22 . . . . 127 A5
Peterborough PE4 . . . . . 220 F5
Davis Dr PE25 . . . . 192 F1
Davis Pl DN35 . . . . 192 B7
Davisons Ave DN17. . . . . 191 D8
Davis's Cl HU10. . . . . . . 178 C8
Davos Way PE25 . . . . . . 206 A7
Davy Ave PE25 . . . . 182 A4
Davy Cl **3** LN11 . . . . .61 F3
Davy Cres DN20. . . . . . . 196 C5
Davy's La **6** LN4 . . . . . . .88 A2
Dawber La
Claxby St Andrew LN13. . . .88 F5
Thimbleby LN9 . . . . .85 C5
Dawes La DN16 . . . . 183 D4
Dawlish Rd DN33. . . . . . 194 E6
Dawnay Dr HU10. . . . . . 179 A6
Dawnhill La DN21. . . . . . .42 E2
Daws Gate
Moulton PE12 . . . . 157 F2
Whaplode PE12 . . . . 158 A2
DAWSMERE PE12. . . . . . 148 F4
Dawsmere Rd PE12 . . . . 148 F4
Dawson Ave **1** PE11 . . . 214 F4
**Dawson City Claypits
Nature Reserve** * DN19 . . .5 C4
Dawson Cl
Lincoln LN6 . . . . 204 F6
5 Newborough PE6 . . . . 174 E4
Dawson Dr **8** PE24 . . . . 102 E7
Dawson Rd **7** NG34 . . . . 212 D6
Dawsons La LN3 . . . . . . 203 F8
Daybell Cl **20** NG13 . . . . 128 A6
Daybrook Cl NG32 . . . . . 139 C8
Day Cl
6 Keadby DN17. . . . . . . .17 D6
Wrawby DN20 . . . . .20 E4
Daymond St PE2 . . . . . . 230 D8
Day's La PE20 . . . . 134 F3
Deacon Dr DN15 . . . . . . 182 B2
Deacon Rd LN2 . . . . 202 C5
Deaconscroft PE3. . . . . . 225 B5
Deacons Sch PE1 . . . . . . 226 B5
Deacon St PE1 . . . . 225 F3
Dealtry Cl DN21 . . . . .53 D5
Dean Cl **3** NG34 . . . . . . 121 B8
Deane Cl **7** NG23 . . . . . . .91 D5
Deane Rd DN40 . . . . 186 D4
Dean Rd
Lincoln LN2 . . . . 202 C5
Scunthorpe DN17. . . . . . 184 E6
Deans Cl **6** DN10. . . . . . .39 F5
Deansgate DN32. . . . . . . 191 D5
Deansgrove DN32. . . . . . 191 D7
Deansway LN4. . . . . .81 D7
Dear Love Gate
1 Gedney PE12 . . . . . . 160 A8
Lutton PE12. . . . . 148 C1
Dearne Ct **9** HU15. . . . . . .2 D5
Dear St **11** LN8 . . . . .57 D8
De Aston Sch LN3 . . . . . . .57 E7
De Aston Sq **2** DN15. . . 182 E3
Deaton La DN16 . . . . 195 C6
Debdale PE2 . . . . 229 E4
Debdale Rd NG32. . . . . . 210 A5
Debdhill Rd DN10. . . . . . .39 F6
De Bec Cl PE1 . . . . 226 C3
Decoy Cl **16** PE11. . . . . . 145 C1
Decoy Rd
Borough Fen PE6. . . . . . . 174 E6
Gorefield PE13. . . . . 169 D2
Dee Cl
1 Grimsby DN34 . . . . . . 190 D4
3 Market Deeping PE6 . . 217 A5
Deene Ct PE3. . . . . 225 C5
**Deep (Aquarium & Marine
Research Centre) The** *
HU1. . . . . 181 A5
Deepdale Dr NG34 . . . . . 212 C7
Deepdale Gr **2** HU9 . . . . 181 E8
Deepdale La LN2 . . . . . . .68 C2
DEEPING GATE PE6 . . . . 217 C3
**Deeping Lakes Nature
Reserve** * PE6. . . . . . . 174 C7
Deeping St James PE6. . . 164 E4
DEEPING ST JAMES
PE6. . . . . 217 D4
Deeping St James Com
Prim Sch PE6. . . . . 217 F4
DEEPING ST NICHOLAS
PE11. . . . . 166 C6

Deeping St Nicholas Prim
Sch PE11 ....166 B6
Deepings Leisure Ctr
PE6 ....217 E4
Deepings Sch The PE6 ..217 E5
Deep La PE23...........87 A5
Deerhurst Way 1 PE6 . 175 A1
Deerleap PE3...........225 A5
Deer Pk Rd 8 PE6......164 F3
Dee St 6 HU3..........180 B4
Defender Dr DN7.......190 B7
De Gravel Dr 8 NG34..107 F1
De Havilland Rd PE13...170 D1
Deira NG34.............212 C1
De la Bere Ave 28 LN12 ..77 A8
De Lacy Ave PE25......206 C8
De Lacy La DN35.......192 F6
De Lacy Way DN15.......9 A5
Delamere Cl PE1.......226 D5
Delamere Ct DN36.....192 F1
Delamore Way PE12 ...216 C5
De la Pole Ave HU3....179 F7
Delapre Ct 11 PE6 .....175 A1
Deldale Rd PE21.......136 D8
Delfield Rd PE21.......136 D8
Delgate Ave 2 PE12 ...157 E7
Delgate Bank PE12 ....157 D2
Delhi Sq 3 NG34......120 D8
Delhi St 7 HU9..........5 D8
De Ligne Dr 6 NG32...139 C7
Delius Cl HU4...........179 B4
Dellfield Ave LN6......200 C1
Dellfield Cl LN6........200 C1
Dellfield Ct 8 LN6.....200 C1
Dell The
  18 Broughton DN20 .....19 E3
  Peterborough PE2 ......230 E7
  Scunthorpe DN17......184 D5
Delph Ct PE12..........231 F6
Delph Fields PE12 .....216 A3
Delph Rd
  18 Lincoln LN6.........93 C8
  Long Sutton PE12 .....216 A3
  Skellingthorpe LN6 ....200 B3
Delves Way PE7 ....230 D2
DEMBLEBY NG34........132 A4
De Montfort Univ LN2...234 B2
Denbigh Ct 11 NG23...91 D5
Denby Cl DN15.........182 D5
Denby Dale LN6........200 C2
Denby Dr DN35.........192 C3
Dene Cl LN6............200 B3
Denehall Rd 14 DN3 ...14 A2
Dene La LN4............109 C7
Dene Rd
  Grimsby DN32..........191 E4
  Skellingthorpe LN6 ....200 B3
Deneshway HU13 ....178 D2
Dene The
  6 Nettleham LN2.......68 C2
  Skellingthorpe LN6 ....200 B3
Denham Cl 3 PE25....206 C2
Denham Wlk 11 PE3 ...225 C4
Denis Dr PE2...........230 A4
Denmark Ct 7 HU9....181 C7
Denmark Dr PE2.......230 A4
Dennett Cl PE23.......100 F8
Dennor Cl 1 LN12....77 A8
Denshire Ct 3 PE6 ...164 E4
DENTON NG32...........139 B7
Denton Ave NG31......210 F1
Denton CE Sch NG32..139 A7
Denton Cl NG31........210 F1
Denton La
  Barrowby NG32.........128 F3
  Belvoir NG32..........138 E6
Denton Rd PE2.........231 C6
Denton's Way 11 DN20 ..31 A5
Depot St LN1............201 D3
Derby Ave PE25........206 D1
Derby Cl
  11 Grantham NG31....210 E4
  28 Grimsby DN32......189 C1
Derby Dr PE1...........226 C5
Derby Rd DN15.........182 B2
Derby St
  Kingston upon Hull
    HU3..................180 D8
  13 Lincoln LN6.......205 E8
Dere Cl 8 PE10........213 C6
Derringham Ave 6
  HU4...................179 B6
Derringham St HU3.....180 C7
DERRYTHORPE DN17....17 C3
Derrythorpe Rd DN17...17 D4
Derry Way DN33.......194 E8
Derwent Ave 48 HU14..3 A4
Derwent Cl LN6........205 A2
Derwent Dr
  11 Humberston DN36....36 C8
  Peterborough PE4.....221 C2
Derwent Rd
  Grantham NG31........210 F3
  Scunthorpe DN16 .....185 E6
Derwent St LN1........201 C4
Derwood Gr 7 PE4....220 F5
Desborough Ave PE2...231 D5
Detuyll St W DN15.....182 F5
Detuyll St DN15........182 F5
Devereux Way LN9......199 D2
Devon La 17 NG13 ....128 A6
Devonshire Ave DN32 ..191 D4

Devonshire Rd
  2 Scampton Airfield
    LN1...................67 E5
  Scunthorpe DN17......184 F6
Devon St
  Kingston upon Hull
    HU4...................179 F3
  8 Lincoln LN2........202 C3
Dewberry Ct HU4.......179 C4
De Wint Ave LN6.......205 A5
De Wint Cl
  Lincoln LN6...........205 B5
  5 Metheringham LN4..95 C4
De Wint Ct LN6.........205 A5
Dewsbury Ave DN15 ...182 C4
Dexter Ave NG31.......210 F3
Deyne Ave DN15........183 A3
Dial Sq 1 DN31........191 E7
Diana Princess of Wales
  Hospl DN33 ....191 C3
Diana St DN15.........183 A5
Dickens Beck La LN11 ..49 D5
Dickens Cl PE6........164 E2
Dickens Dr PE9........218 E5
Dickenson Terr 10
  DN21.................197 D3
Dickens Rd NG31......211 E6
Dickens St PE1.........226 B3
Dickinson's La 7 DN36 ...36 B1
Dickson Hill Rd PE22...114 D7
DICKON HILLS PE22 ...114 D7
Dick Turpin Way PE12 ..216 B5
DIGBY LN4.............108 E5
Digby CE Prim Sch
  LN4...................108 D6
Digby Cl 9 LN6........204 C7
Digby Dri Nature
  Reserve* LN4.........108 F5
Digby Gdns DN34 .....191 A5
Digby Rd LN4..........109 B6
Digby St DN15.........182 F4
Digby Tedder Prim Sch
  LN4...................108 D6
Dimmock Cl NG32.....139 B7
Dingley Ct PE3.........225 C5
Dirty La 4 DN7.........14 D8
Discovery Cl NG34....212 A3
Disney Cl LN6...........92 C2
Ditmas Ave 9 HU4....179 B6
Division Rd 1 HU3....180 B4
Dixon Ave
  14 Broughton DN20 .....19 D3
  Dorrington LN4.......108 E3
  Grimsby DN32.........191 E4
Dixon Cl
  Brigg DN20............196 C4
  Lincoln LN6...........201 D1
  12 Tetney DN36.......36 C4
Dixon Dr LN13..........75 E2
Dixon Pl 5 NG31......211 A3
Dixon's Dro PE14......170 F4
Dixons Rd PE6.........217 C4
Dixon St 11 DN21....201 D1
Dixon Way LN6.........201 D1
Dockholme Gate LN1 ..145 A4
Docking La LN9........199 B8
Docking's Holt PE12...216 B6
Dock Office Row 6
  HU1...................181 A7
Dock St HU1...........180 F6
Dock Terr PE21........209 B7
Dock Twr The* 7 DN31 ..189 B3
Doctor's La PE10......143 A2
DODDINGTON LN6.......79 E5
Doddington Ave LN6...205 A4
Doddington Dr PE3....225 B2
Doddington Hall & Gdns*
  LN6...................79 D5
Doddington La
  Claypole NG23.........117 E7
  Doddington NG23 .....118 B7
  Westborough & Dry
    Doddington NG23....117 E5
Doddington Rd
  Birchwood LN6........204 C6
  Doddington & Whisby LN6 ..79 E3
  Lincoln LN6...........204 F4
Dodswell Gr HU9........5 F8
Doe Cl LN6.............92 D5
Dog and Duck La
  DN21.................197 B8
Dog Dro
  Holbeach PE12........158 C5
  Sutton St James PE12 ...159 A1
Dog Dro N PE12........158 D2
Dog Dro S PE12........168 A2
DOGDYKE LN4..........110 D7
Dogdyke Ppg Sta*
  LN4...................110 D7
Dogdyke Rd
  Coningsby LN4........207 B2
  Wildmore LN4.........111 B6
Dog Holes La DN22 ....52 A1
Dog Kennel Rd DN21...55 A8
Dog Rose Dr PE10.....213 D2
DOGSTHORPE PE1.....226 C7
Dogsthorpe Gr 2 PE1 ..226 A5
Dogsthorpe Jun Sch
  PE1...................226 B7
Dogsthorpe Rd PE1....226 A5
Dolby Vale DN33.......190 F3
Dole Rd DN17...........6 B1
Dole Wood Nature
  Reserve* PE10........164 C7

Doll La 1 DN20........20 F7
Doll's Bank PE12......159 A4
Dolman Cres DN17.....184 F4
Dolphin La 22 PE21 ...208 F5
Dolphin St 4 DN15....192 F6
Dominion Cl 8 DN36 ..195 C6
Donaldson Dr 4 PE4 ..221 C2
Doncaster Gdns 14
  LN5...................107 A8
Doncaster Rd
  Gunness DN15..........17 E6
  Hatfield DN7...........14 D3
  Haxey DN9............26 F2
  Scunthorpe DN15.....182 B3
  Stainforth DN7.........14 B6
  Doncaster St HU3.....180 B6
Donegal Cl PE4.........221 B2
DONINGTON PE11......134 F1
DONINGTON EAUDIKE
  PE20.................135 A3
DONINGTON ON BAIN
  LN11...................59 F1
Donington on Bain Prim
  Sch LN11..............59 E1
Donington Rd
  Bicker PE20...........135 A4
  Horbling NG34.........133 C2
  Kirton PE20...........135 F6
DONNA NOOK LN11 .....38 D2
Donna Nook National
  Nature Reserve*
  Donna Nook LN11 .....38 C2
  North Somercotes LN11 ...51 B7
Donnington Gdns
  DN15.................182 F3
Donnington Pk 1
  PE13.................170 A1
Donnington Rd LN8....59 B2
Donnington St DN32...191 F7
Donville Rd DN17........7 A7
Dooks Cl DN21..........29 C1
Doon Garth 4 HU4....179 A3
Dorado Cl 2 HU3......180 A5
Dorchester Ave PE10...213 E3
Dorchester Cres 6
  PE1...................226 D7
Dorchester Rd DN17...184 C8
Dorchester Way 10 LN6 ..93 B8
Dore Ave LN6..........204 E2
Dormy Ave PE25.......206 D8
Dorothy Ave
  Skegness PE25........206 C3
  Waltham DN37........194 E5
Dorothy Cl PE7........113 A1
Dorothy Cres 1 PE25..206 C3
Dorrigan Cl LN1........201 C7
DORRINGTON LN4......108 E4
Dorset Cl 8 DN15......8 B4
Dorset Cl W 5 DN15....8 B4
Dorset Pl 8 LN1.......67 E5
Dorset St
  Kingston upon Hull
    HU4..................179 F3
  7 Lincoln LN2........202 C3
Dotam's La PE22......126 D4
Double Bank PE22.....126 D6
Double Bridges Rd DN8 ...15 B6
Doubledays La PE24 ...102 D8
Double St LN11........214 D4
Doubletwelves Dro
  PE20.................134 D6
Doughty Cl DN37......194 E5
Doughty Rd DN32......191 E7
Doughty's Cl LN5......234 B2
Doughty St LN5........219 D6
Douglas Ave
  Grimsby DN31.........191 A8
  5 Ingoldmells PE25...90 D3
Douglas Rd
  Cleethorpes DN35.....192 D8
  Market Deeping PE6...217 C4
Doulton Cl 4 LN6......204 D7
Dove Cl
  Louth LN11............198 D7
  6 Sleaford NG34......212 B3
Dovecote
  4 Middle Rasen LN8 ...57 B8
  Rippingale PE10.......143 A3
  Dovecote Cl PE1......226 B7
Dovecote La
  Auburn Haddington & South
    Hykeham LN5.........92 F5
  Coleby LN5............93 F3
  Wainfleet St Mary PE24 ...102 L1
  Yaxley PE7............233 C5
Dovecote Mews 4
  DN20.................196 F6
Dovecotes 8 4 PE6 ...217 A6
Dovecotes 9 LN11.....60 F1
Dove Ct PE21..........214 B5
Dove Dale 8 PE6......204 F2
Dovedale Cl
  Grantham NG31.......211 B8
  2 Winterton DN15 .....9 A6
Dovedale Dr 6 DN33 ..194 E8
Dovedale Gr 1 HU9 ...181 E8
Dovedale Rd DN16.....185 D5
DOVENDALE LN11.......60 F1
Dover Cl NG31.........210 E6
Dove Rd PE4...........221 A2
Dover St
  Grimsby DN31.........191 C8
  Kingston upon Hull HU3 ...180 C8
Doves' La PE22........126 E3
Dowding Mews LN2....202 E4
Dowding Rd LN2.......202 E4
Dowdyke Dro PE20.....146 B8

Dowdyke Rd PE20......145 F8
Dower Rise 11 HU14....3 B7
Dowgate Cl 2 PE11...214 A3
Dowgate Rd 4 PE13...170 B1
Dowlands Bsns Pk LN11..62 C5
Dower Gate St PE3....225 A1
Downing Cl 2 DN14....190 F6
Downing Cres
  Scunthorpe DN16 .....185 A3
  2 Stamford PE9.......219 B7
DOWSBY PE10..........143 B4
DOWSDALE PE6........167 D1
Dowsdale Bank
  Thorney PE6..........176 A8
  Whaplode PE12........167 E2
Dowse Ave DN15.......182 E3
Dowsing Way PE25....206 A6
Dozen's Bank PE11....156 B6
DRAGONBY DN15.......8 E1
Dragonby Rd DN17....184 E4
Drain Bank
  Cowbit PE12...........157 A2
  East Kirkby PE23......99 F3
  Newport HU15...........1 B8
Drain Rd PE6...........221 E7
Drainside PE20.........136 B5
Drainside S PE20......136 C4
Drakards La PE21......209 A3
Drake Ave
  Grimsby DN32.........192 B6
  Heighington/Washingborough
    LN4...................203 B1
Drake Cl 14 PE11.....214 C2
Drake Rd PE25.........103 E4
Drakes Cl
  7 Holbeach PE12.....215 E2
  19 Mablethorpe & Sutton
    LN12.................77 A7
Drakes Mdw LN8.......55 E6
Drake St
  Gainsborough DN21...197 D2
  Lincoln LN1...........201 C4
Drapers Pl 13 PE11...214 D4
Draw Dike PE22........159 D1
Drax Ct 6 LN8..........57 B8
Draycot 6 LN7..........33 A3
Drayton PE20..........225 A4
DRAYTON PE20.........135 C6
Drayton Rd PE20......135 C5
Drew Ave DN32.........191 F4
Drewry La 10 DN9......27 A2
DRIBY LN13............74 E1
Driffield Way PE2......230 D8
Driffil Way DN15........9 A5
Drift Ave PE9..........219 C6
Drift Gdns PE9.........219 C6
Drift Rd PE9...........219 A1
Drift Rd 6 PE9.........219 C6
Drift The
  Barrowby NG32........210 A3
  Belvoir NG32..........138 F5
  Buckminster NG33....151 A4
  Collyweston PE9......171 B1
  Croxton Kerrial NG32...138 F5
  Harlaxton NG32......139 C8
  Ryhall PE9............163 B3
  Skillington NG33.....151 A7
  Syston NG32..........130 A7
  Walcott LN4...........109 D7
  Wansford PE5.........222 F3
Drigh Rd 17 LN8......47 B6
Drill Hall La 5 DN21...197 D5
Dring La DN21..........41 D7
Drinsey Nook La NG23 ..66 B1
Drive The
  Gainsborough DN21...197 E3
  Grantham NG31.......210 D3
  Ingoldmells PE25......206 E8
  7 Kirk Sandall DN3 ...14 A1
  2 Mablethorpe/Sutton on Sea
    LN12.................64 A4
  Peterborough PE3.....225 E2
  Scunthorpe DN17......194 F3
  11 Welton/Dunham LN6
    LN2...................68 D2
Dronfield Ct 8 DN15 ..182 B3
Drove End Prim Sch
  PE12.................148 F3
Drove La
  Coddington NG24.....104 D7
  Sleaford NG34........212 A5
Drove Rd
  Cranland PE12.........167 F3
  Whaplode PE12........168 A3
Drovers Ct DN21.......197 E1
Drovers Rise 11 HU15...2 C6
Drove The
  4 Aubourn Haddington &
    South Hykeham LN6...93 A8
  Collyweston PE9......171 B1
  Osbournby NG34......132 D5
  Sleaford NG34........212 A1
Drummond Rd
  Bourne PE10..........213 E4
  Skegness PE25........206 D4
Drury Cl 1 DN37......194 C4
Drury La
  Bicker PE20...........135 A4
  Lincoln LN1...........234 B3
  New Waltham DN36....60 F1
Drury Pk 8 HU23......117 D3
Drury St LN1...........95 D4
Drydales HU10.........178 C6
Dryden Ave LN2........202 E6
Dryden Cl NG31........211 D6
Dryden Ct 3 LN8......207 B5
Dryden Rd
  Peterborough PE1....225 E7
  Scunthorpe DN17......184 D6

DRY DODDINGTON
  NG23.................117 E8
Dry Leys PE2...........230 F2
Drypool Way HU9......181 A2
Duchess St DN32......191 D
Ducie La DN22..........52 C
Duckpool La LN10......84 A
Duckthorpe La DN35...36 B
Dudley Cl 1 PE21.....209 B
Dudley House Sch
  NG31.................211 A
Dudley Pl DN35........192 C
Dudley Rd
  Brigg DN20...........196 A
  Grantham NG31.......211 A
  Scunthorpe DN16.....185 A
Dudley St DN31........191 C
Dudley Wlk HU4.......179 A
Duesbery St HU3......180 A
Dugard Rd DN32.......192 A
Duke of Bedford Prim Sch
  PE6...................176 A
Duke Rd PE22..........113 A
Duke's Covert Nature
  Reserve* NG32.......120 A
Dukesmead PE4........220 A
Dukesmead Mobile Home
  Pk PE4................220 A
Duke St
  Boston PE21..........208 A
  22 Grimsby DN32.....189 C
  Grimsby DN32.........192 A
  Peterborough PE2.....231 A
  Sleaford NG34........212 A
  14 Stainforth DN7.....14 A
Dunbar Ave DN36.....195 A
Dunbar Cl 5 DN21....197 A
Dunblane Dr PE2......229 A
Duncombe Gdns 1
  DN32.................191 A
Duncombe St DN32....191 A
Dundee Cl PE3.........229 A
Dundee Dr PE9........218 A
Dundee St HU5........180 A
Dunes Family
  Entertainment Ctr The*
  LN12.................64 A
Dunford Rd 8 LN5....234 A
Dunham Cl LN1........65 A
DUNHAM ON TRENT
  NG22.................65 A
Dunham on Trent Prim Sch
  NG22.................65 A
Dunham Rd DN22......65 A
DUNHOLME LN2.......68 A
Dunholme Cl 4 LN2 ..202 A
Dunholme Rd
  Gainsborough DN21...197 A
  9 Welton/Dunholme
    LN2...................68 A
Dunholme St Chads CE
  Prim Sch LN2.........68 A
Dunkirk Rd LN1........201 A
Dunlin Dr PE12........216 A
Dunlin Rd 2 PE9......163 A
Dunlop St LN5.........201 A
Dunlop Way DN16.....185 A
Dunmires La LN4.......6 A
Dunmore Cl LN5.......205 A
Dunmow St DN31......188 A
Dunnegate Way PE11..145 A
Dunnock Cl 3 DN16 ..185 A
Dunns Paddock 3
  DN20.................20 A
Dunoon Ct 4 DN37...190 A
Dunsbury
  Marholm PE6.........221 A
  Peterborough PE3.....224 A
DUNSBY PE10..........143 A
Dunsby Dro PE10......143 A
DUNSCROFT DN7......14 A
Dunstall St DN15......183 A
Dunstall Wlk DN15.....197 A
Dunstan Dr DN8........1 A
Dunstan Hill 26 DN21...30 A
Dunstan Villas 29 DN21...30 A
Dunster Cl NG31......210 A
Dunster Dr HU13......178 A
DUNSTON LN4..........95 A
Dunston Cl 10 LN2...202 A
Dunston Dr HU13......178 A
Dunston Fen La LN4....83 A
Dunston Heath La LN4...94 A
Dunston Rd
  Kingston upon Hull
    HU5..................179 A
  Lincoln LN4............95 A
DUNSVILLE DN7.......14 A
Durban Rd DN32.......192 A
Durham Ave
  Grimsby DN34.........191 A
  Sleaford NG34........212 A
  Thorne/Moorends DN8...15 A
Durham Cl
  Birchwood LN6........200 A
  Grantham NG31.......210 A
Durham Cres LN4......203 A
Durham Rd
  Cleethorpes DN35.....192 A
  Hatfield DN7...........14 A
  Peterborough PE1.....226 A
Durham's Rd PE12.....148 A
Dursley Ave DN36.....195 A
Dutton La PE25........206 A

Dycote La LN5......106 D5
DYKE PE10......154 D5
Dyke Dro PE10......154 E5
Dyke Rd 5 DN36......37 C5
Dykes End NG23......91 D4
Dyke Windmill & Peremill Gallery* PE10......154 D5
Dymoke Cl 3 LN12......64 C3
Dymoke Rd
  Grimsby DN37......190 C6
  Horncastle LN9......199 C2
Dymoke Rd 5 LN12......64 C3
Dysart Rd NG31......210 E4
Dysart Ret Pk NG31......211 A4
Dyson Cl PE1......225 F3

E

EAGLE LN6......79 C2
EAGLE BARNSDALE LN6...92 C7
Eagle Cl 7 LN12......64 A4
Eagle Com Prim Sch LN6......79 B2
Eagle Dr
  5 Sleaford NG34......212 B3
  8 Welton/Dunholme LN2......68 D7
Eagle La LN6......79 D1
EAGLE MOOR LN6......79 C2
Eagle Moor LN6......79 C3
Eagle Rd
  Doddington & Whisby LN6......79 D3
  North Scarle LN6......78 F2
  Spalford NG23......78 D4
Eaglesthorpe PE1......225 F2
Eagle Way
  Bourne PE10......213 E3
  2 Hampton Vale PE7...230 D1
  Yaxley PE7......233 D8
EALAND DN17......16 E6
Ealand Rd 3 DN17......17 C6
Eames Gdns PE1......226 E6
Earl Ave DN36......195 D7
EARLESFIELD NG31......210 F3
Earlesfield La NG31......210 F3
Earle's Rd HU9......181 D7
Earl of Dysart Prim Sch The NG31......210 D3
Earls Cl PE2......231 B6
Earls Dr LN5......205 D8
Earlsfield Cl LN6......204 B5
Earlsgate Gdns 3 DN15...8 F5
Earlsgate Rd DN15......8 F5
Earl Spencer Ct PE2...230 E8
Earl St
  Grimsby DN31......191 C7
  Scunthorpe DN16......183 B1
Earls Wlk 8 DN16......183 B2
Earlswood PE2......229 E5
Earth Cl PE2......231 E5
Ease La LN23......117 F3
Easenby Ave HU10......178 C6
Easenby Cl 4 HU14......3 C7
Eason Rd 8 DN33......191 B2
East Acridge 18 DN18...11 F8
East Ave
  Brant Broughton LN5...105 F5
  Grantham NG31......210 E3
  1 Stainforth DN7......14 C5
East Bank
  2 Stainforth DN7......14 C7
  Sutton Bridge PE12...160 F5
East Banks NG34......212 E4
EAST BARKWITH LN8...71 A8
Eastbeck La LN4......86 A2
East Bight LN2......234 B3
East Boundary Rd DN16......183 F2
Eastbourne St
  Kingston upon Hull HU3......180 A5
Eastbourne Way DN33...194 F7
Eastbrook Rd LN6......205 A5
EAST BUTTERWICK DN17......28 E8
East Camp Rd 8 NG34...120 C8
Eastchurch Rd 4 NG34......120 D8
East Cl 13 NG34......108 E2
Eastcliffe Sq 19 NG32...119 B7
Eastcliff Rd LN2......234 C3
East Cob Gate PE12...157 F6
East Comm La DN16...185 B8
Eastcroft 5 LN1......66 D3
East Croft 10 DN16......203 E7
East Cross St 2 DN21...30 B1
East Dale Dr 3 DN21...30 E2
East Dale Rd HU14......2 C5
East Dr LN4......110 E8
EAST ELLA HU5......179 D7
East Ella Dr HU4......179 C6
East Elloe Ave PE12...215 D3
East End
  3 Burgh le Marsh PE24......102 E7
  Humberside Airport DN39...22 A4
  Langtoft PE6......164 F3
East End Cl DN33......191 D1
Eastern Ave
  Gainsborough DN21...197 F5
  Peterborough PE1......226 C8
Eastern Cl PE1......226 D7
Eastern Dr
  11 Balderton NG24......104 C1
  RAF Cranwell NG34...120 D8

Eastern Ind Est PE1......226 E3
Eastern Inway DN34...191 A4
Eastern Rd PE12......215 F8
Eastern Terr LN5......201 D1
East Fen La PE22......113 B7
EAST FERRY DN21......28 B2
East Ferry Rd
  East Ferry DN21......28 E3
  Laughton DN21......41 B8
  Wildsworth DN21......40 D8
Eastfield
  14 Humberston DN36...36 D8
  3 Market Deeping PE6...217 C5
EASTFIELD PE1......226 D4
Eastfield 1 LN1......66 D7
East Field LN5......92 F2
Eastfield Ave DN33...195 A7
Eastfield Cl
  1 Dunholme LN2......68 E6
  6 Sutterton DN20......136 A2
Eastfield Gr PE1......226 B4
Eastfield Inf & Jun Sch DN40......186 C2
Eastfield Inf Sch LN11...198 D6
Eastfield La
  Manby LN11......62 C7
  Welton LN11......68 E7
Eastfield N Ind Est DN40......12 F3
Eastfield Prim Sch HU4......179 D6
Eastfield Rise
  3 Holton le Clay DN36......195 D2
  Louth LN11......198 D5
Eastfields 2 LN8......43 D3
Eastfield S Ind Est DN40...12 F3
Eastfield St 5 LN2......202 B3
EAST FIRSBY LN8......55 F4
Eastgate
  Bassingham LN5......92 F2
  Bourne PE10......213 E4
  Grimsby DN32......191 E8
  Heckington NG34......122 E3
  Kingston upon Hull HU3......178 E2
  Lincoln LN2......234 B3
  Louth LN11......198 C6
  Market Deeping PE6...217 F3
  Peterborough PE1......226 B2
EASTGATE PE1......226 B2
Eastgate Cl LN2......234 C3
Eastgate Gdns 3 PE12...159 C7
Eastgate La PE34......161 C2
East Gn 30 DN17......29 D7
East Gr
  12 Barton-upon-Humber DN18......3 F1
  6 Colsterworth NG33...151 E6
  Kingston upon Hull HU4...179 D4
Easthall Rd LN7......32 B4
EAST HALTON DN40......12 E6
East Halton Prim Sch DN40......12 D6
East Halton Rd DN40......12 D6
East Hann La DN19......4 E1
EAST HECKINGTON PE20......123 D3
Eastholm LN2......202 E7
Eastholm Cl PE1......226 C3
Eastholme Gdns 10 DN15...8 B4
Easthorpe La HU13......178 B5
Easthorpe Rd
  1 Bottesford NG13...128 B5
  2 Great Gonerby NG31...129 E5
Easthorpe View 2 NG13......128 B5
East Hull Pools* HU9...181 C8
EAST KEAL PE23......100 E7
EAST KEAL FEN SIDE PE23......100 C8
EAST KIRKBY PE23......99 F5
East La
  Corringham DN21......41 E2
  Morton LN6......154 D2
  Stainforth DN7......14 C6
Eastlands 4 PE6......166 F1
Eastlands Bank PE14...161 B1
Eastleigh Cl LN6......200 B1
Eastleigh Rd PE1......226 C3
East Liberty LN2......202 C4
EAST LOUND DN9......27 E2

East Lound Rd
  Haxey DN9......27 D2
  Owston Ferry DN9......28 A3
EAST MARSH DN32......189 B1
East Marsh Rd DN19......5 C3
East Marsh St 3 DN31...191 E8
East Mid Mere Rd DN40...12 F4
East Mill Gate 3 LN3...203 E6
Eastmoor Villas DN9...27 C5
East Mount 12 HU14......3 C4
East of England Showground* PE2......229 C4
East of England Way PE2......229 B4
EASTOFT DN17......7 A3
Eastoft CE Prim Sch DN17......7 A3
Eastoft Rd
  Crowle DN17......16 D8
  Luddington & Haldenby DN17......7 C3
EASTON NG33......140 A2
Easton Garfords Charity Aided Sch PE9......171 D3
Easton La NG33......140 A2
EASTON ON THE HILL PE9......171 C3
Easton Walled Gdn* NG33......140 B2
East Parade DN20......196 C4
EAST RAVENDALE DN37...35 C2
East Ravendale CE Prim Sch DN37......35 C2
East Rd
  Deeping St Nicholas PE11......156 C4
  4 Keadby with Althorpe DN17......17 C6
  Navenby/Wellingore LN5......107 B8
  Northborough PE6......217 E1
  Sleaford NG34......212 F6
  Tetford LN9......73 F1
  Tydd St Mary PE13...170 C8
East Rd Ind Est NG34...212 F5
Eastrea Ct PE2......231 E6
East Row LN11......198 C6
East St Mary's Gate 2 DN31......191 D7
Eastside Rd
  Grimsby DN31......189 B1
  Scunthorpe DN16......183 F2
East St
  Alford LN13......75 F4
  Bole DN22......52 C6
  Crowland PE6......166 E1
  Grantham NG31......211 B4
  Grimsby DN32......191 E7
  Helpringham NG34......133 E7
  3 Hibaldstow DN20......30 F5
  Horncastle LN9......199 B4
  5 Kingston upon Hull HU9......181 B7
  Nettleham LN2......68 C2
  Rippingale NG34......143 A2
  Roxby cum Risby DN15...9 A3
  Scunthorpe DN16......185 B1
  Stamford PE9......219 C5
East Sta Rd PE2......231 B8
EAST STOCKWITH DN21...40 C5
EAST TORRINGTON LN8...58 C2
East View LN4......109 D7
Eastview Cl
  Chapel St Leonard PE24...90 E6
  Louth LN11......107 C1
EASTVILLE PE22......114 B8
Eastville Rd
  4 Grimsby DN33......191 C2
  Toynton St Peter PE23...101 A6
Eastway LN12......68 D2
East Wlk DN15......183 B3
East Wold CE Prim Sch LN11......62 A3
Eastwood Ct 8 LN9......191 D4
Eastwood Ct 5 DN15...182 B2
Eastwood Dr
  2 Bottesford PE21......209 D4
  4 Broughton DN20......19 E4
  4 Grantham NG31......211 D2
Eastwood Rd PE21......209 D5
East Wr Cres PE7......230 C1
Easy Rd PE1......156 E1
Eathwaite Gn PE4......221 C1
Eaton Ct DN14......191 C6
Eaton Rd
  Boston PE21......208 E3
  Immingham DN40......186 D4
Eau Bank LN11......50 D7
Eaudike Rd
  Donington PE20......135 A3
  Quadring PE11......136 A3
Eaudyke Bank 1 PE13...166 F7
Eaugate Rd PE12......157 F1
Ebony Gr LN2......200 C1
Ebrington Cl 3 LN10...97 C6
Eccles Ct 3 DN20......196 F7
Eccleston Rd 15 DN36...14 A3
Ecdystone Dr 3 LN6...205 A1
Eden Cl 13 PE25......206 C1
Edendale Gdns 3 LN1...201 E8
Edendale View LN1......201 E8
Eden Dene DN16......185 D5
Edenfield PE2......230 C6
Eden Field Rd 4 DN3...14 A1
Eden Gr Rd 8 DN3......14 A1
EDENHAM PE10......153 F4
Edenham CE (Controlled) Prim Sch PE10......153 F5

Edenham Rd PE10......154 B6
EDENTHORPE DN3......14 A1
Edenthorpe Hall Prim Sch DN3......14 A1
Edgar Cl DN21......29 C4
Edgar St HU3......180 D5
Egbaston Ave 3 DN17......184 E3
Edgcote Cl PE3......225 C5
Edge Ave DN33......191 D2
Edgefield 4 PE12......157 E7
Edgehill LP LN5......205 D2
Edgehill Dr NG24......104 C4
Edgeworth Ave DN35...182 B3
Edgerley Drain Rd PE1...226 F5
Edinburgh Ave
  Peterborough PE4......220 F3
  3 Skegness PE25......206 D3
Edinburgh Cl 3 PE20...136 C5
Edinburgh Cres
  2 Bourne PE10......213 D6
  2 Kirton PE20......136 C5
Edinburgh Dr
  Holton le Clay DN36...195 C3
  1 Kirton PE20......136 C5
  Spalding PE11......214 E2
  Wisbech PE13......170 D2
Edinburgh Rd
  18 Binbrook Tech Pk LN8......47 B6
  2 Grantham NG31......211 E6
  8 Ruskington NG34......108 E2
  Stamford PE9......219 B6
Edinburgh Sq 4 LN5...94 A7
Edinburgh St HU3......180 A5
Edinburgh Wlk
  Holbeach PE12......215 E2
  Pinchbeck PE11......156 B7
Edington Ct 8 DN21...30 A8
Edis Ct PE2......231 B6
Edison Way 6 PE21...208 F1
Edith Cavell Hosp PE3...225 B4
EDLINGTON LN9......85 B6
Edlington Cl 6 LN2......201 F8
Edmonds Cl 2 PE9......219 D6
Edmonds Way 2 DN31......191 D8
Edmondthorpe Drift LE14......150 D1
Edmondthorpe Rd LE14......150 C1
Edmund Cl DN21......41 D2
Edmund Dr 7 PE9......171 A3
Edmunds Rd 8 NG34...107 F1
Edwalton Ave
  8 Mablethorpe/Sutton on Sea LN12......77 A8
  Peterborough PE3......225 E3
Edward Barker Rd LN4...81 F4
Edward Collins Sq 2 DN31......181 C7
Edward Cres PE25......206 B3
Edward Heneage Prim Sch DN32......191 F7
Edward Rd
  Gainsborough DN21...197 D6
  Spalding PE11......214 B4
  10 Stamford PE9......219 A7
Edward Richardson Prim Sch The LN9......73 F1
Edwards Rd 3 DN15...182 F4
Edward St
  Cleethorpes DN35......192 E5
  Grantham NG31......211 B2
  Grimsby DN32......191 F7
  Kingston upon Hull HU13...178 F1
  1 Lincoln LN5......205 E8
  17 Louth LN11......198 B5
Edwina Ave 6 PE11...156 F8
Edwin Cl 3 NG34......212 D2
Edwin Gdns PE10......213 B5
Edwin St 6 DN21......208 F4
Egar Way PE3......224 F2
Egerton Rd LN2......202 B5
Egginton Cl PE10......178 C7
Egginton St 4 HU2......180 F7
Egret Gr 5 LN6......204 D8
Egton Ave 17 DN17......29 D7
Egton St HU8......181 C8
Eider Cl 3 DN15......18 E8
Eight Acres 10 PE9...219 A5
Eighth Ave DN15......8 A1
Elan Cl PE21......208 E5
Elba St 6 HU9......5 E8
Elbow La PE13......177 F8
Elder Cl
  2 Bourne PE10......213 C6
  Skegness PE25......206 A5
Eldern PE2......230 C4
Elder's Gate PE12......169 E8
Elder St 5 DN15......205 D5
Elder Tree Way LN10...84 D3
Elderwood Ct 6 HU3...180 D5
Eleanor Cl
  Lincoln LN5......205 E7
  Stamford PE9......219 A6
Eleanor St DN32......191 F8
Electric Sta Rd NG34...212 C4
Eleven Acre La PE20...136 D4
Elgar Rd 4 HU4......179 B4
Elgar Way PE9......218 F6
Eliot Cl
  Gainsborough DN21...197 F3

Eliot Cl continued
  9 Sleaford NG34......212 F4
Elizabeth Ave
  Dogdyke LN4......110 D7
  11 Kirk Sandall DN3...14 A2
  6 Lincoln LN6......93 C8
  Lincoln LN6......204 F1
  Wrange PE22......114 C2
Elizabeth Cl
  17 Chapel St Leonard PE24......90 D7
  23 Crowe DN17......16 D7
  Gainsborough DN21...197 C7
  Glentworth DN21......54 F6
  Grimsby DN33......194 D7
  1 Scotter DN21......29 C4
Elizabeth Cres
  6 Ingoldmells PE25......90 E3
  Pinchbeck PE11......144 D1
Elizabeth Ct
  Brigg DN20......196 C5
  18 Chapel St Leonard PE24......90 D7
  Dogsthorpe PE1......226 A5
  Sleaford NG34......212 D3
Elizabeth Dr
  Billingborough NG34......143 B8
  2 Grantham NG31......211 E6
  Peterborough PE2......226 C7
Elizabeth Gr PE25......206 D5
Elizabeth Rd
  Boston PE21......209 B5
  2 Stamford PE9......219 B6
Elizabeth St 3 DN15...183 A4
Elizabeth Way 4 PE10...164 C8
Ella Pk HU10......178 C8
Ella Pk HU10......178 D7
Ellen Cres PE11......214 A3
Ellen Way DN36......195 B7
Ellerby Ct PE23......100 D6
Ellerby Mead NG33......152 D5
ELLERKER HU15......2 A8
Ellesmere Ave 3 LN2...202 D4
Ellesmere Bsns Pk NG31......210 E2
Ellesmere Gr 2 DN34...14 D6
Ellesmere Rise DN34...190 D3
Ellicar La DN10......39 A3
Ellindon PE3......225 B7
Elliot Ave PE3......224 F2
Elliot Cl NG31......211 E6
Elliott Rd LN5......234 C1
Elliott Ave PE9......164 B4
Elliott Way 6 PE24......90 D7
Ellis Mill* LN1......234 A4
Ellison Ave DN16......185 A1
Ellison Boulters CE (Con) Prim Sch LN2......68 F4
Ellison Cl 5 LN2......68 F2
Ellison St
  Lincoln LN5......205 D5
  Thorne/Moorends DN8...15 A7
Ellis St HU9......181 C8
Elliston Jun & Inf Schs DN35......192 C8
Elliston St DN35......192 C8
Ellis Way DN32......191 E8
Ellmore La LN7......32 C3
Eloe Bank PE13......169 B2
ELLOUGHTON HU15......2 B6
Elloughton Cty Prim Sch HU15......2 B7
Elloughton Dale HU15...2 D8
Elloughton Rd HU15......2 C6
Elloughtonthorpe Way 18 HU15......2 B7
Ellwood Ave PE2......231 E5
Ellyslande LN2......140 A5
Elm Ave
  18 Brough HU15......2 C6
  Cherry Willingham/Reepham LN3......203 D5
  Cleethorpes DN35......192 E6
  Grimsby DN34......191 A6
  13 Mablethorpe/Sutton on Sea LN12......64 B3
  Saxilby with Ingleby LN1......57 B8
Elm Cl
  Lincoln LN6......204 F2
  17 Long Bennington NG23......117 D3
  Market Deeping PE6...217 C4
  13 Saxilby LN1......66 D2
  Yaxley PE7......233 F7
Elm Cres
  Burgh le Marsh PE24...102 D8
  Glinton PE6......220 B8
Elmdale 20 DN18......10 E8
Elmdene 5 LN2......68 F4
Elm Dr
  Ingoldmells PE25......206 D8
  Louth LN11......198 D7
  Skegness PE25......90 E1
  3 Sudbrooke LN2......68 F2
Elm Gdns DN35......192 E6
Elm Gr
  Grantham NG31......211 C6
  8 Healing DN41......24 A5
  Scunthorpe DN16......185 B8
Elmhirst Ave PE25......206 D6
Elmhirst Rd 5 DN8......15 B8

Elmhurst La LN9 . . . . 199 B6
Elm La
 Goxhill DN19 . . . . 5 A1
 7 Laceby DN37 . . . . 23 E1
 Low Fulney PE12 . . . . . 157 C6
Elmore Cl 6 NG34 . . . . 212 C4
Elmore Rd PE3 . . . . 225 A3
Elm Rd
 Cleethorpes DN35 . . . . 192 E6
 Waltham DN37 . . . . 194 E3
Elms Dr HU10 . . . . 178 C8
Elm St
 Peterborough PE2 . . . . 230 F7
 Stamford PE9 . . . . 219 C5
Elms View 4 NG31 . . . . 129 D5
Elmswood HU13 . . . . . . 178 C2
Elm Terr PE10 . . . . 213 B6
Elmtree Ave 10 HU14 . . . 3 A4
Elm Tree Cl 11 LN8 . . . . 57 D7
Elm Tree Gr 8 DN8 . . . . 15 B7
Elmtree Rd NG34 . . . . . 108 D1
Elm Way
 Brigg DN20 . . . . 196 B4
 Messingham DN17 . . . . 29 C7
Elmwood Ave 4 PE21 . . 208 F2
Elmwood Cl 6 LN6 . . . . 200 D1
Elmwood Dr 6 PE25 . . . 90 D3
Elsea Dr 8 PE10 . . . . . 164 C8
Elsea Pk Way PE10 . . . 213 D2
Elsenham Rd DN31 . . . . 188 D1
ELSHAM DN20 . . . . 20 F7
Elsham Cl 7 LN6 . . . . . 204 D8
Elsham Cres LN6 . . . . . 204 D8
Elsham Dr DN37 . . . . . . 194 C3
Elsham Gr 1 DN33 . . . . 191 B3
Elsham Hall Ctry & Wildlife
 Pk* DN20 . . . . 20 F6
Elsham Rise HU13 . . . . 178 D1
Elsham Wlk DN21 . . . . . 197 F4
Elsham Wold Ind Est
 DN20 . . . . 21 A8
Elsie Davies Cl NG31 . . 211 C7
Elsiemere Wlk 6 HU4 . . 179 B6
Elsom Way LN9 . . . . . . 199 A4
Elsthorpe Rd
 Edenham PE10 . . . . . . 153 E6
 Hacomby PE10 . . . . . . 154 A7
Elstone PE2 . . . . 230 A4
Elter Wlk PE4 . . . . 221 C3
Elton Cl
 Ermine LN1 . . . . 201 D6
 2 Stamford PE9 . . . . . 218 F6
Elton Rd
 Thorney PE8 . . . . 228 B6
 Wansford PE8 . . . . 222 B2
Elton St 1 NG31 . . . . . . 211 A3
Elveley Dr HU10 . . . . . . 178 A7
Elvin Cl 3 LN2 . . . . 201 F6
Elvington Cl 7 LN6 . . . . 204 B6
Elvington Rd LN6 . . . . . 204 B6
Elwes St DN20 . . . . 196 C2
Elwyn Pl DN35 . . . . 192 D2
Ely Cl PE4 . . . . 220 F3
Ely St
 Lincoln LN1 . . . . 201 D4
 5 Sleaford NG34 . . . . 212 C6
Ely Way 5 NG31 . . . . . . 210 F5
Embankment Rd 4
 PE1 . . . . 226 A1
Embassy Ctr* PE25 . . . 206 E3
Ember La
 Chapel St Leonard PE24 . 77 B1
 Hogsthorpe PE24 . . . . . 90 B8
Embry Rd 2 PE8 . . . . . 172 B1
Emerald Gr 8 HU3 . . . . 180 A4
Emerson Ave DN7 . . . . . 14 C5
Emery La 15 PE21 . . . . 208 F4
Emfield Gr DN33 . . . . . . 194 E7
Emfield Rd DN33 . . . . . 194 D6
Emily St 8 HU9 . . . . . . 181 D7
Eminson Cl 6 DN21 . . . 29 C4
Emlyns Gdns 8 PE9 . . . 219 C6
Emlyns St 2 PE9 . . . . . 219 C6
Emmanual Rd DN16 . . . 185 F6
Emmanuel Ct
 3 Scunthorpe DN16 . . . 185 C6
 Yarborough DN34 . . . . . 191 A6
Emmanuel Dr DN16 . . . 185 A3
Emmanuel Rd PE9 . . . . 219 B7
Emmendingen Ave 2
 NG24 . . . . 104 A6
Emmery Cl 2 DN15 . . . . 19 D4
Emminson Way 1
 NG31 . . . . 210 E8
Emorsgate PE34 . . . . . 161 E3
EMORSGATE PE34 . . . . 161 E3
Empingham Rd
 1 Stamford PE9 . . . . . 219 A5
 Tinwell PE9 . . . . 218 B6
Empringham St 8
 HU9 . . . . 181 D7
Empson Rd PE1 . . . . . . 226 F5
Ena St HU3 . . . . 180 B6
Endcliffe Ave DN7 . . . . . 184 F2
Endeavour Cres 11 HU9 . 5 D8
Endeavour Ct 5 NG34 . . 120 F8
Endeavour Pk Ind Est
 PE21 . . . . 208 A4
Endeavour Way PE20 . . 136 A2
Endell Dr 35 DN21 . . . . 30 B1
Enderby Cl LN4 . . . . . . 203 A2
Enderby Cres DN21 . . . 197 E3
Enderby Rd DN17 . . . . . 184 E4

Enderby Rd Inf Sch
 DN17 . . . . 184 D4
Endsleigh St HU3 . . . . . 180 A7
Enfield Ave DN36 . . . . . 195 D5
Enfield Gdns PE3 . . . . . 225 C4
Enfield Prim Sch
 DN36 . . . . 195 D6
Enfield Rd 8 LN11 . . . . 59 E1
Engaine PE2 . . . . 230 B5
Engine Bank PE12 . . . . 157 F2
Engine Dro NG34 . . . . . 134 B4
Engine Dyke PE12 . . . . 148 B1
Engine St DN20 . . . . . . 196 B3
English Cl HU3 . . . . 180 E4
English Rd PE6 . . . . . . 176 B5
English St
 Kingston upon Hull
  HU3 . . . . 180 A4
 Peterborough PE1 . . . . 225 E5
Ennerdale Cl
 3 Birchwood LN6 . . . . 200 D1
 6 Humberston DN36 . . 192 E1
Ennerdale Rise PE4 . . . 221 B2
Enterprise Rd
 Caistor LN7 . . . . 33 A4
 Mablethorpe/Sutton on Sea
  LN12 . . . . 64 A4
Enterprise Way
 Grimsby DN32 . . . . 192 A6
 Pinchbeck PE11 . . . . . 214 E8
 4 Winterton DN15 . . . . 8 F5
Ephams La DN41 . . . . . 23 E7
Epperstone Residential Cvn
 Pk DN36 . . . . 195 C5
Epsom Cl LN6 . . . . 204 B8
Epsom Pl DN35 . . . . . . 192 F1
Epsom Rd LN6 . . . . 204 B8
EPWORTH DN9 . . . . 27 E7
Epworth Cty Prim Sch
 DN9 . . . . 27 D6
Epworth Leisure Ctr
 DN9 . . . . 27 D6
Epworth Rd
 Hatfield DN7 . . . . 14 F4
 Haxey DN9 . . . . 27 D3
 Owston Ferry DN9 . . . . 28 A4
Epworth Rd (West) 10
 DN7 . . . . 14 E4
EPWORTH TURBARY
 DN9 . . . . 27 C6
Epworth Turbary Nature
 Reserve* DN9 . . . . 27 B6
Epworth View LN1 . . . . 201 E8
Erebus Cl 7 DN23 . . . . 101 A8
Eresbie Rd LN11 . . . . . 198 D3
Eresby Ave 13 PE23 . . . 100 F8
Eresby Specl Sch The
 PE23 . . . . 100 F8
ERMINE LN2 . . . . 202 B8
Ermine Cl
 5 Ancaster NG32 . . . . 120 A3
 6 Bourne PE10 . . . . . 213 C6
 Grantham NG31 . . . . . 211 D5
 8 Lincoln LN1 . . . . . . 201 E8
 Stamford PE9 . . . . 218 F5
Ermine Com Inf Sch
 LN2 . . . . 202 A7
Ermine Ct 10 LN4 . . . . . 81 A1
Ermine Dr 3 LN5 . . . . . 107 B8
Ermine Jun Sch LN2 . . . 202 A8
Ermine Rise PE9 . . . . . 171 B8
Ermine St
 Ancaster NG32 . . . . . . 120 A2
 Appleby DN15 . . . . 9 C1
 Winteringham DN15 . . . 9 B8
Ermine Way
 Market Deeping PE6 . . . 217 E5
 Stamford PE9 . . . . 218 F5
Ernest Terr LN2 . . . . . . 234 B4
Eryholme Cres 1
 DN15 . . . . 182 F2
Escart Ave DN32 . . . . . 192 B6
Escombe View LN1 . . . 201 D8
Eshings The LN2 . . . . . . 68 D7
Esk Cl LN6 . . . . 204 F4
Eskdale Cl 1 PE4 . . . . . 221 C3
Eskdale Rd NG31 . . . . . 211 A7
Eskdale Way DN37 . . . . 190 D8
Eskham Cl DN36 . . . . . . 37 C1
Eskham Cl 1 DN35 . . . . 192 F3
Eslaforde Gdns 18
 NG34 . . . . 212 F4
ESSENDINE PE9 . . . . . 163 D3
Essendine Rd PE9 . . . . 163 C2
Essendyke PE3 . . . . . . 225 A7
Essex Dr 9 DN15 . . . . . 8 B4
Essex Rd 3 PE9 . . . . . 219 B6
Essex St HU4 . . . . 179 E3
Essex Way PE10 . . . . . 213 D4
Estate Ave DN20 . . . . . 19 D3
Estate Rd No 1 DN31 . . 188 B2
Estate Rd No 2 DN31 . . 188 B3
Estate Rd No 3 DN31 . . 188 B3
Estate Rd No 4 DN31 . . 188 B3
Estate Rd No 5 DN31 . . 188 B3
Estate Rd No 6 DN31 . . 188 B2
Estate Rd No 7 DN31 . . 188 B2
Estate Rd No 8 DN31 . . 188 B2
Estcourt Prim Sch
 HU9 . . . . 181 D8
Estcourt St HU9 . . . . . . 181 D8
Estella Way PE11 . . . . . 214 A5
Estuary Way DN1 . . . . . 188 D2
Estwaite Cl LN6 . . . . . . 205 B2
Ethel Ct 3 DN15 . . . . . . 182 E4
Ethelstone Rd 2 DN34 . 191 A7
Etherington St DN21 . . . 197 D4
Eton Cl LN6 . . . . 200 D3

Eton Ct DN17 . . . . 184 F4
Eton Dr DN17 . . . . 184 F3
Eton Rd
 Heighington/
  Washingborough LN4 . . 203 C1
 9 Mablethorpe/Sutton on Sea
  LN12 . . . . 64 C2
Eton St
 Grantham NG31 . . . . . 211 B4
 Kingston upon Hull HU3 . 180 C4
ETTON PE6 . . . . 173 E5
Eudo Rd PE25 . . . . 206 D7
Eugate Rd PE6 . . . . . . 167 F4
Europa Bsns Pk DN31 . 188 C2
Europarc Innovation Ctr
 DN37 . . . . 24 B6
Europa Way
 Brigg DN20 . . . . 196 A4
 Immingham DN41 . . . . 187 B3
Eusden Ct LN4 . . . . . . 207 A5
Euston Ave 5 PE11 . . . 214 B2
Euston Cl LN6 . . . . 200 D2
EVEDON NG34 . . . . 121 F6
Evedon Rd NG34 . . . . . 121 F5
Eve Gdns LN4 . . . . 203 D1
Evelyn Gr N 1 DN32 . . 192 B6
Evelyn Gr S 3 DN32 . . 192 B6
Evendine Ct DN36 . . . . 195 E1
Everard Rd NG31 . . . . . 155 C1
Everdon Way PE3 . . . . . 225 C5
Everest Rd DN36 . . . . . 185 C5
Everingham PE2 . . . . . 229 D5
Everington's La PE25 . . 103 C8
Everthorpe Cl 8 HU15 . . 2 D5
Ever Thorpe Cl 8 HU3 . 180 C5
Eves Cl 9 PE6 . . . . 174 E5
Evesham Ave DN34 . . . 190 E5
Eve St LN11 . . . . 198 B6
Evison Cres 2 LN13 . . . 75 E3
Evison Ct 12 PE22 . . . . 113 B1
Evison Way 1 LN11 . . . 50 E7
Ewart St LN5 . . . . 205 D6
EWERBY NG34 . . . . 122 B6
Ewerby Pond Nature
 Reserve* NG34 . . . . . . 122 E8
Ewerby Rd NG34 . . . . . 122 A5
EWERBY THORPE
 NG34 . . . . 122 D6
Exchange Cl LN6 . . . . . 204 E4
Exchange Pl 5 DN20 . . 196 B3
Exchange Rd LN6 . . . . . 204 C4
Exchange St PE1 . . . . . 226 A2
Exchequergate 5 LN2 . . 234 B3
Exeter Cl
 3 Bourne PE10 . . . . . 213 C5
 Grantham NG31 . . . . . 210 C5
 Heighington/Washingborough
  LN4 . . . . 203 E2
Exeter Ct
 2 Bourne PE10 . . . . . 213 C5
 10 Grimsby DN34 . . . . 190 D4
Exeter Dr
 4 Sleaford NG34 . . . . 212 C6
 Spalding PE11 . . . . . . 214 E4
Exeter Gdns
 10 Bourne PE10 . . . . . 213 C5
 Peterborough PE9 . . . . 218 F4
Exeter Rd
 Peterborough PE1 . . . . 225 F6
 Scunthorpe DN15 . . . . 182 F3
 8 Wittering PE8 . . . . . 172 B1
Exeter St PE10 . . . . . . 213 C5
Exley Sq LN2 . . . . 202 D6
Exmoor Ave DN15 . . . . 182 D7
Exmoor Cl LN6 . . . . . . 204 D1
Exmoor Rd DN17 . . . . . 184 C8
Exton Cl 6 PE6 . . . . . . 218 E5
Eyam Way 3 LN6 . . . . . 204 F1
EYE PE6 . . . . 175 A1
Eyebury Rd
 Eye PE6 . . . . 175 A1
 Peterborough PE6 . . . . 227 A6
Eye CE Prim Sch PE6 . . 175 B1
EYE GREEN PE6 . . . . . 175 A2
Eye Rd PE1 . . . . 174 F1
Eyre Ave DN16 . . . . . . 185 B5
Eyrescroft PE3 . . . . 225 A7
Eyrescroft Prim Sch
 PE3 . . . . 225 A7
Eyre's La LN6 . . . . 78 F1

F

Fagans Way 7 PE25 . . . 206 C1
Fainlight Cl 2 PE24 . . . 206 D8
Fairburn Cl 9 PE24 . . . 90 D7
Fairchild Way PE1 . . . . 226 A7
Fairfax Cl
 Boston PE21 . . . . 208 D7
 Gainsborough DN21 . . 197 F2
 5 Horncastle LN9 . . . . 199 D3
 2 Toft Newton LN8 . . . 56 D5
Fairfax Rd DN31 . . . . . . 191 B7
Fairfax St LN5 . . . . 205 D6
Fairfax Way PE6 . . . . . . 217 E3
Fairfield LN4 . . . . 207 C4
Fairfield Ave
 22 Chapel St Leonard
  PE24 . . . . 90 D7
 Grimsby DN33 . . . . . . 194 E7
Fairfield Cl
 8 Broughton DN20 . . . 19 E3
 3 Spalding PE11 . . . . 214 C6
Fairfield Croft 9 DN9 . . 27 E6
Fairfield Ct 3 DN35 . . . 193 A1

Fairfield Dr
 29 Barton-upon-Humber
  DN18 . . . . 10 F8
 39 Messingham DN17 . 29 C7
Fairfield Ind Est LN11 . . 198 B8
Fairfield Pit Nature
 Reserve* DN19 . . . . . . 4 D3
Fairfield Prim Sch
 DN33 . . . . 194 E8
Fairfield Rd
 Grimsby DN33 . . . . . . 194 E7
 Peterborough PE2 . . . . 231 A8
 Scunthorpe DN15 . . . . 182 C4
Fairfields
 Holbeach PE12 . . . . . . 215 C3
 33 Kirton in Lindsey DN21 . 30 B1
Fairfield View 11 HU15 . 2 D5
Fair Isle Rise DN40 . . . 186 C2
Fairleas LN4 . . . . 81 E2
Fairmead Way PE3 . . . . 225 E2
Fairmont Cres DN16 . . . 183 B2
Fairmont Rd DN32 . . . . 192 A7
Fairtree Wlk 24 DN8 . . . 15 A8
Fair View Ave DN35 . . . 192 E6
Fairview Way PE11 . . . . 214 C6
Fairway DN37 . . . . 194 C3
Fairway Ct DN35 . . . . . 193 C1
Fairways PE10 . . . . 164 A8
Fairways The
 Kirton PE20 . . . . 136 C6
 Scunthorpe DN15 . . . . 182 B2
Fairway The
 Kingston upon Hull
  HU10 . . . . 178 A8
 1 Mablethorpe/Sutton on Sea
  LN12 . . . . 64 A4
Fairweather Ct PE1 . . . . 226 E3
Fakenham Chase PE12 . 215 E3
Falcon Cl LN6 . . . . 79 B2
Falcon Ct
 9 Grantham NG31 . . . . 210 E2
 Kingston upon Hull HU4 . 179 D2
Falconers The DN21 . . . 30 F2
Falcon Rd 1 LN4 . . . . . 108 A7
Falcon Way
 Hampton Vale PE2 . . . . 230 C1
 13 Sleaford NG34 . . . . 212 B3
FALDINGWORTH LN8 . . . 56 F3
Faldingworth Cl 8
 LN6 . . . . 204 C7
Faldingworth Com Prim
 Sch LN8 . . . . 56 F3
Faldingworth Rd LN8 . . 55 F3
Faldos Way 3 LN12 . . . 64 A4
Falkirk Cl 6 PE9 . . . . . 218 E6
Falkland Rd 4 HU9 . . . . 5 F8
Falklands Cl LN1 . . . . . 201 E8
Falklands Rd PE12 . . . . 160 D4
Falkland Way DN18 . . . . 3 F1
Falodan Rd PE2 . . . . . . 229 C3
Fallowfield PE2 . . . . 229 D5
Fallowfield Rd DN33 . . . 194 D7
Fallow Fields 7 PE11 . . 166 C6
Fallow La
 Foston NG32 . . . . 118 A2
 1 Westborough & Dry
  Doddington NG23 . . . . 117 F3
Fall's Dro PE6 . . . . 175 F7
Falsgrave Gr HU5 . . . . . 179 D7
Fane Cl PE9 . . . . 219 B7
Fane Rd PE4 . . . . 221 C1
Fanny Hands La 1 LN8 . 59 A7
Fannystone Rd DN34 . . 191 B7
Fantail Cl 2 PE11 . . . . . 156 E2
Fantasy Island* PE25 . . 90 E3
Fantasy World* DN35 . . 192 F7
Fanthorpe La LN11 . . . . 198 A7
Faraday Cl PE7 . . . . . . 233 D6
FAR BANK DN7 . . . . 14 C8
Far Bank La DN7 . . . . . 14 C8
FARCET PE7 . . . . 231 C2
Farcet CE Prim Sch
 PE7 . . . . 231 C2
Far Comm Rd DN7 . . . . 14 A3
Fardell Rd DN16 . . . . . . 185 D7
Far Dro PE20 . . . . 124 E2
Farebrother St DN32 . . . 191 E6
Far End LN5 . . . . 94 A2
Far Field Rd 2 DN3 . . . . 14 A2
FARFORTH LN11 . . . . . . 73 D5
Far Holme La 5 NG23 . . 91 A8
Far Hurn Dro LN4 . . . . . 110 B7
Faringdon Rd DN10 . . . 189 C2
Far Ings La DN18 . . . . . 3 C1
Far Ings Nature Reserve*
 DN18 . . . . 3 D2
Far Ings Rd DN18 . . . . . 3 D1
Far La
 Coleby LN5 . . . . 93 F3
 Ludborough DN36 . . . . 48 F8
Farleigh Fields PE2 . . . . 229 D6
FARLESTHORPE LN13 . . 76 B1
Farlesthorpe Nature
 Reserve* LN13 . . . . . . 89 A7
Farlesthorpe Rd
 Alford LN13 . . . . 75 F2
 Bilsby LN13 . . . . 76 A2
 Willoughby with Sloothby
  LN13 . . . . 89 B8
Farm Cl
 2 Guinness DN15 . . . . 17 E6
 12 Kirk Sandall DN3 . . 14 A1
Farmers Gate PE12 . . . 215 B2
Farmhouse Cl 12 NG13 . 128 A6
Farmhouse Mews 11
 DN36 . . . . 195 C6
Farm La 10 DN17 . . . . . 28 D8

Farm View
 Castor PE5 . . . . 223 E8
 18 Welton LN2 . . . . . . 68 C2
Farndale Cres 5
 NG31 . . . . 211 A4
Farndale Way
 Grimsby DN31 . . . . . . 191 C2
 1 Winterton DN15 . . . . 9 A7
Farndale La 1 HU13 . . . 180 A3
Far Pasture 4 PE4 . . . . 220 F4
Farrier Rd LN6 . . . . 204 B8
Farriers Ct
 Peterborough PE2 . . . . 230 D2
 Scopwick LN4 . . . . 95 C5
Farriers Fold 13 DN9 . . 27 D5
Farriers Gate 8 NG34 . . 120 F8
Farriers Way
 Carlby PE9 . . . . 163 D3
 6 Market Rasen LN8 . . 57 F8
 2 Tattershall LN4 . . . . 207 A6
Farrier Way PE11 . . . . . 214 A1
Farringdon Cl 2 PE1 . . . 226 C1
Farrington Cres LN6 . . . 200 D1
Farrishes La DN18 . . . . 10 A8
Farrow Ave PE12 . . . . . 215 B2
Farrow Ave PE12 . . . . . 215 B2
Farrows Pond 3 DN19 . . 5 A1
Farthingales PE11 . . . . 214 C2
Farthing Ave DN15 . . . . 182 E6
Farthings Fold PE10 . . . 154 B2
Far Wharf LN6 . . . . 201 C1
Fauconbery Ave 4
 DN33 . . . . 191 C1
Faulding La DN40 . . . . . 12 B2
Faulding Way DN37 . . . 190 C6
Faulkers La PE24 . . . . . 89 E2
Favell Rd 1 LN4 . . . . . . 203 B2
Faversham Ave HU4 . . . 179 B7
Fawcett St DN17 . . . . . 197 C1
Fawsley Cl 6 LN2 . . . . . 202 E7
Fawsley Garth PE3 . . . . 225 C5
FAXFLEET DN14 . . . . . . 1 A7
Faxfleet La DN14 . . . . . 1 A7
Feale Abbey LN4 . . . . . 95 C5
Featherby Pl 7 LN5 . . . 205 B1
Feather La 8 DN19 . . . . 5 A1
Featherworks The*
 PE21 . . . . 209 E6
Felbridge Wlk PE2 . . . . 231 E6
Fellands Gate PE22 . . . 113 E3
Fellowes Gate PE7 . . . . 231 A3
Fellowes Rd PE2 . . . . . 231 A3
Felstead Rd DN34 . . . . 190 F7
Fenbridge Rd PE4 . . . . 221 A3
Fenby Cl DN37 . . . . 190 C7
Fence Bank PE34 . . . . . 161 C3
Fen Cl 2 PE13 . . . . 170 D1
Fen Ct 1 DN18 14
Fendike Bank PE14 . . . 101
Fendike La PE20 135
Fen Dro PE7 . . . . 233 D5
Fendyke End La PE22 . . 126
Fendyke La PE13 170
Feneley Cl PE7 . . . . 231 C2
Fen End La PE12 156
Fen Field Mews PE6 . . . 217
Fengate PE1 . . . . 226 C2
FENGATE PE1 226
Fen Gate PE12 157
Fengate Cl 1 LN6 204
Fengate Dro PE12 157
Fengate Mobile Home Pk
 PE1 226
Fengate Rd
 Pinchbeck PE11 214
 Walsoken PE14 170
Fengate Trad Est PE1 . . 226
FENHOUSES PE20 135
Fenhouses Dro PE20 . . 135
Fenhouses La PE20 . . . 135
Fen La
 Balderton NG24 104
 Bassingham LN5 93
 Beesby with Saleby LN13 . 76
 Conisholme LN11 50
 Dunston LN4 95
 East Keal PE23 100
 Grainthorpe LN11 49
 Lincoln LN6 205
 Long Bennington NG23 . 117
 Mablethorpe & Sutton
  LN12 64
 Maltby le Marsh LN13 . . 63
 Mareham le Fen PE22 . . 98
 North Somercotes LN11 . 50
 North Thoresby DN36 . . 36
 South Carlton LN1 67
 Tydd St Giles PE13 . . . 169
Fenland Airfield PE13 . . 168
Fenland Rd
 13 Thorne/Moorends
  DN8 15
 Wisbech PE13 170
Fenland Wlk PE12 215
Fennell Rd 6 PE11 156
Fenners Ave DN17 184
Fen Rd
 Billinghay LN4 109
 Dowsby PE10 143
 East Kirkby PE23 99
 Frampton PE20 125
 Gosberton PE11 144
 Heighington LN4 81
 Heighington/Washingborough
  LN4 203
 Holbeach PE12 215

Fen Rd *continued*
Little Hale NG34 . . . . . . 133 F8
Metheringham LN4 . . . . . 95 C4
Newton PE13 . . . . 169 E4
Owmby LN8 . . . . 55 F6
Pointon & Sempringham
　NG34 . . . . 143 D6
Ruskington NG34 . . . . . 108 F2
Stickford PE22 . . . . 100 C2
Thurlby PE10 . . . . 154 E1
Timberland LN4 . . . . 96 C1
Toynton St Peter PE23 . . 101 A4
Wisbech St Mary PE13 . . 177 E2
Fenscape* PE12 . . . . . . 157 B7
Fen Sch NG34 . . . . . . 123 C3
Fenside
Halton Holegate PE23 . . 101 C6
Toynton All Saints PE23 . 100 F4
FEN SIDE PE22 . . . . . . 100 A1
Fenside Dr 8 PE6 . . . . 174 E5
Fenside Rd
Boston PE21 . . . . 208 C6
Holland Fen with Brothertoft
　PE21 . . . . 125 C5
FENTON
Fenton LN1 . . . . 65 E3
Fenton NG23 . . . . 105 B1
Fenton Dr PE9 . . . . . . 163 E5
Fenton La DN22 . . . . . 52 C1
Fenton PI LN2 . . . . . . 234 C2
Fenton Rd
Fenton NG23 . . . . 105 B1
Stubton NG23 . . . . 118 B8
Fenton St DN15 . . . . . 183 B3
Fen View
Heighington LN4 . . . . . . 81 F4
Peterborough PE2 . . . . . 231 F6
Fenwick Ct 8 DN36 . . . 195 D1
Fenwick Rd DN33 . . . . 191 B2
Fen Wlk DN36 . . . . . . 37 C5
Ferens Art Gall* HU2 . . . 180 F6
Ferensway HU2 . . . . . 180 E7
Fernbank 2 DN9 . . . . . 27 D7
Fern Croft 10 DN9 . . . . 27 E6
Fern Ct HU13 . . . . 179 A1
Ferndale PE7 . . . . 233 D6
Ferndale CI NG33 . . . . 152 F7
Ferndown 1 DN37 . . . . 188 A1
Ferndown Dr DN40 . . . 186 D4
Fern Dr
Market Rasen LN8 . . . . . 57 D8
Pinchbeck PE11 . . . . . . 214 C7
Ferneries La 3 DN38 . . 21 B4
Fern Gr LN3 . . . . 203 D5
Fernhall CI 15 DN36 . . . 14 A2
Fernhill DN37 . . . . 190 C7
Fernie 11 PE25 . . . . . . 174 E4
Fernland CI 18 HU15 . . . 2 C5
Fernleigh Ave 4 LN4 . . . 81 A1
Fernleigh Way PE21 . . . 209 B6
Fernwood Mews DN21 . 197 F2
Ferriby High Rd HU14 . . 4 C4
Ferriby La DN33 . . . . . 191 C2
Ferry Dr
Barton-upon-Humber
　DN18 . . . . 10 E8
Hessle HU13 . . . . 178 B1
Scunthorpe DN17 . . . . . 184 E5
FERRIBY SLUICE DN18 . . 9 F7
Ferriby Sta HU14 . . . . . 3 A4
Ferry Dr HU9 . . . . 181 D7
Ferry Dr PE6 . . . . 224 D3
Ferry Hill PE5 . . . . 224 B1
Ferry La
Holland Fen with Brothertoft
　PE20 . . . . 124 D6
Newton PE13 . . . . 170 B5
North Kyme LN4 . . . . . . 109 A6
Skellingthorpe LN6 . . . . 200 C5
South Kyme LN4 . . . . . . 109 C1
Sturton le Steeple DN22 . 52 D3
Washingborough LN4 . . . 203 B2
Winteringham DN15 . . . . 2 B1
Ferry Mdws Ctry Pk*
　PE2 . . . . 229 D8
Ferry Mdws Sta PE2 . . 229 E7
Ferry Rd
Bardney LN3 . . . . 83 D1
Barrow upon Humber DN19 . 4 C1
Fiskerton LN3 . . . . 82 D6
Haxey DN9 . . . . 27 D1
Keadby with Althorpe
　DN17 . . . . 17 D4
Kingston upon Hull
　HU13 . . . . 178 E1
Langriville PE22 . . . . . . 124 D8
Scunthorpe DN15 . . . . . 182 E5
Ferry Rd W DN15 . . . . . 182 A6
Ferryside 2 LN3 . . . . . . 82 B6
Ferryside Gdns 3 LN3 . . 82 B6
Ferryview PE2 . . . . . . 229 E6
Festival Ave 3 PE25 . . . 90 D3
Feyzin Dr 40 DN18 . . . . 10 E8
Ffolkes Dr 12 PE34 . . . 161 F3
Field CI
Gosberton PE11 . . . . . . 145 B6
Laceby DN37 . . . . 23 F1
Nettleham LN2 . . . . 68 D2
Ruskington NG34 . . . . . 108 D2
Welton LN2 . . . . 68 D7
Fieldfare CI 8 DN16 . . . 185 B8
Fieldfare Croft PE21 . . 208 C6
Fieldfare Dr PE2 . . . . . 231 E6
Field Farm La 3 LN4 . . . 95 D4
Field Head DN37 . . . . . 23 E1
Fieldhouse Rd DN36 . . 193 A1
Fielding Way DN21 . . . 197 E5

Field La
Bardney LN3 . . . . 83 C5
Eastoft DN17 . . . . 7 A3
Ewerby & Evedon NG34 . 122 C6
Friskney PE22 . . . . 115 A6
Morton DN21 . . . . 197 A8
2 Normanby by Spital
　LN8 . . . . 55 F6
Strubby with Woodthorpe
　LN13 . . . . 63 C1
Wroot DN9 . . . . 26 D5
Field Rd
Billinghay LN4 . . . . 109 E6
Crowle DN17 . . . . 16 D7
Stainforth DN7 . . . . 14 C6
Thorne/Moorends DN8 . . 15 A8
Field Rise PE7 . . . . . . 233 D5
Field CI 3 DN9 . . . . . . 27 D7
Fields End DN39 . . . . . 12 B2
Fieldside
8 Blyton DN21 . . . . 41 C5
11 Crowle DN17 . . . . . . 16 D7
Epworth DN9 . . . . 27 E2
Field Side
Mareham le Fen PE22 . . . 98 F4
Thorne DN8 . . . . 15 A8
Fieldside Cres 1 PE22 . . 99 A4
Fields Rd DN9 . . . . 27 E2
Field St
6 Boston PE21 . . . . 209 A5
Kingston upon Hull HU9 . 181 B7
Field Terr PE7 . . . . 231 C2
Field View PE22 . . . . . 111 F8
Fildes St DN31 . . . . . . 191 D7
Filey CI LN6 . . . . 205 A3
Filey Rd DN32 . . . . 192 A5
FILLINGHAM DN21 . . . . 54 F4
Fillingham Cres
Cleethorpes DN35 . . . . . 192 F3
Scunthorpe DN15 . . . . . 182 B3
Fillingham La DN21 . . . 53 F3
Finch CI LN6 . . . . 204 D8
Finch Dr NG34 . . . . . . 212 B3
Finchfield PE7 . . . . . . 226 F7
Finchley Ct DN31 . . . . . 191 A8
Finchley Gn PE3 . . . . . 225 E4
Findlay Cres DN36 . . . . 195 D6
Fingle St 3 DN22 . . . . . 52 B1
Finisterre Ave PE25 . . . 206 A6
Finkell St DN10 . . . . . . 39 C1
Finkin St NG31 . . . . . . 211 A4
Finkle La 1 DN18 . . . . . 3 F1
Finkle St
Benington PE22 . . . . . . 127 A5
Stainforth DN7 . . . . 14 C7
Finney CI LN4 . . . . 207 D5
Finningley CI 9 LN6 . . . 204 D6
Finningley Rd LN6 . . . . 204 D6
Finns La NG32 . . . . . . 138 C6
Finsbury Dr 3 DN33 . . . 191 E2
Finsbury St 13 LN13 . . . 75 F2
Fir Ave PE10 . . . . 213 A5
Firbeck Ave PE25 . . . . 206 D1
Fir CI DN16 . . . . 185 A4
Fircroft NG31 . . . . 211 C1
Firdale CI 8 PE6 . . . . . 174 A5
Firebeacon La
Grainthorpe LN11 . . . . . 49 E8
Marshchapel LN11 . . . . . 37 D1
Firethorn CI 3 HU3 . . . 180 D5
Fir Hill Quarry Nature
　Reserve* LN11 . . . . . . 61 E1
Fir Rd 1 PE9 . . . . 218 D6
FIRSBY PE23 . . . . 101 F7
Firsby Cres DN33 . . . . 191 A2
First Ave
1 Fixborough Ind Est
　DN15 . . . . 7 F1
Grantham NG31 . . . . . . 211 A6
Grimsby DN33 . . . . 191 C4
6 Scampton Airfield LN1 . 67 E5
Scunthorpe DN17 . . . . . 184 C6
Spalding PE11 . . . . 214 B4
First Dro
Crowland PE6 . . . . 166 E2
Gosberton PE11 . . . . . . 144 C3
Moulton PE12 . . . . 146 E6
Peterborough PE1 . . . . . 226 D1
Firs The 6 NG34 . . . . . 108 D1
First Holme La 2 NG23 . 91 A8
First Hurn Dro LN4 . . . 110 A6
First La HU10 . . . . 179 A5
First Marsh Rd PE13 . . 170 C2
Firth Field Rd DN7 . . . . 14 F4
Firth La DN9 . . . . 26 D6
Firth Rd LN6 . . . . 234 A1
Firtree Ave LN6 . . . . . . 200 C1
Fir Tree Ave 5 LN5 . . . . 93 E8
Fir Tree CI 4 LN2 . . . . . 68 F2
Firtree Dr 8 DN20 . . . . 20 F7
Fir Tree La NG32 . . . . . 119 C5
Fir Trees The HU10 . . . 178 D6
Fish Dock Rd DN31 . . . 189 B2
Fishemore Ave HU13 . . 178 F2
Fisher CI 22 NG23 . . . . 91 D5
Fishergate PE1 . . . . . . 226 B2
Fisherman's Wharf
　DN31 . . . . 191 D8

Fishermans Wlk 2
　HU3 . . . . 180 C4
Fisher PI DN35 . . . . . . 192 D7
Fish Groom's La PE11 . 145 E6
FISHLAKE DN7 . . . . 14 D8
Fishlake Nab DN7 . . . . 14 C7
Fishmere End Rd
Sutterton PE20 . . . . 136 A4
Wigtoft PE20 . . . . 135 F3
Fishmere Gate Rd LN11 . 51 B1
Fishpond La PE12 . . . . 215 E2
Fish St 1 HU1 . . . . 180 F5
FISHTOFT PE21 . . . . . . 126 C1
Fishtoft Dro PE22 . . . . 125 C7
FISHTOFT DROVE
　PE22 . . . . 125 D8
Fishtoft Rd PE21 . . . . . 209 B3
Fishtoft Sch PE21 . . . . 126 C1
Fish Well CI 3 NG23 . . . 151 A8
Fishwick Ave 5 HU13 . . 178 E1
FISKERTON LN3 . . . . . . 82 A6
Fiskerton CE (Controlled)
　Prim Sch LN3 . . . . 82 A6
Fiskerton CI 8 DN34 . . 190 F4
Fiskerton Dr LN2 . . . . . 201 F8
Fiskerton Rd
Cherry Willingham
　LN3 . . . . 203 C4
Cherry Willingham/Reepham
　LN3 . . . . 82 B6
Fiskerton Rd E LN3 . . . 203 E4
Fiskerton Way 2
　DN31 . . . . 188 A3
Fitties La 2 DN36 . . . . . 37 C5
FITTON END PE13 . . . . 169 F3
Fitton End Rd PE13 . . . 169 F3
Fitzgerald Ct 3 LN4 . . . 151 A8
Fitzjames Ct 2 PE23 . . 101 A8
Fitzwilliam Hospl PE6 . . . 224 E2
Fitzwilliam Mews
　DN35 . . . . 192 E2
Fitzwilliam PI 6 LN4 . . . 109 F5
Fitzwilliam Rd 6 LN4 . . 219 A7
Fitzwilliam St
10 Mablethorpe/Sutton on
　Sea LN12 . . . . 64 B4
Peterborough PE1 . . . . . 226 A3
Five Arches PE2 . . . . . 229 C6
Five Bell La PE20 . . . . . 135 C4
Five House La
　Frampton PE20 . . . . . . 136 C8
　Wyberton PE21 . . . . . . 208 B1
Five La Ends NG23 . . . . 79 C8
Five Mile La LN4 . . . . . 82 B5
Flag Bsns Exchange
　PE1 . . . . 226 B1
Flag Fen Bronze Age Mus*
　PE6 . . . . 227 B3
Flag Fen Rd PE1 . . . . . 226 C4
Flag La PE12 . . . . 168 B7
Flamborough CI
　Peterborough PE1 . . . . 225 E1
　6 Skegness PE25 . . . . 206 A6
Flaminian Way 8
　NG32 . . . . 120 A2
Flarepath The DN20 . . . 21 A8
Flaxengate 4 LN2 . . . . 234 B2
Flaxland PE3 . . . . 225 A6
Flaxley Rd HU2 . . . . . . 202 E6
Flaxmill La 6 PE21 . . . . 145 C1
Flaxwell Way 12 NG34 . 121 B7
FLEDBOROUGH NG22 . . 78 A7
FLEET PE12 . . . . 159 B7
Fleetgate 8 DN18 . . . . 3 E1
FLEET HARGATE PE12 . . 159 C7
Fleet Rd
Fleet PE12 . . . . 159 B7
Holbeach PE12 . . . . 215 F2
Fleets La LN4 . . . . 54 A1
Fleets Rd LN4 . . . . 66 D7
Fleet St
Holbeach PE12 . . . . 215 E2
Lincoln LN1 . . . . 201 C4
Fleetway DN36 . . . . . . 37 A3
Fleet Way PE2 . . . . 231 B6
Fleetwood CI 2 DN33 . . 194 C7
Fleetwood Ct LE15 . . . 162 A8
Fleet Wood La Prim Sch
　PE12 . . . . 178 E2
Fleming Ave NG13 . . . . 128 B6
Fleming CI PE7 . . . . . . 233 D6
Fleming Dr
6 Boston PE21 . . . . 208 F1
8 Woodston PE2 . . . . . . 230 D8
Fleming Rd PE11 . . . . . 214 D8
Fleming Wlk HU4 . . . . . 179 D2
Fletcher CI
Kingston upon Hull
　HU13 . . . . 178 E2
3 Scunthorpe DN15 . . . . 182 C6
Fletcher Rd DN34 . . . . 190 F7
Fletcher St LN5 . . . . . . 211 A3
Fletton Ave PE2 . . . . . 231 A8
Fletton Fields PE2 . . . . 231 A7
Fletton Parkway PE2 . . 229 F2
Flinders CI 5 LN4 . . . . . 95 C4
Flinders Rd 13 PE11 . . . 184 C2
Flinders Way LN13 . . . . 203 B6
Flinders Wlk HU4 . . . . . 179 B4
Flint CI PE9 . . . . 163 D1
Flint La LN4 . . . . 54 A1
Flintham Ct 3 LN6 . . . . 160 E4
Flint House Rd PE13 . . . 147 C3
Flinton St HU3 . . . . 180 B3
FLIXBOROUGH DN15 . . . 8 B1
Flixborough Rd DN15 . . 8 B4
FLIXBOROUGH STATHER
　DN15 . . . . 8 A1

Flood Rd The DN21 . . . 197 B3
Flore CI PE3 . . . . 225 C5
Florence Ave HU13 . . . 178 F1
Florence St
Grimsby DN32 . . . . 191 E5
Lincoln LN2 . . . . 202 B3
Florence Way 4 PE6 . . . 217 C5
Florence Wright Ave 6
　LN1 . . . . 198 D4
Floriade CI 4 PE11 . . . . 214 B2
Florins Fold NG34 . . . . 132 F3
Floss La DN22 . . . . 65 B6
Flottergate Mall DN31 . 191 D7
Flour Sq DN31 . . . . 189 A1
Flowerdown Ave 5
　NG34 . . . . 120 D8
Foal Plats La LN13 . . . . 90 A8
FOCKERBY DN17 . . . . . 7 E5
Fodder Dike Bank
　Eastville PE22 . . . . . . 114 C7
　Midville PE22 . . . . 113 E7
FOLD HILL PE22 . . . . . . 115 A6
Fold Hill Rd PE22 . . . . . 114 A2
Fold La
　Moulton PE12 . . . . 157 F7
　5 Tydd St Giles PE13 . . 169 F7
Folds La 2 PE21 . . . . . . 216 B4
Folgate La PE14 . . . . . . 170 F6
FOLKINGHAM NG34 . . . 142 C8
Folkingham CI 11 LN6 . . 204 D8
Folkingham Rd
　Billingborough NG34 . . 133 A1
　1 Morton PE10 . . . . . . 154 C7
　Pickworth NG34 . . . . . 142 A8
FOLKSWORTH PE7 . . . . 232 D1
Folksworth Rd PE7 . . . 232 E1
Folly CI PE7 . . . . 233 C5
Folly La
　Branston & Mere LN4 . . 81 C2
　Hough-on-the-Hill NG32 . 118 F5
　North Kelsey LN7 . . . . 32 C5
　North Scarle NG23 . . . . 91 D8
　West Fen PE22 . . . . . . 99 E1
Folly's Dro PE13 . . . . . 177 F3
Fontwell Cres 9 LN6 . . 205 A5
Fontwell Gdns 2 PE7 . . 219 B5
Foote's Dro PE12 . . . . 167 C8
Forbes Rd PE21 . . . . . 209 C4
Ford CI PE7 . . . . 233 E6
Fordham Dr LN1 . . . . . 201 C7
FORDINGTON LN13 . . . 88 C6
Ford La
　8 Ibaldstow DN20 . . . . 30 F5
　Morton PE10 . . . . 154 C6
Ford's Ave LN7 . . . . . . 32 D5
Ford Way DN41 . . . . . . 23 F5
Foredyke Prim Sch HU9 . 5 D8
Fore La PE20 . . . . 135 A5
Foreman Way 1 PE6 . . . 166 E1
Forest Ave 1 PE20 . . . . 213 B5
Forest CE Prim Sch
　PE7 . . . . 231 C2
Forest Dale PE21 . . . . . 208 F7
Forest Dro DN36 . . . . . 193 B1
Forest Dro PE6 . . . . . . 166 C2
Forge CI
　Freiston PE22 . . . . 126 C4
　South Kelsey LN7 . . . . 32 A1
Forge Cres
　3 Pinchbeck PE11 . . . . 156 E8
　Ulceby DN39 . . . . 12 A1
Forge Ct 12 PE6 . . . . . 217 A6
Forge End PE7 . . . . 229 A4
Forge La LN8 . . . . 56 F8
Forge Way DN36 . . . . . 195 C3
Forkedale DN18 . . . . . 10 E8
Forlander PI LN11 . . . . 198 D6
Forman's La NG34 . . . . 132 F6
Formby's La HU4 . . . . . 211 C7
Forrester St 1 DN20 . . . 196 B3
Forrington PE11 . . . . . . 66 E2
Forstead Hill NG33 . . . . 153 B5
Forster St DN21 . . . . . 197 C5
Forsyth Cres 6 PE25 . . 206 C2
Forsythia Ave 28 DN41 . 23 F5
Forsythia Dr DN33 . . . . 191 C4
Fortescue CI 11 LN4 . . 207 A5
Fortuna Prim Sch LN6 . 204 B7
Fortuna Way DN37 . . . 190 C7
Forty Acre HU10 . . . . . 178 F7
Forty Acre Rd PE1 . . . . 226 D2
Forty Foot La
　Humberside Airport
　　DN20 . . . . 21 F6
　Old Leake PE22 . . . . . . 113 D3
Forty Stps HU10 . . . . . 178 F7
Forum The LN6 . . . . . . 204 F3
Forum Way 7 NG34 . . . 212 F3
FOSDYKE BRIDGE
　PE12 . . . . 146 E7
Fossbank LN1 . . . . 201 D3
Fossdyke Gdns 10 LN1 . 66 C2
Fosse CI 3 PE6 . . . . . . 164 E5
Fosse CI LN6 . . . . 204 D8
Fosse Dr LN6 . . . . 205 A3
Fosse La
　Thistleton LE15 . . . . . 151 B1
　Thorpe on the Hill NG23 . 92 E7
Fosseway 4 DN21 . . . . 197 F5
Fosse Prim Sch
　LN6 . . . . 204 F2

Foss St LN1 . . . . 201 D3
Foster CI 2 LN4 . . . . . . 96 C1
Foster Rd
　27 Collingham NG23 . . 91 D5
　2 Thorne/Moorends
　　DN8 . . . . 15 A8
　Woodston PE2 . . . . . . 230 D8
Fosters CI 3 LN5 . . . . . 107 A8
Foster's Dro PE10 . . . . 155 A3
Foster's Gdns 1 LN4 . . 82 B1
Foster St
　3 Boston PE21 . . . . . . 209 A5
　Heckington NG34 . . . . 122 E3
　Lincoln LN5 . . . . 201 E1
FOSTON NG32 . . . . 117 F2
Foston by Pass NG32 . . 117 F1
Foston Cres LN6 . . . . . 204 F7
Foston La NG32 . . . . . . 128 F7
Foston Rd NG31 . . . . . 210 E3
FOTHERBY LN11 . . . . . 49 A3
Fotherby Rd 5 DN37 . . 184 F4
Fotherby St 3 DN31 . . . 189 A1
Fothergill Dr 17 DN21 . 14 A2
FOUL ANCHOR PE13 . . . 170 D8
Foundry La
　11 Spalding PE11 . . . . 214 D4
　12 Thorne/Moorends
　　DN8 . . . . 15 A8
Foundry Rd
　Bucknall LN10 . . . . . . 84 B3
　Ryhall PE9 . . . . 163 C2
　Stamford PE9 . . . . 219 A5
Foundry Sh Ctr The
　DN15 . . . . 183 B4
Foundry St LN9 . . . . . . 199 C4
Fountain CI
　Kingston upon Hull
　　HU13 . . . . 178 C3
　5 Waltham DN37 . . . . 194 C5
Fountain Hill DN10 . . . . 39 E3
Fountain Hill Rd DN10 . 39 E4
Fountain La 13 PE21 . . 208 F5
Fountain PI 10 PE21 . . . 208 F5
Fountains Ave DN37 . . 188 A1
Fountains PI PE6 . . . . . 175 B1
Fountain St
　2 Caistor LN7 . . . . . . 33 B4
　Kingston upon Hull HU3 . 180 D6
Four Acre CI HU10 . . . . 178 C6
Four Chimneys Cres
　PE7 . . . . 230 C2
Fourfields CE Prim Sch
　PE7 . . . . 136 A2
Fourfields Com Prim Sch
　PE7 . . . . 233 E6
FOUR GOTES PE13 . . . . 170 B7
Fourth Ave
　2 Fixborough Ind Est
　　DN15 . . . . 8 A1
　Grantham NG31 . . . . . 211 F6
　3 Scampton Airfield LN1 . 67 E5
　Scunthorpe DN17 . . . . 184 C6
Fourth Dro
　Gosberton PE11 . . . . . 144 B4
　Peterborough PE1 . . . . 226 F3
Fourways 6 DN36 . . . . 36 D4
Fowler CI LN11 . . . . . . 198 D4
Fowler Rd DN16 . . . . . 185 B8
Foxby Hill DN21 . . . . . . 197 E2
Foxby La DN21 . . . . . . 197 F2
Fox CI
　Boston PE21 . . . . 208 C6
　Little Coates DN34 . . . 190 F6
Fox Covert
　2 Aubourn Haddington &
　　South Hykeham LN6 . . 93 A8
　North Hykeham LN6 . . . 204 B1
　Sudbrooke LN2 . . . . . . 69 A2
Fox Covert La DN10 . . . 40 A4
Foxcovert Rd PE6 . . . . 227 D5
Fox Ct 1 LN17 . . . . 16 C8
Foxdale PE1 . . . . 225 F7
Fox Dale PE9 . . . . 218 F6
Foxe End 10 LN12 . . . . 64 B3
Foxendale Hill LN9 . . . . 72 F1
Foxes Low Rd PE12 . . . 215 F2
Foxfield CI LN6 . . . . . . 200 A5
Foxglove CI
　Brigg DN20 . . . . 196 B4
　1 Spilsby PE23 . . . . . . 101 A8
Foxglove Gdns DN34 . . 190 F6
Foxglove Rd
　16 Market Rasen LN8 . . 57 D8
　1 Stamford PE9 . . . . . 218 C7
Foxgloves PE6 . . . . . . 217 D6
Foxglove Way 8 LN5 . . 205 C2
Fox Headings PE12 . . . 158 E2
Foxhill DN37 . . . . 190 C7
Foxhill Rd HU6 . . . . . . 15 B7
Foxhills Ind Pk DN15 . . 182 F7
Foxhills Rd DN15 . . . . . 182 E5
Foxhills Sch & Tech Coll
　DN15 . . . . 182 E5
Foxhole La PE12 . . . . . 126 D3
Foxley CI PE4 . . . . 221 C8
Foxley Ct 4 PE10 . . . . . 213 C7
Fox St DN15 . . . . 182 F3
Foyle CI LN5 . . . . 205 D2
Fracknall's Row 3
　PE21 . . . . 208 E6
Framlingham Rd PE7 . . 231 F5
FRAMPTON PE20 . . . . . 136 F6
Frampton Bank PE20 . . 136 B8
Frampton La PE20 . . . . 124 E2

Frampton Marsh Nature
  Reserve* PE20 . . . . 137 D5
Frampton Pl PE21 . . . . . . 208 D4
Frampton Roads PE20 . . 136 F6
Frances Askew Prim Sch
  HU4 . . . . 179 F4
Frances Ct 3 DN37 . . . . 194 C5
Frances St DN15 . . . . 183 A3
Francis Bernard Cl 4
  PE21 . . . . 208 D3
Francis Chichester Wlk
  DN21 . . . . 197 F3
Francis Gdns PE11 . . . . . 225 F8
Francis La LN9 . . . . 199 C4
Francis St
  Kingston upon Hull
  HU2 . . . . 180 F7
  Lincoln LN1 . . . . 234 B4
  14 Spalding PE11 . . . . . 214 D4
Franklin Wlk 6 PE12 . . 158 B6
Frankland Cl 1 DN20 . . 196 F6
Frankland Pl DN35 . . . . . 192 D7
Franklin Ave PE25 . . . . . 206 D1
Franklin Cl
  Boston PE21 . . . . 208 C4
  2 Metheringham LN4 . . .95 C4
Franklin Coll DN34 . . . . 191 B5
Franklin Cres
  Peterborough PE1 . . . . . 226 E6
  Scunthorpe DN16 . . . . . 185 E6
  11 Sleaford NG34 . . . . . 212 D5
Franklin Dr PE11 . . . . . . 214 B2
Franklin Gdns 11 PE23 . 101 A8
Franklin Rd 3 DN21 . . . . .29 C4
Franklin St HU9 . . . . 181 C8
Franklin Way
  Humberside Airport
  DN38 . . . . .21 F5
  North Greetwell LN3 . . .203 B6
Frank Perkins Parkway
  PE1 . . . . 226 E6
Frank Perkins Way
  PE1 . . . . 226 D3
Franks Cl 2 PE20 . . . . . 136 D5
Franks La PE13 . . . . 169 F5
Frank Swaby Ct LN5 . . . 205 E6
Frank Walsham Ct
  DN32 . . . . 192 A8
Frank Whittle Cl 1
  NG34 . . . . 120 E8
Frank Wright Ct 4
  LN2 . . . . 202 C7
Fraserburgh Way 2
  PE2 . . . . 229 D4
Fraser Cl PE6 . . . . 217 D5
Fraser St 2 DN32 . . . . . 191 F7
Frederica Rd 12 PE25 . . 103 E4
Frederick Gough Sch
  DN16 . . . . 185 C4
Frederick St
  Cleethorpes DN35 . . . . . 192 E6
  Grimsby DN31 . . . . 191 D8
  Lincoln LN2 . . . . 202 C3
Frederick Ward Way
  DN31 . . . . 191 D7
Freehold St HU3 . . . . . . 180 D7
Freeman Ave 4 HU15 . . . .2 C5
Freeman Cl 10 PE8 . . . . 172 B1
Freeman Ct DN36 . . . . . 195 E2
Freeman Rd LN6 . . . . . . 204 D3
Freemans La 6 DN20 . . . .10 C2
Freeman's La DN22 . . . . .52 A2
Freeman St DN32 . . . . . 191 E8
Freeman Way 9 DN22 . 189 B1
Freeport Wharf DN31 . . 191 E8
Freer Gdns LN11 . . . . . . 198 E6
Freeschool La LN2 . . . . . 234 B2
Freesia Way PE7 . . . . . . 233 F6
Freeston St DN35 . . . . . 192 B8
Freetown Way HU2 . . . . 180 E7
Freightliner Rd HU3 . . . 179 F7
FREISTON PE22 . . . . 126 D2
Freiston Ctr for
  Environmental Ed*
  PE22 . . . . 126 D3
Freiston Rd PE22 . . . . . . 209 B5
FREISTON SHORE
  PE22 . . . . 126 F1
French Dro PE6 . . . . 175 E7
French's Rd PE14 . . . . . . 170 B5
Fresh Fields 8 HU15 . . . .2 C5
Freshney Bog Nature
  Reserve* DN37 . . . . . . 190 E7
Freshney Dr 1 DN31 . . 191 C8
Freshney Pl Sh Ctr
  DN32 . . . . 191 D7
Freshney Way PE4 . . . . . 208 B3
Freston PE4 . . . . 221 D2
Freya Croft DN33 . . . . . 191 B2
Friars Gate PE21 . . . . . . 208 E4
Friars La LN2 . . . . 234 B2
Friars Rd DN17 . . . . 184 E6
Friar Way PE21 . . . . 208 F6
Friary Rd 1 PE24 . . . . . 104 A4
FRIESTHORPE LN3 . . . . . .57 A2
Friest La 11 PE20 . . . . . 135 A4
Frieston NG32 . . . . 119 B6
Frieston Heath La
  NG32 . . . . 119 D6
Frieston Rd NG32 . . . . . 119 B6
Frieston Shore Nature
  Reserve* PE22 . . . . . . 127 A1
Frinkley La
  Honington NG32 . . . . . . 119 B2
  Hougham NG32 . . . . . . 118 D2

Frisby Cl PE6 . . . . 164 D4
FRISKNEY PE22 . . . . 115 A6
Friskney Decoy Wood
  Nature Reserve*
  PE22 . . . . 115 A8
FRISKNEY EAUDYKE
  PE22 . . . . .115 B7
FRITH BANK PE21 . . . . . 125 D5
Frith Bank PE21 . . . . . . 125 D6
Friths La PE20 . . . . 125 B1
FRITHVILLE PE22 . . . . . . 112 D1
Frithville Prim Sch
  PE22 . . . . 112 D1
Frithville Rd PE22 . . . . . 113 A1
Frobisher Ave DN32 . . . 192 B6
FRODINGHAM DN16 . . . 183 C2
Frodingham Footpath 2
  DN15 . . . . 183 B3
Frodingham Inf Sch
  DN16 . . . . 183 B2
Frodingham Rd DN15 . . 183 A4
Frodingham S Rd
  DN16 . . . . 183 D2
Frodsham St 8 HU9 . . . . .5 D8
FROGNALL PE6 . . . . 165 D1
Frognall PE6 . . . . 165 D1
Frog's Abbey Gate
  PE12 . . . . 158 E4
Frome Cl LN6 . . . . 204 D5
Front Rd
  Tydd St Mary PE13 . . . . 160 D1
  Wisbech St Mary PE13 . 177 D6
Front St
  Alkborough DN15 . . . . . . .8 C8
  Barnby in the Willows
  NG24 . . . . 104 F3
  Dunston LN4 . . . . .95 C5
  East Stockwith DN21 . . . .40 B5
  Elsham DN20 . . . . .20 F7
  Gainsborough DN21 . . . 197 B7
  4 Grasby DN38 . . . . . . .32 E7
  Normanby by Spital LN8 . .55 E7
  South Clifton NG23 . . . . .78 C5
  Tealby LN8 . . . . .46 C1
  Ulceby DN39 . . . . .12 A1
Frost Cl DN15 . . . . .2 A1
Frostley Gate PE12 . . . . 158 F3
Frusher Ave DN33 . . . . . 191 C3
Fryston 28 HU15 . . . . .2 C6
Fuchsia Croft 2 DN15 . . 182 F2
Fuchsia Dr HU4 . . . . 179 C6
FULBECK NG32 . . . . 106 C1
Fulbeck Rd DN16 . . . . . . 185 C6
Fulbridge Rd PE4 . . . . . . 221 A3
Fulbridge Rd PE4 . . . . . . 225 F7
Fulford Ct NG31 . . . . . . 211 D8
Fulford Cres
  Kingston upon Hull
  HU10 . . . . 179 A8
  8 New Holland DN19 . . . .4 E2
Fulford Way PE25 . . . . . 206 C6
Fulham Pk 1 DN33 . . . . 191 B2
Fulham Rd PE4 . . . . 225 E4
Fuller St DN35 . . . . 192 D8
Fulmar Dr LN11 . . . . 198 C8
Fulmar Rd LN6 . . . . 204 D8
Fulmen Cl LN1 . . . . 201 C7
FULNETBY LN8 . . . . .69 F6
Fulney Cl PE11 . . . . 157 B6
Fulney Dro PE22 . . . . . . 157 B3
Fulney La PE12 . . . . 157 B6
FULSTOW LN11 . . . . .49 B8
Fulstow Gr 5 DN33 . . . . 191 B3
Fulstow Prim Sch LN11 . . .49 B8
Fulstow Rd LN2 . . . . 202 B8
Fundrey Rd PE13 . . . . . . 170 E1
Fun Farm* PE12 . . . . . . 157 D7
Furlongs La
  Belchford LN9 . . . . .73 B1
  Old Leake PE22 . . . . 114 A1
Furlongs Rd LN12 . . . . . .77 A8
Furlongs The 17 LN8 . . . .57 D8
Furndown Ct LN6 . . . . . 204 B7
Furniss Ct 2 DN18 . . . . . .10 E8
Furrow Cl 18 LN2 . . . . . . .68 D6
Further Old Gate PE12 . 158 D5
Fury Ave LN11 . . . . .62 B6
Furze Hill Nature Reserve*
  PE23 . . . . .87 A3
Furze La LN11 . . . . .62 A5
Furze Ride PE1 . . . . 226 B8
Fussey Gdns PE20 . . . . . .10 C1
Fydell Cres PE21 . . . . . . 208 E4
Fydell Ct PE21 . . . . 208 E6
Fydell St PE21 . . . . 208 E5
Fyson Way PE20 . . . . . . 136 C6

G

Gables The PE10 . . . . . . 213 C2
Gabriel Cres LN2 . . . . . . 202 E6
Gadd's La PE13 . . . . 170 A1
Gainas Ave DN21 . . . . . 197 C6
GAINSBOROUGH DN21 . 197 B4
Gainsborough Central Sta
  DN21 . . . . 197 C4
Gainsborough Coll
  DN21 . . . . 197 C5
Gainsborough Gdns 2
  LN6 . . . . 205 B7
Gainsborough La DN20 . . .30 F8
Gainsborough Lea Rd Sta
  DN21 . . . . 197 D1
Gainsborough Leisure Ctr

Gainsborough Model
  Railway* 15 DN21 . . . . 197 D3
Gainsborough Old Hall*
  DN21 . . . . 197 C5
Gainsborough Rd
  Blyton DN21 . . . . .41 B4
  Bole DN22 . . . . .52 A6
  Girton NG23 . . . . .78 C2
  32 Kirton in Lindsey DN21 . .30 B1
  Kirton in Lindsey DN21 . . .42 D8
  Little Casterton PE9 . . . . 218 F7
  Middle Rasen LN8 . . . . . .57 B7
  Saundby DN22 . . . . .52 B7
  Saxilby with Ingleby LN1 . .66 D2
  Scotter DN21 . . . . .29 B3
  Sturton le Steeple DN22 . .52 B3
  West Rasen LN8 . . . . . . .57 A7
  Willingham DN21 . . . . . . .54 F3
  6 Winthorpe NG24 . . . . 104 B7
  Wiseton DN10 . . . . .39 A1
Gainsthorpe Rd 2 DN21 . .30 C4
Gainsthorpe Rd W
  DN21 . . . . .30 C4
Gallagher Ret Pk
  DN15 . . . . 182 A3
Gallamore Ct 5 LN8 . . . .57 C8
Gallamore La LN8 . . . . . .57 C8
Gallands Cl 11 HU14 . . . . .3 B7
Galletly Cl PE10 . . . . 213 D6
Galley Ct HU9 . . . . 181 C6
GALLEY HILL LN13 . . . . . .75 E6
Gallions Cl 2 PE4 . . . . . 221 B1
Galway Cl 2 PE11 . . . . . 214 A5
Gamlyn Cl 1 PE11 . . . . . 214 D2
Gannet Ct 3 NG31 . . . . 210 E2
Gannocks Cl PE2 . . . . . . 229 F5
Gannocks The PE2 . . . . . 229 F5
Ganton Sch HU10 . . . . . 179 A7
Ganton Way
  Harrowby Est NG31 . . . 211 E7
  Kingston upon Hull HU10 . 178 F8
Garbutt Pl DN35 . . . . . . 193 A4
Garden Cl PE9 . . . . 218 E6
Garden Dr DN36 . . . . . . 195 C7
Garden End Rd PE1 . . . . 226 B6
Gardeners Wlk PE21 . . . 208 D2
Gardenfield LN6 . . . . . . 200 B3
Gardenia Dr DN17 . . . . . 184 F1
Garden St
  5 Brigg DN20 . . . . 196 C3
  Grimsby DN31 . . . . 191 D7
Gardens The
  6 Crowland PE6 . . . . . . 166 F1
  Horncastle LN9 . . . . 199 C3
Gardiner Ave 2 NG24 . . 104 C1
Garfield Cl LN1 . . . . 201 D8
Garfield St DN21 . . . . . . 197 C5
Garfield View LN1 . . . . . 201 D8
Garfit's La PE21 . . . . 208 D1
Garford La 8 PE9 . . . . . 171 D3
Garibaldi St 3 DN32 . . . 189 B1
Garmston St LN1 . . . . . . 234 B3
Garner's La PE34 . . . . . . 161 A4
Garner St DN32 . . . . 191 E6
Garnet Gr 6 HU3 . . . . . 180 A4
Garnett St DN35 . . . . . . 192 D8
GARNSGATE PE12 . . . . . 159 E5
Garnsgate Rd PE12 . . . . 216 A5
Garratt Rd 7 PE9 . . . . . 219 B4
Garrick Cl LN5 . . . . 205 C3
Garrick La DN36 . . . . . . 195 C7
Garrick Wlk PE21 . . . . . 231 B7
Garrison Rd HU9 . . . . . . 181 C6
Garth La DN31 . . . . 191 D8
GARTHORPE
  Garthorpe and Fockerby
  DN17 . . . . .7 F6
  Garthorpe LE14 . . . . . . 150 A4
Garthorpe Rd DN17 . . . . .7 C4
Garth Specl Sch The
  PE11 . . . . 214 E5
Garth The HU10 . . . . . . 179 A4
Garthway 7 DN36 . . . . . 195 D2
Garton Gr
  3 Grimsby DN32 . . . . . 192 A5
  3 Kingston upon Hull
  HU9 . . . . 179 C7
Garton St PE1 . . . . 226 A5
Gartree Com Sch The
  LN4 . . . . 207 B5
Gascoigne 3 PE4 . . . . . 220 E5
Gashouse La 3 DN9 . . . . .28 A3
Gas House La PE12 . . . . 160 E4
Gas La
  2 Navenby/Wellingore
  LN5 . . . . 107 A8
  Stamford PE9 . . . . 219 C5
Gas St
  3 Horncastle LN9 . . . . . 199 C3
  10 Stamford PE9 . . . . . 219 C5
GATE BURTON LN1 . . . . . .53 B2
Gatehouse Rd DN19 . . . . .11 F7
Gateley Cl LN11 . . . . .49 B7
Gateroom La PE22 . . . . . 114 E3
Gate Way DN31 . . . . 188 E2
Gateway The 4 NG24 . . 104 A4
Gatewood La DN22 . . . . . .14 E1
Gatram Rd PE24 . . . . .90 D6
Gaunt Cl 5 PE12 . . . . . . 157 B6
Gauntlet Dro PE20 . . . . 134 F6
Gauntlet Rd
  3 Bicker PE20 . . . . 135 A4
  Grimoldby LN11 . . . . . . .62 B6
Gaunt St LN5 . . . . 234 A1
GAUTBY LN8 . . . . .84 B7
Gautry La DN9 . . . . .28 A4

Gavel St PE7 . . . . 233 C8
Gayle Rd LN4 . . . . 110 E8
Gaysfield Rd 6 PE21 . . . 126 C1
Gayton Ct PE3 . . . . 225 C5
Gayton Ct PE3 . . . . 225 C5
GAYTON ENGINE LN12 . . .63 C6
GAYTON LE MARSH
  LN13 . . . . .62 F3
GAYTON LE WOLD LN11 . . .59 E4
Gayton Rd DN35 . . . . . . 193 A3
Gazeley Gdns PE7 . . . . . 231 B2
Geddington Rd PE2 . . . . 230 E8
GEDNEY PE12 . . . . 159 D7
GEDNEY BROADGATE
  PE12 . . . . 159 D5
Gedney Church End Prim
  Sch PE12 . . . . 159 D7
Gedney Cl
  13 Bicker PE20 . . . . . . 135 A4
  Grimsby DN37 . . . . 190 C8
GEDNEY DROVE END
  PE12 . . . . 149 A4
GEDNEY DYKE PE12 . . . 148 B1
GEDNEY HILL PE12 . . . . 168 D2
Gedney Hill Gate PE12 . 168 F7
Gedney Rd PE12 . . . . . . 216 A6
Gee St HU3 . . . . 180 C5
GEESTON PE9 . . . . 171 A2
Gelder Beck Rd DN17 . . . .29 D6
Gelder's La PE12 . . . . . . 158 A1
GELSTON NG32 . . . . 118 F4
Gelston Rd NG32 . . . . . . 119 A4
Gemshock Cl 3 HU4 . . . 179 D2
Genesis Way
  Great Coates DN37 . . . . .24 B6
  Pyewipe DN37 . . . . 188 A3
Geneva Ave LN2 . . . . . . 202 B6
Geneva St PE1 . . . . 226 A3
Geoff Moulder Leisure
  Complex* PE21 . . . . . . 209 A4
George Ave
  Gedney PE12 . . . . 148 F4
  4 Keadby DN17 . . . . . . .17 D5
  Skegness PE25 . . . . 206 B3
George Butler Cl 23
  DN37 . . . . 190 F8
George Farmer Tech &
  Language Coll PE12 . . 215 D3
George Janney Ct 24
  DN32 . . . . 189 C1
George Mews 2 LN7 . . . . .33 B4
George Sh Ctr The
  NG31 . . . . 211 A4
George St
  2 Barton-upon-Humber
  DN18 . . . . .10 F8
  Boston PE21 . . . . 208 E4
  Bourne PE10 . . . . 213 D5
  Broughton DN20 . . . . . . .19 D3
  Cleethorpes DN35 . . . . . 192 F5
  Gainsborough DN21 . . . 197 B6
  Grantham NG31 . . . . . . 211 B4
  Grimsby DN31 . . . . 191 D7
  Helpringham NG34 . . . . 133 D7
  5 Keadby DN17 . . . . . . .17 D5
  11 Kirton in Lindsey DN21 . .30 B1
  Lincoln LN5 . . . . 234 C1
  Louth LN11 . . . . 198 B5
  Mablethorpe/Sutton on Sea
  LN12 . . . . .76 F4
  1 Market Rasen LN8 . . . .57 D8
  Peterborough PE2 . . . . . 230 F8
  Scunthorpe DN15 . . . . . 183 A4
  Sleaford NG34 . . . . 212 C3
Georgette Ct 7
  PE11 . . . . 214 B5
George Yd 5 HU1 . . . . . 181 A6
Georgian Ct
  Peterborough PE1 . . . . . 225 E1
  6 Spalding PE11 . . . . . 214 D3
Georgina Ct 27 DN18 . . . .10 E8
Gerald's Cl LN12 . . . . . . 202 B5
German's La PE34 . . . . . 161 D2
Gerrard Mews LN4 . . . . 203 D1
Gershwin Ave HU4 . . . . 179 B4
Gertrude St DN32 . . . . . 191 E5
Gervase St DN15 . . . . . . 183 A3
Gibbeson St 5 LN5 . . . . 205 E8
Gibbet La LN8 . . . . .57 A5
Giblin Cotts DN35 . . . . . 182 E5
Gibraltar Hill LN1 . . . . . 234 A3
Gibraltar La 2 DN37 . . . . .23 F1
Gibraltar Point National
  Nature Reserve*
  PE24 . . . . 103 E2
Gibraltar Point Visitor Ctr*
  PE24 . . . . 116 D4
Gibraltar Rd
  Croft PE24 . . . . 103 D1
  5 Hemswell Cliff DN21 . . .55 A8
Mablethorpe/Sutton on Sea
  LN12 . . . . .76 F4
  Seacroft PE24 . . . . 116 D5
Gibson Cl
  Branston LN4 . . . . .81 E2
  1 Sleaford NG34 . . . . . 212 B6
Gibson Gn LN6 . . . . .92 E5
Gibson La LN4 . . . . .95 C6
Gibson Pl 1 PE25 . . . . . 206 A5
Gibson Rd 8 PE25 . . . . . .26 A8
Gibsons Gdn 2 LN11 . . . .50 F7
Giddings Cl PE2 . . . . 229 F4
Gilbert Dr PE21 . . . . 208 A1

Gilberts Gr 4 PE25 . . . . 206 D8
Gilbert Sutcliffe Ct
  DN35 . . . . 192 A2
Gilbey Rd DN31 . . . . 188 D1
Gildale PE4 . . . . 221 B4
Gildenburgh Ave PE1 . . 226 D5
Gilder Way PE21 . . . . . . 209 F2
Gildesburgh Rd LN4 . . . 203 B3
Giles Sch & 6th Form Ctr
  The PE22 . . . . 114 A1
Giles St DN15 . . . . 192 E6
Gillatts Cl 1 DN20 . . . . 196 F7
Gill Ct DN33 . . . . 191 B2
Gillett St HU3 . . . . 180 B4
Gilliatt St DN15 . . . . 183 A4
Gilmores La 18 NG24 . . 104 C1
Gilmorton Dr PE1 . . . . . 226 D7
Gilpin Cl PE10 . . . . 213 E2
Gilpin St PE1 . . . . 225 E6
Gimmel's Gate PE12 . . . 216 C1
GIPSEY BRIDGE PE22 . . 124 F8
Gipsy Bridge Prim Sch
  PE22 . . . . 125 A8
Gipsy Dro
  Friskney PE22 . . . . 114 D7
  Langriville PE22 . . . . . . 124 F8
Gipsy La
  Long Bennington
  Prim Sch PE12 . . . . . . 216 A8
  Holton le Moor LN7 . . . . .32 C1
  Osgodby LN8 . . . . .45 D3
  Owersby LN7 . . . . .44 F8
  Owston Ferry DN9 . . . . . .40 C8
  South Kelsey LN7 . . . . . . .32 C1
  Swineshead PE20 . . . . . 124 A1
  Tydd St Mary PE13 . . . . 160 A2
  Wrangle PE22 . . . . 114 D2
GIPSYVILLE HU4 . . . . . . 179 E3
Girdlestone Wlk 2
  PE6 . . . . 166 F1
GIRSBY LN8 . . . . .59 C6
Girsby La LN8 . . . . .59 B6
GIRTON NG23 . . . . .78 C1
Girton Cl 3 DN16 . . . . . 185 B4
Girton La NG23 . . . . .78 B1
Girton Rd DN17 . . . . .7 C6
Girton Way 3 PE9 . . . . . 219 A7
Gisburn Rd HU13 . . . . . 178 F2
Glade The 8 LN2 . . . . . . .77 A7
Gladiator Rd LN11 . . . . . .62 B6
Gladstone Cotts DN21 . . 197 B8
Gladstone Dr 1 DN16 . . 183 C1
Gladstone Prim Sch
  PE25 . . . . 225 F5
Gladstone St
  Bourne PE10 . . . . 213 C6
  Gainsborough DN21 . . . 197 C5
  Kingston upon Hull HU3 . 180 C6
  Peterborough PE1 . . . . . 225 F3
  NG31 . . . . 211 A5
Glaisdale Gdns NG31 . . 211 B8
Glaisdale Gr HU9 . . . . . 181 F8
Glaisdale Rd 3 DN16 . . 185 D5
Glamis Gdns PE3 . . . . . 225 B2
Glamis Pl LN11 . . . . 198 B5
Glamis Rd HU13 . . . . . . 178 F2
Glanford Gr 12 DN19 . . . .11 D8
Glanford Pk (Scunthorpe
  United FC) DN15 . . . . . 182 A2
Glanford Rd
  Brigg DN20 . . . . 196 D3
  Scunthorpe DN17 . . . . . 184 F3
Glamora Way DN15 . . . 182 B3
Glanville Ave DN17 . . . . 184 F8
Glanville Cres 2 DN17 . 184 F8
Glasgow St HU3 . . . . . . 180 A5
Glastonbury Cl 20 PE6 . 175 A1
Glatton Dr PE2 . . . . 231 D6
Gleanings The 5 LN5 . . 107 B8
Glebe Ave PE25 . . . . . . 229 C4
Glebe Cl
  Burton upon Stather
  DN15 . . . . .8 A5
  3 Donington on Bain
  LN11 . . . . .59 E1
Gorefield PE13 . . . . 169 E3
Holton le Clay DN36 . . . 195 C3
Humberston DN36 . . . . . .36 C8
  8 Ingham LN1 . . . . .54 F2
Scopwick LN4 . . . . .95 C1
  1 Sibsey PE22 . . . . 113 B1
Sleaford NG34 . . . . 212 A2
  2 Spalding PE11 . . . . . 214 A4
Glebe Ct PE2 . . . . 231 B8
Glebe Gdns 2 PE6 . . . . 175 B8
Glebe Rd
  Brigg DN20 . . . . 196 C4
  Cleethorpes DN35 . . . . . 192 E6
  Grimsby DN33 . . . . 191 E1
  Humberston DN36 . . . . . .36 C7
  Peterborough PE2 . . . . . 231 A8
  Scunthorpe DN15 . . . . . 183 B4
  Thorne/Moorends DN8 . . .15 B8
  Wymondham LE14 . . . . 150 B1
Glebe Ret Pk DN15 . . . . 183 B4
Glebe The
  Sturton by Stow LN1 . . . .66 D8
  Upton DN21 . . . . .53 D5
Glebe View 1 PE6 . . . . . 217 B6
Glebe Way
  Barton-upon-Humber
  DN18 . . . . .11 A8
  8 Sutterton PE20 . . . . . 136 A2
Glebe Wlk 18 NG34 . . . 167 B8
Gleedale LN6 . . . . 204 F1
Gleed Ave PE11 . . . . 134 E2
Gleed Boys Sch PE11 . . 214 F4

Gleeds Girl's Tech Coll The
PE11. . . . . .214 F3
Glemsford Rise 2 PE2. . 230 C7
Glenarm Cres 7 LN5. . . 205 D3
Glen Ave 4 PE11. . . . . . .145 B1
Glenbank Cl LN6. . . . . . .204 F3
Glen Cl NG33 . . . . 153 A1
Glencoe Cl 2 DN7. . . . . . .14 D4
Glencoe St HU3 . . . . . . .179 F6
Glencoe Way PE2. . . . . 229 D3
Glen Cres
  7 Essendine PE9 . . . . . 163 D3
  Stamford PE9. . . . . 219 C7
Glendale PE2. . . . . 229 D6
Glendon Cl 5 LN5. . . . . 205 D3
Glen Dr PE21. . . . . .208 B4
Gleneagles
  Grantham NG31. . . . . . 211 D8
  Peterborough PE2. . . . . 229 F6
  10 Waltham DN37. . . . . 194 C4
Gleneagles Cl 3 PE9 . . . 218 E6
Gleneagles Cres 6 DN19. . 4 E2
Gleneagles
  Skegness PE25 . . . . . . 206 D6
  12 Woodhall Spa LN10 . . . .97 C5
GLENEAGLES ESTATE
  PE25. . . . . 206 D6
Gleneagles Gr 4 LN4. . . 203 D1
Glenfield Rd DN37. . . . . 190 D8
Glen Gdns 2 PE11. . . . . 145 E3
Glen Hall Rise 10 DN19. . . .11 C8
Glenham Dr HU10. . . . . .178 F7
Glen Ave 3 PE11. . . . . . 214 C4
Glen Rd
  Castle Bytham NG33 . . . . 152 D1
  Counthorpe & Creeton
  NG33. . . . . 153 A2
  13 Wittering PE8. . . . . . 172 B1
Glenrock Pk HU15 . . . . 2 B6
Glenside NG33. . . . . . . .152 C1
Glenside N PE11. . . . . . 156 C8
Glenside S PE11. . . . . . 156 C8
GLENTHAM LN. 43 E1
Glentham Cl LN6 . . . . . .205 B3
Glentham Rd LN8 . . . . . . 43 F1
Glentham Rd
  Bishop Norton LN8 . . . . . . 43 D3
  6 Gainsborough DN21. . . 53 A8
Glen The PE2. . . . . 231 B7
Glenton St PE1 . . . . 226 C2
GLENTWORTH DN21. . . . .54 E7
Glentworth Cres 4
  PE25. . . . . 206 D4
Glentworth Rd DN21. . . . .53 F4
Glenwood Dr 2 HU4. . . .179 B6
Glenwood Gr 2 PE11. . . 201 D1
GLINTON PE6 . . . . 220 D8
Glinton Rd
  Helpston PE6. . . . . 173 C4
  Newborough PE6. . . . . . 221 C8
Global Ctr Ind Est PE1 . . 226 E4
Gloria Way DN37. . . . . . 190 C7
Glossop Rd DN15 . . . . . .182 B2
Gloucester Ave
  Grimsby DN34 . . . . 191 B4
  Scunthorpe DN16 . . . . . 185 B7
Gloucester Cl
  Skegness PE25 . . . . . . 206 B2
  1 Sleaford NG34 . . . . . 212 C7
Gloucester Ct DN15. . . . 183 A6
Gloucester Rd
  Grantham NG31. . . . . . 210 C5
  Peterborough PE2. . . . . 231 B7
  2 Stamford PE9. . . . . . 219 B6
Gloucester St HU4 . . . . .179 E3
Glover Rd DN17. . . . . . . 184 E8
Glovers Ave 8 DN17 . . . . .17 D4
Glynn Rd LN1. . . . . 201 E8
Glynn View 11 LN1. . . . 201 E8
Goathland Cl HU3. . . . . .180 A6
Goathland Ct 1 DN37. . . 190 E8
Godber Dr LN4 . . . . .205 F3
Goddam's La PE12. . . . . 146 F1
Goddard Cl 7 DN18. . . . . 10 E8
Goddard Cres 12 PE13. . 170 D1
Godfrey Ave 6 PE11. . . . 145 C6
Godfrey Cl 7 PE6 . . . . . .174 E5
Godfrey Rd 11 DN8 . . . . . .15 A8
Godiva Cl 10 PE6 . . . . . .166 F1
Godiva Cres PE10. . . . . . 213 B5
Godman's La HU10. . . . . .178 B8
Godnow Rd DN17. . . . . . . 16 C5
Godric Sq PE2. . . . . 230 D6
Godsey Cres 9 PE6. . . . . 217 C5
Godsey's La PE6 . . . . . . 217 B6
Godson Ave 1 NG34. . . . 122 D3
Godwin Cl PE10 . . . . 213 B6
Godwin Rd 13 PE13. . . . 170 D1
Goffsmill PE2. . . . . 225 A4
Goldcrest Cl
  2 Birchwood LN6. . . . . . 200 E1
  Scunthorpe DN15 . . . . . 182 D6
Golden Drop 2 PE6 . . . . 173 C4
Golden Gr PE20. . . . . . . 135 C5
Golden Harvest Way 6
  PE10. . . . . 158 B6
Goldenholme La 4
  DN22. . . . . .65 A5
Gold Fen Dike Bank
  PE20. . . . . 114 D2
Goldfinch Cl LN6. . . . . . 200 A3
Goldgarth DN32 . . . . . . 192 A5
Goldhay Way PE2. . . . . . 229 F2
Goldie La PE27 . . . . 227 D6
Goldings The 8 DN9. . . . . 27 D2
Gold La LN13 . . . . .63 A1
Goldsmith Ct 1 LN4. . . . 207 A6
Goldsmith Rd NG31. . . . 211 D6

Goldsmith Wlk LN2 . . . . 202 C7
Goldson's La PE22 . . . . . 126 F6
Golf Ct PE17. . . . . .160 F5
Golf Links Dr HU15 . . . . . . 2 B6
Golf Rd 4 LN2 . . . . 64 A4
Gollands La DN9. . . . . 27 B2
Gonerby Hill NG31. . . . . 210 E8
GONERBY HILL FOOT
  NG31. . . . . 210 F8
Gonerby Hill Foot CE Prim
  Sch NG31. . . . . 210 E8
Gonerby La NG32 . . . . . 129 A7
Gonerby Rd NG31. . . . . 210 E8
Goochgate PE2. . . . . 169 A7
Goodacre PE2 . . . . 230 A4
Goodens La PE13 . . . . . . 170 A5
Goodfellows CE Prim Sch
  PE11. . . . . 156 E3
Goodfellows Rd 7
  PE11. . . . . 156 E3
Goodhand Cl DN18. . . . . . 11 A8
Good La LN1. . . . . .234 B4
Goodliff Rd NG31. . . . . . 211 C3
Goodman Cl 6 NG31 . . . 129 E5
Goodson Cl 3 PE21 . . . . 209 B4
Goodwin Dr 8 PE24. . . . . .90 B7
Goodwin Parade 1
  HU3 . . . . 180 D5
Goodwin Wlk PE4. . . . . . 221 A4
Goodwood DN17. . . . . . . 184 D4
Goodwood Cl LN11 . . . . 198 A7
Goodwood La 2 DN35. . . 192 F1
Goodwood Rd 8 PE3 . . . 224 F3
Goodwood Way 19
  LN6. . . . . 204 C7
Goole Rd DN14. . . . . 6 C8
Gooseacre 3 DN17 . . . . . .29 D7
Goosegate La NG32. . . . 118 A2
Goose Gn 10 PE12 . . . . . 160 E4
Goose La PE23. . . . . 87 D2
Goose's La PE14 . . . . . . .161 A1
Gordon Ave PE2 . . . . . . 230 E7
Gordon Boswell Romany
  Mus* PE12. . . . . 214 E1
Gordon Fendick Sch The
  PE13. . . . . 170 D2
Gordon Field 8 LN8. . . . . 57 D7
Gordon Gdns 7 DN33. . . 194 F8
Gordon Rd LN1. . . . . . . .234 B3
Gordon St
  Gainsborough DN21. . . . 197 D2
  4 Kingston upon Hull
  HU3. . . . . 180 B5
Gordon Way PE2. . . . . . 230 C7
Goredike Bank PE13 . . . 169 C2
GOREFIELD PE13. . . . . . 169 E2
Gorefield Cty Prim Sch
  PE13. . . . . 169 F2
Gorefield Rd PE13 . . . . . 169 F2
Gorehall Dr 10 DN7. . . . . 14 C3
Gore La 8 LN8. . . . . 214 D4
Goring Pl DN35. . . . . . . 192 D7
Gorse Cl
  Bottesford DN16 . . . . . . 185 C4
  5 Hatfield DN7. . . . . 14 C3
  4 Woodhall Spa LN10 . . . .97 E6
Gorse Dro NG34 . . . . . . 133 A6
Gorse Gn PE1 . . . . 226 B8
Gorse Hill La
  Caythorpe NG32 . . . . . . 119 A8
  Wellingore LN5. . . . . . . 107 C7
Gorse La
  Gonerby Hill Foot
  NG31. . . . . 211 B1
  Great Ponton NG31. . . . 139 F8
  9 Leasingham NG34 . . . 121 B7
  Scredington NG34 . . . . . 133 A7
  Silk Willoughby NG34 . . . 121 C1
Gorse Rd 1 DN10. . . . . . .39 F6
Gorse Rise NG31. . . . . . 211 C5
Gorton Rd HU10. . . . . . . 178 E7
Gorton St DN31. . . . . . . 189 B2
Gorwick La LN11. . . . . . . .66 B6
GOSBERTON PE11. . . . . 145 B6
Gosberton Bank PE11. . . 145 B6
GOSBERTON CHEAL
  PE11. . . . . 145 A4
Gosberton Clough &
  Risegate Prim Sch
  PE11. . . . . 144 D4
Gosberton House Specl
  Sch PE11. . . . . 145 B6
Gosberton Prim Sch
  PE11. . . . . 145 B6
Gosberton Rd PE11. . . . 145 C4
Goshawk Way LN4. . . . . 207 C6
Goslings Cnr Wood Nature
  Reserve* LN8. . . . . .70 E2
Gospelgate LN11. . . . . . 198 B5
Gospel La LN5. . . . . 106 C3
Gosport Rd DN34. . . . . . 191 A6
Gosport Wlk HU4 . . . . . .179 A4
Gostwick PE2. . . . . 229 D5
Gote La PE13 . . . . 169 E3
Gothic Cl 12 LN6. . . . . . .204 D7
GOULCEBY LN11. . . . . . . .72 D6
Gouldeby La LN11 . . . . . . .72 D6
Goulton St HU3. . . . . . . .180 B3
Gover's Dro PE12 . . . . . . 159 A2
Gower Rd HU4. . . . . .179 B3
Gowt Bank PE22 . . . . . . 126 C3
Gowts La PE12. . . . . 159 E3
GOXHILL DN19. . . . . 12 A8
Goxhill Ave 4 LN1. . . . . 134 E2
Goxhill Ct 14 LN6. . . . . . 204 D7
Goxhill Gdns 4 DN34. . . 190 F4

Goxhill Gr 13 LN6. . . . . . 204 D7
Goxhill Prim Sch DN19. . . .12 A8
Goxhill Rd DN19. . . . . . . .11 E8
Goxhill Sta DN19. . . . . . . 11 F8
GRABY NG34 . . . . .142 F4
Grace Ave LN6. . . . . 204 D3
Grace Cl 4 NG34 . . . . . . 212 E3
Grace Cres PE24. . . . . . . .77 C3
Gracefield La 4 NG23 . . . .78 A4
Grace St LN5. . . . . 201 F1
Graeme Rd PE5 . . . . 222 F2
Grafham Cl PE2 . . . . 231 E4
Grafton Ave PE3 . . . . . . 225 C3
Grafton St
  Grimsby DN32 . . . . 189 C1
  Lincoln LN2 . . . . 202 B3
Graham Ave HU4 . . . . . . 179 C2
Graham Hill Way 4
  PE10. . . . . 213 E4
Graham Rd PE25. . . . . . 206 B4
GRAINSBY DN36. . . . . . . .35 F2
Grainsby Ave
  Cleethorpes DN35 . . . . . 192 D3
  Holton le Clay DN36. . . . 195 E1
Grainsby Cl LN6 . . . . . . 204 C7
Grainsby La DN36. . . . . . .35 E1
Grainthorpe CE Prim Sch
  LN11. . . . . .50 B7
GRAISELOUND DN9. . . . . .27 D1
Graizelound Fields Rd
  DN9 . . . . .27 D1
Grammar Sch La DN20. . . 196 C6
Grammar Sch Rd
  DN20. . . . . 196 C6
Grammar Sch Wlk
  DN16 . . . . 196 C3
Grampian Cl 14 NG34. . . 212 B3
Grampian Way
  Gonerby Hill Foot
  NG31. . . . . 210 D8
  Grimsby DN33 . . . . 194 E8
  Thorne/Moorends DN8 . . .15 A7
Granaries The LN4 . . . . . 108 C8
Granary Cl
  22 Metheringham LN4. . . 95 C4
  5 Waddington LN5. . . . . .93 F6
Granary Croft 7 DN9 . . . . 27 D2
Granary La LN4. . . . . 207 A4
Granary Row LN4 . . . . . . 207 A4
Granary The DN21 . . . . . . 29 C4
Granary Way LN9 . . . . . . 199 A3
Granby Dr 5 NG31. . . . . 211 A6
Granby Rd LN8 . . . . 47 B5
Granby St PE1. . . . . 226 B2
Grand Parade PE25 . . . . 206 D3
Grand Sluice La 1
  PE21. . . . . 209 F6
GRANGE DN34 . . . . 191 F5
Grange Ave
  13 Barton-upon-Humber
  DN18. . . . . .10 E8
  Hatfield DN7 . . . . 14 D4
  24 Laceby DN37. . . . . . . .23 F1
  Misterton DN10. . . . . . . .40 A4
  Peterborough PE1. . . . . 226 A6
  13 Scunthorpe DN15 . . . 183 A5
Grange Cl
  7 Hatfield DN7 . . . . .14 D4
  1 Ingham LN1 . . . . 54 F2
  5 Misterton DN10. . . . . . .40 A4
Grange Cres
  Kingston upon Hull
  HU10. . . . . 178 E6
  Lincoln LN6 . . . . 205 B3
  Peterborough PE2. . . . . 230 A5
Grange Ct 3 LN5. . . . . . . 92 E1
Grange Dr
  Clinton Park LN4 . . . . . . 207 C5
  Lincoln LN6 . . . . 205 B3
  Misterton DN10. . . . . . . .40 A4
  Spalding PE11. . . . . 214 E4
  Stapleford LN6. . . . . . . 105 A7
Grange Farm La DN36 . . 195 D6
Grange Field DN20. . . . . . 20 D8
Grangehill Rd PE12. . . . 169 B6
Grange Ind Est DN16. . . 185 E7
Grange Inf & Jun Sch
  DN34 . . . . 190 F3
Grange La
  Balderton NG24. . . . . . . 104 A1
  Canwick LN4 . . . . 81 A3
  Covenham St Bartholomew
  LN11. . . . . .49 D6
  Garthorpe LE14 . . . . 84 E4
  Heighington LN4 . . . . . . 81 E4
  Hough-on-the-Hill NG32 . . 118 A7
  1 Ingham LN1 . . . . 54 F2
  Keddington LN11 . . . . . . 198 E8
  18 Manby LN11. . . . . . . 62 B6
  North Cockerington LN11 . . 50 A1
  North Kelsey LN7. . . . . . .32 A3
  Stixwould & Woodhall
  LN10. . . . . .97 B6
  Utterby LN11. . . . . .49 A4
  3 Willingham by Stow
  DN21. . . . . .53 E3
Grange La Inf Sch
  DN16 . . . . 185 D5
Grange La Jun Sch
  DN16 . . . . 185 D5
Grange La N DN16 . . . . . 185 C5
Grange Mdws PE22 . . . . 113 A1

Grange Paddock 8
  NG32 . . . . 210 A5
Grange Pk
  2 Brough HU15 . . . . 2 C5
  17 Kirk Sandall DN3 . . . . 14 A3
  Morton DN21 . . . . .40 D3
  6 Swanland HU14 . . . . . . 3 B6
Grange Rd
  Bracebridge Heath
  LN4. . . . . 205 F2
  Gainsborough DN21 . . . . .41 A1
  Garthorpe & Fockerby
  DN14. . . . . 7 E8
  14 Mablethorpe/Sutton on Sea
  LN12. . . . . .77 A7
  4 Metheringham LN4. . . . 95 D4
  Peterborough PE1. . . . . 225 E8
  6 Ruskington NG34 . . . . 108 D1
  Sutton Bridge PE34. . . . 161 B4
  10 Wisbech PE13. . . . . . 170 C1
Grange St LN4. . . . . 109 C7
Grange The 1 NG31 . . . . 211 A4
Grange Wlk
  Grimsby DN34 . . . . 191 A6
  8 Misterton DN10. . . . . . .40 A5
Gransley Rise 3 PE2. . . . 225 C5
Granson Way LN4 . . . . . 203 A2
Granta Cres NG31. . . . . 211 C2
GRANTHAM NG31 . . . . . 211 C3
Grantham Ave DN31. . . . 191 D1
Grantham Canal Nature
  Reserve* NG31. . . . . . 210 D1
Grantham Church VA High
  Sch The NG31. . . . . . . 211 E7
Grantham Coll NG31. . . . 211 B4
Grantham Cricket Gd
  NG31. . . . . 211 B1
Grantham District Hospl
  NG31. . . . . 211 A6
Grantham Dr 2 PE25 . . . 206 B3
Grantham Fun Farm The*
  NG31. . . . . 210 F4
Grantham House*
  NG31. . . . . 211 B5
Grantham Mus* NG31. . . 211 B4
Grantham Prep Sch The
  NG31. . . . . 139 F8
Grantham Rd
  Boothby Graffoe LN5. . . . .94 A1
  Boston PE21. . . . . 208 A3
  Bottesford NG13 . . . . . . 128 A5
  Bracebridge Heath LN4. . 205 F2
  Carlton Scroop NG32. . . . 119 C3
  7 Great Gonerby NG31 . . 129 D5
  Great Gonerby NG32. . . . 210 D8
  Harmston LN5 . . . . 93 F6
  Hough-on-the-Hill NG32 . . 119 A4
  Ingoldsby NG33 . . . . 141 C5
  Navenby/Wellingore
  LN5. . . . . 107 A8
  Old Somerby NG33 . . . . . 140 D8
  Ropsley & Humby NG33 . . 131 A1
  2 Skillington NG33. . . . . 151 A8
  Sleaford NG34. . . . . 212 B2
Grantham St LN2. . . . . . 234 B2
Grantham St NG31 . . . . 211 A3
Granthams The 12
  NG31. . . . . .68 E6
Grantham Town FC
  NG31. . . . . 210 D3
Grantley St NG31. . . . . . 211 A3
Grants La 20 PE21 . . . . . 228 F5
Grant St
  Cleethorpes DN35 . . . . . 192 E7
  Grimsby DN31 . . . . 189 D1
GRANT THOROLD
  DN32. . . . . 192 A7
Granville Ave
  Boston PE21. . . . . 136 D8
  Northborough PE6. . . . . 217 E1
Granville Rd DN15 . . . . . 183 A6
Granville St
  Boston PE21. . . . . 208 D5
  Grantham NG31. . . . . . 211 C3
  Grimsby DN32 . . . . 191 F6
  1 Kingston upon Hull
  HU3. . . . . 180 A6
  Peterborough PE1. . . . . 226 A4
GRASBY DN38 . . . . 32 F7
Grasby All Saints CE Prim
  Sch DN38. . . . . .32 E7
Grasby Cl 4 DN21. . . . . . .53 A8
Grasby Cres DN37 . . . . . 190 D7
Grasby Rd
  Great Limber DN37. . . . . .22 C3
  North Kelsey LN7. . . . . . .32 A2
  Scunthorpe DN17. . . . . . 184 E5
Grasby Wold La DN38 . . . .33 A6
Grasmere Cl 2 DN21. . . . .53 A8
Grasmere Cl 3 PE4. . . . . 221 A4
Grasmere Ct 21 DN37. . . 197 C6
Grasmere Gdns PE4. . . . 221 A4
Grasmere Gr 3 DN36 . . . 192 E1
Grasmere Way LN6. . . . . 204 E7
Grassdale Pk 2 HU15. . . . . 2 B5
Grassgate La PE14 . . . . . 170 E3
Grassmoor Cl 2 LN6. . . . . 93 B8
Grassthorpe Rd NG23. . . 78 A6
Gravecoat La PE11. . . . . 144 E4
Gravel Causeway PE6. . . 166 D1
Gravel Pit Hill Cont DN9. . 27 D1
Gravelpit La LN9. . . . . . . 199 F2
Gravel Pit La 1 LN8 . . . . . 22 A6
Gravel Rd
  Barton-upon-Humber
  DN18. . . . . 3 D1

Gravel Pit Rd continued
  Scotter DN21. . . . . .29 C4
Gravel Pits La PE24. . . . 102 C8
Gravel Rd
  Market Deeping PE6 . . . 165 D3
  Revesby PE22 . . . . .99 B4
Gravel Wlk PE1. . . . . . . 226 A2
Gray Ct PE1 . . . . 225 E8
Graye Dr LN11. . . . . 198 D4
GRAYINGHAM DN21. . . . .42 D7
Grayingham Rd DN21 . . . .42 E7
Grayling Cl 2 DN37. . . . . 190 D7
Graylings The PE21 . . . . 208 B6
Grays Cd DN7 . . . . 184 D6
Grays Ct DN37. . . . . 190 E8
Gray's Ct 4 LN11. . . . . . 198 B6
Gray's Rd 2 LN11. . . . . . 198 B6
Gray St LN1 . . . . .234 A4
GREAT CARLTON LN11. . . .62 E4
GREAT CASTERTON
  PE9. . . . . 171 B8
Great Casterton CE Prim
  Sch PE9 . . . . 171 C8
Great Cl 1 NG33 . . . . . . 151 D2
GREAT COATES DN37 . . . .24 B5
Great Coates Prim Sch
  DN37 . . . . 190 C8
Great Coates Rd
  Grimsby DN37 . . . . 190 C8
  Healing DN41 . . . . 23 F5
  Great Coates Sta DN37. . . 24 B5
Great Field La 1 HU9. . . . . 5 E8
GREATFORD PE9. . . . . . 164 B3
Greatford Gdns PE9. . . . 164 B3
Greatford Rd
  Baston PE6 . . . . 164 F4
  5 Uffington PE9. . . . . . . 172 C6
GREAT GONERBY
  NG31. . . . . 129 C5
Great Northern Ct 12
  NG31. . . . . 211 A4
Great Northern Terr
  LN5. . . . . 234 C1
Great Northern Terr Ind Est
  LN5. . . . . 234 C1
Great N Rd
  Balderton NG24. . . . . . . 117 C8
  Empingham PE9 . . . . . . 162 B2
  Great Gonerby NG32. . . . 129 C6
  Long Bennington NG23 . . 117 D2
  Tinwell PE9 . . . . 218 D5
  Wansford PE8 . . . . 222 D1
GREAT PONTON NG31. . . 140 A5
Great Ponton CE (Aided)
  Prim Sch NG31 . . . . . . 140 A5
GREAT STEEPING
  PE23. . . . . 101 E7
Great Steeping Prim Sch
  PE23. . . . . 101 E7
GREAT STURTON LN9. . . . 71 F3
Great Thornton St
  HU3. . . . . 180 D6
GREAT TOWS LN8 . . . . . . 47 D1
Great Union St HU9 . . . . 181 A7
GREBBY PE23. . . . . .88 D3
Grebe Cl 2 LN6. . . . . . . 204 C1
Greek St HU3. . . . . .179 F5
Greenacre Cl 7 DN7. . . . 14 C2
Greenacres
  6 Donington on Bain
  LN11. . . . . .59 E1
  Peterborough PE4. . . . . 220 E4
  5 Swanland HU14 . . . . . . 3 C7
Green Acres Rd 1 DN8. . 178 C6
Greenacres Dr
  Boston PE21. . . . . 208 D3
  Bourne PE10. . . . . 213 D3
Greenaway Ct LN3 . . . . . 203 E6
Green Bank DN8. . . . . . . 15 D6
Greenbank Dr LN6 . . . . . 205 A5
Green Dro
  Billingay LN4 . . . . 109 F6
  Crowland PE6 . . . . 175 D8
  Helpringham NG34 . . . . . 133 F7
  Little Hale NG34 . . . . . . 134 A7
  Thorney PE6 . . . . 175 F5
Green Dyke PE12 . . . . . . 148 D1
Greendyke La PE13 . . . . 160 A2
Green Farm Ct 2 LN9. . . 199 A2
Green Farm La 12 PE13. . 223 E2
Greenfield Cl 13 DN3. . . . 14 A3
Greenfield La DN13 . . . . . 75 D4
Greenfield Rd
  Coningsby LN4. . . . . 207 D5
  4 Swanland HU14 . . . . . . 3 C7
Greenfields
  8 Glentham LN8. . . . . . . 43 F1
  Holbeach PE12 . . . . 215 C2
  22 Nettleham LN2. . . . . .68 C2
Greenfields La 5
  NG34 . . . . 142 D8
Greenfinch Dr DN35 . . . . 192 E1
Greengarth DN17 . . . . . . 184 F2
Green Gate Cl PE20 . . . . 136 A1
Green Gate PE21 . . . . . . 114 D1
Greengate Cl PE21. . . . . 226 C4
Greengate La 4 DN19 . . . 12 A8
Greengate Rd PE23. . . . . 88 D3
Greenham Cl PE2. . . . . . 229 D5
Green Hill DN35. . . . . . . 192 D3

GREEN HILL NG31.......210 E5
Greenhill Dr **1** LN8......43 D3
Greenhill Rd DN9.........27 C2
Green Hill Rd NG31....210 F5
Greenhoe Rd DN17 ....184 D3
Green La
Algarkirk PE20...........136 B3
Aunsby & Dembleby
NG34..................132 A4
10 Barton-upon-Humber
DN18..................10 F8
Beckingham LN5........105 C4
Belton DN9 ....16 D2
Belton & Manthorpe
NG32..................130 B7
Boston PE21............208 E7
Bottesford NG13 ....128 B5
Bratoft PE24 ....102 C7
Brigsley DN37 ....35 D4
5 Broughton DN20......19 E3
Cherry Willingham LN3 ..203 D5
Collingham NG23........91 D3
Deeping St Nicholas
PE11..................166 C8
Dunham-on-Trent NG22...65 B1
Dunston LN4 ....95 D6
Eagle & Swinethorpe LN6 ..79 C2
Eaton NG32 ....138 A2
Gedney PE12 ....159 A1
Girton NG23............78 C1
Gosberton PE11........145 C7
Grantham NG31........211 D7
Hatfield DN7 ....14 E1
Hemingby LN9 ....72 C3
Heydour NG32 ....131 D5
Hogsthorpe LN13........90 A8
Kingston upon Hull
HU13..................179 A1
Kirton PE20............135 E6
Lea DN21...............52 F5
Leake Commonside PE22 ..113 F3
Leverington PE13 ......169 F2
Lincoln LN6 ....201 D2
Mablethorpe & Sutton
LN12..................63 F4
Marston NG32 ....118 D1
Middle Rasen LN8 ......57 C7
Moulton PE12..........146 E1
13 North Kelsey LN7......32 A4
North Somercotes LN11 ...50 F7
Peterborough PE1.......226 A4
Pilham DN21............41 D4
Pinchbeck PE11.........145 C2
3 Skegness PE25......103 E4
Skellingthorpe LN6 .....200 B5
Spalding PE11 ....214 C3
Stamford PE9...........219 B7
Stickney PE22 ....113 A7
Stixwould & Woodhall
LN10..................97 B8
Struby with Woodthorpe
LN13..................63 B1
Sutterton PE20 ....136 A2
Swinderby LN6..........92 B5
Thimbleby LN9..........85 C5
Threekingham NG34.....132 E3
Wainfleet St Mary PE24 ..102 A1
11 Welton LN2..........68 D6
Westborough & Dry
Doddington NG23......117 F5
Wigtoft PE20...........135 E1
Willoughby with Sloothby
LN13..................89 C5
Witham St Hughs LN6 ....92 D5
Woodhall Spa LN10 .....97 C5
Wyberton PE21.........178 F4
Yaxley PE7..............233 D6
Green La Mid Sch DN8....15 B7
Greenlands Ave **10**
DN36..................195 C6
Green Man La LN4 ......94 F1
Green Man Rd LN5......94 C1
Greenock Way LN6 .....204 B7
Green Pastures **4**
PE12..................158 B7
Green Rd
Aswarby & Swarby
NG34..................131 F7
Newborough PE6........174 F2
Greenrigg Gdns **1**
PE11..................214 D5
Greens Cl DN15.........183 B3
Green's Rd **8** DN7......14 C3
Green St **8** NG31.....129 D5
Greenstiles La HU14 .....3 C7
Greenstock La PE13....170 A6
Green The
3 Allington NG32......128 F7
8 Brough HU15.........2 D6
Castor PE5.............223 E2
Cherry Willingham/Reepham
LN3...................203 F8
11 Coddington NG24....196 C6
Collingham NG23........91 C4
Corby Glen NG33.......152 E2
Dunston LN4 ....95 C5
Gainsborough DN21.....197 F4
2 Glinton PE6..........220 C8
6 Leasingham NG34....121 B8
6 Mablethorpe/Sutton on Sea
LN12..................64 A4
3 Minting LN9 ....84 C8
15 Navenby/Wellingore
LN5...................107 A2
Peterborough PE4.......221 A3

Green The continued
3 Reepham LN3........82 A8
Revesby PE22...........99 B4
6 Scothern LN2.........68 F4
Scotter DN21...........29 C3
Spalding PE11 ....214 E5
4 Swanland HU14 ....3 B7
23 Thorne/Moorends
DN8....................15 A8
11 Thorney PE6........176 A3
Thurlby PE10...........164 C7
Welbourn LN5..........106 E4
Yaxley PE7..............233 E6 E5
Greenway
1 Barton-upon-Humber
DN18..................3 F1
Waltham DN37..........194 E3
2 Welton/Dunholme LN2...68 C7
Greenways **1** HU14........3 A5
Greenway The **1** HU4 ..179 C6
Greenwich House Ind Sch
LN11..................198 C6
Greenwich House Sch
LN11..................198 C6
Green Wlk PE6..........217 A5
Greenwood Cl **1** PE12..215 E2
Greenwood Dr PE21 ....208 F6
Greenwood's Row **5**
NG31..................211 A4
Greestone Mount LN2...234 B3
Greestone Pl LN2.......234 B3
Greestone Strs* LN2...234 B3
GREETHAM LN9..........86 D5
Greetham's La LN2.....192 C5
GREETWELL DN20.........30 C7
Greetwell Cl LN2........234 C3
Greetwellgate LN2.....234 C3
Greetwell Hollow Nature
Reserve* LN2..........202 D5
Greetwell La LN2.......202 F8
Greetwell Pl LN2........202 B5
Greetwell Rd LN2.......234 C3
Gregg Hall Cl **2** LN6...205 B4
Gregg Hall Cres LN6 ....205 B4
Gregg Hall Dr **4** LN6...205 B4
Gregory Cl **1** NG32....139 C7
Gresham St LN1.........201 D4
Gresley Ct **11** NG31...210 E2
Gresley Dr
Lincoln LN6 ....201 D1
1 Stamford PE9........219 B4
Gresley Rd LN11........198 D4
Gresley Way
Immingham DN40.......186 F5
Peterborough PE3.......225 C6
Gretton Cl
1 Claypole NG23......117 E8
Peterborough PE2.......230 C7
Grevel Cl **6** PE11......230 E4
Greyfleet Bank **7** LN11...51 C4
Grey Friars
3 Grantham NG31......211 A4
Grimsby DN37..........190 D7
Greyfriars La **8** LN2....180 D7
Greyfriars Rd **11** DN20...19 E3
GREY GREEN DN9.........16 E2
Greyling Cl **5** LN6.....201 E8
Greyling View **12** LN1...201 E8
Grey St
Gainsborough DN21.....197 B6
Grimsby DN37..........190 D7
Greystone Ave HU5 ....179 E7
Greystones Rd DN21....197 B7
Gride Bank PE22.........126 E8
Gride The PE22 ....113 E1
Griffins Cl **4** PE6......174 E5
Griffiths Ct PE2........229 E5
Grime St DN31..........191 E8
Grimmer's Rd **12** PE13...170 E1
GRIMOLDBY LN11.........62 B7
Grimoldby Prim Sch
LN11..................62 C6
GRIMSBY DN31..........191 B8
Grimsby Auditorium
DN34..................190 F8
Grimsby Docks Sta
DN31..................189 A1
**Grimsby Inst of Higher Educ &
Higher Ed** DN34......191 C4
Grimsby Inst of Higher Ed
(Nunsthorne Com
Campus) The DN33....191 B4
Grimsby Leisure Ctr
DN34..................190 F8
Grimsby Maternity Hospl
DN33..................191 C3
Grimsby Pool DN33....191 D4
Grimsby Rd
2 Binbrook LN8........47 C5
Brackenborough with Little
Grimsby LN11..........61 A8
Cleethorpes DN35......192 D8
Fotherby LN11..........49 A1
Grimsby DN32 ....189 D1
Humberston DN36.......192 E1
Laceby DN37...........190 A4
Louth LN11 ....198 A6
Swallow LN7............34 B6
Waltham DN37..........194 F5
Grimsby Town Sta
DN32..................191 D7
Grimshaw Rd PE1.......226 B6
GRIMSTHORPE PE10....153 E5
Grimsthorpe Castle*
PE10..................153 D5
Grimsthorpe Cl
Grantham NG31........210 E6
12 Market Deeping PE6 ..217 A5

Grimston Rd **5** HU10 ....178 F6
Grindell St HU9..........181 D8
GRINGLEY ON THE HILL
DN10...................39 C1
Gringley Rd DN10.......39 E4
Grinter Cl **3** LN6.......93 C8
Grocock Cl PE12........146 E2
Groose La PE24..........115 D8
Grosvenor Ave
Birchwood LN6 ....200 D2
Bourne PE10............213 C6
Grosvenor Cres
Grimsby DN32 ....191 D6
Louth LN11 ....198 D7
Grosvenor Ct **3** DN7....14 D8
Grosvenor Mews **2**
LN4....................203 D1
Grosvenor Rd
5 Billingborough
NG34..................133 B1
Kirton PE20............136 C6
Louth LN11 ....198 D7
Skegness PE25 ....206 C4
Wisbech PE13 ....170 D1
Grosvenor St N DN15....183 A5
Grosvenor Sq **17** LN5...107 A7
Grosvenor St (South) **2**
DN15..................183 A4
Grosvenor St **4** DN15...183 A4
4 Scunthorpe DN15......183 A4
Grove Cl **10** PE11......145 C1
Grove Cres DN32 ....192 C6
Grove Ct
5 Gainsborough
DN21..................197 C6
Woodston PE2..........230 F8
Grove Dr **3** LN10......97 D5
Grove End Rd **8** NG31...211 B4
Grovefield La PE22......126 D1
Grove Hill HU13.........178 E1
Grove La
Peterborough PE3.......225 A2
Waltham DN37..........194 E4
Grove Leisure Ctr
NG24..................104 B3
Grovenor Ct **5** DN35....193 A1
Grove Pk DN10..........39 F5
Grove Rd
1 Fishlake DN7 ....14 D8
Mablethorpe/Sutton on Sea
LN12...................64 C1
Theddlethorpe All Saints
LN12...................63 D6
Grove St **6** PE21.......209 A5
Grove St W **4** PE21.....209 A5
Grove St The NG24 .....104 B3
Grove St
4 Boston PE21.........209 A5
Heckington NG34.......122 E2
5 Kirton in Lindsey DN21 ...30 B1
Newark-on-Trent NG24 ...104 B3
Peterborough PE2.......230 F8
Groves The PE22........179 B2
Grove The
13 Barrow upon Humber
DN19..................11 C8
2 Beckingham DN10......40 A1
Edlington with Wispington
LN9....................85 B6
6 Gainsborough DN21....53 A5
Grantham NG31........210 E3
Lincoln LN2 ....234 C4
Market Deeping PE6 ....217 B5
Morton PE10............154 B6
Newton on Trent LN1....65 D1
4 Spalding PE11 ....214 C6
4 Welton/Dunholme
LN2....................68 D6
Grove Wood Rd DN10 ....39 F5
Grove Wood Terr **16**
DN10...................39 F5
Grundale HU10..........178 C6
Grundy La LN3...........57 D2
Grundy's La LN9.........84 C8
Grunnill Cl **10** PE25 ....206 A5
Guanockgate Rd PE12 ...169 A2
Guash Way PE9..........219 D7
Gubbole's Dro PE11.....145 A3
Guernsey Gr DN40......186 C2
Guildford Cl **11** NG31...210 E5
Guildford La LN11.......105 F5
Guildford St DN32 ......192 A8
Guildhall Dr **2** PE11....156 E8
Guildhall Mus* PE21....208 F4
Guildhall Rd LN11.......180 F6
Guildhall St
Grantham NG31........211 A4
Lincoln LN1 ....234 A2
Guild Rd PE13 ....170 E1
Guilicarr La LN7.........31 F4
Guilsborough Rd PE6 ....175 B2
Guisefield Rd **8** DN9 ....27 D6
Guiana Rd LN8..........44 D5
Gull Bank
Whaplode PE12 ....167 F5
Wisbech St Mary PE13 ...177 E3
Gull Dro PE13 ....177 D3
Gull La PE13.............170 A2
Gull Rd PE13............177 F2
Gullymore PE13.........224 F6
GUNBY
Candleby with Gunby
PE23..................89 B1
Gunby and stainby NG33...151 C4
Gunby Ave LN6..........204 F6

Gunby Hall* PE23........89 A1
Gunby La PE23..........89 A1
Gunby Pl DN35..........192 E4
Gunby Rd
Gunby & Stainby NG33 ...151 A4
Scunthorpe DN17 ....184 E5
Gunfleet Cl **18** PE20....135 B7
GUNNERBY DN37..........34 F2
Gunners Way DN34 .....190 D4
GUNNESS DN15...........17 E6
Gunness & Burringham CE
Prim Sch DN17.........17 E5
Gunness La
Amcotts DN17..........17 F8
Flixborough DN15 ......182 A7
GUNTHORPE
Owston Ferry DN9.......40 D7
Peterborough PE4.......221 B1
Gunthorpe Prim Sch
PE4...................221 C2
Gunthorpe Rd
Newborough PE6........221 D4
Owston Ferry DN9......40 C8
Peterborough PE4.......221 C2
Sutton Bridge PE14.....160 E1
1 Walpole PE14.........170 F8
Gunthorpe Ridings **2**
PE4...................221 E2
Gunthorpe Rd
PE4...................174 E3
Gurnard Leys PE3.......220 E1
Gurnell St DN15.........183 A4
Gurth Ave **6** DN3.......14 A1
Guthlac Ave **5** PE4.....221 B1
GUTHRAM GOWT PE11...155 E5
GUYHIRN PE13...........177 F2
Guys Head Rd PE12.....160 E7
Guy's Head Rd
Gedney PE12 ....149 C1
Sutton Bridge PE12.....160 F8
Gwash Cl PE9 ....163 C1
Gynewell Gr **4** LN2....202 D7
Gypsy La
Newton PE13............170 C4
Whaplode PE12 ....167 F3

H

Haalam Bank LN12.......63 C4
Haarlem Ct **5** PE11.....214 A2
Habbanya Rise LN4......95 C7
Habblesthorpe Cl DN22...52 C1
Habblesthorpe Rd DN22...52 C1
HABERTOFT PE24........89 E4
HABROUGH DN40.........22 E8
Habrough La DN39.......22 E8
Habrough Rd
Immingham DN40........186 A3
South Killingholme DN40...12 E2
Habrough Rd DN40.......22 E8
Hacconby Dro
Dunsby PE10............144 A1
Haconby PE10..........155 A8
Hacconby La PE10 ......154 C7
HACEBY NG34............34 D3
Hacke Rd **3** PE24......230 D3
Hackness Gr **2** HU5....179 D8
Hack's Dro PE6..........164 F6
HACKTHORN LN2........55 E1
Hackthorn CE (Controlled)
Prim Sch LN2..........55 F1
Hackthorn Pl **4** LN2....201 F8
Hackthorn Rd LN2.......55 F1
HACONBY PE10.........154 D8
HADDINGTON LN5.......92 F6
Haddington La LN6 ......92 F6
HADDON PE7............232 B6
Haddon Cl
Birchwood LN6 ....200 E1
Peterborough PE2.......231 E5
Haddon Rd
Peterborough PE3.......225 E3
Peterborough PE7.......232 C6
Stamford PE9...........218 F6
Haddon St HU3..........179 F4
Hadfield Rd **7** LN6.....205 A5
Hadleigh Cl DN15.......210 F5
Hadleigh Ct DN15.......183 A4
Hadleigh Dr LN6........204 F5
Hadleigh Gn **8** DN17...17 D4
Hadleigh Rd DN40......186 C2
Hadley Rd
Peterborough PE4.......221 B1
Sleaford NG34..........212 E6
Hadrian Dr **10** PE6.....164 E5
Hadrians Ct PE2........231 A6
Hadrians Rd **3** LN4.....81 A1
Half Cl **3** PE70........135 C7
Haffenden Rd LN2.......202 A6
Hagbeach Dro PE12.....168 A5
Hagbeach Gate PE12....168 A5
Hagg Cross Roads PE23...87 A4
Hagg La **1** DN17........16 E3
HAGNABY
East Kirkby PE23 ....100 A5
Hagnaby cum Hagnaby
LN13...................76 C6
Hagnaby Abbey LN13....76 C7
Hagnaby Rd PE22........89 E4
Hagnaby Rd PE22........100 A6
HAGWORTHINGHAM
PE23..................87 A4
Haig Ave DN16..........183 B1
Haigh St **2** DN32......191 D6
Haigh St **4** DN35......193 A5
Haile Rd DN34..........190 D3
HAINTON LN8............58 F3

Hainton Ave DN32.......191 E6
Hainton Cl DN21........197 E1
Hainton Rd
Lincoln LN6 ....205 C5
Haith's La **1** DN36......36 B3
Haldane St DN21........197 B5
Hale Cl **4** LN2..........202 E2
Hale Hill Rd DN7........14 E2
Hale House Rd PE10 ....153 C2
Hale Rd PE22............112 F1
Hale Rd
Heckington NG34.......122 E2
Helpringham NG34......133 E2
Horsington LN10........84 B2
Hales Cl DN16..........185 A2
Hales Entry HU9........181 C2
HALESGATE PE12........146 E1
Haley Cl **6** LN5.........107 B8
Haley Cl **8** PE13.......170 D2
Half Acre Wood **3**
DN2....................17 D7
Halfleet PE6............217 A6
Halford Cl **8** NG33....151 D2
Halfpenny Cl **10** LN2...202 D7
Halfway House La LN6....92 C6
Halfway Houses LN6.....92 D5
Halifax App DN20........21 A8
Halifax Cl
4 Skegness PE25......206 B5
3 Skellingthorpe LN6...200 A4
Halkon Cl LN7...........7 D3
Hallam Cl
3 Alford LN13.........75 E2
Barrow upon Humber
DN19..................11 D8
Hallam Gr LN6..........205 C4
Hallam's Dro PE20......123 F2
Hallam's La **8** LN4......96 B3
Hallaton Rd PE1.........226 D8
Hall Bank **3** PE13.....169 F7
Hallbrook Ct **5** DN16...185 A1
Hall Cl
Heckington NG34.......122 E3
Ropsley NG33...........131 B1
Hallcroft **6** DN39......12 A1
Hallcroft Rd **1** DN9....27 D2
Hallcroft Rd LN7........7 A3
Hall Dr
Canwick LN4............81 A4
Grantham NG31........211 C5
Lincoln LN6 ....205 C2
Swineshead PE20.......135 B4
HALL END PE22 ....114 D1
Hall End Rd PE22 ....114 C1
Haller St HU9...........181 E8
Hall Farm
5 Market Deeping
PE6...................217 B6
5 Newark-on-Trent
NG24..................104 D5
Hall Farm Pk* LN7.......44 D8
Hallfield Cres NG32....119 C2
Hallfields La PE4........221 C1
Hallgarth DN32..........37 B2
Hallgarth Ave DN16.....183 B2
Hallgate PE12 ....159 E6
Hall Gate
Fleet PE12..............159 B6
Holbeach PE12 ....215 C1
Moulton PE12..........157 F5
Wainfleet St Mary PE24 ..102 C3
Weston PE12............146 B1
Hall Gate Rd PE12 .....168 E2
Hall Gdns **8** DN15......9 B5
Hall Hill Rd PE12 ....215 D1
HALLINGTON LN11.......60 F4
Halliwell Cl **5** HU9......5 F8
Hall La
Algarkirk PE20..........136 B3
Benington PE22.........126 F5
Branston & Mere LN4....81 D7
Burgh le Marsh PE24....102 E7
Elsham DN20...........20 F5
Fiskerton LN3...........82 C7
Frampton PE20.........136 E6
Gunby & Stainby NG33 ...151 B5
Hough-on-the-Hill NG32...118 E3
Lenton Keisby & Osgodby
NG33..................141 E8
Moulton PE12..........146 D2
Nettleham LN2..........68 B2
Peterborough PE4.......221 A4
Stainforth DN7..........14 A6
Stenigot LN11...........72 D7
Stickney PE22 ....112 F7
Welbourn LN5..........106 E4
West Keal PE23.........100 C6
Whaplode PE12 ....147 B6
Hall Lea PE23 ....114 D7
Hall Mdw **1** DN20......10 C2
Hall Meadow Rd PE6....217 F7
Hall Orch La **2** LN5....106 E5
Hall Pk
Heckington NG34.......122 F1
Swanland HU14.........3 C7
Hall Pk Rd DN40........186 D5
Hall Pl PE11.............214 D6
Hall Rd
Haconby PE10..........154 D8
Heckington NG34.......122 E2
Hough-on-the-Hill NG32...118 E3
Londonthorpe & Harrowby
without NG31...........211 F6
Hall Rise DN17...........29 D2
Haigh St **2** NG33......151 D2
Halls Cl LN4.............95 C6
Halls Hill LN11...........57 E3

alls La
6 Keelby DN41 . . . . .23 A4
North Kelsey LN7 . . . . . . .32 A4
all's Rd DN10 . . . . .39 D2
all St
  Crowland PE6 . . . . .166 F1
Kingston upon Hull HU2 . .180 D7
16 Navenby/Wellingore
  LN5 . . . . .107 A7
all Wath LN5 . . . . .92 E2
all Way DN38 . . . . .21 F5
all Wlk **1** HU15 . . . . .2 D6
all Yd
  2 Collyweston PE9 . . . . . .171 B1
  20 Metheringham LN4 . . . . .95 C4
almer Gate PE11 . . . . .214 E4
almer Gdns PE11 . . . . .214 F4
almer Paddock **6**
  PE11 . . . . .214 F5
altemprice Leisure Ctr
  HU10 . . . . .178 E7
altemprice St HU3 . . . . . . .179 F5
ALTHAM LN9 . . . . .98 C6
altham Gn DN21 . . . . .197 F4
ALTOFT END PE22 . . . . . .126 C4
altoft End Est PE22 . . . . . .126 C3
alton Cl
  3 Birchwood LN6 . . . . . . .204 B8
  4 Kirton in Lindsey DN21 . .42 F8
ALTON FENSIDE
  PE23 . . . . .101 C6
ALTON HOLEGATE
  PE23 . . . . .101 B8
alton Holegate CE Prim
  Sch PE23 . . . . .101 B7
alton Pl DN35 . . . . .192 D4
alton Rd PE23 . . . . .101 A8
alton Way **3** DN33 . . . . . .191 C2
alyard Croft **8** HU1 . . . . .180 F5
alycon Ave **1** HU13 . . . . .178 E2
ambleton La LN8 . . . . .57 E8
ambleton Rd PE9 . . . . . . .218 E4
AMERINGHAM LN9 . . . . . .86 C2
amerton La **1** LN9 . . . . . .199 C3
amilton Cl
  2 Bourne PE10 . . . . .213 C7
  3 Grimsby DN34 . . . . . . .190 D4
amilton Gr LN6 . . . . .200 B3
amilton Rd
  Alford LN13 . . . . .75 F2
  Grantham NG31 . . . . .211 D6
  4 Lincoln LN6 . . . . .204 D2
  Scunthorpe DN17 . . . . . . .189 D1
amilton Way PE21 . . . . . . .208 F3
amish Wlk **8** DN40 . . . . . .186 B3
am La PE2 . . . . .229 E7
amling Sch PE6 . . . . .167 E4
amling Way HU4 . . . . .179 D2
amlyn Ave HU4 . . . . .179 E7
amlyn Way HU4 . . . . .179 E6
4am Mere Bird Sanctuary*
  PE2 . . . . .229 E7
ammerton Rd DN17 . . . . . .184 E4
ammond Cl PE11 . . . . . . .172 C1
ammond Ct LN12 . . . . .64 B3
amond Rd DN32 . . . . .192 B7
ampden Cl **1** LN6 . . . . . .200 A4
ampden Cres **3** DN7 . . . . .26 A8
ampden Ct **10** NG24 . . . .104 C5
ampden Way
  Sleaford NG34 . . . . .121 A2
  8 Waddington LN5 . . . . . .94 A7
ampshire St HU4 . . . . . . .179 E3
ampson Gdns DN38 . . . . . .14 A2
ampstead Pk DN38 . . . . . .191 B2
ampton Cl
  Humberston DN35 . . . . . .192 F1
  1 Spalding PE11 . . . . . . .214 E2
ampton Coll PE2 . . . . . . .230 D1
ampton Ct PE3 . . . . .225 C6
HAMPTON HARGATE
  PE7 . . . . .230 D2
Hampton Hargate Prim Sch
  PE7 . . . . .230 C2
ampton La PE22 . . . . .127 B7
ampton Rd
  2 Hatfield DN7 . . . . .14 C4
  Scunthorpe DN16 . . . . . .185 C8
ampton St LN1 . . . . .201 D4
HAMPTON VALE PE7 . . . .230 D1
Hampton Vale Prim Sch
  PE7 . . . . .230 C1
anbury PE2 . . . . .229 F3
HANBY NG33 . . . . .141 E7
anby La
  1 Alford LN13 . . . . .75 F2
  Welton le Marsh PE23 . . . .89 B4
andel Cl DN21 . . . . .197 D5
andel House Prep Sch
  DN21 . . . . .197 D5
andley Ct Mews **2**
  NG34 . . . . .212 D3
andley St
  Heckingham NG34 . . . . . .122 E3
  8 Sleaford NG34 . . . . . . .212 D4
ands on History Mus*
  HU1 . . . . .180 F6
angman's Cnr PE6 . . . . . .175 F5
angman's La
  Edenham PE10 . . . . .153 F7
  Haconby PE10 . . . . .154 A7
ankey St PE1 . . . . .225 F3
annah's Est PE34 . . . . . . .161 D1
ANNAH LN1 . . . . .76 E6
annah Cres LN6 . . . . .92 E5
annah Bvd PE11 . . . . .214 A3
annath PE13 . . . . .170 B8

Hanover Ct HU1 . . . . .180 E6
Hanover Dr **28** HU15 . . . . . .2 C5
Hanover Gdns DN16 . . . . . .185 C6
Hanover Hill DN21 . . . . .54 F6
Hanover Sq **1** LN7 . . . . . . .33 B4
Hansard Cres **3** LN7 . . . . .33 B4
Hansards Dr **2** LN8 . . . . . . .70 D5
Hansard Way **8** PE20 . . . .136 C5
Hanson Dr **2** LN12 . . . . . . .76 F8
Hanson Way DN32 . . . . . . .192 B8
HANTHORPE PE10 . . . . . .154 B7
Hanthorpe Rd PE10 . . . . . .154 B7
Ha'penny Bridge Way
  HU9 . . . . .181 B5
Harbour Way HU9 . . . . . . .181 C6
HARBY NG23 . . . . .79 C5
Harby Cl
  Grantham NG31 . . . . .210 E1
  Lincoln LN6 . . . . .205 B3
Harcourt Dr HU9 . . . . .181 C8
Harden's La LN9 . . . . .73 F1
Harding Cl
  9 Mablethorpe & Sutton
  LN12 . . . . .64 C1
  6 Mablethorpe/Sutton on Sea
  LN12 . . . . .76 F8
Harding House Gall*
  LN2 . . . . .234 B3
Hardings La PE23 . . . . .88 B2
Hardings The **20** LN2 . . . . .68 D7
Hardiway PE23 . . . . .209 B5
HARDWICK LN1 . . . . .196 A4
Hardwick Cl
  Louth LN11 . . . . .198 A7
  3 Saxilby with Ingleby
  LN1 . . . . .66 C2
Hardwick Cl PE23 . . . . . . .225 B2
Hardwicke Cl **7** NG31 . . . .211 A3
Hardwick Pl **1** LN2 . . . . . .202 A8
Hardwick Plot La PE20 . . . .124 C1
Hardwick Rd
  5 Kirton PE20 . . . . .136 C5
  1 Stamford PE9 . . . . .218 F6
Hardwick St HU5 . . . . .180 B8
Hardy Rd DN17 . . . . .184 D6
Hardy's Animal Farm*
  PE25 . . . . .90 E5
Hardys Ct DN32 . . . . .192 A6
Hardy's Dro PE10 . . . . .213 F7
Hardy's La PE11 . . . . .167 D4
Hardy's Rd DN35 . . . . .192 F4
Hardell Cl PE11 . . . . .221 F1
HAREBY PE23 . . . . .99 F8
Hareby Hill PE23 . . . . .100 A8
Hare Cl **3** HU4 . . . . .122 E2
Harecroft Rd PE13 . . . . . . .170 C1
Hare St DN32 . . . . .191 F6
Harewood Ave **7** DN3 . . . . .14 A2
Harewood Cres
  Lincoln LN6 . . . . .205 A3
  Louth LN11 . . . . .198 B7
Harewood Gdns PE3 . . . . . .225 B2
Harewood Gr **1** DN35 . . . .192 F1
Harford Gate PE12 . . . . . . .159 C5
Hargate La PE34 . . . . .161 E2
Hargate Way PE7 . . . . .230 D3
Hargon La NG24 . . . . .104 B7
Hargrave St DN31 . . . . . . .188 D1
Hargreaves Way DN35 . . . . .183 B6
Harland Rd **9** HU15 . . . . . . .2 C6
HARLAXTON NG32 . . . . . .139 C7
Harlaxton CE Prim Sch
  NG32 . . . . .139 C7
Harlaxton Cl **2** LN6 . . . . .204 C6
Harlaxton College
  NG32 . . . . .139 D7
Harlaxton Dr **4** LN6 . . . . .204 C6
Harlaxton Manor & Gdns*
  NG32 . . . . .139 D7
Harlaxton Rd **3** NG31 . . . .210 F3
Harlech Grange PE3 . . . . . .225 B1
Harlech Way DN32 . . . . . . .191 F8
Harlech Wlk DN40 . . . . . . .186 D3
Harlequin Dr
  10 Mablethorpe/Sutton on
  Sea LN12 . . . . .64 B3
  6 Spalding PE11 . . . . . . .214 A5
Harlestone Ct DN34 . . . . . .190 C4
Harley St HU2 . . . . .180 E8
Harlow St DN31 . . . . .188 D1
Harlton Cl PE2 . . . . .231 E5
HARMSTON LN5 . . . . .93 F5
Harmston Cl LN2 . . . . .202 A8
Harmston Pk Ave LN5 . . . . .93 F4
Harmston Rd LN5 . . . . .93 A5
Harneis Cres DN37 . . . . . . .23 F1
Harness Dr LN4 . . . . .207 A5
Harn Rd PE7 . . . . .230 E2
Harold's Bank PE13 . . . . . .169 B2
Harold St DN32 . . . . .192 A8
Harome Gr HU5 . . . . .179 C7
Harpe Cl **10** PE11 . . . . . . .156 E8
Harpenden Cl **3** DN7 . . . . .14 D3
Harpenden Dr **18** DN7 . . . .14 D3
Harper Garth LN9 . . . . .85 B5
Harpham Rd
  Gate Burton DN21 . . . . . . .53 A1
  Marshchapel DN36 . . . . . . .37 A5
  Marton DN21 . . . . .65 D8
HARPSWELL DN21 . . . . . . .54 E8
Harpswell Cl **1** NG31 . . . . .53 A8
Harpswell La LN2 . . . . .42 C1
Harpswell Rd LN2 . . . . . . .202 A7
Harrier Rd **3** DN8 . . . . . . .15 A1
Harriet St **5** PE12 . . . . . . .160 E4

HARRINGTON PE23 . . . . . . .87 C7
Harrington Ave **4** LN6 . . . .205 C8
Harrington Croft **8**
  PE12 . . . . .215 E2
Harrington Dr **7** PE1 . . . . .175 C8
Harrington Pl DN16 . . . . . .185 A5
Harrington Rd **7**
  NG33 . . . . .151 D2
Harrington St
  Bourne PE10 . . . . .213 D6
  Cleethorpes DN35 . . . . . .189 D1
Harrington Way **6**
  PE6 . . . . .175 C8
Harris Bvd **2** LN12 . . . . . . .64 B3
Harris Cl **1** PE25 . . . . .206 A5
Harrison Pl
  Lincoln LN1 . . . . .234 A4
  North Hykeham LN6 . . . . .204 A5
Harrison's Dro PE20 . . . . . .124 B2
Harrison's La PE24 . . . . . . .101 F4
Harrison St DN31 . . . . .191 C7
Harris Rd LN6 . . . . .205 B6
Harris St
  Kingston upon Hull
  HU3 . . . . .179 F5
  Peterborough PE1 . . . . . .225 F6
Harris Way NG31 . . . . .211 A2
Harrolds Cl **3** PE13 . . . . . .170 F1
HARROWBY **1** NG31 . . . . .211 F4
Harrowby CE (Aided) Inf
  Sch NG31 . . . . .211 C6
Harrowby Cl
  Digby LN4 . . . . .108 C5
  Grantham NG31 . . . . .211 C6
Harrowby Cres NG31 . . . . .211 D6
Harrowby Est NG31 . . . . . .211 D6
Harrowby La
  Grantham NG31 . . . . .211 D6
  Londonthorpe & Harrowby
  NG31 . . . . .130 C3
Harrowby Rd NG31 . . . . . . .211 C6
Harrow Cl
  Gainsborough DN21 . . . . .197 F6
  Heighington/Washingborough
  LN4 . . . . .203 C1
Harrowdyke DN18 . . . . .10 E8
Harrow Gdns DN17 . . . . . . .184 F4
Harrow Rd
  Deeping St Nicholas
  PE11 . . . . .166 C7
  6 Mablethorpe/Sutton on Sea
  LN12 . . . . .64 B3
Harrow St
  Grantham NG31 . . . . .211 B3
  Kingston upon Hull HU3 . .180 B4
Harrows The **8** LN2 . . . . . .68 D7
Harrox Rd **5** PE12 . . . . . . .157 F7
Harrox Sd **2** PE12 . . . . . . .157 F7
Harrys Dream **3** DN20 . . . .19 E3
HARSTON NG32 . . . . .138 E6
Harston Rd NG32 . . . . .138 F7
Hartford Ct PE7 . . . . .231 D6
Harthill Dr HU3 . . . . .180 C5
Hart La DN15 . . . . .9 B5
Hartland Ave **3** LN6 . . . . .205 A1
Hartle Bridge HU9 . . . . . . .181 C6
Hartley St
  Boston PE21 . . . . .208 F6
  3 Lincoln LN2 . . . . .234 C3
HARTSHOLME LN6 . . . . . .204 B8
Hartsholme Dr LN6 . . . . . . .205 A8
Hartsholme Pk LN6 . . . . . .204 B8
Hartshorne Prim Sch
  LN6 . . . . .204 F7
Hart St DN35 . . . . .192 C8
Hartwell Ct PE3 . . . . .225 D1
Hartwell Way PE3 . . . . .225 D1
Harvard Cl **1** LN4 . . . . . . .203 D1
Harvest Ave **34** DN18 . . . . .10 E8
Harvest Cl
  21 Kirk Sandall DN3 . . . . .14 A2
  2 Metheringham LN4 . . . . .95 C4
Harvest Cres **2** DN37 . . . .194 C4
Harvest Dr NG24 . . . . .104 B5
Harvester Cl **19** DN9 . . . . .27 E6
Harvester Way
  Crowland PE6 . . . . .175 B8
  Peterborough PE1 . . . . . .226 C1
  1 Sibsey PE22 . . . . .113 B1
Harvey Cl
  Bourne PE10 . . . . .213 B4
  11 Wittering PE8 . . . . . . .172 B1
Harvey Kent Gdns **1**
  LN3 . . . . .83 C4
Harveys Cl PE11 . . . . .214 F6
Harvey St LN1 . . . . .201 D3
Harwich Cl **12** LN5 . . . . . .205 D3
Harwood Ave PE22 . . . . . . .215 C1
Harwood Dr **1** HU4 . . . . . .179 B6
Hase Wlk HU1 . . . . .23 H6
Hassall Rd PE25 . . . . .206 A2
Hassock Hill Dro PE13 . . . .169 D3
HASTHORPE LN13 . . . . .89 C5
Hastings Cl **3** PE24 . . . . . .102 E8
Hastings Dr **4** LN4 . . . . . . .81 E4
Hastings Gr HU5 . . . . .179 E7
Hastings Rd PE4 . . . . .221 A2
HATCLIFFE DN37 . . . . .34 F3
Hatcliffe Cl **2** NG31 . . . . .211 A8

Hatcliffe Gdns **11** LN2 . . . .202 A8
Hatcliffe Cl **6** DN33 . . . . . .191 B3
HATFIELD DN7 . . . . .14 D5
Hatfield Crookesbroom
  Prim Sch DN7 . . . . .14 C4
Hatfield High Sch DN7 . . . . .14 D3
Hatfield La DN3 . . . . .14 A4
Hatfield Manor CE Jun Sch
  DN7 . . . . .14 C4
Hatfield Rd
  Hatfield DN7 . . . . .14 F6
  Thorne/Moorends DN8 . . . .15 A7
Harrington Way **6**
  PE6 . . . . .175 C8
Hatfield Woodhouse
  Prim Sch DN7 . . . . .14 C5
HATFIELD WOODHOUSE
  DN7 . . . . .15 A3
Hatfield Wr Pk* DN7 . . . . . .14 E5
Hathersage Ave LN6 . . . . . .204 E2
Hathersage Ct **3**
  DN15 . . . . .182 B2
Hatt Cl **2** PE21 . . . . .157 F7
HATTON LN8 . . . . .71 B3
Hatton Cl **3** LN6 . . . . .205 A7
Hatton Gr **7** DN33 . . . . . .191 B3
Hatton Mdws Nature
  Reserve* LN8 . . . . .71 A2
Haugh LN13 . . . . .75 B2
HAUGHAM LN11 . . . . .73 F8
Haugham Pastures
  LN11 . . . . .61 E2
Haugh La LN13 . . . . .75 A3
Hauser Cl **8** NG34 . . . . . .212 B2
Havelock Dr PE2 . . . . .231 E6
Havelock Mews DN32 . . . . .192 C6
Havelock St
  Kingston upon Hull
  HU3 . . . . .180 A4
  Spalding PE11 . . . . .214 C3
Havelok Cl **4** LN11 . . . . . .198 D4
Haven Ave
  Brough HU15 . . . . .2 B6
Haven Bank
  6 Skidbrooke with Saltfleet
  Haven LN11 . . . . .51 C4
Haven Bank LN4 . . . . .111 B3
Haven Cl
  7 Blyton DN21 . . . . .41 C5
  Fleet PE12 . . . . .159 C7
  Ferry Pk* PE21 . . . . . . .137 C7
Haven Garth **1** HU15 . . . . .2 B5
Haven Gdns DN31 . . . . . . .188 C1
Haven High Tech Coll The
  PE21 . . . . .209 E4
Haven House Rd PE24 . . . .102 F3
Havenhouse Sta PE24 . . . .102 F2
Haven Mdws PE21 . . . . . . .208 C7
Haven Rd
  4 Barton-upon-Humber
  DN18 . . . . .3 E1
  North Killingholme DN40 . . .13 A4
Haven Side **8** PE24 . . . . .102 D1
Havenside Nature
  Reserve* PE21 . . . . .137 A8
Haven The* PE21 . . . . . . .208 E4
Haven The HU10 . . . . .181 B6
Haven Village **3** PE21 . . . .208 F3
Haverfield Rd PE11 . . . . . . .214 D3
Haverholme Cl **10**
  LN4 . . . . .108 C1
Haverholme Dro PE12 . . . . .159 D5
Haverlands The **3**
  NG31 . . . . .210 E8
Haverstoe Pl DN35 . . . . . . .192 C3
Havveswater Cl **4** NG31 . .211 C2
Hawerby Rd **3** DN37 . . . . . .23 F1
Hawker Dr LN11 . . . . .198 D4
Hawkins Dr LN6 . . . . .204 F2
Hawkins Gr DN32 . . . . .192 B6
Hawkins Way **7** DN40 . . . . .12 E3
Hawksdale Cl **3** NG31 . . . .211 A7
Hawkshead Gr LN2 . . . . . . .202 A8
Hawksworth St **2**
  DN21 . . . . .197 D4
Hawksmede Way LN11 . . . .198 D8
Hawksmoor Cl **2** LN6 . . . .204 D1
Hawks Way NG34 . . . . .212 B3
Hawksworth St **2**
  DN21 . . . . .197 D4
Haworth Cl
  Brigg DN20 . . . . .196 C4
  Cherry Willingham LN3 . . .203 B6
  Gainsborough DN21 . . . . .197 D6
  Immingham DN40 . . . . . .186 E5
  Kingston upon Hull HU3 . .179 F5
  Waddington LN5 . . . . . . .205 C1
Hawthorn Bank LN11 . . . . .214 B1
Hawthorn Chase
  Lincoln LN2 . . . . .202 E7
  1 Moulton PE12 . . . . . . .157 F6
Hawthorn Cl
  Beckingham DN10 . . . . . . .52 A8
  Healing DN41 . . . . .23 F6
  4 Market Deeping PE6 . . .217 B6
  2 Newborough PE6 . . . . .174 E5
  2 Ruskington NG34 . . . . .108 E1
Hawthorn Ct **1** HU13 . . . .178 D3
Hawthorn Dr
  1 Mablethorpe LN12 . . . . .64 B3
  Sleaford NG34 . . . . .212 D3
Hawthorne Ave
  Cleethorpes DN35 . . . . . .192 D8

Hawthorne Ave continued
  9 Grimsby DN33 . . . . . . .194 F8
  9 Hatfield DN7 . . . . .14 C2
  Louth LN11 . . . . .198 B6
  New Waltham DN36 . . . . .195 B5
  4 Scunthorpe DN17 . . . . .184 F8
  8 Wisbech PE13 . . . . . . .170 D2
Hawthorne Cl
  2 Bracebridge Heath
  LN4 . . . . .81 A1
  5 Manby LN11 . . . . .62 C6
  6 Scopwick Heath LN4 . . .108 A7
  20 Winterton DN15 . . . . . . .9 A5
  Wroot DN9 . . . . .11 C2
Hawthorne Cres **3**
  DN17 . . . . .184 F8
Hawthorne Ct **4** NG31 . . . .210 D2
Hawthorne Gdns **8**
  DN19 . . . . .12 A8
Hawthorne Rise HU13 . . . . .178 B3
Hawthorn Gate **28** DN18 . . .10 F8
Hawthorn Gdns DN21 . . . . .197 D5
HAWTHORN HILL LN4 . . . .110 F6
Hawthorn Rd
  Bourne PE10 . . . . .213 C6
  Cherry Willingham LN3 . . .203 C6
  4 Old Leake PE22 . . . . . .114 A1
  Peterborough PE1 . . . . . .226 C5
  Skegness PE25 . . . . .206 A2
  Yaxley PE7 . . . . .233 F5
Hawthorn Rise **4** DN19 . . . .12 A8
Hawthorns The **14** LN2 . . . .68 D2
Hawthorn Way **4** LN5 . . . . .92 F3
Hawthorn Wlk **1** LN1 . . . . . .66 D7
HAWTHORPE PE10 . . . . . .142 A2
Hawthorpe Rd NG33 . . . . . .141 F1
Hawton Cl **1** DN21 . . . . . .197 E6
Hawton La NG24 . . . . .104 A2
HAXEY DN9 . . . . .27 C2
Haxey Carr DN9 . . . . .27 B4
Haxey CE Prim Sch DN9 . . .27 D3
Haxey Gate Rd DN10 . . . . . .39 F7
Haxey Grange **3** DN9 . . . . .27 D2
Haxey La DN9 . . . . .27 D1
Haxey Rd DN10 . . . . .39 F7
Haxey Turbary Nature
  Reserve* DN9 . . . . .27 A4
Haycroft Ave **4** DN31 . . . .191 C8
Haycroft La PE22 . . . . .159 B7
Haycroft St DN31 . . . . .191 C7
Haydon Ave PE25 . . . . .206 A4
Haydon Cl HU10 . . . . .178 D8
Haydor Ave LN2 . . . . .202 A8
Hayes Yd **4** LN11 . . . . .72 A8
Hayfield Cl
  7 Barnby Dun DN3 . . . . .14 A4
  5 Haxey DN9 . . . . .27 D2
Hay Gn Rd PE34 . . . . .161 E1
Hay Gn Rd (North)
  PE34 . . . . .161 E2
Hay Gn Rd (South)
  PE34 . . . . .161 D1
HAY GREEN PE34 . . . . . . .161 E1
Hayling Mere **3** DN35 . . . .192 F1
Haynes Cl **3** LN8 . . . . .15 B7
Haynes Gdns **8** DN8 . . . . .15 B8
Haynes Gn **8** DN8 . . . . . . .15 B8
Haynes Gr **1** DN8 . . . . . . .15 B8
Haynes Rd DN8 . . . . .15 B8
Hays Cl **3** DN36 . . . . .195 C2
Hayton Cl **2** DN15 . . . . .9 B5
Hayton Gr HU4 . . . . .179 D4
Haytons La **2** DN15 . . . . . . .9 D1
Haywain Dr **7** PE11 . . . . . .166 C6
Haywardsfield **4** PE23 . . . .225 A1
Haze La **3** LN6 . . . . .204 C6
Hazeland Cl HU10 . . . . .154 C6
Hazel Cl
  Messingham DN17 . . . . . . .29 C7
  North Hykeham LN6 . . . . .204 B1
Hazel Croft
  4 Immingham DN40 . . . . .186 A4
  Peterborough PE4 . . . . . .220 E4
Hazel Ct **29** HU15 . . . . .2 C5
Hazel Dr LN9 . . . . .199 B5
Hazel Gr
  6 Bottesford DN16 . . . . . .185 B2
  2 Kingston upon Hull
  HU3 . . . . .180 D5
  Louth LN11 . . . . .198 E4
  Sleaford NG34 . . . . .212 D6
  Stamford PE9 . . . . .218 D6
  Welton/Dunholme LN2 . . . .68 C6
Hazelnut Cl **3** PE22 . . . . . . .99 A4
Hazel Rd DN14 . . . . .14 C5
Hazelwood Ave LN6 . . . . . .204 C6
Hazelwood Dr PE10 . . . . . .213 B6
Hazelwood Dr PE10 . . . . . .159 A7
Hazelwood Rd NG31 . . . . . .210 F7
Headingley Ave **4**
  DN17 . . . . .184 E3
Headlands Dr LN12 . . . . . . .178 C2
Headland Way
  3 Haconby PE10 . . . . . . .154 D8
  2 Navenby LN5 . . . . .107 B8
Headquarters Cres **5**
  NG34 . . . . .120 C8
Heads La HU13 . . . . .178 C1
Headstead Bank DN22 . . . . .65 B7
Healey Cl **5** NG23 . . . . . . .91 D4
Healey La LN12 . . . . .63 C4
Healey Rd DN16 . . . . .185 C8

HEALING DN41...........23 F5
Healing Moated
  Settlement*
  DN4 ....23 F5
Healing Rd ⑤ DN41......23 D6
Healing Sch DN41........23 F5
Healing Prim Sch DN41 ..23 F5
Healing Sta DN41........23 F6
Heanor Ct DN15 ....182 B3
HEAPHAM DN21 ....53 E7
Heapham Cres DN21 ....197 F4
Heapham La DN21........53 F7
Heapham Rd DN21.......53 E7
Hearfield Terr HU13....178 E1
Heartsease Way PE10 ..213 E3
Heath Cl ① LN2.........68 C7
Heathcote Rd
  Bourne PE10 ....213 E4
  Castle Bytham NG33 ..152 D1
  Coningsby LN4........207 E5
Heather Ave PE1 ....226 A8
Heather Cl
  ① Boston PE1.........208 D3
  ① Woodhall Spa LN10 ..97 E6
Heatherdale Cl
  ⑥ Grimsby DN33 ......194 F2
  Peterborough PE7 ....231 C5
Heather Gr DN16 ....185 E5
Heather Rd PE25 ....206 B2
Heather Rd Ind Est
  PE25.................206 B2
Heath Farm Cl NG32 ...119 F3
Heath Farm Rd NG31 ...130 C2
Heathfield Ave
  Branston LN4..........81 E2
  Spalding PE11 ....214 F2
Heathfield Cl ⑨ DN3...14 A3
Heathfield Ct DN34 ....191 B6
Heathfield Rd NG31 ....210 C3
Heath La
  Ancaster NG32 ....119 F3
  Boothby Graffoe LN5 ..94 B2
  Carlton Scroop NG32 ..119 D4
  Great Ponton NG33 ...139 D4
  Honington NG32 ......119 C2
  Leasingham NG34 ....121 C7
  Normanton NG32.......119 F6
  Syston NG32 ....130 D8
  Welton LN1 ....67 F6
  Wilsford NG32........120 B1
Heathlea ① LN2 ....68 F4
Heath Rd
  Bracebridge Heath
  LN4 ....205 F2
  Coleby LN5............93 F3
  Helpston PE6 ....173 C2
  ⑮ Navenby LN5 ....107 A8
  ① Nettleham LN2......68 C2
  Scopwick LN4 ....108 B8
  Southern LN2 ....68 D4
  Skegness PE25 ....206 B3
Heath's Meadow Nature
  Reserve* PE4 ....102 C7
Heaton Cl PE3 ....225 B3
Heaton St ① DN21......54 F1
Hebden Moor Way ⑧
  LN6 ....93 B8
Hebden Rd DN15 ....182 C4
Hebden Wlk NG31......211 F6
HECKDYKE DN10 ....40 C7
Heckdyke La DN10......40 C7
HECKINGTON NG34 ......122 D3
Heckington Rd NG34...122 C1
Heckington Sta NG34 ..122 C1
Heckington Windmill*
  NG34.................122 E2
Hedda Dr ② PE7.......230 D3
Hedgefield Hurn PE11 ..144 F4
Hedge Field Rd NG32 ..210 A4
HEDGEHOG BRIDGE
  PE20.................124 E5
Hedgehog La PE20.....124 D4
Hedge La LN6 ....92 D4
Hedgelands
  Peterborough PE4 ....221 A5
  ③ Wisbech PE13.....170 D2
Hedgerow Cl ⑤ DN19...11 C8
Hedgerow La ① DN20 ..196 D3
Hedon Rd HU9.........181 B6
HEIGHINGTON LN4 ......81 F4
Heighington Fen LN4....82 A5
Heighington Rd LN4 ....81 C4
Heimdal Rd DN33 ......191 C2
Helen Cres ① DN40....186 A4
Helene Gr DN32 ....192 B7
Helenship La DN22......65 A4
Hell La NG32 ....140 C5
Hellyers Ct HU4 ....179 D2
Helm Dr HU9 ....181 C6
Helmsdale Gdns PE4...220 F2
Helmsley Ct ① HU7....231 F5
Helmsley Gr HU5 ......179 C7
Helmsley Way PE11 ....214 F4
HELPRINGHAM NG34....133 E7
Helpringham Rd
  Burton Pedwardine
  NG34.................122 B1
  Helpringham NG34 ...133 C8
Helpringham Sch
  NG34 ....133 D7
HELPSTON PE6 ....173 C4
Helpston Rd
  Castor PE5............223 D2
  Etton PE6 ....220 A8
Helsby Rd LN5 ....205 D4

HELSEY PE24 ....89 F7
Helsey La PE24 ....89 F7
Helston Wlk DN17 .....184 C8
Heltwate PE3 ....225 B7
Heltwate Sch PE3......225 B7
Heltwate Sch PE3......225 B7
HEMINGBY LN9 ....72 B1
Hemingby La LN9.......199 C6
Hemingby Way LN9 ....199 C5
Hemingford Cres PE2 ..231 E6
Hemington Way ①
  PE20.................136 C5
Hemmingway Wlk
  HU13 ....178 E3
Hempdyke Rd DN15....182 E4
Hemplands The ⑨
  NG23 ....91 D5
Hemswell Ave
  ④ Kingston upon Hull
  HU9 ....5 E8
  Lincoln LN6 ....205 D4
HEMSWELL CLIFF LN8....55 A8
Hemswell Cliff Prim Sch
  LN8 ....43 A1
Henderson Ct DN31 ...190 F8
Hemswell La DN21......42 D1
Henderson Ave DN15 ..182 F4
Henderson Ave Prim Sch
  DN15 ....182 F4
Henderson Cres ②
  DN15 ....182 F4
Henderson Way DN15 ...9 A5
Heneage Rd DN32 .....191 F6
Hengist Cl ① NG34 ...212 B2
Henley Ct
  ② Gainsborough
  DN21.................197 C6
  Lincoln LN5 ....205 D8
Henley St LN5 ....205 D8
Henlow Cl
  ⑥ Birchwood LN6 ....204 B8
  ① Kirton in Lindsey DN21 ..42 F8
Henrietta St ③ PE11..214 C3
Henry Boot Way HU4 ..179 B1
Henry La LN3...........83 D4
Henry St
  Grimsby DN31 ....191 C8
  Lincoln LN5 ....201 F1
  Peterborough PE1 ....226 A4
  Scunthorpe DN15 ....182 F3
Henshaw PE1..........226 E6
Henshaw Ave ① LN12 ..77 A7
Henson Cl
  ⑬ Spalding PE11 .....214 C2
  ⑤ Wisbech PE13 .....170 D2
Henson Dr ⑬ DN15....107 A8
Henton Cl ⑦ LN6 .....104 C5
Hercules Dr ⑦ NG24 ..104 A4
Herdgate La PE11......145 D2
Hereford Ave DN34 ....191 A3
Hereford Ct ① NG34 ..212 C7
Hereford St ① HU4....179 E3
Hereford Tech Sch
  DN34 ....191 B5
Hereford Way ⑧ NG31 ..210 E5
Heren Pl ⑦ PE11 ......214 A2
Hereward Cl ② PE1....226 B2
Hereward Cross ⑥
  PE1..................226 A2
Hereward Pl DN16.....185 E7
Hereward Rd
  Peterborough PE1 ....226 B2
  Spalding PE11 ....214 B4
Hereward St
  ⑤ Bourne PE10 ......213 D5
  Lincoln LN1 ....234 B4
Hereward Way
  ⑪ Crowland PE6 .....166 E1
  Market Deeping PE6 ..217 E4
Herewood Com Coll
  PE1..................226 D5
Herewood Cross Sh Ctr
  PE1..................226 A3
Heritage Pk Prim Sch
  PE7..................231 F5
Herlington PE2.........230 B4
Herlyn Cres ③ PE25....90 E3
Hermes Way NG34.....212 A3
Hermitage The ⑥ PE9 ..219 A5
Hermit St LN5 ....234 B1
Heron Cl
  Grimsby DN32 ....192 B4
  ⑥ Scunthorpe DN15 ..182 C6
  Skegness PE25 ......103 C8
  ⑤ Surfleet PE11 .....145 E3
Heron Dr DN21 ....197 F5
Heron Holt ⑥ DN20....19 D4
Heron Pk PE1 ....226 F6
Heronry Dr PE6 ....224 E2
Herons Ct PE9 ....172 F6
Heron St HU3 ....180 B5
Heron View LN6 ....204 E8
Heron Way
  ⑬ Barton-upon-Humber
  DN18..................10 E8
  Holton le Clay DN36 ..195 C3
  Spalding PE11 ....214 F2
  Wyberton PE21 ......136 F8
Herrick Cl LN5 ....205 D4
Herrick Ct ② LN4 .....207 A6
Herrick Rd DN17.......184 D7

Herring La
  ① Pinchbeck PE11 ...145 B1
  ② Spalding PE11 .....214 D4
Herrington Ave ③ LN2 ..68 C2
Hersey Rd ⑱ LN7 ......33 B4
Hervey Rd NG34 ......212 C2
Hesketh Cres ⑪ PE25 ..103 E4
Hesketh Ct LE15 ......162 A8
Hesketh Dr ⑤ DN3 ....14 A2
HESSLE HU13...........178 C1
Hessle Ave DN14 ......208 D4
Hessle Ct PE21 ....208 C4
Hessle Dr PE21 ....208 C3
Hessle High Sch HU13 ..178 C2
Hessle Mount Sch
  HU13 ....178 C3
Hessle Penshurst Prim Sch
  HU13 ....178 F3
Hessle Rd HU4 ....178 D1
Hessle Sta HU13 ....3 E4
Hessle View ④ DN18....10 E8
Hetley PE2 ....230 A4
Hever Cl NG31.........210 E5
Hewde La DN15 ....2 A1
Hewitt's Ave
  Humberston DN36 ....192 C1
  New Waltham DN36 ..195 D8
Hewitt's Cir DN36.....192 C2
Hewitts Manor ①
  DN35 ....192 D2
Hewitt's Windmill*
  DN21.................53 E7
Hewson Rd
  ⑤ Humberston DN36 ..36 D8
  Lincoln LN1 ....201 C4
Hewson's La NG23 ....91 D3
Hewson St ② DN17 ....29 D7
Hexham Ct ③ PE1 ....226 D3
HEYDOUR NG32 ....131 D6
Heyford Cl PE4 ....221 D2
Heynings Ct DN21 .....53 B4
Heysham Cl ⑧ LN5 ....205 D3
Hey St DN35 ....192 F5
Heythrop Rd ③ DN35 ..192 E3
HIBALDSTOW DN20 ......31 A5
Hibaldstow Cl
  ⑩ Birchwood LN6 ....204 C7
  ⑧ Grimsby DN34 .....190 F4
Hibaldstow Prim Sch
  DN20..................31 A5
Hibaldstow Rd LN6 ....204 C7
Hickling Cl LN6 ....210 E2
Hickling Wlk PE4 .....221 C3
Hickman Cres DN21 ...197 C8
Hickman Ct DN21 .....197 E4
Hickman Gr ② DN21 ...41 B5
Hickman St DN21 .....197 C4
Hickory Rd ⑤ LN6 .....200 C1
Hicks La PE7 ....230 F5
Hide's La
  Addlethorpe PE24 .....90 B1
  Skegness PE25 ....103 B8
Higgins Cl LN6 ....204 E7
Higgins Rd ① LN13 ....75 E2
Higham Way ① HU15 ...2 D5
Highbridge La PE11 ...145 C6
Highbridge Rd LN11 ...49 F2
High Bridge Rd DN8 ...15 C7
High Broadgate PE13 ..169 F7
High Bunning La NG34 ..143 A7
High Burgage DN15 ....2 B1
Highbury St PE1 ....226 A5
Highclere Rd PE7 .....230 D3
Highcliffe ⑤ DN15 ....107 A7
Highcliffe Rd NG31 ....211 B7
Highcliff Gdns DN15 ..182 E3
High Cliff Rd DN35....193 A6
High Cres PE9 ....171 C8
High Ct Way PE7 .....233 D8
Highdales HU10 ......178 C8
High Dike
  Cranwell & Byard's Leap
  NG34.................120 B8
  Easton NG33 ....151 E8
  Great Ponton NG33 ..140 C4
  Navenby/Wellingore LN5 ..94 B1
  North Rauceby NG32 ..120 A5
  Old Somerby NG33 ...130 D2
  Waddington LN5 ....93 F8
  Welby NG31...........130 E5
  Wellingore LN5 ....107 B6
  Wilsford NG32........119 F1
High Dyke Rd ② NG34 ..107 C1
High Fen PE11.........144 B4
HIGH FERRY PE22 .....126 A8
High Ferry La PE22 ...113 A1
Highfield Ave
  ① Immingham DN40 ..186 B3
  ② Lincoln LN6 ....205 B7
  ③ Mablethorpe/Sutton on Sea
  LN12 ....64 C1
  Scunthorpe DN15 ....182 E3
  Wellow DN32.........191 E5
Highfield Cl
  ⑧ Barnby Dun DN3 ...14 A4
  Foston NG32 ....117 F2
  Gainsborough DN21 ..197 E5
  ⑧ North Thoresby DN36 ..36 B1
  Osbournby NG34 .....132 C5
Highfield Cres
  ⑰ Barton-upon-Humber
  DN18..................10 F8
  Croxton Kerrial NG32 ..138 D3
  Westwoodside DN9 ...27 B2
Highfield Dr
  ⑧ Kirton in Lindsey
  DN21..................30 B1
  Stapleford LN6 ....105 A6

Highfield Gr DN20 ....196 C5
Highfield La
  Halton Holegate PE23 ..101 B8
  Reveshy PE22 ....99 B5
Highfield Rd
  ⑦ Donington PE11 ...134 F2
  North Thoresby DN36 ..36 B1
  ⑭ Saxilby LN1.........66 D2
High Field Rd DN20....196 F5
Highfields
  ⑧ Barrowby NG32 ...210 A5
  ① Barrow upon Humber
  DN19..................11 C7
  ⑰ Crowle DN17 ....16 D8
  ② Nettleham LN2......68 D2
High Fields La PE11....156 E8
Highfields Rise ⑤ LN4 ..95 C4
Highfields Sch NG24 ..104 B3
Highfield Terr
  ⑤ Glentham LN8......43 F1
  ⑤ Lincoln LN6 ....205 A2
High Garth DN17.......184 F2
Highgate ① DN15 .....192 F5
High Gate
  Helpringham NG34 ...133 C7
  Mablethorpe & Sutton
  LN12 ....64 A2
  Theddlethorpe St Helen
  LN12 ....63 D5
Highgate Cl ③ LN12 ...64 C1
Highgate La
  Claxby with Moorby
  PE22..................99 B6
  Normanby by Spital LN8 ..56 B7
  Owmby LN8 ....55 F6
Highgrove
  ⑪ Long Sutton PE12 ..216 B5
  ⑨ Messingham DN17 ..29 D7
Highgrove Cres PE21 ..209 C6
Highgrove Gdns PE9 ..218 C5
High Holme Rd LN11 ..198 B6
Highlees Prim Sch
  PE3..................225 C6
High Levels Bank DN8 ..15 F8
High Leys Rd DN17 ...184 F3
HIGH MARNHAM NG23 ..78 B5
High Mdw
  Grantham NG31 ......210 D4
  Heighington/Washingborough
  LN4 ....203 C1
High Mdws
  ① Fiskerton LN3......82 A7
  Kingston upon Hull
  HU10 ....178 C8
High or Main Rd PE12 ..215 A2
High Point Ret Pk
  DN31 ....189 A1
High Rd
  Barrowby NG32 ......210 A5
  Elloughton-cum-Brough
  HU15 ....2 D7
  Gorefield PE13 ....169 F2
  Grantham NG31 ......211 C8
  Hough-on-the-Hill NG32 ..119 A5
  Londonthorpe & Harrowby
  without NG31 ....130 D4
  Moulton PE12 ....158 A7
  ⑧ Saxilby LN1.........66 D2
  Weston PE12 ....157 C7
  Wisbech St Mary PE13 ..177 F2
High Ridge Comp Sch
  DN15 ....182 E3
High Ridge Sch & High
  Ridge Adult Ed Ctr
  DN15 ....182 E3
High Ridge Sports Hall
  DN15 ....182 E3
HIGH RISBY DN15 ....9 A1
High St E DN15 ....183 C3
High St N ⑯ NG16 ....108 E2
High St S ⑰ NG16 ....108 E2
High St St Martin's
  PE9..................219 C3
High St W DN21 ....29 B4
High Side PE13 ....169 D2
High St
  ① Alford LN13 ....75 F3
  Alvingham LN11 ......49 F2
  Barrow upon Humber
  DN19..................11 D8
  ① Barton-upon-Humber DN18 ..3 E1
  Bassingham LN5 ......92 F2
  Baumber LN9 ....85 A4
  ② Beckingham DN10 ..52 B8
  Belton DN9 ....16 E1
  Benniworth LN8 ....71 B8
  Bicker PE20 ....135 A4
  Binbrook LN8 ....47 C4
  Blyton DN21 ....208 F3
  Boston PE21 ....208 F3
  Bottesford NG13 ....128 A6
  Branston LN4..........81 E2
  ⑤ Broughton DN20 ...19 D3
  Burgh le Marsh PE24 ..102 E8
  Burringham DN17 .....17 D4

High St continued
  Caistor LN7 ....33 B3
  Careby PE9...........163 C1
  Carlton-le-Moorland LN5 ..105 E4
  Castle Bytham NG33 ..152 D1
  Castor PE5............223 B1
  Caythorpe NG32 .....119 E1
  Cherry Willingham/Reepham
  LN3 ....203 D6
  Cleethorpes DN35 ....192 E6
  Collingham NG23 ......91 D6
  ③ Collyweston PE9 ..171 E1
  Colsterworth NG33 ...151 C7
  Coningsby LN4........207 A4
  Corby Glen NG33 ....152 C7
  Corringham DN21 ......41 E2
  ⑨ Crowle DN17 ....16 C8
  Donington PE11 ......134 E2
  Eagle & Swinethorpe LN6 ..79 E5
  East Ferry DN21 ......28 E5
  Eastoft DN17 ....7 A2
  ⑫ Easton on the Hill
  PE9..................171 C3
  Elkington LN11 ....60 E5
  Epworth DN9 ....27 C2
  Eye PE6 ....175 A1
  Faldingworth LN8 ......56 F8
  ⑮ Fillingham DN21 ....56 F6
  ② Fiskerton LN3......82 A7
  Flixborough DN15 ......8 B3
  ③ Fulbeck NG32 .....106 C1
  Fulletby LN9 ....86 B1
  Gainsborough DN21 ..197 D3
  Garthorpe & Fockerby
  DN17...................7 E6
  Gate Burton DN21 ....53 A5
  Girton NG23...........78 E8
  Glentham LN8 ....43 F3
  Glinton PE6 ....220 C8
  Gosberton PE11 .....145 B6
  Grainthorpe LN11 ....50 B8
  Grantham NG31 ......211 A5
  Great Gonerby NG31 ..129 D5
  Great Limber DN37 ...22 D1
  Gringoleythorpe PE23 ..87 A1
  Harby NG23 ....79 C4
  Harlaxton NG32 .....139 C7
  Harmston LN5 ....93 F3
  Hatfield DN7 ....7 C1
  Haxey DN9 ....27 C2
  ⑯ Heckington NG34 ..122 E3
  Heighington/Washingborough
  LN4 ....203 B1
  Helpringham NG34 ...133 D7
  Hogsthorpe PE24......90 D7
  Holbeach PE12 ....215 E6
  Horbling NG34 ....133 B3
  Horncastle LN9 ......199 B4
  Humberside Airport DN39 ..22 A3
  Ingham LN1 ....54 F7
  ① Ingoldmells PE25....90 E6
  Ketton PE9 ....171 C1
  Kexby DN21 ....53 E2
  Kingston upon Hull HU1 ..181 A2
  ⑱ Kirton in Lindsey DN21 ..30 B1
  Laceby DN37 ....23 E3
  Leadenham LN5 ......106 D5
  Lincoln LN5 ....234 A2
  ② Little Bytham NG33 ..163 A3
  Long Sutton PE12 ....216 C5
  Luddington & Haldenby
  DN17...................7 D1
  ⑫ Mablethorpe/Sutton on Sea
  LN12 ....64 B4
  Market Deeping PE6 ..217 B5
  Market Stainton LN8 ..72 A4
  Martin LN4 ....96 C3
  Marton DN21 ....65 D8
  Messingham DN17 .....29 D7
  Metheringham LN4 ....95 C4
  Misterton DN10 ....39 F5
  ⑤ Morton PE10 ......154 C2
  Moulton PE12 ....157 F6
  ⑫ Navenby/Wellingore
  LN5 ....107 A2
  Nettleham LN2........68 C2
  Newton on Trent LN1 ..65 D4
  North Ferriby HU14 ....3 A5
  ⑧ North Kelsey LN7 ...32 A4
  Northorpe PE10 ......164 C2
  North Scarle LN6 ......78 E4
  North Thoresby DN36 ..36 A1
  Osbournby NG34 .....132 C5
  Owston Ferry DN9 .....28 B3
  Peterborough PE2 ....231 A3
  Pointon & Sempringham
  NG34.................143 B2
  Redbourne DN21 ......30 F5
  Reepham LN3 ....203 F6
  Rippingale PE10.......142 F2
  Ropsley NG33 ....131 B1
  Roxby cum Risby DN15 ..8 E3
  Saxilby LN1 ....66 D2
  Scampton LN1 ....67 C7
  Scotter DN21 ....29 C3
  Scunthorpe DN15 ....183 A3
  Sixhills LN8 ....59 A4
  Skegness PE25 ......206 C3
  Skellingthorpe LN6 ...200 A4
  Snitterby DN21 ....43 D8
  South Clifton NG23 ...78 C5
  South Ferriby LN11.....10 A4
  South Kyme LN4 ......123 B4
  South Witham NG33 ..151 D1
  Spalding PE11 ....214 C4

gh St continued
Spilsby PE23. . . . . **88** A1
Stamford PE9. . . . . **219** C5
Staunton NG13 . . . . **117** A2
Sturton by Stow LN1 . . . .**66** C7
Sutton Bridge PE12 . . . . **160** F4
Swayfield NG33. . . . . **152** D5
Wainfield NG33 . . . . **132** B7
Swineshead PE20 . . . . **135** B7
Swinstead NG33 . . . . **153** A5
Upton DN21. . . . . **53** D5
Waddingham DN21 . . . . **43** D7
Waddington LN5 . . . . **93** F7
Vainfleet All Saints
PE24 . . . . **102** D1
Walcott LN4. . . . . **109** D7
Walesby LN8 . . . .**46** B5
Walkeringham DN10 . . . . **39** F3
Waltham DN37 . . . . **194** E4
Welbourn LN5 . . . . **106** E5
West/East Butterwick
DN17. . . . .**17** D1
Willingham by Stow DN21. . .**53** E3
Winterton DN15 . . . .**9** A5
Wootton DN39. . . . . **11** E2
Wroot DN9. . . . .**26** D6
gh Thorpe Cres
N35 . . . . **192** D3
gh Thorpe Rd LN13 . . . .**83** D1
GH TOYNTON LN9 . . . .**86** A4
gh Wash Dro **2** PE6 . . . . **166** E1
ghwood Mews DN35 . . . **192** E1
ghwood Rd PE27 . . . . **230** C1
gson Rd **4** LN1. . . . . **201** D7
lary Gr HU4 . . . . **179** B2
lary Rd DN33 . . . . **194** C7
lda Cl **6** NG34. . . . . **212** B2
Idas Ave HU5 . . . . **180** A8
lda St
Boston PE21 . . . . **209** A7
Grimsby DN32. . . . . **189** C1
ldreds Sh Ctr PE25 . . . . . **206** D3
Idyard Ct **1** HU10. . . . . . **178** F6
Idyard St DN32 . . . . **192** B8
les Ave **8** DN21 . . . .**9** A5
ll Abbey LN4 . . . .**95** D7
llary Cl
Spalding PE11 . . . . **214** B2
Stamford PE9 . . . . **219** D6
llary Rd DN16. . . . . **185** B5
llary Way DN37 . . . . **190** E8
ll Ave NG31. . . . . **211** B5
ll Brow HU10 . . . . **178** B6
ll Cl PE1 . . . . **226** D5
ll Cres DN21 . . . . **197** F5
llcrest NG34 . . . . **107** C2
llcrest Ave
Kingston upon Hull
HU13. . . . . **178** C2
Paxley PE7 . . . . **233** E6
llcrest Com Inf Sch
DN21. . . . . **197** F4
llcrest Dr **2** DN15 . . . . **8** A4
llcrest Gdns **3** PE20. . . **135** B7
llcroft **1** LN4. . . . . **205** D2
ll Ct NG31. . . . . **210** D2
LLDYKE PE22 . . . . **126** A6
ll Field **8** PE24 . . . . **102** D2
llfoot Dr DN17 . . . . **184** E3
llgate PE12 . . . . **168** C2
llgate St PE34 . . . . **161** F3
llingford Way NG31 . . . . . **210** E3
ll La PE20 . . . . **136** B5
llman Cl LN4 . . . . **205** F3
llman Rd HU13 . . . . **178** F3
ll Rd DN21. . . . .**41** E1
ll Rise
Broughton HU15 . . . .**2** C6
Coleby LN5. . . . .**93** F3
South LN11 . . . . **198** A7
ll's Ct **9** NG34. . . . . **212** D4
lls Dr **3** DN36. . . . . **36** D4
llside
Ancaster NG32 . . . . **120** A2
Marton DN21. . . . .**65** E8
llside App **6** LN2. . . . . . **202** C3
llside Ave
Lincoln LN2 . . . . **202** C1
Mablethorpe/Sutton on Sea
LN12 . . . .**77** A8
llside Cl PE9 . . . . **172** F2
llside Cres
Barnetby le Wold DN38. . .**21** B5
Grantham NG31 . . . . **211** D2
llside Dr
Barton-upon-Humber
DN18. . . . .**10** E8
Grantham NG31 . . . . **211** D2
llside Est NG34 . . . . **108** F2
llside Rd
Broughton DN20 . . . . **19** E4
Glentworth DN21. . . . .**54** F7
Woolsthorpe by Belvoir
NG32. . . . . **128** D1
llstead Cl **15** DN36. . . . .**36** D4
llsyde Ave **11** DN10 . . . . **39** F5
ll Terr LN11 . . . . **198** C4
ll The
Saltfleet LN11 . . . .**51** C4
Skellingthorpe LN6 . . . . . **200** A4
Worlaby DN20. . . . .**10** E1
ll Top **11** LN6. . . . . **215** B2
lltop Ave DN15 . . . . **182** D5
lltop Cl DN17. . . . .**79** B2
lltop Dr DN17 . . . .**29** C7
ll Top La **1** DN21 . . . .**41** B5
ll Top Pl DN34 . . . . **190** D3

Hill View Cl NG31 . . . . **210** E3
Hill View Rd **14** NG33 . . . **151** D2
Hillward Cl PE2. . . . . **230** C6
Hilton Ave DN15 . . . . **182** B3
Hilton Cl **2** DN9 . . . .**16** E2
Hilton Ct DN35 . . . . **193** B1
Hilton's La PE12 . . . . **136** E1
Hinaidi La LN4. . . . .**95** C7
Hinchcliffe PE2 . . . . **229** E2
Hindon Wlk DN17. . . . . **184** C8
Hine Ave NG24. . . . . **104** B4
Hinkler St DN35 . . . . **192** E5
Hinkley Dr DN40 . . . . **186** B5
Hinman Wlk **9** DN15 . . . . **183** D3
Hipper La PE20 . . . . **135** D2
Hither Old Gate PE12 . . . . **158** D6
Hives La LN6 . . . .**71** E2
Hix Cl PE12. . . . . **215** C2
Hix's La PE13. . . . . **160** A1
Hobart Cl **11** LN5 . . . .**93** E8
Hobart Rd NG31 . . . . **211** D7
Hobart St HU3 . . . . **180** D5
Hobb La **4** DN21 . . . .**29** C3
Hobhole Bank Nature
Reserve* PE21 . . . . **137** C7
Hobson Rd **7** HU15. . . . .**2** C6
Hobsons Gn PE11. . . . . **214** A5
Hobson Way DN41 . . . . **187** E2
Hockland Rd **2** PE13 . . . . **169** F7
Hockle's Gate PE12 . . . . . . **159** B7
Hockney Hole La PE12 . . **158** A7
Hodder Cl **1** NG34. . . . . . . **212** B3
Hoddesdon Cres **20**
DN7 . . . .**14** D3
Hod Fen Dro PE7 . . . . **233** F2
Hodge Ct **8** HU9 . . . . **181** C7
Hodgetoft La LN11 . . . .**63** E1
Hodgson Ave PE4 . . . . **220** E6
Hodgson St HU8 . . . . **181** A7
Hodgson Way **3** LN12 . . . . .**77** A8
Hodney Rd **6** PE6 . . . . **175** A1
Hodson Cl LN16 . . . . **200** B5
Hodson Gn LN9. . . . . **199** C4
Hoe Dr **19** LN6. . . . .**93** A7
Hoekman Dr **8** PE11 . . . . . **214** B2
Hoekman Way PE11. . . . . . **214** B2
HOFFLEET STOW PE20 . . **135** C4
Hogens La HU3 . . . . **170** A5
Hoggard La DN14 . . . .**7** E8
Hogg La HU10 . . . . **178** B8
Hog's Gate PE12. . . . . **158** A6
HOGSTHORPE PE24 . . . .**90** B6
Hogsthorpe Prim Sch
PE24. . . . .**90** B7
Hogsthorpe Rd LN13. . . . . . **76** F1
HOLBEACH PE12. . . . . **215** C3
HOLBEACH BANK
PE12. . . . . **215** C7
Holbeach Bank Prim Sch
PE12. . . . . **215** C7
HOLBEACH CLOUGH
PE12. . . . . **215** C2
Holbeach & District Nature
Reserve* PE12 . . . . **215** E2
Holbeach Dro Gate
PE12. . . . . **168** C4
HOLBEACH DROVE
PE12. . . . . **168** B3
HOLBEACH HURN
PE12. . . . . **147** F2
Holbeach Prim Sch
PE12. . . . . **215** D3
Holbeach Rd
Spalding PE11 . . . . **214** F6
Spalding PE12 . . . . **157** B6
HOLBEACH ST JOHNS
PE12. . . . . **158** C1
HOLBEACH ST MARKS
PE12. . . . . **147** A2
Holbeach St Marks CE Prim
Sch PE12 . . . . **147** A2
HOLBEACH ST MATTHEW
PE12. . . . . **148** A2
Holbeach Tecnology Pk
PE12. . . . . **215** B4
Holbeck Pl **2** DN40. . . . . . **186** B4
Holborn Rd PE11 . . . . **214** B2
Holborn St HU8. . . . . **181** B7
Holcroft PE2. . . . . **230** B3
Holdan Cl DN36. . . . . **193** A1
Holdenby Cl **3** LN2. . . . . . **202** E7
Holden Dr **9** PE24. . . . . . . **102** E7
Holden Way **7** NG31. . . . . **129** E5
Holderness Rd HU9 . . . . . . **181** C8
Holdfield PE3. . . . . **225** B6
Holdich St PE3 . . . . **225** E2
HOLDINGHAM NG34 . . . . . **121** E6
Holdingham La NG34 . . . . **121** E7
Hole Gate PE12 . . . . **101** C8
Holgate La PE4. . . . . **220** F7
Holgate Pl **13** HU14 . . . .**3** B7
Holgate Rd DN16 . . . . **185** D8
Holkham Rd PE2. . . . . **229** D3
Holland Ave
Crowle DN17. . . . .**16** DB
Peterborough PE4 . . . . . . **221** B1
Scunthorpe DN15 . . . . . . **182** B4
Holland Cl
Bourne PE10 . . . . **213** C5
Market Deeping PE6 . . . **174** B4
Holland Dr PE25. . . . . **206** C1
Holland La PE22 . . . . **114** F4
Holland Mkt **18** PE11 . . . **214** D4
Holland Rd
Horbling NG34. . . . . **133** B3
Spalding PE11 . . . . **214** E4
Stamford PE9. . . . . **219** C6

Holland Rd continued
Swaton NG34. . . . . **133** E3
Holland's Chase PE11. . . . **156** A6
Holland St HU9. . . . . **181** D8
Holland Way PE12 . . . . **215** B2
Hollengs La **1** LN11 . . . .**59** E1
Holles St **6** DN32. . . . . . . **191** E8
Hollies The PE12. . . . . **215** E3
Hollin Bridge La DN7 . . . .**15** A3
Hollingworth Ave **1**
DN40 . . . . **186** B4
Hollingworth Cl **6**
DN35 . . . . **192** D2
Hollingsworth La DN9. . . . . . .**27** E6
Hollis' Rd NG31. . . . . **210** F2
Hollowbrook Cl **3**
NG34 . . . . **108** D2
Hollowdyke La NG24 . . . . . **104** C1
Hollowgate Hill DN21 . . . . . **42** E4
Hollowgate La NG23 . . . .**78** A5
Hollows The **4** LN11. . . . . . .**61** F3
Holly Cl
Cherry Willingham/Reepham
LN3. . . . . **203** E5
Horncastle LN9 . . . . **219** A5
Lincoln LN5. . . . . **205** D5
Newborough PE6 . . . . . . **174** E5
Scunthorpe DN16 . . . . . . **185** C4
Sleaford NG34 . . . . **212** D2
Stallingborough DN41 . . . .**23** E6
Holly Dr PE10. . . . . **213** C7
Holly Hill **1** HU15 . . . .**2** E6
Holly Rd PE25. . . . . **206** A2
Holly St LN5. . . . . **205** D5
Hollytree Ave **2** HU5 . . . . **179** B7
Holly Tree Cl **9** LN8 . . . .**57** D7
Holly Way **2** PE6 . . . . **217** D4
Hollywell Rd LN5 . . . . **205** D1
Hollywell Rd (The Rookery)
23 LN3. . . . .**75** F2
Holly Wlk PE7 . . . . **230** D3
Hollywood Dr **8** NG31. . . . **210** F7
HOLME
DN16 . . . .**19** A1
Holme NG23 . . . .**91** A2
Holme Ave DN36. . . . . **195** C6
Holme Cl
Brigg DN20 . . . . **196** D4
Castor PE5. . . . . **223** D2
Thorpe on the Hill LN6. . . .**92** F8
Holme Dene **1** DN9 . . . .**27** C2
Holme Dr
Burton upon Stather
DN15. . . . .**8** B5
Sudbrooke LN2 . . . .**68** F2
Holme Gdns **7** DN7 . . . .**14** C7
Holme Hall Ave DN16 . . . . **185** B3
HOLME HILL DN32 . . . . . . **191** F6
Holme La
Grassthorpe NG23. . . . .**78** A2
Holme DN16. . . . . **185** E2
Marnham NG23 . . . .**78** A4
Messingham DN17 . . . .**29** E8
Ruskington NG34 . . . . . . **108** A1
Scunthorpe DN16 . . . . . . **185** B3
Winthorpe NG24 . . . . **104** B8
Holme Rd PE7 . . . . **233** E4
Holmes Cl
Louth LN11 . . . . **198** B7
Skidbrooke with Saltfleet
Haven LN11 . . . .**51** C4
Holmes Dr **10** PE9 . . . . . . **171** A3
Holmes Field **6** LN5 . . . . . .**92** F3
Holmes La
North Somercotes LN11 . . .**38** A1
Roxby cum Risby DN15 . . . .**9** D5
Welton/Dunholme LN2 . . . .**68** E6
Holmes Rd
Frampton PE20 . . . . **124** F1
Glinton PE6 . . . . **220** D7
Horsington LN10 . . . .**83** F1
Kirton PE20 . . . . **136** A8
Stickney PE22 . . . . **113** A7
Stixwould & Woodhall
LN10. . . . .**84** A1
Holmes Sch DN21 . . . . **191** E7
Holmes Way
Horncastle LN9 . . . . **199** D1
Peterborough PE4 . . . . . . **221** D2
Wragby LN8. . . . .**70** D4
Holme Valley Prim Sch
DN16 . . . . **185** C3
Holme Wlk **1** DN36 . . . . . **197** F5
Holme Wood Cl **5** DN3 . . .**14** A1
Holme Wood La
Claxby with Moorby LN9 . . .**99** B8
Hameringham LN9 . . . .**86** B1
Holmfield LN3 . . . .**82** B7
Holmfirth Rd DN15. . . . . . . **182** C4
Holm La NG23 . . . . **104** F1
Holm Rd DN9. . . . .**27** B2
Holmshaw Cl **2** DN15 . . . . .**14** A2
Holmside LN6 . . . . **185** A2
Holt Cl
Lincoln LN6. . . . .**93** C8
Wittering PE8. . . . . **172** B1
Holt La
Horncastle LN9 . . . . **199** D4
Mareham le Fen PE22 . . . .**99** A3
Holton Ct DN36. . . . . **195** C1
HOLTON CUM BECKERING
LN8. . . . .**70** C8
HOLTON LE CLAY
DN36 . . . . **195** D2
Holton-le-Clay Inf Sch
DN36 . . . . **195** D2

Holton le Clay Jun Sch
DN36. . . . . **195** E1
HOLTON LE MOOR LN7. . . .**45** A8
Holton Mount DN36. . . . . . **195** C2
Holton Rd
Nettleton LN7 . . . .**33** A2
South Kelsey LN7. . . . .**32** D1
Tetney DN36 . . . . **195** F1
Holt Prim Sch The
LN6. . . . . **200** A3
Holt The DN21. . . . . **197** F5
Holy Cross Gdns **12**
NG32 . . . . **119** B7
Holydyke DN18 . . . .**10** E8
Holy Family Prim Sch
DN7 . . . .**14** D7
Holyoake Rd DN32 . . . . **192** C6
Holyroad Dr DN15 . . . . **182** D7
Holyrood Cl PE20 . . . . **134** E3
Holyrood Wlk PE11 . . . . . . **214** D2
Holy Trinity CE Prim Sch
LN4. . . . . **207** A5
Holywell Cl **1** PE25 . . . . . **211** A5
Holy Well La LN11 . . . .**49** A4
Holywell Rd **6** PE6 . . . . . . **162** E8
Holywell Way PE3 . . . . **224** F2
Home Beat Dr DN20 . . . .**19** C3
Home Cl
Bourne PE10 . . . . **213** C7
Bracebridge Heath LN4. . **205** F3
Kingston upon Hull HU4 . . **179** C5
Home Ct **8** LN5 . . . . **205** E3
Home Farm Cl
Great Casterton PE9 . . . . **218** C8
Laughterton LN1. . . . .**65** D2
Homefarm La NG23. . . . .**79** A7
Homefield Ave DN33 . . . . . **191** D3
Home Paddock DN37 . . . . **194** E4
Home Pasture **4** NG24 . . **220** F5
Home Pk **4** NG34 . . . . **120** F8
Homers La PE22 . . . . **126** D4
Home St DN15. . . . . **183** B4
Homestead Garth **11**
DN7 . . . .**14** D4
Honeyhall Rd PE13 . . . . **169** C2
Honeyhill Com Prim Sch
PE4. . . . . **221** E1
Honeyholes La LN2 . . . .**68** D6
Honey Pot Cl LN22 . . . . **202** E7
Honey Pot La NG33 . . . . . . **151** F4
Honeysuckle Cl
11 Lincoln LN6. . . . . **205** C2
14 Mablethorpe & Sutton
LN12 . . . .**76** F8
18 Sutton on Sea Ln11 . . .**76** F8
Honeysuckle Ct
Humberston DN35. . . . . . **192** E1
Peterborough PE2 . . . . . . **230** D7
Scunthorpe DN16. . . . . . **185** C4
HONINGTON NG32 . . . . . . **119** C2
Honington App **5** LN1. . . **201** D7
Honington Cres LN1 . . . . . . **201** D7
Honington Rd **2** NG32. . . **130** B8
Hood Cl NG34 . . . . **212** A3
Hood Rd DN17. . . . . **184** D6
Hood St
Kingston upon Hull
HU8. . . . . **181** A8
8 Lincoln LN5. . . . . **201** F1
Hook's Dro PE13 . . . . **177** C4
Hooks La LN5 . . . . **106** E6
Hoop End DN36. . . . .**36** D4
Hoopers Cl **4** NG13 . . . . . **128** A5
Hoop La LN9 . . . .**70** E2
Hope Gdns PE12 . . . . **215** E3
Hope St
Cleethorpes DN35 . . . . . . **193** A5
Grimsby DN32 . . . . **191** F8
Lincoln LN5 . . . . **201** F1
Hopfield DN20 . . . .**31** A5
Hopgardens **1** DN21. . . . . . .**53** E3
Hopgarth **11** DN9 . . . .**27** D2
Hop Hills La DN7 . . . .**14** F5
Hoplands Rd LN4 . . . . **207** D5
Hoplands The **4** NG34 . . **212** F4
Hopland's Wood Nature
Reserve* LN13 . . . .**88** F6
HOP POLE PE11. . . . . **165** F5
Hopton St LN9 . . . . **199** B3
Hopwood Cl HU3 . . . . **180** D8
Hopyard La
Bassingham LN5 . . . .**93** B1
Normanton on Trent
NG23. . . . .**78** A3
Horace St PE21. . . . . **208** E5
HORBLING NG34 . . . . **133** C2
Horbling Fen Dro
NG34 . . . . **133** D2
Horbling La PE22 . . . . **114** F4
Horbling Lane Nature
Reserve* NG34 . . . . **133** B1
Horbury Cl DN15. . . . . **182** D4
HORKSTOW DN18 . . . .**10** A5
Horkstow Rd DN18 . . . .**10** E7
Hornbeam Ave DN16 . . . . . **185** A5
Hornby Dr **20** LN12 . . . .**77** A7
HORNCASTLE LN9. . . . . . . **199** D3
Horncastle City Prim Sch
LN9 . . . . **199** C4
Horncastle Hill **2** NG34 . . .**87** A1
Horncastle La
Dunholme LN2 . . . .**68** B5
Grange de Lings LN1 . . . . . .**67** F5
Horncastle Rd
Bardney LN3 . . . .**83** C4

Horncastle Rd continued
Boston PE21 . . . . **208** F8
Fishtoft PE21. . . . . **125** E5
Goulceby LN9. . . . .**72** D5
Horsington LN10 . . . .**84** D4
Louth LN11 . . . . **198** A4
Mareham le Fen PE22 . . . . .**98** F4
Raithby cum Maltby LN11 . . .**60** F2
Roughton LN9 . . . .**85** C2
Tathwell LN11 . . . .**73** A8
West Ashby LN9 . . . . **199** C8
Woodhall Spa LN10 . . . .**97** F6
Wragby LN8 . . . .**70** D5
Horne La **3** NG22 . . . .**65** B1
Horner Cl **1** LN5. . . . . **205** C2
Hornsby Cres DN15 . . . . . . **182** F4
Hornsby Rd NG31. . . . . **210** E2
Hornsea Parade **4**
HU9 . . . . **181** C8
Horney Hill Rd DN21 . . . .**28** D1
Horn The **7** PE25 . . . . **206** A7
Horse Fair Gn **28** DN18 . . . .**15** A8
Horse Fayre **7** PE11. . . . . **214** A3
Horsegate PE6 . . . . **217** D4
Horsegate Field Rd DN19 . . .**5** B2
Horseham's La PE20 . . . . . **135** A5
Horse Mkt **24** LN7. . . . .**33** B4
Horsemoor Dro PE12 . . . . **159** B1
Horsemoor La LN9. . . . .**72** C2
Horse Pasture La DN22 . . . .**65** C1
Horseshoe Cl **12** NG14 . . **200** B5
Horseshoe Cl **12** NG14 . . **126** D5
Horseshoe Rd PE11 . . . . . . **214** A2
Horseshoe Terr **5** PE13 . . **170** C1
Horseshoe Way
Hampton Vale PE7. . . . . . **230** D2
Yaxley PE7 . . . . **233** D8
Horseshoes Yd **11** PE6 . . **166** E1
Horsewells St **11** DN9 . . . . .**39** C1
HORSINGTON LN10. . . . .**84** C3
Horstead Ave DN20 . . . . . . **196** D5
Horton St LN2 . . . . **202** C3
Hospital Dro PE12 . . . . **225** C5
Hospital La PE21. . . . . **209** A6
Hospital Rd PE12 . . . . **161** A5
Hotchkin Ave LN1. . . . .**66** E2
Hotham Dr HU5 . . . . **179** B8
Hotham Rd HU5. . . . . **179** A8
Hotham Rd S HU5 . . . . **179** B8
Hotham St HU9 . . . . **181** D7
Hotspur Rd DN21 . . . . **197** C6
HOUGHAM NG32 . . . . **118** C3
Hougham Rd
Hougham NG32 . . . . **118** B4
Westborough & Dry
Doddington NG23. . . . . . **117** F5
Hough La
Carlton Scroop NG32. . . . **119** C4
Claypole NG23. . . . . **117** F7
Hough Rd
Barkston NG32 . . . . **130** B8
Carlton Scroop NG32 . . . **119** A3
Hough-on-the-Hill NG32 . . **118** E7
Houghton Ave PE2 . . . . **231** F5
Houghton Rd NG31 . . . . . . **211** C2
Houlden Way **1** NG34 . . . **122** A5
Hounsfield Cl PE2. . . . . **104** B5
Houps Rd **8** DN8 . . . .**15** B8
Hourne Ct HU13 . . . . **178** E2
Hourne St HU13. . . . . **178** E2
House Ct LN16 . . . . **185** D4
Househams La LN11 . . . .**61** F3
Howard Cl DN34 . . . . **161** F2
Howard Gr DN32. . . . . **192** B6
Howard Rd **10** LN4 . . . . . . **108** A7
Howard St LN1 . . . . **201** C4
Howdale La HU2 . . . . **181** A7
Howden Croft Hill HU15. . . . .**2** A8
Howe La
Ashby with Scremby
PE23. . . . .**88** C3
Goxhill DN19 . . . .**11** F8
HOWELL NG34 . . . . **122** D5
Howell Fen Dro NG34 . . . . **122** E5
Howell Rd NG34 . . . . **122** E3
Howgarth La PE22 . . . . **114** F5
Howland Rd **3** NG13. . . . . **128** A5
Howland PE2 . . . . **230** A3
Howlett Rd DN35 . . . . **193** A4
HOWSHAM LN7 . . . .**32** A6
Howsham La **3** DN20 . . . . . .**14** D3
Howville Ave **2** DN7 . . . . . .**14** F3
Howville Rd **1** DN7 . . . .**14** F3
Hoylake Dr
1 Immingham DN40 . . . . **186** D5
Peterborough PE7 . . . . . . **231** C5
Skegness PE25 . . . . **206** D5
Hoylake Rd DN17 . . . . **184** F6
Hubba Cres PE25 . . . . **206** B6
Hubbard Cl **2** NG34 . . . . . **135** C6
Hubbard's La PE25 . . . . **206** B5
HUBBERT'S BRIDGE
PE20. . . . . **124** F2
Hubberts Bridge Sta
PE20. . . . . **124** F2
Hubert's Cl **1** LN11 . . . .**62** C1
Hub The * NG34. . . . . **212** E4
Huckles Way PE25. . . . . **206** B6
Huddleston Rd DN35 . . . . . **192** B7
Hudson Ave DN15. . . . . **182** B3
Hudson Cl PE23. . . . .**88** B3
Hudson Ct HU13 . . . . **178** D1

Hudson Dr LN4 . . . . .207 E6
Hudson Rd **4** PE11 . . . . . . 214 C2
Hudson's Gdns **5**
PE21. . . . . .209 B4
Hudson St HU3 . . . . .180 D8
Hudson Way
Grantham NG31. . . . . .211 A3
12 Skegness PE25. . . . . . .206 A5
Huggin Carr Rd DN7 . . . . . .14 F1
Hughes Ford Way **20**
LN1. . . . . .66 D2
Hugh Hill La DN7 . . . . .14 D6
Hughson Wlk **3** LN2. . . . . .68 E6
Hulberry Cl **10** DN41 . . . . . .23 A4
Hull Arena* HU1 . . . . .180 E4
Hull Coll
Kingston upon Hull
HU1. . . . . .181 A7
Kingston upon Hull HU2 . .180 D7
Kingston upon Hull HU3 . .179 F7
Hull Collegiate HU10. . . . .178 D5
Hull & E Riding Mus*
HU9 . . . . .181 A6
Hull Maritime Mus*
HU1. . . . . .180 F6
Hull Rd HU13 . . . . .178 F1
Hull Royal Infmy HU3 . . . .180 C6
Hull's Dro PE6. . . . . .167 D3
Hull Sta HU1 . . . . .180 E6
Hull Trinity House Sch
HU1 . . . . .180 F6
Hull Truck Theatre*
HU2 . . . . .180 D7
Humber Bank Factories
DN41. . . . . .187 D4
Humber Bank S DN31 . . . .189 C2
Humber Bridge Rd
DN31 . . . . .189 C1
Humber Cres
6 Brough HU15 . . . . .2 C5
Scunthorpe DN15 . . . . . . .184 F6
Humberdale Cl **8** HU14. . . .3 B6
Humberdale Dr HU14 . . . . . .3 C5
Humber Dock St HU1 . . . .180 F5
Humber Rd
Barton-upon-Humber
DN18. . . . . .3 E1
Immingham DN40 . . . . . . .186 A8
North Ferriby HU14 . . . . . . .3 A4
Humberside Intl Airport
DN38 . . . . .21 F5
Humber St
3 Cleethorpes DN35 . . . .192 F5
Grimsby DN31 . . . . .189 C1
Kingston upon Hull HU1 . .180 F5
HUMBERSTON DN35 . . . . .193 A2
Humberston Ave DN36 . . .195 E6
Humberston CE Prim Sch
DN36 . . . . .36 D8
Humberston Comp Sch
DN36 . . . . .36 C8
Humberston Holt **1**
LN11. . . . . .198 C7
Humberstone Rd DN32. . .192 A6
Humberston Fitties*
Dn36 . . . . .36 F8
Humberston Pk Specl Sch
DN36 . . . . .36 C8
Humberston Rd
Cleethorpes DN36 . . . . . .192 C3
Tetney DN36 . . . . .36 C6
Humber Terr DN31 . . . . . .191 C8
Humber View
3 Barton-upon-Humber
DN18. . . . . .10 E8
Kingston upon Hull
HU13. . . . . .178 C2
4 Swanland HU14 . . . . . . .3 B6
Humberville Rd DN40 . . . .186 D4
HUMBY NG33. . . . . .141 C7
Humby Rd NG33. . . . . . . .141 B8
Hume Brae **6** DN40 . . . .186 B3
Hume St **5** DN31 . . . . . .191 C7
Hunchback La PE13. . . . . .170 E2
HUNDLEBY PE23 . . . . .87 F1
Hundlehouse La LN4 . . . . .111 D4
HUNDLE HOUSES LN4. . . .111 C4
Hundle Houses La LN4 . . .111 D4
Hund Oak Dr **3** DN7 . . . .14 D4
Hundred Acres La
NG24 . . . . .104 B1
Hundreds La
Gringley on the Hill
DN10. . . . . .39 A5
Little Sutton PE12 . . . . . . .216 F1
Hundreds Rd PE6 . . . . . . .175 C6
Hungarton Ct **3** PE1. . . .226 D8
Hungate LN1 . . . . .234 B2
Hun Gate PE11 . . . . .145 D3
Hungate Rd NG32. . . . . . .139 A7
Hungerdike Gate PE12 . . .215 A2
HUNGERTON NG32 . . . . . .140 A7
Hungry Hill Rd **1** HU13 . . .62 C5
Hunsley Cres DN32 . . . . . .192 B4
Hunsley Dr **5** DN41. . . . . .23 E6
Hunstan La PE20 . . . . .113 F4
Hunston Rd **4** LN10 . . . . .97 C5
Huntcliff Sch DN21 . . . . . . .30 C1
Hunter Ave LN11. . . . . .62 C6
Hunter Pl LN11 . . . . .198 B4
Hunter Rd
Brookenby LN8 . . . . .47 A6
Brough HU15 . . . . .2 C6
Hunters Cl **9** PE12 . . . . . .215 E2
Hunter's Croft **1** DN9 . . . .27 D3

Hunters Dr **13** LN4 . . . . .95 C4
Hunter's Dr **6** DN10 . . . . .39 C1
Hunters La
Baumber LN9. . . . . .72 A1
Tattershall LN4 . . . . .207 C5
Hunting Ave PE2 . . . . .230 F7
Huntingdon Cl **2** PE2 . . . .215 E3
Huntingdon Cres **8**
DN15 . . . . .8 B4
Huntingdon St HU4 . . . . . .179 E3
Huntingdon Com Prim
Sch NG31 . . . . .211 A3
Huntingtower Rd
NG31 . . . . .211 A3
Hunt Lea Ave
Grantham NG31. . . . . .210 F1
Lincoln LN6 . . . . .205 C8
Huntly Gr PE1 . . . . .226 A4
Huntly Rd PE2 . . . . .230 E7
Hunt Rd DN16 . . . . .185 C5
Hunts Cl **7** DN20 . . . . .19 E4
Huntsgate PE12 . . . . .159 D4
Hunt's Gate PE12 . . . . . . .159 E1
Hunts La **4** DN20 . . . . .30 F5
Huntsman CI PE1 . . . . .209 D2
Huntsmans Chase
DN36 . . . . .195 B7
Huntsmans Gate PE3 . . . .224 F3
Hurdletree Bank PE12. . . .158 E4
Hurdman Way PE25 . . . . . . .90 E3
Hurd's Farm DN20 . . . . . . .20 D8
Hurford Pl DN37 . . . . .194 D7
Hurle Cres PE21 . . . . .208 D6
Hurlstone Cl **25** DN3 . . . . .14 A2
Hurn Bank PE12 . . . . .147 E2
Hurnbridge Rd LN4 . . . . . .111 A4
Hurn Cl
2 Birchwood LN6. . . . . .204 B8
7 Ruskington NG34 . . . .108 D1
Hurn Dro LN4 . . . . .110 A8
Hurn La PE22. . . . . .126 A7
Hurn Rd
Holbeach PE12 . . . . .147 E1
Marholm PE6. . . . . .220 C3
HURN'S END PE22 . . . . . . .127 C8
Hurn The
5 Billingborough
NG34. . . . . .133 B1
Digby LN4 . . . . .108 E6
Hurst Cres NG32 . . . . .210 A4
Hurst La DN17 . . . . .184 E3
Hurstlea Dr DN36 . . . . . . .193 B1
Hurst The **6** PE25 . . . . . . .206 A6
Hurstwood Cl LN2 . . . . . . .202 D8
Hurton's La LN11 . . . . .49 C6
Hussey Cl **2** NG34 . . . . . .212 E4
Hussey Twr* PE21 . . . . . . .209 A4
Husthwaite Rd **18** HU15. . . .2 D5
Hutchinson Gdns **5**
PE12. . . . . .157 E7
Hutchinson Rd **2**
DN15 . . . . .192 E7
Huteson La DN15 . . . . .8 C8
Hutson Dr LN6 . . . . .204 F2
HUTTOFT LN13. . . . . .76 E3
Huttoft Bank Pit nature
Reserve* LN13. . . . . .77 B6
Huttoft Prim Sch LN13 . . . .76 F3
Huttoft Rd **17** LN12 . . . . . .76 F8
Hutton Cl **3** PE11 . . . . . . .214 F2
Hutton Rd DN31 . . . . .189 B2
Hutt St HU3 . . . . .180 D7
Hyde Gdns PE6 . . . . .164 F3
Hyde Pk Cl
6 Lincoln LN6. . . . . .204 F1
Nunsthorpe DN33 . . . . . . .191 B2
Hyholmes PE3 . . . . .224 F7
Hykeham Rd LN6 . . . . .205 B4
Hykeham Sta LN6. . . . . . . .204 D3
Hymers Ave HU3 . . . . .180 B7
Hymers Coll HU3 . . . . .180 B7
Hyperion St HU9. . . . . .181 A7
Hythegate PE4. . . . . .221 B4

Ingham Cl LN6. . . . . .205 B3
Ingham Cl LN4 . . . . .207 E6
Ingham Hall Gdns
PE13. . . . . .177 D7
Ingham La LN1. . . . . .55 B1
Ingham Prim Sch LN1. . . . .54 F2
Ingham Rd
Coningsby LN4 . . . . .207 E6
3 Stow LN1. . . . . .66 C8
Inghams La **1** DN36 . . . . . .36 D4
Inghams Rd **3** DN36. . . . . .36 D4
Ingleborough **1** PE1. . . . .226 A5
INGLEBOROUGH PE14 . . . .170 E5
INGLEBY LN1. . . . . .66 C4
Ingleby Cres LN2 . . . . .201 F8
Ingleby Cl PE21. . . . . .214 F4
Ingleby Gr DN37 . . . . .190 F8
Ingleby Rd **14** DN17 . . . . . .29 D7
Ingleby St PE21 . . . . .151 D7
Ingledew Cl **8** NG34. . . . .122 E2
Inglenook Dr **2** DN8. . . . . .15 B8
Ingleton Ave HU4 . . . . . . .179 C6
Inglewood Cl DN16 . . . . . .185 A4
Inglewood Dr **4** HU4 . . . .179 B5
Ingmires **1** PE21. . . . . .2 D6
INGOLDMELLS PE25. . . . . .90 E4
Ingoldmells Prim Sch
PE25. . . . . .90 D4
Ingoldmells Rd PE24 . . . .102 E8
INGOLDSBY NG33 . . . . . . .141 D5
Ingoldsby Prim Sch
NG33 . . . . .141 D5
Ingoldsby Rd NG33. . . . . .141 B3
Ingram Cres **9** DN7 . . . . . .14 C4
Ingram Gdns **11** DN20 . . . .30 E8
Ingram Gr DN7 . . . . .14 C4
Ingram La **1** NG23 . . . . . . .78 A1
Ingram Pl DN35. . . . . .192 D2
Ingram Rd
Boston PE21. . . . . .208 D6
Hatfield DN7 . . . . .14 C3
Ingram Row LN9. . . . . .199 B3
Ing Rd PE20 . . . . .134 F4
Ings Bank PE22 . . . . .126 E7
Ings Dro
Butterwick PE22 . . . . .126 D7
Leverton PE22 . . . . .113 E1
Ings La
Belchford LN9 . . . . .73 B2
Brackenborough with Little
Grimsby LN11 . . . . .49 B4
Bratoft PE24 . . . . .102 C6
Brough HU15 . . . . .2 C5
Cumberworth LN13 . . . . . . .89 E7
Ellerker HU15 . . . . .2 A5
2 Hibaldstow DN20. . . . . .31 A5
Horsington LN10 . . . . .84 D2
Immingham DN40 . . . . . . .186 E3
Leverton PE22 . . . . .126 F7
Little Steeping PE23 . . . . .101 E5
North Coates DN36 . . . . . . .37 A3
North Ferriby HU14 . . . . . . .3 A4
Saltfleetby LN11 . . . . .62 F8
Scamblesby LN11 . . . . .71 A8
Skidbrooke with Saltfleet
Haven LN11 . . . . .51 A3
South Cave HU15. . . . . .1 E7
South Somercotes LN11 . . .50 E3
Walkerith DN21 . . . . .40 C3
Waltham DN37. . . . . .194 F4
8 West Ashby LN9 . . . . . . .85 E7
West Ashby LN9 . . . . .199 D8
West Stockwith DN10. . . . . .40 C6
Winterton DN15. . . . . .9 B4
Ings Rd
Benington PE22. . . . . .126 D8
Gringley on the Hill DN10. . .39 B3
Kirton in Lindsey DN21 . . . .29 F1
Mablethorpe & Sutton
LN12 . . . . .76 E7
INGTHORPE PE9 . . . . .218 A8
Inhams Cl PE13 . . . . .177 D5
Inley Dro PE12 . . . . .169 A8
Inner St NG31 . . . . .211 B3
Innings The **1** NG34 . . . .212 D3
Innovation Way
Alwalton PE2 . . . . .229 B5
Great Coates DN37 . . . . . . .24 B6
Inns Cl LN6 . . . . .204 E3
Inshops Ctr DN32 . . . . . . .189 B1
Intax Mews DN32 . . . . . . .191 F6
Inverness Rd **14** DN7 . . . .14 C4
Iona Cl DN21 . . . . .197 E6
Iona Dr DN36. . . . . .36 D8
Ipswich Gdns NG31 . . . . . .210 E5
Irby Cres **9** PE21 . . . . . . .158 B7
Irby Ct DN35. . . . . .192 D3
IRBY IN THE MARSH
PE24. . . . . .102 B6
Irby Pl PE21 . . . . .208 F5
Irby Rd DN17 . . . . .184 E5
Irby St PE21 . . . . .208 E5
IRBY UPON HUMBER
DN37 . . . . .34 D7
Irchester Pl PE3 . . . . .225 D5
Ireland Wlk HU4 . . . . .179 B4
Ireton Ave NG24 . . . . .104 C4
Irish Hill LN1 . . . . .198 A5
IRNHAM NG33 . . . . .141 E1
Irnham Rd
Corby Glen NG33. . . . . . . .141 C1
Stamford PE9 . . . . .219 C2
Iron Bar Dro PE13 . . . . . . .155 F4
Ironestone Cl LN4 . . . . . . .207 D8
Ironmonger St **8** PE9 . . .219 C5
Irvine Rd **2** DN16. . . . . . .185 C5
Irwin Rd DN21. . . . . .41 C6

Isaac Newton Prim Sch The
NG31. . . . . .210 F3
Isaac Newton Way
NG31 . . . . .211 F6
Isaac's Hill DN35. . . . . . . .192 E6
Isaan Newton Ctr **14**
NG31 . . . . .225 D4
Isham Rd **1** PE3. . . . . . . .225 D4
Isis Ct HU9 . . . . .181 B5
ISLAND CARR DN20 . . . . .196 B2
Island Carr Rd DN20 . . . . .196 A3
Island Rd DN17 . . . . .7 E6
Isle Cl **3** DN17 . . . . .16 D8
Islip Ct **2** LN9 . . . . .199 D3
Ison Cl **4** NG34. . . . . . . .120 E8
Itlings La HU13 . . . . .178 F1
Itterby Cres DN35. . . . . . .192 C3
Itter Cres PE4 . . . . .221 C1
Ivanhoe Rd **4** DN16 . . . .183 C1
Ivatt Cl **1** NG34. . . . . . . .122 F2
Ivatt Way **2** PE3 . . . . . . .225 C6
Ivel Cl **6** LN12. . . . . .64 B5
Ivel Gr **4** LN12 . . . . .64 B5
Ivery La PE22 . . . . .114 D4
Ivesdyke Cl **3** PE13. . . . . .170 B2
Ivy Cl PE4. . . . . .14 E4
Ivy Cres PE21. . . . . .208 D3
Ivy Farm Ct **20** DN41 . . . . .23 F5
Ivy Gr PE4 . . . . .221 B2
Ivy La
Coningsby LN4. . . . . .207 F1
Grainthorpe LN11 . . . . .37 C1
Wainfleet St Mary PE24 . . .115 C8

J

Jack Haws La **3** PE9 . . . .172 D4
Jack Hunt Sch PE3 . . . . . .225 B3
Jack Hunt Swimming Pool
PE3. . . . . .225 B3
Jacklin Cl **5** LN11 . . . . . . .50 B8
Jacklin Cres LN12 . . . . .64 A4
Jacklin Dr **3** LN11. . . . . . .51 C4
Jacklin La DN17 . . . . .7 C3
Jacklins App DN16 . . . . . .185 A3
Jack Row La DN7 . . . . .14 B8
Jackson Dr **3** HU3 . . . . . .180 C5
Jackson Mews **6**
DN40 . . . . .14 D4
Jackson Rd **1** DN15 . . . .182 E3
Jackson's Field LN8 . . . . . .57 B7
Jacksons La PE24 . . . . . . .102 E8
Jackson's Pl DN36 . . . . . .192 D1
Jackson St
Grimsby DN31 . . . . .191 C8
Kingston upon Hull HU3 . .180 D4
Jacobean Rd **4** LN6 . . . . .204 D6
Jacobs Ct **2** PE11 . . . . . .214 C6
Jade Gr **1** HU3. . . . . .180 A4
Jaguar Dr LN6. . . . . .204 D6
Jail La PE22 . . . . .126 F2
James Ave
Mablethorpe/Sutton on
Sea LN12 . . . . .64 C2
Skegness PE25 . . . . .206 B6
James Ct
Gainsborough DN21 . . . . .197 D5
Louth LN11 . . . . .198 C6
Jameson Bridge St **8**
LN8. . . . . .57 D8
Jameson St **2** HU1 . . . . .180 F6
James Pl DN39. . . . . .12 B1
James Rd **1** DN21. . . . . . .55 A8
James St
Boston PE21. . . . . .208 E5
Brigg DN20 . . . . .196 C3
Grimsby DN31 . . . . .191 C8
Lincoln LN2 . . . . .234 B3
Louth LN11 . . . . .198 C6
James Way **9** DN40 . . . . .186 B3
Jankin La PE24 . . . . .161 F1
Janton Ct DN36. . . . . .195 C7
Japan Rd DN21 . . . . .197 B5
Japonica Hill **3** DN40. . .186 C3
Jaque's Bank DN40 . . . . . . .16 A5
Jarratt Hill La HU15. . . . . . . .1 D8
Jarratt St HU1. . . . . .180 F6
Jarvis Cl LN6 . . . . .204 F7
Jarvis's Gate PE12 . . . . . .159 C1
Jasmin Cl **9** PE13. . . . . . .170 E1
Jasmine Cl PE10. . . . . . . .213 B7
Jasmine Ct
2 Goxhill DN19 . . . . .12 A8
Peterborough PE2 . . . . . . .229 E2
Spalding PE11 . . . . .214 A2
Jasmine Way
Immingham DN40 . . . . . . .186 C3
Yaxley PE7. . . . . .233 F6
Jason Rd **6** LN6. . . . . . . .205 A5
Javelin Ave **8** LN8. . . . . . .47 B6
Javelin Rd **12** LN11. . . . . .62 C6
Jefferson Cl **8** PE4 . . . . .228 F1
Jefferson Dr **22** HU15. . . . .2 C6
Jeffery Ave **6** PE13 . . . . .170 E1
Jeffrey La DN9. . . . . .16 E1
Jekil's Bank
Holbeach PE12 . . . . .158 C1
Moulton PE12 . . . . .167 B8
Whaplode PE12 . . . . .158 E5
Jekil's Gate PE12 . . . . .159 A5
Jellicoe Ave PE24 . . . . . . .102 D3
Jellicoe Ct DN16. . . . . .183 C1
Jellicoe Dr LN4 . . . . .207 B6
Jenkins Cl
Louth LN11 . . . . .198 C5
5 Skegness PE25. . . . . .206 A7

Jenkins' La PE22. . . . . .127 #
Jenner Ct **2** DN35. . . . . . .192 #
Jenner Dr **1** DN35. . . . . . .192 #
Jenning St HU8. . . . . .181 #
Jenny Brough La HU13. . . .178 #
Jenny Brough Mdws
HU13 . . . . .178 #
Jenny Cl HU13 . . . . .178 #
Jensen Rd LN4 . . . . .205 #
Jericho La DN40. . . . . .12 #
Jermyn Mews LN4. . . . . . .203 #
Jermyn St NG34 . . . . .212 #
Jerusalem LN6 . . . . .79 #
Jerusalem Ave LN6 . . . . . .200 #
Jesmond Ave **5** DN17 . . .184 #
Jesmond View LN1. . . . . . .201 #
Jessop Cl
Beacon Hill NG24. . . . . . . .104 #
Cherry Willingham/Reepham
LN3. . . . . .203 #
Horncastle LN9 . . . . .199 #
9 Leasingham NG34 . . . .121 #
Jessop Way NG24 . . . . . . .104 #
Jiggle's Gate PE12. . . . . . .158 #
Jill Gr HU13 . . . . .178 #
Job's La LN6 . . . . .79 #
Jobson Rd LN9 . . . . .199 #
Jock Hedge PE24 . . . . .102 #
John Adams Way PE21. . . .208 #
John Brown Cl LN9 . . . . . .199 #
John Clare Prim Sch
PE6. . . . . .173 #
John Coupland Hospl
DN21 . . . . .197 #
John Kew Way PE6. . . . . . .217 #
John Fielding Com Specl
Sch PE21 . . . . .209 #
John Foster Cl **9**
NG31 . . . . .211 #
John Gold Ave **6**
NG24 . . . . .104 #
John Harrison CE Prim Sch
DN19 . . . . .11 #
John Harrison's Cl **3**
DN19 . . . . .11 #
John Harrison Way
PE12. . . . . .215 #
John Harrox Prim Sch The
PE12. . . . . .157 #
John Hunt Infants Sch
NG24 . . . . .104 #
John Hunt Jun Sch The
NG24 . . . . .104 #
John Leggott Sixth Form
Coll DN17. . . . . .184 #
John Mansfield Sch
PE1. . . . . .226 #
John Smith Cl LN13. . . . . .199 #
Johnson Ave PE11. . . . . . .214 #
Johnson Cl
3 Belton DN9. . . . . .16 #
3 Skegness PE25. . . . . .206 #
Johnson Ct LN4 . . . . .207 #
Johnson Dr
Bracebridge Heath
LN4 . . . . .205 #
9 Scotter DN21 . . . . .29 #
Johnson Hospl PE11 . . . . .214 #
Johnson's Dro PE13 . . . . . .16 #
Johnson's La **7** DN17. . . . .16 #
Johnsons Rd **8** NG24 . . .104 #
Johnson St DN15 . . . . .182 #
Johnson Way **12** PE2. . . .102 #
Johnson Wlk PE1. . . . . . . .226 #
John Spendluffe Tech Coll
LN13. . . . . .75 #
John St
Lincoln LN2 . . . . .234 #
12 Market Rasen LN8 . . . .57 #
John Swain's Way
PE12. . . . . .216 #
John Wake Cl **2** PE13 . . .170 #
John Wesley Rd PE4 . . . . .220 #
Jolls La LN9 . . . . .86 #
Jolly Comm La LN13. . . . . . .77 #
Jolly Farmer La PE21 . . . .126 #
Jonathan Dr PE25 . . . . . . .206 #
Jonathan Gdns **1**
NG24 . . . . .212 #
Jonquil Ave DN16. . . . . . . .185 #
Jordan Mews PE2 . . . . .97 #
Jordan's Cradge Bank Rd
PE11. . . . . .146 #
Jorose St **4** PE3 . . . . . . .225 #
Jorose Way PE3 . . . . .225 #
Joseph Ogle Cl DN36 . . . .195 #
Joseph Ruston Tech Coll
LN6. . . . . .205 #
Joseph St DN31 . . . . .191 #
Joshua Way **1** DN21 . . . . .43 #
Joy Paine Cl PE21 . . . . . . .208 #
Joy's Bank PE12 . . . . .158 #
Jubilee Ave
Boston PE21 . . . . .208 #
Faldingworth LN8 . . . . .56 #
Grantham NG31 . . . . .211 #
Jubilee Cl
4 Bardney LN3. . . . . .83 #
Cherry Willingham/Reepham
LN3. . . . . .203 #
Coningsby LN4 . . . . .207 #
1 Hogsthorpe PE24. . . . . .90 #
17 Horncastle LN9 . . . . . .199 #
Lincoln LN6 . . . . .204 #
Long Sutton PE12 . . . . . . .216 #
Martin LN4. . . . . .96 #

ibilee Cl continued
🔁 Morton PE10 . . . . 154 C7
Scotter DN21. . . . . 29 B3
🔢 Spalding PE11 . . . . 214 C4
ibilee Cres
Gainsborough DN21 . . . . . 197 D5
outh LN11 . . . . 198 C8
ibilee Ct 🔟 NG34 . . . . . . 212 E4
ibilee Dr
🔁 Bardney LN3. . . . . 83 C4
Wragby LN8 . . . . 70 D4
ibilee Gr NG34 . . . . 212 C6
ibilee Parade 🔟 PE24 . . 90 D7
ibilee Rd LN11. . . . . 50 E7
ibilee St
Peterborough PE2 . . . . . . 230 F8
🔁 Ruskington NG34 . . . . . 108 E1
ibilee Way
Crowland PE6. . . . . 166 F1
Horncastle LN9 . . . . 199 B4
Scunthorpe DN15 . . . . . . 183 B3
dge Gate PE22 . . . . 114 E3
dge Cl 🔁 PE21 . . . . 209 C4
dy Cross PE1 . . . . 145 B8
lian Cl HU5 . . . . 179 A7
lian St DN32 . . . . 192 A7
lian's Wlk 🔟 HU10 . . . . . 178 F6
lia Rd LN4 . . . . 203 D1
lia's Mead 🔁 PE11 . . . . 214 B5
nction Rd DN7. . . . . 14 C6
nella Cl HU3 . . . . 180 A4
ngle Zoo The *
DN35 . . . . 193 B3
nior Cadets Rd
NG34 . . . . 120 B8
niper Cl
Flixborough DN15 . . . . . . 182 C6
🔟 Leasingham NG34 . . . . 121 B7
🔁 Lincoln LN5. . . . . 205 C2
Spalding PE11 . . . . 214 F4
niper Cres
Peterborough PE2 . . . . . . 225 A2
Spalding PE11 . . . . 214 F5
niper Dr 🔢 LN2 . . . . 68 F4
niper Way
Gainsborough DN21 . . . . . 197 D5
Grimsby DN33 . . . . 191 C2
🔁 Sleaford NG34 . . . . . . 212 D2
ury Rd PE7 . . . . 233 C8
ustice Hall La 🔟 DN17 . . 16 D8
ustice La DN14 . . . . 7 B8
utland Ct 🔟 DN36 . . . . . . 195 D7

K

arelia Ct HU4 . . . . 179 B5
aren Ave 🔢 DN41 . . . . . . 23 A4
arsons Way LN2 . . . . 68 D7
atherine Cres PE25 . . . . . 206 D2
athleen Ave
Cleethorpes DN35 . . . . . . 192 D8
Scunthorpe DN16 . . . . . . 185 B5
athleen Gr DN32. . . . . . . 192 C7
aytham Rice CI DN35 . . . 192 A8
aymile CI 🔢 DN16. . . . . . 195 C6
EADBY DN17 . . . . 17 D7
eadby Cl LN6. . . . . 204 F7
eal Carr Nature Reserve *
PE23 . . . . 100 E7
EAL COTES PE23. . . . . . . 100 C4
eal Hill PE23 . . . . 100 B7
ealholme Rd DN17. . . . . . . 29 D7
eaton Cl PE25 . . . . 206 A5
eats Ave
Grantham NG31. . . . . 211 E6
Scunthorpe DN17 . . . . . . 184 D7
eats Cl
Lincoln LN2 . . . . 202 C7
🔢 Mablethorpe/Sutton on Sea
LN12 . . . . 77 A7
eats Dr NG34 . . . . 121 C6
eats Gr 🔢 PE9 . . . . 218 E5
eats Way PE1 . . . . 225 D7
eb La DN15. . . . . 9 D2
eble Cl 🔢 LN4 . . . . 219 A7
eble Ct 🔟 LN4 . . . . 207 B5
EDDINGTON LN11. . . . . . . 198 F8
eddington Ave LN1 . . . . 201 E8
eddington Cres 🔁
LN11. . . . . 198 D7
eddington Rd
Louth LN11 . . . . 198 C7
Scunthorpe DN17 . . . . . . 184 F4
edlestone Rd LN11 . . . . . 210 F1
edleston Rd PE7. . . . . . . 231 F6
eeble Dr LN4. . . . . 203 D1
KEELBY DN41 . . . . 23 A5
eelby Prim Sch DN41 . . . 23 A5
eelby Rd
🔢 Gainsborough DN21. . . . 53 A8
Scunthorpe DN17 . . . . . . 184 F5
Stallingborough DN41. . . . 23 C4
eel Dr 🔟 NG13 . . . . 128 A5
eeling St 🔢 LN11. . . . . . . 50 F7
eepers Cl 🔢 LN2 . . . . 68 D7
eepers Way NG34 . . . . 9 E1
eeper's Way LN8 . . . . 16 E1
eeton Rd PE1 . . . . 225 E7
eightley Rd PE12 . . . . . . 147 B5
eir Hardie Wlk DN32 . . . 191 D7
EIRBY PE10. . . . . 141 F3
eith Cres 🔢 DN37 . . . . . . 23 F1
KELBY NG32. . . . . 131 C8
ELFIELD DN9 . . . . 28 C4
elham Rd
🔢 Great Gonerby
NG31. . . . . 129 E5

Kelham Rd continued
🔁 Great Gonerby NG31. . 210 E8
Grimsby DN32 . . . . 192 D6
Kellet Gate PE12. . . . . . . 157 B5
Kells Cl 🗓 LN5 . . . . 205 D3
Kell's Dro PE20 . . . . 124 E1
Kelly Cl 🔢 PE11 . . . . 156 E8
Kelsey Ave DN15 . . . . 182 B3
Kelsey La 🔟 LN7 . . . . 17 D4
Kelsey Rd LN7 . . . . 32 C2
Kelsey St LN1. . . . . 234 A2
Kelso Ct PE4 . . . . 221 A1
KELSTERN LN11 . . . . 48 A1
Kelstern Cl 🔟 LN6. . . . . . 204 C6
Kelstern Ct 🔟 DN34 . . . . 191 A5
Kelstern Rd LN6 . . . . 204 C6
Kelston Dr 🔁 HU13 . . . . . 179 A3
Kelthorpe Gr PE9 . . . . . . 171 A2
Kemble Cl LN6. . . . . 204 B8
Kemeshame Ct DN37. . . . 194 F4
Kemp Rd
Grimsby DN31. . . . . 189 C3
🔁 Swanland HU14 . . . . 3 B6
Kemp St PE6 . . . . 166 E1
Kempton Cl 🔢 PE11 . . . . 156 E3
Kempton Dr 🔢 PE4 . . . . . . 14 C2
Kempton Rd HU3 . . . . 179 E6
Kempton Vale DN35 . . . . 192 F1
Kempton Way NG31 . . . . . 210 F4
Kendal Cl 🔁 PE4 . . . . 221 D2
Kendal Ct DN16 . . . . 185 C6
Kendale Rd DN16 . . . . 185 E8
Kendal Rd DN40 . . . . 186 E3
Kendal Way HU5 . . . . 179 A3
Kendon Gdns DN8 . . . . 15 B8
Kendrick Ct PE4 . . . . 231 D6
Kenford Ct DN36. . . . . . . 195 C7
Kenilworth Cl 🔁 LN1 . . . . 66 D2
Kenilworth Dr LN6 . . . . . 205 C5
Kenilworth Rd
Cleethorpes DN35 . . . . . . 192 D4
Grantham NG31 . . . . 211 F5
Scunthorpe DN16 . . . . . . 183 C1
Kenlan Rd 🔟 PE13 . . . . . 170 D1
Kenleigh Dr PE21 . . . . . . 209 D4
Kenmare Cres 197 F2
Kenmar Rd 🔟 DN37 . . . . 23 F1
Kennedy Ave
🔢 Alford LN13 . . . . 75 F2
Skegness PE25 . . . . 206 C2
Kennedy Cl LN20 . . . . 196 E3
Kennedy Rd
Bracebridge Heath
LN4. . . . . 205 F3
Holbeach PE12 . . . . 215 C4
Kennedy Way Sh Ctr
DN40 . . . . 186 C4
Kennel La
Doddington & Whisby
LN6. . . . . 79 E5
Reepham LN3 . . . . 203 E8
Kennels Rd PE6. . . . . 224 D4
Kennet Wlk LN3 . . . . 203 F8
Kenner Cl 🔢 LN4 . . . . . . 205 A6
Kennet Gdns PE4 . . . . . . 221 C1
Kenneth Ave
🔁 Burgh le Marsh
PE24 . . . . 102 E8
🔟 Hatfield DN7 . . . . 14 C2
🔢 Stainforth DN7 . . . . 14 C6
Kenneth Campbell Rd 🗓
DN36 . . . . 37 C5
Kenneth St 🔟 LN1. . . . . . 201 F6
Kennington Cl 🔢 LN2 . . . . 68 E5
Kennulphs Cl 🗓 PE6 . . . . 175 C8
Kensington Cl PE12. . . . . 215 F3
Kensington Dr 🗓 PE11. . . 214 B2
Kensington Gdns 🔟
LN12. . . . . 64 B3
Kensington Pl DN33. . . . . 195 A8
Kensington Rd DN15 . . . . 182 B3
Ken Stimpson Com Sch
PE4. . . . . 220 F4
Kent Ave LN12 . . . . 63 F5
Kent Cl
Kingston upon Hull
HU9. . . . . 181 C7
🗓 Sutton Bridge PE12 . . . 160 E4
Kent Dr LN4 . . . . 81 A5
Kentmere Pl 🔢 PE4 . . . . 221 D2
Kent Rd
🔢 Binbrook Tech Pk
LN8. . . . . 47 B6
Leake Commonside PE22 . 113 F3
Peterborough PE2 . . . . . . 225 C2
Kent St
Grimsby DN31 . . . . 189 B1
🗓 Lincoln LN2. . . . . 202 C3
Kenwardby Rd HU10. . . . . 178 E8
Kenwick Cl LN11. . . . . . . 198 D3
Kenwick Dr NG31 . . . . . . 211 D4
Kenwick Gdns LN11 . . . . 198 D3
Kenwick Hill
Legbourne LN11 . . . . 198 E1
Raithby cum Maltby LN11 . . 61 C3
Kenwick Pastures
LN11. . . . . 198 D2
Kenwick Rd LN11 . . . . 198 D2
Kenya Dr DN17 . . . . 184 F2
Kenyon Cl 🔁 DN8 . . . . 15 A8
Kerries Wlk DN17 . . . . . . 184 F2
Kerrison View 🗓 LN2 . . . . 68 D2
Kerr's Cres NG32 . . . . 118 D2
Kerry Dr HU10 . . . . 178 C6
Kerry Pit Way HU10 . . . . 178 C6
Kesgrave St 🔢 DN31. . . . 189 C1
Kesteven Cl 🔟 PE6 . . . . . 217 D4

Kesteven Ct
🔢 Habrough DN40 . . . . . . 22 E8
🔟 Lincoln LN6 . . . . 204 D2
Kesteven Dr 🔟 PE6 . . . . . 217 A6
Kesteven Gr 🗓 DN17. . . . . 16 D8
Kesteven & Grantham Girl's
Sch NG31 . . . . 211 B5
Kesteven Rd PE9 . . . . 219 C7
Kesteven & Sleaford Girl's
High Sch NG34 . . . . 212 D4
Kesteven St
Lincoln LN5 . . . . 234 B1
🔟 Sleaford NG34 . . . . . . 212 E4
Kesteven Way 🔢 PE10 . . 213 C5
Kesteven Wlk 🔢 PE21. . . 226 B2
Kestrel Cl
Grantham NG31 . . . . 210 F2
Longthorpe PE3 . . . . 225 A2
Kestrel Dr
Bourne PE10 . . . . 213 E3
Louth LN11 . . . . 198 D8
Kestrel Rd
🔢 Scopwick Heath
LN4. . . . . 108 A7
Scunthorpe DN17 . . . . . . 184 E6
Kestrel Rise LN6 . . . . 79 B1
Keswick Cl 🔢 PE4 . . . . . . 221 D3
Ketco Ave PE9 . . . . 171 A4
Ketel Ct PE12. . . . . 216 C3
Ketlock Hill La 🔟 DN22 . . 52 B1
KETSBY LN11 . . . . 74 D3
Kettering Rd
Scunthorpe DN16 . . . . . . 183 C2
Wittering PE9 . . . . 219 B2
Kettlebridge La DN40 . . . . 12 E6
Kettleby La DN20 . . . . 20 E3
Kettleby Rd 🔟 DN20 . . . . 196 D4
Kettleby Thorpe La
DN20 . . . . 20 B6
KETTLETHORPE LN1 . . . . . 65 F2
Kettlethorpe Dr 🔢 HU15 . . . 2 D5
Kettlethorpe Rd LN1 . . . . . 65 E3
Kettlewell St DN32. . . . . . 191 E5
KETTON PE9 . . . . 171 A3
Ketton CE Prim Sch
PE9. . . . . 171 A3
Ketton Rd PE9 . . . . 171 B2
Kew Rd DN35 . . . . 192 E6
KEXBY DN21. . . . . 53 C5
Kexby La DN21. . . . . 53 C4
Kexby Mill Cl 🔢 LN6 . . . . 93 B8
Kexby Rd DN21 . . . . 54 D6
Kexby Wlk DN21 . . . . 197 F3
Keyholme La DN36. . . . . . . 37 D2
Key Theatre * 🔢 PE1 . . . . . 226 B1
Khartoum St DN7 . . . . 14 B4
Khormaksar Dr LN4. . . . . . 95 C7
Kiddier Ave DN37 . . . . . . 194 D7
Kidd La HU15 . . . . 2 C6
Kidgate LN11 . . . . 198 B5
Kidgate Mews LN11. . . . . 198 B5
Kidgate Prim Sch
LN11. . . . . 198 C5
Kilburn Cres 🔟 LN6 . . . . 205 A6
Kildare Dr 🔁 DN35 . . . . . 225 C4
Kilham PE2 . . . . 229 E2
Killarney Cl NG31 . . . . . . 211 E7
Killingholme Haven Pits
Nature Reserve *
DN40 . . . . 13 A6
Killingholme Prim Sch
DN40 . . . . 12 E3
Kiln Hill 🔟 LN8 . . . . 59 A7
Kiln La
Brigg DN20 . . . . 196 B3
Fulbeck NG32 . . . . 106 C1
Immingham DN41. . . . . . 187 C2
Immingham DN41 . . . . . . 186 B1
🔟 Stallingborough DN41 . . 186 F1
Kiln La Ind Est DN41. . . . 187 B3
Kiln La Trading Est
DN41 . . . . 187 C2
Kilnwell Rd 🔢 LN8. . . . . . . 57 D8
Kiln Yd LN11. . . . . 198 C5
Kilverstone PE4 . . . . 220 F6
KILVINGTON NG13. . . . . . . 117 A1
Kimberley St HU3. . . . . . . 180 C7
Kimberley Terr NG31 . . . . 210 E7
Kimblewick La PE11 . . . . 214 A2
Kimbolton Ct PE1 . . . . . . 225 F3
Kime Cl NG34. . . . . 142 C8
Kime's La 🔟 PE22 . . . . . . 98 F4
Kinder Ave LN6 . . . . 205 A2
Kinderley Rd PE13 . . . . . . 170 D2
King Charles Cl HU10. . . 178 E7
King Edward Fst Sch
DN8 . . . . 15 B8
King Edward Rd
Thorne/Moorends DN8 . . . 15 A8
🔢 Woodhall Spa LN10 . . . . 97 C6
King Edward St
Belton DN9 . . . . 16 E2
🔟 Grimsby DN31 . . . . . . 189 B1
🔟 Kingston upon Hull
HU1. . . . . 180 F6
Kirton in Lindsey DN21 . . . 30 B1
Scunthorpe DN16 . . . . . . 183 A1
Sleaford NG34 . . . . 212 E4
King Edwards Terr 🔟
HU15 . . . . 2 B5
King Edward VI Sch
Louth LN11 . . . . 198 A5
Spilsby PE23 . . . . 87 F1
KINGERBY LN8. . . . . 44 E3

Kingerby Beck Mdws
Nature Reserve * LN8 . . . 44 E5
Kingerby Cl DN21. . . . . . . 197 E3
Kingerby Rd DN17 . . . . . . 184 E5
Kingfisher Cl
🔁 Birchwood LN6. . . . . . 204 D8
🔁 Brigg DN20 . . . . 196 A4
Scunthorpe DN15 . . . . . . 182 D5
Yaxley PE7 . . . . 233 D5
Kingfisher Ct 🔢 PE11. . . 214 F2
Kingfisher Dr
🔢 Skegness PE25. . . . . . 206 A7
🔢 Surfleet PE11 . . . . 145 E3
Kingfishers PE2 . . . . 229 D6
King George Ave 🔟
LN10. . . . . 97 D6
King Georges Ct 🗓
DN7 . . . . 14 C5
King George V Ave 🔟
PE12. . . . . 215 F3
King George V Stadium
DN32 . . . . 192 B5
King Henry Chase PE3 . . 225 A5
King John Bank
🔁 Sutton Bridge PE14 . . 170 F8
Walpole PE14. . . . . 161 A2
King Johns Rd 🔁 NG26. . 135 A3
Kings Arms Yd 🔁 LN2. . . 234 B2
Kings Ave PE25 . . . . 206 E8
King's Ave
Boston PE21 . . . . 209 C3
Brigg DN20 . . . . 196 D3
King's Bench St HU3. . . . 180 B5
Kingsbridge Ct 🔟 PE4 . . 220 E5
King's Causeway DN14 . . . . 6 E8
Kings Cl PE22 . . . . 112 C8
Kingscliffe Rd NG31. . . . . 211 A8
King's Cres
Boston PE21 . . . . 209 C3
Swineshead PE20 . . . . . . 135 B8
Kings Croft 🔟 DN17 . . . . . 16 E6
King's Cross Cl 🔁 HU3. . 180 C6
Kings Ct
🔢 Kirton PE20 . . . . 136 C5
🔟 Louth LN11 . . . . 198 E7
Old Bolingbroke PE23 . . . 100 A7
🔢 Scawby DN20 . . . . 30 F8
Scunthorpe DN15 . . . . . . 183 B4
Kingsdale PE21 . . . . 184 E2
King's Delph Dro PE7 . . . 231 E2
Kingsdown Rd LN6. . . . . . 204 B7
Kings Dyke Cl PE2 . . . . . 231 E6
Kingsgate PE21 . . . . 159 E2
King's Gdns PE1. . . . . 226 A5
Kings Hill 🔢 NG32 . . . . . 119 B7
Kings Leigh 🔟 HU3 . . . . . 180 C6
Kingsley Ave PE10 . . . . . 213 B5
Kingsley Cl
🔟 Barnack PE9 . . . . 172 D3
🔟 Brough HU15 . . . . 2 B5
Kingsley Gr DN33 . . . . . . 191 C4
Kingsley Rd
🔢 Mablethorpe/Sutton on
Sea LN12 . . . . 64 B4
North Hykeham LN6 . . . . 204 B5
Peterborough PE1 . . . . . . 226 C4
Kingsley St LN1. . . . . 234 A4
Kingsline Cl 🔟 PE6 . . . . . 176 A3
Kings Mews DN35 . . . . . . 193 C1
Kings Parade DN35 . . . . . 193 A5
Kingsport Cl HU3 . . . . 180 A7
Kings Rd
Holbeach PE12 . . . . 215 F3
🔁 Immingham DN40 . . . . 186 E5
Metheringham LN4 . . . . . . 95 C4
Peterborough PE2 . . . . . . 231 B6
Stamford PE9. . . . . 219 B6
King's Rd
Barnetby le Wold DN38 . . . 21 B5
Humberston DN35 . . . . . . 193 B3
Spalding PE11 . . . . 214 D5
Kings Sch PE1. . . . . 226 A4
Kings Sch The NG31. . . . . 211 B5
King St
🔟 Billinghay LN4 . . . . . . 109 F5
Boston PE21 . . . . 208 E4
East Halton DN40 . . . . 12 D7
Gainsborough DN21 . . . . . 197 D3
🔢 Goxhill DN19 . . . . 12 A8
🔢 Keelby DN41. . . . . 23 A5
🔟 Kirton PE20 . . . . 136 C5
Lincoln LN5 . . . . 234 A1
🔢 Mablethorpe/Sutton on Sea
LN12 . . . . 64 B3
Market Rasen LN8. . . . . . . 57 D8
🔟 Peterborough PE1 . . . . 226 A2
Scunthorpe DN15 . . . . . . 183 B4
🔢 Sutton Bridge PE12. . . 160 E4
Thorne/Moorends DN8 . . . 15 A8
Wainfleet All Saints
PE24 . . . . 102 A2
West Deeping PE6 . . . . . . 173 A8
Wilsford NG32 . . . . 120 A1
Winterton DN15. . . . . 9 A5
Yarburgh LN11. . . . . 49 E4
Kingsthorpe Cres
PE25 . . . . 206 C1
Kingston Ave
Grantham NG31. . . . . 210 E4
Grimsby DN34. . . . . 191 A6
Kingston upon Hull HU13 . 178 F1
Kingston Cl 🔢 DN35 . . . . 193 A1

Kingston Communications
Stadium (Hull City AFC
Hull RLFC)* HU3. . . . . . . 180 B7
Kingston Dr PE2. . . . . 231 E5
Kingston Rd
Kingston upon Hull
HU10. . . . . 178 F8
Scunthorpe DN16 . . . . . . 185 A7
Kingston Ret Pk HU1 . . . 180 E5
Kingston St HU1. . . . . 180 E5
Kingston Terr NG34 . . . . 212 E3
KINGSTON UPON HULL
HU1 . . . . 180 F4
Kingston View 🔢 DN18. . . 10 F8
Kingston Wharf 🔟
HU1. . . . . 180 F5
Kingsway
Boston PE21 . . . . 209 B3
Bourne PE10 . . . . 213 D6
🔁 Brigg DN20. . . . . 196 B4
Cleethorpes DN35. . . . . . 193 C5
🔟 Leverington PE13 . . . . 170 E1
Lincoln LN5 . . . . 201 F1
Nettleham LN2. . . . . 68 C2
Scunthorpe DN15 . . . . . . 182 C3
Stainforth DN7. . . . . 14 C6
Tealby LN8. . . . . 46 C1
Kings Way LN2 . . . . 68 C7
Kingsway Sta DN35 . . . . . 193 B4
Kings Wlk 🔟 NG31. . . . . . 211 A4
KINGTHORPE LN8 . . . . 70 F5
King William Cl 🔟
PE34. . . . . 161 F3
Kinloch Way DN40 . . . . . . 186 B2
Kinloss Cl 🔟 LN6 . . . . . . 204 C6
Kinnears Wlk PE2. . . . . . . 229 F2
Kinoulton Ct 🔢 PE10 . . . 210 E2
Kinross Rd NG34 . . . . 120 F2
Kinsbourne Grn 🔟 DN7 . . 14 D4
Kinsley Wlk 🔟 DN15. . . . 183 B3
Kintore Dr NG31. . . . . 211 C4
Kipling Ave 🔟 DN17 . . . . 184 D7
Kipling Cl
🔟 Grantham NG31. . . . . 211 E6
🔢 Stamford PE9 . . . . 218 E5
St Giles LN2. . . . . 202 B7
Kipling Ct PE1. . . . . 225 E8
Kipling Dr
🔟 Mablethorpe/Sutton on
Sea LN12 . . . . 77 A7
🔢 Sleaford NG34 . . . . . . 212 F4
Kiplington Cl HU3 . . . . . . 180 A7
Kipling Wlk 🔟 LN6 . . . . . 179 D2
Kippings The 🔢 PE10 . . . 164 C8
Kirby Cl 🗓 PE11. . . . . 214 F4
Kirby Wlk 🔟 PE21 . . . . . 226 B3
KIRK BRAMWITH DN7. . . . . 14 A6
KIRKBY LN8 . . . . 44 C3
Kirkby Bank PE23 . . . . 99 E3
KIRKBY FENSIDE PE23 . . . . 99 E4
Kirkby Gr DN33 . . . . 191 A3
Kirkby Gravel Pit Nature
Reserve * LN4. . . . . 207 A8
KIRKBY GREEN LN4 . . . . . 108 C8
Kirkby La
Coningsby LN4. . . . . 207 D8
Woodhall Spa LN10 . . . . . 97 D8
KIRKBY LA THORPE
NG34 . . . . 121 F5
Kirkby la Thorpe CE Prim
Sch NG34 . . . . 121 F4
Kirkby Moor Nature
Reserve * LN10 . . . . 98 A5
KIRKBY ON BAIN LN10 . . . . 98 B5
Kirkby on Bain CE Prim Sch
LN10. . . . . 98 C5
Kirkby Rd
Ewerby & Evedon
NG34 . . . . 122 B6
Scunthorpe DN17 . . . . . . 184 E4
Kirkby St LN5. . . . . 201 F1
KIRKBY UNDERWOOD
PE10. . . . . 142 D2
Kirkby Underwood Rd
PE10. . . . . 154 A8
Kirkdale Cl 🔟 NG34. . . . . 121 B8
Kirkden Paddocks DN9. . . 16 C2
KIRK ELLA HU10 . . . . 178 C6
Kirkgate PE13 . . . . 169 F7
Kirk Gate
Waltham DN37. . . . . 194 E4
🔟 Whaplode PE12 . . . . . 158 B7
Kirkgate St PE13 . . . . 170 E1
Kirk Gdns PE21 . . . . 208 D7
Kirkham Ct HU13 . . . . 178 F2
Kirkhouse Gn Rd DN7 . . . 14 A8
Kirklands Rd HU5. . . . . . . 179 E8
Kirkmeadow PE3 . . . . 225 A8
Kirk Rise HU10 . . . . 178 C7
Kirkside DN37 . . . . 194 D4
Kirkstall PE2 . . . . 230 B3
Kirkstall Cl LN2. . . . . 202 E6
Kirkstead Bridge LN10. . . 97 B4
Kirkstead Cres DN33 . . . . 191 B3
Kirkstead Ct 🔟 LN10. . . . 97 D5
Kirkstone House Sch
PE6. . . . . 164 E4
Kirkton Gate PE2 . . . . 225 A1
Kirkway HU10 . . . . 178 B7
Kirkwood Cl PE23. . . . . . . 225 E2
Kirman Cres 🗓 DN17 . . . 184 F3
KIRMINGTON DN39 . . . . . . 22 A6
Kirmington CE Prim Sch
DN39 . . . . 22 A6
Kirmington Ct 🔟 LN6 . . . 204 C6

Kirmington Gdns 🔳
DN34 . . . . 191 A7
KIRMOND LE MIRE LN8 . . . 46 F3
Kirmond Rd LN4 . . . . 47 A4
Kirness Dro LN4 . . . . 109 C6
KIRTON PE20 . . . . 136 D5
Kirton Dro LN4 . . . . 110 F1
KIRTON END PE20 . . . . . . 136 B6
KIRTON HOLME PE20 . . . . 135 E8
Kirton Holme Rd PE20 . . 124 D1
KIRTON IN LINDSEY
DN21 . . . . 30 C2
Kirton La
Hatfield DN8 . . . . 14 E7
🔳 Long Bennington
NG23 . . . . 117 D4
Stainforth DN7 . . . . 14 D6
Kirton Lindsey Prim Sch
DN21 . . . . 30 B1
Kirton Lindsey Sta
DN21 . . . . 30 B2
Kirton Prim Sch PE20 . . . 136 C5
Kirton Rd
Blyton DN21 . . . . 41 D6
Holme DN16 . . . . 19 B2
Manton DN21 . . . . 30 A3
Messingham DN17 . . . . 29 E6
Scawby DN20 . . . . 30 C8
Scotter DN21 . . . . 29 D3
Waddingham DN21 . . . . 43 B7
Kisgate 🔟 LN1 . . . . 66 D7
Kishorn Ct DN40 . . . . . . 186 B2
Kisimul Sch LN6 . . . . 92 A6
Kit Cat La PE20 . . . . 145 F8
Kitty Briggs La LN11 . . . 210 E1
Kitwood Cl 🔳 PE21 . . . . 209 B4
Kitwood Rd PE21 . . . . . . 209 B4
KNAITH DN21 . . . . 53 A3
Knaith Hall La DN22 . . . . 52 E3
Knaith Hill DN21 . . . . 53 A3
KNAITH PARK DN21 . . . . . 53 B4
Knapton Ct LN7 . . . . 33 B4
Knarr Fen Rd PE6 . . . . . . 176 E2
Kneeland 24 LN2 . . . . 68 D6
Knight Cl PE6 . . . . 217 D5
Knighton Cl PE7 . . . . 230 D1
Knight Pl 2 LN5 . . . . 205 E8
Knightsbridge 2
DN36 . . . . 195 C6
Knightsbridge Rd 41
DN17 . . . . 29 D7
Knights Cl
5 Belton DN9 . . . . 16 E2
16 Laceby DN37 . . . . 23 F1
Leverington PE13 . . . . 170 B2
Knight's Ct DN16 . . . . . . 185 A3
Knight St
Grimsby DN32 . . . . 192 B6
4 Lincoln LN5 . . . . 205 E8
2 Pinchbeck PE11 . . . . . . 145 B1
Knight Terr LN5 . . . . 205 E8
Knipe Ave PE11 . . . . 214 C3
KNIPTON NG32 . . . . 138 C6
Knipton La NG32 . . . . . . 138 D6
Knipton Rd NG32 . . . . . . 138 B4
Knole Wlk PE3 . . . . 225 B3
Knoll St DN35 . . . . 192 F6
Knolls The NG32 . . . . . . 210 B5
Knoll The NG31 . . . . 210 D8
Knowle St 20 LN12 . . . . . . 64 B3
Kohima Cl 🔳 PE10 . . . . . 213 E7
Kooreman Ave 🔟
PE13 . . . . 170 D1
Kyme Rd
Boston PE21 . . . . 208 D6
Heckington NG34 . . . . 122 E3

L

Labour in Vain Dro
LN4 . . . . 110 A6
Labrador Dr 🔳 DN20 . . . 19 E4
Laburnham Ave DN37 . . . 194 D4
Laburnham Cl DN37 . . . . 194 D4
Laburnum Ave
Gainsborough DN21 . . . . 197 D6
4 Gunness DN15 . . . . 17 E6
Yaxley PE7 . . . . 233 F6
Laburnum Cl
3 Bourne PE10 . . . . 213 C6
Grantham NG31 . . . . 211 D5
Lincoln LN6 . . . . 205 A2
7 Wisbech PE13 . . . . 170 E1
Laburnum Cres LN11 . . . 198 E4
Laburnum Ct
4 Cherry Willingham/
Reepham LN3 . . . . 82 A8
Hessle HU13 . . . . 178 E1
Laburnum Dr
Cherry Willingham/Reepham
LN3 . . . . 203 D5
Grimsby DN34 . . . . 190 E7
Ingoldmells PE25 . . . . . . 206 D8
3 Scunthorpe upon Hull
HU5 . . . . 179 B7
Morton PE10 . . . . 154 B7
Laburnum Gr
8 Burton upon Stather
DN15 . . . . 8 B5
16 Crowle DN17 . . . . 16 D7
Peterborough PE1 . . . . . . 226 B8
Scunthorpe DN16 . . . . . . 185 B7
Spalding PE11 . . . . 214 F5
Laburnum Rd NG34 . . . . 107 C2

LACEBY DN37 . . . . 23 E1
LACEBY ACRES DN34 . . . 190 C4
Laceby Acres Prim Sch
DN34 . . . . 190 D5
Laceby Rd
Grimsby DN34 . . . . 191 A4
Scunthorpe DN17 . . . . . . 190 C3
Scunthorpe DN17 . . . . . . 184 E5
Laceby St LN2 . . . . 202 B3
Lacey Gdns LN11 . . . . . . 198 D6
Lacey Gdns Jun Sch
LN11 . . . . 198 D6
Lacey's Cl PE22 . . . . 126 F6
Lacey's Dr PE22 . . . . 126 F6
Lacey's La PE22 . . . . 126 E6
Lacy Cl 🔳 LN1 . . . . 68 D2
Ladbroke Cl 🔳 NG34 . . . 133 D7
Ladds Cl 6 PE21 . . . . . . 209 C4
Ladd's Mill Cl 7 LN6 . . . 93 B8
LADE BANK PE22 . . . . . . 113 F5
Lade Bank
Old Leake PE22 . . . . 113 F5
Wrangle PE22 . . . . 114 B6
Lady Bower Cl 9 LN6 . . . 205 A2
Ladybower Way PE4 . . . . 221 C3
Lady Charlotte Rd PE7 . . 230 C3
Lady Fen La LN13 . . . . . . 76 B1
Lady Frances Cres
DN35 . . . . 192 C5
Lady Frances Dr 🔳 LN8 . . 57 D8
Lady Jane Franklin Sch The
PE23 . . . . 87 F1
Lady La PE24 . . . . 102 A2
Lady Lodge Dr PE2 . . . . . 230 A5
Lady Margaret's Ave
PE6 . . . . 217 C5
Lady Matilda's Dr PE25 . . 206 C8
Lady Meers Rd LN3 . . . . 203 E6
Lady Romayne Cl PE9 . . 217 C4
Ladysmith Rd DN32 . . . . 191 F7
Ladysmith Terr NG31 . . . 210 E7
Ladywell Gate 4 HU15 . . . 2 C6
Ladywood Rd PE11 . . . . 214 E6
Lafford Ct NG34 . . . . . . 212 B5
Lafford Dr 2 LN4 . . . . . 109 F6
Lafford High Sch The
LN4 . . . . 109 F6
Laforey Rd DN31 . . . . . . 188 A3
Lagonda Cl LN4 . . . . 205 F1
Lagoon Rd DN17 . . . . . . 184 B6
Laing Cl 2 LN1 . . . . 83 B4
Lakeside
Anderby PE24 . . . . 77 C3
Great Coates DN37 . . . . . . 24 B6
Peterborough PE4 . . . . . . 221 B5
Peterborough PE2 . . . . . . 230 F2
Pyewipe DN37 . . . . 188 A3
Lakeside Gr HU4 . . . . . . 179 D4
Lakeside Leisure Ctr
PE2 . . . . 230 A5
Lakeside Parkway
DN16 . . . . 185 F5
Lakeside Ret Pk DN16 . . 185 F6
Lakeside Sh DN35 . . . . . 193 B2
Lakeview Cl 3 LN6 . . . . 204 C1
Lake View Rd LN6 . . . . . 205 C6
Lakeview Way PE7 . . . . . 230 C2
Lairgate Pl DN35 . . . . . . 192 F1
Lambert Ave 12 HU15 . . . 2 C6
Lambert Bank
Fleet PE12 . . . . 158 D1
Holbeach PE12 . . . . 168 D8
Lambert Mews 5 PE9 . . . 219 C4
Lambert Rd
4 Allington NG32 . . . . . . 128 F7
Grimsby DN32 . . . . 191 D6
Lambeth Wlk 8 PE9 . . . . 219 A6
Lamb Gdns LN2 . . . . 202 B6
Lamb La
Benington PE22 . . . . 127 A4
Newport HU15 . . . . 1 A8
Lambourn Ct 8 DN35 . . . 192 F1
Lambourne Rise DN16 . . 185 A2
Lambourne Way 6
NG34 . . . . 122 D2
Lambs Row 5 PE21 . . . . 208 C6
La Milesse Way 🔳
DN21 . . . . 135 C7
Lammas Leas Rd 4
LN8 . . . . 57 E7
Lammas Rd PE21 . . . . . . 226 A7
Lammin's La 2 PE22 . . . . 99 A4
Lamport Cl 9 PE21 . . . . 217 A6
Lamport Dr NG32 . . . . . . 191 D6
Lanark St 2 HU5 . . . . . . 180 B8
Lancaster App DN40 . . . . 12 C4
Lancaster Ave
Grimsby DN31 . . . . 191 B7
Horncastle LN9 . . . . 199 C5
Skegness PE25 . . . . 206 A5
Lancaster Ct
3 Great Steeping
PE23 . . . . 101 D7
Long Sutton PE12 . . . . . . 216 C4
Stickney PE22 . . . . 113 A7
6 Waddington LN5 . . . . . . 94 A7
Lancaster Dr
6 Coningsby LN4 . . . . . . 207 D4
Long Sutton PE12 . . . . . . 216 C4
Moorland Prison DN7 . . . . 26 A8
6 Scampton Airfield LN1 . . 67 F5

Lancaster Dr *continued*
10 South Killingholme
DN40 . . . . 12 E3
Lancaster Gate DN36 . . . 195 C1
Lancaster Gdns 2
NG31 . . . . 211 D2
Lancaster Gn DN21 . . . . . 54 F8
Lancaster Pl 4 LN5 . . . . 201 F1
Lancaster Rd
11 Beacon Hill NG24 . . . 104 C5
3 Binbrook Tech Pk LN8 . . 47 B6
Gringley on the Hill DN10 . . 39 D1
Scunthorpe DN16 . . . . . . 185 A5
8 Stamford PE9 . . . . 219 B6
Lancaster Sch The
LN6 . . . . 204 C8
Lancaster Way
25 Brough HU15 . . . . 2 C5
Market Deeping PE6 . . . . 217 B7
2 Skellingthorpe LN6 . . . 200 A4
Yaxley PE7 . . . . 233 F6
Lancelot Ct HU9 . . . . . . 181 C6
Lancelot Way 🔳 PE11 . . 214 B3
Lancewood Gdns 3
LN6 . . . . 204 C8
Lancia Cres LN4 . . . . 205 F2
Lancing Cl 7 PE21 . . . . 221 A3
Lancing Way 4 DN33 . . . 194 E8
Land Dike LN11 . . . . 37 A1
Landcare Dr DN34 . . . . . 191 B6
Landing La HU15 . . . . 1 A7
Landmere Gr LN6 . . . . . . 200 D1
Land of Gn Ginger 10
HU1 . . . . 181 A6
Landor Ave 3 DN17 . . . . 184 D7
Landsdowne Cl 22 LN12 . . 77 A8
Landsdowne Ct PE11 . . . 214 F6
Landsdowne Rd 2
PE25 . . . . 206 C4
Landseer Ave PE24 . . . . . 90 D8
LANEHAM DN22 . . . . 65 A3
Laneham Rd NG22 . . . . . . 65 A1
Laneham St
Rampton DN22 . . . . 65 A5
Scunthorpe DN15 . . . . . . 183 A3
Lanes The 10 DN36 . . . . . 36 D4
Lane The
🔳 Easton on the Hill
PE9 . . . . 171 D3
West Deeping PE6 . . . . . . 173 B7
Laney Cl LN2 . . . . 202 C7
Langary Gate Rd PE12 . . 158 E1
Langdale Cl 3 LN4 . . . . 194 D7
Langdale Cres NG31 . . . 211 A8
Langdyke PE1 . . . . 226 F6
Langford Cl 🔳 HU4 . . . . 179 D4
LANGFORD NG23 . . . . 91 C1
Langford Gdns NG31 . . . 211 B6
Langford La NG23 . . . . . . 91 A2
Langford Rd PE2 . . . . 231 A7
Langham Rd 🔳 HU4 . . . . 179 B7
Langhole Dro PE11 . . . . 145 B1
LANGHOLME DN9 . . . . 39 E8
Langhole La LN6 . . . . 27 B1
Langmere Wood Nature
Reserve* DN9 . . . . 39 D8
Langley Cl PE3 . . . . 225 B8
Langley Cl LN11 . . . . 198 E4
Langley Dr DN16 . . . . . . 185 A2
Langley Pl DN35 . . . . . . 193 A4
Langley Rd LN6 . . . . 204 D2
Langley Wlk DN40 . . . . . 186 D3
LANGRICK PE22 . . . . 124 E7
LANGRICK BRIDGE
PE22 . . . . 124 E6
Langrick Rd
Boston PE21 . . . . 208 C6
Coningsby LN4 . . . . 98 C1
Holland Fen with Brotherloft
PE20 . . . . 124 E4
Langthwaite Cl 20 HU15 . . 2 D5
LANGTOFT PE6 . . . . 164 F3
Langtoft Outgang Rd
PE11 . . . . 165 D6
Langtoft Prim Sch PE6 . . 164 F3
LANGTON
Langton by Spilsby PE23 . . 87 F5
Langton LN9 . . . . 85 B3
LANGTON BY WRAGBY
LN8 . . . . 70 F3
Langton Cl
Grimsby DN33 . . . . 191 A3
Horncastle LN9 . . . . 199 A3
Lincoln LN6 . . . . 202 B7
Langton Ct PE25 . . . . . . 206 C5
Langton Dr
Grimsby DN33 . . . . 191 A3
Langton Gdns LN9 . . . . . 199 A3
Langton Hill LN9 . . . . . . 199 A3
Langton La LN9 . . . . 85 C4
Langton Rd
Holton le Clay DN36 . . . . 195 E2
Peterborough PE2 . . . . . . 226 D7
Langwith Dr PE12 . . . . . 215 C2
Langwith Gdns PE12 . . . 215 C1
LANGWORTH LN3 . . . . 69 B4
Langworthgate LN2 . . . . 234 C3
Langworth Rd LN2 . . . . . 69 B4
Lannimore Cl LN5 . . . . . 205 D3
Lansdall Ave 4 DN21 . . . 156 F2
Lansdowne Ave
Grimsby DN32 . . . . 191 D4
Lincoln LN6 . . . . 205 C5
2 LN12 . . . . 77 A8
Lansdowne Rd
8 Navenby/Wellingore
LN5 . . . . 107 A8

Lansdowne Rd *continued*
Yaxley PE7 . . . . 233 F6
Lansdowne St HU3 . . . . . 180 C6
Lansdowne Way PE2 . . . 230 D7
Lansdown Link 🔳
DN35 . . . . 192 E3
Lansdown Rd 4 DN40 . . 186 D4
Lansdown Way 17 LN10 . . 97 C5
Laporte Rd DN40 . . . . . . 187 C5
Lapwater La PE12 . . . . . 147 C6
Lapwing Cl LN6 . . . . 200 A3
Larch Ave 16 LN2 . . . . . . 68 D2
Larch Cl
8 Bourne PE10 . . . . 213 C7
2 Grantham NG31 . . . . . . 210 D2
Immingham DN40 . . . . . . 186 E5
Ruskington NG34 . . . . . . 108 D1
Yaxley PE7 . . . . 233 F6
Larch Ct 9 DN21 . . . . . . 197 E6
Larch Gn NG34 . . . . 107 D1
Larch Gr
Peterborough PE1 . . . . . . 226 C6
8 Scawby DN20 . . . . 30 F8
Scunthorpe DN16 . . . . . . 185 B7
Larchmont Cl 10 HU15 . . . 2 C6
Larch Rd DN35 . . . . 192 D2
Larch Way 8 LN6 . . . . . . 201 E4
Larchwood Cres LN6 . . . 200 D1
Larden Ave DN33 . . . . . . 194 E8
Lark Cl 13 LN8 . . . . 70 D4
Lark Dr 3 LN5 . . . . 107 A7
Larkin Ave LN1 . . . . 203 D5
Larklands PE3 . . . . 225 B1
Lark Rise
8 Market Deeping
PE6 . . . . 217 C5
Scotter DN21 . . . . 29 B3
Larkspur Ave 8 DN41 . . . 23 F5
Larkspur Croft PE21 . . . 208 C6
Larkspur Rd LN2 . . . . . . 202 D7
Larkspur Wlk PE4 . . . . . 221 B3
Larks Rise PE10 . . . . 154 B7
Larmour Rd DN37 . . . . . 190 D7
Larne Cl 12 LN5 . . . . . . 205 C2
Larne Rd LN5 . . . . 205 D2
Larners Fields 8 LN6 . . . 66 C7
Lashbrook Garth HU4 . . . 179 B4
Lassingham 8 LN5 . . . . . . 2 C6
Latham Ave PE2 . . . . 230 C7
Latimer Gdns 12 NG34 . . 122 E3
LAUGHTERTON LN1 . . . . . 65 D2
LAUGHTON DN21 . . . . 41 C8
Laughton Endowed CE Sch
DN21 . . . . 41 C8
Laughton Rd
Blyton DN21 . . . . 40 F5
Boston PE21 . . . . 208 D6
Laughton Way LN2 . . . . . 201 F7
Laughton Way N LN2 . . . 201 F8
Launde Gdns PE9 . . . . . . 218 E4
Launder Terr NG31 . . . . 211 A3
Laundon Rd NG34 . . . . . 132 E3
Laura Ct PE25 . . . . 90 E3
Laureate Gr PE11 . . . . . . 214 B4
Laurel Cl
6 Donington PE11 . . . . . . 134 E2
8 Gainsborough DN21 . . 156 F8
Grimsby DN33 . . . . 191 C2
Kingston upon Hull HU5 . . 179 B7
Lincoln LN6 . . . . 205 D5
Yaxley PE7 . . . . 233 D4
Laurel Dr 7 PE6 . . . . . . 176 A3
Laurels Cl 11 DN40 . . . . 22 E8
Laurel Way DN16 . . . . . . 185 D7
Lauridston Cl 9 DN37 . . 23 E1
Laurier St DN35 . . . . . . 192 D8
Laurold Ave 🔳 DN7 . . . . 15 A3
Laval Pl PE21 . . . . 209 B5
Lavender Cl
Lincoln LN5 . . . . 205 C2
10 Sleaford NG34 . . . . . . 212 D2
Lavender Cres PE1 . . . . . 226 B8
Lavender Ct DN41 . . . . . 214 A2
Lavender Gr DN36 . . . . . 195 B7
Lavender Way
Bourne PE10 . . . . 213 B7
13 Scunthorpe DN15 . . . 183 B3
2 Stamford PE9 . . . . 218 A1
Lavenham Cl HU5 . . . . . . 179 C7
Lavenham Ct LN2 . . . . . . 202 E8
Lavenham Gr LN6 . . . . . . 205 A4
Lavenham Rd DN33 . . . . 191 B3
Lavington Grange PE1 . . 226 E6
Law Ct 1 PE11 . . . . 214 A3
Lawley Cl LN2 . . . . 203 B8
Lawn Ave
Peterborough PE2 . . . . . . 226 A7
Skegness PE25 . . . . 206 D2
Lawn Cres 1 PE25 . . . . . 206 D2
Lawn Ct LN1 . . . . 234 A4
Lawn in Lincoln The*
LN1 . . . . 234 A3
Lawn La LN3 . . . . 152 F2
Lawns The
Collingham NG23 . . . . 91 C5
4 Grimsby DN31 . . . . . . 191 C7
Hibaldstow DN20
HU10 . . . . 178 D7
18 Wisbech PE13 . . . . . . 170 C1
Lawnswood HU3 . . . . . . 178 D3
Lawnswood Ct DN16 . . . 185 A4
Lawn Wood Nature
Reserve* NG33 . . . . 152 E2
Lawrance Way 10
PE10 . . . . 164 C8
Lawrence Ave PE7 . . . . . 231 C2
Lawrence Cl 🔳 LN6 . . . . 205 B7

Lawrence La 8 NG34 . . . 120 C8
Lawrence Rd PE8 . . . . . . 172 C1
Lawrence's Dro PE10 . . . 164 F8
Lawrence St DN31 . . . . . 191 C8
Lawrence's Cl PE6 . . . . . 174 C5
Lawson Ave
Grimsby DN31 . . . . 191 B7
Peterborough PE2 . . . . . . 231 D6
Lawson Ct 15 LN2 . . . . . . 68 C6
Lawson Leas 5 NG32 . . . 210 A5
Laxton Gdns 7 PE11 . . . 156 E8
Laxton Gr DN16 . . . . 185 A2
Laxton La NG33 . . . . 152 E7
Laycock Ave 2 DN10 . . . 39 C1
Laythorpe Ave PE25 . . . 206 D1
Laythorpe Gdns 2
LN4 . . . . 207 C4
LEA DN21 . . . . 52 F5
Leaburn Rd DN21 . . . . . . 29 D7
LEADENHAM LN5 . . . . . . 106 C3
Leadenham CE Prim Sch
LN5 . . . . 106 D3
Leading Dro PE7 . . . . . . 233 D3
Lea Dr DN32 . . . . 191 F5
Leaf Ave PE7 . . . . 230 D3
Leafere Way 🔳 PE13 . . . 170 B2
Lea Fearns Olive
Anderson Prim Sch
DN21 . . . . 53 A5
Lea Garth 8 DN17 . . . . . . 29 D7
Leagate Rd
Coningsby LN4 . . . . 207 F6
Langriville PE22 . . . . 124 F8
Thornton le Fen PE22 . . . 111 F1
Lea Gdns PE3 . . . . 225 F1
Lea Gr 2 LN3 . . . . 83 C4
LEAKE PE22 . . . . 127 C8
LEAKE COMMONSIDE
PE22 . . . . 113 F3
LEAKE FOLD HILL
PE22 . . . . 114 A2
Leakes Row LN11 . . . . . 198 C7
Lealand Cl LN2 . . . . 202 E6
Lealand Way PE21 . . . . . 209 A2
Leame Cl HU3 . . . . 180 A7
Leamington Cl 2
DN16 . . . . 183 C1
Leamington Ct DN16 . . . 183 C1
Leamlands La PE12 . . . . 149 B1
Lea Pk Home Est PE21 . . 209 B4
Lea Rd DN21 . . . . 197 D2
Lea Rd W DN21 . . . . 197 D1
Leas Cl DN37 . . . . 194 E5
Lease La DN40 . . . . 12 D6
LEASINGHAM NG34 . . . . 121 B8
Leasingham La NG34 . . . 108 D1
Leas Jun & Inf Sch The
DN37 . . . . 194 E5
Leas Rd NG34 . . . . 122 F2
Leas The NG34 . . . . 119 B1
Leas The LN4 . . . . 121 B8
Leaver Gate PE24 . . . . . 102 B2
Leaves Lake Dro PE11 . . 155 E7
Lea View 4 PE9 . . . . 163 D1
Lebanon Dr 8 LN3 . . . . . 170 E1
Lechler Cl LN2 . . . . 68 D3
Leconfield Cl 2 LN6 . . . 204 C6
Leconfield Rd 16 LN6 . . 204 C7
Ledbury Dr DN36 . . . . . 195 D7
Ledbury Rd PE3 . . . . 225 C3
Ledham PE2 . . . . 229 D4
Lee Ave
Healdingby/
Washingborough LN4 . . . 203 D1
Sutterton PE20 . . . . 136 B2
Leeder Cl PE7 . . . . 231 D7
Lee Fair Gdns DN37 . . . 184 F2
Leek Hill 18 DN15 . . . . . . 9 A5
Leeming Cl 8 LN6 . . . . . 204 D6
Lee Rd
Grimsby DN32 . . . . 234 C6
Peterborough PE2 . . . . . . 233 E6
Lee Smith St HU9 . . . . . 181 C2
Lees Rest Houses HU4 . . 179 C6
Lees The PE2 . . . . 198 B5
Lees The PE6 . . . . 217 E5
Legard Ave DN16 . . . . . 185 B6
Legard Dr 7 HU10 . . . . . 178 F4
Legbourne CE Prim Sch
LN11 . . . . 61 E5
Legbourne Abbey* LN11 . . 61 E5
Legbourne Cl 8 LN11 . . 201 D3
Legbourne Rd LN11 . . . . 198 E1
Legbourne Wood Nature
Reserve* LN11 . . . . 61 E7
Leggott Way 8 DN41 . . . 23 E4
Leicester Cl 8 LN6 . . . . . 58 A4
LEGSBY LN8 . . . . 191 E1
Legsby Pl DN32 . . . . 191 E4
Legsby Prim Sch LN8 . . . 58 A4
Legsby Rd LN8 . . . . 57 E1
Leicester Cl LN4 . . . . . . 203 C1
Leicester Gr NG31 . . . . . 210 D8
Leicester St
Kingston upon Hull
HU3 . . . . 180 D1
🔳 Sleaford NG34 . . . . . . 212 D
Leiden Fields 2 PE11 . . . 214 B
Leighton Cl PE2 . . . . 230 C
Leighton Cres 2 LN6 . . . 205 B
Leighton Gdns 3 LN6 . . 201 C
Leighton Prim Sch
PE2 . . . . 230 C
Leighton Wlk 4 PE12 . . . 159 D
Leinster Gr 3 DN33 . . . 225 D
Leiston Ct 21 PE6 . . . . . 175 A

.emon Wong La LN5 .... 106 C3
.enham La HU1 ....180 E6
.ENTON NG33 ....141 E5
.enton Gn LN2 ....202 B7
.enton's La
  Friskney PE22 ....115 A5
  Leverton PE22 ....126 F6
.enton Way **2** PE20 ... 136 D6
.eofric Cl **19** PE6 ......166 F1
.eofric Ave PE10 ....213 B5
.eonard Cres DN15 .....182 F3
.eonard St **4** HU3......180 C8
.eopold Cl DN16 ....185 A6
.erowe Rd PE13 ....170 E1
.eslie Ct **5** DN15 ......183 B3
.eslie La
  Blaxton DN9 ....26 A4
  Misson DN10 ....39 A7
.even Rd DN16 ....185 D6
.evens Wlk PE4 ....225 B3
.everett Rd PE21 ....209 B4
.EVERINGTON PE13 ....170 B3
.everington Comm
  PE13 ....169 F1
.everington Cty Prim Sch
  PE13 ....170 B2
.everrs Cl PE21 ....209 F5
.everstock Gn **38** DN2 ...14 D4
.EVERTON PE22 ....126 F6
.EVERTON HIGHGATE
  PE22 ....127 A6
.EVERTON LUCASGATE
  PE22 ....127 B6
.EVERTON OUTGATE
  PE22 ....127 B7
.evington St **3** DN31 ..189 C1
.ewes Gdns PE4 ....221 A3
.ewis Ave **13** LN12 ....77 A8
.ewis Cl NG32 ....210 B4
.eys Farm Jun Sch
  DN17 ....184 F4
.eys The
  Cherry Willingham LN3 ..203 C6
  Peterborough PE3 ......225 A1
.eytonstone La PE10 .....213 D2
.iberty La HU1 ....181 A6
.ichfield Ave
  Peterborough PE4 ......220 F3
  Scunthorpe DN17 ....184 C7
.ichfield Cl NG31 ....210 E4
.ichfield Ct DN32 ....192 B6
.ichfield Rd
  Bracebridge Heath LN4 ...81 A2
  Grimsby DN32 ....192 B6
  12 Hatfield DN7 ......14 D4
.iddell St HU2 ....180 E7
.idgard Rd DN36 ....193 A1
.idgate Cl PE2 ....230 C2
.idgett Cl **10** DN20 .....30 F8
.idgate The **7** DN9 .....27 D6
.ifeboat Ave PE25 ......206 D1
.ighter-than-Air Rd
  NG34 ....107 C1
.ighton Ave **4** PE20 ...136 C5
.ilac Ave DN16 ....183 C1
.ilac Cl
  Birchwood LN6 ....204 C8
  Bourne PE10 ....213 B6
  Wisbech PE13 ....170 E1
  3 Woodhall Spa LN10 .194 D8
.ilac Rd
  9 Elloughton-cum-Brough
    HU15 ....2 C1
  Peterborough PE1 ......226 C7
.ilac Wlk PE7 ....233 F6
.ilacwood Dr **8** NG31 ..210 F7
.ila Dr **18** PE11 ....145 B3
.ilburn Cl **5** NG34 .....121 B8
.ilburn Dr PE11 ....214 C6
.ilford Cl **5** LN2 ......202 E7
.ilford Rd PE2 ....202 E7
.illey St **8** PE13 ....117 D3
.illicrap Ct **2** LN1 .....234 B4
.illian's Carr Nature
  Reserve* PE23 ....100 E6
.illy's La LN2 ....234 B4
.ilywood Rd **2** DN20 ...19 D3
.imber Cl **2** DN21 .....53 A7
.imber Cl DN34 ....191 A6
.imber Hill LN4 ....47 D4
.imber Rd
  Humberside Airport
    DN39 ....22 A6
  Swallow LN7 ....34 A7
.imber Vale DN34 ....191 A6
.imburg Dr **7** PE11 ....214 A2

Lime Ave
  Scunthorpe DN16 ....19 A3
  Wisbech PE13 ....170 D1
Lime Cl
  Burgh le Marsh PE24 ....102 D7
  8 Langtoft PE6 ....164 F3
  3 Old Leake PE22 ....114 A1
  RAF Cranwell NG34 .....107 D1
  Ruskington NG34 ......108 D1
Lime Cres LN5 ....205 C1
Lime Ct PE11 ....214 E3
Limedale View **2** DN3 ..14 A3
Lime Gr
  Bassingham LN5 ....92 F2
  2 Boston PE21 ....209 C2
  2 Bottesford DN16 ...185 A8
  Caythorpe NG32 ....119 C7
  Cherry Willingham/Reepham
    LN3 ....203 D5
  9 Goxhill DN19 ....12 A8
  Grantham NG31 ....211 C6
  Holbeach PE12 ....215 D3
  Holton le Clay DN36 ....195 D1
  Humberston DN36 ....36 C7
  7 Ingoldmells PE25 ...90 D3
  Louth LN11 ....198 C7
  Scunthorpe DN16 ....185 B7
Lime Kiln Cl PE3 ....225 E4
Lime Kiln Way LN2 .....202 C4
Limelands **2** LN2 .....234 C3
Lime St
  Grimsby DN31 ....191 C8
  Kingston upon Hull HU8 ..181 A8
  3 Sutton Bridge PE12 ..160 F4
Limes The
  8 Beckingham DN10 ...40 A1
  Castor PE5 ....223 F1
  4 Stallingborough DN41 ..23 D6
  2 Wittering PE8 ....172 B1
Limetree Ave DN33 .....191 C3
Lime Tree Ave
  Gainsborough DN21 .....197 D5
  Kingston upon Hull HU13 ..178 F2
  2 Market Deeping PE6 ..217 A6
  20 Metheringham LN4 ..95 C4
  Peterborough PE1 ......225 F4
Limetree Cl
  13 Sleaford NG34 .....212 D2
  Yaxley PE7 ....233 F7
Lime Tree Cl
  1 Collingham NG23 ...91 D4
  6 Fulbeck NG32 ......121 B8
  6 Lincoln LN6 ....204 E8
Lime Tree Gr **4** DN8 ...15 A8
Lime Tree Paddock **2**
  NG12 ....68 F4
Limetree Wlk **1** NG34 ..122 E2
Limewalk PE12 ....216 C6
Linchfield Cl PE6 ....217 E5
Linchfield Prim Sch
  PE6 ....217 D6
Linchfield Rd PE6 ......217 D6
LINCOLN LN5 ....234 B3
Lincoln Ass Rm* LN2 ...234 B3
Lincoln Ave LN6 ....205 C8
Lincoln Byd DN31 ....191 B7
Lincoln Castle* LN1 ....234 A3
Lincoln Castle Way DN19 ...4 D2
Lincoln Cath* LN2 ......234 B3
Lincoln Christs Hospl Sch
  LN2 ....202 B6
Lincoln Cl
  4 Crowle DN17 ....16 D7
  Grantham NG31 ....210 F5
  3 Market Deeping PE6 ..217 A6
Lincoln Coll
  Lincoln LN1 ....234 B3
  Lincoln LN2 ....234 C3
Lincoln Cres **2** DN21 ...42 F8
Lincoln Ct
  4 Beacon Hill NG24 ...104 A6
  Brumby DN16 ....185 B7
Lincoln Cty Hospl The
  LN2 ....202 C4
Lincoln Dr
  27 Barton-upon-Humber
    DN18 ....10 F8
  30 Caistor LN7 ....33 B4
  5 Scampton Airfield LN1 ..67 F5
  5 Waddington LN5 .....94 A7
  24 Winterton DN15 .....9 A5
Lincoln Drill Hall*
  LN1 ....234 B2
Lincoln Gate DN36 ......48 D5
Lincoln Gdns DN16 .....185 A6
Lincoln Gdns Prim Sch
  DN16 ....185 A6
Lincoln Gn
  Kingston upon Hull
    HU4 ....179 C7
  Skegness PE25 ....206 B5
Lincoln La
  Boston PE21 ....208 C5
  Holbeach PE12 ....147 D5
  Kettlethorpe LN1 ....65 F3
  Osgodby LN8 ....44 F2
  Thorpe on the Hill LN6 ..92 E8
Lincoln Minst Sch
  LN2 ....234 B4
Lincoln Nuffield Hospl The
  LN2 ....234 B4
Lincoln Rd
  Bassingham LN5 ....92 F2
  10 Binbrook Tech Pk LN8 ..47 B6
  Brant Broughton LN5 ...105 F5
  Brant Broughton &
    Stragglethorpe LN5 ...106 A5
  Canwick LN4 ....81 B3

Lincoln Rd continued
  Caythorpe NG32 ....119 B6
  Cleethorpes DN35 ......192 C5
  Deeping Gate PE6 ......217 C3
  Digby LN4 ....108 D6
  Doddington & Whisby
    LN6 ....204 A6
  Dunholme LN2 ....68 D6
  Dunston LN4 ....95 B5
  Faldingworth LN8 ......56 F3
  Fenton LN1 ....65 E3
  Fiskerton LN3 ....203 F4
  4 Glinton PE6 ....220 C8
  Heighington/Washingborough
    LN4 ....203 A2
  Holton cum Beckering LN8 ..70 B7
  Honington NG32 ....119 C2
  Horncastle LN9 ....199 A4
  Ingham LN1 ....54 F2
  1 Leasingham NG34 ...121 B8
  Lincoln LN6 ....204 E8
  Louth LN11 ....61 B8
  Metheringham LN4 .....95 C4
  Middle Rasen LN8 ......57 B7
  Moorland Prison DN7 ...26 A8
  Nettleham LN2 ....68 B1
  Newark-on-Trent NG24 ..104 A6
  Northborough PE6 ......217 D1
  Peterborough PE6 ......220 D5
  Ruskington NG34 ......108 D2
  Saxilby with Ingleby LN1 ..66 E1
  4 Skegness PE25 ......206 C3
  Skellingthorpe LN6 ....200 B4
  Sleaford NG34 ....212 B7
  Stamford PE9 ....219 C7
  West Barkwith LN8 .....71 A7
Lincoln Rd Bridge
  NG24 ....104 A5
Lincoln Rd Nocton LN4 ..95 F7
Lincoln's Ave LN2 ......168 C2
Lincolnshire Archives*
  LN1 ....234 B3
Lincolnshire Aviation
  Heritage Ctr* PE23 ....99 F5
Lincolnshire Coast Light
  Rly* PE25 ....90 D1
Lincolnshire Rare Breeds
  Poultry* LN11 ....61 F8
Lincolnshire Rd Transport
  Mus* LN6 ....204 D5
Lincolnshire Showground*
  LN1 ....55 F1
Lincolnshire Wolds Rly*
  DN36 ....48 F6
Lincoln Sta
  Gainsborough DN21 .....197 C5
  Kingston upon Hull HU2 ..180 F7
Lincoln Sta LN2 ....234 B1
Lincoln Way **1** PE11 ...214 C5
Linda Cres LN11 ....198 A4
Lindale Gdns PE2 ......185 C7
Lindbergh Dr PE11 .....214 C2
Linden Cl **6** LN4 ......204 D7
Linden Ct LN11 ....214 C5
Linden Dene **1** LN6 ...204 D1
Linden Dr PE24 ....102 D7
Linden Rd LN4 ....199 C4
Linden Rise PE10 ......213 D7
Lindens PE13 ....177 A3
Lindens The NG31 ......211 B2
Linden Terr DN21 ......197 D3
Lindholme
  5 DN21 ....29 C3
Lindholme Bank Rd
  DN7 ....15 B1
Lindisfarne Ave DN36 ...195 B6
Lindisfarne Dr PE6 .....175 A1
Lindisfarne Way NG31 ..210 E5
Lindis Rd PE21 ....209 C5
Lindley St HU3 ....180 A7
Lindley St LN5 ....205 E8
Lindrick Cl **4** NG31 ...211 D7
Lindrick Rd **6** LN4 ....14 F3
Lindrick Wlk **5** DN37 ..194 C4
Lindridge Wlk PE3 .....225 A2
Lindsey Ave PE6 ....217 A6
Lindsey Cl
  6 Bourne PE10 ....213 C5
  Gainsborough DN21 .....197 F2
  Peterborough PE4 ......221 A2
Lindsey Ct **12** DN9 .....27 C3
Lindsey Ctr **4** DN21 ...197 B5
Lindsey Dr
  Crowle DN17 ....16 D8
  3 Healing DN41 ....23 F8
  Holton le Clay DN36 ...195 C2
Lindsey Lower Sch & Com
  Arts Coll DN35 ....192 D6
Lindsey Pl HU4 ....179 C7
Lindsey Rd
  Cleethorpes DN35 ......192 F4
  Stamford PE9 ....219 C6
  8 Uffington DN19 .....12 A8
Lindsey Rise **3** DN33 ..194 F8
Lindsey Sch The DN35 ..192 E4
Lindsey St **3** DN19 ....12 A8
Lindsey St **16** DN21 ...42 F8
Lindsey Way LN11 .....198 D3
Lindum Ave
  8 Immingham DN40 ...186 B3
  Lincoln LN2 ....234 C3
Lindum Cl
  Chapel St Leonard PE24 ..90 E7
  2 Crowle DN17 ....16 C7

Lindum Rd
  Cleethorpes DN35 ......193 A4
  Lincoln LN2 ....234 B3
Lindum Sq **5** PE25 ....206 B5
Lindum St DN15 ....183 B3
Lindum Terr LN2 ....234 C3
Lindum Way **5** PE11 ...134 F2
Linecroft La DN10 ......40 B4
Linga La LN5 ....93 A3
Lingfield Cl **8** LN1 ....66 D3
Ling Garth PE1 ....226 B8
Linghall La LN4 ....111 E5
Ling House La DN7 .....14 A5
Ling La NG33 ....152 C5
Ling Moor Prim Sch
  LN6 ....204 E3
Lings La DN7 ....14 D3
Lingwood Pk **5** PE3 ...225 A1
Linkage Coll PE23 ......100 F7
Link Rd PE1 ....225 F3
Links Ave **2** LN2 .....64 B5
Links Cres **4** PE25 ....103 E4
Linkside PE3 ....220 F1
Links Rd DN35 ....193 A3
Link The
  Bracebridge Heath
    LN4 ....205 F4
  7 Leasingham NG34 ..121 B8
  Louth LN11 ....198 E5
Links
  2 Navenby/Wellingore
    LN5 ....107 A7
Linkway **7** DN7 ......14 F3
Link Way PE11 ....214 E4
Linley Cl **4** NG23 ....91 D4
Linley Dr PE21 ....208 E2
Linnaeus St HU3 ....180 C6
Linnet PE2 ....229 D6
Linnet Cl
  Birchwood LN6 ....204 D8
  7 Market Deeping PE6 ..217 C5
  Scunthorpe DN15 ......182 D6
Linnet Dr PE10 ....143 A3
Linnet Way **11** NG40 ..212 B3
Linthorpe Gr HU10 ....178 E8
Linton **3** HU1 ....2 C6
Linton Cl
  Freiston PE22 ....137 E7
  Westwoodside DN9 ....27 A2
Linton Rise **3** DN15 ...8 A4
Linton St **5** LN5 .....201 F1
Linwood Ave **5** DN33 ..194 F8
Linwood Cl LN6 ....57 D5
Linwood Rd
  Lissington LN8 ....57 D3
  Martin LN4 ....96 B3
Linwood Warren Nature
  Reserve* LN8 ....58 A6
Liquorpond St **11** PE21 ..208 F4
Lissett Cl **6** LN6 .....204 B6
LISSINGTON LN2 ....57 C2
Lissington Rd
  Gainsborough DN21 .....197 E3
  Wickenby LN3 ....57 C1
Lister Rd
  Peterborough PE1 ......225 F7
  Scunthorpe DN15 ......182 C3
Lister St
  Grimsby DN31 ....191 B8
  Kingston upon Hull HU1 ..180 E5
LISTOFT PE24 ....89 F7
Litchfield Cl PE2 ....233 F5
Little Bargate St LN5 ..205 E8
Littlebeck Cl HU3 ......180 A4
Littlebeck Rd **3** DN36 ..36 C8
Little Belt The DN21 ...197 D7
LITTLEBOROUGH DN22 ..52 F1
Littleborough La DN21 ..52 E2
Littleborough Rd DN22 ..52 C2
Littlebury Gdns PE12 ..215 C2
LITTLE BYTHAM NG33 ..163 A8
Little Bytham Rd
  Castle Bytham NG33 ...152 E1
  Counthorpe & Creeton
    NG33 ....153 A2
LITTLE CARLTON LN11 ..62 C4
LITTLE CASTERTON
  PE9 ....171 E8
Little Casterton Rd
  PE9 ....171 E7
LITTLE CAWTHORPE
  LN11 ....61 E2
Littlechild Dr **4** PE13 ..170 B2
Little Cl
  Edenham PE10 ....153 D5
  2 Eye PE6 ....175 A1
LITTLE COATES DN34 ...190 F7
Little Coates Prim Sch
  DN34 ....188 D1
Little Coates Rd DN34 ..190 E4
Little Comm PE12 ......215 B2
Little Dog PE21 ....158 C1
Little Dovegate PE12 ...215 B8
Little Dro PE20 ....124 C2
Littlefair Rd **3** HU9 ...5 D8
LITTLEFIELD DN34 .....191 B6

Littlefield La
  Grimsby DN34 ....191 A6
  Marshchapel DN36 .....37 B2
Little Gate La LN4 .....82 A1
Little George St HU8 ...181 A8
Little Gonerby CE (Aided)
  Infant's Sch NG31 .....211 B5
LITTLE GRIMSBY LN11 ..49 B2
Little Grimsby La LN11 ..49 A1
LITTLE HALE NG34 .....133 E8
Little Hale Dro NG34 ...133 F8
Little Hale Rd NG34 ...122 C1
Little Holme Rd PE34 ..161 C2
Little Johns Cl PE3 ....224 F3
Little John St DN34 ....191 B7
Little La
  Broomfleet HU15 ....1 C6
  12 Collingham NG23 ...91 C4
  Gringley on the Hill DN10 ..39 C1
  Louth LN11 ....198 C5
  Surfleet PE11 ....145 B3
  5 Welbourn LN5 ....106 A5
Little Mason St **3**
  HU1 ....181 A7
Littlemeer PE2 ....229 F4
Little Merebalk La LN9 ..86 B2
Little Michael St DN31 ..191 B7
Littlemoors La PE22 ....113 A3
LITTLE PONTON NG31 ..140 A7
Littleport La **8** PE22 ..113 B1
Little Ramper PE13 ....170 E4
Little Scrubs Wood Nature
  Reserve* LN8 ....70 E1
Little Side Rd PE20 ....135 E8
Little S St **16** LN11 ...198 C5
LITTLE STEEPING
  PE23 ....101 D5
Little Steeping Mud & Stud
  Cottage* PE23 ....101 D6
LITTLE SUTTON PE12 ...160 C5
Little Thorpe La LN6 ...79 F1
LITTLE WELTON LN11 ...60 F6
LITTLE WISBEACH
  NG34 ....143 C6
Little Wlk DN21 ....40 B5
Littlewood Rd DN6 .....15 B8
Littleworth Dro
  Deeping St Nicholas
    PE11 ....156 D1
  Heckington NG34 ......122 F4
  Spalding PE11 ....156 E2
  Sutton St Edmund PE12 ..176 F8
Livermore Gn PE4 .....220 E6
Liverpool Dr LN6 ......200 B6
Liverpool St HU3 ......180 A6
Livesey Rd DN36 ....48 E6
Livingstone Dr PE11 ...214 B2
Lloyd Pl **10** DN9 .....55 A8
Lloyds Ave DN17 ....184 F8
Lobelia Dr **2** DN37 ...185 A1
LOBTHORPE NG33 ......152 A3
Loch Fyne Cl PE22 .....208 D7
Loch Lomond Way
  PE2 ....229 C4
Lockham Gate PE22 ...114 B2
Lockhill DN31 ....189 A2
Lock Hill **30** DN8 .....15 A8
Locking Cl **17** LN6 ...204 C6
Locking Garth LN1 ....49 D5
Lock Keepers Ct HU9 ..181 C6
Lock Keepers Way
  LN11 ....198 D7
Lock La
  Alvingham LN11 ....49 F2
  North Coates DN36 ....37 A3
Locks Cl PE6 ....174 A8
Locksley Christian Sch
  LN11 ....62 C6
Locksley Cl
  6 Boston PE21 ....208 E7
  4 North Somercotes
    LN11 ....50 F7
Locksley Way **5** LN11 ..50 F7
Lockton Cl **4** NG24 ...104 B7
Lockton Ct **10** DN18 ..10 E8
Lockton Gr **1** HU5 ...179 D8
Lockwood Bank DN9 ...27 E6
Lockwood Cl **17** DN8 ..15 A8
Lockwood Ct **8** DN15 ..182 E4
Lockwood St HU2 ......180 F8
Loder Ave PE3 ....224 F2
Lodge Ave PE23 ....100 D4
Lodge Cl
  10 Brough HU15 .....2 C7
  Kingston upon Hull HU13 ..178 F1
  6 Welton/Dunholme
    LN2 ....68 D7
Lodge Ct **3** LN7 .....14 D4
Lodge Dr **8** LN4 .....204 D7
Lodge Cvn Pk LN6 .....207 A4
Lodge Dr LN6 ....105 A8
Lodge Gdns HU13 .....178 C2

Lodge La
Flixborough DN15 . . . . 8 B2
Kirk Bramwith DN7 . . . . 14 A8
Nettleham LN2 . . . . .68 D1
Upton DN21 . . . . .53 D5
Lodge Rd
Bourne PE10 . . . . 213 C7
4 Coningsby LN4 . . . . 207 A5
Scunthorpe DN15 . . . . 182 C2
Tattershall Thorpe LN10 . . 97 E3
Lodge Top Cl LN6 . . . . . .204 E5
Lodge Way NG31 . . . . . . 211 A6
Lodington Ct 5 LN9 . . 199 D3
Loft Ave DN37 . . . . .190 E8
Loganberry Dr HU4 . . . . 179 C4
Loire Ct PE3 . . . . .225 E4
Lomax Dr 2 NG34 . . . . . 212 C6
Lombard St DN34 . . . . . . 191 A7
Lombard Dr PE1 . . . . .226 B8
Lomond Gr DN36 . . . . .36 C8
Lomond Rd HU5 . . . . .179 E8
Londesborough St
HU3 . . . . 180 C7
Londesborough Way 13
LN4 . . . . .95 D4
London Rd
Boston PE21 . . . . 208 E1
Bracebridge Heath LN4 . . 205 F5
Frampton PE20 . . . . 136 D7
Grantham NG31 . . . . .211 B3
Haugham LN11 . . . . .74 A7
Long Sutton PE12 . . . . . . 216 C4
Louth LN11 . . . . .198 C3
Newark-on-Trent NG24 . . 104 B2
Osbournby NG34 . . . . 132 C5
Peterborough PE2 . . . . . . 226 A1
Sleaford NG34 . . . . 212 B1
Spalding PE11 . . . . 214 C2
Tathwell LN11 . . . . .61 C2
Wansford PE8 . . . . 222 B2
Yaxley PE7 . . . . 233 C5
LONDONTHORPE
NG31 . . . . 130 D4
Londonthorpe La
NG31 . . . . .211 E8
Londonthorpe Rd
NG31 . . . . .211 E8
Long Acre 1 LN12 . . . . . . .64 B4
LONG BENNINGTON
NG23 . . . . 117 D3
Long Bennington CE Prim
Sch NG23 . . . . 117 D3
Long Causeway PE1 . . . . 226 A2
Longcliffe Rd NG31 . . . . 211 A8
Long Cl La LN3 . . . . .82 B7
Longcroft Dr 1 NG41 . . 207 C6
Longdales Rd LN2 . . . . . 201 F6
Longden St HU3 . . . . 180 A7
Longdon Cl 6 PE12 . . . .160 E4
Long Dro
Bourne PE10 . . . . 155 B1
Gosberton PE11 . . . . 144 B6
Rippingale PE10 . . . . 143 D3
Thurlby PE10 . . . . .164 E7
Walcott LN4 . . . . .109 E8
Wisbech St Mary PE13 . . 177 D4
Long Farm La PE22 . . . . .52 E2
Long Field Dr 2 DN3 . . . .14 A1
Longfield Gate PE2 . . . . 230 A6
Longfield Rd DN34 . . . . . 190 E4
Long Field Rd 2 DN3 . . . .14 A2
Long Gates LN11 . . . . . . .51 A4
Longhead La PE14 . . . . . 170 D3
Longhedge Dro PE20 . . . .134 E5
Long Hedge La
Greetham with Somersby
LN9 . . . . .86 C5
Swaby LN13 . . . . .74 E4
Long Hollow NG33 . . . . . 131 C3
Longhorn Cl DN37 . . . . . 194 B4
Longhurst Gdns PE21 . . 208 D7
Long La
Auborn Haddington & South
Hykeham LN6 . . . . .93 B7
Barnby in the Willows
NG24 . . . . .104 F4
Fleet PE12 . . . . 168 B3
Ingham LN1 . . . . .54 E2
Leadenham LN5 . . . . 107 A2
Moulton PE12 . . . . 157 E5
Mumby LN13 . . . . .76 E2
Redmile NG32 . . . . 128 A1
2 Westborough & Dry
Doddington NG23 . . . . . .117 F3
Willoughton DN21 . . . . . . .42 E3
Longlands LN13 . . . . .63 D3
Longleat Dr LN1 . . . . 198 A7
Long Leys Rd LN1 . . . . . . 201 C6
Longmeadow Rise 18
DN41 . . . . .23 A4
Longmeadows PE10 . . . . 154 B7
Longmeadows Dr DN37 . . .23 F2
Long Pasture 5 PE4 . . . 220 F5
Long Rd
1 Scunthorpe DN15 . . .182 F4
Terrington St Clement
PE34 . . . . .161 F5
2 Tydd St Mary PE13 . . 170 C8
Longrigg Wlk 17 PE20 . .135 B7
Long St
5 Foston NG32 . . . . . . 117 F1
Great Gonerby NG31 . . . 129 E5
LONG SUTTON PE12 . . . . 216 C4
Long Sutton Butterfly Pk *
PE12 . . . . 216 D6

Long Sutton Cty Prim Sch
PE12 . . . . 216 B5
LONGTHORPE PE3 . . . . . . 225 A1
Longthorpe Cl 3 PE3 . . 225 A2
Longthorpe Gn PE3 . . . . 225 B1
Longthorpe House Mews
11 PE3 . . . . 224 F2
Longthorpe Parkway
PE3 . . . . 225 A2
Longthorpe Prim Sch
PE3 . . . . 225 A2
Longton Rd 4 DN3 . . . . . .14 A2
Longueville St PE4 . . . . 230 B5
Longwater PE2 . . . . 230 B6
Long Wood La LN4 . . . . . .95 C2
Long Wood Rd DN21 . . . . .41 A1
Lonsdale St PE12 . . . . . . 213 E6
Lonsdale Gr PE10 . . . . . . 213 E6
Lonsdale Pl 3 LN5 . . . . . 201 F1
Lonsdale Rd PE9 . . . . . . 218 E5
Lonsdale St 8 HU3 . . . . 180 A6
Loop La 1 PE12 . . . . 157 F7
LOOSEGATE PE12 . . . . . . 158 A8
Loosegate Rd PE12 . . . . 158 A8
Lopham La DN17 . . . . .34 F8
Lord Dr 4 NG31 . . . . 129 E5
Lords La 19 DN19 . . . . . . .11 D8
Lord's La 6 NG33 . . . . . . 151 A8
Lord St
Gainsborough DN21 . . . . 197 C4
Grimsby DN31 . . . . 191 B8
4 Sleaford NG34 . . . . . 212 C3
17 Stainforth DN7 . . . . .14 C6
Lornas Field PE7 . . . . . . 230 D2
Lorne St LN5 . . . . 234 C1
Losecoat Cl 1 PE9 . . . . 219 D7
Lothian Cl 7 LN5 . . . . . . .93 F7
Lotus Cl 5 LN6 . . . . 204 D1
Loughborough Univ of
Peterborough PE1 . . . . . 226 A3
Rough Rd LN9 . . . . .72 F1
Louisberg Rd DN21 . . . . .54 F8
Louis Dr HU5 . . . . .179 B8
Louis St HU3 . . . . 180 C8
LOUTH LN11 . . . . 198 E6
Louth Cty Hospl LN11 . . 198 E6
Louth Mus * LN11 . . . . . . 198 B6
Louth Playgoers Riverhead
Theatre * LN11 . . . . 198 D7
Louth Rd
East Barkwith LN8 . . . . . . .58 E1
Fotherby LN11 . . . . .49 A3
Grimsby DN33 . . . . 191 D1
1 Holton le Clay DN36 . . 195 D2
Horncastle LN9 . . . . .73 A5
New Waltham DN36 . . . . 195 B5
Skidbrooke with Saltfleet
Haven LN11 . . . . .51 C4
2 West Ashby LN9 . . . . .85 E7
Wragby LN8 . . . . .70 D5
Louth Sta Est (Ind)
LN11 . . . . 198 C6
Louth Trading Est
LN11 . . . . 198 C7
Lovat Cl HU3 . . . . 180 D5
Loveden Ct DN35 . . . . . . 193 A3
Loveden View 6 NG32 . .119 B7
Love La
Caythorpe NG32 . . . . 119 C7
Gainsborough DN21 . . . . 197 C6
Louth LN11 . . . . 198 A5
Spalding PE11 . . . . 214 F3
3 Sutterton PE20 . . . . 136 A2
Wrangle PE22 . . . . 114 C4
Lovell Rd DN17 . . . . 184 E3
Lovell Way PE34 . . . . 161 F2
Lovers La PE5 . . . . 222 F2
Love's Hill
Castor PE5 . . . . 223 F1
Peterborough PE5 . . . . . . 224 A1
Loves La LE15 . . . . 162 A1
Lovesey Cl LN4 . . . . 205 D6
Lovett St DN35 . . . . 189 E1
LOW BARLINGS LN3 . . . . . .82 E8
Lowbridge La 4 PE11 . . 145 C6
Low Burgage DN15 . . . . . .2 B1
LOW BURNHAM DN9 . . . . .27 E5
Low Church Rd 2 LN8 . . .57 C8
Low Comm La HU15 . . . . .2 D4
Lowcroft Ave 4 DN9 . . . .27 D2
Lowcroft Cl 8 DN9 . . . . . .27 D2
Low Cross St 6 DN17 . . 16 D8
Low Deeps La DN10 . . . . .26 C1
LOWER BASSINGTHORPE
NG33 . . . . 140 E4
LOWER BITCHFIELD
NG33 . . . . 141 A3
Lower Church Rd LN6 . . 200 B5
Lowerdale 2 HU15 . . . . . .2 C6
Lower High St 9 LN5 . . . .93 F7
DN8 . . . . .15 A8
Lower Kenyon St 10
DN8 . . . . .15 A8
Lower Rd NG22 . . . . 119 A5
Lower Sow Dale Nature
Reserve * LN9 . . . . .86 B6
Lower Spring St 1
DN35 . . . . 189 A1
Low Farm Dr NG34 . . . . 142 C8
Lowfield Cl
4 Barnby Dun DN3 . . . .14 A8
3 Kirton in Lindsey DN21 . .30 B1
Lowfield Cl HU10 . . . . . . 178 F6
Lowfield House HU10 . . 178 F6
Lowfield La
Balderton NG24 . . . . 104 A5
Belchford LN9 . . . . .73 C2
Low Field La HU15 . . . . . . .2 E5

Lowfield Rd HU10 . . . . . . .178 E5
Low Fields Ave 1
PE11 . . . . 214 F4
Lowfields Inf Sch LN5 . 205 C2
Lowfields Jun Sch
LN5 . . . . 205 C2
Lowfields La
Allington NG32 . . . . 128 F7
Butterwick PE22 . . . . 126 E5
Lowfields Rd PE22 . . . . . 126 E6
LOW FULNEY PE12 . . . . . . 157 B4
Low Fulney Est PE12 . . . . 157 C5
Low Garth DN17 . . . . 184 F2
Lowgate
Fleet PE12 . . . . 159 C8
Kingston upon Hull HU1 . 181 A6
Lutton PE12 . . . . 160 A8
Low Gate
Friskney PE22 . . . . 115 A6
Gosberton PE11 . . . . 145 C7
Marshchapel DN36 . . . . . .37 C1
Moulton PE12 . . . . 158 A6
Surfleet PE11 . . . . 145 C3
Tydd St Mary PE13 . . . . . 160 A1
Lowgate Ave 7 PE20 . . . 135 A4
Lowgate Cres PE12 . . . . 159 E8
Lowgate La PE20 . . . . . . 135 A4
Lowgate Rd
Ashby with Scremby
PE23 . . . . .88 D2
Conisholme LN11 . . . . . . .50 C5
Hogsthorpe PE24 . . . . . . .90 B8
Low Holland La DN22 . . . .52 C2
Lowick Gdns PE3 . . . . . . 225 C5
Low La
Croft PE24 . . . . 102 D6
Holbeach PE12 . . . . 215 F4
Kirk Bramwith DN7 . . . . . .14 A6
Middle Rasen LN8 . . . . . . .45 C1
Terrington St Clement
PE34 . . . . .161 E3
Wrangle PE22 . . . . 114 B3
Low Levels Bank DN8 . . .15 D4
Low Leys Rd 6 DN17 . . . 184 E3
LOW MARNHAM NG23 . . . .78 A4
Low Mill La PE20 . . . . . . 136 E1
Lowmoor La LN9 . . . . .85 C3
Low Moor Rd LN6 . . . . . . 204 E5
Low Pk La LN4 . . . . .81 F4
Low Rd
Barrowby NG32 . . . . 210 A4
Besthorpe NG23 . . . . .91 C7
Blyborough DN21 . . . . . . .42 E6
Croft PE24 . . . . 102 F5
Crowland PE6 . . . . 175 A8
Friskney PE22 . . . . 114 F4
Grantham NG31 . . . . 211 B4
Harmston LN5 . . . . .93 D6
Healing DN41 . . . . .23 F5
Holbeach PE12 . . . . 147 F2
Marshchapel DN36 . . . . . .37 A1
Osgodby LN8 . . . . .45 B3
South Kyme LN4 . . . . 123 B8
Spalding PE11 . . . . 214 F4
Wainfleet St Mary PE24 . 102 C1
Walpole Cross Keys
PE34 . . . . 161 D3
Worlaby DN20 . . . . .20 C8
Wyberton PE21 . . . . 136 E7
LOW RISBY DN15 . . . . .9 A2
Low St
Beckingham DN10 . . . . . . .40 A1
Billingborough NG34 . . . . 133 B1
Collingham NG23 . . . . .91 C4
Dunham-on-Trent NG22 . .65 A1
Harby NG23 . . . . .79 B5
Haxey DN9 . . . . .27 D2
North Ferriby HU14 . . . . . . .3 A4
Stow DN20 . . . . .19 A4
Winterton DN15 . . . . .9 A5
Lowther Gdns PE4 . . . . . 221 B2
Lowther St HU3 . . . . 180 A7
Low Thorpe Rd LN7 . . . . .33 B4
LOW TOYNTON LN9 . . . . . 199 F6
Low Toynton Cl LN9 . . . . 199 D5
Low Toynton Rd LN9 . . . 199 D5
Low Wood La LN6 . . . . . . .91 F8
Loxley PE4 . . . . 220 E4
Loxley Gn HU4 . . . . 179 B7
Loxley Way 6 HU15 . . . . . .2 D5
Loyalty La DN18 . . . . .3 E1
Loyd St HU10 . . . . 178 F6
Lucan Cl 13 PE22 . . . . . 113 B1
Lucas Ct 4 DN41 . . . . .23 F5
Lucern Ct LN11 . . . . 198 D6
Lucetta Gdns 9 PE11 . . 214 B5
Lucian Wlk 7 HU4 . . . . . 179 A1
Lucian St LN5 . . . . 234 A2
Luda Terr LN11 . . . . 198 D7
LUDBOROUGH DN36 . . . . . .48 E6
Ludborough Pk DN36 . . . .48 E6
Ludborough Rd
13 North Thoresby
DN36 . . . . .36 B1
North Thoresby DN36 . . . .48 D8
Ludborough Sta DN36 . . . .48 F6
Ludborough Way 8
DN35 . . . . 192 F3
LUDDINGTON DN17 . . . . . . .7 D3
Luddington & Garthorpe
Prim Sch DN17 . . . . .7 C3
Luddington Rd
Garthorpe & Fockerby
DN17 . . . . .7 D5
1 Peterborough PE4 . . 221 B1
LUDFORD LN8 . . . . .59 A8
Ludford CE Sch LN8 . . . . .59 B8

Ludford Cres DN21 . . . . . 197 E3
Ludford Dr 3 LN6 . . . . . . 205 A7
Ludford Rd LN8 . . . . .47 C4
Ludford St DN32 . . . . 191 E6
Ludgate Cl DN37 . . . . 194 D4
Ludgate La DN34 . . . . 191 A7
Ludlow Gdns 4 PE11 . . . 145 A8
Ludlow Pl DN35 . . . . 192 E5
LUDNEY LN11 . . . . .50 C6
Ludney La LN11 . . . . .50 C6
Luffenham Cl 4 PE9 . . . . 218 E5
Lulworth Ave HU4 . . . . . . 179 A3
Lulworth Cl DN17 . . . . . . 184 C8
Lulworth Wlk DN40 . . . . . 186 B2
Lumley Ave PE25 . . . . . . 206 D3
Lumley Cres 3 PE25 . . . 206 D4
Lumley Pl 2 LN1 . . . . 201 F1
Lumley Sq 8 PE25 . . . . . 206 C3
Lunds The HU10 . . . . 178 C6
Lundy Cl DN40 . . . . 186 C2
Luneburg Pl DN35 . . . . . 182 C5
Luneburg Way DN15 . . . . 182 C6
Lunedale Rd DN16 . . . . . 185 D5
Lunn La NG23 . . . . .91 C4
Lunn's Cres 21 DN18 . . . .10 E8
Lupin Rd LN2 . . . . 202 C8
Lurgan Cl LN5 . . . . 205 D3
LUSBY PE23 . . . . .86 F2
Lusher Way PE3 . . . . 225 A1
Luston Cl LN6 . . . . 200 B1
Luton Rd HU5 . . . . 179 F8
LUTTON PE12 . . . . 160 A8
Lutton Bank PE12 . . . . . . 148 D1
Lutton Garnsgate
PE12 . . . . 160 B6
Lutton Gate Rd PE12 . . . 168 E4
Lutton Gowts PE12 . . . . . 216 D7
LUTTON GOWTS PE12 . . . . 216 D8
Lutton Low Rd PE12 . . . . 160 B7
Lutton St PE25 . . . . 225 C6
Lutton Gate La PE12 . . . 149 B2
Lych Gate 10 DN20 . . . . . .19 D3
Lydbrook Rd DN16 . . . . . 183 A1
Lydd Cl LN6 . . . . 204 C6
Lydford Rd DN40 . . . . 186 A4
Lydia Ct 3 DN40 . . . . 186 A4
Lygon St DN16 . . . . 183 B1
Lyle Cl 3 LN4 . . . . .64 A4
Lyme Wlk 9 PE3 . . . . 225 C6
Lymington Garth HU4 . . . 179 A3
Lymn Bank PE24 . . . . 102 C4
Lymn Ct 2 NG31 . . . . 210 E2
Lynchwood PE2 . . . . 229 C5
Lyndale Ave 17 DN3 . . . . 14 A1
Lyndale Pk PE2 . . . . 229 C6
Lynden Ave NG31 . . . . . . 210 E8
Lyndhurst Ave
8 Grimsby DN33 . . . . 191 D3
Skegness PE25 . . . . 206 B5
Lyndhurst Ct 1 PE25 . . 206 B5
Lyndis Wlk PE21 . . . . 215 E1
Lyndon Bsns Pk LN6 . . . 204 B5
Lyndon Cres LN11 . . . . . . 198 D6
Lyndon Way
Louth LN11 . . . . 198 D8
Stamford PE9 . . . . 218 E5
Lyneham Cl LN6 . . . . 204 B7
Lyn Ellis Cl 2 PE21 . . . . 209 C4
Lynmouth Cl 1 LN6 . . . . 205 A1
Lynmouth Dr DN17 . . . . . 184 C8
Lynn Rd
Walpole Cross Keys
PE34 . . . . 161 C3
Walsoken PE13 . . . . 170 E2
Lynnwell Cl PE25 . . . . . . 206 A6
Lynton Ave HU4 . . . . 179 B3
Lynton Cl DN15 . . . . 182 D4
Lynton Parade DN31 . . . 191 B7
Lynton Rd PE1 . . . . 225 F6
Lynton Rise DN35 . . . . . . 192 E4
Lynwood Ave HU10 . . . . . 178 E6
Lyric Cl 1 HU4 . . . . 179 B3
Lysaghts Way DN15 . . . . .8 C1
Lytham Cl
Heighington/
Washingborough LN4 . 203 D1
Londonthorpe & Harrowby
without NG31 . . . . 211 E7
Lytham Dr DN37 . . . . 194 C3
Lythemere PE2 . . . . 230 C4
Lytton St LN2 . . . . 234 C3
Lyvelly Gdns PE1 . . . . . . 226 E6

M

MABLETHORPE LN12 . . . . .64 C3
Mablethorpe Com Prim
Sch LN12 . . . . .64 A4
Mablethorpe Rd
North Coates DN36 . . . . . .37 A3
Theddlethorpe St Helen
LN12 . . . . .63 F5
MacAulay Dr
Lincoln LN2 . . . . 202 B6
Newark-on-Trent NG24 . . 104 B3
Macaulay Jun & Inf Sch
DN31 . . . . 191 B8
MacAulay St DN31 . . . . . 191 B8
MacAulay Way DN31 . . . 191 B8
Mace Rd PE2 . . . . 231 D5
Machray Pl DN35 . . . . . . 192 D7
McInnes St 4 DN21 . . . . 197 B5
Mackender Ct 4
DN16 . . . . 185 C6
Mackenzie Pl 8 DN40 . . 186 B3
Maclure St DN31 . . . . 189 B2

Macmillan Ave LN6 . . . . 204 C6
MacPhail Cres LN1 . . . . . .66 E2
McVeigh Ct 13 DN41 . . . .23 F7
Maddison La PE23 . . . . . . .88 B2
Madeley St HU3 . . . . 180 C4
Madely Gn DN34 . . . . 191 A2
Maegan Way DN35 . . . . . 192 E5
Mafeking Terr PE21 . . . . 209 A2
Maffit Rd HU4 . . . . 179 A3
Magdalen Cl 4 DN16 . . . 185 B4
Magdalene Rd DN34 . . . . 190 F5
Magdalene View NG24 . . 104 B4
Magdalen Mus * PE24 . . 102 D2
Magdalen Rd PE24 . . . . . 102 D2
Magdalen Sch PE24 . . . . 102 D2
Magdellan Ct PE3 . . . . . . 225 C2
Magee Rd PE4 . . . . 221 B3
Magellan Dr 9 PE23 . . . . 101 A4
Magellan Way LN1 . . . . . 214 C2
Magistrates Rd PE7 . . . . 233 D8
Magna Cres 15 NG34 . . . 122 E1
Magna Mile LN8 . . . . .59 B8
Magnolia Ave PE3 . . . . . 225 A2
Magnolia Cl LN4 . . . . .81 D2
Magnolia Dr DN16 . . . . . 195 D2
Magnolia Rd NG34 . . . . . 212 D3
Magnolia Rise 4
DN40 . . . . 186 C5
Magnolia Way DN16 . . . . 185 E4
Magpie Cl LN6 . . . . 200 A1
Magpie Cr 8 NG34 . . . . . 122 B2
Magrath Ct 3 DN20 . . . . 196 C4
Maiden Cl 1 DN40 . . . . . 186 A4
Maiden Ct 10 LN1 . . . . . . .66 D1
Maiden Gr 2 NG34 . . . . . 212 E1
Maiden La
Hogsthorpe PE24 . . . . . . .90 B4
11 Stamford PE9 . . . . . 219 C5
Maidens Rd 10 PE20 . . . 136 A4
Maidenwell La LN11 . . . . .73 D1
Maidenwell La 1 LN7 . . . .32 A
Maiden Well La 5
LN5 . . . . 107 A
Maidment Dr LN1 . . . . . . 201 C
Maidwell Way DN34 . . . . 190 C
Main App Rd DN16 . . . . . 183 C
Main Ave
Bracebridge Heath
LN4 . . . . 205 F
Scunthorpe DN17 . . . . . . 184 C
Maine Ave DN15 . . . . 182 B
Main Rd
Anwick NG34 . . . . 109 B
Ashby cum Fenby DN37 . . .35 D
Barkston NG32 . . . . 130 B
Belchford LN9 . . . . .73 A
Benniworth LN8 . . . . .72 C
Bourne PE10 . . . . 154 C
Carrington PE22 . . . . 112 C
Collyweston PE9 . . . . 171 B
2 Donington on Bain
LN11 . . . . .59 E
Dunsby PE10 . . . . 143 B
East Kirkby PE23 . . . . .99 F
Etton PE6 . . . . 173 E
Friskney Eaudike PE22 . . 115 C
Gedney PE12 . . . . 159 C
Goulceby LN11 . . . . .72 D
Gunby & Stainby NG33 . . 151 B
Haconby PE10 . . . . 154 C
Heighington/Washingborough
LN4 . . . . 203 B
Leadenham LN5 . . . . 106 D
Little Hale NG34 . . . . 122 E
Little Steeping PE23 . . . . 100 A
Long Bennington NG23 . . 117 D
Nocton LN4 . . . . .95 B
North Willingham LN8 . . . .58 D
Parson Drove PE13 . . . . 177 B
3 Potterhanworth LN4 . .82 B
Quadring PE11 . . . . 134 F
Saltfleet LN11 . . . . .51 C
2 Sibsey PE22 . . . . . . 113 B
Spilsby PE23 . . . . .87 F
Stickford PE22 . . . . 100 B
Stickney PE22 . . . . 112 E
Tallington PE9 . . . . 172 E
Thurlby PE10 . . . . 164 D
Toynton All Saints PE23 . 100 F
2 Tydd St Mary PE13 . . 170 C
17 Uffington PE9 . . . . . 172 C
Main St
Ailsworth PE5 . . . . 223 D
Ancaster NG32 . . . . 119 F
Ashby de la Launde & Bloxholm
LN4 . . . . 108 B
Barlings LN3 . . . . .69 F
Barnack PE9 . . . . 172 D
Barrowby NG32 . . . . 210 A
Baston PE6 . . . . 164 E
4 Bishop Norton LN8 . . .43 D
Bonby DN20 . . . . .10 A
Boothby Graffoe LN5 . . . . .94 A
Boothby Pagnell NG33 . . 141 A
Bottesford NG13 . . . . 128 C
Broomfleet HU15 . . . . .1 C
Brough HU15 . . . . .1 C
Buckminster NG33 . . . . . 150 F
Cadney DN20 . . . . .31 D

Main St *continued*
Careby Aunby & Holywell PE9 163 B7
Carlton Scroop NG32 119 C4
Castor PE5 223 D3
Claypole NG23 117 F7
Clipsham LE15 162 C7
Crowle DN17 16 E6
Croxton Kerrial NG32 138 D3
Denton NG32 139 A7
Doddington & Whisby LN6 79 D5
Dorrington LN4 108 E3
Dunham-on-Trent NG22 65 B1
East/West Stockwith DN10 40 C5
Edenham PE10 153 F4
Ellerker HU15 2 A8
Ewerby & Evedon NG34 122 C6
Farcet PE7 231 C2
Fenton NG23 105 C1
Fishlake DN7 14 D8
Foston NG32 117 F1
Fulstow LN11 49 B8
Gedney PE12 148 B1
Graiselound DN9 27 D1
1 Grasby DN38 32 E7
Great Casterton PE9 218 C8
Greatford PE9 164 C2
Gunby & Stainby NG33 151 B4
Hackthorn LN2 55 E1
Haconby PE10 154 D8
Hatfield DN7 14 F3
Honington NG32 119 C1
Horkstow DN18 10 A5
Horsington LN10 84 D3
Hougham NG32 118 C3
Ingoldsby NG33 141 D5
Laneham DN22 65 A3
Mablethorpe & Sutton LN12 64 B1
Mareham le Fen PE22 98 F3
Marston NG32 118 D2
Newark-on-Trent NG24 104 C2
Normanby by Spital LN8 55 F7
North Kyme LN4 109 F3
North Leverton with Habblesthorpe DN22 52 B1
North Rauceby NG34 120 E5
Norton Disney LN6 92 C2
Osgodby LN8 45 A3
RAF Cranwell NG34 120 C8
Ryhall PE9 163 D1
Scawby DN20 30 F7
Scopwick LN4 95 D1
Scothern LN2 68 F4
Scredington NG34 132 F7
Southorpe PE9 172 E1
South Rauceby NG34 120 E4
South Scarle NG23 91 E6
Sproxton LE14 138 F1
Sutton on Trent NG23 91 A8
Swanland HU14 3 B7
Syston NG32 130 A7
Thistleton LE15 151 C1
Thorney NG23 78 F7
Thornton Curtis DN39 11 E5
Thorpe on the Hill LN6 92 E8
1 Timberland LN4 96 B1
Torksey LN1 65 D6
Ufford PE9 172 F3
Upton DN21 53 D5
Welby NG32 130 F5
West Ashby LN9 85 E7
Westborough & Dry Doddington NG23 117 E5
Whitton DN15 1 E3
Wilsford NG32 120 C2
Worlaby DN20 20 D8
1 Wymondham LE14 150 C1
Yaxley PE7 233 E5
Mainwaring Cl 5 LN2 68 E6
Mainwaring Rd LN2 234 C4
Maisdike La PE12 159 B5
Maize Ct 9 NG34 212 F3
Malborne Way PE2 230 B4
Malborough Dr 4 LN12 64 A3
Malcolm Ave NG34 107 C1
Malcolm Rd DN34 190 F4
Malcolm Sargent Prim Sch PE9 218 E5
Maldon Dr HU9 181 C6
Malham Ave HU4 179 C6
Malham Cl LN6 200 C1
Malham Dr LN6 200 C1
Malim Way 3 NG31 210 F8
Malkinson Cl
4 West Halton DN15 8 E7
12 Winterton DN15 9 A5
Mallalieu Ct 2 DN15 182 E4
Mallard Ave 6 DN3 14 A4
Mallard Cl
Birchwood LN6 200 E1
5 Essendine PE9 163 D3
19 Healing DN41 23 F5
Skellingthorpe LN6 200 A4
Spalding PE11 214 E2
Mallard Ct
10 Grantham NG31 210 E2
4 North Hykeham LN6 204 C1
5 Stamford PE9 219 B4
Mallard Dr 6 LN7 33 B4
Mallard Dro PE11 134 B1
Mallard Mews DN32 191 E6
Mallard Rd
Low Fulney PE12 157 C5
Peterborough PE3 220 E1
3 Scunthorpe DN17 184 E6
Mallards Reach 8 PE11 134 F2
Mallards The 5 PE6 174 A5
Mallard Way
Brigg DN20 196 A3
Skegness PE25 103 C7
Malling Wlk DN16 185 B2
Mallory Cl 6 LN6 204 C7
Mallory Dr 3 PE11 214 C2
Mallory La 18 PE9 219 B5
Mallory Rd
1 Ashby de la Launde & Bloxholm LN4 108 A7
Peterborough PE1 226 C2
4 Scunthorpe DN16 185 D5
Mallowfield 2 LN8 57 B8
Mallows La PE22 113 C2
Mall Sh Ctr The LN1 234 B2
Malmesbury Dr 3 DN34 191 C6
Malmsgate La PE20 135 F6
Malm St HU3 180 B6
Malpas Ave 4 DN21 197 D5
MALTBY LN11 60 F3
Maltby Ave DN37 190 C3
Maltby Cl 20 PE8 172 B1
Maltby Dr PE6 164 D4
Maltby La 12 DN18 3 E1
MALTBY LE MARSH LN13 76 A8
Maltby Rd
Scunthorpe DN17 184 E5
Skegness PE25 206 D5
Maltby Way LN9 199 D3
Malten La 8 PE12 158 B7
Malting La PE11 134 E2
Maltings La NG31 210 E7
Malting Sq PE7 233 F6
Maltings The
5 Alford LN13 75 F3
1 Leasingham NG34 121 B7
Long Sutton PE12 216 B5
6 Thorney PE6 176 A3
Wothorpe PE9 219 C2
Maltings Way DN32 191 E8
Maltkiln La
Brant Broughton LN5 105 F5
2 Elsham DN20 20 F7
Malt Kiln La 1 LN5 93 F6
Maltkiln Rd
Barton-upon-Humber DN18 3 F1
Fenton LN1 65 E3
Malton Rd LN6 204 F3
Malus Cl PE7 230 C3
Malvern Ave
Grimsby DN33 191 A3
Heighington/Washingborough LN4 203 D2
Spalding PE11 214 E6
Malvern Cl
Lincoln LN5 205 D4
15 Lincoln LN6 93 C8
20 Lincoln LN6 93 C8
Sleaford NG34 212 B2
Spalding PE11 214 E6
4 Thorne/Moorends DN8 15 A7
Malvern Dr 5 NG31 210 E8
Malvern Rd
5 Mablethorpe/Sutton on Sea LN12 64 B4
Peterborough PE4 221 C2
Scunthorpe DN17 184 F7
Manasty Rd PE2 229 C2
MANBY LN11 62 D6
Manby Hall Bsns Pk DN40 186 D5
Manby Middlegate LN11 62 D7
Manby Rd
Immingham DN40 186 C6
Legbourne LN11 61 E4
Scunthorpe DN17 184 E4
Manby Rd by Pass DN40 186 D6
Manby St LN5 205 D6
Mancetter Sq PE4 220 F1
Manchester Rd 11 LN5 94 A7
Manchester St
Cleethorpes DN35 192 D8
Kingston upon Hull HU3 180 A4
Manchester Way
3 Donington PE11 134 F2
Grantham NG31 210 C5
Mandalay Dr 1 PE10 213 E7
Mandela Link 1 DN31 191 C7
Mandeville PE2 229 F4
Mandike Rd PE20 136 C2
Manifold Rd DN16 185 E5
Manlake Ave DN15 9 A5
Manley Ct 1 DN9 27 D6
Manley Gdns
Brigg DN20 196 B3
11 Cleethorpes DN35 192 F3
Manley St 4 DN15 183 B3
Mannaberg Way DN15 183 B6
Manners Cl 3 PE9 172 C6
Manners Rd NG24 104 B2
Manners St NG31 211 A6
Manning Rd PE10 213 D5
Manningtree Cl DN32 191 E6
Mann La DN9 16 D2
Manor Ave
Grimsby DN32 191 D6
Peterborough PE2 231 B7
Manor Cl
6 Bardney LN3 83 C4
Manor Cl *continued*
11 Baston PE6 164 E5
East Kirkby PE23 99 F4
Farcet PE7 231 C2
3 Great Gonerby NG31 129 E5
11 Keelby DN41 23 A5
Langtoft PE6 164 E3
7 Leasingham NG34 121 B7
Lincoln LN2 234 B4
14 Metheringham LN4 95 D4
15 Ruskington NG34 108 D2
Ryhall PE9 163 C2
7 Sibsey PE22 113 B1
2 Spalding PE11 214 C1
6 Welbourn LN5 106 E5
13 Wittering PE8 172 B1
Yaxley PE7 233 D5
Manor Cliff 1 LN8 55 F6
Manor Ct
9 Bourne PE10 213 C5
2 Carlton-le-Moorland LN5 105 E8
Grimsby DN32 191 D7
17 Nettleham LN2 68 C2
Nocton LN4 95 B7
1 Stallingborough DN41 23 E6
2 Sudbrooke LN2 68 F3
Manor Ct Rd 7 DN9 27 E6
Manor Dr
12 Baston PE6 164 E5
2 Binbrook LN8 47 C4
3 Bonby DN20 10 C2
4 Brough HU15 2 C6
5 Great Gonerby NG31 129 D5
1 Great Gonerby NG31 129 E5
Halton Holegate PE23 101 B7
7 Harlaxton NG32 139 C7
Holbeach PE12 215 D3
1 Long Bennington NG23 117 D3
Peterborough PE6 221 E3
3 Scawby DN20 30 E8
Skegness PE25 206 B5
2 Sudbrooke LN2 68 F2
Waltham DN37 194 E5
7 Wragby LN8 70 D4
Manor Farm Cl 43 DN17 29 D6
Manor Farm Dr 3 LN1 66 D7
Manor Farm La
Castor PE5 223 E2
3 Essendine PE9 163 D3
Manor Farm Rd DN17 184 E6
Manor Gdns
Boston PE21 209 A4
8 Hatfield DN7 14 E4
Peterborough PE2 231 C7
Manor Hill LN11 60 A1
Manor Hill Cnr PE12 169 D7
Manor House Ct PE6 217 E4
Manor House La NG23 117 E5
Manor House Mus* LN13 75 F3
Manor House Rd PE12 146 F2
Manor House St
1 Fulletby LN9 86 B8
5 Horncastle LN9 199 B4
Peterborough PE1 226 A3
Manor La
Aisthorpe LN1 67 C7
4 Barrow upon Humber DN19 11 D8
Bourne PE10 213 C4
Broadholme LN6 66 D1
5 Carlton-le-Moorland LN5 105 E8
Goxhill DN19 11 F8
Hougham NG32 118 C3
Threekingham NG34 132 E3
16 Waddington LN5 93 F7
1 Welton/Dunholme LN2 68 D6
Wrangle PE22 114 B2
Manor Leas Cl LN6 205 B3
Manor Leas Inf Sch LN6 205 B3
Manor Leas Jun Sch LN6 205 B3
Manor Paddock 6 NG32 128 F7
MANOR PARK DN17 184 D6
Manor Pk 7 LN11 61 F3
Manor Pl NG34 212 C5
Manor Rd
Barrowby NG32 210 A5
Bottesford NG13 128 A5
Burton Coggles NG33 152 C8
Carlby PE9 163 E4
2 Collingham NG23 91 D4
Coningsby LN4 110 E8
1 Crowle DN17 16 D7
East Ella HU5 179 B8
Folksworth PE7 232 D1
4 Hagworthingham PE23 87 A4
Hatfield DN7 14 E4
Heighington/Washingborough LN4 203 B1
Kingston upon Hull HU5 179 B8
Kirton PE20 136 B5
Lincoln LN2 234 C4
Northorpe DN21 42 A8
Saxilby LN1 66 D2
Scunthorpe DN16 185 B3
Sleaford NG34 212 B2
5 Stainforth DN7 14 C7
Stretton LE15 162 A6
Swanland HU14 3 B6
Swinderby LN6 92 A5
Twin Rivers DN14 7 E7
Manor Rd *continued*
Wansford PE5 222 F2
Manor Rise LN3 203 F8
Manor St
7 Heckington NG34 122 E3
Keelby DN41 23 A5
8 Kingston upon Hull HU1 180 F6
Ruskington NG34 108 D2
Manor Stables Craft Ctr* NG32 106 C1
Manor Way
Kingston upon Hull HU10 178 F6
6 Langtoft PE6 164 F3
Market Deeping PE6 217 E4
Manrico Dr LN1 201 C7
Manse Ave LN5 205 D4
Mansell Cl 1 PE11 214 B3
Mansel St 3 DN32 189 D1
Mansfield Ct
4 Grimsby DN32 189 C1
Peterborough PE1 226 C5
Mansfield Rd DN15 182 B2
Mansgate Hill LN7 33 B3
Mansion Ct Gdns DN8 15 A8
Manson Cl 11 DN34 190 D4
MANTHORPE
Grantham NG31 211 A8
Toft with Lound and Manthorpe PE10 164 A7
Manthorpe Dro PE10 164 F8
Manthorpe Rd NG31 211 B7
Mantle Gn PE22 115 B6
MANTON DN21 30 B5
Manton PE3 225 A3
Manton Ct DN20 30 F6
Manton La DN20 30 E6
Manton Rd
Lincoln LN2 201 F7
Manton DN21 30 B4
MANTON WARREN DN16 30 B8
Mantree Cross DN21 41 A8
Manwaring Way 15 PE20 135 B7
Maple Ave
15 Crowle DN17 16 D7
Grimsby DN34 190 E7
Keelby DN41 23 A4
Kingston upon Hull HU10 178 F8
13 Northorpe PE10 164 C8
2 Scunthorpe DN15 182 C5
10 Wisbech PE13 170 D1
Woodhall Spa LN10 97 C6
Maple Cl
Brigg DN20 196 E3
Gainsborough DN21 197 B7
9 Keelby DN41 23 A4
5 Kingston upon Hull HU5 179 C7
Leasingham NG34 121 C7
Louth LN11 198 D7
42 Messingham DN17 29 D7
Thimbleby LN9 199 A5
4 Waddington LN5 93 E8
Maple Ct
Gainsborough DN21 197 F5
Yaxley PE7 233 F6
Maple Dr
5 Bassingham LN5 92 F3
1 Sudbrooke LN2 68 F2
Maple Gdns PE10 213 D6
Maple Gr
22 Healing DN41 23 F5
12 Heckington NG34 122 D3
Holbeach PE12 215 A2
Immingham DN40 186 C5
New Waltham DN36 195 B5
Peterborough PE1 226 C7
3 Scopwick Heath LN4 108 A7
Spalding PE11 214 F4
Maple Rd PE21 209 C2
Maple St LN5 205 D5
Maples The PE1 226 F5
Maple Tree Cl E DN16 183 A1
Maple Tree Cl W DN16 183 A1
Maple Tree Way DN16 183 A1
Maple Way 12 PE11 134 E2
Maple Wlk PE7 230 C2
Maplewood Ave HU5 179 B7
Maplewood Cl NG31 210 F7
March Rd PE13 177 F1
March St 13 DN21 30 B1
Marconi Dr PE7 233 D6
Marcus St DN34 191 A6
Mardale Gdns PE4 221 D2
Mareham La
Aswarby & Swarby NG34 132 E7
Pointon & Sempringham NG34 142 F7
Sleaford NG34 212 F2
Threekingham NG34 132 F3
MAREHAM LE FEN PE22 99 A3
Mareham le Fen CE (Controlled) Prim Sch PE22 99 A4
MAREHAM ON THE HILL LN9 86 A2
Mareham Rd LN9 199 D2
MARFLEET HU9 5 E8
Marfleet Ave 4 HU9 5 D8
Marfleet Cnr 9 DN36 36 B1
Marfleet La HU9 5 E8
Marfleet Prim Sch HU9 5 E8
Margaret Ave 1 DN17 17 D5
Margaret Dr PE21 209 B6
Margaret Gr 1 HU13 178 F1
Margaret Pl DN36 195 C6
Margaret St
5 Grimsby DN32 191 F7
Immingham DN40 186 C3
Margrave La
Garthorpe & Fockerby DN17 7 E5
Reedness DN14 6 E7
Marham Cl 4 LN6 204 B8
MARHOLM PE6 220 C1
Marholm Rd
4 Peterborough PE3 220 F1
Peterborough PE6 224 B3
Ufford PE9 172 F2
Marian Ave 22 LN12 64 B3
Marian Rd PE21 208 F7
Marian Way
6 Skegness PE25 206 B3
Waltham DN37 194 B4
Mariette Way PE11 214 B6
Marigold Ave PE10 213 D3
Marigold Cl
Lincoln LN2 202 C8
Stamford PE9 218 C6
Marigolds PE6 217 D5
Marigold Wlk
3 Humberston DN35 192 E1
5 Sleaford NG34 212 F3
Marina Rd 15 LN12 64 B3
Marina View 8 DN8 15 A7
Marine Ave
11 Mablethorpe LN12 64 B3
8 Mablethorpe/Sutton on Sea LN12 64 C1
North Ferriby HU14 3 A4
Skegness PE25 206 D1
Marine Ave W 8 LN12 76 F8
Marine Rd PE11 214 E5
Mariners Arms Flats 2 DN17 17 D6
Mariners Cl HU9 181 C6
Marine Wharf 5 HU1 180 F5
Marisco Ct 2 LN12 77 A8
Marjorie Ave LN6 205 D8
Mark Ave
Horncastle LN9 199 A5
Sleaford NG34 212 F4
MARKBY LN13 76 C5
Market Cl 3 PE24 102 E8
Market Ct
8 Crowle DN17 16 D7
Long Sutton PE12 216 C5
MARKET DEEPING PE6 217 E6
Market Deeping Com Prim Sch PE6 217 C6
Market Hall* LN11 198 B5
Market Hill
Scunthorpe DN15 183 B4
Winteringham DN15 2 B1
Market La
Old Leake PE22 127 C8
Terrington St Clement PE34 161 E2
Market Pl
3 Alford LN13 75 F2
1 Binbrook LN8 47 C4
21 Boston PE21 208 F5
2 Brigg DN20 196 B3
Coningsby LN4 207 A4
2 Epworth DN9 27 E6
Gainsborough DN21 197 C4
2 Grantham NG31 211 A4
4 Horncastle LN9 199 B4
6 Kingston upon Hull HU1 181 A6
36 Kirkby in Lindsey DN21 30 B1
Long Sutton PE12 216 C4
9 Louth LN11 198 B5
Market Deeping PE6 217 B4
10 Market Rasen LN8 57 D8
Owston Ferry DN9 28 B3
4 Sleaford NG34 212 D4
6 Spalding PE11 214 D4
Swineshead PE20 135 B7
4 Wragby LN8 70 D5
MARKET RASEN LN8 57 E8
Market Rasen CE Prim Sch LN8 57 D7
Market Rasen Race Course LN8 57 F7
Market Rasen Rd
Dunholme LN2 68 E6
Holton cum Beckering LN8 70 B8
Lissington LN3 57 E1
Snarford LN8 56 E1
Welton/Dunholme LN2 68 E6
Market Rasen Sta LN8 57 D7
Market Rasen Way PE12 215 E3
Market Sq 17 PE21 208 F5
Market St
Bottesford NG13 128 A5
3 Cleethorpes DN35 192 F6
Gainsborough DN21 197 D4
Grimsby DN31 191 D8
Long Sutton PE12 216 C5
3 Sleaford NG34 212 D4
1 Spilsby PE23 88 A1
31 Winterton DN15 9 A5
MARKET STAINTON LN8 72 B6
Market Way PE11 214 C8
Markham Mews DN37 194 F4
Markham Ret Pk PE9 219 E7
Markhams Orch DN33 194 F7

Markham Way [2]
DN20 ....196 F7
Markillie La PE12....... 160 A3
Marklew Ave DN34....191 B7
Mark Rise [1] DN21.......41 C5
MARLBOROUGH LN5 .....93 B4
Marlborough Ave
  [2] Haxey DN9 ....27 D2
  Heighington/Washingborough
    LN4....................203 C1
  Kingston upon Hull
    HU13...................178 D2
  [2] Spalding PE11 ....214 E2
Marlborough Cl
  [21] Grimsby DN32 ....189 C1
  [5] Lincoln LN2..........202 C8
  Yaxley PE7 ....233 E5
Marlborough Dr [1]
  DN16 ....185 B8
Marlborough Rd [11]
  DN8 ....15 B7
Marlborough St [11]
  DN21 ....197 D3
Marlborough Terr [3]
  HU2....................180 E7
Marlborough Way
  DN35 ....192 F1
Marlowe Dr LN2.........202 B6
Marlowe Gr PE4 ....225 E8
Marlowe Rd DN17 ....184 D7
Marlow Rd DN21.........197 E6
Marmaduke St [3] HU3 . 180 C4
Marmion Dr [7] DN15.......9 A5
Marmion Rd
  Coningsby LN4...........207 E5
  [4] Scunthorpe DN16....185 C8
Marne Ave PE4 ....221 A1
Marne Gdns LN1.........201 E6
Marne St HU3 ....180 A8
Marples Mews DN35.....192 F5
Marquess Dr LN36 ......195 D7
Marrat Cl LN2 ....202 E6
Marratts La NG31.......129 D5
Marriot's Gate [8] PE12. 160 A8
Marriott Ct PE1.........226 E5
Marris Dr [11] DN15.......9 B5
Marr La HU15..............1 A7
Marsden Dr DN15.......182 D3
Marsden Rd DN31 ....189 D1
Marshall Ave
  Grimsby DN34...........191 B7
  Kingston upon Hull
    HU10...................178 E8
Marshall Cl
  [3] Fishtoft PE21 ....126 C1
  [3] Laceby DN37 ....23 E1
Marshall's Bank PE13 ...177 D8
Marshall's Way PE7......231 C2
Marshalls Yard DN21 ...197 D4
Marsham Way [2] DN21...53 A8
Marsham PE2............209 A2
Marsh Ave PE21 ....209 A2
MARSHCHAPEL DN36 .....37 B2
Marshchapel Cl [2]
  DN35 ....192 F3
Marshchapel Prim Sch
  DN36 ....37 B2
Marsh Dro PE11 ....46 A5
Marshfield Rd [4]
  DN16 ....185 C5
Marshfields Sch PE1.... 226 D7
Marsh La
  Algarkirk PE20..........146 B8
  Barnetby le Wold DN38....21 B4
  Barrow upon Humber DN19 ..4 C2
  Barton-upon-Humber DN18...3 F1
  Boston PE21 ....209 A1
  Burgh le Marsh PE24....65 B1
  Carlton-le-Moorland LN5..106 A7
  Dunham-on-Trent NG22.....65 B1
  Grainthorpe LN11 ....50 C7
  Kettlethorpe LN1........65 C2
  Middle Rasen LN8 ....57 B8
  Misterton DN10...........40 A5
  New Holland DN19 ....4 D2
  North Leverton with
    Habblesthorpe DN22 .....52 E1
  North Somercotes LN11 ...38 C1
  Orby PE24 ....89 C2
  Saundby DN22............52 B7
  Skidbrooke with Saltfleet
    Haven LN11.............51 C5
  South Cockerington LN11..62 B8
  South Killingholme DN40....13 B4
  Tattershall LN4..........97 D1
  Winteringham DN15 ....2 A1
  Wyberton PE21 ....136 F8
Marshland High Sch
  PE14...................170 E4
Marshlands Dr PE12.....215 F3
Marshland St [10] PE34..161 F3
Marsh Rd
  [3] Crowle DN17.........16 C8
  Gedney PE12............148 C2
  Holbeach PE12 ....215 F8
  Kirton PE20 ....137 A3
  Orby PE24 ....90 B3
  Spalding PE12 ....157 B7
  Sutterton PE20 ....146 A7
  Tydd St Mary PE13 .....160 C1
  Walkeringham DN10 .....40 B3
  Walpole PE14 ....170 F8
  Weston PE12............145 F1
Marsh The PE14 ....170 E8

Marsh Way [3] DN36......37 C5
MARSTON NG32...........118 C2
Marston Hall & Gdns
  DN40....................118 D2
Marston La NG32 ....129 A7
Marston Moor Rd
  NG24 ....104 C4
MARTIN
  Martin LN4..............96 C3
  Roughton LN9 ....85 B1
Martin Cl
  [2] Bottesford DN16 .....185 B2
  Heighington/Washingborough
    LN4....................81 E4
  Louth LN11 ....198 D8
  Skellingthorpe LN6 .....200 A3
Martin Ct PE4 ....221 A4
Martin Dales Dro [1]
  LN10....................97 B4
Martin N Dro LN4........96 D3
Martin Rd LN4...........96 C2
Martinsbridge PE7.......226 F7
Martin's Cl [5] DN19.....11 D8
Martin S Dro LN4........96 D3
Martins Rd
  Crowland PE6............167 E4
  Ulceby DN39 ....12 B1
Martin St LN5...........201 F1
Martins Way PE2 ....229 F5
Martins Wlk [1] LN12....77 A8
Martn Way
  Ingoldmells PE25........206 C8
  New Waltham DN36.......195 B6
MARTON DN21...........65 D8
Marton Gr
  [5] Grimsby DN33 ....191 A3
  [35] Hatfield DN7.........14 D4
Marton Prim Sch DN21...65 E8
Marton Rd
  Sturton by Stow LN1......66 B7
  Willingham DN21.........53 E2
Martyn Rd DN35 ....192 D7
Marvel St HU9...........181 B7
Marvis Cres PE7 ....230 C3
Mary Armyne Rd PE2 ....230 B5
Mary La LE14 ....138 B1
Marylebone Wlk [2]
  DN33 ....191 B2
Mary St DN15...........182 F3
Mary Sumner Way [3]
  DN15...................182 E4
Mary Walsham Cl PE2...231 E5
Masefield Dr [10] LN12....77 A7
Maskew Ave PE1.........225 E6
Mason Dr DN17.........184 E3
Masonic La [5] PE23......87 F1
Masons Ct PE24 ....10 E8
Mason St HU2...........180 F7
Massey Cl
  [1] Epworth DN9 ....27 D6
  Kingston upon Hull HU3 ..180 A5
Massey Rd LN2 ....234 C4
Massey St HU3 ....180 A4
Mast Dr HU9............181 C6
Master Dike PE12.......159 D1
Masterton Cl [8] PE9 ....219 D7
Masterton Rd PE9 ......219 C7
Mathews St DN35.......192 C7
Matilda Rd LN6.........201 D1
Matley PE2..............229 E5
Matley Prim Sch PE2 ....229 E5
Matlock Ct DN15........182 B2
Matlock Dr
  Grimsby DN37..........190 F8
  Lincoln LN6............204 E2
Matmore Cl PE11 ....214 F3
Matmore Gate PE11.....214 F3
Mat Pitts La PE24.......102 C1
Matthew Flinders Way
  PE21...................228 D3
Matthew Humberstone CE
  Sch DN35 ....192 C4
Mattimore Dr [6] PE12 ..215 E2
Maud Foster Mill
  PE21...................209 A6
Maud St [2] PE21.......209 A5
MAVIS ENDERBY PE23....87 C1
Mavis Enderby Cross Roads
  PE23....................87 E2
Mavis Rd [2] DN17......184 E6
Mawford Cl PE12 ....146 E2
Mawson Gdns PE4......102 E2
MAWTHORPE LN13........88 F8
Mawthorpe Hill Rd
  LN13.....................88 F8
MAXEY PE6..............173 C7
Maxey Cl [1] PE6 ....217 A5
Maxey Ct [1] LN11......198 B6
Maxey Rd
  Maxey PE6..............173 C6
  Northborough PE6.......217 C1
Maxey View PE6 ....217 C3
Maxham's Gn Rd PE6...173 D3
Maxwell Ave LN6 ....205 C8
Maxwell Ct DN34 ....190 D5
Maxwell Dr [1] LN12......64 B3
Maxwell Rd PE2 ....230 D6
Mayall Ct [2] LN5........93 F7
May Blossom Wlk
  PE11...................214 B3
May Cres LN1 ....201 D4
Mayfair Ave LN6 ....205 C7
Mayfair Cres [12] DN37..194 C4
Mayfair Ct DN35........193 A1
Mayfair Dr [4] LN11.....214 B1
Mayfair Dr W DN37......190 C8
Mayfair Gdns PE21......209 B7

Mayfield Ave
  Gainsborough DN21 .....197 B7
  [3] South Killingholme
    DN40....................12 F2
  [3] Stainforth DN7.......14 D6
Mayfield Cl
  [1] Grimsby DN33 ....194 D8
  [15] Pinchbeck PE11 .....156 E8
Mayfield Cres
  Louth LN11 ....198 D4
  [3] Middle Rasen LN8 ...57 C8
Mayfield Gr [1] PE25 ....90 D3
Mayfield Gr [5] PE25 ....206 B3
Mayfield Rd HU1........226 A6
Mayfield St HU3 ....180 C8
Mayflower Cl DN40 .....186 C3
Mayflower Cl
  [2] Gainsborough DN21...52 F6
  [6] South Killingholme
    DN40....................12 E3
Mayflower Dr NG34.....122 D2
Mayflower Pl PE2........209 C3
Mayflower Way [2] LN12...64 B3
May Gr HU13 ....178 D2
Mayland Ave HU5.......179 A8
Mayner's Dike PE12.....169 F8
Mayor's Wlk PE3 ....225 E3
Maypole House Sch
  LN13....................88 E8
Maypole St DN21........42 D2
Maysfield Ct [10] DN20...31 A5
Maysfield Dr [3] PE13 ...170 B2
Mays La LN1............66 E2
May's La PE13 ....170 D2
May St DN35 ....192 D8
Maythorpe Cl HU3 ......180 A7
Maytime Ct [7] PE11.....214 A5
Maytime Ct PE12 ....216 D5
Mead Cl
  [8] Lincoln LN6..........205 A5
  Peterborough PE3.......220 F1
Meadenvale PE1.........226 F5
Mead Garth DN15.......182 B6
Meadow Ave DN39.......12 A2
Meadowbank [5] DN9 ...16 E1
Meadow Bank PE22.....126 F6
Meadow Bank Ave [1]
  LN3.....................82 B6
Meadowbank Rd HU3....179 E7
Meadowdraw
  [9] Ancaster NG32......120 A3
  [4] Ruskington NG34 ...108 D2
Meadow Cl
  [1] Bourne PE10 ....213 D5
  [7] Cherry Willingham/
    Reepham LN3...........82 A8
  [4] Colsterworth NG33 ..151 E6
  [5] Goxhill DN19 ....5 A1
  Lincoln LN6.............93 C8
  [3] Louth LN11..........198 C4
  [2] Manby LN11..........62 C6
  [6] Metheringham LN4...95 D4
  [2] Pinchbeck PE11 .....145 C1
  [4] Scothern LN2 ....68 F4
  Spalding PE11 ....214 E6
Meadowcroft [7] LN11....59 E1
Meadow Croft
  [1] Kirk Sandall DN3 .....14 A1
  Waltham DN37..........194 E5
Meadow Ct
  Grimsby DN34..........190 E7
  [2] Hibaldstow DN20.....30 F5
Meadowdale Cres [3]
  NG31 ....211 A8
Meadow Dr
  Barton-upon-Humber
    DN18...................10 F8
  [4] Binbrook LN8 ....47 C5
  [2] Grimsby DN33 ....194 D8
  [1] Healing DN41........24 A5
  [3] Misterton DN10.......39 F5
Meadow Dro PE10 ......213 F7
Meadow End NG31......211 D2
Meadowfield
  [4] Middle Rasen LN8 ...57 C8
  Sleaford NG34..........212 C5
Meadow Field Rd [6]
  DN3......................14 A3
Meadowgate PE9 ....172 F5
Meadow Gate PE10 ....213 D6
Meadowgate La [3]
  PE11...................214 A3
Meadow La
  Auburn Haddington & South
    Hykeham LN6 ....93 B7
  Benniworth LN8..........59 B1
  Girton NG23.............78 C2
  Leasingham NG34 ......121 B7
  Lincoln LN6.............93 C8
  Normanton on Trent NG23..78 B3
  North Cockerington LN11 ..50 A1
  North Kelsey LN7.........31 C7
  North Scarle LN6.........78 F1
  Pointon & Sempringham
    NG34..................143 C6
  [9] Ryhall PE9 ....163 C1
Meadowlake Cl LN6......200 D1
Meadow Rd
  Dunston LN4............95 C5
  Langtoft PE6............217 A8
  Newark-on-Trent NG24...104 B2
  Newborough PE6........221 B8
  Scunthorpe DN17 ....184 C6
Meadow Rise
  [8] Barnby Dun DN3 .....14 A4
  Blyton DN21.............41 C6
  [1] Gainsborough DN21...53 A5
  [7] Saxilby LN1..........66 D2

Meadows Cl [7] NG23 ...117 D3
Meadows La
  Lincoln LN4.............202 E2
  Reepham LN3...........69 A1
Meadows Rise [1] LE14..150 B1
Meadows The
  [2] Beckingham DN10 ...52 B8
  Burringham DN17 ....17 C4
  [6] Long Bennington
    NG23...................117 D3
  Mablethorpe/Sutton on Sea
    LN12...................64 C2
  [6] Market Deeping PE6 .217 C5
  [2] Messingham DN17 ...29 D8
  [7] Pinchbeck PE11 .....145 C1
  Skegness PE25 ....206 A4
  Westwoodside DN9 ......27 A2
Meadowsweet [2] PE13 ..218 C7
Meadow Vale LN7 ....33 B4
Meadow Vale LN20......30 F8
Meadow View
  Humberston DN35.......192 F1
  [4] Morton PE10 ....154 D6
  Swinderby LN6...........92 A5
Meadow View Bsns Units
  PE9.....................219 F6
Meadow Way
  Billinghay LN4...........109 E6
  Bracebridge Heath LN4...81 A1
  [1] Grimsby DN33 ....114 A1
  Spalding PE11 ....214 A2
  [6] Welton/Dunholme
    LN2.....................68 D6
Meadow Wlk
  [10] Kirk Sandall DN3 ....14 A2
  [6] Swanland HU14......3 B7
Mead The
  [11] Laceby DN37 ....23 F1
  [4] Lincoln LN6..........205 A5
  Peterborough PE4.......221 A1
Meadway
  Cherry Willingham/Reepham
    LN3....................203 F8
  [11] Market Deeping PE6 .217 A6
  [2] Spalding PE11 ....214 A4
Mead Wlk HU4 ....179 C6
Meakers Way LN13.......76 F3
Meals Gate PE14 ....221 D2
Measham Dr [4] DN7.....14 D7
Measures Cl [10] PE10...154 D6
Mechanic La [4] DN3 ...180 D5
Medbourne Gdns [1]
  PE1.....................226 D8
Meden Ave [2] HU15......2 D5
Medeswell PE2 ....230 C3
Medforth La PE21........208 E8
Medina Gdns [1]
  Gainsthorpe* DN21......30 D4
Medina Gdns LN12......64 B2
Medium Section Rd
  DN16 ....19 A4
MEDLAM PE22...........112 D7
Medlam Cl PE22 ....112 C7
Medlam La PE22........112 D7
Medlam Rd PE21 ....208 C3
Medlar Dr [4] HU15......3 B7
Medlock Cres [5] PE11 ..214 F5
Medway [1] HU6.........66 D7
Medway Cl [3] PE11 ....145 C6
Medway Cres LN6.......205 B2
Medway Pl [5] DN34.....191 A5
Medworth PE2...........229 F3
Meeres' La PE20 ....136 A5
Meering Cl [8] NG23....91 D5
Meering La NG23 ....78 C4
Meers Bank LN12........64 A6
Meeting House La LN5...105 F5
Meggan Gate PE3........225 A1
Meggitt La DN15.........2 A6
Megs La [10] LN5 ....107 A8
Melbourne Ave [4]
  DN33 ....191 D3
Melbourne Dr [4] PE25...206 A4
Melbourne Rd
  Birchwood LN6 ....204 C8
  Grantham NG31.........211 D7
  [4] Stamford PE9 ....219 D6
Melbourne Way [9] LN5 ..93 E8
Melbury Wlk DN17......184 C8
Melbury Way PE3........197 E1
Melford Cl PE3 ....222 A8
Melford Ct DN16........185 E5
Melholme La LN11.......50 A2
Mellows Cl
  Cherry Willingham/Reepham
    LN3....................203 F8
  Peterborough PE1 ......226 B5
Melwood View DN9......28 A3
Melrose Cl
  [3] Stamford PE9 ....218 E6
  [6] Woodhall Spa LN10 ..97 C6
Melrose Dr PE2 ....231 A7
Melrose Rd DN21 ....197 C6
Melrose St HU3.........180 C8
Melrose Way DN37 .....188 A1
MELTON HU14 ....2 F5
Melton Bottom HU14......2 F6
Melton Fields HU14......2 E5
Melton Old Rd HU14.....2 E5
Melton Rd
  North Ferriby HU14......3 A5
  Wrawby DN20............20 F4
  Wymondham LE14......150 B2
MELTON ROSS DN38......21 D5
Melville St LN5..........234 A1
Melwood Hill DN9 ......27 F6
Melwood View [18] DN9...27 E6

Memorial Hall Dr [9]
  LN8.....................107 A7
Menasha Way DN16......185 E7
Mendip Ave
  Grimsby DN33 ....191 C1
  Scunthorpe LN6..........93 C8
Mendip Cl
  [6] Gonerby Hill Foot
    NG31...................210 E8
  [2] Lincoln LN5..........205 D3
  Spalding PE11 ....214 B6
Mendip Gr PE4 ....221 C2
Mendip Rd DN11........132 A6
Menson Dr DN7..........14 D4
Mentmore Gdns PE21...208 B4
Mercer Dr LN1 ....201 D6
Mercer Rd DN21.........197 B6
Mercer Row LN11.......198 B5
Mercia Ave [14] NG34...212 B2
Mercia Dr [3] NG32.....120 A2
Mercia Gdns [2] PE10 ...63 A6
Mercia Gr [4] PE6 ....164 E5
Mercian Ct PE2..........231 D7
Merebalk La LN9........86 B2
Mere Balk La LN9........85 A7
Mere Booth Rd PE22....125 A7
Mere La DN6.............185 D7
Meredith Ave DN17 .....184 D6
Mere Dro
  Old Leake PE22.........113 F4
  Yaxley PE7 ....233 F4
Meredyke Rd DN17 ....7 D3
Mere La
  Edenthorpe DN3 ....14 A3
  Heydour NG32..........131 D6
  Winterton DN15..........9 A7
Merelade Gr [4] PE4....220 E5
Mere Rd
  Branston & Mere LN4....81 E1
  Waddington LN5.........93 F7
Meres Leisure Ctr &
  Swimming Pool
  NG31 ....210 D3
Meres Rd NG31.........210 C3
Mereway The NG33 .....141 A5
Meridian Cl [1] PE21 ...209 D4
MERIDIAN POINT
  DN35 ....193 B3
Meridian Point Ret Pk
  DN35 ....193 B3
Meridian Rd PE21.......209 C4
Meridian View LN11.....198 B4
Meridian Wlk [2] PE12...215 B2
Meriton PE2.............229 F3
Merlewem LN2...........68 C2
Merlin Dr [7] PE10......213 E3
Merlin Dr [2] DN20.......21 A8
Merlin Rd
  [14] Binbrook Tech Pk
    LN8......................47 B6
  Scunthorpe DN17 ....184 E6
Merrick Cl [13] NG31....129 E5
Merrick St HU9..........181 B2
Merriemeade Dr
  PE25...................206 D7
Merrifield Rd [7] PE24...102 E2
Merryweather Ct [7]
  DN16 ....185 B2
Mersey Way DN37 ......190 D8
Merton Rd DN16.........185 A3
MESSINGHAM DN17......29 D7
Messingham La DN20...30 D8
Messingham Nature
  *Reserve** DN17 ....29 F6
Messingham Prim Sch
  DN17 ....29 D7
Messingham Rd
  East Butterwick DN17....28 D8
  Scotter DN21.............29 C4
  Scunthorpe DN17 ....184 F4
Met La LN11.............62 C6
METHERINGHAM LN4.....95 D4
Metheringham Airfield
  *Visitor Ctr** LN4 ....96 A2
Metheringham Cl [1]
  LN6.....................95 C8
Metheringham Delph
  *Nature Reserve** LN4 ...96 D2
Metheringham Fen La
  LN4.....................95 E5
Metheringham Heath La
  LN4.....................94 E1
Metheringham Prim Sch
  LN4.....................95 C4
Metheringham Sta LN4...95 D4
Metro Ctr The PE2 ......230 D6
Mews The HU3 ....180 B8
Mew Gull Dr [2] LN12....77 A7
Meynell Ave [3] LN6.....205 C8
Meynell Dr DN21..........40 D8
Meynell Wlk PE3 ....225 B1
Michael Foale La LN11...198 C2
Michaelgate LN2 ....234 B3
Mickle Gate PE3 ....225 A1
Middle Barn Hill DN20...10 D8
Middlebridge Rd DN10...39 B3
Middle Broad Dro
  PE13...................169 D5
Middlebrook Cl LN6.....205 A5
Middlebrook La [1]
  DN6......................15 A2
Middlebrook Rd [4]
  LN6.....................205 A5
Middle Dro
  Gedney PE12............148 C2

Middle Dro continued
Holland Fen with Brothertoft
 PE21 . . . . 208 A7
Kirton PE20 . . . . 124 D2
Newton PE13 . . . . .169 E4
Middle Fen Dro PE20 . . 134 D4
Middle Fen La LN4 . . . . .82 C5
Middlefield PE7 . . . . . 230 D3
Middlefield La
 Gainsborough DN21 . . . . .197 E2
 1 Glentham LN8 . . . . .43 F1
Middlefield Sch of Tech
 The DN21 . . . . .197 E3
Middlegate LN5 . . . . . .92 F2
Middlegate Cl 12 DN19 . .11 C8
Middlegate La
 Bonby DN20 . . . . .10 C3
 Elsham DN20 . . . . .21 A7
 Orby PE24 . . . . .89 D2
 South Ferriby DN18 . . . . .10 B7
Middlegate Rd DN20 . . 136 C6
Middlegate Rd E PE20 . 136 D5
Middlegate Rd (West) 1
 PE20 . . . . 136 D6
Middleham Cl
 3 Kingston upon Hull
 HU9 . . . . .181 E8
 2 Peterborough PE7 . . .231 F5
Middle Holme La 3
 NG23 . . . . .91 A8
Middle La
 Amcotts DN17 . . . . .7 E1
 Sturton le Steeple DN22 . . .52 E3
 Thorpe on the Hill LN6 . . . .92 F8
Middlemarsh Rd PE24 . . 103 A7
Middle Marsh Rd PE12 . . 146 F7
Middlemere Bank
 PE22 . . . . .126 E7
Middlemore Yd 1
 NG31 . . . . .211 B4
Middle Pasture 3 PE4 . . 220 F5
Middleplatt Rd DN40 . . 186 E5
MIDDLE RASEN LN8 . . . . .57 B8
Middle Rasen Prim Sch
 LN8 . . . . .57 B8
Middle Rd
 Crowland PE6 . . . . .166 E1
 Newborough PE6 . . . . . .221 E7
 Terrington St Clement
 PE34 . . . . .161 D4
 Tydd St Mary PE13 . . . . . .160 B1
 2 Whaplode PE12 . . . . .158 B7
Middle St
 Aisthorpe LN1 . . . . .67 D7
 Cammeringham LN1 . . . . . .55 A1
 Corringham DN21 . . . . . . .41 E2
 Croxton Kerrial NG32 . . . . 138 D4
 Dunston LN4 . . . . .95 C5
 Farcet PE7 . . . . .231 C2
 Fillingham DN21 . . . . . . .55 A5
 Gunby & Stainby NG33 . . . 151 B5
 5 Lincoln LN6 . . . . . . .93 C8
 7 Metheringham LN4 . . . .95 D4
 14 North Kelsey LN7 . . . .32 A4
 5 Potterhanworth LN4 . . .82 B1
 Rippingale PE10 . . . . . . .142 F2
 Scampton LN1 . . . . .67 C6
 Scotton DN21 . . . . .29 C6
 5 Skillington NG33 . . . .151 A8
 South Carlton LN1 . . . . . .67 D3
 Willoughton DN21 . . . . . . .42 E3
Middlesykes La LN11 . . .62 C7
Middlethorpe Prim Sch
 DN35 . . . . 192 D3
Middle Thorpe Rd
 DN35 . . . . 192 D3
Middleton Cl 3 . . . . . 225 A4
Middleton Ct 9 DN21 . . .29 D7
Middleton Ct HU5 . . . . 180 B8
Middleton Prim Sch
 PE3 . . . . 225 A4
Middleton Rd
 Newark NG24 . . . . 104 B6
 Scunthorpe DN16 . . . . . . 185 B4
Middleton's Field LN2 . . 234 B4
Middleton's Rd PE7 . . . 233 E5
Middleton St HU3 . . . . 180 C8
Middleton Way NG34 . . . 121 C7
Midfield Pl 18 DN36 . . . .36 D8
Midfield Rd DN36 . . . . . .36 D8
Midfield Way 14 DN41 . . .23 A4
Midgate PE1 . . . . 226 A2
Mid Gate PE22 . . . . . . 113 E3
Midgate (East) PE22 . . . 113 E1
Midgate La PE22 . . . . . 113 E1
Midgley Cl HU3 . . . . . . 180 C5
Midholm LN3 . . . . 203 E5
Midia Cl LN1 . . . . 201 C7
Midland Ind Est DN16 . . 185 D8
Midland Rd
 Peterborough PE3 . . . . . .225 E3
 Scunthorpe DN16 . . . . . .183 D1
Midsummer Gdns
 PE12 . . . . .216 A4
Midthorpe La 3 LN9 . . . .85 E7
MIDVILLE PE22 . . . . . . 113 E8
Midville Cl 10 LN1 . . . . 201 E8
Midville La PE22 . . . . . 100 B1
Midville Rd
 Midville PE22 . . . . .113 B7
 Toynton All Saints PE23 . . .100 F4
Midway Cl 3 LN1 . . . . . .68 D2
Midway Gr HU4 . . . . . . 179 E4
Milcroft Cres DN7 . . . . . .14 D4
Mildenhall Dr LN6 . . . . 204 B8
Mildmay Rd PE4 . . . . . 225 D8
Mildmay St LN1 . . . . . . 234 A4
Mile Dro PE6 . . . . .173 F5

Mile End Ave 19 DN7 . . . .14 D3
Mile La LN12 . . . . .64 A2
Miles Bank PE11 . . . . . 214 C7
Miles Cross Hill LN13 . . . .75 D1
Miles Hawk Cl 28 LN12 . . .77 A7
Milestone La PE11 . . . . 145 C1
Milford La 11 PE12 . . . .167 B8
Milford Ct 3 DN32 . . . . 189 C1
Milford Ctr Bsns Pk
 LN11 . . . . .198 A8
Milkinghill La PE20 . . . . 135 A5
Milking Nook Dro
 PE10 . . . . .154 F3
Milking Nook Rd PE6 . . . 221 C8
Millard Ave DN7 . . . . . . .14 D4
Millard Nook 50 DN7 . . . .14 D4
Mill Bank PE12 . . . . . . 159 A5
Mill Baulk Rd 3 DN10 . . . .39 F3
Millbeck Bank HU15 . . . . .1 E8
Millbeck Dr LN2 . . . . . . 202 B8
Millbrook Cl 3 LN6 . . . . .93 B8
Millbrook La LN8 . . . . . .70 C4
Millbrook Sch DN16 . . . . 185 B6
Millbrook Way 50 DN18 . . .10 F8
Mill Cl
 7 Alford LN13 . . . . . . .75 F3
 Billinghay LN4 . . . . .109 E5
 6 Brigg DN20 . . . . . . 196 A3
 4 Croft PE24 . . . . . . .102 E2
 6 Marshchapel DN36 . . . .37 C2
 Murrow PE13 . . . . .177 D5
 2 North Leverton with
 Habblesthorpe DN22 . . . . .52 B1
 Waltham DN37 . . . . .194 E3
 28 Wisbech PE13 . . . . . 170 D1
Mill Cres
 Peterborough PE2 . . . . . .229 E4
 20 Scotter DN21 . . . . . .29 C3
Mill Croft
 3 Scawby DN20 . . . . . .30 F8
 2 Scunthorpe DN16 . . . .185 D7
Mill Ct
 Lincoln LN1 . . . . .234 A4
 1 Waddingham DN21 . . . .43 D7
Mill Dr NG31 . . . . 211 C2
Mill Dro
 Bourne PE10 . . . . .213 E7
 Cowbit PE12 . . . . .157 B2
 Crowland PE6 . . . . .175 A8
 Deeping St Nicholas
 PE11 . . . . .155 D1
Millennium Fst Coll
 PE25 . . . . .206 B3
Miller Ave DN32 . . . . . . 192 C6
Miller Cl 12 DN36 . . . . . .15 B7
Miller La DN8 . . . . .15 B7
Miller Rd DN21 . . . . .41 A1
Millers Brook DN9 . . . . . .16 E1
Millers Cl
 Heighington/
 Washingborough LN4 . . . . .81 E4
 4 Sleaford NG34 . . . . .212 C7
Miller's Cl PE10 . . . . . . 143 A3
Millers Ct LN11 . . . . . . 198 C6
Millers Dale 2 LN6 . . . . 204 F2
Millers' Gate PE22 . . . . 113 A2
Millers Quay 6 DN20 . . . 196 A3
Millers Rd LN5 . . . . .93 F6
Millers Rest PE12 . . . . 158 C7
Millers Way
 6 Alford LN13 . . . . . . .75 F3
 6 Heckington NG34 . . . .122 E2
Mill Farm Est LN4 . . . . 207 B5
MILLFIELD PE1 . . . . . . 225 F5
Mill Field 1 LN12 . . . . . .64 C2
Millfield Ave
 Grimsby DN33 . . . . .191 D3
 8 Saxilby LN1 . . . . . . .66 D2
Mill Field Cl 6 PE6 . . . . 173 C4
Millfield Cres NG34 . . . . 119 B6
Mill Field Ct 11 DN3 . . . .14 A3
Millfield Gdns 6 PE6 . . .166 F1
Millfield La E PE20 . . . . 136 D7
Millfield La W PE20 . . . 136 D7
Millfield Prim Sch LN4 . . .81 F4
Millfield Rd
 Bratoft PE24 . . . . .102 C7
 3 Market Deeping PE6 . . .217 A6
 21 Metheringham LN4 . . . .95 C4
 7 Morton PE10 . . . . . . .154 C7
 South Somercotes LN11 . . . .50 F5
 Thorne/Moorends DN8 . . . . .15 A8
Mill Field Rd
 8 Donington PE11 . . . . .134 E2
 Fishlake DN7 . . . . .14 C8
 Scunthorpe DN16 . . . . . . .183 E3
Millfields
 22 Barton-upon-Humber
 DN18 . . . . .10 E8
 18 Caistor LN7 . . . . . . .33 B4
Millfields Way 9 DN19 . . .11 C8
Millfield Terr NG34 . . . . 212 D5
Millfield The 1 DN20 . . . .31 A5
Mill Garth DN35 . . . . . . 192 D3
Millgate 10 LN5 . . . . . . 107 A7
Mill Gate PE12 . . . . . . 158 B1
Mill Gn Rd PE11 . . . . . 214 A7
Millgood Cl LN11 . . . . . 198 D5
MILL HILL PE24 . . . . . . 103 B8
Mill Hill
 Ellerker HU15 . . . . .2 A8
 Friskney PE22 . . . . .114 F6
 Gringley on the Hill DN10 . . .39 B1
 Nettleham LN2 . . . . .68 C2
Mill Hill Cres DN35 . . . . 192 E5
Mill Hill Dr DN16 . . . . . 185 C3
Millhill La 12 PE20 . . . . 135 B7
Mill Hill Rd DN7 . . . . . . .14 E3

Mill Hill Way LN11 . . . . .62 A8
Mill House La 1 DN15 . . . .9 B5
Millhouse St Rise 5
 DN40 . . . . .186 A4
Mill House Windmill*
 DN17 . . . . .7 C4
Mill La
 Addlethorpe PE25 . . . . . . .90 D1
 Ashby with Scremby PE23 . . .88 D3
 Aubourn Haddington & South
 Hykeham LN5 . . . . .92 F5
 8 Barrow upon Humber
 DN19 . . . . .11 C8
 Beesby with Saleby LN13 . . .75 F5
 Bicker PE20 . . . . .135 B4
 Billinghay LN4 . . . . .109 E5
 Boston PE21 . . . . .208 E4
 Brant Broughton &
 Stragglethorpe LN5 . . . . .105 E5
 Bratoft PE24 . . . . .102 C7
 Brigg DN20 . . . . .196 B2
 Brough HU15 . . . . .2 C1
 6 Broughton DN20 . . . . .19 E3
 Burgh on Bain LN8 . . . . . .59 C5
 Butterwick PE22 . . . . . . .126 E4
 Caistor LN7 . . . . .33 C4
 Castor PE5 . . . . .223 F1
 7 Croxton Kerrial
 NG32 . . . . .138 D4
 Donington PE11 . . . . .134 E2
 Eagle & Swinethorpe LN6 . . .79 C2
 East Halton DN40 . . . . . . .12 D6
 Firsby PE24 . . . . .102 A7
 Fleet PE12 . . . . .168 C2
 Fosdyke PE20 . . . . .136 D1
 Friskney PE22 . . . . .115 C7
 Gainsborough DN21 . . . . . .197 B8
 Gorefield PE13 . . . . .169 E1
 Gosberton PE11 . . . . .145 C6
 4 Goxhill DN19 . . . . . . .5 A1
 Grainthorpe LN11 . . . . . . .50 B8
 Great Ponton NG33 . . . . . .140 A5
 Hackthorn LN2 . . . . .56 B1
 Haxey DN9 . . . . .27 B2
 Heighington/Washingborough
 LN4 . . . . .81 E4
 Hemingby LN9 . . . . .72 B1
 Heydour NG32 . . . . .131 B5
 Hogsthorpe PE24 . . . . . . .90 B7
 Holbeach PE12 . . . . .215 B5
 Holton le Clay DN36 . . . . .195 C4
 Horbling NG34 . . . . .133 B3
 Horncastle LN9 . . . . .58 A1
 Huttoft LN13 . . . . .76 E4
 Immingham DN40 . . . . .186 A4
 6 Keelby DN41 . . . . . . .23 A4
 5 Ketton PE9 . . . . . . .171 A3
 Kingston upon Hull
 HU10 . . . . .178 C6
 Kirton in Lindsey DN21 . . . .30 C1
 Kirton PE20 . . . . .136 A7
 Legbourne LN11 . . . . .61 F3
 Lincoln LN1 . . . . .201 E1
 Little Steeping PE23 . . . . .101 A6
 Louth LN11 . . . . .198 B7
 Maltby le Marsh LN13 . . . . .75 F8
 Manby LN11 . . . . .62 C2
 4 Marschapel DN36 . . . . .37 C2
 Marston NG32 . . . . .118 D2
 Martin LN4 . . . . .96 C3
 Middle Rasen LN8 . . . . . . .57 B8
 Minting LN9 . . . . .71 B2
 Mumby LN13 . . . . .76 E5
 Newton PE13 . . . . .169 F5
 North Clifton NG23 . . . . . .78 C7
 3 North Kelsey LN7 . . . .32 A4
 Osgodby LN8 . . . . .45 A3
 Owmby LN8 . . . . .56 A8
 Peterborough PE5 . . . . . .228 F7
 Pickworth NG34 . . . . .132 A1
 Saltfleetby LN11 . . . . . . .51 C1
 Saxilby LN1 . . . . .66 E2
 Scamblesby LN11 . . . . . . .72 F5
 Scawby DN20 . . . . .30 F8
 Skegness PE25 . . . . .206 A8
 Skidbrooke with Saltfleet
 Haven LN11 . . . . .51 C4
 10 South Ferriby DN18 . . .10 A7
 South Somercotes LN11 . . . .50 F5
 South Witham NG33 . . . . . .151 C1
 Sturton by Stow LN1 . . . . . .66 C2
 Sutterton PE20 . . . . .136 C2
 14 Sutton Bridge PE12 . .160 E4
 Swineshead PE20 . . . . . . .135 A8
 Tallington PE9 . . . . .172 F7
 Tetford LN9 . . . . .73 E1
 Thorney PE8 . . . . .228 B7
 Tydd St Mary PE13 . . . . . . .160 B4
 Wainfleet All Saints
 PE24 . . . . .102 C1
 Walkeringham DN10 . . . . . .39 F3
 Welbourn LN5 . . . . .106 F4
 Welton le Marsh PE23 . . . . .89 B4
 Welton LN7 . . . . .68 E8
 West Keal PE23 . . . . .100 B6
 West Walton PE14 . . . . . . .170 F4
 Whaplode PE12 . . . . .168 B7
 Wigsley NG23 . . . . .78 F4
 Wildmore LN4 . . . . .111 A7
 Willoughby with Sloothby
 LN13 . . . . .89 C6
 Woodhall Spa LN10 . . . . . .97 E7
 Wrangle PE22 . . . . .114 D1
 Wrawby DN20 . . . . .196 F7
Mill La Cl PE24 . . . . . . .90 D7
Mill La W NG23 . . . . . . .2 B6
Mill Marsh Rd PE12 . . . . 146 D2

Mill Mere Rd
 Corringham DN21 . . . . . . .41 D2
 5 Waddington LN5 . . . . .93 F7
Mill Moor Way 3 LN6 . . . 204 D1
Millom Way DN32 . . . . . . 191 F8
Mill Pl DN35 . . . . 192 F6
Millport Dr HU4 . . . . . . 179 B2
Mill Race DN36 . . . . .36 E4
Mill Rd
 Addlethorpe PE24 . . . . . . .90 D2
 Boston PE21 . . . . .209 B3
 Claypole NG33 . . . . .117 E2
 Cleethorpes DN35 . . . . . . .192 E5
 Crowle DN17 . . . . .16 C8
 Donington on Bain LN11 . . . .59 E2
 Hibaldstow DN20 . . . . .30 E2
 2 Keadby DN17 . . . . . .17 D5
 Lincoln LN1 . . . . .234 A4
 Luddington & Haldenby
 DN17 . . . . .7 C4
 Market Rasen LN8 . . . . . . .57 D7
 Maxey PE6 . . . . .173 C7
 Pilsgate PE9 . . . . .172 C7
 Swanland HU14 . . . . .3 A6
 Walpole PE14 . . . . .170 F6
 Wisbech St Mary PE13 . . . .177 D5
Mill Rise
 6 Navenby/Wellingore
 LN5 . . . . .107 A7
 14 Scothern LN2 . . . . . .68 F4
 Swanland HU14 . . . . .3 A6
Mill Row
 Barrowby NG32 . . . . .129 B3
 2 Lincoln LN1 . . . . . .234 A4
Mills Cl 15 NG23 . . . . . 117 D3
Mills Dr DN7 . . . . .26 A8
Mills Service Rd DN16 . . .19 A4
Mill St
 Kingston upon Hull
 HU1 . . . . .180 E6
 Ryhall PE9 . . . . .163 C2
 Scamblesby LN11 . . . . .73 A4
 Sibsey PE22 . . . . .113 A7
Millstone Cl LN1 . . . . . 199 A3
Millstone La 3 PE9 . . . . 172 D3
Millstream Rd LN4 . . . . . .81 E4
MILLTHORPE NG34 . . . . . 143 B6
Millthorpe Dro NG34 . . . 143 E5
Millthorpe Rd NG34 . . . . 143 B5
Mill View
 Peterborough PE7 . . . . . .229 A5
 5 Waltham DN37 . . . . .194 E4
Mill View Cl 3 DN7 . . . . .27 D7
Millview Ct LN9 . . . . . . 199 B4
Mill View Ct 12 LN8 . . . . .70 D4
Millview Gdns 3 DN20 . . . 20 D3
Millview Rd
 11 Heckington NG34 . . . .122 E2
 Ruskington NG34 . . . . .108 D2
Milman Rd LN2 . . . . 202 B4
Milne Gn 4 PE20 . . . . . . 135 B7
Milners Ct 22 PE9 . . . . . 219 C5
Milner's La 3 PE23 . . . . .87 F1
Milnyard Sq PE2 . . . . . . 229 C2
Milson Cl
 8 Barton-upon-Humber
 DN18 . . . . .10 E8
 7 Broughton DN20 . . . . .19 D4
Milson Rd 17 DN41 . . . . . .23 A4
Milton Cl
 Branston LN4 . . . . .81 D2
 Cherry Willingham LN3 . . . .203 E5
 2 Gainsborough DN21 . . .197 E6
Milton St
 Lincoln LN5 . . . . .205 E7
 Newark-on-Trent NG24 . . . .104 A3
Milton Way
 Kirkby la Thorpe NG34 . . . .121 E4
 Peterborough PE2 . . . . . .224 E3
 2 Sleaford NG34 . . . . .212 F3
Mimosa Ct DN16 . . . . . . 185 E4
Mina Cl PE2 . . . . 231 D4
Minden Pl 4 DN21 . . . . . .55 A8
MININGSBY PE22 . . . . . . .99 D7
Minnett's Hill NG32 . . . . 130 D7
Minnow Cl 1 DN21 . . . . . 190 D7
Minshull Rd DN35 . . . . . 192 F4
Minster Dr
 Cherry Willingham/Reepham
 LN3 . . . . .203 D2
 2 Lincoln LN1 . . . . . .198 D4
Minster Precincts 9
 PE1 . . . . .226 A2
Minster Rd
 16 Misterton DN10 . . . . .39 F5
 Scunthorpe DN15 . . . . . . .182 B2
Minster Yd LN2 . . . . . . 234 B3
MINTING LN9 . . . . .84 D8
Minting Cl 9 LN1 . . . . . 201 E8
Minting La LN9 . . . . .71 D1
Mint La LN1 . . . . 234 A2
Mint St LN1 . . . . 234 A2
Misfield Rd
 Grimsby DN32 . . . . .191 F4
 Scunthorpe DN15 . . . . . . .182 C4
Misson Bank DN9 . . . . . . .26 C3
MISTERTON PE10 . . . . . . .39 F5
Misterton Cty Prim Sch
 DN10 . . . . .39 F4

Mitchell Cl
 Eastgate PE1 . . . . .226 C2
 3 Hatfield DN7 . . . . . .14 D5
 2 Skellingthorpe LN6 . . .200 A4
Mitchell Dr LN1 . . . . . . 201 C6
Mitchell Rd LN4 . . . . . . 207 F6
Mitre La 16 PE21 . . . . . 208 F5
Moat House Rd 22 DN21 . . .30 B1
Moat La
 Bolingbroke PE23 . . . . . . .100 A8
 Old Leake PE22 . . . . .114 B1
 8 South Killingholme
 DN40 . . . . .12 E3
 4 Welbourn LN5 . . . . . .106 E5
Moat Rd
 Scunthorpe DN15 . . . . . . .8 C1
 Terrington St Clement
 PE34 . . . . .161 F1
Moat Wlk LN1 . . . . 211 E6
Modder St 1 LN6 . . . . . . 181 B6
Moggsville La PE2 . . . . . 230 B4
Moira Cl 5 DN7 . . . . .14 D7
Mole Dro PE12 . . . . 168 C1
Mollison Ave DN35 . . . . . 192 F5
Mollison Rd HU4 . . . . . . 179 A3
Monarch Ave PE2 . . . . . . 231 A6
Monarchs Rd PE22 . . . . . 136 A3
Monce Cl LN2 . . . . .68 C7
Monckton Way LN2 . . . . . .68 C5
Mondemont Cl 4
 PE12 . . . . .215 E3
Money Bridge La PE11 . . . 144 F1
Moneys Yd 7 NG34 . . . . . 212 D4
Monic Ave HU13 . . . . 178 F2
Monkfield Coll LN5 . . . . . 106 C2
Monkhouse Ct 6
 LN5 . . . . .214 A3
Monks Abbey Prim Sch
 LN2 . . . . .202 B4
Monks Ave LN11 . . . . 198 C6
Monks Cl
 4 Hatfield DN7 . . . . . .14 D5
 New Quarrington NG34 . . . .212 A2
Monks Dr 22 PE6 . . . . . . 175 A1
Monks Dyke Rd LN11 . . . . 198 D5
Monks Dyke Tech Coll
 LN11 . . . . .198 D5
Monks Gr PE4 . . . . 220 E8
Monks House La 5
 PE11 . . . . .214 A4
Monkshouse Prim Sch
 PE11 . . . . .214 A4
Monks Leys Terr LN2 . . . . 234 C3
Monks Manor Ct LN2 . . . . 202 B5
Monks Manor Dr LN2 . . . . 202 B4
Monks Mdw 3 PE5 . . . . . . 222 E6
Monks Rd
 Lincoln LN2 . . . . .234 B3
 Scunthorpe DN17 . . . . . . .184 F6
 8 Swineshead PE20 . . . .135 B7
MONKSTHORPE PE23 . . . . . 101 E8
Monksthorpe La PE23 . . . . .88 F1
Monks Way Ind Est
 LN2 . . . . .202 D3
Monks Wlk 4 PE11 . . . . . 214 A4
Monkton 3 HU15 . . . . .2 D6
Monkwood Cl 17 NG23 . . . . .91 D5
Monmouth La PE12 . . . . . 216 E8
Monmouth St HU4 . . . . . . 179 E3
Monsal Dale LN6 . . . . . . 204 F2
Monson Cl LN5 . . . . 201 C5
Monson Pk DN21 . . . . .42 A8
Monson Rd LN5 . . . . 234 A1
Monson St LN5 . . . . 201 E6
Montague St
 Cleethorpes DN35 . . . . . . .189 D1
 Lincoln LN2 . . . . .234 C2
Montagu Rd PE4 . . . . 225 D8
Montagu Terr 1 LN2 . . . . 234 C2
Montaigne Cl 3 LN2 . . . . 202 D7
Montaigne Cres LN2 . . . . 202 D7
Montaigne Gdn LN2 . . . . . 202 D7
Montbretia Dr 2
 DN17 . . . . .185 A1
Monteith Cres PE21 . . . . 209 B5
Montgomery Rd
 Cleethorpes DN35 . . . . . . .192 D5
 Skegness PE25 . . . . .206 A3
Montrose Cl
 8 Grantham NG31 . . . . .211 D7
 1 Lincoln LN6 . . . . . .204 E1
 10 Stamford PE9 . . . . .218 E6
Montrose Gr NG34 . . . . . . 121 A2
Montrose St DN31 . . . . . . 188 D1
Monument St LN1 . . . . . . 234 A3
Moody La DN31 . . . . 188 A5
Moon's Gn 3 PE12 . . . . . 157 F6
Moor Bank PE22 . . . . 113 C3
Moor Cl DN36 . . . . 195 D5
MOORBY PE22 . . . . .99 B6
Moorby Cl LN1 . . . . 201 E8
Moor Closes Nature
 Reserve* NG32 . . . . . .120 A2
Moor Dike Rd DN7 . . . . . . .26 A8
Moore Cl NG23 . . . . 117 F7
Moor Edges Rd DN8 . . . . . .15 B8
Moore's La 1 PE11 . . . . . 175 A1
Moor Farm Nature
 Reserve* LN10 . . . . . .98 A6
Moorfield Rd 2 PE22 . . . . 225 D3
Moorfields La DN14 . . . . . .6 F7
Moor Gate PE12 . . . . 159 A4

Moorgate Cl PE10 . . . . . . 154 D7
Moor Gn HU4 . . . . 179 B7
Moorhen Cl LN6 . . . . .92 D4
Moorhouse Rd HU5 . . . . . 179 B8
MOORHOUSES PE22 . . . . 112 A8
Moorhouses Rd PE22 . . . 111 F8

Moorings The
Broughton DN20 . . . . 196 A3
Burton LN1 . . . . 200 D7

Moor La
Ashby de la Launde &
Bloxholm LN4 . . . . 108 C3
Besthorpe NG23 . . . . .91 D7
Blankney LN4 . . . . .95 E4
Braceby & Sapperton
NG34 . . . . 131 E1
Branston & Mere LN4 . . . . .81 F2
Caistor LN7 . . . . .33 A5
5 Cherry Willingham/
Reepham LN3 . . . . .82 A8
Hatfield DN8 . . . . .15 D3
Horsington LN10 . . . . .84 D2
Kirkby on Bain LN10 . . . . .97 F6
Laneham DN22 . . . . .65 A3
Leasingham NG34 . . . . . 121 C7
Lincoln LN6 . . . . 204 E1
Long Bennington NG23 . . 117 C3
Marlborough LN5 . . . . .93 A4
Martin LN4 . . . . .96 A2
North Clifton NG23 . . . . . .78 D6
Potter Hanworth LN4 . . . . .82 B2
Reepham LN3 . . . . .69 B1
Roughton LN10 . . . . .98 B7
South Clifton NG23 . . . . . .78 E5
South Witham NG33 . . . . 151 B2
Stapleford LN6 . . . . 105 B8
Thorpe on the Hill LN6 . . .79 E1
Thurlby LN6 . . . . .92 E4
Wroot DN9 . . . . .26 C6

Moorland Ave
1 Lincoln LN6 . . . . 205 A5
4 Walkeringham DN10 . .39 F3
Moorland Cl
8 Carlton-le-Moorland
LN5 . . . . 105 E8
Moray LN3 . . . . .89 F3
Moorland Cres **5** LN6 . .205 B6
Moorland Dr DN36 . . . . . 195 C7
Moorland Inf Sch LN6 . . .205 B7
Moorlands **9** DN9 . . . . . .27 A2
Moorlands The **22** LN4 . . .95 D4

Moorland Way
5 Epworth DN9 . . . . .27 E6
Lincoln LN6 . . . . 204 F5
Moor Owners Rd DN8 . . . .15 D8
Moor Pk **5** NG34 . . . . . 108 D1
Moor Pk Dr **9** LN10 . . . . .97 C5

Moor Rd
Bottesford DN17 . . . . . . 184 C2
15 Collingham NG23 . . . .91 D5
Crowle DN17 . . . . .16 C8
Newborough PE6 . . . . . . 174 C5
Owersby LN8 . . . . .45 A5
Snitterby DN21 . . . . .43 B5
Thorne DN8 . . . . .15 C7
Walesby LN8 . . . . .45 E3
Moorside PE22 . . . . .98 E3
Moor Side PE22 . . . . 111 C8
Moorside Cl LN6 . . . . . . 204 E1
Moors Rd DN15 . . . . 182 C3
Moor St LN1 . . . . 201 D4
Moorswood Gate PE12 . . 159 D3
MOORTOWN LN7 . . . . .32 C2
Moortown Cl **6** NG31 . . .211 D7
Moortown Rd LN7 . . . . . . .33 A3
Moorwell Bsns Pk
DN17 . . . . 184 D3
Moorwell Rd DN17 . . . . . 184 E2
Moray Cl **8** PE9 . . . . . . 218 D6
MORBORNE PE7 . . . . 232 B3
Morborne Cl PE2 . . . . . . 231 D6
Morborne La PE7 . . . . . . 232 D4
Morborne Rd PE7 . . . . . . 232 C2
Morborn Rd PE7 . . . . 230 C2
Mordaunt Ave DN33 . . . . 194 D7
Morden Cl **12** LN4 . . . . . .95 D4
Morecambe Ave DN16 . . 185 A4
Moreland Ave **1** LN12 . . .77 A8
Morfield Gr **8** DN9 . . . . . .27 D6
Morgan Cl PE7 . . . . 233 E6
Morgans Cl **2** NG24 . . . . 104 D5
Morgan Way **5** DN19 . . . . .4 E2
Morkery La
Castle Bytham NG33 . . . 152 B2
North Witham NG33 . . . . 151 F2
Morley La DN36 . . . . 195 C6
Morley Rd DN17 . . . . 184 F5
Morley's La NG33 . . . . . . 152 F7
Morley St **3** DN21 . . . . . 197 C5
Morley Way PE2 . . . . 230 D5
Morpeth Cl PE2 . . . . 230 C6
Morpeth Rd PE3 . . . . 225 C3
Morpeth St HU3 . . . . 180 D7
Morpeth Wlk DN34 . . . . . 191 A7
Morris Cl **2** LN2 . . . . .68 D6
Morris Ct PE7 . . . . 233 E6
Morris Gdns **2** PE25 . . . 206 B5
Morrison Cl **10** LN12 . . . . .76 F8
Morris Rd HU3 . . . . 179 E7
Morris St PE1 . . . . 226 A4
Mortal Ash Hill DN16 . . . .19 C2
Mortimer Dr HU10 . . . . . 178 F6
MORTON
Morton DN21 . . . . 197 C8

MORTON continued
Morton PE10 . . . . 154 C6
Thorpe on the Hill LN6 . . .92 C6
Morton CE (Controlled)
Prim Sch PE10 . . . . . . 154 D7
Morton Cl
Gainsborough DN21 . . . . 197 B8
Immingham DN40 . . . . . . 186 B5
Morton Dr LN6 . . . . 204 F7
Morton Dro PE10 . . . . . . 155 A6
Morton Front DN21 . . . . . 197 B7
Morton La LN6 . . . . .92 C8
Morton N Dro PE10 . . . . .155 B7
Morton Rd
Gainsborough DN21 . . . . 197 C7
Grimsby DN34 . . . . 191 B7
Laughton DN21 . . . . .41 B8
Swinderby LN6 . . . . .92 B7
Morton St HU3 . . . . 180 C8
Morton Terr DN21 . . . . . . 197 C6
Morton Trentside Prim Sch
DN21 . . . . 197 B8
Morton Way LN9 . . . . 199 C1
Morus Cl PE10 . . . . 213 C6
Mosscroft La DN7 . . . . . . .14 F3
Mossdale Cl NG31 . . . . . 129 F5
Moss Dr PE25 . . . . 206 C2
Mossop Dr PE6 . . . . 164 E3
Moss Rd
Kirk Bramwith DN7 . . . . . .14 A8
Motherby La LN1 . . . . . . 234 A2
MOULTON PE12 . . . . 157 F7
MOULTON CHAPEL
PE12 . . . . 157 E1
Moulton Chapel Prim Sch
PE12 . . . . 157 F1
Moulton Chapel Rd
PE12 . . . . 157 C1
Moulton Cl **1** DN34 . . . . 190 D4
MOULTON EAUGATE
PE12 . . . . 167 F8
Moulton Gr PE3 . . . . 225 C6
Moulton Marsh Nature
Reserve* PE12 . . . . . . 146 F8
Moulton Mere Bank
PE12 . . . . 157 E7
MOULTON SEAS END
PE12 . . . . 146 E2
Mount Ave
14 Barton-upon-Humber
DN18 . . . . .10 E8
Kingston upon Hull
HU13 . . . . 178 D2
19 Winterton DN15 . . . . . .9 B5
Mountbatten Ave
11 Pinchbeck PE11 . . . . .156 E8
Stamford PE9 . . . . 219 A6
Yaxley PE7 . . . . 233 D5
Mountbatten Cl **5**
DN16 . . . . 185 B4
Mountbatten Dr **2**
PE13 . . . . 170 C1
Mountbatten Way
Bourne PE10 . . . . 213 E7
Peterborough PE3 . . . . . 225 B6
Mount La
Burton Pedwardine
NG34 . . . . 122 A2
Kirkby la Thorpe NG34 . . 121 F3
Legsby LN8 . . . . .58 A3
Mount Olivet LN11 . . . . . 198 A6
Mount Pleasant
9 Alford LN13 . . . . .75 F2
Bishook LN8 . . . . .47 B4
1 Holton le Clay DN36 . .195 D1
Kingston upon Hull HU9 . 181 C8
Louth LN11 . . . . 198 C5
8 New Holland DN19 . . . . .4 E2
Peterborough PE2 . . . . . 231 C7
Sleaford NG34 . . . . 212 E5
6 Wainfleet All Saints
PE24 . . . . 102 D2
Waltham DN37 . . . . 194 D5
Mount Pleasant Cl
DN21 . . . . .53 B1
Mount Pleasant Rd
PE13 . . . . 170 D1
Mount Pleasant Windmill*
DN21 . . . . .30 B2
Mount Rd LN4 . . . . 205 F3
Mount Royale Cl DN39 . . .12 A1
Mount St Inf Sch LN1 . . .201 E6
Mount St
9 Grantham NG31 . . . . . 211 A5
Lincoln LN1 . . . . 201 E6
Mountsteven Ave PE4 . . 221 B1
Mount The **15** DN3 . . . . . .14 A1
Mount Tumbledown Cl
PE12 . . . . 160 E4
Mount View **5** HU14 . . . . .3 A5
Mourne Terr **8** LN5 . . . . 205 D2
Mowbray Cl **3** DN9 . . . . .27 D3
Mowbray Ct **23** DN9 . . . . .27 E6
Mowbray Rd
Bretton PE3 . . . . 220 D1
14 Thorne/Moorends
DN8 . . . . .15 B7
Mowbray St
Epworth DN9 . . . . .27 E6
Gainsborough DN21 . . . . 197 C6
Moxon's La LN1 . . . . .93 F7
Mrs Mary Kings CE
(Controlled) Prim Sch
LN4 . . . . .96 B3
Mrs Smith's Cottage*
LN5 . . . . 107 B8
Much La LN1 . . . . 234 A2

MUCKTON LN11 . . . . .74 D8
Muckton Wood Nature
Reserve* LN11 . . . . .74 E8
Muirfield
Grantham NG31 . . . . 211 D8
11 Waltham DN37 . . . . . 194 C4
Muirfield Cl **6** PE11 . . . . 214 C2
Muirfield Croft DN40 . . . . 186 C4
Muirfield Dr PE25 . . . . . . 206 D5
Mulberry Ave **3** LN6 . . . 204 F2
Mulberry Cl
5 North Thoresby
DN36 . . . . .36 B1
Sleaford NG34 . . . . 212 D2
Waddington LN5 . . . . 205 C1
Mulberry Ct **6** PE20 . . . 135 B6
Mulberry Dr DN17 . . . . . . .16 D7
Mulberry Gdns
Bottesford DN16 . . . . . . 185 E4
Paston PE4 . . . . 221 C1
Mulberry Rd LN8 . . . . .45 E5
Mulberry Way
Skegness PE25 . . . . 206 B6
Spalding PE11 . . . . 214 E3
Mulberry Wlk **11** NG34 . .122 D3
Mulgrave Cl DN37 . . . . . 190 F8
Mulgrave St S DN15 . . . . 183 A4
Mulgrave St HU8 . . . . . . 181 A8
Mull Way DN40 . . . . 186 C2
Multon Ings La PE20 . . . . 136 B7
MUMBY LN13 . . . . .76 F1
Mumby Mdws LN13 . . . . . .76 F1
Mumby Rd LN13 . . . . .76 F2
Mumby's Bridge Rd
PE22 . . . . .98 F2
Munday Way PE13 . . . . . 170 B2
Munster Ct **6** DN31 . . . . 189 C1
Munton Fields NG33 . . . . 131 A1
Murdock Rd LN5 . . . . 205 E6
Murray St **8** DN31 . . . . . 189 B2
MURROW PE13 . . . . 177 D5
Murrow Bank PE13 . . . . . 177 D6
Murrow Cty Prim Sch
PE13 . . . . 177 D5
Murrow La PE13 . . . . 177 F5
Museum of Lincolnshire
Life* LN1 . . . . 234 A4
Musgraves Orch LN2 . . . .68 C7
Muskham PE3 . . . . 224 F4
Mussons Cl NG33 . . . . . . 152 E7
Muster Roll La PE21 . . . . 209 A3
Musticott Pl **17** PE13 . . .170 E1
MUSTON NG13 . . . . 128 C5
Muston La NG13 . . . . 128 B5
Muston Meadows National
Nature Reserve* NG13 . . . . 128 B3
Muston Rd NG31 . . . . 210 E2
Muswell Rd PE3 . . . . 225 E4
Mutton La DN10 . . . . .39 F1
Myers Cl NG32 . . . . 120 C1
Myle Cross Jun Sch
LN2 . . . . 202 C6
Myles Way **15** PE13 . . . . 170 D2
Myrtle Ave PE1 . . . . 226 C7
Myrtle Ct PE1 . . . . 226 C7
Myrtle Gr PE1 . . . . 226 C7
Myrtle House Cvn Pk
PE1 . . . . 226 F5
Myrtle Rd **5** DN7 . . . . . . .14 C4
Myrtle St **8** HU15 . . . . .2 C5
Myton St HU1 . . . . 180 E6

N

Naam Gr LN1 . . . . 234 A4
Naam Pl LN1 . . . . 234 A4
Nab La DN7 . . . . .14 C8
Nags Head Pas **10**
NG34 . . . . 234 A4
Nairn Rd PE9 . . . . 218 E6
Nandike Cl **4** HU10 . . . . 178 F6
Nan Sampson Bank
DN9 . . . . .26 B4
Nansicles Rd PE2 . . . . . . 230 D6
Napier Pl PE2 . . . . 229 C6
Napier St LN2 . . . . 234 C2
Narrow Boats The **3**
DN20 . . . . 196 A3
Narrow La
Belchford LN9 . . . . .73 B2
Twin Rivers DN14 . . . . .7 C8
Whaplode PE12 . . . . 158 C4
Naseby Cl
21 Hatfield DN7 . . . . . . .14 D3
Peterborough PE3 . . . . . 225 C1
Naseby Dr DN37 . . . . 191 B8
Naseby Gr DN31 . . . . 191 C8
Nash La **2** LN6 . . . . 204 E1
Natal View LN1 . . . . 201 D8
Nathan Cl PE3 . . . . 225 B2
National Ave HU5 . . . . . . 179 F8
National CE Jun Sch The
NG31 . . . . 211 B3
National Fishing Heritage
Ctr* DN31 . . . . 191 E8
National Parrot Sanctuary
The* PE22 . . . . 114 D7
Natural World Ctr* LN6 . . .79 F1
Natureland Seal
Sanctuary*
PE25 . . . . 206 E4
NAVENBY LN5 . . . . 107 A8
Navenby CE Prim Sch
LN5 . . . . 107 B8

Navenby La
Ashby de la Launde &
Bloxholm LN4 . . . . 107 F6
Bassingham LN5 . . . . .93 A1
Navensby Cl DN31 . . . . . 188 A2
Navigation House* **8**
NG34 . . . . 212 C4
Navigation La **8** LN7 . . . .33 B4
Navigation Way HU9 . . . . 181 C6
Naylors Dr **5** LN8 . . . . . .57 B8
Naylor's Row **3** HU9 . . . . 181 B7
Ndola Dr LN9 . . . . 199 C2
Neale Rd **18** LN6 . . . . . . .93 C8
Neal's Gate PE12 . . . . . . 158 E2
Neap House Rd
Flixborough DN15 . . . . . 182 A7
Gunness DN15 . . . . .17 E6
Neatgangs La DN19 . . . . . .5 A3
Neath Rd HU5 . . . . 179 A8
Neaverson Rd **2** PE6 . . . 220 D7
Needham Dr PE12 . . . . . . 159 C1
Needham Rd PE10 . . . . . 154 C6
Needhams Mdw LN13 . . . .76 B3
Needham The **8** PE25 . . . 206 A7
Neile Cl LN2 . . . . 202 D7
Nelson Cl
5 Crowland PE6 . . . . . . 166 F1
4 Skegness PE25 . . . . . 206 A7
Nelson Dr LN4 . . . . 203 B2
Nelson Gdns **51** PE13 . . 170 C1
Nelson Rd
Fiskerton LN3 . . . . .82 A6
Kingston upon Hull HU5 . 179 B7
4 Mablethorpe/Sutton on Sea
LN12 . . . . .64 B3
Nelson St
Gainsborough DN21 . . . . 197 C6
Grimsby DN31 . . . . 189 B1
Kingston upon Hull HU1 . 181 A5
Lincoln LN1 . . . . 201 D3
Nelson Way
9 Boston PE21 . . . . 208 E4
6 Grimsby DN34 . . . . . 190 D4
Nelthorpe Cl **3** DN39 . . . .12 A1
Nelthorpe St LN5 . . . . . . 201 E1
Nene Cl
10 Ruskington NG34 . . . 108 D2
Wansford PE8 . . . . 222 A3
4 Wittering PE8 . . . . . . 172 B1
Nene Ct
4 Grantham NG31 . . . . . 210 E2
5 Spalding PE11 . . . . . . 214 F5
Nenelands **8** PE12 . . . . . 160 F4
Nene Mdws **17** PE13 . . . 170 F4
Nene Parade **9** PE13 . . . 170 C1
Nene Parkway PE3 . . . . . 224 F1
Nene Pk **6** LN6 . . . . 204 C1
Nene Rd LN1 . . . . 201 E8
Nene St PE1 . . . . 226 B2
NENE TERRACE PE6 . . . 175 D6
Nene Valley Prim Sch
PE2 . . . . 230 D8
Nene Way PE5 . . . . 222 F2
Neptune St
Cleethorpes DN35 . . . . . 192 C7
Kingston upon Hull HU1 . 180 E4
Neslam Rd NG34 . . . . . . 143 C7
Ness La DN17 . . . . .7 B8
Netherfield PE12 . . . . 215 B2
Nethergate DN9 . . . . .27 B2
Netherlands Way
DN41 . . . . 187 B3
Netherton Rd HU4 . . . . . 179 B4
NETTLEHAM LN2 . . . . . . .68 D2
Nettleham CE (Aided) Jun
Sch
Nettleham LN2 . . . . 202 A6
Nettleham Inf Sch LN2 . . .68 C2
Nettleham Rd
Lincoln LN2 . . . . 234 C4
Scothern LN2 . . . . .68 E3
Nettleholme **10** DN7 . . . . .14 D4
NETTLETON LN7 . . . . .33 A3
Nettleton Cl LN4 . . . . .81 E2
Nettleton Dr LN6 . . . . .92 E5
Nettleton Prim Sch LN7 . .33 A3
Nettleton Rd LN7 . . . . . . .33 B3
Neustadt Cir **7** LN2 . . . . 234 B3
Neville Ave PE11 . . . . . . 214 F4
Neville Cl
5 Keadby with Althorpe
DN17 . . . . .17 D4
Kingston upon Hull HU3 . 180 D5
Neville Cres DN15 . . . . . . .9 A5
Neville La DN7 . . . . .14 A8
Neville Rd DN35 . . . . 183 C2
Neville St DN35 . . . . 192 D8
Neville Turner Way
DN37 . . . . 194 D4
NEWARK PE1 . . . . 226 E6
Newark Ave PE1 . . . . . . 226 C6
Newark Hill
Foston NG32 . . . . 117 F1
Great Gonerby NG31 . . . 129 D6
Newark Hill Prim Sch
PE1 . . . . 226 D6
Newark Hospl NG24 . . . . 104 A4
Newark La NG32 . . . . 119 C4
Newark N Gate Sta
NG24 . . . . 104 A5
Newark & Nottinghamshire
Agricultural Society's
Showground* NG24 . . . 104 C7
NEWARK-ON-TRENT
NG24 . . . . 104 B4

Newark Rd
Barnby in the Willows
NG24 . . . . 104 E8
Bassingham LN5 . . . . .92 E
Fenton LN1 . . . . .65 D
Leadenham LN5 . . . . 106 C
Lincoln LN6 . . . . 204 F
Newark-on-Trent NG24 . . 104 C
Norton Disney LN6 . . . . . .91 F
Peterborough PE1 . . . . . 226 E
Stapleford LN6 . . . . 105 B
Swinderby LN6 . . . . .92 A
Newark Rd Ind Est
PE1 . . . . 226 E
NEW BALDERTON
NG24 . . . . 104 A
NEWBALL LN3 . . . . .69 D
NEW BARNETBY DN38 . . .21 D
New Beacon Rd NG31 . . . 211 C
Newbey Cl PE3 . . . . 225 B
Newbigg
1 Crowle DN17 . . . . .16 C
Westwoodside DN9 . . . . . .27 B
NEW BOLINGBROKE
PE22 . . . . 112 D
Newbolt Ave DN17 . . . . . 184 D
Newbolt Cl **11** LN7 . . . . . .33 A
Newborn Ave DN15 . . . . . 182 E
Newborn Cl PE22 . . . . . . 231 E
NEWBOROUGH PE6 . . . . 174 E
Newborough CE Prim Sch
PE6 . . . . 174 E
Newborough Rd PE4 . . . . 174 E
Newboults La **2** PE9 . . . . 219 A
Newbridge Hill LN11 . . . . 198 C
Newbridge La LN11 . . . . . .49 E
New Bridge Rd HU9 . . . . 181 C
Newbury Ave DN37 . . . . . 188 A
Newbury Gr **2** DN34 . . . 190 E
Newbury Rd **18** NG24 . . . 104 C
Newbury Terr DN37 . . . . . 188 A
Newby Rd DN31 . . . . 191 C
New Cartergate 1
DN31 . . . . 191 D
Newcastle Dr PE2 . . . . . . 230 D
Newcastle Rd **4** NG31 . . 210 D
New Chapel La **8** DN37 . .23 F
New Cl DN33 . . . . 191 C
New Clee Sta DN31 . . . . . 189 D
New Cleveland St HU8 . . 181 A
New Coll PE9 . . . . 219 C
Newcomb Ct
2 Sleaford NG34 . . . . . 212 B
16 Stamford PE9 . . . . . .219 B
Newcombe Way PE2 . . . . 229 D
Newcot La LN4 . . . . .81 F
New Cres LN3 . . . . 203 D
New Cross Rd **8** PE9 . . . 219 C
New Cut PE6 . . . . 176 B
Newdike Gate PE12 . . . . 158 C
Newdown Rd DN17 . . . . . 184 D
New End
Hemingby LN9 . . . . .72 B
5 Wainfleet All Saints
PE24 . . . . 102 D
New England
Croft PE24 . . . . 102 E
Peterborough PE1 . . . . . 225 E
New Est
1 Little Bytham NG33 . . 163 A
Swinstead NG33 . . . . 153 A
New Fen Dike PE12 . . . . . 169 A
New Fen Dro PE12 . . . . . 168 B
Newfield Cl **10** DN3 . . . . . .14 A
Newfield Dr LN4 . . . . 109 F
Newfields PE13 . . . . 169 D
NEW FLETTON PE2 . . . . 231 B
Newgate La NG31 . . . . . . 130 D
Newgate Rd PE13 . . . . . . 169 F
Newgates **3** PE9 . . . . . . 219 C
New Gdn St **5** HU1 . . . . . 180 F
New George St HU2 . . . . 180 F
New Green **3** DN7 . . . . . .14 C
Newhall Rd
13 Kirk Sandall DN3 . . . .14 A
3 Kirk Sandall DN3 . . . . .14 A
NEWHAM PE22 . . . . 112 A
Newham La PE22 . . . . . . 112 A
New Hammond Beck Rd
PE21 . . . . 208 A
Newham Rd **2** PE9 . . . . . 219 A
Newhaven Dr LN5 . . . . . . 205 D
New Haven Terr DN31 . . . 188 F
New Ings La DN22 . . . . . . .52 E
Newington Ave HU4 . . . . 179 E
Newington Prim Sch
HU3 . . . . 180 A
Newington St HU3 . . . . . 179 F
New Inn La **3** DN7 . . . . . .14 C
New La
Girton NG23 . . . . .78 D
Great Carlton LN11 . . . . . .62 E
Reedness DN14 . . . . .6 E
Tathwell LN11 . . . . .61 A
Toynton St Peter PE23 . . 101 A
Wansford PE8 . . . . 222 C
Newland LN1 . . . . 234 A
New Land Ave DN15 . . . . 182 E
Newland Dr DN15 . . . . . . 182 D
Newlands DN21 . . . . 197 E

ewland St W **2** LN1 . . . 234 A2
ewlands Ct DN21 . . . . . . .197 E5
ewlands Pk DN36 . . . . . . .193 B1
ewlands Rd
  2 Haconby PE10 . . . . .154 D8
  Deeping St Nicholas PE6 . .166 D5
  arson Drove PE13 . . . . . .177 D7
  urfleet PE11 . . . . .145 F4
  ewland View **17** DN9 . . . .27 E6
  ewland Wlk DN15 . . . . . .182 E3
  W LEAKE PE22 . . . . .114 A8
  w Leake Prim Sch
    E22 . . . . .113 F7
  ewlyn Cl
    3 Kingston upon Hull
      HU13 . . . . .179 A2
  ew Waltham DN36 . . . . . .195 C7
  ewman Cl **19** PE8 . . . . . .172 B1
  ewmarch Ct DN33 . . . . . .191 B2
  ewmarket LN11 . . . . .198 C4
  ewmarket Cl PE1 . . . . . . .226 B6
  ewmarket St **4** DN21 . . . . .53 C1
  EW MEADOW PE7 . . . . . . .231 F2
  ew Meadow Dro PE7 . . . . .231 F2
  ew Mill Field Rd DN7 . . . .14 E3
  ewnham Cres DN16 . . . . . .185 A4
  ew Options Barton Sch
    N18 . . . . .11 A8
  ew Pk Est **1** DN7 . . . . .14 D7
  ewport LN2 . . . . .234 B4
  ewport Ave DN15 . . . . . . .210 D4
  ewport Cl **4** HU3 . . . . . .180 D5
  ewport Cres **2** LN5 . . . . .93 F7
  ewport Ct **1** LN5 . . . . . .234 B4
  ewport Dr DN15 . . . . .9 A6
  ewport St DN18 . . . . .3 F1
  ewport Wlk DN40 . . . . . . .186 D3
  EW QUARRINGTON
    NG34 . . . . .212 A2
  ew Rd
    lankney LN10 . . . . .96 F5
    irmingham HU15 . . . . . . .2 C8
    leethorpes DN35 . . . . . . .192 F6
    lipsham LE15 . . . . .162 B7
    1 Collyweston PE9 . . . . .171 B1
    roft PE24 . . . . .103 C3
    Deeping St Nicholas PE6 . .166 D5
    5 Easton on the Hill
      PE9 . . . . .171 D3
    3 Eye PE6 . . . . .175 A1
    olksworth PE7 . . . . .232 E6
    aceby DN37 . . . . .35 A3
    angtoft PE6 . . . . .164 F3
    Peterborough PE1 . . . . . . .226 B2
    Quadring PE11 . . . . .145 C8
    ryhall PE9 . . . . .163 C1
    cunthorpe DN17 . . . . . . .184 B6
    ilk Willoughby NG34 . . . . .121 A1
    palding PE11 . . . . .214 D4
    taunton NG13 . . . . .117 B2
    utton Bridge PE12 . . . . . .160 F5
    winefleet DN14 . . . . .6 C4
    histleton LE15 . . . . .151 D1
    Wainfleet All Saints
      PE24 . . . . .101 E2
    Waltham DN37 . . . . .194 E4
    Worlaby DN20 . . . . .10 D1
  ew River Dro
    PE12 . . . . .156 F3
    3 Spalding PE12 . . . . . .214 C1
  ew River Gate PE12 . . . . .168 D8
  ew Roman Bank
    E34 . . . . .161 D3
  ew Row
    Gonerby Hill Foot
      NG31 . . . . .210 E7
    1 Market Deeping PE6 . . .217 D4
    3 Messingham DN17 . . . . .29 D7
  ewsham Dr DN34 . . . . . . .191 A7
  Helpringham NG34 . . . . . .133 D7
  6 Louth LN11 . . . . .198 B5
  Jsbournby NG34 . . . . .132 D5
  Sleaford NG34 . . . . .212 E4
  2 Stamford PE9 . . . . . . .219 C6
  ewstead Ave
    Cherry Willingham/Reepham
      LN3 . . . . .203 E5
    olton le Clay DN36 . . . . .195 E2
  ewstead Cl PE6 . . . . .175 A2
  ewstead Dr
    Cleethorpes DN35 . . . . . .192 E4
    1 Mablethorpe/Sutton on Sea
      LN12 . . . . .64 C3
  ewstead PE9 . . . . .219 F6
  ryhall PE9 . . . . .163 D1
  ewstead St HU5 . . . . .180 A8
  EWTOFT LN11 . . . . .56 E5
  EWTON
    ewton and Haceby
      NG34 . . . . .132 A3
    ewton PE13 . . . . .170 A5
    ewton Bar NG34 . . . . . . .132 A3
  EWTON BY TOFT LN8 . . . . .56 E6
  ewton Cl
    2 Metheringham LN4 . . . . .95 C4
    winderby LN6 . . . . .92 A5
    5 Wragby LN8 . . . . . . .79 D4
  ewton Ct **6** NG33 . . . . .151 E7

Newton Dr LN3 . . . . .203 C6
Newton Gr DN33 . . . . .191 C4
Newton La
  Binbrook LN8 . . . . .47 D5
  15 Ruskington NG34 . . . . .108 E2
Newton Marsh La DN36 . . . .36 F6
NEWTON ON TRENT
  LN1 . . . . .65 D1
Newton-on-Trent CE Prim
  Sch LN1 . . . . .65 C1
Newton Pk **10** NG23 . . . . .117 D3
Newton Rd DN16 . . . . .185 E6
Newton St
  5 Grantham NG31 . . . . . .211 B4
  3 Kingston upon Hull
    HU3 . . . . .180 A4
  Lincoln LN5 . . . . .234 B1
  Newark-on-Trent NG24 . . . .104 A4
Newton Terr LN11 . . . . . . .198 C5
Newton Way
  5 Colsterworth NG33 . . .151 D7
  Sleaford NG34 . . . . .212 D5
New Town **6**
  3 Spilsby PE23 . . . . . . .101 A8
  Stamford PE9 . . . . .219 D5
New Town **6** PE9 . . . . . .171 D3
Newtown Ct HU9 . . . . .181 E7
Newtown Sq HU9 . . . . .181 E7
New Trent St DN17 . . . . . .16 E6
NEW WALTHAM DN36 . . . . .195 D7
New Waltham Prim Sch
  DN36 . . . . .195 C7
New Wlk HU14 . . . . .3 A4
NEW YORK LN4 . . . . .111 C5
New York Prim Sch
  LN4 . . . . .111 C4
New York Rd LN4 . . . . .110 F6
Nicholas Ct **26** DN18 . . . . .10 E8
Nicholas Taylor Gdns **1**
  PE3 . . . . .225 B1
Nicholas Way LN11 . . . . . . .41 E2
Nichol Hill **2** LN11 . . . . .198 B5
Nicholls Ave PE3 . . . . .225 E3
Nicholson Rd
  1 Healing DN41 . . . . . . .24 A5
  Immingham DN40 . . . . .12 E4
Nicholson St **8** DN35 . . . .192 F5
Nicholson Way **7** DN9 . . . .27 D7
Nicolette Way LN8 **10** PE11 . .214 B5
Nicolgate La DN20 . . . . . . .196 D4
Nicolson Dr **8** DN18 . . . . .10 F8
Nidd's La PE20 . . . . .136 E4
Nightingale Cl DN15 . . . . . .182 C7
Nightingale Cres **1**
  LN6 . . . . .204 E8
Nightingale Ct PE4 . . . . . . .221 E2
Nightingale Dr PE7 . . . . . .233 D6
Nightingales **18** PE6 . . . . .217 C5
Nightleys Rd DN22 . . . . . . .65 B8
Ninescores La DN9 . . . . . . .26 B4
Ninth Ave
  3 Fixborough Ind Est
    DN15 . . . . .8 A1
  Grantham NG31 . . . . .211 F5
NINTHORPE PE25 . . . . .206 D6
Nipcut Rd PE6 . . . . .175 C2
NOCTON LN4 . . . . .95 B7
Nocton Com Prim Sch
  LN4 . . . . .95 C7
Nocton Dr LN2 . . . . .201 F8
Nocton Fen La LN4 . . . . . . .83 A1
Nocton Rd
  7 Potterhanworth LN4 . . .82 B1
  Potter Hanworth LN4 . . . . .95 B8
Nooking La DN37 . . . . .23 D7
Nookings Dr **3** DN20 . . . . .31 A5
Nooking The DN9 . . . . .27 C3
Nookin The **1** LN5 . . . . . .106 E5
Nook The
  Croxton Kerrial NG32 . . . . .138 D3
  7 Easton on the Hill
    PE9 . . . . .171 D3
  1 Helpston PE6 . . . . . . .173 C4
  Sproxton LE14 . . . . .150 C7
Norbeck La LN11 . . . . .68 C6
Norburn
  2 Peterborough PE3 . . . .220 F1
  Peterborough PE3 . . . . . . .225 B8
Norfolk Ave DN15 . . . . .8 A4
Norfolk Bank La HU15 . . . . .1 F8
Norfolk Cl **1** LN8 . . . . . . .47 B6
Norfolk Cres
  Bracebridge Heath
    LN4 . . . . .205 F4
  1 Scampton Airfield LN1 . .67 F5
Norfolk La DN35 . . . . .192 F4
Norfolk Rd **19** DN20 . . . . .189 C1
Norfolk La DN35 . . . . .192 E7
Norfolk Pl **4** PE21 . . . . . .208 F6
Norfolk St Ind Est
  PE21 . . . . .208 F7
Norfolk Sq **5** PE9 . . . . . . .219 B6
Norfolk St
  Boston PE21 . . . . .208 F6
  Kingston upon Hull HU2 . . .180 E7
  Lincoln LN1 . . . . .201 C4
  Peterborough PE1 . . . . . . .225 F4
Norland Ave HU4 . . . . .179 C6
Norman Ave **5** DN20 . . . . .208 F5
NORMANBY DN15 . . . . .8 B3
NORMANBY-BY-SPITAL
  LN8 . . . . .55 E7
NORMANBY BY STOW
  DN21 . . . . .179 A2
Normanby Cliff Rd LN8 . . . .55 D7
Normanby Hall Cntry Pk*
  DN15 . . . . .8 C3

NORMANBY LE WOLD
  LN7 . . . . .45 F5
Normanby Pk Farming
  Mus* DN15 . . . . .8 C3
Normanby Prim Sch
  LN8 . . . . .55 E7
Normanby Rd
  Burton upon Stather
    DN15 . . . . .8 C3
  Nettleton LN7 . . . . .33 B2
  3 Owmby LN8 . . . . .55 F6
  Scunthorpe DN15 . . . . . . .183 A5
  Stow DN21 . . . . .53 F1
Normanby Rise LN8 . . . . . . .45 E5
Norman Cl
  8 Barton-upon-Humber
    DN18 . . . . .10 F8
  30 Metheringham LN4 . . . .95 C4
NORMAN CORNER
  DN37 . . . . .194 C2
Norman Cres **3** DN7 . . . . .184 F8
NORMAN CROSS PE7 . . . . . .232 F2
Norman Dr **8** DN7 . . . . . .14 D4
Normandy Cl LN11 . . . . . . .198 E6
Normandy Rd DN35 . . . . . . .192 D5
Norman Mews **3**
  PE10 . . . . .213 D5
Norman Rd
  Grimsby DN34 . . . . .191 B7
  Hatfield DN7 . . . . .14 D3
  Peterborough PE1 . . . . . . .226 C4
Norman St **1** LN5 . . . . . .234 B1
NORMANTON
  Bottesford NG13 . . . . .128 A3
  Normanton NG23 . . . . .119 D5
Normanton La NG13 . . . . . .128 A6
Normanton Rd
  3 Beacon Hill NG24 . . . .104 B5
  1 Crowland PE6 . . . . . . .166 F1
  Peterborough PE1 . . . . . . .226 C4
Normanton Rise HU4 . . . . . .179 C7
Normanby Cl **3** HU8 . . . . .181 C8
Norris Cl **10** NG34 . . . . . .122 D3
Norris St LN5 . . . . .201 F1
Norsefield Ave DN37 . . . . . .194 E5
Nortcote Heavy Horse Ctr*
  PE23 . . . . .101 D7
Northam Cl PE6 . . . . .175 B3
Northampton Rd DN16 . . . . .183 C1
North Ave PE10 . . . . .155 D3
North Axholme Comp Sch
  DN17 . . . . .16 D7
North Bank
  Crowland PE6 . . . . .166 E1
  Thorney PE6 . . . . .227 D1
North Bank Rd **4** PE1 . . . .226 D3
NORTHBECK NG34 . . . . . . .132 F8
North Beck La PE23 . . . . . . .87 E1
NORTHBOROUGH PE6 . . . . . .217 F2
Northborough Prim Sch
  PE6 . . . . .173 F6
Northborough Rd PE6 . . . . .174 C5
North Bracing PE25 . . . . . . .206 E3
NORTH CARLTON LN1 . . . . .67 C4
NORTH CARR DN9 . . . . .27 C3
North Carr La DN20 . . . . . . .9 F3
North Carr Rd
  Misterton DN10 . . . . .39 F7
  Scotter DN17 . . . . .28 E5
  West Stockwith DN10 . . . . .40 B6
Normanby Rise HU4 . . . . . . .179 C7
North Church Side **12**
  HU1 . . . . .180 F6
Northcliffe Rd NG31 . . . . . .211 A7
North Cliff Rd DN21 . . . . . .30 C2
NORTH CLIFTON NG23 . . . . .78 C7
North Clifton Prim Sch
  NG23 . . . . .78 C6
North Coates Rd DN36 . . . . .37 A4
NORTH COCKERINGTON
  LN11 . . . . .50 A1
North Cockerington CE
  Prim Sch LN11 . . . . .50 A1
Northcote Heavy Horse
  Ctr* PE23 . . . . .101 D7
NORTH COTES DN36 . . . . . .37 A3
North Cotes CE
  (Controlled) Prim Sch
  DN36 . . . . .37 A3
North County Prim Sch
  DN21 . . . . .197 B6
North Court **10** LN6 . . . . .68 C2
North Cres **3** NG23 . . . . .128 A5
Northcroft **4** LN1 . . . . . . .66 D3
Northcroft La NG23 . . . . . . .91 C5
North-dale Ct **2** DN21 . . . .30 B2
Northdale Pk **1** HU14 . . . . .3 B7
North Dales Rd LN4 . . . . . . .82 A5
North Dr
  2 Ancaster NG32 . . . . . .120 A3
  5 Balderton NG24 . . . . .104 C1
  Kingston upon Hull
    HU10 . . . . .178 E6
  RAF Cranwell NG34 . . . . . .107 D1
  Swanland HU14 . . . . .3 B7
North Dro
  Bicker PE20 . . . . .134 E6
  Deeping St Nicholas
    PE11 . . . . .155 F1
  Luton PE12 . . . . .133 E7
  Quadring PE11 . . . . .144 C8
  Swaton NG34 . . . . .133 D4
North Eastern Rd DN8 . . . . .15 A8
NORTH ELKINGTON
  LN11 . . . . .48 D1
North Elkington La
  LN11 . . . . .48 E1

North End LN11 . . . . .49 E3
North End **5** DN19 . . . . . .12 A8
NORTH END LN11 . . . . .62 F8
North End DN18 . . . . .10 A8
NORTH END PE20 . . . . .135 B8
North End PE13 . . . . .170 C1
North End Cres **9**
  DN36 . . . . .36 D4
North End La
  2 Fulbeck NG32 . . . . . .106 C1
  Saltfleetby LN11 . . . . .62 F8
  South Cockerington LN11 . . .50 F1
  South Kelsey LN7 . . . . .32 A2
  3 Tetney DN36 . . . . . . .36 D4
North End Rd **7** DN36 . . . .36 D4
Northern Ave DN20 . . . . . . .196 C5
Northern Rd NG24 . . . . . . .104 A5
Northern's Cl NG33 . . . . . . .151 D5
Northey Rd PE6 . . . . .227 C2
North Farm Rd DN17 . . . . . .184 D3
Northfield Rd DN11 . . . . . . .52 E4
North Fen Dro PE20 . . . . . .134 E4
North Fen Rd
  8 Glinton PE6 . . . . . . .220 C8
  Helpringham NG34 . . . . . . .133 D7
NORTH FERRIBY HU14 . . . . .3 B4
North Ferriby CE Prim Sch
  HU14 . . . . .3 A5
Northferry La **2** DN9 . . . . .26 D1
NORTHFIELD HU13 . . . . . . .178 F2
Northfield HU14 . . . . .3 B7
Northfield Ave
  Kingston upon Hull
    HU13 . . . . .178 E3
  3 Sudbrooke LN2 . . . . . .68 F3
Northfield Cl
  19 Ruskington NG34 . . . .108 E2
  1 Scunthorpe DN16 . . . .185 C6
  1 Tetney DN36 . . . . . . .36 D4
  West Butterwick DN17 . . . . .17 D1
Northfield La
  Amcotts DN17 . . . . .7 E2
  North Clifton NG23 . . . . . .78 D7
  Thornton Curtis DN39 . . . . .11 D5
  Willoughton DN21 . . . . .42 C4
Northfield Rd
  Ashby wi Scremby
    PE23 . . . . .88 D1
  Kingston upon Hull HU3 . . .179 F6
  Messingham DN17 . . . . . . .185 A1
  North Leverton with
    Habblesthorpe DN22 . . . . .52 D1
  Peterborough PE1 . . . . . . .225 F7
  4 Ruskington NG34 . . . .108 E2
  Welton LN2 . . . . .68 D7
North Field Rd PE6 . . . . . . .217 B7
Northfield Rise **1** LN1 . . . .66 C2
Northfields
  Bourne PE10 . . . . .213 D7
  Stamford PE9 . . . . .219 C6
Northfields Ct PE9 . . . . . . .219 C6
North Foreland Dr **3**
  PE25 . . . . .206 D8
North Forty Foot Bank
  PE21 . . . . .208 A6
Northgate
  Kingston upon Hull
    HU13 . . . . .178 E2
  Lincoln LN2 . . . . .234 B4
  Louth LN11 . . . . .198 B5
NORTHGATE PE11 . . . . .144 D1
North Gate
  Gosberton PE11 . . . . .145 A6
  Newark-on-Trent NG24 . . . .104 A5
  Pinchbeck PE11 . . . . .144 D1
  Sleaford NG34 . . . . .212 D5
Northgate Ct LN11 . . . . . . .198 B6
Northgate Sch LN34 . . . . . .212 D5
North Greetwell
  LN2 . . . . .203 B8
North Halls **1** LN8 . . . . . .47 C5
NORTH HARBY NG23 . . . . . .79 C7
North Heath La NG32 . . . . . .106 D3
North Holme **8** DN36 . . . . .36 D4
North Holme Rd LN11 . . . . .198 B5
NORTH HYKEHAM
  LN6 . . . . .204 D2
North Ing Dro PE11 . . . . . . .134 C4
Northing La LN7 . . . . .68 F5
Northing Lane LN13 . . . . . . .77 A5
North Ings Rd DN7 . . . . . . .14 E5
Northings The **1**
  NG32 . . . . .210 B4
North Intake La DN9 . . . . . .40 C8
NORTH KELSEY LN7 . . . . . . .32 A4
NORTH KELSEY MOOR
  LN7 . . . . .32 D4
North Kelsey Prim Sch
  LN7 . . . . .32 A4
North Kesteven Ctr*
  LN6 . . . . .204 D1
North Kesteven Sch
  LN6 . . . . .204 D1
NORTH KILLINGHOLME
  DN40 . . . . .12 D3
NORTH KYME LN4 . . . . .109 F4
North Kyme Cty Prim Sch
  LN4 . . . . .109 E3
North La
  Coningsby LN4 . . . . .207 D4
  Marshchapel DN36 . . . . . . .37 C2
  2 Navenby/Wellingore
    LN5 . . . . .107 A8
  Reepham LN3 . . . . .68 F1

North La continued
  Swaby LN13 . . . . .74 E4
NORTHLANDS PE22 . . . . . . .113 A4
Northlands Ave **3** DN15 . . . .9 A5
Northlands La PE22 . . . . . . .113 A4
Northlands Rd
  Glentworth DN21 . . . . .54 E6
  Winterton DN15 . . . . .9 A6
Northlands Rd S **10** DN15 . . .9 A5
NORTH LEVERTON CE Sch
  DN22 . . . . .52 B1
NORTH LEVERTON WITH
  HABBLESTHORPE
  DN22 . . . . .52 B1
North Leys Rd DN22 . . . . . . .52 E1
North Lincoln Rd DN16 . . . .183 F2
North Lincolnshire Mus*
  DN15 . . . . .183 A2
North Lindsey Coll
  DN17 . . . . .184 E8
Northminster PE1 . . . . .226 A3
North Moor Dr **2** DN10 . . . .39 F3
North Moor Rd
  Martin LN4 . . . . .96 B3
  Messingham DN17 . . . . .29 B8
Northmoor Rd DN17 . . . . . . .6 C1
North Moss La
  Scotter DN17 . . . . .29 C5
  Walkeringham DN10 . . . . . .39 F3
North Moss La DN41 . . . . . .187 B1
Northolme
  Gainsborough DN21 . . . . . .197 D5
  Sutton St Edmund PE12 . . . .168 E5
Northolme Circ **2**
  HU13 . . . . .178 E2
Northolme Cres
  Kingston upon Hull
    HU13 . . . . .178 E3
  Scunthorpe DN15 . . . . . . .182 F3
Northolme Ct HU13 . . . . . . .198 C2
Northolme Rd HU13 . . . . . . .178 E3
Northon's La PE12 . . . . .215 C3
NORTH ORMSBY LN11 . . . . .48 E4
NORTHORPE
  Donington PE20 . . . . .134 E3
  Northorpe DN21 . . . . .42 A8
  Thurlby PE10 . . . . .164 C8
Northorpe Cl LN6 . . . . .204 F7
Northorpe La PE10 . . . . . . .164 C8
Northorpe Rd
  Donington PE20 . . . . .134 D3
  Halton Holegate PE23 . . . . .101 B8
  Scunthorpe DN15 . . . . .41 F8
NORTH OWERSBY LN8 . . . . .44 E5
North Parade
  Gainsborough DN21 . . . . . .197 F4
  Grantham NG31 . . . . .211 A6
  Holbeach PE12 . . . . .215 E3
  Lincoln LN1 . . . . .234 A3
  Scunthorpe DN16 . . . . .185 D6
  Skegness PE25 . . . . .206 D3
  2 Sleaford NG34 . . . . . .212 C7
North Parade Extension
  PE25 . . . . .206 E3
North Prom DN35 . . . . .192 E7
North Quay DN31 . . . . .189 C3
North Ramper DN21 . . . . . . .44 A7
NORTH RAUCEBY
  NG34 . . . . .120 E5
North Rd
  Bourne PE10 . . . . .213 D4
  Bratoft PE24 . . . . .102 B8
  7 Cranwell NG34 . . . . . .107 F1
  Gedney Hill PE12 . . . . . . .168 B7
  1 Keadby with Althorpe
    DN17 . . . . .17 C6
  Kingston upon Hull HU4 . . .179 E4
  Leadenham LN5 . . . . .106 D3
  Mablethorpe & Sutton
    LN12 . . . . .64 E3
  Sleaford NG34 . . . . .212 A4
  Sturton le Steeple DN22 . . . .52 B4
  Tattershall Thorpe LN4 . . . .97 F3
  Tetford LN9 . . . . .73 F1
  Tydd St Mary PE13 . . . . . .160 B2
NORTH RESTON LN11 . . . . .62 B2
North Scaffold La NG23 . . . . .91 D3
NORTH SCARLE LN6 . . . . . . .78 F2
North Scarle Miniature
  Railway* LN6 . . . . .78 F1
North Scarle Prim Sch
  LN6 . . . . .78 F2
North Scarle Rd NG23 . . . . . .91 F8
North Sea La DN35 . . . . . . .193 A3
North Shore Rd PE25 . . . . . .206 D6
Northside **2** DN20 . . . . . . .27 C2
Northside La DN22 . . . . .52 C1
North St
  1 Barrow upon Humber
    DN19 . . . . .11 D8
  2 Boston PE21 . . . . . . .208 F6
  Bourne PE10 . . . . .213 D5
  Caistor LN7 . . . . .33 A4
  Cleethorpes DN35 . . . . . . .192 F6
  6 Crowland PE6 . . . . . . .166 E1
  9 Crowle DN17 . . . . . . .16 D8
  Digby LN4 . . . . .108 E6
  Folksworth PE7 . . . . .233 A1

North St *continued*
Gainsborough DN21 . . . . 197 C5
7 Grantham NG31 . . . . 211 A5
Horncastle LN9 . . . . 199 C4
Kingston upon Hull
  HU10 . . . . 178 E6
Middle Rasen LN8 . . . . 57 B8
Morton DN21 . . . . 197 C8
8 Nettleham LN2 . . . . 68 C2
Osbournby NG34 . . . . 132 C5
Owston Ferry DN9 . . . . 28 B3
Peterborough PE1 . . . . 226 A2
Roxby cum Risby DN15 . . . . . 9 A4
Scunthorpe DN15 . . . . 183 B4
Stamford PE9 . . . . 219 B5
Sturton le Steeple DN22 . . . . 52 B3
Thimbleby LN9 . . . . 85 B5
West Butterwick DN17
  West/East Butterwick
  DN17 . . . . 28 D8
Winterton DN15 . . . . 9 B6
North Terr PE1 . . . . 226 E7
NORTH THORESBY
  DN36 . . . . 36 B1
North Thoresby Prim Sch
  DN36 . . . . 36 A1
Northumberland Cl
  13 Scampton Airfield
  LN1 . . . . 67 E5
  8 Stamford PE9 . . . . . . 219 A6
Northumberland Cl
  DN34 . . . . 191 B6
Northumbria Rd NG34 . . 212 B2
North Walls HU1 . . . . . . 181 A6
North Warren Rd
  DN21 . . . . 197 B6
Northway 3 LN11 . . . . . . 49 B8
North Way
  6 Lincoln LN6 . . . . 204 D2
  Marshchapel DN36 . . . . 37 B2
NORTH WILLINGHAM
  LN8 . . . . 58 D7
NORTH WITHAM NG33 . . 151 D4
North Witham Bank
  LN1 . . . . 234 A2
North Witham Rd
  NG33 . . . . 151 D3
Northwood Dr
  Hessle HU13 . . . . 178 B3
  Sleaford NG34 . . . . 212 C6
NORTON DISNEY LN6 . . . . 92 C2
Norton Disney Rd LN5 . . . . 92 D1
Norton Gr HU4 . . . . 179 D4
Norton La
  Bishop Norton LN8 . . . . 43 C2
  Thurlby LN6 . . . . 92 C4
Norton Rd
  Peterborough PE1 . . . . 225 F6
  Scunthorpe DN16 . . . . 185 B5
  Stapleford LN6 . . . . 105 C8
Norton St NG31 . . . . 211 A3
Norwell La NG23 . . . . 91 C1
Norwich Ave DN34 . . . . . . 191 A4
Norwich Cl
  Heighington/
  Washingborough LN4 . . . . 203 E1
  3 Sleaford NG34 . . . . . 212 C7
Norwich Dr LN4 . . . . 81 A2
Norwich Rd PE13 . . . . 170 C1
Norwich Way 7 NG1 . . . . 210 E5
Norwood Ave DN15 . . . . . 182 F2
Norwood Cl 3 HU10 . . . . 178 E7
Norwood La
  Borough Fen PE6 . . . . 174 E1
  Peterborough PE4 . . . . 221 F2
Norwood Prim Sch
  PE4 . . . . 221 C3
Norwood Rd
  7 Hatfield DN7 . . . . 14 C5
  3 Skegness PE25 . . . . . 103 E4
Norwood St HU3 . . . . 180 C7
Nostell Rd DN16 . . . . 183 D1
Nottingham Rd 1
  NG13 . . . . 128 A5
Nottingham Terr 3
  LN2 . . . . 234 C3
Nottingham Way PE1 . . . . 226 C6
Novello Garth HU4 . . . . . . 179 B4
Nowells La 6 PE10 . . . . . 213 D5
Nuffield Cl 6 DN16 . . . . . 185 B4
Nunburnholme Ave 5
  HU14 . . . . 3 A4
Nunburnholme Pk
  HU5 . . . . 179 B7
Nunnerley Pl DN37 . . . . . 194 F5
Nuns Cnr DN33 . . . . 191 C4
Nuns Rd DN17 . . . . 184 F6
NUNSTHORPE DN33 . . . . 191 B4
Nunsthorpe & Bradley Pk
  Children's Ctr DN33 . . . . 191 A4
Nunthorpe Cl 10 DN7 . . . . 14 D4
Nursery Cl
  4 Barton-upon-Humber
  DN18 . . . . 3 F1
  14 Dunholme LN2 . . . . . 68 E6
  Peterborough PE1 . . . . 226 A4
  10 Saxilby LN1 . . . . 66 D2
  Scunthorpe DN17 . . . . . . 184 F3
Nursery Gdns
  25 Alford LN13 . . . . 75 F2
  6 Holton le Clay DN36 . . 195 D2

Nursery Gr LN2 . . . . 202 A6
Nursery La
  Belvoir NG32 . . . . 138 C6
  Morton DN21 . . . . 40 D3
  Peterborough PE1 . . . . 226 D2
Nursery Rd
  Boston PE21 . . . . 209 B2
  Cranwell & Byard's Leap
  NG34 . . . . 120 C8
Nursery St 2 LN8 . . . . 57 D7
Nurses La
  Skellingthorpe LN6 . . . . . . 200 A5
  4 Wymondham LE14 . . . 150 C1
Nutfields Gr 7 DN7 . . . . . . 14 C6
Nut La PE22 . . . . 114 C1
Nutwood View 4
  DN16 . . . . 185 D4

O

Oak Ave
  13 Brough HU15 . . . . 2 C6
  Grimsby DN32 . . . . 191 E4
  8 Scawby DN20 . . . . 30 F8
  11 Welton/Dunholme LN2 . 68 E6
Oak Cl
  8 Ingoldmells PE25 . . . . . 90 D3
  Louth LN11 . . . . 198 E4
  14 Sudbrooke LN2 . . . . . 68 F2
  5 Woodhall Spa LN10 . . . 97 E6
Oak Cres
  Boston PE21 . . . . 208 E7
  Bourne PE10 . . . . 213 B6
  Cherry Willingham/Reepham
  LN3 . . . . 203 D5
Oak Ct 1 PE11 . . . . 214 E3
Oakdale Ave
  3 Kingston upon Hull
  HU10 . . . . 178 E8
  Peterborough PE2 . . . . 231 D4
Oakdale Cl 4 NG31 . . . . . . 211 A8
  Oakdale Prim Sch PE7 . . . 231 C4
Oak Dr HU5 . . . . 179 B7
Oak Farm Paddock
  LN6 . . . . 204 C1
Oakfield 16 LN1 . . . . 66 D2
Oakfield Cl 4 DN16 . . . . . 196 E3
  Oakfield Prim Sch
  DN16 . . . . 185 A5
Oakfield St LN2 . . . . 202 B3
Oakford DN17 . . . . 184 D8
Oak Gr
  3 Barnetby le Wold
  DN38 . . . . 21 B4
  3 Barrow upon Humber
  DN19 . . . . 11 C7
  6 Market Deeping PE6 . . 217 B6
Oakham Ave 5 LN12 . . . . . . 64 A3
Oakham Cl 1 NG31 . . . . . . 210 E6
Oakham Terr 12 PE21 . . . . 208 F3
Oakham Wlk DN40 . . . . . . 186 E3
Oak Hill LN4 . . . . 203 B2
Oak House La PE22 . . . . . 126 C4
Oakhurst Cl NG31 . . . . . . 211 D2
Oakland Ave 39 DN7 . . . . . 14 D4
Oakland Cl 3 LN1 . . . . 201 D7
Oaklands
  8 Beckingham DN10 . . . . . 40 A1
  8 Collingham NG23 . . . . . 91 D4
  Eastfield PE1 . . . . 226 E7
  5 Woodhall Spa LN10 . . . 97 D5
Oaklands Dr
  Kingston upon Hull
  HU13 . . . . 178 D3
  4 Wisbech PE13 . . . . . . 170 E1
Oaklands Rd DN40 . . . . . . 186 C5
Oaklands The 11 LN8 . . . . . 70 D4
Oakland Way 11 PE11 . . . . 145 C1
Oakleaf Rd PE1 . . . . 226 C6
Oakleigh DN16 . . . . 185 C3
Oakleigh Dr
  Canwick LN1 . . . . 201 C6
  Peterborough PE2 . . . . 230 C6
Oakleigh Rd NG31 . . . . . . 210 C3
Oakleigh Terr LN1 . . . . . . 201 C6
Oakley Dr PE11 . . . . 214 E6
Oakley Pl PE21 . . . . 147 F2
Oak Rd
  Glinton PE6 . . . . 220 B8
  1 Healing DN41 . . . . 24 A5
  Scunthorpe DN16 . . . . . . 185 B7
  Sleaford NG34 . . . . 212 D2
  Stamford PE9 . . . . 218 D7
Oakroyd Cres 22 PE13 . . . 170 D1
  Oakside Pk Ind Est
  NG34 . . . . 212 F6
Oaks La DN10 . . . . 39 F2
Oaks The
  Balderton NG24 . . . . 104 C2
  15 Nettleham LN2 . . . . . . 68 D2
  1 Scothern LN2 . . . . 68 F3
Oak Tree Ave DN21 . . . . . 197 F6
Oaktree Cl 3 PE11 . . . . . . 145 B7
Oak Tree Cl
  3 Long Bennington
  NG23 . . . . 117 D3
  7 Market Rasen LN8 . . . . 57 D7
Oak Tree Dr LN6 . . . . 92 D4
Oak Tree Mdw LN9 . . . . . 199 C5
Oak Tree Wlk 29 DN17 . . . 16 D7
Oak View
  18 Dunholme LN2 . . . . . . 68 E6
  Peterborough PE3 . . . . 224 F4
Oak Way
  Cleethorpes DN35 . . . . . . 192 D2
  3 Heckington NG34 . . . . 122 D3
Oakwell Cl DN16 . . . . 185 D4

Oakwood Ave 4 LN6 . . . . . 204 C8
Oakwood Cl HU10 . . . . . . 179 A7
Oakwood Dr DN7 . . . . 190 C7
Oakwood Glade PE12 . . . . 215 C3
Oakwood Pk PE12 . . . . . . 146 E2
Oakwood Rise 2
  DN16 . . . . 185 B4
OASBY NG32 . . . . 131 C6
Oasby Rd NG32 . . . . 131 C7
Oat Dr NG34 . . . . 212 E3
Oatfield Way NG34 . . . . . . 122 D2
Oban Ave PE21 . . . . 218 E6
Oban Cl 7 DN40 . . . . 186 C3
Oberon Cl LN1 . . . . 201 C6
OBTHORPE PE10 . . . . 164 C6
Obthorpe La PE10 . . . . . . 164 C7
Occupation La
  Anderby PE24 . . . . 77 C3
  Carrington PE22 . . . . 99 C1
  6 North Kelsey LN7 . . . . . 32 A4
  Swanland HU14 . . . . 3 B8
Occupation Rd
  Great Gonerby NG32 . . . . . 129 C6
  Lincoln LN1 . . . . 234 A4
  Peterborough PE1 . . . . 225 F4
Ocean Ave PE25 . . . . 206 D1
Ocean Bvd HU9 . . . . 181 B6
Octagon Dr 14 PE13 . . . . . 170 C1
Octavia Cl 22 PE13 . . . . . 170 E1
Odecroft PE3 . . . . 225 C7
Odin Ct DN33 . . . . 191 B2
Off Haydons Ave PE25 . . . 206 A4
Ogilvy Dr DN17 . . . . 184 F3
Ogrey PE10 . . . . 164 C7
O'Hanlon Ave DN20 . . . . . 196 D3
Old Annandale Rd
  HU10 . . . . 178 C8
Old Bailey Rd PE7 . . . . . . 233 C8
Old Barn Ct
  Fleet Hargate PE12 . . . . . . 159 C8
  Ludford LN8 . . . . 59 A7
Old Barracks The
  NG31 . . . . 211 C4
Old Black Dro NG34 . . . . . 109 D1
OLD BOLINGBROKE
  PE23 . . . . 100 B8
Old Boston Rd LN4 . . . . . . 207 D3
Old Bowling Gn 4 LN13 . . . 75 F2
Old Brickkiln La LN5 . . . . . . 92 F2
Oldbrook PE3 . . . . 220 E1
Old Brumby St DN16 . . . . 185 A8
Old Carpenter's Yd 1
  DN7 . . . . 14 B6
Old Chapel Ct 2 DN21 . . . . 43 D7
Old Chapel La
  2 Burgh le Marsh
  PE24 . . . . 102 C7
  9 Laceby DN37 . . . . 23 F1
Old Chapel Rd LN6 . . . . . . 204 D8
Old Church La 1 PE23 . . . . 101 D7
Old Church Rd PE24 . . . . . . 90 D4
OLD CLEE DN32 . . . . 192 C6
Old Clee Infants & Jun Sch
  DN32 . . . . 192 B6
Old Courts Rd 2 DN20 . . . 196 C3
Old Courtyard The 1
  DN21 . . . . 65 D6
Old Crosby DN15 . . . . 183 A5
Old Dairy 11 DN10 . . . . . . 11 D8
Old Dairy The PE21 . . . . . 209 A1
Olde Curiosity Mus★
  LN12 . . . . 64 C3
Old Epworth Rd (East) 1
  DN7 . . . . 14 F4
Old Farm Ct 4 DN37 . . . . . . 24 A1
Old Fen Bank
  Wainfleet All Saints
  PE24 . . . . 101 F2
  Wainfleet St Mary PE24 . . . 102 A1
Old Fen Dike
  Gedney PE12 . . . . 158 F1
  Sutton St James PE12 . . . . 169 B8
Old Fendike Rd PE12 . . . . . 157 B3
Old Fen La
  Coningsby LN4 . . . . 207 E1
  Pinchbeck PE11 . . . . 145 A1
  Old Fen Rd PE22 . . . . 115 A8
Oldfield Cl
  3 Barnby Dun DN3 . . . . . . 14 A4
  1 Stainforth DN7 . . . . . . 14 B6
Oldfield Cres 18 DN7 . . . . . 14 C6
Oldfield La PE22 . . . . 127 C6
Old Field La DN7 . . . . 14 A5
Oldfield Rd BD8 DN8 . . . . . 15 B7
Old Fleet DN37 . . . . 190 C6
OLD FLETTON PE2 . . . . . . 231 A6
Old Fletton Prim Sch
  PE2 . . . . 230 F6
Old Forge Rd 7 DN10 . . . . . 39 F5
Old Forty Foot Bank
  NG34 . . . . 123 C1
OLD GATE PE12 . . . . 159 F3
Old Great N Rd
  Stamford PE9 . . . . 218 C8
  Thorney PE8 . . . . 228 B7
  Wansford PE8 . . . . 222 C2
  Wothorpe PE9 . . . . 219 B2
Old Hall Gdns 5 NG24 . . . 104 C5
Old Hall La 6 PE11 . . . . . . 145 D2
Old Hall Spinney NG32 . . . 119 C2
Oldham Dr 8 PE11 . . . . . . 145 C1
Old Hammond Beck Rd
  PE21 . . . . 208 A2
Old Haxey Rd DN9 . . . . 39 F6
Old Hill The NG32 . . . . . . 138 C6
Old Hundred La PE12 . . . . 167 F2
Old Inn La PE22 . . . . 146 E7
Old Ironside Rd DN16 . . . 183 D3

Old Knarr Fen Dro
  PE6 . . . . 176 C2
Old Lane DN14 . . . . 6 F7
Oldlane Gate DN14 . . . . 6 D4
OLD LEAKE PE22 . . . . 114 A1
Old Leake Prim Sch
  PE22 . . . . 114 A1
Old Leicester Rd PE8 . . . . 222 A3
Old Leys La DN21 . . . . 43 A3
Old Lincoln Rd NG34 . . . . 119 B7
Old Lynn Rd 2 PE13 . . . . . 170 E1
Old Main Rd
  2 Barnetby le Beck
  DN37 . . . . 35 B6
  Fleet Hargate PE12 . . . . . . 159 C7
  Fosdyke PE20 . . . . 146 D8
  Irby DN37 . . . . 34 D7
  Leake PE22 . . . . 114 B1
  Scambleby LN11 . . . . 72 F5
Old Market Ave
  4 Hundleby PE23 . . . . . . 87 F1
  12 Spilsby PE23 . . . . 87 F1
Old Market Pl DN31 . . . . . 191 D7
Old Mill La
  10 Broughton DN20 . . . . . 19 E3
  Grimoldby LN11 . . . . 62 B6
  Horncastle LN9 . . . . 199 C3
  Whitton DN15 . . . . 1 E3
  Wrawby DN20 . . . . 196 F7
Old Mill Pk LN11 . . . . 198 C6
Old Nick Theatre
  DN21 . . . . 197 D4
Old North Rd PE8 . . . . 222 A3
Old Oak Pl PE10 . . . . 213 E4
Old Orchard NG32 . . . . . . 210 A5
Old Paddock Ct 1
  LN9 . . . . 199 B4
Old Place 3 DN34 . . . . . . 212 F4
Old Plumtree La 3
  DN36 . . . . 36 B1
Old Pond Ct 7 LN6 . . . . . . 200 D1
Old Pond La PE5 . . . . 223 E2
Old Pond Pl HU14 . . . . 3 A4
Old Post La NG33 . . . . . . 151 D6
Old Post Office La
  8 Barnetby le Wold
  DN38 . . . . 21 B4
  Butterwick PE22 . . . . 126 E4
  4 South Ferriby DN18 . . . 10 A7
Old Rectory Dr
  7 Tallington PE9 . . . . . . 172 F7
  Wansford PE8 . . . . 222 A6
Old Rectory Gdns
  DN16 . . . . 185 A6
Old Rectory The★ DN9 . . . . 27 E6
Old Road
  Grimsby DN37 . . . . 190 C8
  Healing DN37 . . . . 24 B5
Old Roman Bank
  3 Skegness PE25 . . . . . . 206 D6
  Terrington St Clement
  PE34 . . . . 161 E3
Old School Dr 14 DN20 . . . 30 F5
Old School La
  4 Billinghay LN4 . . . . . . 109 F6
  6 Cranwell NG34 . . . . . . 120 F8
  Donington on Bain LN11 . . . 59 E2
  2 Fishtoft PE21 . . . . . . 126 C1
  8 North Kelsey LN7 . . . . . 32 A4
  Scunthorpe DN16 . . . . . . 185 B3
Old School Mews 12
  PE23 . . . . 88 A1
Old School Yd 17 DN21 . . . 30 B1
Old Showfields DN15 . . . . 197 D6
Old Sluice Rd PE12 . . . . . 215 B8
Old Smithy Ct 11 LN7 . . . . 33 B4
Old Smithy & Heritage Ctr
  The★ DN9 . . . . 23 B3
OLD SOMERBY NG33 . . . . 140 D8
Old South Eau Bank
  PE12 . . . . 168 A1
Old Stack Yd The 3
  DN20 . . . . 196 F6
Old Station Yd
  Bottesford NG13 . . . . 128 B6
  Morton PE10 . . . . 154 D6
Old Thorne Rd DN7 . . . . . . 14 E4
Old Trent Rd DN21 . . . . . . 197 A5
Old Upper Ings La DN22 . . . 52 D3
Old Vicarage La
  12 Lutton PE12 . . . . . . 160 A8
  Lutton PE12 . . . . 216 C8
Old Vicarage Pk 2
  DN20 . . . . 30 E8
Old Village St DN15 . . . . . 17 E6
Old Wainfleet Rd 1
  PE25 . . . . 206 B3
Old Warp La 11 DN18 . . . . 10 A7
Old Wharf Rd 9 NG31 . . . . 211 A4
Old Wood 1 LN6 . . . . 200 C1
Old Wood Cl LN6 . . . . 200 C1
OLD WOODHALL LN9 . . . . . 85 A2
Oliver Cl 8 NG24 . . . . 104 A4
Oliver Ct DN31 . . . . 191 D8
Olive Rd PE1 . . . . 226 C7
Oliver Quibell Cty Infants
  Sch NG24 . . . . 104 A3
Oliver Rd 18 NG23 . . . . . . 117 D3
Oliver St DN35 . . . . 192 D8
Olivier Ct HU4 . . . . 179 C5
Olivier Ave PE13 . . . . 170 D1
Olsen Rise LN2 . . . . 202 D6
Omega Bvd DN8 . . . . 14 F8
On Hill 17 HU14 . . . . 3 B7
Ontario Rd DN17 . . . . 184 A3
Onyx Gr 2 HU3 . . . . 180 A4
Oole Rd DN35 . . . . 192 F6

Oosterbeek Cl 5 PE10 . . . 213
Opporrune Rd 23 PE13 . . . 170
Orangawood Cl 7
  NG31 210
Orange Row 3 PE34 161
ORANGE ROW PE34 161
Orange Row Rd 1
  PE34 161
Orby Cl DN15 183
ORBY PE24 89
Orby Bank PE24 89
Orby Gr DN33 191
Orby Holme Field La
  PE24 89
Orby Rd
  Addlethorpe PE24 90
  Burgh le Marsh PE24 89
Orchard Ave 8 DN21 29
Orchard Cl
  4 Barrow upon Humber
  DN19 11
  22 Barton-upon-Humber
  DN18 3
  Bassingham LN5 92
  Billinghay LN4 109
  4 Blyton DN21 41
  6 Bourne PE10 213
  6 Burringham DN17 17
  9 Burton upon Stather
  DN15 8
  Cherry Willingham/Reepham
  LN3 203
  11 Donington PE11 134
  4 Gonerby Hill Foot
  NG31 210
  Great Hale NG34 122
  2 Hatfield DN7 14
  6 Helpringham NG34 . . . 133
  Kingston upon Hull HU10 . . 178
  1 Kirton in Lindsey DN21 . . 30
  Leverington PE13 170
  Louth LN11 198
  2 Mablethorpe/Sutton on Sea
  LN12 64
  4 Market Deeping PE6 . . 217
  12 Messingham DN17 . . . 29
  2 Metheringham LN4 95
  2 Morton PE10 154
  4 Moulton PE12 157
  Peterborough PE3 225
  9 Pinchbeck PE11 156
  8 Scothern LN2 68
  5 Scunthorpe DN16 185
  2 Sleaford NG34 212
  13 Stamford PE9 219
  7 Welton/Dunholme
  LN2 68
  Whaplode PE12 215
Orchard Croft
  6 Epworth DN9 27
  5 Owston DN9 193
Orchard Ct
  3 Thorney PE6 175
  Waltham DN37 194
Orchard Dr
  7 Burton upon Stather
  DN15 8
  3 Gunness DN15 17
  15 Hatfield DN7 14
  3 Heckington NG34 122
  Kingston upon Hull
  HU13 178
  1 Rampton DN22 65
  Walton Highway PE14 170
  Winteringham DN15 2
Orchard Garth 18 LN5 93
Orchard Gr
  Boston PE21 209
  1 Hatfield DN7 14
  Misterton DN10 40
Orchard La 13 LN1 66
Orchard Mews PE2 230
Orchard Pk 4 LN11 62
Orchard Rd
  Barnack PE9 172
  5 Fiskerton LN3 82
  Kingston upon Hull HU4 . . . 179
  4 Stamford PE9 219
  Orchard Sch NG24 104
Orchard St
  Boston PE21 208
  Lincoln LN1 234
  Peterborough PE2 230
  2 Spalding PE11 214
  2 Thorne/Moorends
  DN8 15
Orchards The
  Harrowby Est NG31 211
  Immingham DN40 186
  8 Middle Rasen LN8 57
  Peterborough PE2 229
Orchard The
  Market Deeping PE6 217
  New Waltham DN36 195
  Peterborough PE4 221
  Washingborough LN4 203
Orchard Way
  4 Coningsby LN4 207
  10 Cowbit PE12 167
  Easton on the Hill PE9 171
  11 Mablethorpe/Sutton on Sea
  LN12 64
  8 Market Rasen LN8 57
  6 Nettleham LN2 68
Orchid Cl PE7 233
Orchid Rd LN5 205
Orchid Rise DN15 182
Orchid Way PE25 206

rdoyno Gr **2** NG24 .... 104 C5
re Blending Rd DN16 .. 19 A4
rford Rd LN8........... 47 B5
ribi Cl HU4 .... 179 C2
riole Rd DN17.........184 E6
rion Cl **8** HU3 ....180 B5
rion Way **4** DN34 .... 190 D4
rkney Pl DN40........ 186 C2
rme La LN11 .... 198 C6
rme Rd PE3........... 225 D4
rmsby DN35 .... 192 D3
rmsby House Dr **7**
PE22................... 99 A4
rmsby Rd DN17........184 E5
rmsby Ring LN11......74 C1
rton Brick Works
PE7...................233 B8
RTON BRIMBLES
PE2...................233 B8
RTON GOLDHAY PE2...229 F3
RTON LONGUEVILLE
PE2...................230 B5
rton Longueville Sch
PE2...................230 A5
RTON MALBOURNE
PE2...................230 A4
rton Mere PE2........230 B7
rton Parkway PE2 ....229 D4
RTON SOUTHGATE
PE2...................229 C2
RTON WATERVILLE
PE2...................229 E4
RTON WISTOW PE2....229 C6
rton Wistow Prim Sch
PE2...................229 C6
rwell Gr PE4...........221 D1
rwell St DN31 ....189 C1
sborne Cl **3** LN1...... 201 E6
sborne Dr DN36...... 195 D1
sborne Pk **1** PE13 .. 170 C2
sborne Rd
Immingham DN41.......187 B2
Wisbech PE13 ....170 C2
sborne St **1**
Cleethorpes DN35 ....192 F6
Grimsby DN31 ....191 D7
Kingston upon Hull HU1 ..180 E6
sborne Way DN34.....199 A4
sborn Way **9** NG34... 122 D3
SBOURNBY NG34...... 132 C4
sbournby Prim Sch
NG34..................132 C5
sbourne Cl PE4........221 D1
sbourne Way **7** PE6...217 A5
se **3** PE25..............206 B6
seby La NG34.........133 A1
SGODBY
Lenton Keisby and Osgodby
NG33..................141 E3
Osgodby LN8...........45 A3
sgodby Prim Sch LN8...45 A3
sgodby Rd LN8.........44 E5
sier Gr PE4 ....230 D2
sier Rd PE11..........214 E5
slear Cres DN35 ......192 E5
slear's La LN11........73 D5
slinc Ostrich Farm*
PE12....................99 B7
sprey Cl LN2...........229 F2
sprey Cl **1** NG32......212 B3
sric Ct PE1............226 C5
ster Fen La NG23......104 F1
ster Cl **8** NG31........210 F8
ster Dr PE10..........213 B4
stler's La DN18........10 A5
swald Rd
Scunthorpe DN15......183 A3
1 Woodston PE2......230 D7
swim Cl **1** NG34......212 C2
RBY LN8...............46 A4
xby La LN8............46 A3
ttawa Rd DN17........184 E4
tter Ave **1** LN1........66 D2
tterbrook PE2.........229 D5
tterburn St **6** HU3 .. 180 A5
tters Cotts LN5.......205 D7
ulton Cl LN6 ....205 A2
undle Cl
Heighington/
Washingborough LN4 .. 203 C1
Scunthorpe DN16 .....185 C3
undle Rd
5 Mablethorpe/Sutton on
Sea LN12..............64 C1
or Lady of Lincoln Cath
Prim Sch LN2..........202 A7
usemere Cl **4** NG34...133 B1
uter Circ Dr LN2 .....202 C7
uter Circ Gn LN2 .....202 C6
uter Circ Ind Est LN2..202 D5
uter Circ Rd LN2 .....202 D5
utfield PE3............220 C1
utgang La DN22........45 A6
utgang The HU15......2 B7
utgate DN17 ....16 E7
st Holme La DN36.....36 E3
val App LN2...........202 B7
val The
1 Brough HU15 ....2 C5
Grimsby DN33 ....191 C1
5 Hatfield DN7.......14 C5
Kingston upon Hull
HU10..................178 B8
Lincoln LN2...........202 B7
Scopwick LN4.........108 B7
2 Scunthorpe DN17...184 E3

Overcoat La DN22.......65 B7
Overgate Rd NG33.....152 D5
Overstone Ct PE3.....225 D6
Overton Ave HU10 ....178 E8
Overton Cl **5** LN5.....107 B8
Overton Ct **9** DN18....3 E1
Overton Rd LN4.......207 D4
Overton Way PE2......229 F4
Owen Ave HU13........179 A1
Owen Cl **7** PE9........172 D3
Owe's La LN11.........51 A5
Owl Cl LN6............92 D5
Owl Dr PE20...........135 B7
Owl End PE7...........233 D5
Owl End Wlk PE7......233 D5
OWMBY DN38..........32 D7
OWMBY-BY-SPITAL
LN8....................55 F6
Owmby Cliff Rd LN8 ...55 C5
Owmby Hill DN38.......32 D8
Owmby La LN7.........32 C5
Owmby Rd
4 Searby cum Owmby
DN38...................32 B8
Spridlington LN8......55 F7
Owmby Wold La DN38..21 E1
OWSTON FERRY DN9.....28 B3
Owston Ferry Rd DN9...27 F1
Owston Rd DN10.......40 B6
Oxburgh Cl
8 Peterborough PE7 ..231 F5
1 Wisbech PE13......170 C1
Oxby Cl **17** NG34......122 E2
Oxclose PE3...........225 A8
OXCOMBE LN9.........73 D4
Oxcombe Cl DN33.....194 D7
Oxcroft Bank
Moulton PE12.........157 F1
Whaplode PE12.......158 A2
Oxeney Dr **2** LN3......69 C3
Oxford Cl LN4.........203 C1
Oxford Ct **1** NG34....212 D7
Oxford Rd
Peterborough PE1.....225 F5
5 Stamford PE9.......219 A7
Oxford St
Boston PE21..........208 F3
Cleethorpes DN35 ....192 F5
Grantham NG31.......211 B3
Grimsby DN32 ....189 B1
Kingston upon Hull HU2 ..181 A8
2 Lincoln LN5........234 B1
Market Rasen LN8.....57 D8
Scunthorpe DN16......185 D6
Oxlands La PE24......102 B7
Oxmarsh La DN19.......4 E2
Oxney Rd PE1.........226 D5
Oxney Rd Ind Est PE1..227 A6
Oyster Ct DN35.......192 C5

P

Pacey Cl LN6...........92 A6
Packhorse Gdns PE20..135 B6
Packman La LN11.....178 B8
Paddington Way PE10..154 D7
Paddock Cl
6 Ancaster NG32.....120 A2
12 Bracebridge Heath
LN4....................81 A1
Ropsley NG33.........131 B1
Paddock Cl **5** DN20...186 C3
Paddock Gn **8** PE11...214 D5
Paddock Gr **6** PE21...208 F4
Paddock La
5 Blyton DN21........41 C5
1 Metheringham LN4...95 D4
West Butterwick DN17 ..17 C1
Paddock Rd NG34...120 C8
Paddock Rise
11 Barrow upon Humber
DN19...................11 C8
Ingoldsby NG33.......141 C5
Paddocks The
1 Barnetby le Beck
DN37...................35 B6
8 Beckingham DN10 ...40 A1
6 Bottesford NG13 ...128 A5
7 Burgh le Marsh PE24..102 E7
Carlton Scroop NG32...119 C3
Gedney PE12.........159 E2
Great Hale NG34......122 E4
1 Hemswell PE12.....215 E3
Paddock The
8 Barkston NG32.....130 B8
4 Burton on Stather
DN15...................8 B4
4 Cherry Willingham
LN3....................203 E6
10 Collingham NG23...91 D4
Kingston upon Hull HU4 ..179 B5
Louth LN11...........198 A5
Manby LN11..........74 A5
1 Market Deeping PE6..217 A6
2 Marton DN21.......53 D8
2 Morton PE10.......154 C7
2 North Ferriby HU14...3 A5

Paddock The *continued*
16 Ruskington NG34 .. 108 D2
Skellingthorpe LN6 ... 200 A4
5 Sleaford NG34......212 F4
5 Stamford PE9.......219 A5
16 Sudbrooke LN2......68 F2
5 Swanland HU14 ......3 C7
Paddock View PE22....100 B2
Pademoor Terr DN17....7 A2
Padholme Rd E PE1....226 C3
Padholme Rd E PE1....226 D3
Padley Rd LN2.........202 E6
Padleys La PE23 ......100 C4
Padmoor La DN21......53 C5
Pado La LN13...........74 E4
Padstow Wlk DN17.....184 C8
Pagehall Cl DN33.....191 D1
Paignton Ct DN33.....194 C6
Pain La PE22..........113 E3
Painshall Cl **11** LN12...68 D7
Painters Way **20** LN12..76 F8
Paisley Prim Sch HU4..180 A6
Paisley St HU3.........180 A7
Palace Theatre*
NG24..................104 A4
Palma Ct **2** PE24.......90 D7
Palm Ct HU1...........226 B8
Palmer Ave HU10 .....178 D8
Palmer Ct **3** NG34....212 B6
Palmer La **15** DN19 ....11 D8
Palmer Rd NG32......129 C6
Palmers Rd PE1.......226 F5
Palmerston Rd PE2....230 F7
Palmwood Cl **3** NG31..210 F7
Pamela Cl DN40.......186 D4
Pamela Rd DN40......186 D4
Pandyke La PE22......113 F3
PANTON LN8...........71 B5
Panton Cl **6** PE6 .....217 D5
Panton Rd LN8........71 B8
Papermill La
Ewerby & Evedon
NG34..................121 E7
Tealby LN8............46 D2
Pape's La PE24 ....101 F4
Papyrus Rd PE4......220 D3
Parade The LN3.......203 E6
Paradise La
5 Fulletby LN9........86 B8
Northborough PE6....173 F6
Paradise Pl
8 Brigg DN20........196 B3
Lincoln LN6 ....199 C3
5 Scawby DN20.......30 F8
Paradise Row LN9.....199 C4
Paragon St HU1.......180 A6
Parish Church Prim Sch
DN21..................197 C5
Parishes Sh Ctr The
DN15..................183 B3
Parish Mews **3** DN21..197 C5
Parish's La PE22......115 A4
Park Ave
Allington NG32........128 F7
19 Barrow-upon-Humber
DN18...................10 F8
Billinghay LN4.........109 F5
17 Crowle DN17.......16 D7
Grimsby DN32 ....191 E4
Heighington/Washingborough
LN4....................203 D2
Kingston upon Hull
HU13..................178 B3
Lincoln LN6 ....204 F7
Louth LN11...........198 E6
21 Mablethorpe/Sutton on Sea
LN12...................64 B3
Misterton DN10........39 E6
Scunthorpe DN17 ....184 F3
Skegness PE25.......206 D4
Sleaford NG34........212 F4
Spalding PE11........214 C6
3 Spilsby PE23........87 F1
Sutterton PE20.......136 A2

Paddock Cres PE7.....231 F5
Park Farm Rd
Peterborough PE6.....224 E5
Scunthorpe DN15 ....182 F7
Park Farm Way PE7...231 F6
Parkfield Ave **14** HU14..3 A4
Parkfield Dr HU3 .....179 F6
Parkfield Rd
5 Ruskington NG34...108 C2
18 Ryhall PE9 ....163 C1
Park Gate **7** PE21.....208 F5
Park Gdns PE12.......215 E3
Park Hill
Cherry Willingham/Reepham
LN3....................203 E5
28 Kirton in Lindsey DN21..30 B1
Parkhill Cres **3** DN3....14 A4
Parkhill Rd **2** DN3.....14 A4
Parkhill Rise **7** DN15...9 B5
Park Home Ave PE7...230 D1
Park Home Rd PE7....230 D1
Parkin Rd
7 Cowbit PE12.......167 B8
Scunthorpe DN17 ....184 F4
Parkinson Ave **1**
DN15..................183 A3
Parkinson's Way **6**
LN12...................64 C2
Park La
12 Alford LN13........75 F3
Billinghay LN4........109 F5
5 Boston PE21........208 F6
Bracebridge LN5......205 D6
Burton LN1...........200 D7
Coningsby LN4........207 C4
Denton NG32.........139 A7
2 Donington PE11....134 E2
East Kirkby PE23......99 E5
Ewerby & Evedon NG34..122 B7
Freiston PE22.........126 D3
Gorefield PE13........169 F3
Heighington/Washingborough
LN4....................203 C2
Holbeach PE12.......215 E3
Humberston DN35.....192 F1
Leverington PE13.....170 A3
Long Sutton PE12....216 C5
Manby LN11...........62 C5
Peterborough PE1.....226 C4
Pinchbeck PE11.......145 D3
Redbourne DN21.......30 F3
Saxby All Saints DN20..10 A3
9 Skillington NG33...151 A8
Spalding PE11........214 C5
Stamford PE9.........219 C4
Swineshead PE20 ....135 A7
Westwoodside DN9.....27 A2
Wigsley NG23.........78 F5
Parklands
2 Fleet Hargate PE12...159 C7
Mablethorpe/Sutton on Sea
LN12...................64 B3
1 Mumby LN13........76 F1
4 West/East Butterwick
DN17...................28 D8
Parklands Ave LN6.....95 B7
Parklands Cl **4** NG24..104 C5
Parklands Cres **11** HU14..3 A5
Parklands Dr
4 Harlaxton NG32....139 C7
10 North Ferriby HU14...3 A5
Parkland Way LN6.....70 C4
Park La E HU4.........179 C5
Park La W HU4.........179 C5
Park-lea **6** DN22......102 A2
Park Rd
11 Alford LN13........75 F3
1 Allington NG32.....128 F7
Boston PE21..........208 E2
Buckminster NG33....150 E6
Claxby LN8............45 E4
Grantham NG31.......211 D2
Holbeach PE12.......215 D2
1 Horncastle LN9 ....199 C4
Long Sutton PE12....216 C5
Mablethorpe/Sutton on Sea
LN12...................64 C1
Market Deeping PE6..217 C1
Spalding PE11........214 C4
St James PE12.......169 D7
Swineshead PE20 ....135 A7
1 Weston PE12.......157 E7
Park Rd E LN12.......64 C1
Park Rd W LN12......64 C1
Park Row
Kingston upon Hull
HU3...................180 D7
Louth LN11...........198 D7
Northfield HU13.......178 E2
Parks Cl **4** DN39......12 A1
Parksgate Ave LN6....204 F5
Parkside
1 Nettleham LN2.....68 D2
Peterborough PE2.....230 B6
Parkside Cres PE11...214 C4
Parkside Dr **4** LN2 ....90 D7
Parkside The **4** NG33..151 D2
Park Springs Rd DN21..197 F2
Park Sq DN15.........183 A2
Park St **3** DN7.........14 C4
Park St
Cleethorpes DN35 ....189 D1

Ord–Pas 269

Park St *continued*
Grimsby DN32 ....192 B8
Kingston upon Hull HU3 .. 180 D6
Lincoln LN1...........234 A2
11 Messingham DN17...29 D7
Peterborough PE2.....230 F7
Swinefleet DN14.......6 D8
Winterton DN15........9 B5
Parkstone Gr **28** DN7 ...14 D4
Park Terr PE1.........226 A6
Park The
Coningsby LN4........207 D5
Lincoln LN1...........234 A2
Potter Hanworth LN4...95 B8
Park View
22 Barton-upon-Humber
DN18...................10 F8
Cleethorpes DN35 ....192 C8
Crowle DN17..........16 D6
Kingston upon Hull HU4..179 E4
Mablethorpe/Sutton on Sea
LN12...................64 C1
10 Messingham DN17...29 D7
10 Northorpe PE10....164 C8
13 Thorne/Moorends
DN8....................15 A7
Park View Ave LN4.....81 D2
Park View Cl **7** DN19...11 C7
Park View Terr DN17...28 C8
Parkway The
Kingston upon Hull
HU10..................178 E8
Spalding PE11........214 A2
Park Wlk
Easton on the Hill PE9...171 D3
Kingston upon Hull HU3..180 B8
Parkwood Prim Sch
DN17..................184 D8
Parkwood Rise **14** DN3..14 A3
Parliament St
3 Brough HU15........2 D6
Kingston upon Hull
HU1...................180 F6
Peterborough PE1.....225 F5
Parnell St **3** LN2......197 C5
Parnwell Prim Sch
PE1...................226 F7
Parnwell Way PE1 ....226 F6
Parr Cl DN35..........192 D7
Parry Rd PE2 LN12....64 B3
Parslins The PE6......217 F5
Parsonage La PE12...159 F1
Parson Dro
Billinghay LN4........109 F7
Pinchbeck PE11.......144 B2
Parson Dro La PE13...178 D2
PARSON DROVE PE13..177 D7
Parson's Drove
Parsons La DN15......106 C8
Parsons Dr **3** PE25...208 E7
Parson's Dro
Holland Fen with Brothertoft
PE20..................124 A8
Swaton NG34.........133 D4
Parsons Halt **1** LN11..198 C6
Parsons La **18** LN13....75 F2
Parsons Rd LN12......168 B4
Parthian Ave PE12....136 D8
PARTNEY PE23........88 A3
Partney CE (Aided) Prim
Sch PE23.............88 B3
Partney Rd PE23......87 C3
Partridge Cl
4 Caistor LN7........33 B4
Scunthorpe DN17.....184 E6
Yaxley PE7............233 D6
Partridge Dr LN7......33 F2
Partridge Gn PE4.....220 E5
Pashley Rd DN8.......15 B7
PASTON PE4...........221 D1
Paston Farm Adventure
Ctr* PE4..............221 E2
Paston La PE4.........221 B1
Paston Parkway PE4...221 C4
Paston Ridings PE4...221 C1
Paston Ridings Prim Sch
PE4...................221 D1
Pasture Ave **9** DN17...17 D4
Pasture Cl
7 Colsterworth NG33 ..151 E2
Grantham NG31.......211 D1
Pasture Dr DN11......198 D4
Pasture Dr PE10......154 F7
Pasture La
Amcotts DN17..........7 D1
Bassingham LN5.......93 B2
Belvoir NG32.........138 C6
Garthorpe & Fockerby
DN17...................7 D6
Market Rasen LN8.....57 E8
Northborough PE6....173 F6
Pasture Rd DN21.....197 F4
Pasture Rd N DN18...3 F1
Pasture Rd S DN18....4 A1
Pastures Rd **38** DN32....29 D7
Pastures Rd DN32....191 E7
Pastures The
8 Cowbit PE12.......167 B8
12 Long Bennington
NG33..................117 D3
Old Somerby NG33...140 E8
12 Rampton DN22.....65 A5
12 Welton LN2.........68 C5
Pasture The PE6......217 C6

Pasture Wharf Nature
Reserve* DN18 . . . . .4 A2
Patchett Cl DN33 . . . . .191 B2
Patch Rd LN6 . . . . .92 D4
Pateley Moor Cl **13** LN6 . . .93 C8
Patman's La PE22 . . . . . . .114 E4
Patricks Cl **5** LN7 . . . . .32 A4
Patrick St DN32 . . . . .191 E5
Patriot Cl PE11 . . . . .214 C4
Patten Ave **2** PE24 . . . . .102 D1
Patterdale Rd
 Kingston upon Hull
 HU5. . . . . .179 E8
 3 Peterborough PE4 . . . .221 E2
Paul Cres **4** DN36 . . . . . . .36 C8
Paulette Ct **11** PE11. . . . .214 B5
Paul La **1** DN15 . . . . .9 D1
Paulsgrove PE2 . . . . .229 D5
Paul's La LN6. . . . . .207 C7
Paul's Wlk DN17. . . . . .184 B7
Pavilion Gdns
 3 Scunthorpe DN17. . . .182 F2
 5 Sleaford NG34 . . . . .212 D3
Pavilion Way DN36. . . . . . .195 C7
Paving Way LN6. . . . . .204 C4
Pawlett Cl PE6 . . . . .217 D5
Paxton Rd PE2. . . . . .229 D4
Payne Ave PE13 . . . . .170 D1
Paynell **22** LN2 . . . . .68 D6
Paynells PE2 . . . . .230 A3
Payne Sch PE13 . . . . .177 D7
Paynesholm PE4. . . . . .221 E1
Peace Haven **2** DN37 . . .194 C5
Peach Tree Cl **5**
 DN16. . . . . .185 D4
Peach Tree Ct **5** HU3 . .180 D5
Peachwood Cl **4**
 NG31. . . . . .210 F8
Peacock Cl **5** NG34 . . . .212 E3
Peacock's Rd PE22 . . . . . .112 B1
Peacock St DN17 . . . . .184 F5
Peacocks The NG23 . . . . .117 D3
Peacock Way PE3. . . . . . . .224 F2
Peak Dale LN6. . . . . .204 A2
Peake Cl PE2 . . . . .230 F6
PEAKIRK PE6 . . . . .174 A5
Peakirk-cum-Glinton CE
 Prim Sch PE6 . . . . .220 C8
Peakirk Rd
 Deeping Gate PE6 . . . . . .217 F3
 Glinton PE6 . . . . .220 D8
 Peterborough PE6. . . . . .174 A7
Peaks Ave DN16 . . . . .195 C7
Peaksfield Ave DN32 . . . . .191 F5
Peaks La
 Grimsby DN36. . . . . .191 F2
 New Waltham DN36. . . . .195 D7
Peaks Parkway
 Grimsby DN32. . . . . .191 E5
 New Waltham DN36. . . . .192 A1
Pearces La **5** PE10 . . . . .154 C7
Pearces Rd PE6. . . . . .227 B5
Pearl Cl **8** PE25 . . . . .206 C4
Pearl Ct PE22. . . . . .215 D3
Pearl Leisure Ctr PE5 . . . .223 E1
Pea Rm Craft Ctr &
 Heckington Village Trust
 Sta Mus* NG34 . . . . . . .122 F2
Pearson Prim Sch
 LN11 . . . . .180 D8
Pearson Rd DN35. . . . . . . .192 F3
Pearson St **5** HU2. . . . . .180 E7
Peartree Cl **5** LN6. . . . . .200 D1
Pear Tree Cl
 4 Epworth DN9 . . . . . . .27 D6
 Sleaford NG34. . . . . .212 D2
 Waltham DN37. . . . . .194 D4
Pear Tree Cres **2**
 PE13. . . . . .170 B1
Peartree Hill Rd PE12. . . . .168 B8
Peartree House Rd
 PE12. . . . . .215 F7
Pear Tree La
 Covenham St Bartholomew
 LN11 . . . . .49 B6
 Great Hanworth DN7 . . . .14 A8
 Utterby DN36. . . . . .48 E5
Pear Tree Rd PE20 . . . . . .136 D5
Peascliffe Dr NG31. . . . . . .211 A8
Peaseholme HU13 . . . . . . .178 C1
Peasgate La
 Toynton All Saints
 PE23. . . . . .100 F6
Peaslin St Peter PE23. . . . .101 A7
Peashill La NG32 . . . . .139 B8
Peat Carr Bank DN9 . . . . . .26 C3
Peatlings La PE13. . . . . . . .170 C1
Pebble Cl **4** PE12 . . . . . .160 E4
Peck Ave PE21. . . . . .208 D4
Peck Hill NG33 . . . . .131 B1
Peckover Cl **4** PE7 . . . . .231 F5
Peckover Prim Sch
 PE13. . . . . .170 C1
Pecks Dro W **4** LN6. . . .78 A1
Peddars Ct **18** LN4. . . . . .81 A1
Peddars Way PE13 . . . . . . .225 A2
Pedlar La LN11 . . . . .62 A7
Pedley La **15** PE13 . . . . .170 C1
Peel Castle Rd **10** DN6 . .15 D7
Peele Sch The PE12. . . . . .216 D6
Peel Hill Rd **9** DN8. . . . . .15 B7
Peel St
 Kingston upon Hull
 HU3. . . . . .180 D8

Peel St continued
 Lincoln LN5 . . . . .201 E1
Pegasus Gr **6** PE10. . . . .213 E7
Pegasus Rd DN20 . . . . .21 A8
Pelham Ave DN33. . . . . . . .191 C1
Pelham Cl
 20 Barton-upon-Humber
 DN18. . . . . .10 E8
 Peterborough PE3 . . . . . .224 F2
 7 Sudbrooke LN2. . . . . .68 F2
Pelham Ct **1** DN41 . . . . . .23 A4
Pelham Dr **1** HU9. . . . . . .181 C7
 Pelham Ind Est DN40 . . . .186 D6
Pelham Pl DN33 . . . . .191 C1
Pelham Rd
 Claxby LN8. . . . . .45 D6
 Cleethorpes DN35. . . . . .192 D7
 Grimsby DN31. . . . . .191 C1
 2 Holton le Clay DN36. .195 C2
 Immingham DN40 . . . . . . .186 B3
 1 Skegness PE25. . . . .206 C4
Pelham Sq **8** DN35 . . . . .192 E7
Pelham St LN5 . . . . .234 B1
Pelham View **3** DN20. . . .30 F5
Pell Pl **7** PE21 . . . . .209 C4
Pell's Dr **5** PE20 . . . . . . .136 D5
Pemberton Dr DN36 . . . . . .195 B4
Pemberton St **1** HU8. . . .181 B7
Pembrey Cl **18** LN6 . . . . .204 C7
Pembroke Ave
 Peterborough PE2 . . . . . .229 F5
 Scunthorpe DN16. . . . . . .185 A3
 Yarborough DN34 . . . . . . .191 A7
Pembroke Cl **1** PE6 . . . . .220 D8
Pembroke Rd
 Grimsby DN34 . . . . .191 A5
 Stamford PE9. . . . . .219 A7
Pendeen Cl
 6 Gainsborough
 DN21. . . . . .197 E6
 New Waltham DN36. . . . .195 C7
Pendine Cres LN6 . . . . . . .205 A1
Pendlebury Dr **4** PE6. . .217 D5
Pendleton DN35. . . . . .225 B6
Pendred Ave LN6. . . . . .94 D4
Pendreth Pl DN35. . . . . . . .192 D7
Pendula Rd PE13 . . . . .170 E1
Penfold La **1** LN4 . . . . . .203 C2
Pengleton Cl **2** NG33. . .151 D2
Penistone Ct **2** HU9. . . .181 D7
Pennell St LN5 . . . . .201 E1
Pennine Rd **7** DN8 . . . . . .15 A7
Pennine Way
 Gonerby Hill Foot
 NG31. . . . . .210 E7
 Peterborough PE2 . . . . . .221 B2
 Spalding PE11. . . . . .214 E6
Pennington Cl PE2. . . . . . .229 E3
Pennington St **1** HU8. . .181 B7
Pennycress Cl LN2. . . . . . .202 C8
Pennyfield **16** PE11. . . . .156 E8
Pennygate PE11 . . . . .214 A4
Penny Gdns **6** PE20. . . .136 C5
PENNY HILL PE12 . . . . . . .215 D6
Pennyhill Cl PE11 . . . . .214 C6
Penny Hill Rd PE12 . . . . . .215 E3
Penny Toft La PE11 . . . . . .214 B8
Penrose Cl **19** LN6. . . . . .93 C8
Penshurst Ave HU13 . . . . .178 F3
Penshurst Rd DN35 . . . . . .192 D4
Penswick Gr **6** NG24 . . .104 C5
Pentelow Ct CF13. . . . . . . .177 D5
Pentland Dr
 20 North Hykeham LN6. . .93 B8
 Sleaford NG34. . . . . .121 A2
Pentlands The **2** PE4 . . .221 C2
Penwald Ct **7** PE6. . . . . .175 B8
Penway Dr PE11. . . . . .214 B8
Penwith Dr HU10 . . . . .178 F7
Peover Cl **4** DN9 . . . . . . .225 A1
Peploe Cres **10** DN19. . . . .4 B2
Peploe La **3** DN19. . . . . . .4 A2
Peppercorn Cl
 3 Lincoln LN6. . . . . . . .201 D1
 Peterborough PE7 . . . . . .230 A2
Peppercorn Wlk
 5 Grimsby DN32 . . . . .191 E7
 8 Holton le Clay DN36. .195 D2
Peppermint Gr **7**
 PE25. . . . . .206 D2
Pepper's La NG34. . . . . . . .133 C4
Peppin La LN11. . . . . .49 A2
Perceron Dr **4** PE11. . . . .214 A2
Percival St
 Peterborough PE3. . . . . .225 E2
 Scunthorpe DN15 . . . . . .183 A4
Percy St
 8 Kingston upon Hull
 HU2. . . . . .180 E7
 1 Lincoln LN2. . . . . . . .202 B3
 3 Scunthorpe DN16. . .183 B2
Peregrine Cl
 Kingston upon Hull
 HU4. . . . . .179 D2
 6 Sleaford NG34 . . . . .212 B3
Peregrine Dr **2** PE6. . . . .175 B8
Peregrine Pl PE10 . . . . . . .213 E3
Peregrine St **7** LN6 . . . . . .93 C8
Perkin Field PE4. . . . . .161 F2
Perkins Cl **2** DN37. . . . . .190 F8
Perkins La PE12 . . . . .173 C6
Permain Cl DN33 . . . . .191 E1
Perney Cres **17** LN6. . . . . .93 C8
Pernys Cl PE7 . . . . .230 D3
Perrin Ave **6** PE25 . . . . . .206 A5
Perriwinkle Way PE10. . . . .213 D3
Perry Rd PE13 . . . . .170 B2
Perry St HU3 . . . . .180 A6

Pershore Ave DN34 . . . . . .190 D4
Pershore Way
 Birchwood LN6 . . . . .204 C6
 Eye PE6 . . . . .175 B2
Perth Ave **1** PE25. . . . . . .206 A4
Perth Rd PE9 . . . . .218 E6
Perth St W HU5 . . . . .180 A8
Perth St HU5 . . . . .179 F8
Perth Way DN40 . . . . .186 B2
Pescod Sq **27** PE21 . . . .208 F5
Petchell Way **2** DN32. . .191 F8
PETERBOROUGH PE3. . . .225 D5
Peterborough Cath*
 PE1 . . . . .226 A2
Peterborough Dr **10**
 NG31. . . . . .210 E5
Peterborough Coll of Adult
 Ed PE1. . . . . .226 B3
Peterborough District
 PE3. . . . . .226 A3
Peterborough Dr PE6 . . . . .224 E2
Peterborough Her Ctr*
 PE3. . . . . .225 A1
Peterborough High Sch
 PE3. . . . . .225 D2
Peterborough Mus & Art
 Gall* PE3. . . . . .225 F2
Peterborough NV Sta
 PE2. . . . . .225 F1
Peterborough Rd
 Castor PE5. . . . . .223 E1
 10 Collingham NG23 . . .91 D5
 23 Eye PE6 . . . . .175 A1
 Langtoft PE6 . . . . .217 A8
 Newborough PE6 . . . . . . .174 E4
 Peterborough PE7 . . . . . .231 C3
 Scunthorpe DN16 . . . . . .185 B7
 Wansford PE8 . . . . .222 A3
Peterborough Regional
 Coll PE1 . . . . .226 B5
Peterborough Sta PE3 . . . .225 F2
Peterborough Way
 NG34 . . . . .212 C7
 Grimsby DN37 . . . . .188 A1
 Holbeach PE12. . . . . .215 C3
 Lincoln LN1. . . . . .201 E8
 4 Sleaford NG34 . . . . .212 D3
 Stamford PE9. . . . . .219 B5
 7 Waddington LN5. . . . .93 E8
Peterhouse Cl
 Peterborough PE3 . . . . . .225 E3
 1 Stamford PE9. . . . . .219 B7
Peterhouse Ct **14** DN4. .185 A4
Peterhouse Rd DN34 . . . . .190 F6
Peter Paine Cl PE22 . . . . . .126 F4
Peter Paine Sports Ctr
 PE21. . . . . .208 B5
Peter Seadike La PE11. . . .145 D5
Petersfield Cl LN6. . . . . . . .204 B7
Peter's La LN13. . . . . .63 B2
Petersport PE12 . . . . .160 D3
Pethley La NG34 . . . . .143 A6
Petticoat La **15** PE21. . . .208 F5
Pettit Way **5** PE21 . . . . . .209 C4
Petts Cl **5** PE13 . . . . .170 E1
Petts La PE12. . . . . .160 F5
Petuaria Cl HU15 . . . . .2 B6
Petworth Cl **2** PE6 . . . . .217 A5
Peveril Ave DN17. . . . . .184 F8
Peveril Rd PE1 . . . . .225 F6
Pheasant Cl **5** DN17. . . .184 E6
Pheasant St **1** LN7. . . . . . .33 B4
Pheasant Gr **4** PE24 . . . .220 E5
Pheasant Way PE7 . . . . . . .233 D5
Phelps Pl DN32 . . . . .192 C5
Phelps St DN35. . . . . .189 D1
Philip Ave
 Cleethorpes DN35. . . . . .192 D4
 Waltham DN37. . . . . .194 E5
Philip Ct **4** DN33. . . . . . . .204 F1
Philip Gr
 Cleethorpes DN35. . . . . .192 D4
 Skegness PE25 . . . . .206 B4
Philips Cres DN15 . . . . . . .182 F3
Phillips Ct **6** PE9. . . . . . .219 C4
Phillips La **6** DN37 . . . . . .23 F1
Phoenix Clayton Sch
 PE2. . . . . .230 B4
Phoenix Ct DN21. . . . . .197 F3
Phoenix Parkway
 DN15. . . . . .182 E7
Phoenix St **6** DN32. . . . .191 D7
Phorpres Cl PE7 . . . . .230 D3
Phorpres Way PE7 . . . . . . .230 E3
Phyllis Ave DN34. . . . . .191 B7
Phyllis Taylor Gdns
 DN32 . . . . .191 D7
Piccadilly **4** DN36. . . . . .195 C6
Piccadilly Way **1**
 PE10. . . . . .154 C6
Pickards Way PE13 . . . . . .170 C1
Pickathorpe La LN11. . . . . . .50 E6
Pickering Ct **6** DN37 . . . .190 F8
Pickering Gr **15** DN8 . . . .15 A7
Pickering High Sch Sports
 Coll HU4. . . . . .179 C1
Pickering's Meadow Nature
 Reserve* LN2. . . . . .68 F4
Pickerings The **19** HU14 . .3 A4
Pick Hill La
 Grimoldby LN11. . . . . .62 C8
 South Cockerington LN11. .50 C1
Picksley Cres DN35 . . . . . .195 D1
PICKWORTH
 Pickworth NG34. . . . . . . .142 A8
 Pickworth PE9 . . . . .162 E4
Pickworth Rd PE9 . . . . .162 F2
Pickworth Rd DN16 . . . . . .155 A3
Pidgeon Cote La **20**
 DN16. . . . . .12 A8
Pied Bull Cl **8** PE9 . . . . .171 A3

Pier St **9** HU1. . . . . .180 F5
Pietermaritz St **1** LN1. . .201 E8
Pieter Maritz View **15**
 LN1. . . . . .201 E8
Pike Dam La PE12 . . . . . . .159 A6
Pilgrim Ave DN40. . . . . . . .186 D3
Pilgrim Hospl PE21 . . . . . .209 A8
Pilgrim Rd PE21 . . . . .209 A4
Pilgrim's Cl **5** DN40 . . . . .12 E3
Pilgrims Way DN40 . . . . . . .186 A4
Pilgrim's Way PE11 . . . . . .214 A4
PILHAM DN21. . . . . .41 D4
Pilham Ct DN21. . . . . .197 F3
Pilham Cl DN21. . . . . .41 C4
Pilley's La PE21. . . . . .125 F5
Pilmore La PE12 . . . . .157 B6
Pilots View DN18. . . . . .3 E2
Pilots Way HU9. . . . . .181 B5
PILSGATE PE9 . . . . .172 C4
Pilton Cl PE4 . . . . .221 D1
Pimpernel Way **2**
 DN16. . . . . .185 D4
PINCHBECK PE11. . . . . . . .156 E8
Pinchbeck Ave **1**
 DN16 . . . . .183 C2
Pinchbeck E CE Prim Sch
 PE11. . . . . .156 E8
Pinchbeck Engine Mus*
 PE11 . . . . .145 E1
Pinchbeck Fen Slipe
 Nature Reserve*
 PE11 . . . . .156 A6
Pinchbeck La PE24 . . . . . . .102 F4
Pinchbeck Rd
 5 Butterwick PE22 . . . .126 E3
 Spalding PE11 . . . . .214 D5
PINCHBECK WEST
 PE11. . . . . .156 A7
Pinder La **10** PE11 . . . . . .134 F2
Pinder Dr **2** PE22 . . . . . . .114 B5
Pine Cl
 14 Balderton NG24 . . . .104 C3
 Grimsby DN37 . . . . .188 A1
 Holbeach PE12. . . . . .215 C3
 Lincoln LN1. . . . . .201 E8
 4 Sleaford NG34 . . . . .212 D3
 Stamford PE9. . . . . .219 A7
 7 Waddington LN5. . . . .93 E8
Pine Ct
 8 Cleethorpes DN35. . .192 D7
 Spalding PE11 . . . . .214 F4
Pinefield Ave **4** DN3. . . . .14 A3
Pinefield Rd **3** DN3 . . . . . .14 A3
Pine Hall Rd DN3 . . . . .14 A3
Pine Mdws HU10. . . . . .178 B8
Pines The DN21. . . . . .197 F2
Pinetree Ave **1** DN21. . . .29 E4
Pine Tree Cl PE11 . . . . .214 E4
Pinetrees St **4** NG34 . . . .212 E4
Pine Wlk
 5 Brough HU15 . . . . .2 C6
 4 Healing DN41. . . . . . .24 A5
Pinewood Ave PE8. . . . . . . .172 B1
Pinewood Cl
 Bottesford DN16 . . . . . . .185 A4
 4 Bourne PE10 . . . . . . .213 B5
Pinewood Cres DN33. . . . .190 F3
Pinewood Dr NG31. . . . . . .210 F8
Pinewood Gr **2** HU5. . . . .179 C2
Pinfold **15** DN9 . . . . .27 E6
Pinfold Cl
 7 Bottesford NG13 . . . .128 A6
 8 Collingham NG23 . . . .91 D5
 13 Northorpe PE10 . . . .164 C8
 Osbournby NG34 . . . . . . .143 B6
 Pointon & Sempringham
 NG34 . . . . .143 B6
 4 Ruskington NG34 . . . .108 E4
 South Rauceby NG34. . . .120 E4
 2 Stallingborough DN41. .23 D6
 Stamford PE9 . . . . .219 C3
 Stickney PE22 . . . . .113 A6
 Swaby LN13 . . . . .74 E4
 Walcott LN4 . . . . .109 C7
 Weston PE12 . . . . .157 D8
Pinfold Rd
 Bourne PE10 . . . . .213 F5
 Castle Bytham NG33 . . . .152 D1
Pinfold The LN4 . . . . .108 A3
Pinfold Way **11** NG34. . . .108 E4
Pinfold Way **2** DN20. . . . .20 E8
Pingle La
 Bishop Norton LN8 . . . . . .43 D3
 20 Wellingore LN5. . . . .107 A7
Pingle Nature Reserve
 The* LN4. . . . . .207 D5
Pingles The **9** PE10 . . . . .164 C8
Pingle The **2** DN34 . . . . .133 B1
Pingley La DN20 . . . . .196 D2
Pingley Mdw DN20. . . . . . .196 D2

Pinney's Ct DN41 . . . . .23 F1
Pinnings La DN21. . . . . .43 D
Pinstock La **10** PE12 . . . .159 C2
Pioneer Way LN6 . . . . .201 E
Pipistrelle Ct **4** PE4 . . . . .221 A
Pippin Cl **1** DN21. . . . . . .198 C
Pippin Ct **1** DN15 . . . . . .182 C
Pippin Dr DN16. . . . . .185 B
Pipwell Gate PE12 . . . . . . .146 E
Pitcher Row La PE7. . . . . . .136 B
Pit La
 Gedney PE12 . . . . .149 A
 Great Ponton NG33 . . . . .140 B
 Ketton PE9 . . . . .171 A
Pitman Ave **22** DN16 . . . .10 E
Pitmoor La **3** DN39. . . . . . .12 A
Pitt La DN10. . . . . .39 C
Pittneys PE4 . . . . .221 D
Pitts Rd LN4. . . . . .203 C
Pitt St HU3 . . . . .179 F
Pk Com Prim Sch
 DN21. . . . . .208 E
Plains La DN8 . . . . .15 F
Plane St HU3 . . . . .180 A
Planet Ice PE3. . . . . .220 E
Plank Dro PE6. . . . . .175 B
Plantain Cl **1** DN16 . . . . .185 D
Plantation Dr HU14 . . . . .2 F
Plantation Rd
 Cranwell & Byard's Leap
 NG34. . . . . .107 C
 20 Thorne/Moorends
 DN8. . . . . .15 A
Planting Rd NG33. . . . . . . .140 B
Plash Dro PE13 . . . . .177 F
Plassey Rd **6** DN21. . . . . .55 A
Platform Dr PE12 . . . . .216 A
Platts La
 Bucknall LN10 . . . . .84 B
 Tetford LN9 . . . . .72 A
Platt's La NG12 . . . . .118 B
Playgarth Est LN4 . . . . .108 E
Playhouse The* NG34 . . . .212 D
Playhouse Yd **3** NG34 . . .212 D
Playing Field La **2** LN8 . . .59 A
Playtowers* DN35 . . . . .193 B
Pleasance Way LN11. . . . . .62 C
Pleasant Ave LN11. . . . . . .198 D
Pleasant Gr **2** PE4. . . . . .198 C
Pleasant La LN6. . . . . .105 E
Pleasant Pl **1** LN6. . . . . .205 E
Pleasure Island Theme
 Pk* DN35. . . . . .193 C
Plimsoll Way HU9. . . . . . . .181 B
Plot La NG23 . . . . .91 E
Plough Dr **18** LN8. . . . . . .57 D
Plough Hill **22** LN7. . . . . . .33 B
Plough La
 1 Cherry Willingham/
 Reepham LN3 . . . . .82 A
 6 Fiskerton LN3. . . . . . .82 A
 6 Newborough LN6 . . . .174 E
Plover Ct **15** DN18. . . . . . . .3 E
Plover Dr **15** HU15 . . . . . . .2 C
Plover Gr LN6 . . . . .204 E
Ploverly **2** PE4. . . . . .221 A
Plover Rd **1** PE9 . . . . . . .163 D
Plover Sq **12** LN7 . . . . . . .33 B
Plowden Rd HU3 . . . . .179 F
Plowright Theatre*
 DN15. . . . . .183 A
Plum Tree Dr **3** DN36 . . . .37 C
Plumtree Hill Rd DN7 . . . . . .14 C
Plumtree La **2** DN36 . . . . .36 B
Plum Tree Way DN16. . . . . .185 A
Plymouth Cl **7** DN15. . . . . .9 A
Plymouth Rd DN17. . . . . . .182 C
Poachers Brook LN6. . . . . .204 A
Poacher's Croft **8** DN9 . . .16 E
Poachers Ct **22** LN1. . . . .66 D
Poachers Gate **4**
 PE11. . . . . .145 B
Poachers Hide **2**
 PE11. . . . . .145 B
Poachers La LN2 . . . . .68 D
Poachers Mdw **20** LN2 . . .68 D
Poachers Rest **3** LN1 . . . .66 D
Pocklington Cres **2**
 NG24 . . . . .104 B
Pocklington Rd **24**
 NG23 . . . . .91 D
Pocklington Way **10**
 NG34. . . . . .122 E
PODE HOLE PE11 . . . . .156 C
Pode La PE22. . . . . .113 F
Poffinder Wood Rd DN7 . . .14 E
POINTON NG34 . . . . .143 B
Pointon Rd NG34 . . . . .143 B
Point Rd PE25. . . . . .90 F
Poles Bank PE10 . . . . .53 C
Policemans La **2** LN4 . . .203 C
Pollam Cl **3** DN35 . . . . . .192 D
Pollyatt La PE11 . . . . .67 E
Pollyplatt Prim Sch LN1. . . .67 F
Polton Cl **3** DN41 . . . . . . .23 A
Polton Toft **2** DN7. . . . . . .14 D
Polyanthus Dr **4** NG34. . .212 F
Polygon Wlk **4** NG31. . . . .211 F
Pond La **4** PE10. . . . . .213 E
Pond Side DN19 . . . . .11 C
Pond St
 Great Gonerby NG31. . . . .129 D
 8 Harlaxton NG32 . . . . .139 C
Ponds Way **10** DN18. . . . . .3 E
Ponsonby Dr PE24 . . . . . . .230 D
Ponton Ave NG31. . . . . . . .211 E
Ponton Rd NG33. . . . . .140 D
Poolbank La HU15 . . . . .2 E

ool Dr DN17............184 F4
oole's La **8** PE23......87 F1
ooley Way PE7.........233 D6
ools La **8** PE20........136 A2
oor Gdn Rd NG34.......132 F6
oor Plat La LN13 ......62 F3
ope's La
Leverington PE13 .... 170 A2
Terrington St Clement
  PE34...................161 E2
op Way PE1...........225 E8
oplar Ave
Lincoln LN6........... 201 C3
Mablethorpe/Sutton on Sea
  LN12...................64 A5
Peterborough PE1 ...... 226 C8
oplar Cl
Anlaby with Anlaby Common
  HU4................. 179 A5
Boston PE21 .... 208 D2
Ruskington NG34........108 E2
oplar Cres PE10 ......213 B6
oplar Ct
5 Old Leake PE22 ...... 114 A1
Spalding PE11 ....214 B4
oplar Dr
Brigg DN20 .... 196 C5
6 Broughton DN20..... 19 D3
2 Gosberton PE11....145 C6
Humberston DN36....... 193 B1
oplar Gdns DN16 ......185 B7
oplar Gr
5 Cleethorpes DN35 ...192 E7
3 Scotter DN21.........29 C3
oplar La DN21.........41 D2
oplar Rd
Bucknall LN10 ....84 A3
3 Cleethorpes DN35....192 E7
6 Hatfield DN7..........14 C4
3 Healing DN41.........23 F5
oplar Rd Bsns Units
DN35..................192 E7
oplars Mobile Homes
DN15..................182 B5
oplar St LN5 ....205 D5
oplar Dro PE13 ....169 D1
opple St HU9..........181 B6
opplewell Cl **3** DN9 ....16 E2
opplewell Terr **13** DN9 ..27 E6
oppy Cl
Boston PE21...........208 B4
1 Scunthorpe DN15 .... 182 C6
oppyfield Way DN20 ..196 B4
oppy Pl PE10...........213 D3
orcher Way PE21.......208 C6
ortal Gn **8** PE25 ......206 A5
ortchester Cl PE2 .....231 F5
orter's La **4** PE9 .....171 D3
orter St
Kingston upon Hull
  HU3.................180 E5
Scunthorpe DN15 ......183 A4
orthcawl Cl **12** NG31...211 D7
ort La PE5 ....223 E1
ortland Ave
Grimsby DN32 ....191 E4
Peterborough PE1......225 F7
ortland Dr **6** PE25 ....206 A7
ortland Manor DN32...191 E4
ortland Pl
Grimsby DN32..........191 E4
9 Kingston upon Hull
  HU2.................180 E7
ortland St
Boston PE21...........208 E5
Kingston upon Hull HU2 .180 D7
Lincoln LN5 ....234 B1
ortland Terr **5** DN21...197 D3
ortman Cl PE3 ....225 C4
ortman Rd DN35.......182 E6
ortsmouth Cl **1**
HU3..................210 F5
ortsmouth Wlk HU4 ..179 B4
ORT SUTTON BRIDGE
PE12..................160 F4
ostergate HU1 ....180 F6
ostland Rd PE6........166 F1
ost Office Hill NG33 ..151 B5
ost Office La
Ashby cum Fenby DN37....35 D3
Burton Coggles NG33 ... 152 C8
2 Humberside Airport
  DN39..................22 A6
5 Spilsby PE23..........88 A1
3 Sutterton PE20....... 136 A2
Whitton DN15 .... 1 E3
osts The NG32.........129 B3
otesgrave Way **8**
NG34 .... 122 D3
ot La PE20 ....146 E8
ottergate LN2 ....234 B3
ottergate Cl **1** LN5....93 F7
ottergate Rd
Ancaster NG32 .... 120 A3
Caythorpe NG32....... 119 E7
Fulbeck NG32..........106 E1
Normanton NG32......119 E5
Welbourn LN5..........106 F4
OTTERHANWORTH
LN4...................82 B1
OTTERHANWORTH
BOOTHS LN4.........82 C2
otterhanworth CE
(Controlled) Prim Sch
LN4...................82 B1
otterhanworth Rd
Branston & Mere LN4......82 A1
Heighington LN4 ....81 F3

Potterhanworth Rd *continued*
Potter Hanworth LN4 ......95 B8
Potters Cl **2** PE10.......213 E4
Potter's Lodge Meadows
  Nature Reserve*
  NG33..................152 B2
Potters Way PE1........226 B1
Pottinger Gdns **5** LN7...33 A3
Potts La DN17...........16 D7
Poulter Ave PE2 ....231 D5
Pound Rd LN4..........96 C2
Poverty La LN11 ....61 B2
Powells Cres DN16.......185 B6
Powell St PE2 ....209 C2
Pratt Ave PE4...........221 D2
Prebend La LN11 ....68 C7
Precinct Cres
2 Skegness PE25.......103 B4
5 Skegness PE25.......103 A4
Precincts The **5** PE6 ....217 B5
Precinct The DN17 ......184 D7
Premier Ct **6** NG31......211 A5
Prenton Cl **8** LN6........205 A5
Prescott Ave **11** HU15.....2 C5
Prescott Gr **3** DN7 ......14 D4
Prestland PE6 ....217 A6
Preston Dr DN20........196 C4
Prestongate HU13 ....178 E1
Preston La **18** DN18 ......10 F8
Prestwick Cl
2 Birchwood LN6........200 B1
Londonthorpe & Harrowby
  without NG31..........211 E7
Pretoria Rd NG31........210 E7
Pretoria St HU3..........179 F5
Pretymen Cres DN36.....195 C5
Prial Ave LN6...........205 B6
Prial Cl LN7 ....205 C6
Pride Parkway NG34......212 F7
Pridmore Rd NG33.......152 E8
Priestfield Dro **1**
  PE12..................159 D7
Priestgate
1 Barton-upon-Humber
  DN18 ....10 F8
4 Peterborough PE1.....226 A2
Priestley Cl **7** PE20.....136 C5
Priest's House* PE9 ....171 C3
Primitive Chapel La **1**
  DN40 ....12 F2
Primrose Cl
8 Healing DN41.........23 F5
5 Lincoln LN5..........205 C2
6 Morton PE10 ....154 D6
11 North Hykeham LN6....93 A8
Peterborough PE1......226 A8
9 Skegness PE25.......206 A5
Primrose Cres
Boston PE21...........208 B4
4 Pinchbeck PE11......156 E8
Primrose Dr
8 Kingston upon Hull
  HU5..................179 D3
Yaxley PE7............233 F7
Primrose La **4** NG34.....107 C1
Primroses **1** PE6 ....217 D5
Primrose St DN21.......197 D3
Primrose Way
6 Grantham NG31 ......211 D2
Humberston DN35 ......192 E1
Scunthorpe DN15 ......182 C6
5 Spalding PE11 ......214 A2
Stamford PE9...........218 C2
Prince Albert Gdns **2**
  DN32 ....189 A1
Prince Alfred Ave **1**
  PE25..................206 D3
Prince Ave **8** PE24 ......90 D7
Prince Charles Ave **1**
  LN8....................70 D4
Prince Charles Dr **32**
  DN18 ....10 F8
Prince George St PE25..206 C3
Prince of Wales Cl **12**
  PE13..................170 D2
Prince Philip Dr DN18 ...10 F7
Princes Ave
Grimsby DN31 .... 191 C7
Kingston upon Hull
  HU3..................178 E1
Princes Ct **15** LN6 ......213 D6
Prince's Dock St **16**
  HU1..................180 F6
Princes Gate PE1.......226 B1
1 Stamford PE9........219 C4
Prince's Rd DN17........213 D6
Princess Alexandra Ct **1**
  DN17..................197 C6
Princess Anne Rd
  PE21..................209 C6
Princess Ave DN7........14 C6
Princess Dr
34 Barton-upon-Humber
  DN18 ....10 F8
Grantham NG31.........211 A5
Princess Margaret Ave **3**
  LN4....................95 C4
Princess Rd PE20.......136 C4
Princess Royal Cl **4**
  LN2 ....234 C3
Princess Sq LN4 ....109 C4

Princess St
Boston PE21 .... 208 D5
1 Immingham DN40 ..... 186 C3
Lincoln LN5 ....201 E1
Princes St
Brigg DN20 .... 196 C3
Holbeach PE12 ....159 A7
Prince's St
Metheringham LN4 ....95 C4
Peterborough PE1.......226 A4
Sutton Bridge PE12 .....160 E4
Princess Wlk DN21 .....197 F4
Prince St **13** HU1 ....180 F6
Prince William Dr **8**
  PE22..................126 E3
Prince William Rd **8**
  LN8....................56 D5
Pringle Cl LN4..........207 D5
Prins Ave PE23 ....170 D1
Prins Ct **10** PE13.........170 D1
Printing Office La **14**
  DN17 ....16 D8
Priors Cl DN36..........195 D5
Priors Gate PE4.........220 D4
Priors St LN5 ....201 E1
Priory Cl
Gainsborough DN21 .....197 F4
Louth LN11 ....198 C5
Market Deeping PE6......217 F4
10 Northorpe PE10 ......164 C8
11 Ruskington NG34.....108 E1
12 Swanland HU14 ....3 B7
Priory Dr **5** LN3.........82 B6
Priory Farm Dr **4**
  HU4..................179 D2
Priory Gr HU4 ....179 D3
Priory La
6 Barrow upon Humber
  DN19...................11 D8
Dunston LN4 ....95 D5
Manby LN11............62 C6
Scunthorpe DN17 ....184 F6
Priory La Inf Sch DN17...184 F6
Priory La Jun Sch
  DN17..................184 E6
Priory Pk HU4 ....179 B1
Priory Rd
Boston PE21...........209 F5
Fishtoft PE21 .... 126 C2
Grimsby DN37 ....190 D6
Louth LN11 ....198 C5
Peterborough PE3.......225 E3
Ruskington NG34........108 E1
Scunthorpe DN17 ....185 A6
Spalding PE11 ....214 D3
Stamford PE9...........219 D5
Priory Sch The PE11 ....214 F4
Priory Way
2 Gainsborough DN21....53 A5
Kingston upon Hull HU4..179 A1
Sleaford NG34.........212 A2
Private La LN8..........55 F7
Proby Cl PE7 ....233 D5
Procters Dr DN21.........78 C1
Proctors Cl **6** PE12......159 C7
Proctors Rd DN36.......202 D5
Proctor's Way **6** DN20....31 A5
Progress Way NG31......211 A6
Promenade
Mablethorpe/Sutton on Sea
  LN12...................64 D1
Prospect Ctr **13** PE12....180 E7
Prospect Pl
1 Grantham NG31 ......211 A5
Kingston upon Hull HU9 ..181 B7
4 Market Rasen LN8 .....57 E7
Prospect St
Horncastle LN9 ....199 B5
Kingston upon Hull HU2 ..180 E7
Prospect Terr **17** PE7 ...197 D3
Prospero Cl PE2 ....230 F6
Proudfoot La PE12.......159 B6
Providence Cres **17**
  DN18 ....10 E8
Providence Pl **3** LN4 ...207 C4
Provost Rd **8** LN11 ......62 A6
Prunus Ave HU10 ....185 C8
Pryme Rd DN16.........185 C8
Pryme St HU10 ....178 A1
Prystie Pl DN35.........192 D2
Psalter Rd LN3..........82 B6
Puddiners La DN14 ....6 E7
Pudding and Dip La **8**
  DN7....................8 B5
Pudding Bag La **6** PE7....172 C4
Puddingpoke La **8**
  PE12..................160 A8
Pulcroft Rd HU13 ....178 D2
Pullan Cl **9** LN4.........95 D4
Pullman Cl **11** LN6.......95 D4
Pullover La PE24 ....90 F7
Pullover The PE24 ....90 E7
Pulman St HU3..........180 D4
Pulvertoft La **12** PE21 ...208 F4
Pump Hill DN20..........31 D6

Pump La
Fenton NG23 .... 105 C1
5 Skidbrooke with Saltfleet
  Haven LN11 ....51 C4
Pump Sq **18** PE21........208 F5
Punchbowl La
Boston PE21...........208 B7
Holland Fen with Brothertoft
  PE22..................126 E3
Purbeck Rd
9 Grimsby DN33 ....194 E8
Scunthorpe DN17 ......182 C1
Purcell Cl **1** NG31......211 D6
Puritan Way PE21.......208 C7
Puttock Gate PE20......146 D7
Pyecroft PE1...........226 B6
PYEWIPE DN31 ....188 C1
Pyewipe Bglws DN31....188 C1
Pyewipe Rd DN31.......188 C1
Pyhill PE3..............225 B7
Pyke Rd LN6............204 D5
Pymoor La PE22 ....113 B2
Pynder Cl LN4..........203 A2
Pyruss Dr HU4..........179 B2
Pytchley Wlk DN35......192 E2

Q

QUADRING PE11 ....145 A8
Quadring Bank PE11 ....144 E6
Quadring Cowley & Browns
  Prim Sch LN1 ....135 A1
QUADRING EAUDIKE
  PE11..................145 C8
Quadring Rd
Donington PE11 ....134 F2
Quadring PE11..........145 B7
Quaker La
7 Boston PE21..........208 F4
Spalding PE11 ....214 A3
Quantock Cl
7 Kingston upon Hull
  HU3..................180 D5
3 Scunthorpe DN17 ....184 D8
Quantock Ct **9** NG34....212 B3
Quantock Rd DN33......194 E8
QUARRINGTON NG34 ...212 B1
Quarry La PE6 ....173 C7
Quarry Rd LN11 ....198 C7
Quarryside LN11 ....198 B4
Quart La DN14 ....6 D6
Quay La DN14 ....179 D2
Quayside Ctr* NG34 ....212 E4
Quayside E **6** PE10 .....213 E2
Quayside W **7** PE10 .....213 E2
Quays The DN21 ....197 B5
Quebec Rd
Mablethorpe/Sutton on Sea
  LN12...................64 B4
Scunthorpe DN17 ......184 D3
Queen Eleanor Prim Sch
  NG23...................79 B6
Queen Eleanor Tech Coll
  PE9..................219 B7
Queen Elizabeth Ave **3**
  DN18 ....10 A7
Queen Elizabeth Gram Sch
  NG34 .... 199 A4
Queen Elizabeth Rd
  Lincoln LN6 ....201 D8
Queen Elizabeth's Gram
  Sch LN13 ....75 E2
Queen Elizabeth's High Sch
  DN21.................197 C7
Queen Elizabeth Way **33**
  LN8....................70 D8
Queen Headland La LN5..92 F1
Queen Mary Ave DN35..192 C7
Queen Mary Ave Inf Sch
  DN32 .... 192 C7
Queen Mary Rd LN1.....201 D8
Queen St Pl **1** LN1 .....198 C5
Queen Street
5 Barton-upon-Humber
  DN18...................3 F1
Market Deeping PE6.....217 C6
2 Spalding PE11 ....157 B6
Queen's Bank PE12.....167 C5
Queensbury Way **2**
  HU14 ....3 B6
Queen's Cl **2** DN17......17 D6
Queen's Cres
Lincoln LN6 ....201 D5
15 Stainforth DN7 ....14 A5
Queen's Ct **3** LN11......198 D4
Queens Ct **3** DN18.......15 A8
Queens Dock Ave **4**
  HU1..................180 F6
Queen's Dr PE25.......206 B8
Queen's Dr W PE1.......226 A5
Queen's Gdns DN35.....192 A5
Queen's Gdns **6** HU3....180 D4
Queens Parade DN1......191 C7
Queen's Parade DN35...192 F5
Queens Pk **1** LN12.......64 C3

Poo-Rai 271

Queens Pk Specl Sch
  LN5..................205 E8
Queens Rd
Immingham DN40 ......187 A4
8 Mablethorpe/Sutton on Sea
  LN12...................77 A8
Peterborough PE2......231 B7
Skegness PE25.........206 B4
Spalding PE11 ....214 F5
Queen's Rd
9 Barnetby le Wold
  DN38...................21 B4
1 Boston PE21.........209 A5
Bourne PE10 ....213 D6
6 Heckington NG34 ....122 E2
Newark-on-Trent NG24 ..104 A5
Queen's Royal Lancers Mus
  The * NG32 ....138 C8
Queens St PE9..........219 B6
Queen St
6 Bardney LN3..........83 B4
3 Barton LN3............83 C4
Barton-upon-Humber DN18...3 F1
Boston PE21...........208 E5
Bottesford NG13 ....128 A6
Brigg DN20 ....196 C3
4 Collingham NG23 .....91 D5
Epworth DN9 ....27 E6
Gainsborough DN21 ....197 D3
4 Grantham NG31 ......211 A3
Grimsby DN32 ....191 E8
Horncastle LN9 ....199 C3
Kingston upon Hull HU1 ..181 A5
Kirton in Lindsey DN21 ...30 B1
Lincoln LN5 ....201 E1
Louth LN11 ....198 B5
9 Market Rasen LN8 .....57 D8
2 Peterborough PE1 ....226 A2
3 Scunthorpe DN16 .....183 C2
Sleaford NG34.........212 C3
4 Spilsby PE23.........88 A1
17 Sutton Bridge PE12 ..160 E4
Thorne/Moorends DN8 ...15 A8
15 Winterton DN15 ....9 A5
20 Wisbech PE13........170 D1
Yaxley PE7............233 F6
Queen's View Cres
  DN16 .... 185 D7
Queensway
Gainsborough DN21 ....197 F4
3 Grantham NG31 ......211 E6
Kingston upon Hull HU9 ..181 E3
1 Ingoldmells PE25 .....90 E3
Lincoln LN2 ....202 B5
Long Sutton PE12 ......216 C6
Louth LN11 ....198 E5
13 Mablethorpe/Sutton on Sea
  LN12...................64 B4
Pointon & Sempringham
  NG34 .... 143 B6
2 Potterhanworth LN4...82 B1
13 Ruskington NG34 ....108 D2
21 Saxilby LN1..........66 C6
Scunthorpe DN16 ......185 C7
Skellingthorpe LN6 ....200 A3
Stainby by Stow LN1....66 C6
Queens Wlk PE2........230 F8
Queen's Wlk PE1 ......226 A5
Queenswood Rd DN16 ..185 C3
Queen Victoria Sq
  HU1..................180 F6
Quick La PE12 ....168 A7
Quilter Ave HU4 ....179 B5
Quinton Cl LN4.........203 A4
Quinton Rd LN42.......191 E4
Quorn Cl **7** PE6.........174 E4
Quorn Dr **3** SLN6.......205 C8
Quorn Gdns **1** LN11 ....198 C4
Quorn Mews **2** DN35...192 E3
Quorum The HU4 ....179 D2

R

Rabbithill La NG23.......78 D3
Racecourse Rd PE9......171 E3
Raceground The
  Bourne PE11 ....214 A1
2 Spalding PE11 ....156 F2
Race La DN39 ....11 C3
Rachel Cl DN21.........197 C7
Radcliffe Cl **3** PE10 ....219 B5
Radcliffe Ct DN16.......185 D8
Radcliffe Rd
3 Healing DN41.........24 A5
3 Stamford PE9........219 B5
Radford Cl PE8 ....172 C1
RAF Digby Ops Mus *
  LN4..................108 A7
Ragdale Cl PE2 ....226 E7
RAGNALL NG22 ....78 A8
Railway Cl **17** NG31.....151 D1
Railway La PE12 ....160 E3
Railway Pk Cl **6** LN6 ....201 D4
Railway Pk Mews LN6...201 D4
Railway St DN31........189 B2
Railway St
Barnetby le Wold DN38...21 B4
Grimsby DN32 ....189 B1
Kingston upon Hull HU1 ..180 F5
Railway Terr
3 Grantham NG31 ......211 A3
5 Peterborough PE1 ....226 A2
Railwild* PE3...........225 F1
Rainsbutt Rd DN17.......6 C1

Rainton Ct **3** PE11 . . . . .214 F4
Rainwall Ct **2** PE20 . . . . 136 A2
Rainwall's La PE20 . . . . 136 A3
RAITHBY LN11 . . . . .60 F3
Raithby Ave **20** DN41 . . . . . . .23 A4
RAITHBY BY SPILSBY
PE23 .87 D2
Raithby Cross Roads
PE23 .87 C2
Raithby Gr **6** DN33 . . . . . 191 A3
Raithby Hill PE23 . . . . .87 D1
Raithby Rd PE23 . . . . .87 D1
Rake Bridge Bank DN7 . . . .14 D2
Raleigh Cl **2** PE11 . . . . . . .214 C2
Raleigh Dr HU9 . . . . 181 D6
Raleigh Way PE3 . . . . .225 B6
Ralphs La PE20 . . . . 136 C7
Ram Bvd DN15 . . . . .182 E7
Ramper La LN1 . . . . .65 E4
Ramper Rd DN20 . . . . .152 B7
Ramper The **6** PE11 . . . . . 156 E3
RAMPTON DN22 . . . . .65 A4
Rampton Rd DN22 . . . . .65 A4
Ramsay Cl PE25 . . . . 206 C1
Ramsden Ave **8** DN18 . . . . .10 E8
Ramsey Way PE2 . . . . .231 F6
Ramsgate LN11 . . . . 198 C6
Ramsgate Rd LN11 . . . . 198 C6
Ramskir La DN7 . . . . .14 C7
RANBY LN8 . . . . .72 B5
Ranby Rd DN17 . . . . .184 E5
RAND LN8 . . . . .70 A5
Randall Bank PE12 . . . . 158 A2
Rand Farm Pk* LN8 . . . . . . .70 A5
Randolph Rd PE20 . . . . 146 D7
Randsfield Ave **20** HU15 . . . 2 C5
Rangefield PE2 . . . . .229 E4
Rangell Gate PE12 . . . . .157 B5
Range Rd NG31 . . . . 211 C5
Rangoon Way **4** PE10 . . . .213 E7
Ransom Ct **8** DN20 . . . . . . .22 A6
Ransome Way **17** HU15 . . . 2 C6
Ranters Row **8** LN13 . . . . . .75 F2
Ranville Ct **11** PE11 . . . . . . 145 C1
Ranworth Cl **1** PE25 . . . . 206 D7
Ranyard La LN11 . . . . .72 E5
Rase La **5** LN8 . . . . .57 D8
Rasen Ct **3** LN8 . . . . .57 B8
Rasen Ct **1** PE11 . . . . 226 D3
Rasen La LN1 . . . . 234 A4
Rasen Rd
Tealby LN8 . . . . .46 B1
Walesby LN8 . . . . 45 F1
Rason's Ct **8** PE21 . . . . . . 209 A5
Rasper Rd Pools Nature
Reserve* DN40 . . . . 186 A8
Rat Abbey DN15 . . . . .9 C4
Ratcliffe Ct **1** PE1 . . . . . . 226 D7
Rathkenny Cl PE12 . . . . 215 E2
Rats Pen La LN11 . . . . .62 C1
Ratten Row PE22 . . . . .127 A5
Rauceby CE Sch NG34 . . . .120 E5
Rauceby Dro NG34 . . . . .120 F3
Rauceby Sta NG34 . . . . .120 F3
Rauceby Terr LN1 . . . . 234 A2
Rauceby Warren Nature
Reserve* NG34 . . . . 120 F2
Ravel Cl PE6 . . . . .218 F6
Raven Cl **1** DN20 . . . . .19 D4
Ravencroft La DN10 . . . . .40 A1
Ravendale Cl **31** DN18 . . . .10 F8
Ravendale Cl
Gonerby Hill Foot
NG31 . . . . 211 A8
Holton le Clay DN36 . . . . . 195 E1
Ravendale Dr LN2 . . . . .202 A7
Ravendale Rd
Cleethorpes DN35 . . . . . . .193 A3
Gainsborough DN21 . . . . .197 E3
Ravendale St N **3**
DN15 . . . . .183 B3
Ravendale St S DN15 . . . . .183 B3
Ravenhill Cl DN35 . . . . .192 D3
Ravens Bank PE12 . . . . .158 B2
Ravenscar Rd **5** DN37 . . .188 A1
Raven's Dro PE12 . . . . 159 A3
Ravensfleet Rd DN21 . . . . . .40 C6
Raven's Gate
Fleet PE12 . . . . .159 A3
Holbeach PE12 . . . . 159 A3
Ravensmoor Cl **4** LN6 . . .204 E1
Ravenspurn Way DN31 . . . .191 D8
Raven St HU9 . . . . .181 D7
RAVENSTHORPE PE3 . . . .225 C6
Ravensthorpe Prim Sch
PE3 . . . . 225 C7
Ravens View LN6 . . . . .92 D4
Ravenwood LN4 . . . . .203 A2
Rawcliffe Gr HU4 . . . . .180 C5
Rawling Way HU3 . . . . .180 C5
Rawnsley Rd **44** LN7 . . . . . .33 B3
Rawnsley Cl **8** LN13 . . . . . .75 F2
Rawsons La PE21 . . . . .125 E5
Raybrook Cl **5** PE21 . . . . .208 E7
Raymond Mays Way
PE10 . . . . 213 D2
Raymond Rd DN16 . . . . .185 C7
Rayner Ave PE2 . . . . .231 E5
Raynor's La PE22 . . . . .114 A2
Rayton Cl LN4 . . . . .203 A2
Raywell Cl HU10 . . . . .178 F7
Raywell St HU2 . . . . 180 E7
Reaches The PE6 . . . . .175 C3
Read Cl **2** NG24 . . . . .104 C1
Reading Cl LN4 . . . . .203 E1

Reading Gate DN14 . . . . .6 C4
Reading Rm Yd **2** HU14 . . .3 A4
Reads La **4** NG33 . . . . 151 D7
Read Way LN4 . . . . .207 D5
Reams Cl **4** PE21 . . . . 209 D4
Reapers Cl **1** PE12 . . . . . . 215 B2
Reaper's Rise **20** DN9 . . . .27 E6
Reaper's Way **8** DN9 . . . . .27 D2
REASBY LN1 . . . . .69 C6
Recreation Gd Rd PE9 . . . . 219 B6
Recreation Rd **2** PE10 . . .213 D5
Recto Ave DN32 . . . . .191 F5
Rectors Way **6** PE4 . . . . . 221 D2
Rectory Cl
1 Barrowby NG32 . . . . 210 A5
2 Binbrook LN8 . . . . .47 C5
2 Fishtoft PE21 . . . . 126 C1
Rectory Gdns
2 Beckingham DN10 . . . .40 A1
4 Glinton PE6 . . . . 220 C8
Peterborough PE2 . . . . .231 B7
Rectory La
Addlethorpe PE24 . . . . .90 C4
Barrowby NG32 . . . . 210 A5
Bottesford NG13 . . . . 128 A6
Claypole NG23 . . . . .117 F8
Etton PE6 . . . . 173 D5
3 Fulbeck NG32 . . . . . . 106 C1
Gainsborough DN21 . . . . . .52 F5
6 Gedney PE12 . . . . . . 159 D7
Glinton PE6 . . . . .220 C8
Harlaxton NG32 . . . . 139 C7
Leadenham LN5 . . . . 106 C2
2 Mareham le Fen PE22 . .98 F4
North Witham NG33 . . . . .151 D4
4 Ownby LN8 . . . . .55 F6
2 Peakirk PE6 . . . . 174 A5
22 Waddington LN5 . . . . .93 F7
Woolsthorpe by Belvoir
NG32 . . . . 138 D8
Rectory Lea DN21 . . . . .54 F4
Rectory Rd
Anderby PE24 . . . . .76 F2
Boston PE21 . . . . .209 B3
Coleby LN5 . . . . .93 F3
Newton PE13 . . . . 170 B5
Ruskington NG34 . . . . .108 D1
Tydd St Mary PE13 . . . . . . 160 B1
Rectory St
Beckingham LN5 . . . . .105 B4
Epworth DN9 . . . . .27 E6
Red Barn La PE22 . . . . 136 B3
Redbourn Cl **2** DN16 . . . .183 B1
REDBOURNE DN21 . . . . .30 F3
Redbourne Dr LN2 . . . . .202 A8
Redbourne Mere DN21 . . . .30 E2
Redbourne Rd
Grimsby DN33 . . . . .191 B3
Hibaldstow DN20 . . . . .30 F4
Waddingham DN21 . . . . . . .43 C7
Redbourne St **8** DN16 . . . .19 A6
Redbourne St
Kingston upon Hull
HU3 . . . . .180 B5
1 Scunthorpe DN16 . . . .183 C2
Redbourn Terr **4**
PE21 . . . . .208 F3
Redbourn Way DN16 . . . . . .183 B2
Redbridge PE4 . . . . .220 D6
Red Cap La PE21 . . . . .208 E8
Redcar Cl LN6 . . . . .204 F4
Redcar Gr DN32 . . . . .192 A5
Redcar St HU8 . . . . .181 A8
Redcliff Dr **22** HU14 . . . . . . .3 A4
Redcliffe Rd NG31 . . . . .211 B7
Redcombe La DN20 . . . . . . .196 B4
Redcote Dr LN6 . . . . .204 F4
Redcot Gdns PE9 . . . . .219 B6
Red Cow Dro PE12 . . . . 146 F6
Redcross St NG31 . . . . 211 B5
Redfern Cl HU3 . . . . .180 D5
Redgate Ct **5** PE21 . . . . . .226 E2
Redgate Rd PE13 . . . . .170 C8
Red Hall* PE10 . . . . .213 D4
Redhall Cl **9** DN3 . . . . .14 A2
Red Hall Dr LN4 . . . . .205 F4
Red Hall Farm La LN4 . . . . .205 F4
Redhill La LN8 . . . . .59 A8
Redmile CE Prim Sch
LN11 . . . . .72 E7
Red La
South Ferriby DN18 . . . . . . .9 F7
Welby NG32 . . . . .130 E5
Redland Cres **1** DN8 . . . . .15 B8
Red Leas La LN11 . . . . .62 A8
Red Lion Sq **19** PE9 . . . . .219 B5
Red Lion St
6 Bicker PE20 . . . . 135 A4
2 Boston PE21 . . . . 208 F5
5 Spalding PE11 . . . . . . 214 D4
3 Stamford PE9 . . . . . . .219 B5
Redman Cl DN21 . . . . .197 E5
Redmile CE
Bourne PE10 . . . . 154 D5
Pinchbeck PE11 . . . . .214 C8
Redmile's La **2** PE9 . . . . . 171 A3
Redmile Wlk **5** PE21 . . . . 226 D7
Red Rd DN21 . . . . .84 B8
Redshank Way PE7 . . . . .230 C1
Redstone Ind Est PE21 . . . .208 E3
Redstone Rd PE21 . . . . .208 E3
Redthorne Cl **2** PE11 . . . .214 F5
Redvers Dr HU13 . . . . .117 F7
Redwing Cl
Peterborough PE2 . . . . .231 E2
Skellingthorpe LN6 . . . . . .200 A3
Redwing Gr **1** LN6 . . . . . . 204 D8
Redwood Ave **11** NG34 . . 212 D2

Redwood Ct DN16 . . . . 185 D3
Redwood Dr
Cleethorpes DN35 . . . . . . .192 D2
Waddington LN5 . . . . .205 D1
REEDHAM LN4 . . . . 111 C7
Reedham Garth HU4 . . . . . . 179 A3
Reedham La LN4 . . . . .207 F2
Reedings Cl NG32 . . . . .210 B5
Reedings Rd NG32 . . . . .210 B5
Reedland Way PE7 . . . . .230 C1
Reedmace Cl **3** PE6 . . . . .174 E4
Reedmans Cl **5** PE6 . . . . .164 F3
REED POINT LN4 . . . . .110 E2
Reepham PE2 . . . . .229 D4
REEPHAM LN3 . . . . .203 F8
Reepham CE (Controlled)
Prim Sch LN3 . . . . .203 F8
Reepham Rd LN3 . . . . .203 F8
Reet **8** DN21 . . . . .189 B1
Reeves Way PE11 . . . . 226 D5
Refinery Rd DN16 . . . . .183 F2
Reform Pl **2** NG34 . . . . . . 212 C4
Reform St
9 Crowland PE6 . . . . . . .166 E1
Kingston upon Hull HU2 . .180 F7
Stamford PE9 . . . . .219 F5
Regal Gdns **2** NG33 . . . . .162 E8
Regal Pl PE2 . . . . .231 A8
Regency Ct **3** DN18 . . . . . . .3 E1
Regency Gdns NG31 . . . . . . 211 D5
Regency Way PE3 . . . . .225 E1
Regent Ave LN2 . . . . .200 C1
Regent Dr **18** DN17 . . . . . . .16 D7
Regent Gdns DN31 . . . . .191 C5
Regent Rd **11** LN2 . . . . . . .64 B4
Regent St Sh Arc
DN32 . . . . .191 D7
Regents Cl
6 Collingham NG23 . . . . .91 D4
4 Skegness PE25 . . . . . 206 C1
Regents Pk Cl **7** LN6 . . . .204 F1
Reginald Rd DN15 . . . . 182 C6
Regina Wlk **10** PE24 . . . . . .90 D7
Reginald Rd DN15 . . . . 182 C6
Reindeer Cl LN9 . . . . 199 A4
Rein The DN9 . . . . .27 A2
Reldene Dr HU5 . . . . .179 B7
Rembrandt Way PE11 . . . . .214 B3
Remigius Gr LN2 . . . . 202 C7
Remple Ave **2** DN7 . . . . . . .15 A3
Remple Comm Rd DN7 . . . .14 F2
Remple La **8** DN7 . . . . .14 F2
Renault Dr LN4 . . . . .205 F1
Rendel St DN31 . . . . 188 F1
Renew's Dro PE6 . . . . .166 D3
Renfrew Cl **2** LN5 . . . . . . 205 C2
Renfrew Dr NG34 . . . . .121 A2
Renfrew Rd LN5 . . . . .205 C2
Renton Ct HU10 . . . . .178 F5
Reporto Ave LN2 . . . . .202 D6
Repton Cl LN4 . . . . .203 D1
Repton Dr DN16 . . . . .185 B3
Repton Rd **7** LN12 . . . . . . .64 B4
Reservation The NG34 . . . . 212 F7
Reservoir Rd PE11 . . . . .145 F4
Reservoir St LN1 . . . . 234 A4
Resolute Cl **6** PE23 . . . . . 101 A8
Resolution Ct PE21 . . . . . . .208 A4
Response Ave DN17 . . . . . . .191 F5
Reston Ct DN35 . . . . .193 A3
Reston Gr LN1 . . . . .201 B8
Retief Cl LN1 . . . . .201 D8
Retief View LN1 . . . . 201 D8
Retreat The
Easton on the Hill PE9 . . . .171 C3
4 Maxey PE6 . . . . 173 C6
REVESBY PE22 . . . . .99 C3
Revesby Abbey PE22 . . . . . .99 C5
Revesby Ave
Boston PE21 . . . . .208 D4
Grimsby DN34 . . . . .190 F4
Scunthorpe DN16 . . . . . . .185 A7
Revesby Bank
Carrington DN22 . . . . .99 B1
Revesby PE22 . . . . .112 B8
REVESBY BRIDGE PE22 . . .99 C3
Revesby Cl
Boston PE21 . . . . .208 D4
Lincoln LN6 . . . . .204 F6
Revesby Cnr **5** PE22 . . . . . .99 A4
Revesby Dr DN35 . . . . .185 A8
Revesby Dr PE25 . . . . .206 A4
Revigo Ave DN10 . . . . .191 F5
Revill Cl
3 Claypole NG23 . . . . . .117 E8
17 Scotter DN21 . . . . . . .29 C3
Reynard Ct LN2 . . . . .53 E3
Reynard St **3** PE23 . . . . . . .88 A1
Reynolds Dr HU14 . . . . .2 F5
Reynolds Dr **1** LN6 . . . . . .205 B6
Reynolds Gdns **6**
PE12 . . . . .157 F7
Reynolds Jun & Inf Sch
DN35 . . . . .192 D7
Reynold's Paddock **2**
LN5 . . . . .93 A5
Rhodes Ave **2** NG34 . . . .212 C3
Rhodes St HU3 . . . . .179 F5
Rialto Ave DN32 . . . . .191 F5
Ribble St **4** HU3 . . . . .180 B5
Riber Cl **2** NG31 . . . . .210 E5
Ribes Cl **1** PE7 . . . . .230 D3
Ribston Cl DN16 . . . . .185 A2
RIBY DN37 . . . . .23 C2
Riby Cl **3** DN21 . . . . .53 A7

Riby Cross Roads DN37 . . .23 C3
Riby Ct DN36 . . . . .195 E2
Riby Rd
Cabourne LN7 . . . . .33 D6
Keelby DN41 . . . . .23 A4
Scunthorpe DN17 . . . . .184 E5
Stallingborough DN41 . . . .23 C4
Swallow LN7 . . . . .34 A7
Riby Sq DN31 . . . . .189 B1
Riby St DN31 . . . . .189 B1
Richard Busby Way **14**
PE12 . . . . .160 A8
Richards Ave LN6 . . . . .204 F4
Richardson Cl **18** DN36 . . .36 D8
Richard St DN31 . . . . .191 C8
Richard Young Cl **4**
PE13 . . . . .170 D2
Richdale Ave **1** DN41 . . . .30 B2
Richmond Ave PE4 . . . . .221 A2
Richmond Cl
Boston PE21 . . . . .209 A5
Caythorpe NG32 . . . . .119 B6
2 Sleaford NG34 . . . . . .212 B2
Richmond Ct **1** PE25 . . . .206 C2
Richmond Dr
Green Hill HU5 . . . . .210 E5
Lincoln LN6 . . . . .204 F3
Scunthorpe DN16 . . . . . . .185 C4
Skegness PE25 . . . . .206 A4
Richmond Leisure Complex
PE25 . . . . .206 B1
Richmond Rd
Cleethorpes DN35 . . . . . . .192 E5
Gainsborough DN21 . . . . .197 F4
Grimsby DN34 . . . . .191 A6
Kingston upon Hull
HU13 . . . . .178 E2
Lincoln LN1 . . . . .201 D4
Richmond Sch The
PE25 . . . . .206 C2
Richmond Way PE13 . . . . . .170 B2
RIDDINGS DN17 . . . . .184 E4
Riddings Inf Sch
DN17 . . . . .184 F4
Riddings Jun Sch
DN17 . . . . .184 F4
Rider Gdns PE21 . . . . 209 D2
Rides The **7** PE6 . . . . .164 F3
Ridge Cl **14** LN2 . . . . .68 D6
Ridge View
2 Brigg DN20 . . . . .196 D4
Ermine LN1 . . . . .201 D8
Fillingham DN21 . . . . .54 F4
Harmston LN5 . . . . .93 F4
Ridge View Rd LN4 . . . . .205 F4
Ridgeway **11** LN2 . . . . .68 D2
Ridge Way
Peterborough PE2 . . . . . . .231 B8
Scunthorpe DN17 . . . . . . .182 E1
Ridgeway Rd HU5 . . . . .179 B7
Ridgeway The DN34 . . . . . . .190 D3
Ridgewell Cl **10** LN6 . . . . .204 D8
Ridgewood Ave **14** DN3 . .14 A1
Ridgewood Dr **3** DN15 . . . .8 A4
Ridings The
Bourne PE10 . . . . 213 C3
Kingston upon Hull HU5 . . 179 A8
Market Rasen LN8 . . . . .57 E7
17 Rothwell PE21 . . . . . . .3 A4
Ridley Ave PE25 . . . . .206 D2
Rightwell E PE3 . . . . .225 A6
Rightwell E PE3 . . . . .225 A5
Rightwell W PE3 . . . . .225 A5
RIGSBY LN13 . . . . .75 D2
Rigsby Wood Nature
Reserve* LN13 . . . . .75 C3
Rigsmoor Cl **2** LN6 . . . . . .93 C8
Rileston Pl HU16 . . . . .185 B2
Riley Cl
Bracebridge Heath
LN4 . . . . .205 F2
Yaxley PE7 . . . . .233 D6
Rimac Rd LN11 . . . . .51 D2
Rimes La DN22 . . . . .65 A7
Rime's La LN10 . . . . .98 C6
Rimington Rd **4** PE21 . . . 126 C1
Ring Beck La HU15 . . . . .2 A8
Ringers La PE13 . . . . .170 B2
Ring Moor Cl **3** LN4 . . . . .109 F5
Ringrose St HU3 . . . . .179 F5
Ringstead Rd PE4 . . . . .221 D1
Ringstone Chase PE10 . . . .142 F1
Ringwood PE3 . . . . .224 F3
Ringwood Cl
4 Birchwood LN6 . . . . . .200 D1
1 Scunthorpe DN16 . . . .185 B4
Rinks La LN5 . . . . .92 E1
Rio Dr NG23 . . . . .91 D5
Ripley Cl DN15 . . . . .182 B2
Ripley Ct DN15 . . . . .205 A3
Riplingham Rd HU10 . . . . . .178 A4
Ripon Cl
1 Bracebridge Heath
LN4 . . . . .81 A2
Grantham NG31 . . . . .210 F5
Peterborough PE4 . . . . . . .220 F3
Scunthorpe DN17 . . . . . . .184 D2
Ripon Dr NG34 . . . . .212 C6
Ripon Pl **7** LN12 . . . . .64 B3
Ripon St
Grimsby DN31 . . . . .191 C8
Lincoln LN5 . . . . .201 F1
Ripon Way HU9 . . . . .181 C8
RIPPINGALE PE10 . . . . .142 F3
Rippingale CE (Controlled)
Prim Sch PE10 . . . . .142 F2
Rippingale Rd PE10 . . . . . . .142 D2
Rippons Dro PE6 . . . . .217 E2
Risby PE3 . . . . .225 B8

RISBY LN8 . . . . .46 E
Risby Gn LN6 . . . . .204 E
Risby Rd DN15 . . . . .9 A
Risedale **28** LN7 . . . . .33 E
RISEGATE PE11 . . . . .144 E
Risegate Rd PE11 . . . . .144 E
Riseholme PE2 . . . . .229 E
Riseholme La LN2 . . . . .67 E
Riseholme Rd
Gainsborough DN21 . . . . .197 E
Lincoln LN2 . . . . .201 E
Rise The
18 Navenby/Wellingore
LN5 . . . . .107 A
8 North Ferriby HU14 . . . .3 E
Scunthorpe DN17 . . . . . . .184 E
South Ferriby DN18 . . . . . .10 A
Risegate La NG33 . . . . .130 E
Riston St HU3 . . . . .180 C
Rivan Ave DN33 . . . . .194 E
Rivehall Ave **7** NG34 . . . . . .68 C
Rivelin Cres DN16 . . . . .185 A
Rivelin Pl DN16 . . . . .185 A
Rivelin Rd DN16 . . . . .185 A
Rivendale PE4 . . . . .220 A
River Bank PE12 . . . . .214 C
River Bank PE7 . . . . .217 E
Riverbank Rise **17** DN18 . . .3 E
Riverbank Studios*
PE11 . . . . .214 E
River Cl PE11 . . . . .214 C
Riverdale **8** LN2 . . . . .68 C
Riverdale Rd DN16 . . . . .185 A
Rivergate
3 Peterborough PE1 . . . .226 A
5 Spalding PE11 . . . . . . 214 E
Rivergate Sh Ctr PE1 . . . . .226 A
River Gr LN11 . . . . .179 E
Riverhead Rd LN11 . . . . .198 C
Riverhead Terr LN11 . . . . . .198 C
River La
Anwick NG34 . . . . .109 E
Kedington LN11 . . . . .198 E
Moulton PE12 . . . . .158 A
Peterborough PE3 . . . . . . .225 E
River Mdw DN20 . . . . .196 A
Rivermead LN6 . . . . .205 C
Rivermead Cl LN6 . . . . .205 C
River Rd
West Burton DN22 . . . . . . .52 C
West Walton PE14 . . . . . . .170 C
Riverside
2 Brigg DN20 . . . . .196 A
Grantham NG31 . . . . .211 E
Market Deeping PE6 . . . . .217 C
5 Scotter DN21 . . . . .29 C
1 Spalding PE11 . . . . . . 214 E
Riverside App DN21 . . . . . . .197 C
Riverside Cl
14 Bottesford NG13 . . . .128 A
5 Sleaford NG34 . . . . . .212 C
Riverside Ct
Louth LN11 . . . . .198 C
South Field HU13 . . . . .3 E
Riverside Dr DN35 . . . . .193 C
Riverside Gdns
Parson Drove PE13 . . . . . .177 C
Peterborough PE3 . . . . . . .225 C
Riverside Ind Est PE21 . . . .209 A
Riverside Mead PE2 . . . . . . .231 E
Riverside Pk
Grantham NG31 . . . . .211 E
Spalding PE11 . . . . .214 D
Riverside Pk Homes
PE21 . . . . .208 E
Riverside Spinney PE8 . . . .222 A
Riverside The **11** NG34 . . .212 C
Riverside Wlk
8 Bottesford NG13 . . . . 128 A
Grantham NG31 . . . . .211 E
River Terr **4** PE13 . . . . . . .170 C
Riverton Cl LN11 . . . . .201 C
Riverton View LN1 . . . . .201 C
Riverview NG23 . . . . .117 C
River View
21 Barton-upon-Humber
DN18 . . . . .10 A
Northfield HU13 . . . . .178 A
Riverview Ave HU14 . . . . .3 A
River Way PE21 . . . . .209 C
Roadwood La NG23 . . . . .78 E
Robden Ct PE2 . . . . .225 E
Roberta Cl **10** PE25 . . . . . .206 A
Robert Ave PE21 . . . . .225 E
Robert Cl DN40 . . . . .186 A
Robert Dukeson Ave
NG24 . . . . .104 A
Robert Manning Tech Coll
The PE10 . . . . .213 E
Robert Pattinson Sch
LN6 . . . . .204 E
Robert Rayner PE2 . . . . .230 E
Robert's Field Nature
Reserve* PE9 . . . . .162 A
Robert's Gr PE25 . . . . .206 C
Robertson Ave **6**
NG34 . . . . .121 E
Robertson Cl **14** LN5 . . . . . .93 E
Robertson Dr NG34 . . . . . . .120 C
Robertson Rd
3 Grantham NG31 . . . . .210 A
Lincoln LN6 . . . . .204 E
Roberts St DN32 . . . . .192 A
Roberts St DN35 . . . . .183 A
Robert Tressell Wlk **2**
LN2 . . . . .202 C

Robey St LN5 . . . . .205 E8
Robin Dr
  Bottesford DN16 . . . . .185 B2
  8 Market Deeping PE6 . . .217 C5
  12 Sleaford NG34 . . . . .212 B3
Robin Hood Cl PE3 . . . . . .224 F2
Robin Hood Cres **13**
  DN3 . . . . .14 A1
Robin Hood Rd
  11 Kirk Sandall DN3 . . . . . .14 A1
  Skegness PE25 . . . . .206 C3
Robin Hood's Wlak
  PE21 . . . . .208 E7
Robin Hood's Wlk
  PE21 . . . . .208 F6
Robinia Dr HU4 . . . . .179 C2
Robins Cl PE2 . . . . .230 E8
Robins Cres LN6 . . . . .92 D5
Robins Field PE8 . . . . .222 A4
Robinson Ave **4** LN13 . . . .75 E2
Robinson Cl DN15 . . . . . . .182 E4
Robinson La
  Grimsby DN31 . . . . .189 C2
  Louth LN11 . . . . .198 C5
Robinson Pl LN6 . . . . .105 F5
Robinson Rd DN40 . . . . . . .186 F6
Robinson St E DN32 . . . . .191 E7
Robinson's Gr **8** DN20 . . . .31 A5
Robinson's La **1** DN36 . . . .36 B1
Robins Wood PE8 . . . . .222 A4
Robson Rd DN35 . . . . .192 D7
Rochdale Rd DN16 . . . . . . .185 A5
Rochester Ave HU4 . . . . . .179 B3
Rochester Cl
  1 Bracebridge Heath
  LN4 . . . . .81 A2
  1 Scunthorpe DN17 . . . .184 C7
Rochester Ct
  2 Bourne PE10 . . . . .213 C2
  Humberston DN35 . . . . . . .193 A1
Rochester Dr
  Birchwood LN6 . . . . .200 D2
  9 Grantham NG31 . . . . .210 E5
Rochford Cres PE21 . . . . . .209 B5
Rochford Twr* PE21 . . . . . .209 E5
Rochford Twr La PE21 . . . .209 D6
Rockingham Cl **8** PE6 . . .217 A6
Rockingham Cres
  DN34 . . . . .190 D4
Rockingham Dr **9**
  DN34 . . . . .190 D4
Rockingham Gr PE4 . . . . . .221 A2
Rockingham Rd **4**
  PE9 . . . . .218 E6
Rockley Ct HU10 . . . . .178 F6
Rock Rd
  Peterborough PE1 . . . . . . .225 F6
  Peterborough PE2 . . . . . . .219 B5
Rock The NG32 . . . . .138 B4
Rod Mill Rd DN16 . . . . . . .183 E1
Roegate La PE12 . . . . .159 F1
Roeze Cl **14** LN10 . . . . . . .97 C5
Rogues Alley PE13 . . . . . . .177 C4
Rokeby Ave HU4 . . . . .179 B5
Rokeby Cl HU4 . . . . .179 B5
Rokeby Pk HU4 . . . . .179 B5
Rokeby Pk Prim Sch
  HU4 . . . . .179 B4
Rolleston St **3** LN2 . . . . .201 F7
Rolleston Garth PE1 . . . . . .226 C8
Rolls Cl PE7 . . . . .233 E7
Roman Bank
  Bourne PE10 . . . . .213 E4
  Holbeach PE12 . . . . .215 D8
  Huttoft PE24 . . . . .77 C4
  1 Ingoldmells PE25 . . . . .206 D8
  Moulton PE12 . . . . .146 E2
  Newton PE13 . . . . .170 B4
  6 Skegness PE25 . . . . . .206 C3
  Spalding PE11 . . . . .214 F6
  Stamford PE9 . . . . .219 A5
Roman Cl
  6 Metheringham LN4 . . . .95 D4
  Navenby LN5 . . . . .107 B8
Roman Dr PE8 . . . . .222 D2
Roman Pavement LN2 . . . .202 C4
Roman Rd
  Moulton PE12 . . . . .157 D1
  Scawby DN20 . . . . .30 D8
Roman Way
  7 Ancaster NG32 . . . . . .120 A2
  Aubourn Haddington & South
   Hykeham LN6 . . . . .92 E6
  Horncastle LN9 . . . . .199 D3
  Riddings DN17 . . . . .184 F6
Roman Wharf LN1 . . . . . . .201 C3
Romany Gdns DN21 . . . . . .231 D5
Romney Cl **3** LN6 . . . . . . .205 B6
Romney Cl **6** NG34 . . . . .212 D5
Romney Dr LN6 . . . . .205 B5
Romney St DN34 . . . . .190 D5
Romulus Way LN1 . . . . .93 B8
Ronald Cl **3** PE25 . . . . . .206 C4
Rood's La PE12 . . . . .157 C8
Rookery Ave
  2 Grimsby DN33 . . . . . .191 D3
  Sleaford NG34 . . . . .212 B3
Rookery Cl LN11 . . . . .198 D8
Rookery Croft **14** DN9 . . .27 E6
Rookery La
  Ancaster NG32 . . . . .119 F2
  13 Leasingham NG34 . . .121 B7
  Wildmore LN4 . . . . .111 E2
  Wymondham LE14 . . . . . . .150 B1
Rookery Rd
  2 Bicker PE20 . . . . .135 A4
  8 Healing DN41 . . . . .23 F5

Rookery Rd continued
  Sutton Bridge PE12 . . . . . .160 D7
Rookery The
  14 Collingham NG23 . . . . .91 D5
  Peterborough PE2 . . . . . . .229 C7
  2 Scawby DN20 . . . . .30 F8
  Yaxley PE7 . . . . .233 D5
Rooklands **10** DN21 . . . . . .29 C3
Rook's La DN10 . . . . .39 F6
Roosdyke La PE22 . . . . . . .137 D7
Roper's Bridge La
  PE20 . . . . .136 A4
Roper's Gate
  Gedney PE12 . . . . .159 F8
  2 Lutton PE12 . . . . .160 A8
Roper's La PE12 . . . . .159 D1
Ropery La **2** DN18 . . . . . . .3 E1
Ropery Rd DN21 . . . . .197 B7
Ropery St
  Grimsby DN32 . . . . .191 F7
  Kingston upon Hull HU3 . . .180 D4
Ropery The LN1 . . . . .234 A3
Ropewalk **8** LN8 . . . . .70 D5
Ropewalk Gall* DN18 . . . . . .3 F1
Ropewalk The
  1 Caistor LN7 . . . . .33 B4
  3 Colsterworth NG33 . . .151 E6
Rope Wlk
  Lincoln LN6 . . . . .234 A1
  15 Thorne/Moorends
   DN8 . . . . .15 A8
ROPSLEY NG33 . . . . .131 B1
Ropsley CE (Controlled)
  Prim Sch NG33 . . . . .131 A1
Ropsley Rd NG33 . . . . .140 E8
Rosaire Pl DN33 . . . . .195 A8
Rosalind Ave DN34 . . . . . . .191 B7
Rosamond St **7** HU3 . . . . .180 B4
Rose Ave PE8 . . . . .231 C7
Rosebank DN21 . . . . .197 B7
Rosebery Ave
  2 Hatfield DN7 . . . . .14 D4
  Skegness PE25 . . . . .206 D1
Rosebery Ave
  Boston PE21 . . . . .208 C5
  Lincoln LN1 . . . . .201 D4
Rose Cottage Gdn Ctr &
  Tropical Forest*
  PE11 . . . . .156 D8
Rose Cottage La LN5 . . . . . .94 A3
Rose Cres PE12 . . . . .158 D3
Rosedale
  Scunthorpe DN17 . . . . . . .184 E2
  Waltham DN37 . . . . .194 C5
Rosedale Cl **4** LN6 . . . . . .204 F3
Rosedale Dr DN31 . . . . . . .211 B8
Rosedale Gr HU5 . . . . .179 D7
Rosefields DN21 . . . . .197 E5
Rosegar Ave PE10 . . . . . . .135 F2
Rosegarth St **14** PE21 . . .208 F4
Rose Gr **1** PE25 . . . . .206 D5
Rosehill Cl **8** LN7 . . . . . . .66 D2
Rosehip Rd **8** PE10 . . . . .154 D6
Rose La
  Beesby with Saleby
   LN13 . . . . .75 F5
  Pinchbeck PE21 . . . . .156 E8
Roselea Ave **8** LN2 . . . . . .68 D6
Rose Leigh Way **1** LN4 . .214 C7
Rosemary Ave
  Grimsby DN34 . . . . .190 F6
  11 Market Deeping PE6 . .217 C5
Rosemary Cres NG31 . . . . .210 E1
Rosemary Gdns
  12 Bourne PE10 . . . . . . .213 C6
  4 Skegness PE25 . . . . . .206 B8
Rosemary La LN2 . . . . .234 B2
Rosemary Rise NG35 . . . . .141 D5
Rosemary Way DN35 . . . . .192 E1
Rose Mdws 208 B4
Rosemount Dr DN16 . . . . . .185 B6
Rosemount Grange
  HU13 . . . . .178 C3
Rosemount La **5** DN21 . . . .43 D7
Rose Pl PE21 . . . . .209 A3
Roseum Cl LN6 . . . . .204 E5
Roseveare Ave DN31 . . . . .191 A4
Roseway **6** DN21 . . . . . . .197 D5
Rose Wlk
  Scunthorpe DN15 . . . . . . .183 C3
  11 Wisbech PE13 . . . . . .170 C1
  Wittering PE9 . . . . .172 B1
Rosewood Cl
  2 Birchwood LN6 . . . . . .204 C8
  4 Kingston upon Hull
   HU3 . . . . .179 B7
Rosewood Dr **5** NG34 . . . .212 D2
Rosewood Way **1**
  DN16 . . . . .185 B3
Rosey Row **4** HU1 . . . . . .181 C7
Rosina Gr N **2** DN32 . . . .192 B6
Rosina Gr S **4** DN32 . . . .192 B6
Roslyn Rd HU3 . . . . .145 A7
Rosmead St HU9 . . . . .181 D8
Rosper Rd DN40 . . . . .186 A8
Rosper Road Pools Nature
  Reserve* DN40 . . . . .186 A8
Rossall Cl
  7 Mablethorpe/Sutton on
   Sea LN12 . . . . .77 A7
  Scunthorpe DN16 . . . . . . .185 C3
Rossa Rd LN13 . . . . .76 D7
Ross Cl
  5 Coddington NG24 . . . .104 B6
  St Giles LN2 . . . . .202 D6
Rossetti St NG31 . . . . .211 E5
Rossington St **18** NG34 . . .95 C4

Ross La **6** DN15 . . . . .9 B5
Ross Rd DN31 . . . . .189 D1
Rostrop Rd LN4 . . . . .95 C7
Rosyth Ave PE22 . . . . .115 A5
Rothbart Way **2** PE7 . . . .230 C3
Rothbury Rd DN17 . . . . . . .184 F7
Rotherby Gr **8** PE1 . . . . .226 E7
Rothschild Cl PE21 . . . . . . .208 B4
ROTHWELL LN7 . . . . .33 F2
Rothwell Ave **8** DN33 . . .191 B3
Rothwell Cl DN21 . . . . .197 E4
Rothwell Rd
  Cabourne LN7 . . . . .33 C3
  4 Lincoln LN2 . . . . .201 F7
  Scunthorpe DN15 . . . . . . .182 D4
Rothwell Way PE2 . . . . . . .230 C7
Rotten Row
  Pinchbeck PE11 . . . . .156 E8
  Theddlethorpe St Helen
   LN12 . . . . .63 E5
Rotten Sykes La DN15 . . . . .1 F2
ROUGHTON LN10 . . . . .98 B7
Roughton Ct **5** LN2 . . . . .202 A8
ROUGHTON MOOR
  LN10 . . . . .98 A7
Roughton Moor Wood
  Nature Reserve*
  LN10 . . . . .97 F6
Roundhouse Cl PE1 . . . . . .226 D3
Roundway
  Grimsby DN34 . . . . .191 C5
  3 Immingham DN40 . . . .186 C3
Roundway The HU4 . . . . . .179 C5
Routland Cl **8** LN8 . . . . . . .70 D7
Roval Dr DN40 . . . . .186 A4
Rowan Ave
  Peterborough PE1 . . . . . . .226 C6
  Spalding PE11 . . . . .214 E5
Rowan Cl
  6 Barrow upon Humber
   DN19 . . . . .11 C8
  6 Healing DN41 . . . . .23 A4
  10 Wisbech PE13 . . . . . .170 C1
Rowan Cres DN16 . . . . . . .185 C3
Rowan Ct
  3 Goxhill DN19 . . . . . . .12 A8
  11 Heighington/
   Washingborough LN4 . . . .203 D1
Rowan Dr
  5 Healing DN41 . . . . .23 A4
  Silk Willoughby NG34 . . . .121 B2
Rowan Rd
  Lincoln LN6 . . . . .204 F3
  Waddington LN5 . . . . .93 B8
Rowans The
  Gainsborough DN21 . . . . . .197 F5
  Holbeach PE12 . . . . .159 A7
  6 Nettleham LN2 . . . . . . .68 C2
  4 Westwoodside DN9 . . .27 A2
Rowan Way
  1 Boston PE21 . . . . . . .208 B5
  2 Bourne PE10 . . . . . . .213 B6
  16 Metheringham LN4 . . .95 D4
Rowanwood Dr **2**
  NG31 . . . . .210 F7
Rowe Ave PE2 . . . . .230 D7
Rowgate Rd LN11 . . . . .73 A5
Rowland Ct **1** PE4 . . . . . .220 F5
Rowland Rd DN14 . . . . . . .183 B2
Rowlandson St **3**
  DN31 . . . . .191 C7
Rowley Rd PE21 . . . . .209 A4
Rowmills Rd **2** DN16 . . . .185 D8
ROWSTON LN4 . . . . .108 E7
Rowston Cl DN21 . . . . .197 C6
Rowston St DN35 . . . . .193 A1
Roxborough Cl LN6 . . . . . .200 E2
Roxburgh Rd PE7 . . . . .230 B8
Roxburgh St **1** HU5 . . . . .180 B8
ROXBY DN15 . . . . .9 C4
Roxby Ave DN15 . . . . .9 C4
Roxby Cl LN6 . . . . .204 F6
Roxby Rd DN15 . . . . .9 A4
Roxholm Cl **3** NG34 . . . . .108 D1
Roxholme Rd NG34 . . . . . .121 B6
Roxton Ave DN41 . . . . .23 A5
Roxton Hall Dr **15** HU14 . . .3 A4
Royal Air Force Coll The
  NG34 . . . . .120 C8
Royal Arthur Cl **5**
  PE25 . . . . .206 C1
Royal Cl **12** PE12 . . . . . . .168 C4
Royal Ct DN15 . . . . .193 B1
Royal Hull Hospitals NHS
  Trust HU3 . . . . .180 C6
Royal Mews HU3 . . . . .180 C6
Royal Oak Ct
  18 Heckington NG34 . . .122 E3
  18 Louth LN11 . . . . .198 B5
Royal Oak La **3** LN5 . . . . .93 A5
Royal St SN11 . . . . .30 B6
Royalty Bank PE22 . . . . . . .101 B3
Royal Way PE21 . . . . .208 E8
Royce PE7 . . . . .233 C6
Royce Rd
  Peterborough PE1 . . . . . . .226 D3
  Spalding PE11 . . . . .214 B2
Roydon Gr LN6 . . . . .205 B6
Royden Cl PE23 . . . . .101 B3
Royle Cl PE7 . . . . .233 C6
Royston Ave PE2 . . . . .230 D7
Ruards La DN19 . . . . .5 A1
RUCKLAND LN11 . . . . .72 A5
Ruckland Ave LN1 . . . . .201 F7
Rudgard Ave LN2 . . . . .202 A7
Rudgard La DN21 . . . . .234 A3
Rudham Ave DN32 . . . . . . .191 D6
Rudkin Dr **5** NG34 . . . . . .212 D6

Rudyard Cl **7** LN12 . . . . . .77 A7
Rudyard Gr PE4 . . . . .221 C3
Rue de L'yonne **1**
  NG23 . . . . .91 D5
Rue de Nozay **3** DN20 . . .19 E4
Rufford Cl **2** LN6 . . . . . . .205 C8
Rufford Rd DN35 . . . . .192 E4
Rugby Ct **1** NG31 . . . . . . .211 B3
Rugby Rd
  4 Mablethorpe/Sutton on
   Sea LN12 . . . . .64 B4
  Scunthorpe DN16 . . . . . . .185 A8
Rugby St **5** HU3 . . . . .180 B4
Rumbold La **8** PE24 . . . . .102 D1
Runcorn Garth HU4 . . . . . .179 B3
Runcorn Rd LN6 . . . . .204 B5
Running Post La PE20 . . . .135 B4
Runswick Cl LN6 . . . . .205 A3
Runswick Ct DN32 . . . . . . .192 B6
Runswick Rd DN32 . . . . . . .192 B6
Rupert Rd **1** DN33 . . . . . .191 D3
Rural Ave PE11 . . . . .144 D1
Rural Villages Sch Bucknall
  LN10 . . . . .84 B3
Rushcarr La DN17 . . . . .17 C1
Rushcliffe Rd NG31 . . . . . .211 A7
Rush Furlong Nature
  Reserve* DN9 . . . . .27 E3
Rushmere PE2 . . . . .229 C3
Rushmere Ctry Pk*
  LN11 . . . . .61 F8
Ruskin Ave PE6 . . . . .220 E4
Rushtons Way **12** DN20 . . .30 F5
Rusky Dro PE11 . . . . .145 C8
Ruskin Ave LN2 . . . . .202 B6
Ruskin La DN2 . . . . .202 B6
RUSKINGTON NG34 . . . . . .108 E1
Ruskington Cl DN37 . . . . . .188 A2
Ruskington Sta NG34 . . . . .108 E1
Ruskin St **1** NG31 . . . . . . .211 B3
Ruskin St
  2 Gainsborough
   DN21 . . . . .197 D2
  Kingston upon Hull HU3 . . .180 B6
Russell Ave
  Lincoln LN6 . . . . .93 C8
  Newark-on-Trent NG24 . . .104 A2
Russell Cl **12** PE6 . . . . . . .176 A3
Russell Cres DN34 . . . . . . .190 F7
Russell Ct DN35 . . . . .193 A1
Russell Dr **8** PE7 . . . . . . .167 B8
Russell Hill PE8 . . . . .222 A6
Russell Rd **7** NG34 . . . . .121 B8
Russell Read Almshouses
  13 NG31 . . . . .211 A4
Russell St
  Kingston upon Hull
   HU2 . . . . .180 E7
  Lincoln LN6 . . . . .205 D6
  Peterborough PE1 . . . . . . .225 F3
Russell Wlk **2** DN7 . . . . . .14 C5
Russet Cl **4** DN15 . . . . . .182 C5
Russet Dr LN11 . . . . .198 C4
Russet La DN20 . . . . .196 F6
Rustic La DN7 . . . . .41 C6
Ruston Rd NG31 . . . . .211 F7
Ruston Way LN6 . . . . .202 D8
Rutland Cl **15** NG33 . . . . .151 D2
Rutland Dr **1** HU5 . . . . . .179 A7
Rutland La **15** NG13 . . . . .128 A5
Rutland Rd
  Ryhall PE9 . . . . .163 C1
  1 Scampton Airfield LN1 . .67 E5
Rutland St **2** DN32 . . . . . .189 D1
Rutland Terr PE9 . . . . .219 A4
Rutland Way
  Ryhall PE9 . . . . .163 C1
  1 Stamford PE9 . . . . . . .219 D3
Ryall Rd
  Great Casterton PE9 . . . . .171 C8
  Stamford PE9 . . . . .219 D1
Ryhall Rd Ind Est PE9 . . . . .219 D3
Ryhall CE Prim Sch
  PE9 . . . . .163 C1
Ryhall Rd
  Great Casterton PE9 . . . . .171 C8
  Stamford PE9 . . . . .219 D1
Ryland Bridge LN2 . . . . .68 E6
Ryland Gdns **10** LN2 . . . . .68 D6
Ryland Rd LN2 . . . . .68 D6
Rymac Cres PE25 . . . . .90 E4
Rymer Pl DN35 . . . . .193 A4
Ryton Rd PE21 . . . . .208 B3

S

Sable Cl HU4 . . . . .179 C2
Sabre Way PE1 . . . . .226 F4
Sackville Cl DN40 . . . . .186 D4
Sackville Rd DN40 . . . . . . .186 D4

Sackville St **2** DN31 . . . .191 C7
Sacred Heart RC Prim Sch
  PE3 . . . . .225 A5
Sacrewell Farm & Ctry
  Ctr* PE8 . . . . .222 C5
Saddleback Rd
  Skidbrooke with Saltfleet
   Haven LN11 . . . . .51 A3
  South Cockerington LN11 . . .50 E1
Saddle Cl PE4 . . . . .225 E8
Saddle Row NG34 . . . . . . .120 B8
Saddlers Cl
  Glinton PE6 . . . . .220 D8
  Osbournby NG34 . . . . .132 D5
Saddler's Cl **11** LN4 . . . . . .95 C4
Saddlers Mead **10**
  PE11 . . . . .214 A2
Saddlers Way
  Fishtoft PE21 . . . . .209 C2
  7 Sutton PE12 . . . . .216 B5
  9 Middle Rasen LN8 . . . . .57 E7
Saddler's Way **2** DN9 . . . .27 D3
Sadler Cl **3** PE25 . . . . . . .206 C1
Sadler Rd LN6 . . . . .204 B5
Saffrondale HU10 . . . . .178 E7
Saffron Wlk **12** PE10 . . . .213 C5
Sage Ct LN6 . . . . .205 D8
Sagefield Cl **3** DN33 . . . .194 D8
Sage's La PE4 . . . . .225 C8
Sailors Wharf HU9 . . . . . . .181 C6
Sainsbury Way HU4 . . . . . .179 A1
St Abbs Cl **3** DN33 . . . . .181 A5
St Aiden's Rd **5** LN6 . . . .204 E2
St Albans Ave DN31 . . . . . .191 A8
St Albans Cl
  8 Grantham NG31 . . . . .210 D5
  9 Hibaldstow DN20 . . . . .30 F5
  8 Scunthorpe DN17 . . . .184 C7
St Alban's Dr **16** PE25 . . .175 A1
St Andrews Ave **2**
  DN17 . . . . .184 F2
St Andrews CE Prim Sch
  Heckington NG34 . . . . . . .122 E3
  Immingham DN40 . . . . . . .186 A4
  Woodhall Spa LN10 . . . . . . .97 C6
St Andrews Cl **5** DN17 . . .201 F1
St Andrew's Cl
  4 Helpringham NG34 . . .133 D7
  Redbourne DN21 . . . . .30 F3
St Andrews Com Prim Sch
  HU10 . . . . .178 C7
St Andrew's Cres **6**
  DN34 . . . . .121 B7
St Andrews Ct
  Immingham DN40 . . . . . . .186 A4
  4 Timberland LN4 . . . . . . .96 C1
St Andrews Dr **6** LN1 . . . . .96 C1
St Andrew's Dr
  1 Burton upon Stather
   DN15 . . . . .8 B4
  Grimsby DN32 . . . . .192 B4
  Lincoln LN6 . . . . .205 C8
  Skegness PE25 . . . . .206 D5
St Andrews Gdns LN6 . . . . .205 C8
St Andrews Gr **33** DN7 . . .14 D4
St Andrews Rd DN40 . . . . .186 B5
St Andrew's Mount
  HU10 . . . . .178 C8
St Andrew's Pl **3** LN1 . . .234 B1
St Andrew's Rd
  1 Mablethorpe/Sutton on
   Sea LN12 . . . . .64 B4
  Northborough PE6 . . . . . . .217 E1
St Andrew's Rd
  8 Butterwick PE22 . . . . .126 E3
  Spalding PE11 . . . . .214 C1
St Andrew's St
  10 Heckington NG34 . . .122 E3
  18 Kirton in Lindsey DN21 .30 B1
St Andrews Wlk **5**
  LN10 . . . . .97 C5
St Annes NG31 . . . . .50 F7
St Anne's CE (Cont) Prim
  Sch NG31 . . . . .211 C1
St Annes Cl
  Lincoln LN2 . . . . .202 A4
  Skegness PE25 . . . . .206 C6
  1 Sleaford NG34 . . . . . .212 C6
  3 Spalding 214 C6
St Anne's Dr
  5 Barnby Dun DN3 . . . . .14 A3
  Epworth DN9 . . . . .27 E4
  4 RAF Cranwell NG34 . .120 C8
St Anne's Gdns LN6 . . . .?
St Anne's La NG31 . . . . . . .130 F7
St Ann's Ave DN34 . . . . . . .191 B6
St Ann's La PE12 . . . . .158 F3
St Anns Wharf **1** 181 F4
St Aubins Cres LN4 . . . . . . .81 F4
St Audrey Cl PE2 . . . . .229 D5
St Augustine Ave
  DN32 . . . . .191 E5
St Augustine Cres
  DN16 . . . . .185 B5
St Augustine LN2 . . . . .202 F6

St Augustines CE Jun Sch
PE2. . . . . .230 F8
St Augustine's CE Sch
PE13. . . . . 170 D2
St Augustine's CE (Aided)
Prim Sch PE9 . . . . 219 C7
St Augustine's Wlk
PE2. . . . . .230 E8
St Augustine Webster Cath
Prim Sch DN15. . . . . .182 D4
St Barbara's Cres **7**
DN15 . . . . 8 B4
St Barnabas CE Prim Sch
DN38 . . . . .21 B4
St Barnabas Ct **4** HU3. . .180 C4
St Barnabas Dr **1** HU14. . . 3 C7
St Barnabas Rd DN38 . . . .21 B4
St Bartholomews CE Prim
Sch PE11 . . . . 156 A8
St Bartholomew's Cl **4**
DN41 . . . . .23 E5
St Bede Ct HU4. . . . . .179 E5
St Bedes Cath Science Coll
PE21. . . . . .209 B6
St Bedes RC Comp Sch
DN16 . . . . .185 B6
St Bee's Dr **10** PE6. . . . . .175 A1
St Benedict Ct **19** PE6. . . .166 F1
St Benedicts Cl **2** PE6. . .220 D8
St Benedict's Cl **2**
LN6. . . . . .204 D2
St Benedicts Sq LN5. . . . .234 A2
St Benet's Gdns **2**
PE6. . . . . .175 A1
St Bernadettes RC Prim
Sch DN16 . . . . .185 C6
St Bernards Ave LN11. . . .198 D6
St Bernards Cl LN11. . . . .198 E6
St Bernard's Cl **6** DN20. . .19 E4
St Bernard's Sch LN11. . . .198 E5
St Botolph La PE2. . . . . . .230 C6
St Botolphs CE Prim Sch
Peterborough PE2. . . . . . .230 B6
Sleaford NG34. . . . . .212 B3
St Botolphs Cl **2** LN1. . . .66 D3
St Botolph's Cres **8**
LN5. . . . . .205 E8
St Botolphs Ct **16** LN5. . .205 E8
St Botolphs Gate LN1. . . .66 D3
St Botolphs Infants Sch
LN5. . . . . .205 D8
St Botolphs Mews **31**
PE21. . . . . .208 F5
St Botolphs Rd **7**
NG34 . . . . .212 C6
St Botolph's Rd DN16 . . .185 C7
St Botolph's Way PE6. . . .176 A2
St Catherine Ct PE12. . . . .215 F3
St Catherines **18** LN5 . . .205 E8
St Catherines Cres
DN16 . . . . .185 A4
St Catherines Ct
Ashby DN16. . . . . .185 D6
Grimsby DN34 . . . . .190 F6
St Catherine's Ct LN5. . . .205 D7
St Catherine's Dr **8**
DN7 . . . . .14 C2
St Catherine's Gr LN5. . . .205 D7
St Catherine's Rd
Grantham NG31. . . . . .211 B4
Lincoln LN5 . . . . .205 E7
St Chads Cl **2** LN2 . . . . . .68 E6
St Chads Gate DN37. . . . .188 A1
St Chad's Rd DN16. . . . . .185 D7
St Chads Wlk S **20**
DN37 . . . . .190 E8
St Charles RC Prim Sch
HU2 . . . . .180 E8
St Christophers Cl **11**
NG34 . . . . .107 F1
St Christopher's Rd **11**
DN36 . . . . .36 C8
St Christophers Specl Sch
LN6. . . . . .205 B4
St Claire's Ct **6** LN6. . . . .204 C8
St Clares Wlk DN20 . . . . .196 C2
St Clement's Cl **7** PE9 . . .219 A5
St Clements Cl LN14. . . . .108 E7
St Clements Coll PE25 . . .206 C5
St Clement's Ct **3** LN1. . .234 B4
St Clement's Dr **1** LN3. . . .82 B6
St Clements Gn PE25 . . . .206 B4
St Clements Rd **17**
NG34 . . . . .108 D2
St Clement's Rd
3 Lincoln LN6. . . . . . . .204 E2
2 Skegness PE25. . . . . . .206 B4
St Clements Way
DN36 . . . . .195 C4
St Crispins Cl **2** DN40. . . .12 E4
St Crispin's Cl **3** LN6. . . .204 D2
St Cuthberts Ct **14** LN1. .234 B3
St Davids Cl **2** PE25. . . . .206 D6
St David's Cl **2** LN3 . . . .203 E7
St Davids Cres DN17 . . . .184 E3
St David's Rd LN6. . . . . . .204 D2
St David's Sch PE25. . . . .206 D1
St David's St **13** LN8 . . . . .47 B6
St Denys Ave NG34 . . . . .212 B6
St Deny's Cl **2** DN40. . . . .12 E3
St Edith Gate **6** LN11. . . .62 C6
St Edmonds CE PE24 . . . .115 D8
St Edmonds Cl **3**
NG31 . . . . .210 D5
St Edmunds Ct DN34 . . . .190 F6
St Edmunds Rd NG34 . . . .212 C3
St Edward's Dr **15** LN2 . . . .68 F2
St Edwins Cl **18** DN7 . . . . .14 D4
St Edwins Dr **17** DN7. . . . .14 D4
St Faith & St Martin CE Jun
Sch LN1 . . . . .201 D4
St Faiths CE Inf Sch
LN1. . . . . .201 D4
St Faith's Sch **6** LN1. . . . .201 D4
St Firmin's Way PE10 . . . .164 D7
St Frances Ct PE25. . . . . .206 B6
St Francis Ave DN31 . . . . .191 A8
St Francis Cl **5** LN6. . . . .204 D2
St Francis Gdns **2**
LN12. . . . . .77 A7
St Francis Gr **1** DN37. . . .23 E1
St Francis Sch LN1. . . . . .201 E7
St George Ave PE2. . . . . . .231 E6
St George's Ave **3**
PE9. . . . . .219 D6
St George's Ave **5** PE14. .14 C2
St George's CE Aided Prim
Sch PE9 . . . . .219 C7
St George's CE Com Prim
Sch DN21. . . . . .197 F2
St Georges Cl
2 Cranwell NG34. . . . . .107 F1
22 Thorne/Moorends
DN8. . . . . .15 B7
St George's Cl LN6 . . . . .204 E2
St Georges Coll of Tech
NG34 . . . . .212 C4
St George's Ct DN21. . . . . .30 F3
St Georges Dr **3** LN10. . . .97 C5
St George's Hill DN21. . . . .54 F7
St Georges Hospl LN1. . . .201 C4
St Georges La LN2. . . . . . .67 F1
St Georges Prim Sch
HU3 . . . . .180 A6
St Georges Rd **21** DN8 . . . .15 B7
St George's Rd
Kingston upon Hull
HU3 . . . . .180 A5
17 Wittering PE8. . . . . . . .172 B1
St George's Sq **13** PE9 . .219 C5
St George's St **8** PE9 . . .219 C5
St Georges Way **11**
NG31 . . . . .211 D7
St Gilbert of Sempringham
CE Prim Sch NG34. . . . . .143 B7
St Gilberts CE Prim Sch
PE9. . . . . .219 A5
St Gilbert's Cl NG34. . . . .143 B6
St Gilbert's Rd PE10 . . . . .213 C6
St GILES LN2 . . . . .202 C7
St Giles Ave
Lincoln LN2 . . . . .234 C4
1 Sleaford NG34. . . . . . .212 F4
St Giles' Ave DN33 . . . . . .191 D1
St Giles Inf Sch LN2 . . . . .202 B6
St Guthlac Ave **1** PE6. . .217 B5
St Guthlac Sch PE6. . . . . .166 F1
St Guthlac's Cl **3** DN3 . . .16 C1
St Guthlac's Way **1**
PE21. . . . . .126 C1
St Helenas CE Prim Sch
LN13. . . . . .89 A7
St Helens Ave DN33. . . . . .191 D3
St Helen's Ave LN6. . . . . .205 B7
St Helen's Cl NG31. . . . . .210 D4
St Helen's Cres DN37 . . . .194 D1
St Helen's Dr **14** HU15 . . .2 D6
St Helens Rd DN20. . . . . .196 D3
St Helier's Rd DN35. . . . . .192 E7
St Hilary's Cl **1** LN6. . . . .204 D2
St Hilda's Ave DN34. . . . . .191 B6
St Huberts Cl PE25 . . . . . .206 B6
St Hughes Cl PE11. . . . . . .226 C4
St Hugh's Ave DN35. . . . . .192 E6
St Hughs Cl LN6. . . . . . . .204 B7
St Hugh's Cl **7** LN3. . . . .203 E7
St Hugh's Cres DN16. . . . .185 C8
St Hugh's Dr
3 Barlings LN3. . . . . .69 C3
Lincoln LN6 . . . . .204 E2
St Hugh's Hospl DN32. . . .191 F4
St Hugh's Maths & Comp
Sch NG31. . . . . .210 E3
St Hughs Sch
Scunthorpe DN16. . . . . . .183 B1
Woodhall Spa LN10. . . . . . .97 D5
St Hugh St LN2 . . . . .234 C2
St Hugh's Terr **3** LN1. . . .66 C7
St Hybald's Gr **2** DN20 . .30 F7
St Ives Cres DN34. . . . . . .190 E5
St James Ave
Grimsby DN34 . . . . .191 A6
7 Hatfield DN7. . . . . .14 C3
Peterborough PE1. . . . . . .225 F7
St James Cl
19 Crowle DN17 . . . . .16 D7
Newton PE13. . . . . .170 A5
St James Ct **3** DN15. . . .183 A3
St James' Ct **2** DN34 . . .191 C6
St James Rd
Brigg DN20 . . . . .196 D3
Long Sutton PE12 . . . . . .216 A1
Welton HU14 . . . . .2 F5
St James's Sch DN34 . . . .191 C6
St James's Rd **6** DN20. . .30 E8
St James's St HU3. . . . . . .180 D5
St James's Way **5**
PE11. . . . . .214 D4
St James View LN11. . . . .198 B4
St James Way **2** PE12 . . .158 E5
St Joan's Dr **5** DN20 . . . . .30 E7
St John Fisher RC Sch
PE1. . . . . .226 C4
St John's Ave
3 Cherry Willingham/
Reepham LN3 . . . . .203 E7
1 Lincoln LN6. . . . . .204 E2
St Johns CE Prim Sch
PE2. . . . . .231 C7
St Johns Church Sch
PE2. . . . . .229 F3
St Johns Cl
2 Baston PE6. . . . . .164 E5
Brigg DN20 . . . . .196 D3
2 Goxhill DN19 . . . . .12 A8
Scampton LN1. . . . . .67 C6
St Johns Ct
Grange DN34. . . . . .191 A5
6 Grantham NG31. . . . . .211 A3
St John's Dr
Corby Glen NG33. . . . . . . .152 F7
Ingoldmells PE25. . . . . .90 E4
6 Spalding PE11 . . . . .214 B3
St Johns Mews PE12. . . . .215 E2
St Johns Rd PE2. . . . . .231 B7
St John's Rd
Boston PE21 . . . . .209 A3
Bracebridge Heath LN4. . .205 F2
9 Humberston DN36 . . . . .36 C8
Lincoln LN2 . . . . .201 F6
Scunthorpe DN16 . . . . . . .185 C6
Spalding PE11 . . . . .214 C3
Weston PE12. . . . . .157 C2
2 Wittering PE8. . . . . .172 B1
St John's St
3 Holbeach PE12. . . . . . .215 E2
Peterborough PE1. . . . . . .226 B2
2 Stamford PE9. . . . . . . .219 B5
St John St **11** PE2 . . . . . .102 D1
St John's Terr **13**
DN21 . . . . .197 D3
St John the Baptist CE
Prim Sch PE11. . . . . .214 C2
St Joseph Dr HU4 . . . . . . .179 C5
St Josephs RC Prim Sch
DN35 . . . . .192 D4
St Judes Cl PE3 . . . . .225 C4
St Julian's Wells HU10 . . .178 D7
St Kyneburgha Cl PE5. . . .223 E2
St Lamberts Gr **4**
PE12. . . . . .157 D7
St Lawrence CE
(Controlled) Prim Sch
LN6. . . . . .200 B4
St Lawrence Rd **3** LN3 . . .83 C4
St Lawrence Rd DN7. . . . . .14 C4
St Lawrence Specl Sch
LN9. . . . . .199 D4
St Lawrence's Pl **2**
DN16 . . . . .185 D7
St Lawrence's Rd
DN16 . . . . .185 D6
St Lawrence St LN9. . . . . .199 B4
St Lawrence Way **3**
PE9. . . . . .172 F7
St Leodegar's Cl PE20 . . .136 D7
St Leonard's Ave DN31. . .191 A8
St Leonards Dr PE24. . . . . .90 D7
St Leonards Pl **3** LN10 . . .97 D5
St Leonard's La
4 Lincoln LN2. . . . . .234 C3
South Cockerington LN11 . . .62 B7
St Leonard's Rd **2**
PE13. . . . . .170 B2
St Leonard's St **8** PE9. . .219 C5
St Luke's Cl
Cherry Willingham/Reepham
LN3. . . . . .203 F7
1 Hatfield DN7. . . . . .14 C2
St Luke's Cres **8** DN36. . . .36 C8
St Lukes Ct HU10 . . . . . . .178 F8
St Luke's Ct **7** DN32. . . . .191 F8
St Lukes Sch DN16. . . . . .185 D8
St Luke's St HU3. . . . . . . .180 D6
St Margaret's **6** PE11. . . .145 A8
St Margaret's Ave
PE25. . . . . .206 A4
St Margarets CE
(Controlled) Prim Sch
LN13. . . . . .63 A1
St Margaret's Cl
17 Laceby DN37 . . . . .23 F1
6 Lincoln LN6. . . . . .205 B4
St Margaret's Cres **6**
DN40 . . . . .22 E8
St Margaret's Gdns
LN6. . . . . .205 A4
St Margarets Mews
DN34 . . . . .190 F6
St Margaret's Pl **2**
PE2. . . . . .230 F6
St Margarets Rd **1**
PE2. . . . . .230 F6
St Margaret's Wlk **5**
DN16 . . . . .185 C6
St Mark's Ave **3** LN3 . . . .203 E7
St Mark's Cl
North Hykeham LN6 . . . . .204 E3
Skegness PE25. . . . . .206 B6
St Mark's Ct **3** PE1. . . . . .226 A3
St Marks Dr **6** PE6. . . . . .166 E1
St Marks Rd HU13. . . . . . .169 E3
St Mark's Rd
Holbeach PE12 . . . . .147 D6
10 Humberston DN36. . . . . .36 C8
St Marks Sh Ctr LN5. . . . .234 A1
St Mark's Sq
Kingston upon Hull
HU3. . . . . .180 D4
Lincoln LN5 . . . . .234 A1
St Marks St PE1 . . . . .226 A3
St Mark St
Kingston upon Hull
HU8. . . . . .181 A8
Lincoln LN5 . . . . .234 A1
St Marks Terr **22** PE21. . .208 F5
St Martins NG33 . . . . .152 E1
St Martins Ave **2** LN4 . . .179 E6
St Martins CE Prim Sch
DN9 . . . . .28 A3
St Martins Cl **2** NG34. . .107 F1
St Martin's Cl
2 Blyton DN21. . . . . .41 C5
4 Stamford PE9 . . . . .219 C4
Stubton NG23 . . . . .118 B7
St Martin's Cres
Grimsby DN33. . . . . .191 C3
7 Scawby DN20. . . . . .30 E8
St Martin's La LN1. . . . . . .234 B3
St Martin's Pl **8** DN41. . . .23 A4
St Martins Prep Sch
DN32. . . . . .191 D5
St Martin's Rd
Newborough PE6 . . . . . . .221 F8
4 Scawby DN20. . . . . .30 E8
1 Wisbech PE13. . . . . . . .170 E2
St Martin's St
Lincoln LN2 . . . . .234 B3
Peterborough PE1. . . . . . .225 F5
St Martin's Way **4**
NG32 . . . . .120 A3
St Mary CI **12** PE6. . . . . .166 E1
St Mary's Abbey*
PE20 . . . . .135 C7
St Mary's Ave
4 Barnetby le Wold
DN38. . . . . .21 B4
2 Pinchbeck PE11. . . . . .156 E8
12 Welton/Dunholme
LN2. . . . . .68 D7
4 Wittering PE8 . . . . .172 C1
St Marys Cath Prim Sch
NG31 . . . . .211 C5
St Marys CE (Controlled)
Prim Sch LN2. . . . . .68 C6
St Marys Ct
South Field HU13. . . . . .3 E4
Weston PE12 . . . . .157 D7
St Mary's Ct
1 Bottesford HU13. . . . . .128 A6
2 Brough HU15. . . . . .2 C7
Farcet PE7. . . . . .231 C2
Grimsby DN34 . . . . .192 C6
Peterborough PE1. . . . . . .226 B4
Thorney PE6 . . . . .176 A2
Wilsford NG32 . . . . .120 C1
St Mary's Cres
1 Manby LN11. . . . . .62 C6
9 Stow LN1. . . . . .66 D4
Swineshead PE20 . . . . . . .135 B6
St Mary's Ct **5** DN15 . . . .182 C6
St Marys Dr
6 Sleaford NG34. . . . . . .212 C6
3 Sutterton PE20. . . . . . .136 B5
St Mary's Dr
3 Hatfield DN7. . . . . .14 C2
Peterborough PE2. . . . . . .229 F4
St Mary's Gdns
6 Cowbit PE12. . . . . .167 B8
Long Sutton PE12 . . . . . .216 C5
12 Whaplode PE12 . . . . . .158 B7
St Mary's Hill **17** PE9. . . .219 C5
St Mary's La
4 Barton-upon-Humber
DN18. . . . . .10 F8
Binbrook LN8 . . . . .47 F7
Claxby LN8. . . . . .45 E5
Louth LN11 . . . . .198 C5
St Mary's Mdws **2**
PE12. . . . . .159 D7
St Mary's Pk LN11. . . . . . .198 A6
St Mary's Pl **3** PE9. . . . . .219 C5
St Mary's RC (Aided) Prim
Sch PE21 . . . . .209 B6
St Mary's RC High Sch
DN33 . . . . .191 A3
St Mary's Rd
DN20 . . . . .196 C5
St Mary's St
DN32 . . . . .191 F8
St Mary's Way
Farcet PE7. . . . . .231 C2
Lincoln LN5 . . . . .234 A1
6 Stamford PE9. . . . . . . .219 C5
St Mary's Way **2** PE22. . .114 A1
St Mathews Cl **2** LN6. . .201 D1
St Matthews Cl **11**
PE25. . . . . .206 A6
St Matthew's Cl
5 Cherry Willingham/
Reepham LN3 . . . . .203 E7
4 Holbeach PE12. . . . . . .215 D2
St Matthew's Dr **13**
PE12. . . . . .160 E4
St Matthew's Rd **12**
DN34 . . . . .36 C8
St Matthew St HU3. . . . . .180 B5
St Mawes Cres DN34. . . . .191 A7
St Mellion Dr NG31. . . . . .211 E7
St Michael Cl **23** LN5. . . . .93 F7
St Michael's Ave PE13 . . .170 D1
St Michaels CE Prim Sch
LN6. . . . . .92 E8
St Michael's CE Sch
LN11. . . . . .198 D5
St Michaels Cl **18** DN8. . .15 B7
St Michael's Cl **15** DN8 . .15 B7
St Michael's Cres **5**
DN16 . . . . .185 C8
St Michael's Ct **7** DN8 . . .15 B7
St Michael's Gate PE1 . . .226 C7
St Michael's La
PE24 . . . . .102 D1
Wainfleet St Mary PE24 . .115 D8
St Michaels Mount **18**
HU14 . . . . .3 B7
St Michael's Rd
Grimsby DN34 . . . . .190 D4
3 Louth LN11. . . . . .198 C5
18 Wittering PE8. . . . . . . .172 B1
St Michaels Terr **7**
LN1. . . . . .234 B3
St Michael's Way **1**
NG34 . . . . .120 C8
St Michaels Wlk **8**
NG34 . . . . .212 C6
St Nectan Cl **9** HU3. . . . .180 A4
St Nicholas Ave HU4 . . . .179 C2
St Nicholas CE (Controlled)
Prim Sch PE21. . . . . .209 B4
St Nicholas CE Sch
DN39. . . . . .12 A1
St Nicholas Cl
4 Barkston NG32. . . . . . .130 B8
Boston PE21. . . . . .209 B3
St Nicholas Dr DN37 . . . .190 C6
St Nicholas Gdns HU4. . .179 C2
St Nicholas Prim Sch
PE12. . . . . .160 A8
St Nicholas Rd
Boston PE21. . . . . .209 B3
Thorne/Moorends DN8. . . .15 A8
St Nicholas St LN1. . . . . .234 A4
St Nicholas Way
10 Lincoln LN6. . . . . .160 AE
5 Spalding PE11. . . . . . . .214 A5
St Norberts RC Prim Sch
DN17. . . . . .16 D7
St Norbett's Cath Prim Sch
PE12. . . . . .214 C4
St Olaf's Dr DN32. . . . . . .191 D6
St Olave's Dr **17** PE6. . . .175 A3
St Pauls Ave **6** LN3 . . . .197 B2
St Paul's Ave **6** LN9. . . . .203 E7
St Pauls Cl PE13 . . . . .169 E2
St Paul's Cl PE13. . . . . . . .170 D1
St Pauls Gdns DN16. . . . .185 B5
St Paul's Gdns PE10 . . . . .213 D4
St Paul's La **2** LN1 . . . . .234 B3
St Pauls Prim Sch
PE21. . . . . .214 F6
St Paul's Rd
Gainsborough DN21 . . . . .197 B7
Peterborough PE1. . . . . . .225 F7
Scunthorpe DN16 . . . . . . .185 B6
Spalding PE11. . . . . .214 F5
St Pauls St HU2 . . . . .180 E8
St Paul's St PE9 . . . . .219 C5
St Paul's Sq **17** PE6. . . . .166 F1
St Pega's Rd
Glinton PE6. . . . . .174 A6
Peakirk PE6. . . . . .220 B8
St Peter at Arches **6**
LN2. . . . . .234 B2
St Peter at Gowts CE
(Controlled) Prim Sch
LN5. . . . . .201 E1
St Peter in-Eastgate CE
(Cont) Inf Sch LN2 . . . . .234 C3
St Peter & St Paul CE Prim
Sch PE24 . . . . .102 D2
St Peter & St Paul Lincs
Cath High Sch LN6 . . . . .205 B2
St Peter's Ave
8 Cherry Willingham/
Reepham LN3 . . . . .203 E7
Cleethorpes DN35. . . . . . .192 C6
Kingston upon Hull
HU10. . . . . .178 E6
Lincoln LN6 . . . . .204 D2
Scunthorpe DN16 . . . . . . .185 B3
St Peter's CE Jun Sch
PE13. . . . . .170 C1
St Peters CE Prim Sch
Cleethorpes DN35. . . . . . .192 F6
Dunston LN4 . . . . .95 C6
St Peters Cl **2** DN21. . . . . .40 B5
St Peter's Cl
Burgh le Marsh PE24 . . . .102 D1
2 Holton le Clay DN36. . .195 D
St Peter's Cres **5** DN36. . .36 C
St Peters Ct **9** PE9 . . . . .219 B

St Peters Dr 4 LN10 . . . . .97 D5
St Peters Gr 2 DN37 . . . . .23 E1
St Peter's Gr 14 DN21 . . . . .29 C3
St Peter's Hill
🔲 Grantham NG31 . . . . . .211 A4
14 Stamford PE9 . . . . .219 B5
St Peter's Rd
🔲 Bourne PE10 . . . . .213 C5
Peterborough PE1 . . . . . . .226 A2
St Peter's Rd 12 DN21 . . . . .29 C3
St Peter's Sch DN10 . . . . . .39 B1
St Peter's Way PE6 . . . . . .176 A2
St Pierre Ave NG31 . . . . . .211 E7
St Polycarp's Dr PE12 . . . .168 B3
St Quintins Cl 8 HU9 . . . .181 C8
St Rumbold's St LN2 . . . . .234 B2
St Sebastians CE (Aided)
Prim Sch LN2 . . . . .129 E5
St Simon's Dr 8 LN1 . . . .203 E7
St Stephen's Sh Ctr
HU1 . . . . .180 D6
St Stephens St HU2 . . . . . .180 D6
St Swithins Cl 1 PE20 . . .135 A4
St Swithins Sq LN2 . . . . . .234 B2
St Thomas CE Prim Sch
PE21 . . . . .208 F1
St Thomas Ct
Boston PE21 . . . . .208 F2
Long Sutton PE12 . . . . . . .216 B5
St Thomas Dr PE21 . . . . . .208 E2
St Thomas Moore RC Prim
Sch PE1 . . . . .226 D4
St Thomas Moore Rd
HU6 . . . . .179 A4
St Thomas More RC Prim
Sch HU4 . . . . .179 A4
St Thomas Rd 2 DN31 . . . .191 B8
St Thomas' Rd 13 DN36 . . . .36 C8
St Tibba Way 15 PE9 . . . . .163 C1
St Valentines Way
PE25 . . . . .206 B6
ST VINCENT NG31 . . . . . . .211 D3
St Vincent Cl 2 PE25 . . . .206 A6
St Vincent's Ave DN15 . . . .183 A6
St Vincent's Rd NG31 . . . . .211 C3
St Wilfrid's Cl 8 LN4 . . . . .95 D4
St William Cl PE12 . . . . . .215 F3
Salacon Way 12 DN32 . . . .189 C1
Saladine Ct 24 DN41 . . . . . .23 F5
Salamander Cl DN31 . . . . . .191 B8
SALEBY LN13 . . . . .75 F6
Salem St 5 PE11 . . . . .145 B6
Salisbury Ave 2 LN8 . . . . . .47 B6
Salisbury Cl
🔲 Grantham NG31 . . . . . .210 D5
Morton DN21 . . . . .40 D3
🔲 Saxilby with Ingleby
LN1 . . . . .66 D2
2 Scunthorpe DN17 . . . . .184 C7
Salisbury Dr
2 Canwick LN4 . . . . .81 A2
Waltham DN37 . . . . .194 D4
Salisbury Rd PE4 . . . . .220 F3
Salisbury St
Gainsborough DN21 . . . . . .197 C3
Kingston upon Hull
HU3 . . . . .178 D1
Salix App 11 LN6 . . . . . . .204 C8
Sallie Bank La LN1 . . . . . . .65 D2
Sallows Rd PE1 . . . . .226 B6
SALMONBY LN9 . . . . .86 E8
Salmonby Rd DN17 . . . . . .184 E4
Saltash Rd HU4 . . . . .179 A2
Saltburn Gr 5 DN32 . . . . .192 A5
SALTBY LE14 . . . . .138 F1
Saltby Rd
Croxton Kerrial NG32 . . . . .138 D3
Sproxton LE14 . . . . .150 C7
Saltergate
Lincoln LN2 . . . . .234 B2
Peterborough PE1 . . . . . . .226 E7
The Willows DN37 . . . . . . .188 A1
Salter Gate LN11 . . . . .51 A1
Saltergate Rd 28 DN17 . . . . .29 D7
Saltern Dr PE11 . . . . .214 B5
Saltersford Gr NG31 . . . . . .211 D1
Saltersford Rd NG31 . . . . . .211 D2
Saltersgate HU1 . . . . .226 F7
Salters' La LN11 . . . . .48 B4
Saltersway NG34 . . . . .132 F3
Salters Way 14 PE11 . . . . .134 E2
SALTFLEET LN11 . . . . .51 B4
Saltfleetby ·
Theddlethorpe Dunes
National Nature
Reserve* LN11 . . . . .51 E3
Saltfleet La PE11 . . . . .145 B4
Saltfleet Rd
Saltfleetby LN12 . . . . .51 D1
Theddlethorpe All Saints
LN12 . . . . .51 D1
SALTFLEETBY ALL SAINTS
LN11 . . . . .51 C1
Saltfleetby CE Prim Sch
LN11 . . . . .51 B1
SALTFLEETBY ST CLEMENT
LN11 . . . . .51 C2
SALTFLEETBY ST PETER
LN11 . . . . .63 B8
Salthouse La HU1 . . . . .181 A6
Saltings The 6 PE34 . . . . .161 F3
Saltmarsh PE2 . . . . .230 C4
Saltney Gate PE12 . . . . . . .215 A6

Salts Rd PE14 . . . . .170 F4
Salvesen Rd DN35 . . . . . . .189 D1
Salvesen Way HU3 . . . . . . .180 A3
Samman Cl HU10 . . . . .178 D6
Sampey Way 13 NG34 . . . .133 B1
Samphire Cl 8 DN36 . . . . . .37 C5
Sampson St DN17 . . . . .7 A2
Sam Scorer Gall* LN1 . . .234 B3
Samuel Ave DN32 . . . . .192 B6
Samworths Cl PE5 . . . . . . .223 F2
Sanbeds La DN9 . . . . .27 B2
Sanctuary Way DN37 . . . . . .190 C6
Sandars Rd DN21 . . . . .53 A8
Sandbach Arc PE25 . . . . . .206 D3
Sandback Ave PE25 . . . . . .206 C2
Sandbeck La DN21 . . . . .41 B6
Sandcliffe Rd NG31 . . . . . .211 D7
Sanderlings The 6
PE6 . . . . .174 A5
Sanders Cl
Lincoln LN1 . . . . .201 D8
15 Mablethorpe & Sutton
LN12 . . . . .77 A7
Meering NG23 . . . . .91 C8
Sanderson Cl 1 DN16 . . . .183 B1
Sanderson's Bank DN10 . . . .26 C2
Sanders View LN1 . . . . . . .201 D8
Sandfield Cl DN17 . . . . . . .184 D5
Sandfield Dr 8 HU15 . . . . . .2 C5
Sandford PE3 . . . . .225 B5
Sandford St 8 DN31 . . . . .188 D1
Sandhill La 1 DN22 . . . . . .52 B3
Sandhill Rd DN14 . . . . .7 B6
SANDHOLME PE20 . . . . . . .136 F4
Sandholme La PE20 . . . . . .136 E5
Sandhouse Cres
2 Scunthorpe DN16 . . . . .183 C1
Scunthorpe DN16 . . . . . . .185 C8
Sandhurst Cres 5
NG34 . . . . .212 B2
Sandhurst Ct 6 LN12 . . . . .77 A7
Sandhurst Rd
8 Hampton Vale PE7 . . . .230 D1
5 Mablethorpe/Sutton on Sea
LN12 . . . . .77 A7
SANDILANDS LN12 . . . . .77 A8
Sandilands 22 LN12 . . . . . .77 A7
Sandilands Pit Nature
Reserve* LN12 . . . . .77 A7
Sand La
Barkston NG32 . . . . .129 F8
Besthorpe NG23 . . . . .91 C8
Broadholme LN6 . . . . .66 D1
8 Broughton DN20 . . . . . .19 D3
Caistor LN7 . . . . .32 E4
Fenton LN1 . . . . .65 D3
Great Steeping PE23 . . . . .101 C7
Hougham NG32 . . . . .118 C5
Marton DN21 . . . . .30 A5
Marston NG32 . . . . .118 E1
Messingham DN17 . . . . . . .29 A7
Osgodby LN8 . . . . .45 B3
Spalford NG23 . . . . .78 D4
Thorney NG23 . . . . .79 B8
Torksey LN1 . . . . .66 C5
Wroot DN9 . . . . .26 C6
Sandlees La NG34 . . . . . . .123 B4
Sandlemere Cl 8 HU3 . . . .180 A5
Sandon Cl NG31 . . . . .211 C5
Sandon St NG31 . . . . .211 B5
Sandon Specl Sch
NG31 . . . . .211 C5
Sandown Cl 5 PE11 . . . . . .156 E3
Sandpiper Dr
Kingston upon Hull
HU4 . . . . .179 B1
Peterborough PE2 . . . . . . .231 E6
Sandpit Rd 14 PE6 . . . . . . .176 A3
Sandra Cres LN4 . . . . .203 D1
Sand Rd DN17 . . . . .28 B8
Sandringham Ave 29
PE13 . . . . .170 D1
Sandringham Cl
🔲 Stamford PE9 . . . . .219 B7
8 Whaplode PE12 . . . . . .158 B6
Sandringham Cres
DN17 . . . . .184 F3
Sandringham Ct 4
PE12 . . . . .215 F3
Sandringham Dr
Londonthorpe & Harrowby
without NG31 . . . . .211 E5
Louth LN11 . . . . .198 B7
13 Mablethorpe & Sutton
LN12 . . . . .76 F8
Wragby LN8 . . . . .70 D4
Sandringham Gdns
PE21 . . . . .209 C6
Sandringham Rd
Cleethorpes DN35 . . . . . . .192 D4
Peterborough PE4 . . . . . . .225 C8
Sandringham St 2
HU3 . . . . .180 A6
Sandringham Way 3
PE6 . . . . .217 A5
Sandringham Wlk 6
PE13 . . . . .214 D2
Sands Cl 8 DN17 . . . . .17 D5
Sands Ct 1 HU14 . . . . .3 A4
Sandsfield La DN21 . . . . . .197 D2
Sands La
Brantingham HU15 . . . . . . .1 F7
Broughton HU15 . . . . .2 C6
Carlton-le-Moorland LN5 . . . .92 E1
Ellerker HU15 . . . . .2 B4
Scotter DN21 . . . . .29 B3
2 South Ferriby DN18 . . . .10 A7

SANDTOFT DN8 . . . . .16 A3
Sandtoft Cl LN6 . . . . .204 D6
Sandtoft Rd
Hatfield DN7 . . . . .15 A4
Sandtoft DN9 . . . . .16 B3
Sandtone Gdns PE1 . . . . . .214 D5
Sandwell Dr LN6 . . . . .200 D1
Sandy Bank PE22 . . . . .98 C1
SANDY BANK LN4 . . . . .111 E6
Sandy Bank LN4 . . . . .111 D6
Sandy Cl 1 DN36 . . . . .37 C5
Sandyford La PE22 . . . . . . .113 E3
Sandy Gate
Quadring PE11 . . . . .144 F7
Sutton St James PE12 . . . .169 A7
Sandy La
Anderby PE24 . . . . .77 C3
Belchford LN9 . . . . .73 A2
Candlesby with Gunby
PE23 . . . . .88 F1
Chapel St Leonard PE24 . . . .90 E7
Great Steeping PE23 . . . . .101 D7
Lusby with Winceby PE23 . . .86 F1
North Willingham LN8 . . . . .58 C5
Tealby LN8 . . . . .46 C1
Tydd St Giles PE13 . . . . . .170 A7
5 West Ashby LN9 . . . . . . .85 E7
Woodhall Spa LN10 . . . . . .97 E7
Saner St HU3 . . . . .180 B6
Sansford Gn 5 LN6 . . . . . .205 A6
SANTON DN15 . . . . .19 B7
SAPPERTON NG34 . . . . . . .141 E8
Sapperton PE4 . . . . .220 F6
Sapphire Cl PE24 . . . . .89 D2
Sapphire Gr 7 HU3 . . . . . .180 A4
Saracen Cl DN21 . . . . .197 F2
SARACEN'S HEAD
PE12 . . . . .215 A7
Sarah Gate PE11 . . . . .145 B8
Sargeants Cl 6 PE22 . . . . .113 B1
Sargent Cl 4 LN4 . . . . .95 C4
Sargent's Cl 5 PE9 . . . . . .219 A6
Sargon Way 3 DN31 . . . . . .188 A1
Sarthe Cl 5 PE20 . . . . . . .135 B7
Sassaby Cl HU4 . . . . .179 C3
Satinwood Cl 10 LN6 . . . . .200 C1
Saunby Gr DN35 . . . . .192 E7
SAUNDBY DN22 . . . . .52 B7
Saundergate La PE21 . . . . .136 D8
Saundergate Pk 11
PE21 . . . . .136 D8
Saunders St 3 DN31 . . . . .191 C8
SAUSTHORPE PE23 . . . . . . .87 E4
Sausthorpe Rd
Partney PE23 . . . . .88 A3
Sausthorpe PE23 . . . . .87 F3
Savile St HU1 . . . . .180 F6
Saville Rd PE3 . . . . .225 D4
Saville Rd Ind Est PE3 . . . .225 D5
Saville St LN5 . . . . .205 D7
Savory Rd 4 PE13 . . . . . . .170 D1
Savoy Ct 2 DN36 . . . . . . .195 C6
Sawmill La LN8 . . . . .70 C5
SAXBY LN1 . . . . .55 F5
SAXBY ALL SAINTS
DN20 . . . . .10 A3
Saxby Ave PE25 . . . . .206 D2
Saxby Cliff Rd LN8 . . . . .55 D4
Saxby Gdns PE1 . . . . .226 C8
Saxby Gr DN33 . . . . .191 A3
Saxby Hill DN20 . . . . .10 A4
Saxby Rd
Bonby DN20 . . . . .10 B2
Scunthorpe DN17 . . . . . . .184 E5
SAXILBY LN1 . . . . .66 D3
Saxilby CE Prim Sch
LN1 . . . . .66 E2
Saxilby Rd
Lincoln LN1 . . . . .201 A7
Skellingthorpe LN6 . . . . . .200 A6
Sturton by Stow LN1 . . . . . .66 B4
Saxilby Sta LN1 . . . . .66 D2
Saxon Cl
8 Barton-upon-Humber
DN18 . . . . .10 F8
🔲 Metheringham LN4 . . . . .95 D4
Spalding PE11 . . . . .214 F2
Saxon Cres DN35 . . . . .192 C6
Saxon Ct
2 Blyton DN21 . . . . .41 C5
Scunthorpe DN16 . . . . . . .185 B3
Saxondale HU4 . . . . .179 C7
Saxonfield LN7 . . . . .33 A4
Saxon Gate 15 PE20 . . . . . .136 F3
Saxon Rd
8 Barnack PE9 . . . . .172 D3
Peterborough PE1 . . . . . . .226 C3
Saxon St 8 LN1 . . . . .234 A4
Saxon Way
2 Ancaster NG32 . . . . . . .120 A3
Bourne PE10 . . . . .213 C6
17 Caistor LN7 . . . . .33 B4
3 Horncastle LN9 . . . . . . .199 C4
8 Ingham LN1 . . . . .54 F2
Kingston upon Hull HU13 . .178 F1
Saxon Wik 10 DN21 . . . . . .30 B1
Saxony Way 6 LN6 . . . . . .134 F2
Sayer Ct PE2 . . . . .229 F4
Scalby Ho HU5 . . . . .179 D8
Scald Gate PE22 . . . . .99 A3
Scale La HU1 . . . . .181 A6
Scalesgate Rd PE12 . . . . . .159 B1

Scalford Dr PE1 . . . . .226 C8
Scallow La DN17 . . . . .29 D6
Scalp Rd PE21 . . . . .137 B7
SCAMBLESBY LN11 . . . . . . .72 F5
Scamblesby CE
(Controlled) Prim Sch
LN11 . . . . .72 F5
Scamblesby Hill LN9 . . . . . .72 E4
SCAMPTON LN1 . . . . .67 D6
Scampton Airfield LN1 . . . .67 E6
Scampton Ave LN6 . . . . . .204 F6
Scampton CE Prim Sch
LN1 . . . . .67 D6
Scampton St 3 DN34 . . . . .191 A5
Scampton Way
Gainsborough DN21 . . . . . .197 E3
Scampton LN1 . . . . .67 F5
Skegness PE25 . . . . .206 A5
Scandinavian Way
DN41 . . . . .187 B3
Scarborough Bank
PE23 . . . . .100 B1
Scarborough Cl 10 PE10 . . .142 B7
Scarborough St 3 DN31 . . .188 A4
Scarborough Ave PE25 . . .206 D4
Scarborough Espl PE25 . . .206 E3
Scargate La LN4 . . . . .108 F8
Scarle Cl 1 LN6 . . . . .205 A2
Scarle La LN6 . . . . .79 B2
Scarrington Cres HU4 . . . .179 B6
Scarrow CI HU3 . . . . .180 A7
Scartho CI DN33 . . . . .194 E8
Scartho Jun & Inf Sch
DN33 . . . . .191 D2
Scartho Pk DN33 . . . . .191 B2
Scartho Rd DN33 . . . . .191 D2
SCAWBY DN20 . . . . .30 E8
Scawby Cres LN6 . . . . .204 F7
Scawby Prim Sch DN20 . . . .30 E8
Scawby Rd
Brigg DN20 . . . . .196 A2
Broughton DN20 . . . . .19 E2
Grimsby DN33 . . . . .191 A3
Scawby DN20 . . . . .31 A7
Scunthorpe DN17 . . . . . . .184 E5
Schiphol Way DN38 . . . . . . .21 E5
Schofield CI 7 DN19 . . . . . .11 C8
School CI
🔲 Maxey PE6 . . . . .173 C7
🔲 Scothern LN2 . . . . .68 F4
5 Surfleet PE11 . . . . .145 E4
School Croft DN9 . . . . .27 B2
School Dr
27 Messingham DN17 . . . . .29 D7
6 Welton/Dunholme LN2 . . .68 C6
School Hill LN4 . . . . .150 C7
Schoolhouse La 1
LN11 . . . . .198 B5
School House La 6
DN10 . . . . .39 F3
School Houses 9 DN20 . . . .19 E4
School La
Addlethorpe PE24 . . . . .90 D3
Appleby DN15 . . . . .9 D1
🔲 Baston PE6 . . . . .164 E4
Beckingham LN5 . . . . .105 B4
8 Bicker PE20 . . . . .135 A4
Binbrook LN8 . . . . .47 B5
2 Bonby DN20 . . . . .10 C2
Boothby Pagnell NG33 . . . .140 F5
Brigsley DN37 . . . . .23 E3
Butterwick PE22 . . . . .126 E3
Cabourne LN7 . . . . .33 E2
Canwick LN4 . . . . .81 A4
Claypole NG23 . . . . .117 E8
5 Croxton Kerrial
NG32 . . . . .138 D4
8 Donington PE11 . . . . . .134 F2
Edenham PE10 . . . . .153 F4
8 Glinton PE6 . . . . .220 C8
Grayingham DN21 . . . . .42 E7
Great Steeping PE23 . . . . .101 E7
Hainton LN8 . . . . .58 E3
3 Harmston LN5 . . . . .93 E6
Heighington/Washingborough
LN4 . . . . .203 C2
8 Huttoft LN13 . . . . .76 E2
2 Irby DN37 . . . . .34 D7
Kingston upon Hull
HU10 . . . . .178 E7
5 Lutton PE12 . . . . .160 A8
Maltby le Marsh LN13 . . . . .76 A4
8 Mareham le Fen PE22 . . .99 A4
8 Messingham DN17 . . . . .118 D2
5 Maxey PE6 . . . . .173 C7
🔲 New Holland DN19 . . . . .4 E2
North Cockerington LN11 . . .49 F1
4 North Ferriby HU14 . . . . .3 A4
North Scarle LN6 . . . . .78 E1
3 North Somercotes LN11 . .50 F7
Old Leake PE22 . . . . .114 A6
Old Somerby NG33 . . . . . .140 B8
Raithby PE22 . . . . .113 B4
Redbourne DN21 . . . . .30 F3
Ropsley NG33 . . . . .131 B1
Rothwell LN7 . . . . .33 C2
2 Scampton Airfield LN1 . . .67 F6
Sedgebrook NG32 . . . . . . .128 F4
Silk Willoughby NG34 . . . .121 A1

School La continued
Snitterby DN21 . . . . .43 D5
South Carlton LN1 . . . . . . .10 A7
7 South Ferriby DN18 . . . .10 A7
Springthorpe DN21 . . . . . . .53 E8
2 Sturton by Stow LN1 . . . .66 C7
17 Tetney DN36 . . . . .36 D4
Thistleton LE15 . . . . .151 C1
Thorpe on the Hill LN6 . . . .92 E8
6 Uffington PE9 . . . . .172 C6
Walcott LN4 . . . . .109 C7
3 West/East Butterwick
DN17 . . . . .28 D8
2 Willingham by Stow
DN21 . . . . .53 E3
Wilsford NG32 . . . . .120 C1
School Rd
🔲 Barnack PE9 . . . . .172 D3
Newborough PE6 . . . . .174 E5
Scunthorpe DN16 . . . . . . .185 B6
8 South Killingholme
DN40 . . . . .12 E3
West Walton PE14 . . . . . . .170 E4
Winteringham DN15 . . . . . . .2 A1
School View NG13 . . . . . . .128 A5
School Wlk DN35 . . . . .192 C5
School Yd Mews DN20 . . . .196 C4
Schooner Ct HU4 . . . . .179 B3
Schrimshaw Ct 6
PE25 . . . . .206 C4
Schrimshire's Rd DN22 . . . .52 A1
Scoggins Way 4
NG34 . . . . .122 D3
Scoldall La PE11 . . . . .145 E4
Scolding Dro PE6 . . . . .176 E5
SCOPWICK LN4 . . . . .95 D1
Scopwick Pl 3 LN2 . . . . . .201 F1
Scorer St LN5 . . . . .201 F1
Scotenson PE2 . . . . .229 E3
Scotgate PE9 . . . . .219 A5
SCOTHERN LN2 . . . . .68 E4
Scothern La
Dunholme LN2 . . . . .68 E5
10 Welton/Dunholme LN2 . .68 E6
Scothern Rd LN2 . . . . .68 D3
Scotia Rd PE21 . . . . .209 F2
Scotia Way PE21 . . . . .209 F2
SCOTLAND NG33 . . . . .141 C5
Scotland La NG33 . . . . . . .141 B5
Scotney Dr NG31 . . . . .211 F5
Scotney St PE1 . . . . .225 E7
Scott Ave DN17 . . . . .184 C6
Scott Cl
8 Claypole NG23 . . . . . . .117 E8
Grimsby DN37 . . . . .190 F8
Peterborough PE2 . . . . . . .231 E6
Scotten Dike Dro PE10 . . . .154 E6
SCOTTER DN21 . . . . .29 B3
Scotter Prim Sch DN21 . . . .29 C3
Scotter Rd
Laughton DN21 . . . . .41 C8
Messingham DN17 . . . . . . .29 D5
Scunthorpe DN17 . . . . . . .182 C1
Scotter Rd S DN17 . . . . . .184 C3
Scotterthorpe Rd DN21 . . . .29 A5
Scotterthorpe Rd PE10 . . .153 D3
SCOTTLETHORPE DN21. . . .29 A5
Scottlethorpe Rd 2 . . . . . .202 C6
Scottlethorpe Rd PE10 . . .153 E4
SCOTTON LN21 . . . . .29 C2
Scotton Comm Nature
Reserve* DN9 . . . . .27 B1
Scotton Dr 7 LN6 . . . . .205 A7
Scott's Cr PE26 . . . . .164 E3
Scott's Hill 4 NG32 . . . . . .106 C1
Scotts Rd PE2 . . . . .220 D8
Scott St
Gainsborough DN21 . . . . . .197 C5
Kingston upon Hull PE2 . . .180 F7
SCOTT WILLOUGHBY
NG34 . . . . .132 B4
SCRAFIELD LN9 . . . . .86 C3
SCRANE END PE22 . . . . . . .137 F8
Scrap Bay Rd DN16 . . . . . . .19 A3
SCREDINGTON NG34 . . . . . .132 E7
Scredington Rd
Burton Pedwardine
NG34 . . . . .122 B1
Helpringham NG34 . . . . . .133 C7
SCREMBY PE23 . . . . .88 E2
SCRIVELSBY LN9 . . . . .98 E8
Scrivelsby Ct DN35 . . . . . .193 A3
SCRUB HILL LN4 . . . . .111 B6
Scrub La
Authorpe LN11 . . . . .75 A8
East Halton DN40 . . . . .12 E5
Withern with Stain LN11 . . .75 C7
Scullery La NG33 . . . . .141 A5
SCUNTHORPE DN15 . . . . . .183 B5
Scunthorpe CE Prim Sch
DN15 . . . . .183 A4
Scunthorpe General Hospl
DN15 . . . . .183 B3
Scunthorpe Leisure Ctr
DN15 . . . . .183 B4
Scunthorpe Sta DN16 . . . .183 A2
Seabank Rd PE13 . . . . .170 E1
Sea Bank Rd PE24 . . . . .90 E7
Seabrook Dr DN16 . . . . . . .185 A2
SEACROFT PE25 . . . . .103 E4
Seacroft Cl 13 NG31 . . . . .211 D7
Seacroft Dr 10 PE25 . . . . .206 C1

Seacroft Espl PE25......103 E4
Seacroft Rd
  Cleethorpes DN35.......193 A5
  Mablethorpe/Sutton on Sea
  ....64 B3
Seacroft Sq
  10 Skegness PE25......103 E4
  11 Skegness PE25......116 E8
SEADYKE PE20.............136 E3
Sea Dyke PE22............114 B2
Seadyke Rd
  Kirton PE20..............136 E3
  Wisbech St Mary PE13 ...177 F6
Sea Dyke Way **1** DN36....37 C2
Sea End Rd PE22..........127 A4
Seafield Rd **5** PE13......170 B2
Seaford Rd DN35...........193 B1
Sea Front Rd
  10 Skegness PE25......103 E4
  9 Skegness PE25.......103 E4
Seagate Rd PE12..........216 D2
Seagate Terr PE12........216 D4
Seagull Cl HU4............179 E2
Seaholme Rd LN12.........64 B2
Sea La
  Benington PE22..........127 B4
  Butterwick PE22.........126 F3
  Friskney PE22............115 C5
  Hogsthorpe PE24..........90 C7
  Huttoft LN13...............77 A4
  Ingoldmells PE25.........90 E3
  Leverton PE22............127 B6
  Mablethorpe/Sutton on Sea
  ....LN12..77 A7
  North Coates DN36........37 B4
  Old Leake PE22...........114 C1
  Saltfleet LN11.............51 C5
  Theddlethorpe St Helen
  ....LN12..63 E7
  Wrangle PE22.............114 E1
Sealey's La PE13..........177 D8
Seal Sanctuary & Nature
  Ctr The* LN12..............64 B5
Seamer Gr **3** DN32......192 A5
SEARBY DN38...............32 C8
Searby Hill DN38...........32 C8
Searby Rd
  Lincoln LN2...............202 B8
  Scunthorpe DN17.........184 E4
Searby Wold La DN38......21 E1
Sea Rd
  Anderby PE24..............77 B2
  19 Chapel St Leonard
  ....PE24..90 D7
  Cleethorpes DN35.........192 F6
Seargeants Cl **1** PE4....174 E4
Searjeant St PE1..........225 E5
Searson Cl PE7............172 F7
Seascale Wlk DN32........191 F8
Seas End Prim Sch
  ....PE11..145 D3
Seas End Rd
  Moulton PE12.............146 D1
  Surfleet PE11............145 E3
SEATHORNE PE25...........206 E8
Seathorne Cres PE25......90 F1
Seathorne Prim Sch
  ....PE25..206 D7
Seaton Cl PE7.............233 D6
Seaton Gr
  Grimsby DN32............192 A5
  Kingston upon Hull HU4 ..179 E5
Seaton Rd
  Kingston upon Hull
  ....HU13..178 F2
  Scunthorpe DN17.........184 D8
  6 Stamford PE9.........219 B4
Sea View LN11.............51 D3
Sea View Rd DN35.........206 D5
Sea View St DN35.........192 F5
Seawall La DN36...........37 C5
Sebrights Way PE3........224 F3
Second Ave
  Crowland PE6............166 E3
  Gosberton PE11..........144 C3
  Peterborough PE1........226 D1
Second Dro Ind Est
  ....PE1..226 D1
Second Marsh Rd
  PE14.......................170 C3
SEDGEBROOK NG32........128 F5
Sedgebrook Cl **1** NG32..201 F8
Sedgebrook Rd NG32......128 F6
Sedge Cl
  6 Barton-upon-Humber
  ....DN18..3 F1
  Leasingham NG34........121 C7
Sedge Hole Cl Nature
  Reserve* DN9.............27 F2
Sedgemoor Cl **3** LN6....204 E1
Sedgemoor Pl **2** PE12...167 B8
Sedgewood Way LN5.......182 C6
Seed Cl La **4** DN37......23 F1
Seedlands Cl PE21........209 B7
Sefton Ave PE13...........170 C1
Sefton St **3** HU3.........180 E4
Segmere St **3** DN35....193 A5
Segrave Gr HU5............179 D8

Selbourne Rd **4** DN34...190 E4
Selby Cl LN6...............205 A3
Selby Ct DN17.............184 D7
Selby Dr DN8................14 F8
Selby St HU3..............180 A5
Selge Way DN33...........190 F3
Selkirk St HU5.............180 A8
Sellers Grange PE2........224 B2
Sellwood Ct NG34.........212 F7
Sellwood Gdns LN9........199 B3
Selmeston St DN34.......191 C6
Selwyn Ave **16** HU14.....3 A4
Selwyn Ct DN34...........190 F6
Selwyn Rd PE9.............219 A7
Sempers Cl LN6............92 E8
Sennefleet Rd DN21.......29 B4
Sentance Cres PE20......136 C6
Sequana Ct HU9...........181 B6
Seraphin App Rd
  ....DN16..183 E1
Seraphim Rd DN16.........183 F1
Serena Rd **5** PE25.......206 D2
Serlby Gdns PE1...........225 B3
Serpentine Gn Sh Ctr
  ....PE7..230 D3
Serpentine St **1** LN8.....57 D7
Serpentine The PE7........230 D3
Service Rd DN37...........190 D8
Service Rd 1 **10** DN37...190 E8
Service Rd 2 **17** DN37...190 E8
Service Rd 3 **13** DN37...190 E8
Service Rd 4 **6** DN37.....190 E8
Service Rd 5 **13** DN37...190 E8
Service Rd 6 **4** DN37.....190 F8
Service Rd 7 **12** DN37...190 F8
Service Rd 8 **3** DN37.....188 A1
Service Rd 9 **7** DN37.....188 A1
Service Rd 10 **5** DN37...188 A1
Service Rd 12 **2** DN37...188 A1
Service Rd 13 **4** DN37...188 A1
Service Rd 14 **3** DN37...188 A1
Service Rd 15 **18** DN37..190 E8
Service Rd 16 DN37........190 D8
Service Rd 17 DN37........190 F8
Service Rd 19 **14** DN37..190 F8
Service Rd 20 **19** DN37..190 E8
Service Rd 21 **1** DN37...190 D8
Service Rd 22 **3** DN37...190 D8
Service Rd 23 DN37........190 D8
Service Rd 25 **11** DN37..190 D8
Service Rd 26 **9** DN37....190 D8
Service Rd No 1 **3**
  ....DN37..189 B1
Service Rd No 2 **4**
  ....DN37..189 B1
Setchfield Pl PE2..........230 F7
Setterwood Garth **2**
  ....HU10..178 E8
Setts Gn PE10.............213 C2
Sevenacres PE7...........229 E5
Seven Quay Rd DN40.......186 E7
Seventh Ave **8** NG31....211 F6
Severn Cl PE4.............221 C1
Severn Rd PE11...........214 F5
Severn St LN1.............201 C4
Severn Way **2** DN37.....190 E8
Sewell Cl NG34...........234 C3
Sewell Ct PE1..............234 C3
Sewell's Wlk LN5..........201 E1
Sewer La **3** HU1.........180 F5
SEWSTERN NG33...........150 F4
Sewstern Rd NG33.........151 B4
Seymour Ave LN11.........198 C4
Seymour La **14** LN13.....75 F2
Seymour Pl PE4...........221 F2
Seymour St HU3...........179 F5
Sezanne Wlk **10** PE11...214 C6
Shackleton Cl
  Market Deeping PE6.......217 B7
  10 Spalding PE11.......214 C2
Shaddys Wlk LN13.........88 E6
Shaftesbury Ave
  Birchwood LN6............200 D2
  Grimsby DN34............191 B7
Shaftesbury Mews **6**
  DN36......................195 C6
Shaftesbury Way **2**
  DN35........................91 D5
Shakespeare Ave
  Grantham NG31..........211 E6
  Peterborough PE1........225 F7
  4 Scunthorpe DN17....184 C6
Shakespeare Cl **6**
  HU3........................180 D8
Shakespeare St
  5 Gainsborough
  ....DN21..197 D2
  Lincoln LN5...............205 E8
Shamfields Rd **3**
  ....PE23..101 A8
Shamrock Cl PE2..........231 C7
Shanklin Dr NL11..........210 E4
Shannon Ave LN6..........205 A5
Shannon Cl **2** LN6.......205 A5
Shannon Rd **8** LN4.......207 D4
Shardloes LN4.............81 E2
Shardloes Rd **5** PE25...103 E4
Sharma Leas PE4..........220 E3
Sharmans Cl **11** LN12....77 A7
Sharman Way PE11........214 B5

Sharnbrook Ave **1**
  PE7........................230 C1
Sharpe Cl **15** DN18.......10 E8
Sharpe Rd NG31...........211 C6
Sharpe's Rd PE6...........165 C3
Sharp's Cl PE10...........213 B6
Sharp's La PE22...........127 A6
Sharp Wlk LN6..............93 C8
Shawbury Ct **2** DN16.....204 C6
Shaw Dr DN33..............191 E1
Shawfield Cl **10** DN15....14 A3
Shaw La PE22.............127 B8
Shaw Rd
  Boston PE21.............208 C7
  Grantham NG31..........210 D2
  Gringley on the Hill DN10 .39 C2
Shaws La PE12............160 B3
Shaws Mews LN11.........198 B5
Shaw St HU9...............181 B7
Shaw Way **4** LN2.........68 C2
Shays Dr **1** LN6..........205 A7
Shearers Dr **12** PE11....214 A2
Shearman's Wath
  Thimbleby LN9.............85 C6
  West Ashby LN9..........199 A8
Shears Ct DN37...........194 F4
Shearwater Cl PE22.......229 D6
Shearwater Cl
  3 Birchwood LN6.......200 E1
  Louth LN11...............198 D8
Shearwater Rd LN6........200 E1
Sheep Cote La DN7........14 D2
Sheep Dip La DN7..........14 D4
Sheepdyke La **2** DN36...10 C2
Sheepfold St PE2..........193 C6
Sheepgate PE22...........127 A6
Sheep Marsh La DN36......37 B3
Sheep Mkt
  2 Spalding PE11.......214 D4
  11 Stamford PE9.......219 B5
Sheepwalk
  Auburn Haddington & South
  Hykeham LN5..............92 E5
  Peterborough PE4........221 E1
Sheepwash La LN4.........81 E4
Sheffield Pk Ave DN15....182 F5
Sheffield St (East) **1**
  ....DN15..183 A4
Sheffield St (West) **4**
  ....DN15..182 F4
Sheila Cres **4** PE11......214 A3
Sheldrake Rd **1** NG34...212 B3
Shelford St DN15...........183 A4
Shelley Ave
  Grantham NG31..........211 D6
  Grimsby DN33............191 B4
Shelley Cl
  3 Mablethorpe/Sutton on
  Sea LN12...................77 A7
  New England PE1.........225 F8
  12 Stamford PE9.......218 E6
Shelley Dr
  Lincoln LN2...............202 B6
  1 Sleaford NG34.......212 F4
Shelroy Cl DN15...........182 C5
Shelton Rd PE2............231 D6
Shenley Cl **10** DN7........14 D3
SHEPEAU STOW PE12......167 F3
Shepeau Stow Prim Sch
  ....PE12..167 F3
Shepherds Cl PE4.........221 A4
Shepherd's Croft **1**
  DN9........................27 D7
Shepherd's La NG34.......133 E7
Shepherd's Wlk PE9.......163 D1
Sheppard's Dro PE6.......167 B1
Shepperson's Ave
  PE11.......................144 F5
Shepton La NG34..........142 A8
Sheraton Cl **15** LN6......204 D7
Sheraton Dr **13** DN36....36 D8
Sherborne Rd PE1.........226 D6
Sherborne Way **16**
  ....PE20..135 B7
Sherbrooke St **2** LN2....202 D4
Sherburn Cres DN15......182 D4
Sherburn St
  Cleethorpes DN35.........192 F4
  Kingston upon Hull HU9 ..181 D8
Sheridan Cl **1** LN2........202 C7
Sheridan Rd PE21..........225 F8
Sheriff Way PE21..........208 E2
Sheringham Way PE2......230 C6
Sherwood Ave
  Boston PE21.............208 E7
  Newark-on-Trent NG24...104 A4
  4 Peterborough PE2....230 F7
  7 Wisbech PE13.......170 D1
Sherwood Cl
  1 Louth LN11..........198 C4
  Stamford PE9.............218 F5
Sherwood Dr
  Kingston upon Hull
  ....HU4..179 A7
  Spalding PE11............214 D6
  Waddington LN5..........205 D1
Sherwood Rd
  10 Coningsby LN4.......207 D4
  Grimsby DN34............190 F5
  5 Mablethorpe/Sutton on Sea
  ....LN12..64 B4
Sherwood Rise **7**
  NG32........................119 B7
Sherwood Vale DN15......182 D3
Shetland Way DN40........186 C2
Shillaker Cl PE10..........213 D4
Shipton Rd DN16...........185 C5

Shire Ave PE11............214 A5
Shiregate **12** LN4.........95 C4
Shire Gr PE1..............226 C5
Shire La NG31.............117 D8
Shires Orch **6** NG32.....138 D4
Shirley Cres DN16.........185 B8
Shivean Gate **5** PE21....157 F7
Shodfriars La **4** PE21....208 F4
Shoe La LN9................135 A7
Shoemaker's La DN21......29 E5
Shoff Dro PE11............134 D1
Shoff Rd PE11.............134 D1
Sholt's Gate PE12.........158 C7
Shop Hill **7** PE22..........98 F4
Shop La LN11..............72 D6
Shore Rd
  Freiston PE22............126 D2
  Garthorpe & Fockerby
  ....DN17..7 F5
Shortacres Rd PE2........230 F7
Short Dro
  Gosberton PE11..........144 C5
  Pointon & Sempringham
  ....NG34..143 F4
  Thurlby PE10............164 E8
Shortfen PE2...............230 C4
Short Ferry Rd LN3.........82 F6
Shortfield La PE21.........159 F7
Short Furrow LN5..........107 B8
Short Hollow NG33.........131 C1
Short La
  Fotherby LN11............49 A2
  Ingham LN1................54 F3
  Lincoln LN1...............234 A2
  1 West Halton DN15.....8 E8
  3 Wisbech PE13........170 A1
Shortleys Rd DN22.........65 B5
Short's Cnr PE22..........112 D3
Short St
  2 Cleethorpes DN35....192 F6
  4 Spalding PE11.......214 C4
Short Wheatley La
  ....NG23..91 D3
Shortwood La
  Bullington LN8............69 F4
  Friesthorpe LN3...........57 A2
Shorwell Cl **3** NG31......210 E4
Shotbolt La PE11..........214 D8
Shrewsbury Ave PE2......230 D5
Shropshire Rd **9** LN1.....67 E5
Shrubberies Nature
  Reserve* PE12...........216 B5
Shrub Rd PE2..............216 B5
Shrubwood Cl **3**
  NG34......................122 E2
Shuttlefield La PE20......135 F4
Shuttleworth Ct **12** LN6 ..93 C8
Sibelius Rd HU4...........179 B4
SIBSEY PE22..............113 B2
Sibsey Ct DN37...........188 A2
Sibsey Drain Bank
  ....PE22..126 A6
Sibsey Free (Controlled)
  Prim Sch PE22...........113 A2
Sibsey La **3** PE21........208 F4
Sibsey Rd
  Boston PE21.............209 B8
  Fishtoft PE21............125 F5
Sibsey Trader Windmill*
  ....PE22..113 A2
Sibthorpe Dr LN2..........68 F2
Sibthorp St LN5...........201 E1
Sickling Gate Rd PE22....115 B7
Sidebar La NG34...........123 C4
Side La DN33..............195 A7
Side Row NG24............104 A4
Side St **2** NG32.........128 F7
Sidings Ct **3** HU15.......2 B5
Sidings The
  Hodbeach PE12...........215 D1
  Horncastle LN9...........199 A3
  Lincoln LN6...............234 A1
  Long Sutton PE12........216 B4
  2 Louth LN11..........198 B5
  14 Mablethorpe/Sutton on Sea
  ....LN12..77 A8
  2 Morton PE10.........157 B6
  6 Moulton PE12.......157 F6
  25 Ruskington NG34...108 E1
  25 Saxilby LN1..........66 D2
Sidlaw Gr LN5..............204 D7
Sidney Chase LN1.........54 F1
Sidney Ct **3** DN35.......192 B8
Sidney Pl DN35............192 B8
Sidney Rd
  Grimsby DN34............191 B7
  5 Scunthorpe DN17....184 D4
Sidney St
  4 Cleethorpes DN35....189 D1
  Cleethorpes DN35........192 B8
  Grantham NG31..........211 A6
  Lincoln LN5...............205 E8
Sidney Terr **17** DN35....205 E8
Sidney Way DN35.........192 B8
Signal Rd HU1.............211 C5
Signhills Ave DN35........193 A4
Signhills Inf & Jun Sch
  ....DN35..193 A4
Silica Cres DN17...........184 C5
SILK WILLOUGHBY
  ....NG34..121 C1
Silt La PE20...............136 E3
Silt Pit La PE21...........137 A7
Siltside PE11..............144 D4
Silverbell DN16............185 E4
Silver Birch Rise DN16....185 B3
Silvergarth DN32..........192 B5
Silver Hill PE7............230 D3

Silverines Mdws Nature
  Reserve* LN11............72 E5
Silver La **20** PE9.........219 B5
Silversides La DN20.......196 A2
Silversides La Cvn Site
  ....DN20..196 A2
Silver's La PE13...........177 E1
Silver St
  Bardney LN3..............83 C4
  Barnetby le Wold DN38...21 B4
  Barrow upon Humber
  ....DN19..11 C2
  Baumber LN9.............72 A1
  Benniworth LN8...........71 F8
  Branston LN4............81 E2
  Coningsby LN4............207 C4
  Gainsborough DN21......197 C6
  Holton le Clay DN36......195 D3
  1 Kingston upon Hull
  ....HU1..180 F6
  Lincoln LN2..............234 B2
  Minting LN9...............84 C8
  North Clifton NG23.......78 C1
  Owston Ferry DN9........28 B2
  Peterborough PE2........230 F7
  1 Ruskington NG34....108 E1
  Stainforth DN7...........14 C0
  Theddlethorpe St Helen
  ....LN12..63 E5
  3 Waddingham DN21....43 D2
  1 Wainfleet All Saints
  ....PE24..102 D3
  Winteringham DN15......2 B1
  Wisbech PE13............170 D3
  5 Wragby LN8..........70 D5
Silverstone Rd **17** LN6...204 C2
Silvertoft La PE7...........136 E8
Silverwood Rd
  8 Bottesford DN16.....128 A5
  Bottesford PE1............225 F5
Silvester Rd PE5...........223 E2
Silvester St HU2...........180 F7
Simons Cl
  4 Donington on Bain
  ....LN11..59 E3
  5 Louth LN11...........198 D4
Simon's Gn LN6............205 C4
Simons Pl DN35...........192 D7
Simon Weir La PE20.......135 D8
Simpson Cl
  7 Barrow upon Humber
  ....DN19..11 D8
  8 St Leonard PE24......90 D7
Sincil Bank LN5...........234 B2
Sincil Bank (Lincoln City
  FC) LN5...................201 E1
Sincil St LN5..............234 B2
Sinclair Cl PE21...........208 E8
Sinderson Rd DN36........36 D8
Singerfire Rd PE5..........223 D2
Sir Francis Hill Prim Sch
  ....LN6..205 C3
Sir Isaac Newton Cl **3**
  ....PE21..215 E3
Sir Isaac Newton Dr **3**
  ....PE21..208 F1
Sirius Cl **3** HU3..........180 B5
Sir John Nelthorpe Sch
  ....DN20..196 C3
Sir William Robertson High
  Sch LN5...................106 E4
Siskin Cl **10** LN11.......143 A3
Siskin Cres DN16..........185 B2
Sissley PE2...............229 C2
Sitwell St HU8.............181 A8
Sixfields Cl LN6...........205 A7
SIXHILLS LN8..............58 E6
Sixhills La LN8.............59 A7
Sixhills Rd LN8............58 D6
Sixhills St DN32...........191 E7
Six House Bank PE11......144 D1
Six Hundreds Dro
  ....PE20..123 E3
Six Score Rd PE6..........165 C4
Sixth Ave
  Fixborough Ind Est DN15 ..8 A7
  2 Grantham NG31......211 F6
  Scunthorpe DN17.........184 B6
Skaters Way PE4..........221 A4
Skayman Fields **7**
  ....LN5..105 D8
SKEGNESS PE25...........206 E4
Skegness Bsns Ctr
  ....PE25..206 B3
Skegness Coll of
  Vocational Ed PE25......206 C2
Skegness & District Hospl
  ....PE25..206 B3
Skegness Gram Sch
  ....PE25..206 C2
Skegness Inf Sch PE25 ..206 C4
Skegness (Ingoldmells)
  Aerodrome PE25..........90 D7
Skegness Jun Sch
  ....PE25..206 C4
Skegness Motor Racing
  Stadium PE25.............90 A2
Skegness Rd
  Burgh le Marsh PE24.....103 A7
  Chapel St Leonard PE24 ..90 D6
  Ingoldmells PE25.........90 E3
  Partney PE23.............88 B3
  8 Wainfleet All Saints
  ....PE24..102 E2
Skegness Ret Pk PE25....206 C3
Skegness Sports Ctr
  ....PE25..206 B5
Skegness Sta PE25.......206 C3

egness Wr Leisure Pk*
PE25 . . . . .90 E1
ELDYKE PE20 . . . . . . .136 F4
eldyke Rd PE20 . . . . . .136 D5
ellingthorpe LN6 . . . . .200 B4
ellingthorpe Rd LN6 . . .200 D2
elton Dr PE12 . . . . . . .216 C3
elton Rd DN17 . . . . . . .184 C7
ENDLEBY PE23 . . . . . . .88 D4
endleby Nature
  Reserve* LN13 . . . . . .88 E6
errie Cl 5 LN6 . . . . . . .205 A1
erry La NG13 . . . . .128 C5
IDBROOKE LN11 . . . . . .51 B3
illings La HU15 . . . . .2 C5
ILLINGTON NG33 . . . . .151 B8
illington Rd NG33 . . . .151 B6
INNAND LN5 . . . . .106 C8
innand La LN5 . . . . . . .106 D7
inners La
  6 South Ferriby DN18 . . .10 A7
  Waltham DN37 . . . . . . .194 E4
ipmarsh La
  Middle Rasen LN8 . . . . . .45 C1
  South Kyme LN4 . . . . . .110 B1
ipmarsh La
  everton PE22 . . . . .126 E8
  Old Leake PE22 . . . . . .113 E1
ippingdale Ind Pk
DN15 . . . . .182 C7
ippingdale Rd DN15 . . .182 F6
ipwith Cres 20 LN4 . . . .95 D4
ipworth Way PE25 . . . .206 C8
IRBECK NG21 . . . . . . .209 B3
irbeck Dr 15 LN1 . . . . .66 D2
irbeck Gdns PE21 . . . .209 B3
IRBECK QUARTER
PE21 . . . . .208 D2
irbeck Rd PE21 . . . . . .209 A3
irmore Rd PE22 . . . . . .114 E5
irth Rd LN4 . . . . .109 F6
itter Rd DN40 . . . . .5 D1
ylark Dr DN14 . . . . . . .185 B2
ylarks Cl 6 PE7 . . . . . .230 D3
ack The 2 HU7 . . . . . . .16 D8
ash La LN9 . . . . .86 D3
ate Drift 2 PE9 . . . . . .171 C2
ate Mill Pl NG31 . . . . .211 B5
ate Mill The NG31 . . . .211 B5
ay Pit Cl 3 DN7 . . . . . .14 F4
ay Pit La DN7 . . . . .14 F3
ea Cotts 18 NG34 . . . .212 B4
EAFORD NG34 . . . . . . .212 D4
eaford (Aided) RC Prim
  Sch NG34 . . . . .212 C5
eaford Art Studio*
  NG34 . . . . .212 D5
eaford Coll NG34 . . . .212 E4
eaford Joint Sixth Form
  NG34 . . . . .212 D5
eaford Leisure Ctr
  NG34 . . . . .212 E4
eaford Lollypocks Field
  Nature Reserve*
  NG34 . . . . .212 E2
eaford Mareham Nature
  Reserve* NG34 . . . . .212 E2
eaford Rd
  Ancaster NG32 . . . . . .120 A2
  Barnby in the Willows
    NG24 . . . . .104 F5
  Boston PE21 . . . . . . .208 B4
  Bracebridge Heath LN4 . .81 A1
  Coningsby LN4 . . . . . .207 A4
  Cranwell NG34 . . . . . .120 F8
  East Kirkby PE23 . . . . .99 E4
  Folkingham NG34 . . . .142 C8
  Heckington NG34 . . . .122 D3
  Honington NG32 . . . . .119 C2
  Leadenham LN5 . . . . .106 D2
  14 Leasingham NG34 . .121 B7
  Metheringham LN4 . . . .95 A4
  13 Navenby/Wellingore
    LN5 . . . . .107 A7
  Newark-on-Trent NG24 . .104 A5
  North Kyme LN4 . . . . .109 E2
  Ruskington NG34 . . . .108 L1
  Tattershall LN4 . . . . . .110 D7
  Walcot near Folkingham
    NG34 . . . . .132 D2
eaford Sta NG34 . . . . .212 D3
eaford Virtual Mus* 7
  NG34 . . . . .212 C4
edge La LN8 . . . . .59 B8
edmere Gr HU4 . . . . . .179 E5
eepers Cl 1 PE12 . . . .216 B4
eights Cl HU3 . . . . . . .180 A7
eights Dr 2 PE14 . . . .170 F1
eights La HU15 . . . . .1 B6
essor St 2 LN5 . . . . . . .94 A7
ipe Dro PE11 . . . . .155 F5
ipe The PE10 . . . . .213 F4
ippery Gowt La PE21 . .136 F8
ipway DN35 . . . . .193 A6
LOOTHBY LN13 . . . . . . .89 D5
oothby High La
  Hogsthorpe PE24 . . . . . .90 A6
  Willoughby with Sloothby
    PE24 . . . . .89 F6
uice La DN18 . . . . .9 E8
uice Rd
  Holbeach PE12 . . . . . .215 B8
  South Ferriby DN18 . . . .9 F8
  Sutton Bridge PE12 . . .161 A6
  Whaplode PE12 . . . . . .147 B4
mall Dro PE12 . . . . . . .157 E7
mall Dro La PE11 . . . .144 E1
mall End Rd PE22 . . . .114 E6

Smalley Rd PE25 . . . . . .209 D4
Smallwood PE3 . . . . . . .225 B5
Smeeton Ct 6 NG34 . . .212 D6
Smeeton's La PE20 . . . .146 C7
Smithdale Cl 9 PE11 . . .214 C6
Smithfield PE6 . . . . .176 B3
Smith Field 10 DN36 . . .36 B1
Smithfield Rd DN16 . . . .185 D6
Smith St
  Lincoln LN5 . . . . .201 E1
  Scunthorpe DN15 . . . .182 F4
Smithy La
  6 Barnetby le Wold
    DN38 . . . . .21 B4
  Friskney PE22 . . . . . . .115 A6
Smooting La LN8 . . . . . .82 A8
Smooting The LN8 . . . . .46 C1
Smythe La DN22 . . . . . . .52 D1
Snaffer's La PE12 . . . . .158 C5
Snainton Gr 4 LN6 . . . .179 D8
Snaith Ave PE20 . . . . . .146 D7
Snaith Cl 9 LN6 . . . . . .204 B6
SNARFORD 56 D1
Snarford Rd LN3 . . . . . . .69 D8
SNELLAND LN3 . . . . .69 D7
Snelland Rd LN3 . . . . . . .69 E8
Snetterton Cl 1 LN6 . . .204 C7
Snipe Dales Ctry Pk*
  PE23 . . . . .86 F3
Snipe Dales Nature
  Reserve* LN9 . . . . .86 E3
SNITTERBY DN21 . . . . . .43 D5
Snitterby Carr La DN21 . .43 F5
Snitterby Rd DN21 . . . . .43 D6
Snowberry Gdns 7
  LN6 . . . . .204 C8
Snowden Cl 1 PE6 . . . .175 C8
Snowdon Cl 4 LN6 . . . .205 D3
Snowdonia Ave DN16 . .182 D7
Snowdon Rd 3 NG23 . . .91 D4
Snowdrop Cl 10 DN41 . . .23 E6
Snowdrop Pl 8 PE11 . . .214 A5
Snowhills PE7 . . . . .233 E5
Sods La PE11 . . . . .145 D5
Soff La DN19 . . . . .12 A6
Soke Parkway PE1 . . . . .221 E1
Soke Rd PE6 . . . . .174 D5
Solhem Ave 13 PE21 . . .136 D8
Solomon Ave DN35 . . . .192 D5
Solway Ave PE21 . . . . . .136 E8
Solway Ct 5 DN37 . . . . .190 E8
SOMERBY DN38 . . . . . . .21 B1
Somerby Cl
  8 Moulton PE12 . . . . .157 F7
  7 Stamford PE9 . . . . .219 B7
Somerby Garth 4 PE1 . .226 D8
Somerby Gn PE21 . . . . .211 D2
Somerby Hill NG31 . . . .211 C2
Somerby Pl NG31 . . . . .211 E1
Somerby Rd
  Gainsborough DN21 . . .197 F5
  Ropsley & Humby NG33 . .141 A8
  Scunthorpe DN17 . . . .184 D5
Somerby Wold La DN38 . .21 C1
Somerden Rd HU9 . . . . . .5 F8
Somerfield Dr 9 LN11 . . .50 F7
SOMERSBY PE23 . . . . . . .87 A7
Somersby Ave 9 LN12 . . .64 B4
Somersby Cl LN6 . . . . . .205 C4
Somerset Ct
  1 South LN11 . . . . . .198 B5
  North Carlton LN1 . . . . .67 C4
Somersby Gn PE21 . . . .209 B7
Somersby Gr 2 PE25 . . .206 D1
Somersby St 5 DN31 . . .191 D8
Somersby Way 5 PE21 . .209 B7
Somerset Dr 4 DN15 . . . .8 B4
Somerset St HU3 . . . . . .180 A5
Somerton Dr 3 DN7 . . . .14 F3
Somerton Gate La LN5 . .93 D7
Somerton Rd DN40 . . . .186 D3
Somervell Rd DN16 . . . .185 C4
Somerville PE4 . . . . .220 E5
Somerville Cl 15 LN5 . . .93 E8
Somerville Ct 14 LN5 . . .93 E8
Somerville Rd 1 PE9 . . .219 A6
Somerville St 1 PE9 . . .172 C6
Somme Cl LN1 . . . . .201 E7
Sonia Crest DN40 . . . . .186 B4
Sophia Ave DN33 . . . . . .191 C1
Sorbus Cl 8 HU7 . . . . . .230 D3
Sorbus Ct 5 HU3 . . . . . .180 D6
Sorbus View 4 HU5 . . . .179 C7
Sorby Cl PE25 . . . . .206 E8
Sorrel Cl
  3 Binbrook LN8 . . . . . .47 C5
  5 Market Deeping PE6 . .217 D6
  4 Stamford PE9 . . . . .218 D6
Sorrel Ct LN6 . . . . .204 C8
Sorrel Dr PE11 . . . . . . .214 A5
Sorrel Way DN15 . . . . . .182 C6
Soss La DN10 . . . . .40 A5
SOTBY LN8 . . . . .71 E5
SOTS HOLE LN4 . . . . . . .96 C7
Soulby La PE12 . . . . . . .114 C2
Sour La DN7 . . . . .14 E8
Soutergate 13 DN18 . . . .3 F1
South Airfield Rd
  NG34 . . . . .120 E4
South Axholme Com Sch
  DN9 . . . . .27 D6
South Bank 8 DN17 . . . .17 D6
SOUTH BRAMWITH
  DN7 . . . . .14 A6
South Brick Lines
  NG34 . . . . .120 B8

South Bridge Rd 2
  HU9 . . . . .181 A5
Southburn Ave HU5 . . . .179 E7
SOUTH CARLTON LN1 . . .67 D3
South Carr Rd DN20 . . . .31 A4
South Church Side 14
  HU1 . . . . .180 F6
Southcliffe Rd 10 DN21 . .29 C3
South Cliff Rd 2 DN21 . . .30 B1
SOUTH CLIFTON NG23 . . .78 B5
Southcoates La HU9 . . . .181 E8
SOUTH COCKERINGTON
  LN11 . . . . .62 A8
South Cres
  11 Bottesford NG13 . . .128 A5
  1 Chapel St Leonard
    PE24 . . . . .90 D7
South Dale LN7 . . . . . . .33 B4
South-Dale Cl 3 DN21 . .30 B2
Southdown LN5 . . . . . . .205 D1
Southdown Rd PE7 . . . . .233 F5
South Dr
  12 Balderton NG24 . . .104 C1
  4 Stow LN1 . . . . .66 C8
South Dro
  Bicker PE20 . . . . .134 E4
  Helpringham NG34 . . .133 E6
  Lutton PE12 . . . . .149 A1
  Quadring PE11 . . . . . .144 A8
  Spalding PE11 . . . . . .156 C2
SOUTH ELKINGTON
  LN11 . . . . .60 E7
South Ella Dr HU10 . . . .178 D7
South Ella Way HU10 . . .178 D7
South End
  Boston PE21 . . . . .208 F4
  Collingham NG23 . . . . .91 C4
South End La
  Hogsthorpe PE24 . . . . . .90 B6
  Thorne/Moorends DN8 . .15 A7
South End La DN22 . . . . .52 E3
Southern Cl 7 LN4 . . . . .207 A5
Southern La LN6 . . . . . . .92 B7
Southern Rd DN40 . . . . .186 D7
Southern Wlk DN35 . . . .194 F7
South Fen Rd
  Bourne PE10 . . . . .213 F4
  Helpringham NG34 . . .133 D6
SOUTH FERRIBY DN18 . . .10 B8
South Ferriby Prim Sch
  DN18 . . . . .10 A7
Southfield
  7 Belton DN9 . . . . .16 E1
  4 Kingston upon Hull
    HU13 . . . . .3 E4
SOUTH FIELD DN33 . . . .194 F7
Southfield Cl
  Thorne/Moorends
    DN8 . . . . .15 B7
  Ulceby DN39 . . . . .12 B1
Southfield Dr
  10 Epworth DN9 . . . . . .27 D6
  2 Louth LN11 . . . . . .198 C4
  21 North Ferriby HU14 . . .3 A4
Southfield La
  Fishtoft PE21 . . . . . . .137 C8
  6 Old Leake PE22 . . . .114 A1
  Old Leake PE22 . . . . . .127 A8
  Willoughton DN21 . . . . .42 D3
Southfield Pl LN9 . . . . .199 C3
Southfield Rd
  1 Broughton DN20 . . . .19 D3
  13 Crowle DN17 . . . . . .16 D7
  Grimsby DN33 . . . . . . .194 F7
  Holton le Clay DN36 . . .15 D6
  North Kelsey LN7 . . . . .31 F3
  Scunthorpe DN16 . . . .185 C5
  Thorne/Moorends DN8 . .15 B7
  1 Winterton DN15 . . . . .8 F5
Southfields
  3 Binbrook LN8 . . . . . .47 C5
  3 Sleaford NG34 . . . . .212 D3
Southfields Ave PE2 . . . .231 D5
Southfields Cl 10 PE13 . .170 D2
Southfields Dr 7 PE21 . .231 D6
Southfields Inf Sch
  PE2 . . . . .231 D5
Southfields Jun Sch
  PE2 . . . . .231 D5
South Furlong Croft 22
  DN9 . . . . .27 E6
Southgate
  Kingston upon Hull
    HU13 . . . . .178 E1
  12 Pinchbeck PE11 . . . .156 E6
  Scunthorpe DN15 . . . .183 B3
South Gate NG34 . . . . . .212 D4
Southgate Spinneys 5
  NG34 . . . . .120 E4
Southgate Way PE2 . . . .229 C2
South Gn PE34 . . . . .161 F2
South Heath La LN6 . . . .106 D1
South Holland Ctr*
  PE11 . . . . .214 D4
South Humberside Ind Est
  DN31 . . . . .191 D8
South Hunsley Sch HU14 . .2 E5
SOUTH HYKEHAM LN6 . . .93 A5
South Hykeham Com Prim
  Sch LN6 . . . . .93 B7
South Ing Dro PE11 . . . .134 E1
South Ings La PE24 . . . .90 B5
South Intake La DN9 . . . .40 C7

SOUTH KELSEY LN7 . . . . .32 A1
South Kesteven Works
  NG31 . . . . .210 F3
SOUTH KILLINGHOLME
  DN40 . . . . .12 E3
South La
  Kingston upon Hull
    HU13 . . . . .178 E1
  Willingham DN21 . . . . .54 A3
Southland Cl DN37 . . . .188 A1
Southland Dr 5 LN6 . . .205 B4
Southlands Ave
  Gainsborough DN21 . . .197 B8
  Louth LN11 . . . . .198 D3
  Peterborough PE1 . . . .226 A6
Southlands Dr
  Grantham NG31 . . . . . .211 C4
  Morton DN21 . . . . .197 B8
Southlands Gdns DN21 . .197 B8
South Leys Sch DN17 . . .184 D4
South Marsh Rd
  Immingham Power St
    DN41 . . . . .187 F1
  Stallingborough DN41 . . .23 F7
South Marsh Rd Ind Est
  DN41 . . . . .187 F2
South Mkt Pl 7 LN13 . . .75 F2
Southmoor La
  Newton on Trent LN1 . . .78 D8
  Snitterby DN21 . . . . . . .43 E5
Southmoor Rd
  Crowle DN17 . . . . .16 C8
  Newton on Trent LN1 . . .78 D8
South Moor Rd DN10 . . .39 F3
Southolme DN21 . . . . . .197 D4
SOUTH ORMSBY LN11 . . .74 D2
SOUTHORPE PE9 . . . . . .172 E2
Southorpe La DN21 . . . .42 A7
Southorpe Paddock Nature
  Reserve* LN8 . . . . . .172 E1
SOUTH OWERSBY LN8 . . .44 E4
South Parade
  Boston PE21 . . . . .208 C4
  11 Caythorpe NG32 . . .119 B7
  Gainsborough DN21 . . .197 F3
  Grantham NG31 . . . . . .211 B2
  Grimsby DN31 . . . . . . .191 D8
  7 Lincoln LN1 . . . . . .201 D4
  Peterborough PE3 . . . .225 E3
  5 Saxilby LN1 . . . . . . .66 D2
  Skegness PE25 . . . . . .206 D2
  South Kyme LN4 . . . . .123 B8
  Spalding PE11 . . . . . .214 C3
  Thorne/Moorends DN8 . .15 A7
South Parade Jun & Inf Sch
  DN31 . . . . .191 D8
South Pk Ave
  Bracebridge Heath
    LN4 . . . . .205 F8
South Pk Rd DN17 . . . . .184 D3
South Ramper DN21 . . . .44 A5
SOUTH RAUCEBY
  NG34 . . . . .120 E4
South Rd
  Bourne PE10 . . . . .213 D4
  Chapel St Leonard PE24 . .90 E6
  4 Keadby with Althorpe
    DN17 . . . . .17 C6
  Mablethorpe/Sutton on Sea
    LN12 . . . . .64 C1
  North Somercotes LN11 . .50 E7
  Sturton le Steeple DN22 . .52 C4
  Tetford LN9 . . . . .73 F1
SOUTH RESTON LN11 . . .62 D1
SOUTHREY LN3 . . . . . . .83 D1
South Ridge Cres 2
  DN17 . . . . .184 F3
South Rise 6 LN6 . . . . . .47 C4
South St Mary's Gate 4
  DN31 . . . . .191 E7
South Scaffold La NG33 . .91 E3
SOUTH SCARLE NG23 . . .91 E6
South Scarle La LN6 . . . .78 E1
South Scarle Rd NG23 . . .91 E6
South Sea La DN36 . . . . .36 D7
South Side DN15 . . . . . . .2 A1
SOUTH SOMERCOTES
  LN11 . . . . .50 E5
South St
  10 Alford LN13 . . . . . .75 F2
  5 Alford LN13 . . . . . . .75 F2
  10 Barnetby le Wold
    DN38 . . . . .21 B4
  Bole DN22 . . . . .52 C5
  Boston PE21 . . . . .208 F4
  Bourne PE10 . . . . .213 D4
  Caistor LN7 . . . . .33 B4
  1 Cleethorpes DN35 . . .193 A5
  20 Crowland PE6 . . . . .166 F1
  Horncastle LN9 . . . . . .199 B3
  Keelby DN41 . . . . .23 A5
  Louth LN11 . . . . .198 D5
  Morton DN21 . . . . .197 C8
  15 North Kelsey LN7 . . . .32 A4
  Owston Ferry DN9 . . . .28 B2
  Peterborough PE3 . . . .225 E3
  Roxton cum Risby DN15 . .8 F3
  Scamblesby LN11 . . . . .72 F5
  Swineshead PE20 . . . .135 B7
  West Butterwick DN17 . .28 D8
  17 Winterton DN15 . . . . .8 F5

Ske–Spe 277

South Terr
  Boston PE21 . . . . .208 F3
  4 Louth LN11 . . . . . .198 C5
SOUTH THORESBY
  LN13 . . . . .75 A3
South View
  Anlaby HU4 . . . . .179 B6
  Broughton DN20 . . . . . .19 D4
  Holton le Clay DN36 . . .195 E1
  Humberston DN36 . . . .193 A1
  Peterborough PE2 . . . .230 F7
  Yarborough DN34 . . . .191 A6
South View Ave
  Brigg DN20 . . . . .196 C5
  Burringham DN17 . . . . .17 D4
South View Cl 4 PE25 . . .206 D2
South View Com Prim Sch
  PE6 . . . . .166 E1
South View La LN11 . . . .62 A7
Southview Leisure Ctr
  PE25 . . . . .103 C8
South View Rd 4 PE25 . .225 D8
South Wood Dr 10 LN4 . .68 E6
Southwell Ave
  HU9 . . . . .5 F8
  Peterborough PE4 . . . .220 E4
Southwell Cl NG31 . . . .210 C5
Southwell's Dr 4 PE25 . .206 D1
Southwell's La 1 LN9 . . .199 C4
Southwick Cl PE4 . . . . .221 C1
SOUTH WILLINGHAM
  LN8 . . . . .59 A7
SOUTH WITHAM NG33 . . .151 E2
South Witham Nature
  Reserve* NG33 . . . . . .151 F2
South Witham Prim Sch
  NG33 . . . . .151 D2
Southwold Cres DN33 . . .194 E8
Sovereign Cl
  12 Grimsby DN34 . . . . .190 D4
  13 Wisbech PE13 . . . . .170 C1
Sovereign Pl PE3 . . . . . .225 E2
Sow Dale Nature Reserve*
  PE23 . . . . .87 A1
Sowers La DN15 . . . . .9 A5
Spa Bldgs LN2 . . . . .234 B2
Spalford Cl 3 DN21 . . . .65 E8
Spa Hill 9 DN21 . . . . . . .30 B1
Spain Ct 5 PE21 . . . . . .208 F4
Spain La 5 PE21 . . . . . .208 F4
Spain Pl PE21 . . . . .209 A4
SPALDING PE11 . . . . . . .214 E6

Spalding Bulb Mus*
  PE11 . . . . .145 C1
Spalding Comm 6
  PE11 . . . . .214 B1
Spalding Dro
  Cowbit PE12 . . . . .157 A3
  Spalding PE12 . . . . . .214 E1
Spalding FE Ctr PE11 . . .214 D4
Spalding Gate PE12 . . . .158 B8
Spalding Gram Sch
  PE11 . . . . .214 D3
Spalding High Sch
  PE11 . . . . .214 D3
Spalding Parish CE Day
  Sch PE11 . . . . .214 E2
Spalding Prim Sch
  PE11 . . . . .214 E3
Spalding Rd
  Boston PE21 . . . . .208 E3
  Bourne PE10 . . . . .213 E1
  Deeping St James PE6 . .165 D1
  Gosberton PE11 . . . . .217 C5
  Holbeach PE12 . . . . . .215 A2
  Market Deeping PE6 . . .217 E5
  Pinchbeck PE11 . . . . .214 C8
  Scunthorpe DN16 . . . .185 B8
  Wigtoft PE20 . . . . .135 E1
Spalding Sta PE11 . . . . .214 C4
SPALFORD NG23 . . . . . .78 D4
Spalford La LN6 . . . . . . .78 A3
Spalford Rd LN6 . . . . . . .78 A3
Spalford Warren Nature
  Reserve* NG23 . . . . . .78 D2
SPANBY NG34 . . . . .132 F4
Spanning Dr 22 PE13 . . .75 F2
Spa Rd
  Lincoln LN5 . . . . .234 C2
  2 Woodhall Spa LN10 . . .97 C6
Spark's La PE12 . . . . . . .158 A4
Spark St DN34 . . . . .191 A7
Sparrowgate Rd PE14 . . .170 F1
Sparrow La
  8 Long Bennington
    NG23 . . . . .117 D3
  Marnham NG23 . . . . . .78 A5
  Newball LN8 . . . . .69 F2
Sparrow Rd 1 PE21 . . . .230 D1
Spa St LN2 . . . . .202 B3
Spaw La 5 LN11 . . . . . .198 B6
Spayne Rd PE21 . . . . . .209 A4
Speechley Rd PE7 . . . . .233 F6
Speechley's Dro PE6 . . .174 F7
Speedwell Cres DN35 . . .182 C6
Speedwell Ct 7 PE6 . . . .217 D6
Speight Cl 5 NG24 . . . .104 B7
Spencer Ave
  Peterborough PE2 . . . .231 D5

Spencer Ave continued
Scunthorpe DN15 . . . .**182** F4
Spencer Cl
 3 Long Sutton PE12. . . . . .**216** B5
 West Walton PE14. . . . .**170** E4
Spencer Gdns
 7 Butterwick PE22. . . . . . .**126** E3
 Holbeach PE12 . . . .**215** F3
Spencer St
 Grimsby DN31 . . . .**189** D1
 6 Kingston upon Hull
 HU2. . . . .**180** E7
 9 Lincoln LN5. . . . .**205** E8
Spence St 10 PE23. . . . .**87** F1
Spendla's La PE12 . . . .**159** F3
Spendluffe Ave 3 LN13. . . .**75** F3
Spennymoor Cl 1 LN6. . . . . .**93** B8
Sperrin Cl 5 LN5. . . . .**205** D2
Speyer Ave PE11. . . . .**214** C5
Speyside Cl 1 PE2 . . . .**229** D4
Spice Ave PE21. . . . .**136** C8
Spicer's La PE22. . . . .**127** B5
SPILSBY PE23 . . . .**101** A8
Spilsby Cl 3 LN6 . . . .**204** D8
Spilsby Hill PE23. . . . .**100** B8
 Spilsby Prim Sch PE23 . . . . .**88** A1
Spilsby Rd
 Boston PE21 . . . .**209** A6
 Eastville PE22 . . . .**101** A1
 High Toynton LN9. . . . .**86** B4
 Horncastle LN9. . . . .**199** E4
 Scunthorpe DN17 . . . .**184** E5
 Spilsby PE23 . . . .**101** A8
 Thorpe St Peter PE24 . . . . .**102** B4
Spindlewood Dr PE10. . . . .**213** D3
Spindles The PE10 . . . .**213** D7
Spindlewood 1 HU15. . . . . .**2** C7
Spinnaker Cl HU9. . . . .**181** C6
Spinners 3 NG34. . . . .**212** E3
Spinney Cl
 Immingham DN40 . . . .**186** C4
 2 Manby LN11 . . . .**62** C6
 4 Ryhall PE9 . . . .**163** C1
Spinney Croft Cl 14 HU14 . .**3** A5
Spinney La
 10 Ryhall PE9 . . . .**163** C1
 2 Scopwick Heath LN4 . . .**108** A7
Spinneys The 5 LN2. . . . . .**68** D7
Spinney The
 1 Barnby Dun DN3 . . . . . .**14** A3
 6 Barrow upon Humber
 DN19. . . . .**11** D8
 Brigg DN20 . . . .**196** D2
 3 Gainsborough DN21. . . .**197** F5
 3 Grimsby DN31 . . . .**191** C7
 3 Market Deeping PE6 . . . .**217** B5
 3 Swanland HU14 . . . .**3** B7
 7 Winthorpe NG24. . . . . .**104** B7
Spinney Wlk
 Kingston upon Hull
 HU4. . . . .**179** C6
 Longthorpe PE3 . . . .**225** B2
Spion Kop La PE20. . . . . . .**135** E3
Spirea App LN6. . . . .**204** C8
Spires The 15 PE20. . . . . . .**136** A2
Spire View
 1 Bottesford NG13 . . . . . .**128** A6
 4 Grantham NG31 . . . . . .**211** A5
 3 Kingston upon Hull
 HU13. . . . .**178** E1
 Sleaford NG34. . . . .**212** A2
Spire View Rd LN11. . . . . .**198** D5
Spirewic Ave PE25. . . . . . .**206** D8
Spitalgate CE (Controlled)
 Prim Sch NG31. . . . .**210** D3
Spital Hill
 Gainsborough DN21 . . . . . .**197** E5
 4 Louth LN11 . . . .**198** B5
SPITAL IN THE STREET
 LN8. . . . .**43** B1
Spital La LN8 . . . .**55** B8
Spital St LN1 . . . .**234** B4
Spital Terr DN21 . . . .**197** D4
Spitfire Ave LN11 . . . .**62** B6
Spittal Hill Rd PE22. . . . . .**126** D4
SPRIDLINGTON LN8 . . . .**55** F3
Spridlington Rd LN8. . . . . . .**56** D3
Spriggs Cl NG34 . . . .**212** C3
Spignall PE3. . . . .**224** F4
Springbank DN20 . . . .**196** C5
Spring Bank
 5 Binbrook LN8 . . . .**47** C4
 Grimsby DN34 . . . .**191** A7
 Kingston upon Hull HU3 . . .**180** D7
Spring Bank W HU5. . . . . .**179** D7
Springbok Cl HU4 . . . .**179** D2
Springburn St HU3 . . . . . .**180** A5
Spring Cl 9 LN2. . . . .**68** E6
Spring Ct
 Dunston LN4 . . . .**95** C5
 Louth LN11 . . . .**198** C5
 1 Welton/Dunholme
 LN2. . . . .**68** D7
Springdale Cl
 2 Kingston upon Hull
 HU9. . . . .**5** D8

Springdale Cl continued
 Kingston upon Hull HU10 . . .**178** F8
Spring Dr
 9 Balderton NG24 . . . . . .**104** C1
 Farcet PE7. . . . .**231** B2
Spring End 3 NG31. . . . . . .**129** D5
Springfield PE2 . . . .**231** A7
Springfield Ave
 Brough HU15 . . . .**2** C6
 1 Hatfield DN7. . . . .**14** E4
Springfield Cl
 Branston LN4. . . . .**81** E2
 Gainsborough DN21 . . . . . .**197** E4
 Lincoln LN2 . . . .**234** B4
 2 Scunthorpe DN16. . . . .**185** C6
Springfield Est LN4 . . . .**95** D1
 Springfield Prim Sch
 DN33 . . . .**194** D7
Springfield Rd
 2 Brigg DN20. . . . .**196** D3
 Grantham NG31. . . . .**211** A2
 Grimsby DN33 . . . .**191** C1
 Kingston upon Hull HU3 . . .**179** F6
 Parson Drove PE13 . . . . . .**177** D7
 Peterborough PE1 . . . .**225** F5
 6 Ruskington NG34 . . . . .**108** D2
 Yaxley PE7 . . . .**233** F5
Springfield Rise 1
 DN20. . . . .**196** E3
Springfields LN8. . . . .**46** B1
 Springfields Sh & Events
 Ctr PE12 . . . .**157** B7
Springfield Way HU10. . . . .**178** E7
Spring Gdns
 Gainsborough DN21 . . . . . .**197** D4
 Grantham NG31. . . . .**211** B2
 Long Sutton PE12 . . . .**216** B4
 13 Louth LN11. . . . .**198** B5
 Sleaford NG34. . . . .**212** C5
 Spalding PE11 . . . .**214** C3
Spring Gdns E HU4 . . . . . .**179** B6
Spring Gdns S HU4 . . . . . .**179** B5
Spring Gdns W HU4. . . . . .**179** B6
Spring Gr
 Kingston upon Hull
 HU3. . . . .**180** A7
 Terrington St Clement
 PE34 . . . .**161** F2
Springhead Ave HU5. . . . . .**179** A7
Springhead Ct HU10 . . . . .**179** A6
Springhead Gdns
 HU10 . . . .**179** A7
Springhead La HU5 . . . . . .**179** A7
 Springhead Prim Sch
 HU10 . . . .**178** E7
Spring Hill
 3 Binbrook LN8 . . . .**47** C4
 Cherry Willingham/Reepham
 LN3 . . . .**203** F8
 Grantham NG31 . . . .**211** D3
 Lincoln LN1 . . . .**234** A3
Spring La
 Balderton NG24 . . . .**104** C2
 4 Colsterworth NG33 . . . .**151** D7
 4 Folkingham NG34 . . . . .**142** D8
 Horbling NG34. . . . .**133** B2
 14 Laceby DN37 . . . .**23** F1
 5 Leasingham NG34 . . . . .**121** B7
 4 Wymondham LE14 . . . . .**150** B1
Springs La DN22. . . . .**52** A2
Springs Parade DN20 . . . . .**196** B3
Springs Rd DN10 . . . .**26** C1
Spring St
 Immingham DN40 . . . .**186** D4
 Kingston upon Hull HU2 . . .**180** D7
 Spalding PE11 . . . .**214** D3
Springs Way DN20 . . . .**196** B3
SPRINGTHORPE DN21 . . . . . .**53** E8
Springthorpe Rd
 Corringham DN21 . . . .**41** E1
 Gainsborough DN21 . . . . . .**197** F4
Spring View 4 LN4. . . . .**47** C4
Springville Ave HU13. . . . .**178** F2
Springway Cres DN33. . . . .**191** A7
Springwood Cres
 DN33. . . . .**194** D7
Sprite La LN4. . . . .**109** D5
Spruce Cl PE12. . . . .**215** C4
Spruce La DN39 . . . .**12** A1
Spurn Ave DN33 . . . .**194** F8
 Spurn Lightship* HU1 . . . .**180** F5
Spur The 7 LN5. . . . .**107** A7
Spyvee St HU8. . . . .**181** A7
Square The
 2 Barnack PE9 . . . .**172** D3
 Barrowby NG32 . . . .**129** B3
 12 Goxhill DN19 . . . .**12** A8
 Kingston upon Hull
 HU13. . . . .**178** A1
 18 Kirton PE20 . . . .**136** C5
 4 Leasingham NG34 . . . . .**121** B7
 North Thoresby DN36 . . . . .**36** B1
 5 Ryhall PE9 . . . .**163** C1
 Toynton All Saints PE23 . . .**100** F6
Squires Gate PE21 . . . . . .**208** D4
Squires Mdw 10 LN11. . . . .**50** F7
Squires The PE2 . . . .**230** F8
Squirrel Chase LN6. . . . . . .**92** D5
Stable La 3 DN18 . . . .**3** E1
Stable Mews DN21 . . . .**53** B8
Stable Way 3 LN8 . . . .**57** E7
Stacey Cl 2 PE25. . . . .**90** D3
Stackyard The PE2. . . . . . .**229** E5
Stafford Ave NG24 . . . .**104** A2

Staffordshire Cres 6
 LN6. . . . .**204** D7
Stafford St
 3 Boston PE21. . . . .**208** F6
 Kingston upon Hull HU2 . . .**180** E8
Stagsden PE2. . . . .**229** F4
Stagshaw Dr PE2 . . . .**231** B8
STAINBY NG33 . . . .**151** C5
Stainby Rd
 Buckminster NG33 . . . .**150** F5
 Gunby & Stainby NG33 . . . .**151** C4
Staindale Rd DN16. . . . . . .**185** D5
Stainesway LN11. . . . .**198** E7
STAINFIELD
 Haconby PE10 . . . .**154** A8
 Stainfield LN8 . . . .**83** B8
Stainfield Rd
 Kirkby Underwood
 PE10. . . . .**142** D1
 Morton PE10 . . . .**154** B7
STAINFORTH DN7. . . . .**14** C6
 Stainforth Inf Sch DN7. . . . .**14** C6
 Stainforth Kirton La Prim
 Sch DN7. . . . .**14** C7
Stainforth Moor Rd
 DN7. . . . .**15** C3
 Stainforth Rd DN7 . . . .**14** A5
Stain La LN12. . . . .**63** E3
STAINSBY LN9. . . . .**86** F6
Stainton Ave 6 DN21 . . . . . .**43** D7
STAINTON BY LANGWORTH
 LN3. . . . .**69** C4
Stainton Cl 5 DN21 . . . .**53** A5
Stainton Dr
 Grimsby DN33 . . . .**191** A3
 8 Immingham DN40 . . . . .**186** B4
Stainton Gdns LN1. . . . . . .**201** E7
Stainton La LN2 . . . .**69** B4
STAINTON LE VALE LN8. . . . .**46** E5
Stallebrass Cl PE2 . . . .**231** E5
STALLINGBOROUGH
 DN41 . . . .**23** E6
 Stallingborough CE Prim
 Sch DN41 . . . .**23** E6
Stallingborough Rd
 Immingham DN40 . . . .**186** B2
 Keelby DN41 . . . .**23** A5
 Stallingborough Sta
 DN41 . . . .**23** E6
STAMFORD PE9. . . . .**219** D4
 Stamford Bsns Pk PE9 . . . .**219** E6
Stamford Cl 6 PE7. . . . . . .**217** B5
 Stamford High Sch
 PE9. . . . .**219** C4
 Stamford Jun Sch PE9 . . . .**219** B3
 Stamford Leisure Ctr
 PE9. . . . .**219** D6
Stamford Lodge Rd
 PE6. . . . .**224** C5
 Stamford Mus* PE9 . . . . . .**219** C5
Stamford Rd
 Barnack PE9 . . . .**172** C4
 Buckminster NG33 . . . .**151** A4
 Collyweston PE9 . . . .**171** C2
 Colsterworth NG33 . . . . . .**151** E5
 Easton on the Hill PE9 . . . .**219** A1
 Essendine PE9 . . . .**163** D2
 Helpston PE6 . . . .**173** C1
 Ketton PE9. . . . .**218** A2
 Marholm PE6 . . . .**220** E6
 Market Deeping PE6 . . . . .**217** A4
 Tinwell PE9 . . . .**218** A6
 West Deeping PE9 . . . . . .**173** A7
 Stamford Ret Pk PE9 . . . . .**219** D6
 Stamford & Rutland Hospl
 PE9. . . . .**219** D6
 Stamfords Art Ctr*
 PE9 . . . .**219** C6
Stamford St NG31. . . . .**211** B2
Stamford Sta PE9 . . . .**219** C4
Stamford Wlk 25 PE9 . . . . .**219** C5
Stamp End LN2 . . . .**234** C2
Stamper St 2 PE3. . . . .**224** F3
Standish Cl PE7 . . . .**230** D8
Standish Gr PE21 . . . .**209** B7
Standish La DN40. . . . .**186** B5
Stane Dr 12 LN4 . . . .**81** A1
Stanfield Rd 2 DN9 . . . .**27** D6
Stanford Cl 1 DN37 . . . .**23** F1
 Stanford Jun & Inf Sch
 DN37. . . . .**23** F1
Stanford Wlk 4 PE23 . . . . .**225** C4
Standard La LN5. . . . .**205** F3
STANGROUND PE2 . . . .**231** C5
 Stanground Coll PE7. . . . . .**231** C5
Stanholme La DN36 . . . .**36** A1
Stanhope Ave LN2 . . . .**202** A6
Stanhope Gdns 1
 PE21 . . . .**209** C4
Stanhope Pl DN35 . . . .**192** C2
Stanhope Rd LN9 . . . .**199** C4
Stanhope St LN9 . . . .**199** C4
Stanhurst La DN7 . . . .**15** A5
 Staniland Prim Sch
 PE21 . . . .**208** D4
Staniland Rd PE21 . . . .**208** D3
Staniland Way
 1 Humberston DN36 . . . . .**36** D8
 Peterborough PE4 . . . .**221** A5
Stanley Ave NG31 . . . .**211** B3
Staniwells Dr 13 DN20 . . . . .**19** D3
Stanley Cl 2 PE24 . . . .**102** D2
Stanley Cres LN4 . . . .**205** F4

Stanley Dr
 11 Sutterton PE20. . . . . . .**136** A2
 Sutton Bridge PE12 . . . . . .**160** E4
Stanley Gdns 13 DN7. . . . . .**14** C6
Stanley Pl 1 LN5. . . . .**201** F1
Stanley Rd
 Peterborough PE1 . . . .**226** A3
 Scunthorpe DN15 . . . .**182** C3
 18 Stainforth DN7. . . . . . .**14** C6
Stanley St
 Bourne PE10. . . . .**213** C6
 Gainsborough DN21 . . . . . .**197** D2
 Grimsby DN32 . . . .**189** C1
 Kingston upon Hull HU3 . . .**180** C7
 Lincoln LN5. . . . .**205** D7
 1 Stamford PE9 . . . .**219** C5
Stan Rowing Ct PE2 . . . . . .**231** C7
Stansfield Gdns DN14. . . . . .**6** A5
Stansted St 3 DN31 . . . . . .**188** D1
Stanthaket Ct 2 LN1. . . . . .**234** B3
Stanton Cl PE10 . . . .**213** E5
Stanton Rd 4 LN12. . . . . . .**77** A8
 Stanton's Pit Nature
 Reserve* PE10. . . . .**163** C8
Stanton Sq PE7 . . . .**230** D2
Stanton St 7 NG31 . . . .**211** A4
Stanwick Ct PE1 . . . .**225** F2
Stapes Garth 1 LN11. . . . . .**50** B8
Stapledon Rd PE2. . . . .**229** D7
Staple Way LN4 . . . .**81** D4
STAPLEFORD LN6 . . . .**105** B8
Stapleford Cl LN2 . . . .**201** F8
Stapleford La
 Coddington NG24. . . . .**104** E6
 Collingham NG23. . . . .**91** E1
Staple La NG24 . . . .**104** B1
Staple Rd DN40. . . . .**12** F3
Staples La 1 LN5 . . . .**93** F7
Star Carr La DN20 . . . .**196** D8
Star Cl PE1. . . . .**226** C3
Starella Gr HU4 . . . .**180** A4
Star Fen Dro NG34. . . . . . .**123** A4
Starham Rd LN7. . . . .**31** C4
Starks La LN8 . . . .**58** D7
Star La
 Holbeach PE12 . . . .**215** C7
 2 Stamford PE9 . . . .**219** C5
Star La Mews 26 PE9 . . . . .**219** C5
Star Lode Dro PE11. . . . . . .**144** B1
Star Mews PE1 . . . .**226** C2
Star Rd PE1 . . . .**226** C2
Stathern Rd PE1. . . . .**226** A3
Stathern Wlk NG31 . . . . . .**210** E2
Stathers Wlk 3 HU10. . . . .**178** F6
Station App
 6 Ancaster NG32. . . . . . .**120** A3
 Boston PE21 . . . .**208** E4
 Cleethorpes DN35 . . . .**192** F7
 11 Donington PE11 . . . . . .**134** E2
 Louth LN11 . . . .**198** C6
Station Ave
 New Waltham DN36. . . . . .**195** D6
 3 South Witham NG33. . . .**151** D2
 Wisbech St Mary PE13 . . . .**177** D5
Station Cl 9 NG23. . . . .**91** D4
Station Ct 7 DN7. . . . .**14** D4
Station Field LN6 . . . .**200** B3
Station La
 Horncastle LN9 . . . .**199** A3
 Scawby cum Ownby DN38 . . .**32** D7
Station Rd
 Ailsworth PE5 . . . .**223** C1
 Alford LN13. . . . .**75** C3
 Algarkirk PE20. . . . .**146** A5
 Bardney LN3 . . . .**83** B4
 Barkston NG32 . . . .**130** C8
 Barlings LN3 . . . .**69** B3
 Barnack PE9 . . . .**172** C4
 Beckingham DN10 . . . .**52** B8
 8 Billingborough NG34 . . .**133** B1
 Blyton DN21. . . . .**41** C5
 Bottesford NG13 . . . .**128** A6
 Bourne PE10 . . . .**155** C3
 Branston LN4. . . . .**81** E2
 Brough HU15. . . . .**2** B5
 Burgh le Marsh PE24. . . . .**102** C8
 Burringham DN17 . . . .**17** E4
 Candlesby with Gunby
 PE24. . . . .**89** B1
 Careby Aunby & Holywell
 PE9. . . . .**163** A8
 Castle Bytham NG33 . . . . .**152** D1
 6 Cherry Willingham/
 Reepham LN3 . . . .**82** A8
 Cherry Willingham/Reepham
 LN3 . . . .**203** F8
 Cleethorpes DN35 . . . .**192** F7
 Collingham NG23. . . . .**91** D4
 Corby Glen NG33 . . . .**152** D7
 Deeping St James PE6 . . . .**174** B7
 Digby LN4 . . . .**108** E5
 Donington on Bain LN11 . . . .**59** E1
 East Halton DN40 . . . .**12** D2
 Epworth DN9 . . . .**27** D7
 Fulstow LN11 . . . .**49** A7
 Garthorpe & Fockerby
 DN17. . . . .**7** E6
 Gedney Hill PE12. . . . .**168** C1
 Gosberton PE11. . . . .**145** A5
 Grantham NG31. . . . .**211** B3
 Grasby DN38 . . . .**32** E6
 Great Steeping PE23 . . . . .**101** F6
 Grimsby DN37 . . . .**190** E8
 Gunness DN15 . . . .**17** E5
 Habrough DN40. . . . .**12** F1
 Halton Holegate PE23. . . . .**101** B8

Station Rd continued
 Harby NG23 . . . .**79** B1
 Harmston LN5 . . . .**93** E6
 Hatfield DN7 . . . .**14** C1
 Haxey DN9 . . . .**27** E1
 Healing DN41 . . . .**23** F6
 Heckington NG34. . . . .**122** E6
 Heighington LN4 . . . .**81** E1
 Helpringham NG34 . . . . . .**133** D2
 9 Hibaldstow DN20 . . . . . .**30** E8
 Holbeach PE12 . . . .**215** C6
 Holton le Clay DN36 . . . . . .**36** A2
 Hubbert's Bridge PE20 . . . .**124** E1
 Keadby with Althorpe
 DN17. . . . .**17** E1
 6 Ketton PE9 . . . .**171** A4
 Kingston upon Hull
 HU13. . . . .**178** E1
 Kirton in Lindsey DN21 . . . .**30** E4
 Kirton PE20 . . . .**136** C5
 Knaith DN21 . . . .**53** F2
 Legbourne LN11 . . . .**61** E7
 Lincoln LN6 . . . .**204** D2
 Little Steeping PE23 . . . . .**101** C1
 5 Long Sutton PE12. . . . .**216** B6
 Ludborough DN36 . . . .**48** E2
 18 Mablethorpe & Sutton
 LN12 . . . .**76** F2
 20 Mablethorpe/Sutton on Sea
 LN12 . . . .**77** A8
 Metheringham LN4 . . . .**95** D2
 Midville PE22 . . . .**113** B1
 1 Misterton DN10 . . . .**40** A7
 Misterton LN13 . . . .**89** A7
 Morton PE10 . . . .**154** D1
 Moulton PE12 . . . .**157** F8
 Mumby LN13 . . . .**76** E4
 North Kelsey LN7. . . . .**32** E1
 Northorpe PE10 . . . .**164** A4
 North Thoresby DN36 . . . . .**36** B1
 Owston Ferry DN9 . . . .**28** A7
 Peterborough PE3 . . . .**225** C4
 Potter Hanworth LN4 . . . . . .**82** A6
 Ruskington NG34 . . . .**108** E3
 Scawby DN20 . . . .**30** F8
 Scredington NG34 . . . .**132** E3
 Scunthorpe DN15 . . . .**183** A3
 Sibsey PE22 . . . .**113** C5
 Sleaford NG34. . . . .**212** C1
 South Kelsey LN7 . . . .**32** C1
 South Killingholme DN40. . . .**12** F3
 South Willingham LN8 . . . . . .**59** A4
 Stallingborough DN41. . . . . .**23** E8
 Stamford PE9. . . . .**219** E6
 Stixwould & Woodhall
 LN10. . . . .**97** A4
 Sturton le Steeple DN22 . . . .**52** E1
 Surfleet PE11. . . . .**145** E8
 Sutterton PE20 . . . .**136** A4
 Swinderby LN6. . . . .**92** A7
 Swineshead PE20 . . . .**135** B7
 Theddlethorpe All Saints
 LN12 . . . .**63** C5
 Thorney PE6 . . . .**176** A8
 Thornton Curtis DN39 . . . . .**11** F5
 Thorpe on the Hill LN6 . . . . .**79** E1
 Thorpe St Peter PE24 . . . .**102** B4
 Timberland LN4 . . . .**96** E5
 Torksey LN1. . . . .**65** C5
 Tumby Woodside PE22 . . . . .**98** F1
 Tydd St Mary PE13 . . . . . .**170** C1
 Ulceby DN39 . . . .**12** E1
 Wainfleet All Saints
 PE24 . . . .**102** D7
 Walkeringham DN10 . . . . . .**40** A3
 Waltham DN36. . . . .**195** A7
 Waltham LE14 . . . .**138** A2
 Whitton DN15 . . . .**1** D7
 Wickenby LN3 . . . .**57** D8
 Woodhall Spa LN10 . . . .**97** C5
Station Rd N 6 LN4 . . . . . .**161** C2
Station Rd S PE34 . . . .**161** C2
Station Rd (West)
 NG31 . . . .**211** A2
Station St
 Boston PE21 . . . .**208** E4
 Donington PE11. . . . .**134** E2
 Lincoln LN5 . . . .**234** B2
 Rippingale PE10 . . . .**143** A2
 1 Spalding PE11. . . . .**214** D3
Station Terr LN5 . . . .**106** C7
Staunton Cl LN1. . . . .**201** D7
STAUNTON IN THE VALE
 NG13. . . . .**117** F5
Staunton St 3 LN1 . . . .**201** D7
Staveley Rd PE4 . . . .**220** F2
Staveley Rd 6 LN13. . . . . . .**75** B4
Staverton Cres LN6 . . . . . .**200** B1
Staverton Rd PE4 . . . .**220** E6
Staves Ct 5 DN36 . . . .**36** C8
Staxton Cl PE6 . . . .**220** A4
Staxton Dr HU9 . . . .**181** C7
Steadfold La PE9 . . . .**218** A4
Steadings The DN15. . . . . . .**8** B3
 Steaner Point Rd LN4 . . . . .**95** C5
Steapas Cl 2 PE23 . . . .**100** F6
Steeles Dr NG24 . . . .**104** C1
Steepers The 4 LN6. . . . . . .**68** C7
Steep Hill LN2 . . . .**234** B3
Steeping Ct LN1. . . . .**201** E8
Steeping Dr DN40 . . . .**186** A4
Steeping Rd PE23. . . . .**101** C6
Steeple Leas 18 NG31. . . . .**211** A5
Steeton Ct 4 LN6 . . . .**204** D1
STENIGOT LN11. . . . .**72** E3
Stenigot Cl 3 LN6. . . . .**204** D1
Stenigot Gr LN6 . . . .**204** D1

Stenigot Rd 1 LN6 204 D6
Stenner Rd LN4 207 F6
Stennett Ave 1 PE11 156 E2
STENWITH NG32 128 D3
Stephen Cl 3 DN39 12 A1
Stephen Cres
 16 Barton-upon-Humber DN18 10 F8
 Grimsby DN34 190 E4
 Humberston DN36 36 C8
Stephen Rd NG24 104 A6
Stephenson Ave
 Gonerby Hill Foot NG31 210 F8
 Pinchbeck PE11 214 E8
Stephenson Cl
 9 Alford LN13 75 E2
 4 Boston PE21 208 F1
 Yaxley PE7 233 D6
Stephenson Ct 5 PE1 226 B2
Stephenson Way PE10 213 D7
Stephens Way 4 PE6 217 F4
Stephen's Way NG34 212 F3
Sterling Cres DN37 194 C4
Sterling Pl 8 LN10 97 E6
Sterne Ave 9 DN20 19 D3
Stevenson Pl 1 DN35 192 D5
Stevenson's Way 33 DN18 10 E8
Stevern Way PE1 226 F4
STEWTON LN11 61 E5
Stewton Gdns LN11 198 D4
Stewton La LN11 198 E4
Steyning La PE20 135 A7
Steynings The PE4 221 A3
STIBBINGTON PE8 222 C2
STICKFORD PE22 100 B2
STICKNEY PE22 113 A8
Stickney CE (Aided) Prim Sch PE22 113 A8
Stickney Farm Pk* PE22 112 F8
Stickney La PE22 112 D7
Still Cl PE6 217 B5
Still The PE13 170 B1
Stirling Cl 4 DN21 197 E6
Stirling Ct
 14 Grantham NG31 210 E2
 Heckington NG34 122 D2
Stirling Dr 12 NG24 104 C5
Stirling Rd PE9 218 F5
Stirling St
 Grimsby DN31 189 D1
 Kingston upon Hull HU3 179 F6
Stirling Way
 Market Deeping PE6 217 C7
 Peterborough PE3 220 E1
 4 Skellingthorpe LN6 200 A4
STIXWOULD LN10 97 B8
Stixwould Rd LN10 97 C7
Stockbridge Pk 3 HU15 2 C7
Stockbridge Rd HU15 2 C7
STOCKHOLES TURBARY DN9 16 B2
Stockhouse La PE11 145 B3
Stocking Way LN2 202 F6
Stockman's Ave 2 PE12 215 F3
Stockmoor La LN8 57 A8
Stocks Hill
 4 Belton DN9 16 E1
 Castor PE5 223 F1
Stockshill Rd DN16 185 C6
Stocks La LN8 56 F3
Stockwell Gate PE12 215 A4
Stockwell Gr 6 HU9 5 F8
Stockwell Prim Sch HU9 5 F8
Stockwith Mill* PE23 87 B5
Stockwith Rd
 Haxey DN9 27 E1
 Walkeringham DN10 40 A3
STOKE ROCHFORD NG33 139 F2
Stoke Rochford Hall Con & Leisure Ctr* NG33 139 F2
Stokesay Ct 8 PE3 225 B1
Stokes Dr NG34 212 B6
Stoksley Wlk DN37 190 F8
Stonebow Ctr LN2 234 B2
Stonebridge PE2 230 C5
Stonebridge Lea PE2 230 C5
Stonebridge Rd NG31 211 B4
Stone Cl 8 PE10 213 C6
Stonecross Rd NG34 107 E1
Stone Dr LE15 152 A1
Stonefield Ave LN2 234 B4
Stonefield Pk LN2 68 C7
Stonegate
 Gedney PE12 159 D6
 Spalding PE11 214 E3
 28 Thorne/Moorends DN8 15 A8
Stone Gate
 Cowbit PE12 157 B1
 Weston PE12 145 F2
STONE HILL DN7 14 F4
Stone Hill DN7 15 A4
Stone Hill Rd DN7 15 A4
Stonehouse Rd PE7 233 E5
Stone La
 Aubourn Haddington & South Hykeham LN5 92 E6
 Burringham DN17 17 E4
 Peterborough PE1 225 F5
 Sutterton PE20 135 F1
 6 Waddington LN5 93 F7
Stoneleigh Ct PE3 225 B2
Stonemasons Ct 4 NG31 211 B4
Stone Moor Rd 14 LN6 93 B8
Stonepit La
 Marston NG32 118 C2
 8 Skillington NG33 151 A8
Stone Pit La
 Skendleby PE23 88 D4
 Willingham DN21 53 F3
Stonepit Rd HU15 2 E6
Stonesby Rd LE14 138 E1
Stones Cl 4 PE24 90 B7
Stones La
 13 Spilsby PE23 88 A1
 West Keal PE23 100 C5
Stone's La PE24 77 C1
Stones Pl 1 LN6 200 E1
Stone Way NG34 212 B6
Stonewell Row LN9 199 C4
Stoney La DN21 54 F7
Stoney Way 15 DN36 36 D4
Stoney Yd LN6 200 A5
Stong's Dro PE11 144 F8
Stool Cl Rd 2 DN9 16 E1
Storbeck Rd 15 PE13 170 D1
Storey's Bar Rd PE6 227 A3
Storey's La PE24 102 E7
Storrington Way PE4 221 A3
Stortford St 7 DN31 188 D1
Story St 11 HU1 180 E7
Stothards La 7 DN19 12 A8
Stoton's Gate PE12 158 E2
Stour Ct 7 NG31 210 E2
Stourton Pl LN9 199 B4
Stove Ct LE15 162 A8
Stovin Cres DN15 9 A5
STOW LN1 66 C8
Stow Cl DN37 190 D8
Stowehill Rd PE4 221 D2
Stowe Rd PE6 164 E2
Stowgate Rd PE6 174 A8
Stow Hill LE14 150 C7
Stow La NG34 133 A1
Stow Pk Rd
 Marton DN21 65 E8
 Stow LN1 66 B8
Stow Rd
 Scunthorpe DN16 185 B7
 Sturton by Stow LN1 66 C8
 Willingham DN21 53 E2
 Wisbech PE13 170 E1
Strafford St DN21 197 D2
STRAGGLETHORPE LN5 105 E3
Stragglethorpe La
 Caythorpe NG32 118 E8
 Fulbeck NG32 105 E2
Strahane Cl LN5 205 C3
Straight Dro PE7 231 E1
Strait Bargate 26 PE21 208 F5
Strait The LN2 234 B3
Strand Cl
 Kingston upon Hull HU2 180 E8
 8 Mablethorpe/Sutton on Sea LN12 64 B3
Strand Infants Sch DN32 189 B1
Strand Jun Sch DN32 189 B1
Strand St DN32 189 B1
Strand The LN12 64 B3
Stratford Ave DN34 191 A4
Stratford Dr 5 DN16 183 C1
Stratten Cl 5 NG34 107 C1
Stratton Pk 1 HU14 3 C6
Strawberry Cl 13 PE13 170 C1
Strawberry Fields Dr PE12 147 D6
Strawberry Gdns HU9 181 B7
Strawberry Hill DN37 194 B4
Strawberry St HU9 181 B7
Strayfleets La PE22 126 D5
Stray Gn 12 NG34 108 E2
Street La
 North Kelsey LN7 32 B4
 North Leverton with Habblesthorpe DN22 65 A8
Street La Rd DN22 52 C1
Street Life Mus of Transport* HU9 181 A6
Streetway PE21 136 E7
Stretham Way 5 PE10 213 C7
Stretton Cl 4 LN1 66 C7
Stretton Rd LE15 162 B6
Strickland Rd DN17 7 A3
Stricklands Dr 4 PE6 175 C8
Strickland St HU3 180 C4
Strong's Bank PE12 158 F4
Strong's Gate PE12 158 F3
STROXTON NG33 139 E5
Stroxton La NG33 139 F5
Stroykins Cl DN34 190 F6
STRUBBY LN13 63 C1
Strubby Airfield LN13 75 E8
Strubby Cl
 9 Birchwood LN6 204 D8
 Cleethorpes DN35 193 A4
Strugg's Hill La PE20 136 B3
Stuart Cl
 Peterborough PE2 231 C6
 Scunthorpe DN17 184 F2
Stuart Ct PE1 226 B4
Stuart St NG31 211 C3
Stuart Wortley St 1 DN31 189 B2
Stubbs Cl 21 HU15 2 D5
STUBTON NG23 118 B7
Stubton Hall Sch NG23 118 B7
Stubton Rd NG23 117 F7
Studcross DN9 27 D6
Studio Ct 26 LN12 77 A8
Studley St HU8 181 B8
Stukeley Cl
 Lincoln LN2 202 E6
 Peterborough PE2 231 D5
Stukeley Gdns 2 PE12 215 C2
Stukeley Hall Dr PE12 215 D2
Stukeley Rd PE12 215 D2
Stumpacre PE3 225 A8
Stump Cross Hill NG34 212 C1
Stumpcross La PE20 135 B6
Stumps La PE12 157 B7
Sturdy Hill LN11 62 E4
STURGATE DN21 53 F8
Sturgate Airfield DN21 53 E6
Sturgate Cl 15 LN6 204 C7
Sturgate Wlk DN21 197 F3
Sturmer Ct 1 DN16 185 B2
Sturrock Ct 12 NG31 210 E2
Sturrock Way PE3 225 C8
STURTON DN20 30 F7
STURTON BY STOW LN1 66 C7
Sturton by Stow Prim Sch LN1 66 D8
Sturton CE Prim Sch DN22 52 C2
Sturton Cl 1 LN2 201 F7
Sturton Gr 2 DN33 191 B4
Sturton La DN20 30 E7
STURTON LE STEEPLE DN22 52 B3
Sturton Rd
 North Leverton with Habblesthorpe DN22 52 B1
 Stow LN1 66 C8
Sturton Way PE12 216 B5
Stutte Cl LN11 198 E3
Styles Croft 6 HU14 3 C6
Subway St HU3 180 B3
Subway The DN16 19 A4
Sudbeck La 17 LN2 68 D6
SUDBROOK NG32 119 E3
SUDBROOKE LN2 68 F2
Sudbrooke Dr LN2 202 A7
Sudbrooke La LN2 68 E2
Sudbrooke Rd LN2 68 F3
Sudbrook Rd NG32 119 D4
Sudbury Cl LN6 205 A5
Sudbury Ct PE7 231 F5
Sudbury Pl LN11 198 B4
Suddle Way 19 DN41 23 A4
SUDTHORPE NG32 119 C8
Sudthorpe Hill 8 NG32 106 C1
Suffolk Cl PE3 225 B2
Suffolk Ct DN32 189 C1
Suffolk Rd 10 LN1 67 E5
Sugar Way PE2 230 D8
Suggitt's Ct DN35 192 D8
Suggitt's La DN35 192 D8
Suggitt's Orch DN35 192 D8
Sullivan Rd HU4 179 B4
Summerdale 28 DN18 10 E8
Summerfield Ave DN37 194 E5
Summerfield Cl
 Waltham DN37 194 E5
 16 Wisbech PE13 170 C1
Summerfield Ct 3 NG34 212 D6
Summerfield Dr 4 NG34 212 D6
Summerfield Rd PE1 225 F4
Summerfields PE22 114 B1
Summergangs La DN21 197 D1
Summergates La PE24 102 C7
Summergroves Way HU4 179 B2
Summer Hill DN21 197 E5
Summer Lesure La PE12 159 F2
Sunbeam Ave LN6 204 D1
Sunbeam Rd HU4 179 D5
Suncastle* PE25 206 E4
Sunderfleet La LN11 51 A5
Sunderland Cl 6 LN6 200 A4
Sunfield Cres LN6 200 D1
Sunfields Cl PE12 157 C3
Sunflower Way PE21 208 B4
Sunningdale
 Grantham NG31 211 C8
 Peterborough PE2 229 E6
 8 Waltham DN37 194 C4
Sunningdale Ave
 Brigg DN20 196 C5
 Spalding PE11 214 C2
Sunningdale Cl
 Chapel St Leonard PE24 90 E7
 1 Skegness PE25 206 D4
 6 Woodhall Spa LN10 97 C5
Sunningdale Cres 2 PE25 206 D4
Sunningdale Dr
 Boston PE21 208 C6
 Chapel St Leonard PE24 90 E7
 4 Immingham DN40 186 D5
 Lincoln LN5 205 D8
 Skegness PE25 206 D4
Sunningdale Gr LN4 203 D1
Sunningdale Rd
 5 Hatfield DN7 14 F3
 Kingston upon Hull HU13 178 F2
 Scunthorpe DN17 184 D4
Sunningdlae Way DN21 197 E6
Sunnybank 11 DN18 10 E8
Sunny Bank HU3 180 B7
Sunny Bank Gdns DN10 39 C2
Sunny Cnr DN33 191 D1
Sunnydale Cl 1 PE11 145 D2
Sunny Hill 8 DN21 30 B1
Sunnymead PE4 220 E6
Sunway Gr DN16 185 B5
SURFLEET PE11 145 C3
Surfleet Bank PE11 145 F5
Surfleet Lows Nature Reserve* PE11 145 D3
Surfleet Rd 5 PE11 145 D2
SURFLEET SEAS END PE11 145 F3
Surfside 5 LN12 77 A8
Surrey Ct 20 DN32 189 C1
Surrey Garth HU4 179 B4
Surtees St DN31 189 B2
Sussex Ave PE21 208 B4
Sussex Cl 7 LN8 47 B6
Sussex Ct DN32 189 C1
Sussex Gdns 16 LN1 67 E5
Sussex Rd PE9 219 B6
Sussex St DN35 192 B8
SUSWORTH DN17 28 D5
Susworth Rd DN17 28 E4
Sutcliffe Ave DN33 191 A3
Sutherland Way PE9 218 F5
SUTTERBY PE23 87 E7
SUTTERTON PE20 136 A3
SUTTERTON DOWDYKE PE20 146 A8
Sutterton Dro LN4 110 E1
Suttling Dales La PE22 126 B8
SUTTON
 Beckingham LN5 105 B3
 Sutton PE5 222 F2
Sutton Branch Line Walkway & Conservation Area* LN12 76 F6
SUTTON BRIDGE PE12 160 D4
Sutton Cl
 Heighington/Washingborough LN4 203 A1
 15 Nettleham LN2 68 C2
SUTTON CROSSES PE12 216 C1
Sutton Ct 2 PE25 206 C3
Sutton Gate PE12 159 D1
Sutton Mdws PE13 170 C2
SUTTON ON SEA LN12 76 F8
Sutton on Sea Prim Sch LN12 77 A8
SUTTON ON TRENT NG23 91 A8
Sutton Pl 4 DN20 30 F7
Sutton Rd
 Beckingham LN5 105 B4
 Bilsby LN13 76 C4
 16 Kirk Sandall DN3 14 A3
 Mablethorpe/Sutton on Sea LN12 64 C2
 Newton PE13 170 B6
 Sutton St James PE12 159 D2
 Terrington St Clement PE34 161 F2
SUTTON ST EDMUND PE12 168 F4
SUTTON ST JAMES PE12 159 D1
Sutton St James Prim Sch PE12 159 C1
Sutton's La PE6 217 D4
Svenskaby PE2 229 B6
SWABY LN13 74 E4
Swaby Cl LN2 202 A8
Swaby Cres 4 PE25 206 B4
Swaby Dr DN35 192 D3
Swaby Valley Nature Reserve* LN13 74 F4
Swadales Cl 11 NG31 129 E5
Swain Ct PE2 230 F8
Swain's Dro PE13 170 C8
Swale Ave PE4 221 C1
Swale Bank PE11 144 D5
Swaledale 10 HU15 2 D6
Swaledale Pl 2 DN16 185 E6
Swale Rd 14 HU15 2 D5
Swales Rd 12 DN36 36 D8
SWALLOW LN7 34 B5
Swallow Ave LN6 200 A3
SWALLOW BECK LN6 205 B5
Swallowbeck Ave LN6 205 A4
Swallow Cl
 5 Chapel St Leonard PE24 90 D7
 4 Gainsborough DN21 53 A7
 1 Sleaford NG34 212 C3
Swallow Ct 6 DN9 27 D7
Swallow Dr
 3 Claypole NG23 117 E8
 15 Healing DN41 23 F5
 Louth LN11 198 D8
Swallowfield PE4 220 E4
Swallowfield Dr HU4 179 B2
Swallowfields Ct 2 PE25 206 A4
Swallow Gate Rd LN11 51 B2
Swallow Hill PE10 164 B7
Swallow La
 Tydd St Giles PE13 170 B8
 Wootton DN39 11 E2
Swallow's Cl NG31 210 E7
Swallow Wlk 3 PE6 217 D5
Swanage Wlk HU4 179 B4
Swan Cl PE11 214 F2
Swan Ct DN21 197 F5
Swan Dr
 Skegness PE25 103 C7
 6 Sturton by Stow LN1 66 D7
Swanella Gr HU3 180 A4
Swan Gdns
 Newark PE1 226 E6
 Parson Drove PE13 177 C7
Swanhill PE8 222 A4
Swanhole La PE22 126 D4
Swanholme Cl LN6 204 E5
SWANLAND HU14 3 A7
Swanland Butts Cl HU10 178 C6
Swanland Cl 25 DN8 15 B7
Swanland Ct 24 DN8 15 B7
Swanland Dale HU14 3 B8
Swanland Garth 6 HU14 3 A5
Swanland Hill HU14 3 B5
Swanland Prim Sch HU14 3 B6
Swanland Rd HU13 178 C2
Swan Moor Bank PE22 114 C3
Swannacks View 3 DN20 30 F7
Swan's La LN5 105 F5
Swanspool PE3 225 B6
Swan St
 1 Lincoln LN2 234 B2
 Spalding PE11 214 D4
Swapcoat La PE12 216 B5
Swapcoat Mews PE12 216 B5
SWARBY NG34 132 A7
Swarby La NG34 132 A7
SWATON NG34 133 D4
Swaton La NG34 133 C3
SWAYFIELD NG33 152 D5
Swayne Cl LN2 202 D7
Swaythling Cl LN6 204 E5
Sweetbriar 3 PE9 218 C7
Sweet Briar Cl 6 DN37 194 C5
Sweetbriar La PE4 220 F6
Sweet Cl 2 PE6 217 D5
Sweet Dews Gr HU9 181 D8
Sweetlands Way PE11 145 B5
Swen Cl 17 LN2 68 D7
Swift Ave LN11 62 C6
Swift Cl PE6 217 D4
Swift Ct 1 PE11 214 F2
Swift Dr DN20 196 A3
Swift Gdns LN2 202 C7
Swift Gn LN2 202 B7
Swift Rd DN17 184 D6
Swiftsure Cres DN34 190 D4
Swift Way PE10 164 B7
Swinburne La DN17 184 D7
Swinburne Rd DN17 184 D7
Swin Cl PE20 135 C6
SWINDERBY LN6 92 A5
Swinderby Cl 1 NG24 104 B5
Swinderby Gdns 2 DN34 191 A5
Swinderby Rd
 Collingham NG23 91 E4
 Eagle & Swinethorpe LN6 79 B1
 North Scarle LN6 78 F1
 Norton Disney LN6 92 C2
 South Scarle NG23 91 F7
Swinderby Sta LN6 92 B7
Swindler's Dro PE12 157 C6
Swinefleet Rd DN14 6 B8
Swinegate
 Grantham NG31 211 A5
 Kingston upon Hull HU13 178 E1
Swine Hill NG32 139 C7
SWINESHEAD PE20 135 B7
SWINESHEAD BRIDGE PE20 123 F1
Swineshead Rd
 Boston PE21 208 A3
 Frampton PE20 124 E1
Swineshead St Marys Prim Sch PE20 135 C7
Swineshead Sta PE20 123 F1
Swine's Meadow Rd PE6 217 D8
SWINETHORPE LN6 79 B4
Swingbridge Rd NG31 210 D2
SWINHOPE LN8 47 C7
Swinhope Hill LN8 47 C5
Swinhope Rd LN8 47 B6
SWINSTEAD NG33 153 A5
Swinstead Rd
 Corby Glen NG33 152 F7
 Counthorpe & Creeton NG33 153 A3
 Irnham NG33 141 E1
Swinster La DN40 12 E6
Switchback LN8 47 C2
Swithin Cl HU13 179 A2
Swynford Cl LN1 65 D2
Sybil Rd 18 PE13 170 D1
Sycamore Ave
 Grimsby DN33 191 C3
 Peterborough PE1 226 C6
Sycamore Cl
 1 Barnetby le Wold DN38 21 B4
 4 Birchwood LN6 204 E8
 Bourne PE10 213 A5
 2 Broughton DN20 19 D3
 Cherry Willingham/Reepham LN3 203 D5

Sycamore Cl continued
Croft PE24 . . . . .102 E4
Hessle HU13 . . . . .178 C3
Kingston upon Hull HU5 . .179 C7
5 Scopwick Heath LN4 . .108 A7
Sycamore Cres **5** LN6 . . .204 E8
Sycamore Ct **3** NG31. . . .210 D2
Sycamore Dr
7 Gainsborough
. . . . .197 E6
Louth LN11 . . . . .198 E5
Sleaford NG34 . . . . .212 D6
3 Waddington LN5. . . . . .93 E8
Sycamore Gr LN4 . . . . .81 A1
Sycamore La **2** LE14 . . .150 B1
Sycamores The 5
PE1. . . . . .214 B1
Sycamore View PE12 . . . .168 C2
Sydney Dr **3** PE25 . . . . .206 A4
Sydney Rd PE2 . . . . .231 D5
Sydney Smith Sch
HU10 . . . . .179 A5
Sydney St PE21 . . . . .208 D5
Syd Wilson Ct LN1. . . . . .201 D7
Syerston Way NG23 . . . .104 B5
Sykemouth Dro PE20. . . .124 C1
Sykes Cl
6 Kingston upon Hull
HU10 . . . . .178 F6
15 Swanland HU14 . . . . . .3 B7
Sykes La
Goxhill DN19 . . . . .5 A2
Saxilby with Ingleby LN1. .66 C3
Sykes St **3** HU2 . . . . . . .180 F7
Sylvan Ave **5** LN10 . . . . .97 D6
Sylvden Dr **20** PE13 . . . .170 E1
Sylvester St **2** DN21. . . . .30 B1
Symmington Cl PE2. . . . . .230 F8
Sympson Cl LN2. . . . . . . .202 E6
Syne Ave **5** PE25. . . . . .206 C5
Syringa Cl LN6. . . . . .200 C1
SYSTON NG32. . . . . .130 A7
Syston Gr LN5 . . . . .205 D4
Sywell Cl **18** LN6. . . . . . .204 C6

T

Tabor Ct PE7 . . . . .230 D2
Tadman St HU3 . . . . .180 D4
Taggs Dr **7** PE25 . . . . . .206 A6
Tait Cl PE21 . . . . .226 C5
Talbot Ave PE2 . . . . .230 D6
Talbot Cl **4** PE23 . . . . . .101 A8
Talbot Rd
Immingham DN40 . . . . . .186 D3
Skegness PE25 . . . . .206 C4
Talisman Dr DN16. . . . . . .185 A2
Tallert Way DN17 . . . . . . .190 F3
Tall Gables **2** NG32. . . . .65 B1
TALLINGTON PE9. . . . . . .172 E7
Tallington Dry Ski Ctr*
PE9 . . . . .172 F7
Tallington Lakes Leisure
Pk* PE9 . . . . .173 A8
Tallington Rd PE9 . . . . . .172 F6
Tall Trees HU13 . . . . .178 C3
Tamar Ct **5** NG31. . . . . .210 E2
Tamar Dr **4** DN36 . . . . .195 D7
Tamarisk Way DN16. . . . .185 D5
Tamar Way **3** LN6. . . . . .205 A2
Tamar Wlk DN17. . . . . . . .184 C8
Tame Ct **4** NG34 . . . . . .212 D5
Tamson Way **5** LN4. . . .212 D5
TAMWORTH GREEN
PE22. . . . . .126 E1
Tanglewood PE4. . . . . . . .220 F6
Tanglewood Cedar Falls 1
PE11. . . . . .214 B1
Tanhouse PE2 . . . . .230 C5
Tanners Ct LN5 . . . . .234 A1
Tanners' La NG33 . . . . . .152 E8
Tanner's La LN5 . . . . .234 A1
Tannery Cl
Boston PE21 . . . . .208 C4
2 Bourne PE10 . . . . . . .213 E4
Tansley Ave **3** NG34 . . .142 D8
Tansley Ct **1** DN15 . . . .182 B2
Tansor Garth PE3 . . . . . . .225 C5
Tantallon Ct **6** PE3. . . . .225 B1
Tapin Cl LN1. . . . . .201 C6
Tarleton Ave **1** NG40. . . .97 E6
Tarleton Ct **2** DN3. . . . . .14 A2
Tarragon Way PE10 . . . . .213 C6
Tarrant PE4 . . . . .220 E6
Tarran Way PE25. . . . . . . .206 B5
Tasburgh St DN32. . . . . . .191 F6
Tasman Cl **5** PE11. . . . . .214 B2
Tasman Rd **5** PE23 . . . .101 A8
TATHWELL LN11 . . . . .61 B2
Tattersall Cl DN17 . . . . . .184 D5
TATTERSALL LN4 . . . . . . .207 A5
Tattershall Ave DN34. . . .190 F4

Tattershall Rd
Billinghay LN4 . . . . .109 F5
Boston PE21 . . . . .208 D7
Fishtoft PE21 . . . . .125 C5
Woodhall Spa LN10 . . . . . .97 D5
Tattershall Sta Gall &
Pottery* LN4 . . . . .110 E7
TATTERSHALL THORPE
LN4 . . . . .207 B8
Tattershall Way LN4 . . . .198 A8
Tatwin Dr **8** PE6 . . . . . .175 B8
Taunton Cl **4** LN4 . . . . .212 D7
Taunton Rd HU4 . . . . .179 A3
Taunton Way DN33 . . . . .194 E8
Tavella Ct **1** DN9. . . . . . .27 B2
Tavern Cl LN13 . . . . .89 A6
Taverner Rd PE21. . . . . . .208 D6
Taverners Rd PE1. . . . . . .225 F4
Tavern La **5** PE24 . . . . . .90 B7
Tavistock Cl **18** PE6 . . . .176 A3
Tavistock Rd PE11 . . . . . .214 B2
Tawney St PE21. . . . . . . .208 F6
Taylor Cl
6 Belton DN9. . . . . .16 E2
Boston PE21 . . . . .209 D4
Taylor's Ave DN35. . . . . .192 E4
Taylor's Dro LN4 . . . . . . .159 C1
Taylor St DN35. . . . . .189 D1
TEALBY LN8 . . . . .46 C1
Tealby Cl **1** DN21 . . . . . .53 A7
Tealby Gr DN33. . . . . .191 B3
Tealby Rd
Middle Rasen LN8 . . . . . . .57 E8
Scunthorpe DN17 . . . . . .184 D5
Tealby Sch LN8 . . . . .46 C1
Tealby St **11** LN5. . . . . . .205 E8
Teal Cl
4 Brigg DN20. . . . . . . .196 A3
3 Skegness PE25. . . . . .206 A6
Teal Dr DN18 . . . . .10 E8
Teale St DN15 . . . . .183 A4
Teal Gr **10** PE12. . . . . . .167 B8
Teal Pl LN7 . . . . .33 A4
Teal Rd LN4 . . . . .110 E8
Team Gate DN37. . . . . . . .190 C6
Teanby Ct **5** DN33 . . . . .224 F3
Teanby Dr **8** DN15 . . . . . . .9 A5
Teasel Dr DN16. . . . . .213 D3
Teasles **8** PE6. . . . . .217 D6
Tedder Dr **3** LN5 . . . . . . .93 F7
Teddy's Farm* LN5 . . . . .105 C4
Tee La DN15. . . . . .8 B5
Tees Ct DN37 . . . . .190 E8
Teesdale Cl LN6 . . . . .200 C2
Teesdale Rd NG31. . . . . . .211 A7
Telford Dr
Newark NG24 . . . . .104 B6
Yaxley PE7. . . . . .233 D6
Telford Pl DN34. . . . . . . .191 A7
Temperance Ave 5
DN17 . . . . .29 D7
Temperance La 5
NG23 . . . . .91 C4
Temper Rd DN16. . . . . . . .185 F8
Temperton's La **5** DN9 . .28 A3
Tempest St LN2. . . . . . . .202 B3
Templar Ct DN16. . . . . . . .185 B3
Templars Way 2
NG33 . . . . .151 D2
Temple Bruer Templar
Preceptory* LN5 . . . . .107 C4
Temple Cl
1 Alford LN13 . . . . .75 E2
1 Belton DN9. . . . . .16 E2
1 Brough HU15 . . . . . . .42 D4
Templefield Rd DN21. . . . .42 D4
Temple Gdns LN2 . . . . . . .234 B3
Temple Grange PE4. . . . . .220 F6
Temple La DN37 . . . . .23 E1
Temple Pk DN37 . . . . .163 E5
Templeman La DN36. . . . . .36 A1
Templemeads Cl 3
PE10. . . . . .154 D6
Temple Pk
Aslackby & Laughton
NG34. . . . . .142 E5
Welbourn LN5. . . . . .107 A4
Westcliffe DN17 . . . . . . .184 F6
Temples Ct **3** PE6. . . . . .173 B4
Temple Terr LN11 . . . . . . .198 B6
Templeway Cl **5** NG32. . .119 B7
Templeway Sq 8
NG32. . . . . .119 B7
Temple Wlk **2** HU15. . . . . .2 E6
Ten Acre Dro PE11. . . . . .135 C1
Ten Acre La
Pinchbeck PE11. . . . . . . .145 C1
Wyville cum Hungerton
NG32. . . . . .139 B5
Tenens Way PE21. . . . . . .209 A1
Tennyson Ave
Grantham NG31. . . . . . . .211 E5
1 Mablethorpe/Sutton on Sea
LN12. . . . . .64 B4
Sleaford NG34 . . . . .212 D5
1 Thorne/Moorends
DN8. . . . . .15 B8
Tennyson Cl
Benniworth LN8. . . . . .59 B1
Brigg DN20 . . . . .196 D2
2 Caistor LN7 . . . . .33 A4
12 Mablethorpe/Sutton on Sea
LN12. . . . . .77 A7
4 Metheringham LN4. . . .95 C4
Tennyson Dr
Bourne PE10 . . . . .213 D3
22 Welton/Dunholme
LN2. . . . . .68 D6

Tennyson Gdns LN9. . . .199 D2
Tennyson Gn **3** PE25 . . .206 C2
Tennyson High Sch The
LN12. . . . . .64 C3
Tennyson Rd
Cleethorpes DN35. . . . . .192 E7
Louth LN11 . . . . .198 C4
17 Mablethorpe/Sutton on Sea
LN12. . . . . .64 B4
Peterborough PE1. . . . . .225 F7
2 Ruskington NG34. . . . .108 E2
Scunthorpe DN16 . . . . . .185 D7
Tennyson St
Gainsborough DN21 . . . .197 D5
Grimsby DN31. . . . . .191 D8
1 Lincoln LN1. . . . . .201 D4
Tennyson Way **1** PE9 . . .218 E5
Tennyson Wlk LN3 . . . . . .203 C6
Tensing Rd DN16 . . . . . . .185 C5
Tentercroft St LN5 . . . . . .234 A1
Tenter La **5** LN5 . . . . . . .107 A8
Tenters The PE12 . . . . . . .215 E2
Tern Rd PE7 . . . . .230 C2
Terrace La PE22 . . . . .99 C5
Terrace The
Great Ponton NG33 . . . . .140 A5
Louth LN11 . . . . .198 D4
10 Spilsby PE23. . . . . . . .88 A1
Terrington Pl DN35 . . . . .192 D4
TERRINGTON ST CLEMENT
PE34. . . . . .161 E3
Terry O'Toole Theatre*
LN6 . . . . .204 D1
TETFORD LN9 . . . . .73 F1
Tetford Hill LN9 . . . . .73 E3
Tetford Rd LN9 . . . . .86 A5
Tethering La DN10. . . . . . .39 A2
TETLEY DN17. . . . . .16 D6
Tetley Rd DN16 . . . . .185 C7
Tetley View **8** DN17. . . . .16 E6
TETNEY DN36. . . . . .36 C2
Tetney Blow Wells Nature
Reserve* DN36 . . . . .36 A3
Tetney Cl **6** LN1. . . . . . . .201 E8
Tetney La DN36 . . . . .195 E2
TETNEY LOCK DN36. . . . .36 E4
Tetney Lock Rd DN36 . . . .36 E4
Tetney Marshes Nature
Reserve* DN36 . . . . .37 C7
Tetney Rd DN36 . . . . .36 C2
Tewkesbury Dr 4
DN34 . . . . .191 C6
Thackeray Cl DN37. . . . . .190 E8
Thacker Bank LN12. . . . . .63 B7
Thackers Cl PE8 . . . . .222 A4
Thackers La LN4 . . . . .81 D2
Thacker's Rd PE22. . . . . .112 B2
Thackers Way PE6 . . . . . .217 D5
Thames Cl **3** PE24 . . . . . .90 B7
Thames Cres **3** PE24 . . . .90 B7
Thames Ct DN37. . . . . . . .190 E8
Thames Meadow Dr 2
PE24. . . . . .90 B7
Thames Rd
Grantham NG31. . . . . . . .210 E2
Spalding PE11 . . . . .214 F5
Thames St
Hogsthorpe PE24. . . . . . .90 B7
Louth LN11 . . . . .198 D4
Thary La PE11 . . . . .145 E4
Thatchers Wlk PE22 . . . . .113 B2
Theaker Ave DN17 . . . . . .197 F5
THEALBY DN15 . . . . .8 D4
Thealby La DN15. . . . . .8 E5
Theatre Royal* LN2 . . . .234 B2
THEDDLETHORPE ALL
SAINTS LN12. . . . . .63 D7
Theddlethorpe Com Prim
Sch LN12. . . . . .63 D6
Theddlethorpe Rd LN12. . .63 F4
THEDDLETHORPE ST
HELEN LN12. . . . . .63 E8
Theodore Rd DN15. . . . . .182 E4
Theodore St LN1. . . . . .1 A4
THE PARKS DN7 . . . . . . .14 C4
Theresa Cl **8** PE25 . . . . .206 A4
Thesiger St
2 Grimsby DN32. . . . . .189 B1
Lincoln LN5 . . . . .201 F1
Thesiger Wlk **8** DN31 . . .189 B1
THETFORD PE6 . . . . .164 E5
Thetford Ave PE6 . . . . . . .164 E5
THE WILLOWS DN37 . . . .190 E7
THIMBLEBY LN9 . . . . .85 B5
Thimbleby Hill LN9 . . . . . .85 C5
Thinholme La DN9. . . . . . .27 A1
Third Ave
1 Fixborough Ind Est
DN15. . . . . .8 A1
Grantham NG31. . . . . . . .211 F7
2 Scampton Airfield LN1. .67 E5
2 Scunthorpe DN17. . . .184 A4
Spalding PE11 . . . . .214 A4
Third Dro
Gosberton PE11. . . . . . . .144 B4
Moulton PE12 . . . . .146 F7
Peterborough PE1. . . . . .226 E2
Third Hill Rd LN4 . . . . . . .110 F3
Third La DN37 . . . . .35 D3
Third Marsh Rd PE14 . . . .170 C3
Thirkleby Cres DN33 . . . .192 B4
Thirlmere Ave DN33 . . . .194 E7
Thirlmere Cl **3** LN6 . . . . .205 A2
Thirlmere Gdns 3
PE4. . . . . .221 C3
Thirlmere Cl **1** LN6 . . . . .200 D1
Thirsk Dr LN6 . . . . .204 F4

Thistle Cl LN2 . . . . .202 C8
Thistle Dr PE2 . . . . .231 C7
Thistlemoor Rd PE1. . . . .225 F7
Thistleton La LE15 . . . . . .151 D1
Thistle Way LN4 . . . . .81 A1
Thomas Cowley High Sch
The PE11 . . . . .134 F2
Thomas Dr **13** NG34. . . . .212 D4
Thomas Gibson Dr
LN9. . . . . .199 D3
Thomas Kitching Way **8**
LN3. . . . . .83 C4
Thomas Magnus Sch
NG24 . . . . .104 A4
Thomas Mid Cott Dr 20
PE20. . . . . .136 C5
Thomas Rd
10 Balderton NG24 . . . . .104 C1
Scunthorpe DN17 . . . . . .184 F8
Thomas St
Grimsby DN32 . . . . .191 F7
Kingston upon Hull HU9 . .181 B7
Lincoln LN2 . . . . .234 C2
Sleaford NG34 . . . . .212 D4
Thomas Sully Cl LN9. . . . .199 A4
Thomas Sumpter Sch
DN17 . . . . .184 E7
Thompson Cl
Skegness PE25 . . . . .206 C5
Spalding PE11 . . . . .214 C3
2 Thorne DN8 . . . . .14 D4
Thompson Gd PE7 . . . . . .230 D3
Thompson's La
Fosdyke PE12 . . . . .146 E8
Hough-on-the-Hill NG32 . .119 A5
Thompson St **10** DN15 . .183 B3
Thonock Cl LN2. . . . . .201 F7
Thonock La LN8 . . . . .44 A1
Thonock Rd DN21. . . . . . . .30 E8
Thoresby **1** DN15 . . . . . .192 E4
Thoresby Prim Sch
HU5 . . . . .180 B8
Thoresby Rd
Fulstow LN11 . . . . .49 A8
Scunthorpe DN17 . . . . . .184 D5
Tetney DN36. . . . . .36 B5
Thoresby St HU5. . . . . . . .180 B8
THORESTHORPE LN13 . . .75 F4
THORESWAY LN8 . . . . .46 D7
Thoresway Dr LN2 . . . . . .202 A2
Thoresway Gr **5** DN33 . .191 A3
Thorgam Ct DN31. . . . . . .191 C7
THORGANBY DN37. . . . . . .47 B8
Thorganby Rd DN35. . . . .193 A3
Thorlby Haven **12**
PE20. . . . . .135 A4
Thorley Cres PE2 . . . . . . .230 D8
Thorn Bank DN9. . . . . .26 E4
Thornbury Rd DN40. . . . .186 D3
Thorndale Way DN21. . . .113 A5
Thorndike Way DN21. . . .197 D3
Thorndyke Mews 7
DN21. . . . . .197 D3
THORNE DN8. . . . . .15 B8
Thorne N Sta DN8 . . . . . . .14 F8
Thorne Rd
Edenthorpe DN3 . . . . .14 A2
Sandtoft DN8. . . . . .16 A3
8 Stainforth DN7 . . . . . .14 C6
Thorne S Sta DN8 . . . . . . .15 B7
Thorne Swimming Baths
DN8. . . . . .15 B8
Thorne Waste Drain Rd
DN8 . . . . .15 D8
Thorne Way DN20 . . . . . .136 C4
THORNEY
Thorney NG23 . . . . .78 F8
Thorney PE6 . . . . .176 A3
Thorney Heritage Mus*
PE6 . . . . .176 A3
Thorney Rd
2 Crowland PE6. . . . . . .175 C8
Newborough PE6. . . . . . .174 D5
Wisbech St Mary PE13 . . .177 C2
THORNEY TOLL PE13 . . . .177 A2
Thorngarth La DN19 . . . . .11 D8
Thorngate LN5 . . . . .234 B2
Thornham's Way 8
HU15 . . . . .2 D5
Thornhill Cres 4
DN17 . . . . .184 F3
Thornhill Gdns DN34. . . .191 A7
Thornhill La DN22 . . . . . . .52 E1
Thornholme Dr DN16 . . . .185 A4
Thorniman La PE20 . . . . .136 E6
Thorn La DN19 . . . . .12 A8
Thorn Leigh **3** HU3 . . . . .180 C6
Thornleigh Dr PE2 . . . . . .230 C6
Thornmead PE4 . . . . .220 E6
Thorn Rd PE7 . . . . .230 C2
Thorns La NG32 . . . . .210 A8
Thornton **20** HU15 . . . . . . .2 C6
THORNTON LN9 . . . . .85 E5
Thornton Abbey* DN39 . .12 B5
Thornton Abbey Sta
DN39. . . . . .12 A5
Thornton Ave
Boston PE21 . . . . .208 D3
Scunthorpe DN15 . . . . . .185 A7
Thornton Cl
3 Heighington/
Washingborough LN4 . . . .203 A2
Kingston upon Hull
HU13. . . . . .178 D1
Langriville PE22. . . . . . . .124 F8
6 Lincoln LN6. . . . . . . .205 A7
Peterborough PE4. . . . . .221 C3

Thornton Cres
Cleethorpes DN35. . . . . .192 E4
Horncastle LN9 . . . . .199 C2
Thornton Ct DN36 . . . . . .195 D8
THORNTON CURTIS
DN39 . . . . .11 E4
Thornton Gdns **21** DN41. . .23 A4
Thornton Gr **15** DN41 . . . .23 A4
THORNTON LE MOOR
LN7. . . . . .44 E7
Thornton Pl DN40. . . . . . .186 B3
Thornton Rd
Barrow upon Humber
DN19. . . . . .11 D6
7 Collingham NG23 . . . . .91 D4
Goxhill DN19 . . . . .11 F6
Owersby LN7. . . . . .44 E7
South Kelsey LN7. . . . . . .32 A1
Spalding PE11 . . . . .214 F3
Thornton Curtis DN39 . . . .11 E4
Thornton St
Barrow upon Humber
DN19. . . . . .11 C7
6 Gainsborough DN21. . .197 D3
Thornton Way LN11 . . . . .203 E6
Thornwell La **2** PE23. . . . .87 A4
Thornwick Ave HU10. . . . .178 E8
Thornwick Cl **3** LN3 . . . .180 C5
Thorold Ave
Cranwell & Byard's Leap
NG34. . . . . .107 E1
6 Cranwell NG34. . . . . .120 E8
Thorold Cl **1** NG32 . . . . .130 B8
Thorold Pl **1** LN3 . . . . . . .14 A2
Thorold Rd NG22 . . . . . . .210 A4
Thorolds Charity CE
(Aided) Prim Sch
NG32 . . . . .118 D2
Thorold St
Boston PE21 . . . . .208 F6
Grimsby DN31. . . . . .189 C1
Thorolds Way PE5 . . . . . .223 D2
Thorold Way LN5 . . . . .93 F4
THORPE LN12. . . . . .64 A1
Thorpe Ave
Lincoln LN1 . . . . .201 D8
Moulton PE12 . . . . .157 E2
Peterborough PE3 . . . . . .225 C2
Thorpe Bank PE22 . . . . . .101 B3
Thorpe Camp Visitor Ctr*
LN4 . . . . .207 B8
Thorpe Cl **3** NG24. . . . . .104 D5
THORPE CULVERT
PE24. . . . . .102 A3
Thorpe Culvert Sta
PE24. . . . . .102 B3
Thorpe Dr NG34 . . . . .120 E2
Thorpe Dro NG34 . . . . . . .120 E3
THORPE FENDYKES
PE24. . . . . .101 F3
Thorpehall Rd **12** DN3 . . .14 A2
Thorpe La
Aubourn Haddington & South
Hykeham LN6. . . . . .93 A8
1 Brattleby LN1. . . . . . . .67 B7
Eagle & Swinethorpe LN6. .79 C1
Tealby LN8 . . . . .46 B1
THORPE LATIMER
NG34 . . . . .133 C6
Thorpe Lea Rd **1** DN8 . . .225 C6
THORPE LE VALE LN8 . . .47 B1
Thorpe Mdws PE3 . . . . . .225 C2
THORPE ON THE HILL
LN6. . . . . .92 E8
Thorpe Pk Rd PE3 . . . . . .225 C2
Thorpe Pl LN4 . . . . .207 B6
Thorpe Prim Sch PE3 . . . .225 B3
Thorpe Rd
Doddington & Whisby
LN6. . . . . .79 E2
Ewerby & Evedon NG34. . .122 C6
Peterborough PE3 . . . . . .225 B1
Tattershall LN4 . . . . .207 C2
THORPE ST PETER
PE24. . . . . .102 A3
Thorpes La **3** NG32 . . . . .138 D4
Thorpe's La PE12 . . . . . . .158 B6
THORPE TILNEY LN4 . . . .109 C8
Thorpe Tilney Dro
Timberland LN4. . . . . .97 A1
Walcott LN4. . . . . .109 C8
Thorpe Wood PE3 . . . . . .224 F1
Thorsby Cl LN5 . . . . .205 D1
Thorseby Ct PE3 . . . . .225 B3
Threadneedle St **9**
PE21. . . . . .208 F5
Three Bridge La LN11. . . . .63 A7
Three Bridges LN11. . . . . .63 A7
THREEKINGHAM NG34. . . .132 E3
Threekingham Bar
NG34 . . . . .132 D3
Three Leys La DN22 . . . . .52 B2
THROCKENHOLT PE12. . . .177 B8
Throstlenest PE2 . . . . . . .231 C3
Thrumber Marsh La
LN13. . . . . .76 F1
Thrunscoe Inf Sch
DN35. . . . . .192 F5
Thrunscoe Jun Sch
DN35. . . . . .192 F5
Thrunscoe Rd **7** DN35. . .192 F5
Thrush Cl **10** NG34. . . . . .212 B3
Thurlaston Cl PE3. . . . . . .225 B2
THURLBY
Bilsby LN13 . . . . .76 D2
Thurlby LN11 . . . . .92 E4
Thurlby PE10 . . . . .164 C8
Thurlby Cl **4** LN4. . . . . . .203 A2

ıurlby Com Prim Sch
PE10. . . . . .164 C8
ıurlby Cres LN2 . . . . .202 B8
ıurlby Fen Nature
Reserve* PE10. . . . . .164 F7
ıurlby Rd
Bassingham LN5 . . . . .92 F3
Bilsby LN13 . . . . .76 B3
Gainsborough DN21 . . . . . .197 E4
ıurlow Ct 1 LN2. . . . . . . .202 E7
ıurning Ave PE2. . . . . . . 231 C6
ıuro Gr PE2. . . . . 230 A3
ıursfield PE4. . . . . 221 A4
ıurstan Ct PE10 . . . . .213 B6
ıurston Gate 2 PE3. . . 225 A1
ıyme Ave
Bourne PE10 . . . . 213 C5
12 Market Deeping PE6 . . 217 C5
ıyme Ct LN6 . . . . 205 D8
ber Rd LN6 . . . . 204 C1
chbourne Cl 6 HU3. . . 180 C5
CKENCOTE PE9 . . . . 171 A8
deswell Ct DN15 . . . . . . .182 B2
lbury Prim Sch HU4. . . .179 B3
lbury Rd HU4 . . . . .179 B3
lebarn La PE20 . . . . .134 F7
lia Cl
Kingston upon Hull
HU4. . . . . .179 B2
Scunthorpe DN16 . . . . 185 D4
lia Way 5 PE10. . . . . . . .213 E2
ll Bridge La
Marton LN1 . . . . .65 F8
Scampton LN1 . . . . .67 A6
Stow LN1 . . . . .66 A8
llbridge Rd LN1. . . . . .66 D7
lley Gate LN11 . . . . .51 B3
lney Ave PE21. . . . . 208 D6
lney The 10 PE12. . . . . . .158 B7
lton Ct PE1 . . . . 226 C8
mber Hill NG33 . . . . 151 A4
mberland DN16 . . . . 185 C4
MBERLAND LN4. . . . . .96 C1
mberland Dro LN4 . . . . . . .96 E2
mberland Rd LN4 . . . . . . .96 C2
mberley Dr DN37 . . . . . 190 C7
me Trap Mus* DN32 . . . .191 E7
mm's La 18 LN5. . . . . .93 F7
mms's Dro PE20 . . . . .134 E8
mson Ct 5 DN10 . . . . .52 B8
ndale Bank Rd DN9 . . . . .39 C8
ndall Cl 2 PE13 . . . . 170 D2
ndall Way 10 PE24 . . . . 102 D1
nkermere Cl 3 LN2. . . . . .68 D6
nker's Dro PE13. . . . . . . 170 D1
nker's La
Girton NG23. . . . . .91 C8
2 Waddington LN5. . . . . . . .93 F6
nkle St LN11. . . . . .62 C7
n La PE10 . . . . 213 C5
nsley Cl NG23. . . . . .117 F7
ntagel Ct 7 PE3 . . . . . . .225 B1
ntagel Way DN36 . . . . . 195 C7
ntern Rise 4 PE6. . . . . 175 A1
ntern Wlk DN37. . . . . . . 188 A1
nus Ave PE7 . . . . 230 C1
NWELL PE9 . . . . 218 D3
nwell Rd PE9 . . . . 219 A4
nwell Rd La PE9 . . . . . . .218 F4
p La PE24 . . . . .102 B4
rrington PE3. . . . . 225 A3
son Garth HU10. . . . . . . .178 F6
the Barn La 8 DN8 . . . . .15 B8
verton Rd PE3 . . . . 225 C3
verton St DN35 . . . . .189 E1
voli Gdns DN32 . . . . .191 F8
LS Com Arts Coll
DN35 . . . . 192 D4
obias Gr 4 PE9 . . . . 218 C7
obruk Cl LN1 . . . . 201 D8
oby's Hill Nature
Reserve* LN11. . . . . .51 C5
odd La DN21 . . . . .41 C4
odds Cl
1 Swanland HU14 . . . . .3 C6
18 Tetney DN36. . . . . .36 D4
odds Ct 26 DN17. . . . . .29 D7
odds La 1 DN15. . . . . .8 A4
odd's La HU15. . . . . .2 A8
odkill's La 7 PE12. . . . . .160 F4
OFT PE10. . . . . .163 F8
oft Cl PE24 . . . . 115 D8
oft Field La PE22 . . . . . . 114 A3
OFT HILL PE22. . . . . .98 D5
oft Hurn 1 PE22 . . . . .98 F4
oft La
17 Sleaford NG34 . . . . 212 D4
Toft Newton LN8 . . . . .56 E7
oftland PE2. . . . . 230 C5
OFT NEXT NEWTON
LN8. . . . . .56 C7
ofts Rd 10 DN18 . . . . .10 E8
oft Tunnel Nature
Reserve* PE10. . . . . 154 A1
olethorpe Hall* PE9 . . . .163 B1
olethorpe Sq 6 PE9 . . . .219 B6
OLL BAR PE9 . . . . 218 C8
oll Bar Ave
6 Bottesford NG13 . . . . . 128 A6
New Waltham DN36. . . . . . .195 B6
ollbar Rd
Great Gonerby NG32. . . . . .129 B8
Marston NG32. . . . . 118 C1
oll Bar Rd
Croft PE24 . . . . 103 D3
Grantham NG31. . . . . 211 C3
oll Bar Sec Sch DN36 . . 195 A5

Tollemache Fields 9
NG33 . . . . 151 D2
Tollemache Rd (North)
NG31 . . . . .139 F8
Tollemach Rd (South)
NG31 . . . . .139 F8
Tollesby La 34 DN7 . . . . . . .14 D4
Tollfield Rd PE21 . . . . .209 B7
Tollgate
Peterborough PE3. . . . . . . 225 A5
Spalding PE11 . . . . 214 C4
Toll House Rd PE2 . . . . . . 230 C7
Toll's La PE12 . . . . .215 E5
Tom La NG34 . . . . .120 E5
Tomline Rd 5 DN41 . . . . . . .23 A5
Tomline St DN31. . . . . .189 B1
Tomlinson Ave 4
DN15 . . . . .182 E3
Tomlinson Cl 3 LN4 . . . . 207 A5
Tomlinson Way 5
NG34 . . . . .108 E2
Tom Otter's La LN1 . . . . . . .66 B1
Tonbridge 1 DN33 . . . . . . 194 E8
Tonbridge Wlk DN33. . . . . .194 E8
Toneham La PE6. . . . . .175 F2
Tonglet Cl 3 PE25. . . . . . 206 C1
Tonnant Way DN34. . . . . . 190 D5
Tooley La PE22 . . . . 114 C2
Tooley St
Boston PE21 . . . . 209 A3
Gainsborough DN21 . . . . . . 197 D3
Toothill Gdns DN34 . . . . . .190 F6
Toot La PE21 . . . . 209 D4
Topaz Gr 3 HU3. . . . . 180 A4
Topham Cres 13 PE6. . . . 176 A3
Top La
Goulceby LN11. . . . . .72 C6
Kirk Bramwith DN7 . . . . .14 A6
Topmoor Way PE4 . . . . . . 221 D1
Top Rd
4 Croxton Kerrial
NG32. . . . . 138 D4
Little Cawthorpe LN11. . . . . .61 E2
Osgodby LN8 . . . . .45 A2
South Killingholme DN40. . . .12 E3
Thorney NG23 . . . . .78 F7
Winterton DN15. . . . . .8 F6
Worlaby DN20 . . . . .10 D1
Topsgate PE12. . . . . 159 C7
Torbay Dr DN33. . . . . .194 E6
Torchil Cl HU10. . . . . 178 C6
Torfrida Dr PE10. . . . . .213 B6
Torfrid Cl 14 PE6 . . . . .166 F1
Torgate Ave LN5 . . . . .92 F2
Torgate La LN5 . . . . .93 A2
Torkington Gdns 9
PE9. . . . . .219 B5
Torkington St PE9 . . . . 219 A5
TORKSEY LN1. . . . . .65 E5
Torksey Ave LN1. . . . . .66 C2
Torksey Dr DN33. . . . . .191 B3
Torksey Ferry Rd DN22. . . . .65 B5
TORKSEY LOCK LN1. . . . . . . .65 E5
Torksey Pl 8 DN33 . . . . . . .191 B3
Torksey St
14 Kirton in Lindsey
DN21. . . . . .30 B1
Rampton DN22 . . . . .65 A5
Torold Dr PE7 . . . . 230 D2
Tor-o-Moor Gdns 2
LN10. . . . . .97 E6
Tor-o-Moor Rd 9 LN10. . .97 E6
Toronto St 2 LN2 . . . . 202 C3
Torpel Way 5 PE6. . . . . . . 173 C7
Torrington La
East Barkwith LN8. . . . . .71 A8
Fleet PE12. . . . . .159 B5
Legsby LN8 . . . . .58 C1
Torrington Rd
Lincoln LN2 . . . . .201 F8
Scunthorpe DN17 . . . . 184 C8
Torrington St DN32 . . . . . . .191 F5
Torr St DN21 . . . . 197 D4
Torskey Castle* LN1. . . . . . .65 D5
Tortoiseshell Wood Nature
Reserve* NG33 . . . . .152 B2
Tossey La LN11 . . . . .50 B2
Tothby Cl 1 LN13 . . . . .75 E3
Tothby La LN13. . . . . .75 E2
Tothby Mdws LN13. . . . . .75 E3
TOTHILL LN11. . . . . .62 E1
Tothill Cl LN6. . . . . .204 F7
Totnes Rd DN33 . . . . 194 E6
Tottermire La 5 DN9 . . . . . .27 D7
Touthill Cl PE1 . . . . 226 A2
Towell Cl PE21. . . . . .209 B3
Tower Ave
Bracebridge Heath
LN4. . . . . .205 F3
Lincoln LN2 . . . . 202 D4
Tower Cl
9 Mablethorpe & Sutton
LN12. . . . . .64 B3
Woodhall Spa LN10 . . . . .97 F7
Tower Cres LN2. . . . . 202 D4
Tower Ct PE2. . . . . .230 F8
Tower Dr
Lincoln LN2 . . . . 202 D4
Woodhall Spa LN10 . . . . .97 F7
Tower Espl PE25. . . . . 206 D3
Tower Flats 4 LN2 . . . . 202 D4
Tower Gdns
Boston PE21 . . . . 209 A4
1 Lincoln LN2. . . . . 202 D4
Tower Hill
Kingston upon Hull
HU13. . . . . .178 E1
Westwoodside DN9. . . . . .27 B2

Tower Hill Dr HU13 . . . . . .178 E1
Tower Hill Mews 2
HU13 . . . . .178 E1
Tower House La 7 HU12. . . 5 F8
Tower La
Harmston LN4 . . . . .94 B4
Spalding PE11 . . . . 214 D3
Tower Rd PE21 . . . . 209 A5
Tower Rd Prim Sch
PE21. . . . . 209 A6
Tower St
14 Boston PE21. . . . . .208 F5
Gainsborough DN21 . . . . . 197 D5
1 Kingston Dock Village
HU9. . . . . 181 A5
Towers The 2 PE25. . . . . 206 D5
Tower View
Kingston upon Hull
HU10. . . . . 178 C5
Sleaford NG34. . . . . .212 B3
Tow La 5 NG32 . . . . .117 F1
Towler St PE1 . . . . 226 A3
Town Bridge 22 PE21 . . . .208 F5
Town Dam Dro PE11 . . . . .144 F8
Town Dam La PE11 . . . . . .134 F2
Town Dro PE11 . . . . .144 F8
Town End NG32. . . . . .120 B2
Town Farm Cl 1 PE11 . . . .156 F8
Townfield La 5 PE20 . . . 135 C7
TOWNGATE PE6. . . . . .164 F1
Towngate E PE6 . . . . 217 C7
Towngate W PE6 . . . . 217 A6
Town Hall Sq DN31 . . . . . .191 E7
Town Hall St 4 DN31 . . . .191 E7
Town Hill DN20 . . . . .19 E4
Town Hill Dr DN20 . . . . .19 E4
Towning Cl 9 PE6. . . . . . . 217 D6
Townley Cl LN9 . . . . 199 D1
Town Rd
Sleaford NG34. . . . . .212 B1
Tetney DN36 . . . . .36 D4
Townsend Cl DN36. . . . . . . 193 C1
Townsend Rd 6 PE8. . . . .172 B1
Townsend Way LN4 . . . . . . .95 C4
Townside DN40 . . . . .12 D6
Town St
Cottam DN22. . . . . .65 B6
Immingham DN40 . . . . .12 E4
South Somercotes LN11 . . . .50 E4
Westborough & Dry
Doddington NG23 . . . . . . .117 F3
TOYNTON ALL SAINTS
PE23. . . . . .100 F6
Toynton All Saints Prim
Sch PE23 . . . . .100 F6
Toynton Cl 3 LN6 . . . . . . .205 B4
TOYNTON FEN SIDE
PE23. . . . . .100 F5
Toynton La PE23 . . . . .101 B6
Toynton Rd DN33. . . . . . . .191 B3
TOYNTON ST PETER
PE23. . . . . 101 A6
Trader Bank
Frithville PE22 . . . . .125 F8
Sibsey PE22. . . . . 113 A2
Trafalgar Ave
Grimsby DN34 . . . . 190 D5
Skegness PE25 . . . . 206 D1
Trafalgar Ct 2 LN4 . . . . . .203 B2
Trafalgar Pk DN36 . . . . . . 195 D7
Trafalgar Pl 8 PE21 . . . . .208 E4
Trafalgar Sq
Long Sutton PE12 . . . . .216 B4
4 Sutton on Trent NG23. . . . .91 A8
Trafalgar St 5 HU3. . . . . . 180 D7
Trafford Est PE14 . . . . . . .170 F4
Trafford Pk 25 PE13. . . . .170 E1
Trafford Rd
Kingston upon Hull
HU10. . . . . .178 E8
13 Wisbech PE13. . . . . . . .170 E1
Trafford St DN15. . . . . .183 B4
Traffords Way DN20. . . . . . .30 F6
Train Gate 23 DN21 . . . . . . .30 B1
Tramway Dr 21 LN12 . . . . . .76 F8
Tranby Ave HU13. . . . . 178 D2
Tranby Croft HU10 . . . . . . 178 C5
Tranby Dr DN32. . . . . .192 B4
Tranby La
Anlaby with Anlaby Common
HU10. . . . . .178 B5
Swanland HU14. . . . . .3 C6
Tranby Lodge Gdns
HU13 . . . . 178 C1
Tranby Mdws Pk HU13 . . 178 C3
Tranby Ride HU10. . . . . . . 178 C5
Tranmere Cl HU3 . . . . .180 B5
Travellers Rest Cvn Site
NG31 . . . . .211 B1
Travis Ave 16 DN8. . . . . .15 B8
Travis CE Fst Sch DN7 . . . .14 E4
Travis Cl 14 DN8. . . . . .15 B8
Travis Gr 15 DN8. . . . . .15 B8
Traviss Cl 2 DN16 . . . . . . .185 B8
Treadgold Ave 10
NG31 . . . . .129 E5
Treading Bank PE13. . . . . 169 C4
Treasure La LN11 . . . . .49 F5
Treece Gdns 10 DN18 . . . . . .3 F1
Tree Cl PE25. . . . . 206 A5
Trefoil Dr PE25 . . . . 103 C6
Trehampton Dr 4
DN21 . . . . .53 A5
Trelawney Cres 2
LN1. . . . . .201 E8
Tremayne Ave 1 HU15. . . . .2 C5
Trenchard Cl DN40. . . . . . .186 E5

Trenchard Rd
9 Ashby de la Launde &
Bloxholm LN4 . . . . 108 A7
3 Mablethorpe/Sutton on Sea
LN12. . . . . .64 B3
Trenchard Sq
2 Scampton Airfield
LN1. .67 F5
1 Waddington LN5. . . . . .94 A7
Trent Ct 6 DN37. . . . . .190 E8
Trentholme Dr 37 DN17 . . .29 D7
Trent La
Beacon Hill NG24. . . . . 104 A5
Besthorpe NG23 . . . . .91 B7
Girton NG23. . . . . .78 B1
Newton on Trent LN1. . . . . . .65 C1
South Clifton NG23 . . . . .78 B5
Trenton Ave HU4. . . . . .179 B6
Trent Port Rd DN21 . . . . . . .65 D8
Trent Rd
Grantham NG31. . . . . 210 D2
Keadby with Althorpe
DN17. . . . . .17 D6
Trentside
Gainsborough DN21 . . . . . . .197 B8
Keadby with Althorpe
DN17. . . . . .17 C3
Trent Side DN17 . . . . .7 F1
Trent St
Gainsborough DN21 . . . . . 197 D3
Scunthorpe DN16 . . . . .183 B2
Trentvale Prep Sch
DN17 . . . . .17 D6
Trent View
Ermine LN1 . . . . 201 D8
Keadby DN17. . . . . .17 D5
5 Marton DN21 . . . . .65 E8
Trent Wlk 13 HU15 . . . . .2 D5
Tresham Rd PE2 . . . . 229 D3
Trevitt Cl 1 NG34 . . . . .212 B7
Trevor Cl 22 DN37. . . . . .23 F1
Trevose Dr 2 LN6 . . . . 205 A1
Triangle Dr 9 HU14 . . . . .3 A4
Triangle The 13 HU14 . . . . . .3 A4
Trienna PE2 . . . . .230 B5
Trinity Cl
10 Crowland PE6. . . . . .166 E1
10 Goxhill DN19 . . . . .12 A8
Trinity Ct 9 DN20 . . . . .19 D4
Trinity Gr HU13 . . . . .178 E2
Trinity House La 17
HU1 . . . . .180 F6
Trinity La LN11 . . . . 198 D6
Trinity Rd
Cleethorpes DN35 . . . . .192 E5
Newark-on-Trent NG24 . . . 104 A2
Scunthorpe DN16 . . . . 185 A4
Stamford PE9. . . . . 219 A6
Wisbech PE13 . . . . .170 E1
Trinity St
Boston PE21 . . . . .208 E4
Gainsborough DN21 . . . . . 197 D3
14 Grimsby DN31 . . . . 189 C1
Kingston upon Hull HU3 . . 180 C7
3 Peterborough PE1 . . . . . 226 A2
Trinity Wlk 1 DN18. . . . . .3 F1
Tritton Rd LN6. . . . . 201 D2
Trollope St LN5. . . . . .234 B1
Trollybus Mus at Sandtoft
The* DN8 . . . . .16 A3
Trondheim Way DN41 . . . 187 A2
Troon Cl
Grantham NG31. . . . . 211 D8
7 Heighington/
Washingborough LN4 . . . 203 D1
11 Stamford PE9. . . . . .218 E6
Troon Rd DN7 . . . . .14 D4
Trotters La 2 NG32. . . . . . 139 C7
Troughton Way 10
PE13. . . . . .170 B2
Troutbeck Cl
6 Lincoln LN2. . . . . 202 A8
1 Peterborough PE4 . . . . 221 D3
Troutsdale Gr HU9. . . . . . . .181 F8
Truesdale Gdns PE6. . . . . .164 E3
Trunch La PE24. . . . . .90 D5
Trundle La 2 DN7 . . . . .14 D8
Trunkass La DN37. . . . . .34 D7
Truro Cl
6 Grantham NG31 . . . . . . .210 F5
5 Sleaford NG34 . . . . 212 C7
Truro Dr LN6 . . . . .204 B8
Truro Way 2 PE11. . . . . . . 214 C4
TRUSTHORPE LN12 . . . . .64 B2
Trusthorpe Rd 2 LN12. . . .64 C1
Tuckers Nook PE6 . . . . . . 173 C7
Tucker's Yd PE2 . . . . 231 C7
Tudor Ave PE7. . . . . 230 C1
Tudor Cl
Beacon Hill NG24. . . . . 104 A4
23 Brough HU15 . . . . .2 C5
Northorpe PE10. . . . . 164 C7
Peterborough PE4 . . . . 221 C2
4 Sutterton PE20. . . . . 136 A2
1 Toft Newton LN8. . . . . . . .56 D5
Tudor Cl (Doglands)
LN8. .56 C5
Tudor Dr
4 Boston PE21. . . . . .208 E7
Gainsborough DN21 . . . . . .197 B8
Louth LN11 . . . . 198 C4
Tudor La 24 HU15. . . . . .2 C5
Tudor Pk LN9. . . . . 199 D4
Tudor Pl PE6 . . . . .217 E5
Tudor Rd LN6. . . . . 204 D6
Tudor Way PE12 . . . . 215 D1
Tudworth Field Rd DN7 . . .15 B5
Tudworth Rd DN7. . . . . .15 A5

Tulip Fields PE12 . . . . 158 C7
Tulip Rd DN15 . . . . 183 C3
Tulipwood Ave 11 LN6 . . 200 C1
Tumby PE22 . . . . .207 F8
Tumby La PE22 . . . . .98 D2
Tumby Rd LN4. . . . . .207 E6
TUMBY WOODSIDE
PE22. . . . . .111 F8
Tummel Ct DN40. . . . . .186 B2
Tunnard St
Boston PE21 . . . . .208 F6
Grimsby DN32 . . . . .192 B8
Tunnel Bank PE10 . . . . . . .213 F3
Tunnel Rd DN20 . . . . .196 F7
Turbary Rd DN9 . . . . .27 B6
Turf Moor Rd 4 DN7 . . . . . .15 A3
Turnberry App DN37 . . . . 194 C4
Turnberry Cl 1 NG31 . . . 211 D7
Turnberry Dr 4 LN10 . . . . .97 C6
Turnbury Cl LN6 . . . . .204 B7
Turner Ave 3 LN6 . . . . . . 205 A6
Turner Cl 2 LN5. . . . . .107 B8
Turner Ct LN6 . . . . .204 B8
Turner's La 17 HU14 . . . . . . .3 A5
Turner St
15 Kirton in Lindsey
DN21. . . . . .30 B1
Lincoln LN1 . . . . 234 A4
Turnor Cl 5 NG33 . . . . . . .151 E6
Turnor Cres NG31. . . . . . . 211 C5
Turnor Rd NG31 . . . . .211 F4
Turnpike Cl
Great Gonerby NG31. . . . . 210 D1
14 Wisbech PE13. . . . . .170 E1
Turnpike Rd PE9. . . . . 163 C2
Turnpole Cl 2 PE9 . . . . . 219 D7
Turnstone Way PE2 . . . . . 231 D7
Turpin Cl DN21 . . . . .197 F5
Turves Rd PE6 . . . . 175 A2
Tut Hole PE23 . . . . .100 F7
Tuxhill Rd PE34. . . . . .161 E1
Tweed Cl LN9. . . . . 199 D2
Twelve Foot Bank LN4 . . .109 F5
Twelvetree Ave PE4 . . . . .220 E5
TWENTY PE10 . . . . 155 C3
Twenty Dro PE10. . . . . 155 C3
Twenty Foot Bank LN4 . . 110 C6
Twitchell 4 LN1. . . . . .66 D7
Two Plank La PE11. . . . . . .214 B6
Two Pole Dro PE7 . . . . . . .231 F1
Two Sisters Cl 8 PE12. . . .160 E4
Twyford Cl 2 NG33 . . . . . .151 E6
Twyford Gdns 3 PE1 . . . 226 D7
Twyning Pl DN35. . . . . 192 D7
Tydd Low Rd
Long Sutton PE12 . . . . 160 A3
Sutton Cross PE12. . . . . . . .216 B1
Tydd Rd PE11. . . . . 156 C6
TYDD ST GILES PE13. . . . .169 F7
Tydd St Giles Sch
PE13. . . . . .169 F6
TYDD ST MARY PE13. . . . .160 B1
Tydd St Mary CE (Aided)
Prim Sch PE13 . . . . 160 A1
Tydeman Cl DN16. . . . . . . 185 A2
Tyesdale PE3 . . . . 225 A4
Tye's Dro PE6 . . . . 165 D2
Tyghes Cl PE6 . . . . .217 F5
Tyler Ave DN31 . . . . 191 A7
Tyler Cres 2 PE22. . . . . . . .126 E3
Tylers Cl 30 PE24 . . . . .90 D7
Tylers Mews PE4. . . . . .220 F3
Tyndal Rd NG31. . . . . .210 F5
Tyne Cl 4 LN6. . . . . 205 A2
Tynedale Ct 5 DN3 . . . . . . .14 A2
Tyne St HU3. . . . . .180 B4
Tyne Way 7 DN37 . . . . .190 E8
Tyrrell Pk PE1 . . . . 226 D2
Tyson Cl NG31 . . . . 211 C6
Tytton Cl 2 PE21 . . . . 136 D8
Tytton La E PE21. . . . . 136 D8
Tytton La W PE21 . . . . 136 D8

U

UFFINGTON PE9 . . . . 172 C6
Uffington Ave LN6 . . . . 205 A6
Uffington CE (Cont) Prim
Sch PE9 . . . . 172 C6
Uffington Cl 10 LN6. . . . . 205 A7
Uffington Rd
2 Barnack PE9. . . . . 172 D4
Stamford PE9. . . . . .219 E6
UFFORD PE9. . . . . .172 F3
UK Coll DN31. . . . . .191 B8
ULCEBY
Ulceby DN39 . . . . .12 B1
Ulceby with Fordington
LN13. . . . . .88 C7
Ulceby Cross LN13. . . . . .88 B8
Ulceby Rd
Scunthorpe DN17 . . . . 184 D5
South Killingholme DN39. . . .12 C2
Wootton DN39. . . . . .11 F3
ULCEBY SKITTER DN39. . . .12 C2
Ulceby Sta DN39. . . . . .12 C2
Uldale Cl LN6. . . . . 200 C2
Uldale Way PE4. . . . . 221 D2
Ullswater Ave PE4 . . . . . . .221 B2
Ullswater Cl 6 LN6 . . . . . . 205 A2
Ulster Ave DN33 . . . . 191 D2
Ulster Rd DN21. . . . . 197 D6
Ulverston Rd HU4. . . . . 179 A3
Ulyett La DN17 . . . . .28 C8

Unicorn Row 10 DN21......30 B1
Union Pl 1 PE21 ......208 F5
Union Rd
 Lincoln LN1 ....234 A3
 Thorne/Moorends DN8 ...15 A8
Union St
 2 Boston PE21.......208 F5
 Grantham NG31.......211 A5
 Holbeach PE12 ....159 A7
 Louth LN11 ....198 B6
 14 Market Rasen LN8 .....57 D8
Unity Ave HU13 ....178 F1
Unity Rd DN30..........192 C6
Unity Sq 5 LN2.........234 B2
University Ct 2 NG31....211 B3
University of Lincoln
 Brayford (Main Campus)
 LN6.................234 A2
University of Lincoln Derek
 Crothall Building
 HU1................180 E6
University of Lincoln
 Holbeach Campus
 PE12................215 D4
University of Lincoln
 Riseholme Campus
 LN2..................68 A2
Upgate LN11............198 B5
Upland Cl LN9 ....199 A5
Uplands PE4............221 A5
Uplands St 9 LN4......234 C3
Upper Burgess St 2
 DN31...............191 E8
Upper Cl The 8 LN1 ....66 D7
Upper Ings La DN22....52 D2
Upper Kenyon St 9
 DN8.................15 A8
Upper Lindum St LN2 ..234 C3
Upper Long Leys Rd
 LN1.................234 A4
Upper Row NG22.........65 A1
Upper Saxon St LN1....234 A4
UPPERTHORPE DN9......27 B3
Upperthorpe Hill DN9...27 A2
Uppingham Rd 6 LN12 ...64 C1
Upsall Rd 9 PE22 .....126 E3
UPTON
 Upton DN21............53 E5
 Upton PE6 ....223 B6
Upton Cl
 Peterborough PE2.....231 E5
 Peterborough PE3.....225 A2
Upton Rd DN21..........53 B4
Upton Wlk DN21.......197 F3
Urban St LN5..........205 D6
Uredale Pl DN16.......185 E5
Usher Gall* LN2........234 B3
Usher Gn
 4 Lincoln LN6.......205 B6
 6 Lincoln LN6.......205 B6
Usher Jun Sch The
 LN6.................205 B7
USSELBY LN8............45 C4
Utgard Way 4 DN33....191 B2
UTTERBY LN11...........48 F4
Utterby Dr DN34.......191 C6
Utterby Prim Sch DN36 ..48 E5

V

Vacherie La LN4........109 F3
Vagarth Cl 15 DN18......3 E1
Valda Vale DN40.......186 A4
Vale Ct PE23...........101 A8
Vale Dr
 Hampton Vale PE7.....230 C1
 Yaxley PE7...........233 D8
Valence Rd PE21.......229 F4
Valentine Cl
 Boston PE21 ....209 C3
 1 Kingston upon Hull
 HU4................179 A2
Valentine Rd LN6......201 C1
Vale of Ancholme Sch
 DN20................196 B4
Vale Rd
 Gonerby Hill Foot
 NG31...............210 F8
 10 Spilsby PE23 .....101 A8
Vale The HU10 ....178 B7
Vale View NG23 ....117 F5
Vale Wood DN16.......185 C3
Valiant Dr
 18 Coddington NG24 ..104 C5
 Manby LN11...........62 C5
Valletta St HU9 ....5 E8
Valley Dr HU10 ....178 B7
Valley La
 Long Bennington NG23...117 B4
 Swaby LN13...........74 E4
Valley Pk View PE2....230 D8
Valley Rd
 Grantham NG31........210 C4
 1 Waddington LN5.....93 B8
Valley View 8 NG24....104 D5
Valley View Dr DN16....185 A2
Valliant St 7 LN5.......94 F1
Vampire Rd LN11.........62 C5
Vancouver Cres DN17...184 E4
Vanessa Dr DN12.......197 C7
Vanessa Rd LN11......198 A4
Vane St HU3 ....180 D7
Van Gogh Dr 8 PE11...214 B3
Vanguard Ct 4 NG34...212 A3

Vanwall Dr 8 LN5.......93 F7
Varah Cl 30 DN18......10 E8
Varlow Rd 8 LN7.......33 B4
Varsity Cl 4 DN7.......26 A8
Vasey Cl LN1...........66 E2
Vaughan Ave
 Bottesford NG13......128 B6
 Grimsby DN36........192 B4
Vauxhall Rd
 2 Boston PE21.......209 A5
 Bracebridge Heath LN4...205 F2
Veall Ct LN4 ....207 C4
Veal St DN31...........191 C7
Velden Way 5 LN8......57 D7
Venables Cl 13 PE24....102 E7
Venables Way LN2.....202 D6
Vence Cl 1 PE9.......219 A5
Venom Rd LN11..........62 C5
Ventnor Ave NG31.....210 E4
Ventura Bsns Pk DN31...188 D2
Venture Way NG31.....210 D2
Verdun Cl LN1.........201 E7
Vere Rd PE1...........225 F7
Vere St LN1...........201 F6
Vere Terr DN31........191 C8
Vergette Rd PE6.......220 E8
Vergette St PE1.......226 B3
Vermont Gr PE21......225 E1
Vermuyden Villas DN8...16 A3
Vernatts Gn PE11......214 C7
Vernon Ave NG31......210 F8
Vernon Rd PE25.......206 C4
Vernon St LN5.........201 D1
Vicarage Av 2 DN20...196 F6
Vicarage Cl
 2 Collingham NG23....91 D5
 6 Cowbit PE12.......167 B8
 Holbeach PE12 ....158 D1
Vicarage Cres 4 DN15...8 B5
Vicarage Ct 18 NG34 ..212 D4
Vicarage Dr LN6.......200 B3
Vicarage Dro PE20....134 D5
Vicarage Farm Rd 5
 PE1.................226 D3
Vicarage Gdns
 2 Brough HU15........2 C6
 5 Littlefield DN34 ...191 C6
 Scunthorpe DN15.....182 F2
 1 Wrawby DN20......20 E3
Vicarage La
 Beckingham DN10 ......40 B1
 Broughton DN20 ....19 E1
 Cadney DN20..........31 D6
 3 Carlton-le-Moorland
 LN5................105 E8
 Dunston LN4..........95 C6
 Elsham DN20..........20 F7
 Grasby DN38..........32 E7
 Harmston LN5.........93 F5
 1 Helpringham NG34..133 D7
 1 Immingham DN40....12 E4
 3 Kingston upon Hull
 HU3................178 E1
 4 Long Bennington
 NG23..............117 D3
 Long Sutton PE12 ....216 D2
 17 Lutton NG23......160 A8
 21 Nettleham LN2......68 C2
 1 Scawby DN20........30 E8
 Scopwick LN4..........95 C1
 5 Sothern LN2........68 F4
 4 Sibsey PE22.......113 B1
 South Clifton NG23....78 C5
 Wainfleet All Saints
 PE24...............102 D1
 13 Wellingore LN5....107 A7
 Wootton DN39.........11 E3
Vicarage Lawn DN21...191 C6
Vicarage Pk 4 DN15.....9 D1
Vicarage Rd
 8 Heckington NG34...122 E3
 Willoughton DN21......42 E4
 Wrawby DN20........196 F6
Vicarage Way PE7......233 D5
Vicar La 2 HU1........180 F5
Vicars Ct LN2.........234 B3
Vicar's Wlk 8 DN17...116 D7
Viceroy Dr PE1........156 F8
Vickers La 4 LN11....198 B5
Victor Dr 1 LN6.......204 C1
Victoria Ave
 1 Hatfield DN7.......14 E4
 Sleaford NG34.........12 C1
 1 Woodhall Spa LN10 ..97 D5
Victoria Bank NG34...133 B1
Victoria Cl
 Gainsborough DN21...197 F2
 2 Marschapel DN36....37 C2
 2 Stainforth DN7.....14 C5
 Wike Well End DN8....15 B7
Victoria Ct 5 DN15....8 B5
Victoria Dock Prim Sch
 HU9................181 B6
VICTORIA DOCK VILLAGE
 ....181 C5
Victoria Dr 5 DN18.....3 F7
Victoria Gr
 Heighington/
 Washingborough LN4...203 D1
 Morton PE10.........154 D7
Victoria Mews 18
 PE11...............214 D4
Victoria Pier* HU1....181 A5
Victoria Rd
 8 Boston PE21.......208 F4
 5 Bourne PE10.......213 E4
 Peterborough PE1.....225 F4

Victoria Rd
 Barnetby le Wold DN38...21 B4
 10 Keelby DN41.......23 A5
 Louth LN11..........198 C7
 Mablethorpe/Sutton on Sea
 LN12................64 B3
 2 Market Rasen LN8...57 E8
 Scunthorpe DN16.....185 A5
 Skegness PE25.......206 B4
 Stamford PE9 ....219 B6
Victoria St Pk DN31....189 A1
Victoria St N DN31....189 A1
Victoria St S 4 DN31..191 E7
Victoria St W DN31....191 E7
Victoria St
 Billingborough NG34...133 B1
 8 Billinghay LN4.....109 F6
 2 Grantham NG31......211 A2
 4 Holbeach PE12.....215 E2
 Kingston upon Hull
 HU3................179 A1
 Lincoln LN1.........234 A3
 Peterborough PE1.....226 A5
 Peterborough PE2....230 F6
 10 Spalding PE11.....214 D4
 3 Wrawby LN8........70 D5
Victoria Terr LN1.....234 A3
Victoria Terr DN31....188 D2
Victor St
 Grimsby DN34........189 C1
 Kingston upon Hull HU9 ..181 C8
Victor Way
 Bourne PE10.........213 E3
 10 Waddington LN5....94 A7
Victory Ct 6 PE12....157 F6
Victory Ct 8 PE11....214 C3
Victory Way
 2 Barton-upon-Humber
 DN18...............3 F1
 8 Grimsby DN34......190 D4
 6 Sleaford NG34......212 A3
Viersen Platz PE1.....226 A1
Vigo Cl LN1...........201 C7
Viking Cl
 6 Bourne PE10.......213 C6
 Immingham DN40......186 A4
 7 Swineshead PE20...135 B7
 11 Waddington LN5.....93 F7
Viking Sch The PE25...206 B4
Viking Way
 32 Metheringham LN4...95 C3
 6 Northorpe PE10....164 C8
 Spalding PE11.......214 F2
Villa Cl PE2...........216 A5
Village Farm Dr 5 LN1 ..66 C7
Village St
 Burton Coggles NG33...152 C8
 Easton NG33.........139 F2
 Pickworth NG34.......142 A8
 Sedgebrook NG32....128 F4
 Woolsthorpe by Belvoir
 NG32...............128 D1
Village The PE2.......230 B5
Villa La PE20..........135 B7
Ville Rd DN16.........185 D6
Vincent Cl 3 HU4......179 A2
Vincent Rd DN31......191 B2
Vine Cl 13 NG13......128 A5
Vine Cres 8 PE21.....208 F8
Vine Ct 8 NG34.......133 B1
Vinegarth 13 DN9......27 E6
Vinehall Rd 3 DN9.....27 C2
Vine Rd 2 PE25.......103 E4
Vine St
 Billingborough NG34...133 C1
 12 Grantham NG31....211 A5
 Lincoln LN2.........234 C2
 Spalding PE11.......214 D4
 Stamford PE9........219 C5
Vine Wlk PE1..........225 B4
Vineyard Rd PE1.......226 B2
Viney Cl PE1..........226 D5
Vinters Way PE22.....126 E3
Vintners Cl PE13.......225 D3
Violet Cl
 4 Humberston DN35..192 E1
 Morton PE10.........154 D6
Virginia Cl 8 PE3.....225 A2
Virginia Dr LN11......198 E5
Viscount Rd PE2......231 A6
Viscount Way 6 DN36...36 D8
Vista The 3 PE1......214 D3
Visual Arts Ctr* DN15...183 C3
Vivian Ave DN32......192 B5
Vivian Cl 1 NG31.....210 D8
Viven Cl PE7..........233 F6
Voases Cl HU10.......178 E6
Voases La HU10.......178 E6
Vokes St PE2 ....230 D8
Vulcan Cres LN6......204 C2
Vulcan Dr 4 LN1.......67 F5
Vulcan St 9 LN5.......94 A7
Vulcan Way LN7........15 A1
Vyner Cl 18 LN12......64 B3

W

Waby Cl DN37.........190 D7
WADDINGHAM DN21.....43 D7
Waddingham Pl
 5 Habrough DN40 .....22 E8
 New Waltham DN36...195 D5
Waddingham Prim Sch
 DN21................43 D7
Waddington Rd LN7...31 F1
WADDINGTON LN5.......93 F7

Waddington Dr 1
 DN17...............184 E3
Waddington La NG23...91 C7
Waddington Pl 4
 DN34...............184 E3
Waddington Redwood Cty
 Prim Sch LN5.........93 E8
WADDINGWORTH LN10...84 C6
Waddingworth Gr LN2...202 A8
Wade Pk Ave PE6......217 C4
Waggoners Cl 1 DN21...29 C4
Waggoners Way PE10...154 C6
Waggoners Wlk PE22...113 B1
Waggons Way 4 DN7.....14 C5
Waincroft 2 DN21......102 C2
Wainer Cl LN4........204 C5
WAINFLEET ALL SAINTS
 PE24...............102 D2
WAINFLEET BANK
 PE24...............102 B1
Wainfleet Rd
 Boston PE21 ....209 D7
 Croft PE24...........102 D7
 Firsby PE23..........101 F6
 Fishtoft PE21........209 D7
 Grimsby DN33........191 B3
 Irby in the Marsh PE24...102 B6
 Skegness PE25.......206 A3
 Thorpe St Peter PE24...102 C3
Wainfleet Rd Industrial Est
 PE25................206 A2
WAINFLEET ST MARY
 PE24...............115 E8
Wainfleet Sta PE24....102 D1
WAINFLEET TOFTS
 PE24...............115 C8
Wainman Rd PE24.....230 D5
Wainwell Mews 3
 LN2.................234 C3
Wainwright PE4.......220 E5
WAITHE DN36...........36 A3
Waithe La DN37........35 E4
Wakefield Ave DN21...29 D4
Wakefield Cl NG31....210 C4
Wake Rd PE1..........226 B2
Wakerley Dr PE2......230 C7
Wakerley Rd 6 DN21...29 C3
Wakes Cl 1 PE10.....213 E4
Wake St LN1..........234 A4
Walbury Cl 4 LN5.....205 D2
WALCOT
 Alkborough DN15.......8 B8
 Walcot Near Folkingham
 NG34...............132 C1
Walcot Bar NG34......132 D2
Walcot Cl LN6........204 F6
Walcot La NG34.......142 C8
Walcot Rd
 Alkborough DN15......8 B8
 Ufford PE9..........172 F3
Walcott Cl LN4........109 D7
Walcott Rd LN4.......109 E6
Walcott St HU3.......180 C4
Walcot Way 2 PE9....218 E6
Walcot Wlk PE1.......225 B4
Waldeck St LN1.......234 A4
Walden Gdns 1 PE21...208 E4
Waldo Rd LN4........205 F5
Waldorf Rd DN35......193 A1
Waldo Way DN15.......8 A1
WALESBY LN8...........46 A3
Walesby Cl DN33......194 D8
Walesby Hill LN8......46 B3
Walesby La LN6.......46 B2
Walesby Rd
 Market Rasen LN8.....57 D8
 Middle Rasen LN8.....45 E1
 Scunthorpe DN17.....184 E4
Walford Cl 2 NG13....128 A5
Walford Dr LN6.......205 A6
Walgrave PE2.........230 B4
Walker Ave DN33......194 F8
Walker Cl 1 DN15.....8 F7
Walker Dr 4 DN15.....9 A5
Walkergate 14 LN11...198 B5
WALKERINGHAM DN10...39 F3
Walkeringham Nature
 Reserve* DN10.......39 F3
Walkeringham Prim Sch
 DN10................39 F3
Walkeringham Rd
 Beckingham DN10......40 A2
 Gringley on the Hill DN10 ..39 D2
WALKERITH DN21.......40 B4
Walkerith Rd
 East Stockwith DN21...40 B5
 Gainsborough DN21...197 B8
 Morton DN21.........40 D3
Walker Rd PE6........220 D7
Walkers Cl
 4 Bottesford NG13...128 B5
 Scunthorpe DN15....183 B3
Walker's Cl 3 DN38...21 B4
Walkers Ct 20 DN17...29 D7
Walker St LN2........180 C5
Walkers Way
 Barrowby NG32......210 A3
 Peterborough PE3....224 F3
 Ulceby DN39.........12 B2
Walkington Way 18
 LN3.................77 A7
Walk La
 Humberston DN36......36 C7
 Irby DN37............34 D7
 Langton by Wragby LN8 ..70 F4
Walks Rd LN4.........120 F1
Walks The 4 PE9.....171 B1

Walk The DN21.........197 F1
Wallace's Dro PE6.....176 C2
Walled Gdn The 8 LN5...93 F7
Waller St HU9 ....181 C6
Walliker St HU3 ....180 A7
Wallingfen La HU15.....1 E
Wallis Ave LN6........205 E
Wallis Cl DN33........191 E
Wallisgate PE12......158 C
Wallis Rd LN1........198 D
Walls Ave 8 PE24.....102 E
Wall's La PE25.........90 E
Wall St
 Gainsborough DN21 ...197 D
 Grimsby DN34.......191 A
Walmer La 1 LN2......202 C
Walmsgate DN36......192 B
WALMSGATE LN11.......74 C
Walmsgate Gdns DN33...191 B
Walmsgate Pl 3 DN33...191 B
Walmsgate Wlk DN33...191 B
Walmsley St HU3 ......180 D
Walnut Cl
 5 Newborough PE6....174 E
 14 Ruskington NG34..108 E
 10 Waltham DN36......36 B
Walnut Cres DN35.....192 C
Walnut Dr 1 DN20.....30 F
Walnutgarth 8 NG34...212 F
Walnut Gr 3 NG33....151 E
Walnut Pl LN5........234 B
Walnut Rd
 8 Bottesford NG13...128 A
 Kirton PE20.........136 C
 Walnut Way DN17......29 C
Walpole Bank PE14....170 F
WALPOLE CROSS KEYS
 PE34...............161 C
WALPOLE MARSH
 PE14...............170 F
Walsall Garth HU4.....179 E
Walsham Rd PE7.......233 C
Walsham Cl 7 DN33....191 E
Walsingham Ct 3
 PE13...............170 C
Walsingham Dr NG33...152 F
Walsingham Way 13
 PE6.................170 C
WALSOKEN PE13........170 E
WALTHAM DN37.........194 C
Waltham Cl
 8 Birchwood LN6.....204 C
 2 Dogsthorpe PE1....226 C
Waltham Grange 5
 DN35...............192 E
Waltham Mus of Rural
 Life* DN37..........194 C
Waltham Rd
 Barnoldby le Beck
 DN37...............194 A
 Birchwood LN6.......204 C
 Brigsley DN37.......194 A
 Croxton Kerrial NG32...138 A
 Grimsby DN33........194 E
Waltham St 1 HU1.....180 E
Waltham Windmill*
 DN37...............194 C
Walton Cl NG34.......221 A
Walton Corn Sch PE4...221 A
Walton Gdns NG31....211 A
Walton Girls High Sch The
 NG31...............210 F
Walton Gr DN32.......192 B
Walton Heath Cl 2
 NG31...............211 D
WALTON HIGHWAY
 PE14...............170 A
Walton Infants Sch
 PE4.................221 A
Walton Jun Sch PE4....221 A
Walton Pk PE4........221 A
Walton Rd
 7 Leverington PE13..170 C
 Marholm PE6.........220 C
 Wisbech PE13........170 C
Walton St Leisure Ctr
 HU3................180 A
Walton St HU3.........180 A
Walton Way 3 NG32....139 C
Wandell's View HU15.....2 C
Wansbeck Rd 8 NG34...128 F
WANSFORD PE8.........222 A
Wansford Rd PE8......222 A
Wanton La PE34.......161 C
Wanton's Cross Gate
 PE22...............126 F
Wanton's La PE22.....159 A
Wapping La 8 DN9......65 C
Warbon Ave PE1.......226 C
Warburton Ct DN36....192 F
Wardall St DN35......192 F
Ward Cl PE1..........226 E
Ward Cres PE21.......208 A
Wardentree La PE11...157 A
Wardour Dr NG31.....211 A
Ward's La PE22.......114 A
Ward St DN35.........192 F
Wareley Rd PE2.......225 F
Wares Way DN15......182 E
WARGATE PE11.........145 C
Wargate Field La PE11...145 C
Wargate Way PE11.....145 C
Waring St LN1.........199 B
Warley Ave 1 DN16....185 C
Warley Dr DN16.......185 C
Warley Rd DN16.......185 C
Warneford Gdns HU5...180 A
Warneford Rd DN35....192 D

arping Way DN15 . . . . . .**182** B3
arren Cl DN21 . . . .**197** B6
arren Ct PE7 . . . . **230** C2
arrendale **12** DN18 . . . . . .**10** E8
arren Farm Cl DN40 . . . . . .**12** D7
arren La LN6 . . . . **92** D4
arren Ct PE7 . . . .**14** D4
arrenne Keep **8**
PE9. . . . .**219** B4
arrenne Rd DN7 . . . .**14** D4
arren Rd
North Somercotes LN11 . . . **51** A6
Scunthorpe DN17 . . . .**183** B5
11 Thorne/Moorends
DN8. . . . .**15** B7
Wothorpe PE9 . . . .**219** C1
arren Way NG31 . . . . . . **211** F7
arth La PE25. . . . .**206** A5
arwick Dr DN33 . . . . . .**191** A4
arwick Cl
3 Grantham NG31. . . . . .**210** D5
1 Hatfield DN7. . . . .**14** F3
8 Saxilby with Ingleby
LN1. . . . .**66** C2
arwick Dr **24** DN18 . . . . . .**10** E8
arwick Rd
8 Chapel St Leonard
PE24 . . . .**90** D7
Cleethorpes DN35 . . . . . .**192** D4
Louth LN11 . . . .**198** B8
Newark-on-Trent NG24. . .**104** B2
Peterborough PE4 . . . . . .**221** A2
Scunthorpe DN16 . . . . . .**183** C1
arwick St HU9 . . . .**181** A1
ascana Cl HU4 . . . .**179** B3
asdale Cl **2** LN6. . . . . .**200** C1
asdale Farm **1** PE4 . . .**221** E2
ash Bank PE12. . . . .**167** A5
ashdike Dro PE11 . . . . .**135** C1
ashdike La
Croft PE24 . . . .**102** E4
Donington PE11. . . . .**135** A1
Stoke Rochford NG33 . . . .**140** A3
Toynton St Peter PE23. . .**101** B6
Wainfleet St Mary PE24 . .**102** C1
ash Dike La PE22 . . . . .**115** A6
ashdike La
Algarkirk PE20. . . . .**136** B1
Kirton PE20 . . . .**136** A6
ashdyke La
Melton & Manthorpe
NG32. . . . .**130** A6
Boston PE21 . . . .**208** B7
Cumberworth LN13 . . . . . .**89** E8
Elsham DN20 . . . .**20** D6
2 Glentham LN8. . . . .**43** F1
Immingham DN40 . . . . . .**186** B5
Leasingham NG34 . . . . . .**121** B7
Mumby LN13 . . . .**76** F1
Nettleham LN2. . . . .**68** B2
Old Leake PE22 . . . .**113** F4
Osgodby LN8. . . . .**45** A3
ashdyke Rd **7** NG32 . .**106** C1
ashdyke Ret Pk
DN40 . . . .**186** C4
ASHINGBOROUGH
LN4. . . . .**203** D2
ashingborough Prim Sch
LN4. . . . .**203** D2
ashingborough Rd
Heighington/
Washingborough LN4 . . . .**81** E4
Lincoln LN4 . . . .**202** D1
ashinghall La DN17 . . . . .**7** A2
assand St HU3 . . . .**180** C4
ass La LN4. . . . .**71** E5
aside Gn La PE20 . . . . . .**146** C7
ater Bank PE10 . . . .**26** E5
aterbelly La PE20 . . . . .**136** A1
ater End
Marholm PE6 . . . .**220** B1
Peterborough PE7 . . . . . .**229** A5
ater Gate
Quadring PE11. . . . .**145** B8
Sleaford NG34. . . . .**212** D4
ater Hill LN3. . . . .**82** B7
aterhouse La HU1 . . . . .**180** C4
atering Dyke Houses
LN2. . . . .**67** F4
ater La
1 Ancaster NG32. . . . . .**120** A2
Bourne PE10 . . . .**213** D2
Castle Bytham NG33 . . . .**152** D1

Water La continued
Castor PE5. . . . .**223** F1
6 Colsterworth NG33 . . .**151** D7
Gunby & Stainby NG33 . . .**151** B5
5 Hagworthingham PE23. .**87** A4
Lincoln LN1 . . . .**234** A2
4 Lincoln LN6. . . . .**93** C8
1 Long Bennington
NG23. . . . .**117** D4
12 South Witham NG33. . .**151** D2
4 Spalding PE11 . . . . . .**214** D2
Threekingham NG34 . . . .**132** F3
Thurlby LN5 . . . .**92** E3
Thurlby HU9 . . . .**164** C8
2 West Halton DN15 . . . .**8** E7
Waterlees Rd PE13. . . . .**170** D1
Water Lilly Way PE10 . . .**213** D3
Waterloo Cl **1** NG32. . .**119** F7
Waterloo Dr
4 Barton DN33 . . . . . .**191** B2
6 Morton PE10 . . . . . .**154** D6
Waterloo La LN6. . . . . .**200** B3
Waterloo Paddock
LN5. . . . .**106** D3
Mablethorpe/Sutton on Sea
LN12 . . . .**64** B4
Peterborough PE1 . . . . . .**226** A5
Waterloo St
Kingston upon Hull
HU2. . . . .**180** E8
Lincoln LN6. . . . .**201** D2
4 Market Rasen LN8. . . .**57** D8
Waterlow Dr **22** DN15 . . . .**9** A5
Watermill La PE23 . . . . .**100** F6
Water Mill La LN9 . . . . .**199** B4
WATER NEWTON PE8. . . .**223** A4
Waters' Edge Ctry Pk*
DN18 . . . .**3** F2
Waterside **5** LN5. . . . . .**109** F5
WATERSIDE DN8 . . . .**14** E8
Waterside
3 Ryhall PE9 . . . .**163** C1
Thorne DN8. . . . .**14** F8
Water Side DN15. . . . . . .**8** E4
Waterside Bsns Pk HU13 . .**3** F4
Waterside Cl **10** PE10 . .**213** C7
Waterside Dr **4** DN31. .**191** D8
Waterside Gdns **5**
PE12. . . . .**215** E2
Waterside N LN5. . . . . .**234** B2
Waterside Rd DN18 . . . . .**3** E2
Waterside S LN5. . . . . . .**234** B2
Waterside Sh Ctr LN2 . . .**234** B2
Watersdale Rd PE7 . . . . .**233** C4
Water St PE9 . . . .**219** C4
Waterton Cl PE6. . . . . . .**217** E4
Waterton La DN7 . . . .**14** D2
Waterwell La NG32 . . . . .**118** F8
Waterworks La PE6 . . . . .**220** B6
Waterworks St
1 Gainsborough
DN21. . . . .**197** D3
Immingham DN40 . . . . . .**186** D5
Watery La
Asterby LN11. . . . .**72** F5
Butterwick PE22 . . . .**126** F3
Goulceby LN11. . . . .**72** D6
Lissington LN3. . . . .**57** D1
Little Cawthorpe LN11. . . .**61** E2
Mareham le Fen PE22 . . . .**98** F4
Swaby LN13. . . . .**74** E4
4 Welton/Dunholme LN2. .**68** E6
1 West Ashby LN9 . . . . .**85** E7
Wickenby LN3 . . . .**70** A8
Watford Ave DN34 . . . . .**190** F4
Watkin St N DN31. . . . . .**188** F1
Watkin St S **2** DN31. . .**188** F1
Watkin St **2** DN22. . . . .**52** B3
Watling Cl
6 Bourne PE10 . . . . . .**213** C6
8 Bracebridge Heath
LN4. . . . .**81** A1
Watson Pk **4** DN10 . . . . .**52** B8
Watsons Croft DN7. . . . . .**14** D6
Watt Cl PE4 . . . .**221** C2
Watts La LN11. . . . .**198** C4
Wauldby Cl **4** HU10 . . . .**178** E7
Wauldby View **2** HU14 . . .**3** B7
Waumsley Way **1** LN13 . .**75** E2
Wavell Dr LN2 . . . .**202** A4
Waveney Cl **1** DN15 . . . . .**8** B5
Waveney Gr PE4 . . . .**221** C2
Waverley Ave LN6. . . . . .**204** F3
Waverley Gdns
5 Leverington PE13. . . .**170** B4
Stamford PE9 . . . .**218** F6
Waverley St HU1. . . . . . .**180** E5
Waverly Cl LN6. . . . .**201** D4
Wayet Rd **6** PE11 . . . . .**156** E8
Wayford ST PE3. . . . . . .**225** A2
Wayside Cl
5 Holton le Clay
DN36. . . . .**195** D3
Wayside Dr DN15 . . . . . .**185** A3
Weatherthorn PE2 . . . . .**230** C5
Weaver Rd LN6. . . . .**204** F3
Weavers Croft **11** DN9. . .**27** A2
Webb Cl **38** DN18 . . . . . .**10** E8
Webb St LN5 . . . .**205** D4
Webster Cl **3** LN5. . . . .**205** A5
Websters Ct LN6 . . . .**204** C8
Webster Way NG31 . . . . .**210** F4

Wedgewood Cl **10** LN6 . .**204** D7
Wedgwood Dr **4**
PE11. . . . .**214** B5
Wedgewood Rd **1**
LN6. . . . .**204** D7
Wedgewood Rd LN6 . . . .**204** D7
Wedland La PE24 . . . . . .**102** D3
WEECAR NG23. . . . .**78** D1
Weedon Cl PE4 . . . .**221** D2
Weekes Rd DN35. . . . . .**192** F4
WEELSBY DN32. . . . . . .**192** A5
Weelsby Ave DN32 . . . . .**191** F4
Weelsby Gr DN32 . . . . . .**191** E4
Weelsby Prim Sch
DN32. . . . .**192** A8
Weelsby Rd DN32. . . . . .**192** A8
Weelsby St DN32. . . . . .**191** D5
Weelsby St S DN32. . . . .**192** A7
Weelsby St
15 Grimsby DN31 . . . . .**189** C1
Grimsby DN32 . . . .**192** A8
Weelsby View DN36. . . . .**195** D8
Weeping Elm Way **6**
DN16 . . . .**185** D4
Weeton Way **5** HU10 . . .**178** E7
Wegberg Rd LN4. . . . .**95** C7
Weir Cl **3** DN9 . . . .**27** A2
Weir Farm **1** LN2 . . . . . .**68** F4
Weir La PE22 . . . .**126** D4
Weir St LN5 . . . .**205** D8
Weir The HU13. . . . .**178** E1
Welbeck Dr PE11 . . . . . .**214** C5
Welbeck Pl **3** DN34 . . . .**190** E4
Welbeck Rd DN35. . . . . .**192** C5
Welbeck St HU5 . . . .**180** B8
Welbeck Way
Louth LN11 . . . .**198** B6
Peterborough PE2 . . . . . .**230** D7
WELBOURN LN5 . . . .**106** F5
Welbourn CE (Cont) Prim
Sch LN5 . . . .**106** E5
Welbourn PE4 . . . .**221** A4
Welbourne Cl **6**
NG23. . . . .**202** A8
Welbourn Prim Sch
PE4. . . . .**221** A4
Welbourn Rd LN5 . . . . . .**106** A5
Welbourn Wlk HU4 . . . . .**179** B6
WELBY HU13 . . . .**234** B4
Welby Cl NG34. . . . .**212** B4
Welby **3** PE11 . . . .**145** B6
Welby-Everard Ct
NG31 . . . .**211** B4
Welby Gdns
Grantham NG31. . . . .**211** A6
Holbeach PE12 . . . .**215** B2
Welby St **6** NG31. . . . .**211** A4
Weldon Rd DN21. . . . .**42** E1
Wel Fen La NG23 . . . . . .**117** E8
Welham St NG31. . . . . . .**211** B4
Welholme Jun & Inf Sch
DN32. . . . .**191** D5
Welholme Rd DN32 . . . . .**191** E6
WELL LN13 . . . .**88** E8
Welland Ave DN34 . . . . .**190** F4
Welland Bank PE6 . . . . .**166** C1
Welland Cl
Peterborough PE1 . . . . . .**226** A4
2 Ruskington NG34 . . . .**108** D2
1 Spalding PE11 . . . . . .**214** C2
Welland Ct **3** DN15 . . . . .**8** B5
Welland Dr **3** NG31. . . .**210** E2
Welland Hospl PE11 . . . .**214** F6
Welland Mews PE9 . . . . .**219** C4
Welland Prim Sch PE1 . . .**226** C8
Welland Rd
Borough Fen PE6. . . . . . .**174** E1
Boston PE21 . . . .**208** B3
Lincoln LN1 . . . .**201** D1
Spalding PE11 . . . .**214** C2
1 Wittering PE8 . . . .**222** B1
Welland Way PE6 . . . . . .**217** E4
Wellbeck Cl **4** DN20 . . .**196** D4
Welldale Ct DN34. . . . . .**190** E4
Wellesley Cl **3** LN8. . . . .**57** D7
Wellfield Cl **6** NG33 . . .**151** D2
Wellgarth DN32 . . . .**192** B5
Wellhead La LN11 . . . .**95** B7
Well High La LN13 . . . . . .**75** D1
WELLINGORE LN5 . . . . . .**107** A7
Wellingore Rd **5** LN2 . .**201** F8
Wellingore Rd **4** **11** LN2 .**64** F4
Wellington Cl
7 Heckington NG34 . . . .**122** C2
Skellingthorpe LN6 . . . . . .**79** F4
9 South Killingholme
DN40. . . . .**12** E3
Wellington Dr **1**
NG31 . . . .**211** D2
Wellington La HU3 . . . . .**180** D8
Wellington Rd
1 Beacon Hill NG24 . . . .**104** A4
Boston PE21 . . . .**209** B4
Mablethorpe/Sutton on Sea
LN12 . . . .**64** B4
Wellington St Wes
HU1 . . . .**180** E5

Wellington Sq **12** LN5 . . . .**94** A7
Wellington St
12 Gainsborough
DN21. . . . .**197** D3
Grimsby DN32 . . . .**191** F8
Kingston upon Hull HU1 . .**180** F5
Lincoln LN1 . . . .**201** D4
4 Louth LN11. . . . .**198** C6
Peterborough PE4 . . . . . .**226** B2
7 Scampton Airfield LN1. .**67** E5
Wellington Way
1 Elsham Wold Ind Est
DN20. . . . .**21** A8
Market Deeping PE6 . . . .**217** B7
8 Skegness PE25 . . . . .**206** A5
Wellington Yd **4** PE23 . . .**88** A1
Well La LN2 . . . .**234** B3
WELLOW DN32. . . . .**191** E5
Wellowgate DN32. . . . . .**191** D7
Wellowgate Mews
DN32 . . . .**191** D6
Wells Cl
Grantham NG31. . . . .**210** C5
Heighington/Washingborough
Peterborough PE4 . . . . . .**220** F3
Wells Ct PE2 . . . .**231** D6
Wells Dr
Bracebridge Heath LN4 . . .**81** A2
6 Market Rasen LN8 . . . .**57** E7
Wells La DN22 . . . .**65** B7
Wells Rd DN37. . . . .**23** D4
Wells St
Grimsby DN31 . . . .**191** B7
Kingston upon Hull HU3 . .**180** C4
Scunthorpe DN15 . . . . . .**183** B4
Well St
1 Bishop Norton LN8. . . .**43** D3
Messingham DN17 . . . . . .**29** C7
Wellstead St HU3 . . . . . .**180** C5
Wells The **13** LN2 . . . . . .**68** D6
Wellsyke La LN10 . . . .**98** A6
Well Turn LN13 . . . .**75** F1
Well Vale **3** DN33. . . . . .**194** D8
Well Vale Cl **29** PE24 . . . .**90** D7
Welsby Ave DN33 . . . . . .**194** C7
Welsdale Rd LN11 . . . . . .**59** E2
WELTON
Welton HU15. . . . .**2** E6
Welton LN2. . . . .**68** C3
Welton Cl **32** DN18 . . . . .**10** E8
Welton Gdns **2** LN2. . . .**201** F8
WELTON HILL LN2. . . . . .**69** A8
WELTON LE MARSH
LN11. . . . .**89** B3
WELTON LE WOLD
LN11. . . . .**71** B7
Welton-le-Wold Nature
Reserve * LN11 . . . .**60** D7
Welton Low Rd HU15 . . . . .**2** C6
Welton Old Rd HU15 . . . . .**2** E6
Welton Rd
Brough HU15 . . . .**2** C5
Nettleham LN2. . . . .**68** C3
Welton Wold View **9**
HU14 . . . .**3** B7
Welwyn Cl NG31. . . . . . .**210** E1
Wembley Cl LN11. . . . . . .**50** F7
Wembley St DN21. . . . . .**197** C4
Wendan Rd **9** DN8 . . . . .**15** A7
Wende The PE11. . . . . . .**214** A3
Wendover Cl
12 Humberston DN36 . . .**36** D8
Messingham DN17. . . . . .**29** D7
Rippingale PE10. . . . .**142** F2
Wendover Rd **13** DN17 . . .**29** D7
Wendover Rise DN35. . . .**192** E3
Wenlock St HU3 . . . .**180** C7
Wenslydale Cl **1**
NG31 . . . .**211** A8
Wensleydale Rd DN16. . .**185** E6
Wensum Ct **2** PE11. . . . .**214** F5
Wentworth Cl
Heighington LN4 . . . .**203** E1
4 Skegness PE25 . . . . .**206** D1
1 Spalding PE11 . . . . . .**214** C2
Willerby HU10 . . . .**178** F8
Wentworth Cres **2** DN19. .**4** E2
Wentworth
Dunholme LN2 . . . .**68** C5
Grantham NG31. . . . .**211** D8
25 Messingham DN17 . . .**29** D7
4 Saxilby with Ingleby
LN1. . . . .**66** D2
Wentworth Rd
Grimsby DN31 . . . .**191** B7
Scunthorpe DN17 . . . . . .**184** B7
Wentworths The PE12 . . .**216** A4
Wentworth Way
Kingston upon Hull
HU9. . . . .**181** C7
7 Woodhall Spa LN10 . . .**97** D5
Werneth Rd **2** DN17 . . . .**29** D7
WERRINGTON PE4 . . . . .**220** F4
Werrington Bridge Rd
PE6. . . . .**221** B6
Werrington Cl PE4 . . . . .**221** A3
Werrington Gr Cvn Pk
PE4. . . . .**220** F4
Werrington Mews **5**
PE4. . . . .**221** A3
Werrington Parkway
PE4. . . . .**220** C5

Werrington Pk Ave **2**
PE4. . . . .**221** A3
Werrington Prim Sch
PE4. . . . .**221** A3
Werry's La **1** PE10 . . . .**213** C6
Wesleyan Ct LN2. . . . . . .**234** B2
Wesleyan Rd PE1 . . . . . .**226** A7
Wesley Ave **5** PE34 . . . .**161** F3
Wesley Cl
4 Epworth DN9 . . . .**27** E6
15 Metheringham LN4 . . .**95** C4
Sleaford NG34. . . . .**212** C2
11 Terrington St Clement
PE34. . . . .**161** F3
2 Winterton DN15 . . . . .**9** A5
Wesley Cres **2** DN35. . .**192** E3
Wesley St
8 Grimsby DN31 . . . . .**189** C1
Kingston upon Hull
HU3. . . . .**180** C5
Wesley Rd
Brigg DN20 . . . .**196** C3
Scunthorpe DN16 . . . . . .**185** E2
9 Terrington St Clement
PE34. . . . .**161** F3
Wesley St **10** HU13 . . . . .**158** C7
Wesley Way LN9 . . . .**199** D3
Wesselow Rd LN4. . . . . .**207** F6
Wessex Cl
Peterborough PE2 . . . . . .**231** D7
Sleaford NG34. . . . .**212** B1
West Acridge **16** DN18 . . .**3** E1
WEST ASHBY LN9 . . . . . .**85** E7
West Ave
Cranwell & Byard's Leap
NG34. . . . .**120** B8
Grantham NG31. . . . .**211** B6
6 Stainforth DN7. . . . . .**14** C6
West Bank
Crowland PE6 . . . .**166** E1
Saxilby with Ingleby LN1. . .**66** C3
Stainforth DN7 . . . .**14** B7
Strubby with Woodthorpe
LN13 . . . .**75** B2
West Bank Rd PE12 . . . .**161** A8
West Banks NG34 . . . . . .**212** C4
Westbeck **2** LN1. . . . . . .**66** F7
Westbeck La DN21. . . . . .**42** C5
WESTBOROUGH NG23 . . .**117** E3
Westborough La NG23 . . .**117** D4
Westbourne Way
HU4 . . . .**179** B6
Westbourne Ave **3**
HU13 . . . .**178** A2
Westbourne Dr
2 Crowle DN17. . . . . . .**16** D7
6 Glinton PE6 . . . .**220** C8
Westbourne Gdns **5**
PE11. . . . .**214** D3
Westbourne Gr
6 Grimsby DN31 . . . . .**194** F8
Kingston upon Hull
HU13. . . . .**178** D2
6 Lincoln LN1. . . . .**201** D3
Westbourne Pk PE10 . . .**213** B5
Westbourne Pl **2**
NG31 . . . .**210** E4
Westbourne St **5** HU3 . .**180** A4
Westbrecks La DN22 . . . .**65** A3
Westbrook Ave **1** PE2 . .**230** F7
Westbrooke Cl LN6 . . . . .**205** A7
Westbrooke Rd LN6 . . . . .**205** A7
West Brook La NG23 . . . .**91** D3
Westbrook Pk Cl **2**
PE2. . . . .**230** F7
Westbrook Pk Rd PE2 . . .**230** F7
Westburn Ave **2** DN19. . .**4** E2
Westbury Dr **2** DN35 . . .**193** A1
Westbury Rd DN35. . . . .**193** A1
WEST BUTTERWICK
DN17. . . . .**28** D6
West Butterwick CE Prim
Sch DN17 . . . .**28** D6
WESTBY NG33 . . . .**140** F3
Bitchfield & Bassingthorpe
NG33. . . . .**140** F2
Burton Coggles NG33 . . . .**152** C8
WESTCLIFF DN17 . . . . . .**184** E7
Westcliffe Prim Sch
DN17. . . . .**184** D6
Ruskington NG34. . . . . . .**108** C2
3 Scotter DN21. . . . . . .**29** C3
Westcliffe St LN1. . . . . . .**201** D6
Westcliff Gdns DN17 . . . .**184** D6
West Coates Rd DN31 . . .**188** D2
West Cob Gate PE12 . . . .**157** F6
Westcombe Sq PE1 . . . . .**226** C5
West Comm Cres
DN17. . . . .**184** F8
West Comm Gdns
DN17. . . . .**184** F7
West Comm La DN17. . . .**184** F7
West Comm N Rd DN17 . .**29** A8
West Comm Sports Hall
DN17. . . . .**184** F8
Westcroft Dr **3** LN1. . . . .**66** D3
West Cross St **24** DN21. . .**30** B1

West Ct 🔟 DN8...........15 A7
West-Dale Cres 🔁
  DN21.....................30 B2
Westdale Dro PE11....134 C2
WEST DEEPING PE6....173 B8
West Dock Ave HU3....180 B4
West Dock St HU3......180 B3
West Dr
  Coningsby LN4..........110 E8
  Sudbrooke LN2..........68 F3
West Dro PE12...........168 C2
West Dro PE12...........168 C3
West Dro S PE12........168 C1
WEST ELLA HU10.......178 A8
West Ella Rd
  Kingston upon Hull
  HU10...................178 A7
  Swanland HU14...........3 C7
West Ella Way HU14......3 C7
West Elloe Ave PE11...214 E6
WEST END PE22.........126 C6
West End
  Burgh le Marsh PE24...102 D8
  Garthorpe & Fockerby
  DN17....................7 E5
  Gorefield PE13.........169 E3
  Harlaxton NG32.........139 E3
  Hogsthorpe PE24.........90 B7
  Holbeach PE12..........215 D2
  Ingham LN1.............54 F2
  Langtoft PE6...........164 E3
  🔽 Spilsby PE23..........87 F1
  Swanland HU14...........3 B6
  Walcott LN4............109 C7
  Winteringham DN15.......2 A1
  Yaxley PE7.............233 D4
West End Cl
  🔟 Bottesford NG13.....128 A6
  Laughton DN21..........41 B8
West End Cres 🔟 PE23...87 F1
West End La DN36........37 B1
West End Rd
  Boston PE21............136 D8
  Epworth DN9............27 C8
  🔁 Habrough DN40.......22 E8
  Kirton PE20............136 B7
  Maxey PE6.............217 A1
  Ulceby DN39............11 F1
  Wyberton PE21.........208 B2
West End Villas 🔟
  PE9...................219 A5
Westerdale 🔟 HU14......3 B7
Westerdale Gr HU9.....181 E8
Westerdale Rd
  🔁 Grantham NG31......211 A7
  Scunthorpe DN16........185 D5
Westerdale Way DN37...190 E8
Westerley Cl 🔁 PE23....225 C4
Westerly Way 🔟 PE11...214 A5
Western Ave
  Brigg DN20.............196 C5
  Easton on the Hill PE9..171 C3
  Holbeach PE12..........215 C7
  Lincoln LN6............205 C7
  Peterborough PE1.......226 B7
  🔁 Saxilby LN1..........66 C2
Western Cres LN6......205 C8
Western Dr
  Balderton NG24.........104 C1
  🔟 Barton-upon-Humber
  DN18...................3 E1
  🔟 RAF Cranwell NG34...120 C8
Western Gn DN15.........2 A1
Western Outway DN34...191 A4
Western Prim Sch
  DN34..................190 E5
Western Tech Sch The
  DN34..................190 F5
West Fen Drain Bank
  PE22..................112 D1
West Fen La PE22.......100 A1
WEST FIELD DN40........12 C6
Westfield App LN2.....203 A8
Westfield Ave
  Boston PE21............208 D4
  Greetwell LN2..........203 B8
  Grimsby DN33..........191 C3
Westfield Cl
  🔟 Metheringham LN4....95 C4
  Yaxley PE7.............233 D5
Westfield Dr
  Greetwell LN2..........203 A8
  🔁🔁 Messingham DN17....29 D7
  🔟 Pinchbeck PE11......156 B8
  🔁 Skegness PE25.......206 B4
  🔟 Swineshead PE20.....135 B7
Westfield Garth 🔁
  DN17...................16 E6
Westfield Gr DN35.....192 D6
Westfield La
  Collingham NG23........91 B4
  Cumberworth LN13........89 D8
  Kirk Bramwith DN7......14 B8
West Field La
  🔟 Swanland HU14........3 B6
  Thorpe on the Hill LN6...92 E8
West Field La HU15.....2 C6
Westfield Rd
  Bardney LN3............83 D1
  Barton-upon-Humber DN18...3 C1
  Fishlake DN7...........14 B8
  🔟 Goxhill DN19........12 A8
  🔟 Hatfield DN7........14 E4
  Kingston upon Hull HU4..179 D5
  Newton PE13...........169 F5

Westfield Rd continued
  Peterborough PE3......225 E4
  Scunthorpe DN17.......184 B6
  Waltham DN37..........194 C4
  🔁 Wisbech PE13.......170 E2
  Yarburgh LN11..........49 D3
  Yaxley PE7.............233 D5
Westfield Rise HU13...178 D2
Westfields
  🔟 Alford LN13.........75 F2
  Easton on the Hill PE9..171 C3
Westfield St 🔟 LN1....201 D3
Westfield Villas 🔟 DN7..14 E4
Westfield Way PE6.....164 E2
WESTGATE DN9...........16 D2
Westgate
  Grantham NG31..........211 A4
  Grimsby DN31..........188 F1
  Kexby DN21.............53 E4
  Lincoln LN1............234 A3
  Louth LN11............198 A5
  Peterborough PE1.......225 F2
  Scotton DN21...........29 C1
  Sleaford NG34.........212 C4
West Gate
  🔟 Ruskington NG34.....108 E2
  Wainfleet All Saints
  PE24..................101 E2
  Weston PE12...........157 D2
Westgate House*
  LN11..................198 A5
Westgate Jun Sch LN1..234 A4
Westgate Pk 🔟 NG34...212 C4
Westgate Pl 🔁 LN11...198 B5
Westgate Rd DN9........16 D2
West Gn
  Kingston upon Hull HU10..3 C8
  🔁🔁 Messingham DN17...29 D7
West Gr
  🔟 Colsterworth NG33...151 E6
  Kingston upon Hull HU4..179 D4
Westhall Cl 🔟 LN5......92 E1
Westhall Rd 🔟 LN2......68 D7
WEST HALTON DN15.......8 E8
West Hann La DN19......4 C1
Westhaven 🔁 PE9......171 C3
West Haven Way DN40...186 B8
Westhawe PE3..........224 F7
West Hill 🔟 HU13......3 E4
Westhill Rd DN34......191 A5
Westholm 🔁 LN1.......203 E5
Westholme Cl 🔟 DN15....8 A4
Westholme La DN38......21 C5
WESTHORPE PE11.........144 F5
Westhorpe Rd PE11.....144 F5
Westhouses PE22.......112 F5
WEST KEAL PE23........100 C6
Westkirke Ave DN33....191 D1
West La
  Baumber LN9............72 A1
  Girton NG23............78 C1
  Haltham LN9............98 C6
  🔟 Keelby DN41..........23 A4
  Skidbrooke with Saltfleet
  Haven LN11.............51 A2
  🔟 Winterton DN15.......9 B5
Westlaby La LN3........69 E8
Westlake Ave PE7......230 C1
Westland Rd
  Kingston upon Hull
  HU10..................178 B7
  🔟 Westwoodside DN9....27 B2
Westlands Ave
  Grimsby DN34...........191 C5
  🔟 Tetney DN36.........36 D4
Westlands Rd HU5......179 B8
West Lea DN33..........194 F7
West Leys Pk 🔟 HU14....3 B6
West Leys Rd HU14......3 B6
Westlode St PE11......214 D4
WEST MARSH DN31.......188 D1
West Marsh Ind Est
  DN31..................188 F1
West Marsh La
  Barrow upon Humber
  DN19...................4 B1
  Goxhill DN19...........5 A3
West Marsh Rd
  Pinchbeck PE11........145 E1
  Spalding PE11.........214 D6
Westmere Prim Sch
  PE12..................160 E4
West Mid Mere Rd
  DN20..................12 D3
West Mill 🔟 PE9......171 C2
West Mill Gate 🔁 LN3..203 E6
Westminster Way 🔁
  NG31..................210 F5
Westminster Cl DN21...40 D3
Westminster Dr
  Grimsby DN34..........191 C6
  🔟 Hatfield DN7.......14 C2
  🔟 Spalding PE11......214 B1
Westminster Gdns 🔁🔁
  PE6...................175 A1
Westminster La 🔟
  PE10..................213 C5
Westminster Pl PE11...226 F5
Westminster Rd
  🔟 Broughton DN20.....19 D4
  Lincoln LN6...........204 D4
Westmoor La LN1........65 E2
West Moor Rd 🔟 DN10...39 F3
Westmoreland Ave 🔟
  LN1....................67 E5

Westmoreland Cl 🔟
  DN9....................27 A2
Westmoreland Gdns 🔁
  PE1...................226 B2
Westmoreland Rd 🔁
  PE12..................157 F6
Westoby La DN19.........11 C7
WESTON PE12...........157 D7
Weston Gr DN40........186 B5
WESTON HILLS PE12....157 C3
Weston Hills CE Prim Sch
  PE12..................157 D2
Weston Hills Rd PE12..157 B4
Weston Miller Dr 🔟
  PE13..................170 D1
Weston St Mary CE Prim
  Sch PE12..............157 E7
Westonville 🔟 PE9....171 B1
Westover Dr 🔟 DN15....8 A4
West Parade
  Grimsby DN31..........191 C7
  Kingston upon Hull HU3..180 C7
  Lincoln LN1...........234 A3
  Peterborough PE3......225 D3
  Spalding PE11.........214 B4
  Wisbech PE13..........170 C1
West Parklands Dr 🔟
  HU14...................3 A5
Westport Rd 🔟 DN35...193 A1
WEST RASEN LN8.........56 E8
WEST RAVENDALE
  DN37...................35 A2
West Rd
  Billingborough NG34...133 B1
  Bourne PE10...........213 B4
  Deeping St Nicholas
  PE11..................156 D3
  Haconby PE10..........154 C8
  🔁 Keadby with Althorpe
  NG34..................143 A6
  🔁 Ruskington NG34....108 D1
  🔁 Tallington PE9.....172 F7
  Tetford LN9............73 E1
  Thorney NG23...........78 F8
  🔟 Tydd St Mary PE13..170 C8
  West Riverside DN40...186 E8
  West Row 🔁 PE21.....208 E4
  WESTRUM DN20..........196 C1
  Westrum La DN20.......196 D2
Westry Cl
  Barrowby NG32.........210 A3
  🔟 Leverington PE13...170 F1
Westry Cnr NG32.......210 A4
West St Gdns 🔟 PE9...219 A5
West St Mary's Gate 🔁
  DN31..................191 D7
Westside Ave NG31....139 E8
Westside Rd
  Cranwell & Byard's Leap
  NG34..................107 E1
  Grimsby DN31..........188 F2
West Sq DN20..........196 C4
West St
  Alford LN13............75 E2
  Barkston NG32.........119 A1
  Barnetby le Wold DN38..21 B4
  Billinghay LN4........109 F6
  Boston PE21...........208 E4
  Bourne PE10...........213 C5
  Brant Broughton LN5...105 F5
  Cleethorpes DN35......192 F6
  Clipsham LE15..........71 B8
  🔁 Crowland PE6.......166 E1
  Easton on the Hill PE9..171 C3
  Folkingham NG34.......142 C8
  Gainsborough DN21.....197 B8
  Hagworthingham PE23....87 A4
  Helpston PE6..........173 B4
  Hibaldstow DN20........30 F5
  Horncastle LN9........199 A3
  Kingston upon Hull HU1..180 E6
  Long Sutton PE12......216 B4
  🔟 Navenby/Wellingore
  LN5...................107 A7
  North Kelsey LN7.......32 A4
  Osbournby NG34.......132 A4
  🔟 Roxby cum Risby DN15..8 F3
  Scawby DN20............30 E5
  Scunthorpe DN15.......183 A3
  Stamford PE9..........219 A4
  Swaton NG34...........133 C4
  Thorne/Moorends DN8...15 A2
  🔁 Timberland LN4......96 B1
  West/East Butterwick
  DN17...................28 C8
  West Halton DN15........8 E7
  Winterton DN15..........9 A5
WEST STOCKWITH
  DN10...................40 C6
West Stonebridge PE2..230 C5
West Syke La LN1.......66 B7
West Terr DN20........196 B3
West Terr St 🔟 DN17...16 D7
WEST TORRINGTON
  LN8....................58 A1
West Town Prim Sch
  PE3...................225 E3
West View
  🔟 Ancaster NG32......120 A3
  🔟 Bardney LN3.........83 B4
  Messingham DN17........29 C7
  🔟 North Ferriby HU14...3 A4
  Scunthorpe DN17.......184 E3
West View Cl 🔟 DN41...23 A5
West View Cres 🔁🔁
  PE24...................90 D7

Westville Rd PE22......112 B2
WEST WALTON PE14.....170 E4
Westward Cl DN34......191 C5
Westward Ho DN34......191 C5
Westward Row LN4.....207 A5
Westway 🔟 LN12.........68 D2
West Way PE25.........206 D7
West Wells La 🔟 DN10...39 C1
Westwick Dr DN34.....205 A4
Westwick Gdns LN6....205 B6
WEST WILLOUGHBY
  NG32..................119 E2
Westwinds Gdns 🔟
  DN9....................9 A5
Westwold Rd 🔁 LN7....33 B4
Westwood 🔟 DN20......19 D4
WESTWOOD PE3.........225 D4
Westwood Cl PE3......225 C4
Westwood Cl LN6......205 A8
Westwood Dr
  Bourne PE10...........213 B4
  🔟 Kingston upon Hull
  HU4...................179 B6
  Lincoln LN6...........205 A8
Westwood Ind Est PE3..225 D7
Westwood Pk Cl PE3...225 C3
Westwood Pk Rd PE3...225 D2
Westwood Rd 🔟 DN41...23 F5
WESTWOODSIDE DN9......27 A2
Wetherby Cl
  🔟 Bourne PE10........213 C7
  🔟 Market Rasen LN8....57 E7
Wetherby Cres LN6....204 F4
Wetherby Way 🔟 PE1...226 D3
Wetmoor La LN2........56 C1
Weydike Bank PE12....159 A4
Weymouth Ave 🔟 DN35..193 A1
Weymouth Cl 🔟 LN5....205 D3
Weymouth Cres DN17...182 C1
Weymouth Way PE1.....226 D6
Whalebone La NG31....140 B7
Whale Dro
  Holbeach PE12.........168 A1
  Whaplode PE6..........167 E1
Whalley St PE1........226 B3
WHAPLODE PE12.........158 A7
Whaplode CE Prim Sch
  PE12..................158 C2
WHAPLODE DROVE
  PE12..................168 B4
WHAPLODE ST CATHERINE
  PE12..................158 C2
Wharfdale Cl DN16......17 E6
Wharfdale Dr 🔁 LN6...204 F3
Wharfedale Pl 🔟
  DN16..................185 E6
Wharfe La
  Kirkby on Bain LN10....98 C5
  Tattershall LN4.......207 D6
Wharf Rd
  Crowle DN17............16 D7
  Grantham NG31.........211 A4
  🔟 Horncastle LN9.....199 B4
  🔁 Misterton DN10......39 F5
  Stamford PE9..........219 C4
Wharfside Mews 🔟
  NG34..................212 D4
Wharf St 🔁🔟 PE12....160 E4
Wharf The DN36.........37 A5
Wharncliffe Rd DN31..189 C3
Wharncliffe Rd N
  DN31..................189 B3
Wharncliffe St HU5....180 A8
WHARTON DN21..........41 B4
Wharton Rd DN21.......41 A5
Wharton St DN31......191 B7
Whattoff Way PE6.....164 D2
Whatton's Cl NG32....128 F5
Wheatdale PE2.........230 A3
Wheatfield Cl
  🔟 Barnby Dun DN3.....14 A3
  Epworth DN9...........27 F6
  🔟 Kingston upon Hull
  HU4...................179 D2
Wheatfield Dr 🔟
  DN37..................194 C5
Wheatfield Rd LN6....200 C1
Wheatfields 🔟 PE12...158 B7
Wheatfield PE6........164 E2
Wheat Gr 🔟 NG34.....212 F3
Wheatgrass La NG32...119 B7
Wheatholme La NG23...78 D6
Wheatley Bank PE14...170 F1
Wheatley La
  🔟 Carlton-le-Moorland
  LN5...................105 E8
  Collingham NG23.......91 D2
Wheatley Rd DN22......52 A3
Wheatmere Dro PE2....157 B5
Wheatsheaf Ave 🔟
  NG34..................104 A6
Wheatsheaf Cl
  🔟 Holbeach PE12......213 B2
  Sibsey PE22...........113 B2
Wheatsheaf Ct 🔟
  PE11..................166 C6
Wheatsheaf La 🔟
  NG23..................117 D4
Wheeldon St 🔟 PE11...197 D3
Wheeler Cl PE21.......209 A4
Wheeler Prim Sch
  HU3...................179 F5
Wheeler St HU3........179 F5
Wheelwright Cl PE10...154 C6
Wheelwrights Ct NG34..109 B1

Wheel Yd PE1...........226 A4
Whelpton Cl LN9.......199 C2
Whetstone Ct 🔟 PE1...226 E2
Whichcote Rd PE6.....174 C2
Whimbrel Way
  🔟 Long Sutton PE12...216 B4
  New Waltham DN36......195 D2
Whin Moor La HU15......2 A4
Whins Gate DN17........7 A4
Whipchicken Rd PE6...167 B4
WHISBY LN6.............79 E
Whisby Cl DN36........195 E
Whisby Nature Pk*
  LN6....................79 F
Whisby Rd LN6.........204 A
Whisby Way LN6.......204 C
Whiston Cl 🔟 PE4.....221 C
Whiston Way 🔟 DN18....3 F
Whitacre PE1..........226 E
Whitby Dr DN32........192 A
Whitby St HU8.........181 B
Whitcross La 🔁
  PE11..................145 E
Whitcross St 🔁 DN18...10 F
Whitefriargate HU1...180 F
Whitefriars Cl LN2....202 E
Whitefriars Rd LN2....202 F
White Gate LN9.........73 E
Whitegate Hill LN7.....33 C
Whitehall 🔁 PE11.....145 C
Whitehall Cres LN4...205 F
Whitehall Clry Cotts
  DN35..................192 A
Whitehall Gr LN1......204 B
Whitehall Rd 🔟 DN35..193 A
Whitehall Terr 🔟 LN1..234 A
White Hart La 🔟 NG23..91 C
Whitehead Cl 🔟 LN12...64 B
Whitehorse La 🔟 PE21..208 F
White House Cl
  🔁 Hatfield DN7.......14 C
  🔟 Stainforth DN7.....14 C
White House Garth 🔟
  HU14...................3 A
White House La
  Boston PE21...........209 C
  🔟 West Halton DN15....8 E
White House Mews 🔟
  HU14...................3 A
Whitehouse Rd 🔟
  NG34..................108 C
White La
  Harmston LN5...........93 F
  Thorne DN8.............15 A
White Leather Sq
  NG34..................133 C
Whitemoor La NG23......91 C
WHITE PIT LN13..........74 C
Whitepit Way LN13......74 D
Whitepost Rd PE6.....174 F
White Row La LN12......64 C
White's La LN5.........92 E
White's Rd HU3........179 F
White St HU3..........179 F
Whitestone Rd PE7....184 C
White's Wood La
  🔟 Corringham DN21....53 A
  Gainsborough DN21.....197 A
Whitethorn Gr 🔟 LN6..200 D
Whitewater PE2........229 D
Whiteways PE3.........229 C
Whitewell Cl 🔟 DN21...30 6
White Wlk HU10........178 C
Whitfield Rd DN17.....184 C
Whitgift Cl DN37.......23 F
Whitgift Way DN37.....190 D
Whiting Sq PE21.......208 F
Whitley Cl 🔟 LN6......200 A
Whitley St 🔟 LN1......67 E
Whitsay PE6...........157 D
Whitman Cl 🔟 PE9.....172 C
Whitman Rd PE7.......184 C
Whitsed Rd 🔟 PE6.....174 E
Whitsed St PE1........226 B
Whittington NG34.....114 E
Whittle Cl 🔁 PE21....208 F
Whittlesey Rd
  Peterborough PE2......231 E
  Thorney PE6...........175 F
WHITTON DN15............1 D
Whitton Rd
  Alkborough DN15.........1 D
  Whitton DN15............1 E
Whitwell PE4..........221 B
Whitworth Way 🔁 LN6...57 D
Whyalla Cl 🔟 LN11....199 C
Whyche The LN4.......109 E
WICKENBY LN3...........57 F
Wickenby Airport LN3...69 F
Wickenby Cl
  🔟 Grimsby DN34.......190 F
  Lincoln LN6...........205 A
Wickenby Cres LN1....201 E
Wickenby Rd LN3.......57 D
Wicken La PE22.......113 F

Vicken Way PE3....... 225 C6
Vickham Rd DN31...... 189 C2
Vicke Bargate 8 PE21..208 F5
Vidford Gn 8 DN7 ....14 D3
Vidow Fen La LN13......76 C3
Vigeon Cl 14 PE12.....167 B8
Vigford LN5............ 234 A1
Vigford Way LN5 ...... 234 A2
Viga La PE24...........90 C8
Vigmore Dr PE7........231 F5
Vignall's Gate PE12 ... 215 A2
VIGSLEY NG23 ....78 F5
Vigsley Cl 7 LN6 ...... 204 D6
Vigsley Rd
  6 Birchwood LN6....... 204 D6
  Harby NG23.............79 B5
  North Scarle LN6........78 E3
VIGTOFT PE20...........135 D5
Vigtoft Bank PE20..... 135 D1
Vigtoft Rd PE20....... 135 F2
Vike Gate Cl 4 DN8......15 B7
Vike Gate Gr 2 DN8.....15 B7
Vike Gate Rd DN8.......15 B8
VIKE WELL END DN8 ......15 B7
Vilberforce Dr 8 HU1...180 F7
Willoughby House*
  HU1................... 181 A6
Vilberforce Rd HU1.....225 E7
Vilberforce St HU3.....180 D6
Vildfowlers Way PE12 ..148 F4
Vidlake PE2.............230 C5
Vildmore Cl LN4 .... 111 C6
Vildmore Cres PE22....114 F6
Vildshed La PE24.......102 D7
VILDSWORTH DN21........40 E8
Vilies Ave 8 PE12.......157 E1
Viles's La PE20.........135 B4
Vilford Gr PE25 .... 206 C1
Vilfred Ave NG24.......104 B2
Vilkie Cl DN15 .... 182 C3
Vilkie Dr NG34......... 142 C8
Vilkinson Dr 9 LN8......57 B8
Vilkinson Rd 7 NG32 .. 117 E1
VILKSBY PE22.............99 A5
Villan Cl PE2...........230 F8
Villders Garth PE12 .. 215 F2
Villerby Rd HU5........179 C8
Villerton Rd 8 LN11.....50 F7
Villesby Rd PE11....... 214 E5
Villesden Ave PE4..... 225 D8
Villey's La PE24 ....90 B8
Villiam Alvey CE Sch
  NG34..................212 C5
Villiam Barcroft Jun Sch
  DN32..................192 C7
Villiam Farr CE Comp Sch
  LN2....................68 D6
Villiam Gn Cl 9 LN12 ..76 F8
Villiam Harrison Sch
  DN21..................197 E2
Villiam Hildyard CE
  (Aided) Prim Sch
  PE6...................217 B5
Villiam Law CE Prim Sch
  PE4...................220 F5
Villiam Lovell CE Sch
  PE22..................113 A7
Villiams Cl 1 PE6......174 E5
Villiams Dr DN39........12 B1
Villiamson Ave PE3....225 E3
Villiamson's Dro LN4...110 A7
Villiam St
  Kingston upon Hull
    HU9.................181 C7
  Lincoln LN2...........234 B4
Villiam Stukeley CE Prim
  Sch PE12..............215 D2
Villiam Tow Cl 7 LN12..76 F8
Villiam Way PE25 ......206 B3
Villiam Wright Dock
  HU3...................180 C3
Villingham Ave 2......201 F8
Kingston upon Hull
VILLINGHAM BY STOW
  DN21...................53 F3
Villingham Hill LN8....58 E7
Villingham La LN8......57 F6
Villingham Rd
  East Barkwith LN8.....58 E1
  Fillingham DN21.......54 D4
  Lea DN21..............53 A5
  Market Rasen LN8......57 E7
  Marton DN21...........53 B1
  Tealby LN8............71 B2
Villingham St DN32....191 E6
Villington Rd PE20 ....136 A7
Villing Way DN32......191 F8
Villis Cl LN1...........234 A4
Villis Terr LN1.........234 A4
Villonholt PE3..........225 C7
Willoughby Meadow Nature
  Reserve* LN13.........89 B6
VILLOUGHBY LN13........89 B7
Villoughby Ave 2
  PE6...................217 C5
Willoughby Branch Line
  Nature Reserve*
  LN13..................89 A7
Villoughby Chase
  DN21..................197 E1
Villoughby Cl
  Corby Glen NG33......152 F7

Willoughby Cl continued
  Helpringham NG34......133 E7
  Silk Willoughby NG34 ..121 B1
Villoughby Ct PE1......226 E8
Villoughby Dr 1 PE3.....88 A1
Willoughby Gall The*
  NG33..................152 F8
Villoughby Gr 5
  DN34..................190 F4
WILLOUGHBY HILLS
  PE21..................209 E7
Villoughby La
  Authorpe LN11.........74 F8
  Muckton LN11..........62 C1
  Waddington LN5.......205 C1
Willoughby Meadow
  Nature Reserve*
  LN13...................89 B6
Willoughby Mem Trust
  Gall* NG33............152 F7
WILLOUGHBY MOOR
  NG32..................119 F2
Villoughby Rd
  16 Alford LN13.........75 F2
  Ancaster NG32.........119 E2
  Aunsby & Dembleby
    NG34................132 B4
  Boston PE21...........209 A7
  Bourne PE10...........213 E4
  Cumberworth LN13.....89 E8
  14 Hibaldstow DN20....31 A5
  7 Mablethorpe/Sutton on Sea
    LN12.................64 C1
  Scunthorpe DN17......184 E5
  Sleaford NG34.........120 F3
  Stamford PE9..........219 C7
Villoughby Sch PE10 ..213 D3
Villoughby St 1
  DN21..................197 D3
WILLOUGHTON DN21.......42 D4
Willoughton Prim Sch
  DN21...................42 D4
Villoughton Rd 3
  PE25..................206 D2
Villow Ave
  4 Misterton DN10......39 F5
  Peterborough PE1......226 E3
Villowbrook Dr DN20...196 E3
Villow Cl
  12 Barnetby DN38......21 B4
  Gainsborough DN21....197 B8
  10 Heckington NG34...122 E3
  Horncastle LN9........199 A5
  1 Saxilby LN1..........66 D2
  Scopwick LN4..........95 D1
  Skellingthorpe LN6....200 B3
Villow Ct
  3 Bracebridge Heath
    LN4..................81 A1
  Heighington/Washingborough
    LN4.................203 C2
  4 Sleaford NG34.......212 A3
Villow Dr
  14 Barton-upon-Humber
    DN18..................3 F1
  8 Bourne PE10.........213 C4
  27 Brough HU15.........2 C5
  2 Coningsby LN4......207 D4
  Kingston upon Hull
    HU10.................178 D8
    Louth LN11...........198 C8
    33 Messingham DN17...29 D7
Villow Dro PE6.........174 E6
Villowfield Ave 12 LN2..68 D2
Villow Gdns 2 DN19.....11 D8
Villow Gr
  1 Keadby with Althorpe
    DN17..................17 D6
  7 Scawby DN20.........30 F8
  Scunthorpe DN16......185 C7
Villow Hall La PE6.....227 D6
Villow Holt PE7........230 C3
Villow La
  Billinghay LN4........109 E6
  3 Cranwell NG34.......120 F8
  Dunston LN4...........95 C6
  32 Goxhill DN19.........5 A1
  Grantham NG31........210 F2
  Ruskington LN4........109 B3
Villowmead Cl DN15....182 E8
Villow Pk DN37.........194 B4
Villow Rd
  Lincoln LN6...........204 F2
  Stamford PE9..........218 D2
Villow Row PE11........214 E5
Villow Row Bank LN11...62 F6
Villows Cl PE13........160 A3
Villows Ct LN4.........207 A4
Villows La PE22........125 F7
Willows Prim Sch
  DN37..................190 D8
Villows The
  6 Cranwell NG34......107 F1
  8 Crowland PE6........166 E1
  Grimoldby LN11........62 F3
  Kingston upon Hull
    HU13.................178 E4
Villow Tree Cl DN40...186 C4
Villow Tree Gdns LN6..204 C8
Villow Wlk PE11........214 E5
Will Row LN12...........63 C5
WILL ROW LN12..........63 C5
Wilmington Dr 18 LN12..77 A8
WILSFORD NG32.........120 C1
Wilsford La NG32.......120 A3
Wilson Cl
  Ingoldmells PE25......90 D3

Wilson Cl continued
  8 North Ferriby HU14....3 A4
Wilson Ct LE15.........162 A8
Wilsons Cl DN15........183 B3
Wilson St
  Cleethorpes DN35......192 D8
  Gainsborough DN21....197 B7
  4 Kingston upon Hull
    HU9.................181 B7
  Kingston upon Hull
    HU10.................178 E6
  Lincoln LN1...........234 A4
WILSTHORPE PE9.........164 C4
Wilton Ave PE24........90 D7
Wilton Cl PE3..........225 C4
Wilton Ct PE3..........225 C4
Wilton Rd DN36.........192 D1
Wilton Rd Ind Est
  DN36..................195 F8
Wilton Road Ind Est
  DN36..................192 D1
Wilton St HU8..........181 B8
Wiltshire Ave HU4......8 B4
Wiltshire Rd HU4......179 E2
Wilyman Cl 21 LN12.....77 A7
Wimberley Cl 3 PE12...157 D7
Wimberley Way
  5 Pinchbeck PE11......156 E8
  3 South Witham NG33..151 D2
Wimbisthorpe Cl 3
  NG13..................128 A6
Wimborn Ave DN34......191 B6
Wimborne Dr 7 PE21....226 F2
WINCEBY PE23...........86 E3
Winceby Ave DN31......191 B8
Winceby Gdns LN9......199 D4
Winchcombe Ave
  DN34..................190 E4
Winchelsea Rd The
  NG34..................108 D1
Winchelsea Rd 14
  LN4...................108 C1
Winchester Ave DN31...191 A3
Winchester Cl 3 LN4....81 A2
Winchester Cl 9 LN6...193 B8
Winchester Dr
  Bottesford DN16......185 C3
  Heighington/Washingborough
    LN4.................203 C1
  6 Mablethorpe/Sutton on Sea
    LN12.................64 A3
Winchester Rd
  Grantham NG31........210 E4
  4 Hatfield DN7.........14 D4
  14 Wainfleet All Saints
    PE24................102 D2
Winchester Way
  Peterborough PE3......225 C4
  Sleaford NG34.........212 C7
Wincolmlee HU2.........181 A7
Windass Cl HU13........178 E1
Windermere Ave
  4 Grimsby DN33........194 E7
  Lincoln LN6...........205 A2
Windermere Cres
  DN36..................192 E1
Windermere Rd LN2.....202 D8
Windermere Way PE4...221 C3
Windgate Way PE8......222 A6
Windlass Cl 16 DN6.....15 A8
Windsbaen Ave DN34...194 D7
Windle Dr PE10.........213 E2
Windmill Cl
  Holbeach PE12.........215 B2
  4 Waddington DN7......93 F6
Windmill Dr
  Burgh le Marsh PE24...102 D8
  13 Heckington NG34...122 E3
Windmill Gdns 3
  PE13..................170 E2
Windmill La
  5 Alford LN13..........75 F2
  Gosberton PE11........144 F6
Windmill St PE1........225 F5
Windmill View 3 LN1...234 A4
Windmill Way LN4......178 F1
Windrush Dr PE4.......221 D1
Windsmoor Rd 18 LN4...47 B6
Windsor Ave
  Holbeach PE12.........215 E2
  Kingston upon Hull
    HU10.................178 D7
  2 Peterborough PE4....225 C8
Windsor Bank PE21.....209 A3
Windsor Cl
  Collingham NG23.......91 D4
  5 Keelby DN41.........212 B2
  4 Stamford PE9........219 B7
  6 Sudbrooke LN2.......68 C2
Windsor Cres
  Boston PE21...........209 A4
  1 Crowle DN17.........16 C7
  4 Ingoldmells PE25....90 D3
  Scunthorpe DN17......184 F7
Windsor Ct
  7 Grimsby DN31.......189 C1
  12 Hatfield DN7........14 C2
Windsor Dr
  19 Caistor LN7.........33 B4
  Grantham NG31........211 E5
  Peterborough PE7......231 D6
  Spalding PE11.........214 D2
  Wisbech PE13.........170 D2
Windsor Gdns PE12.....216 D5
Windsor Gr 1 DN19......5 A1
Windsor La LN11........16 C7
Windsor Mews LN11....198 C5

Windsor Pk Cl 5 LN6...204 F1
Windsor Rd
  Cleethorpes DN35......192 C5
  Crowle DN17...........16 C7
  Lincoln LN6...........198 B8
  Yaxley PE7............233 F6
Windsor Terr 11 PE21..209 A5
Windsor Way
  Barnetby le Wold DN38...21 B5
  Broughton DN20........19 E4
Wine Hill La LN11.......51 B5
Winfrey Ave PE11.......214 D4
Wingate Parade DN37...190 E8
Wingate Rd DN37.......190 D8
Wingate Way PE10......213 E7
Wingfield PE2...........229 F3
Winn Cl DN35...........192 E5
Winniffe Gdns LN2......202 D7
Winn La 4 LN9..........86 B8
Winnowsty La LN2......234 C3
Winn St
  Lincoln LN2...........234 C2
  2 Scunthorpe DN16....183 B2
Winship Cl 4 HU3.......180 C5
Winslow Dr DN40.......186 B5
Winslow Gate PE12.....159 B8
Winslow Gr 2 DN34.....190 F4
Winslow Rd
  Boston PE21...........214 B3
  Winston Ave DN34.....191 B6
  Winston Dr PE25.......206 B6
  Winston Gdns PE21....209 A7
  Winston Rd PE23......100 F8
Winston Way
  5 Brigg DN20..........196 C4
  Farcet PE7............231 C2
Winterbeck Cl 5
  NG13..................128 A6
Wintergold Ave PE11...214 A5
Winteringham Foreshore
  Nature Reserve* DN15....2 A1
Winteringham La DN15....8 E8
Winteringham Prim Sch
  DN15...................9 B6
Winteringham Rd DN15....9 B6
Winter's La 7 DN21.....197 D2
Winter's La
  4 Long Bennington
    NG23................117 D9
  Stamford PE12.........160 A3
WINTERTON DN15.........9 A5
Winterton Cl 41 DN15....9 A5
Winterton Comp Sch
  DN15...................9 A6
Winterton Cty Jun Sch
  DN15...................9 A6
Winterton Rd
  Roxby cum Risby DN15....8 F2
  Scunthorpe DN15......183 B4
  Winteringham DN15.....9 B8
WINTHORPE
  Langford NG23.........104 B8
  Skegness PE25.........206 C8
Winthorpe Ave PE25....206 B8
Winthorpe Cl 17 LN6...204 D7
Winthorpe Gr 17 LN6...204 D7
Winthorpe Prim Sch
  NG23..................104 C8
Winthorpe Rd
  Birchwood LN6........204 D7
  Grimsby DN33.........191 B3
  4 Kingston upon Hull
    HU13.................179 A3
  8 Newark NG24.........104 B7
Winthorpe Way
  Ingoldmells PE25......206 D8
  Skegness PE25.........90 E1
Winton Rd 11 LN5.......107 A8
Wintringham 28 PE25...2 C6
Wintringham Rd DN32..191 E6
Wintringham Sch
  DN32..................191 E4
Winwick Pl PE3.........225 C5
Winyates PE2...........229 F3
Winyards Prim Sch
  PE2...................230 A3
Wire Hill La LN8........70 E5
Wirral Ave 7 DN34.....190 F4
WISBECH PE13...........170 B1
Wisbech Rd
  Long Sutton PE12......216 E1
  Thorney PE6............176 E6
  Walpole PE14.........161 C1
  Walsoken PE14........170 E2
  Wisbech St Mary PE13..177 A2
Wiseholme Rd LN6......200 B2
Wiseman's Gate 1
  PE12..................157 D7
Wiske Ave 7 HU15......2 B6
WISPINGTON LN9.........84 E6
Wisteria Rd PE13.......170 E1
Wisteria Ave LN6.......81 D2
Wisteria Dr DN41.......23 F5
Wisteria Rd PE7........233 D4
Wisteria Way
  Bourne PE10...........213 B7
  Scunthorpe DN16......185 E4
  Wisbech PE14.........221 B3
Wistow Gr HU4.........179 D5
Wistow Rd LN4..........81 C8
Witchford Cl 2 LN6....204 B6
Witchford Rd LN6......204 B6
Witham HU9.............181 B7

Witham Bank
  Dogdyke LN4...........110 D8
  Timberland LN10........97 C3
Witham Bank E 4
  PE21..................208 E6
Witham Bank W PE21...208 E6
Withambrook Pk NG31...211 F7
Witham Cl
  Lincoln LN6...........205 D5
  11 Ruskington LN4.....108 D2
  Stamford PE9..........219 C6
Witham Ct
  2 Boston PE21.........208 E6
  Lincoln LN6...........201 D1
Witham Dr 6 DN15.......8 B5
Witham Gdns PE21......208 E6
Witham Gn PE21........208 E6
Witham Hall Prep Sch
  PE10..................163 D7
Witham/Haven Mouth
  Nature Reserve*
  PE22..................137 F6
WITHAM ON THE HILL
  PE10..................163 D7
Witham Pl
  Boston PE21...........208 E5
  Grantham NG31........211 C2
Witham Rd
  Gunby & Stainby NG33..151 C4
  5 Long Bennington
    NG23................117 D4
  Thistleton LE15.......151 C1
  Woodhall Spa LN10.....97 B5
WITHAM ST HUGHS
  LN6....................92 D5
Witham St Hughs Prim Sch
  LN6....................92 D5
Witham St 3 PE21......208 F6
Witham Town PE21......208 E6
Witham View LN4........93 A3
Witham Way
  Peterborough PE4......221 D1
  Westborough NG23.....117 F3
WITHCALL LN11..........60 C2
WITHERN LN13...........63 A1
Withern Rd DN33.......191 A3
Withington St 1 PE12..160 E4
WITTERING PE8..........172 B1
Wittering Airfield PE8..171 F1
Wittering Cl 5 LN6.....204 D6
Wittering Prim Sch
  PE8...................172 B1
Wittering Rd 9 PE9.....172 D3
Witty St HU3...........180 A3
Wivell Dr 1 DN41.......23 A5
Woad Farm Rd PE21....209 B4
Woad La
  Fishtoft PE22..........137 C7
  Grimsby DN31.........188 A2
  Long Sutton PE12......216 E5
Woburn Ave LN1........201 E6
Woburn Cl
  Louth LN11............198 B7
  4 Market Deeping PE6..217 A5
  Peterborough PE3......225 A1
Woburn Dr
  Grantham NG31........211 F5
  Thorney PE6...........176 A2
Woburn Gr 1 LN10......97 C5
Woburn St HU3.........179 F4
Wolfindin Cl 8 NG31...129 E5
Woldcarr Rd HU3.......179 F4
WOLD NEWTON LN8......47 F7
Wold Rd
  Barrow upon Humber
    DN19.................11 D7
  Kingston upon Hull HU5..179 C8
  Wootton DN39...........11 C2
  Worlaby DN20...........10 E1
Wolds Cl 8 DN17........16 D7
Wolds Leisure-De Aston
  Sports Ctr LN8.........57 E7
Wolds The DN21.........43 D6
Wold View
  1 Brigg DN20..........196 D4
  2 Brough HU15..........2 C6
  Caistor LN7............49 A2
  Fotherby LN11..........49 E6
  Holton le Clay DN36...195 C3
  3 Nettleton LN7........33 B2
  Rothwell LN7...........33 F2
Wolf La PE13...........178 F1
Wolfreton Ct HU10.....178 B8
Wolfreton Garth HU10..178 B8
Wolfreton La HU10.....178 B8
Wolfreton Mews HU10..178 F7
Wolfreton Rd HU10....178 F7
Wolfreton Villas HU10..178 F7
Wolla Bank Nature
  Reserve* PE24.........77 D1
Wollaston Rd
  Cleethorpes DN35......192 E6
  Peterborough PE3......225 C6
Wolseley Cl PE7........233 D6
Wolsey Dr 6 DN19.......11 C7
Wolsey Rd NG24........104 A6
Wolsey Way LN2........202 D8
Womersley Rd DN31....188 C1
Wong Gdns NG32.......210 A4
Wong Row 10 NG32.....211 A5
Wong The LN9..........199 B3
Woodale Cl 2 DN15....182 C6

Woodapple Ct 4 DN41....23 E6
Woodbank
1 Deeping St Nicholas
PE11..............166 C6
Skellingthorpe LN6......200 A5
Woodbine Ave DN20 .... 196 C4
Woodbine Contemporary Arts* PE12............168 A3
Woodbine St PE2........231 A8
Woodbridge Rd NG34....212 E6
Woodbridge Rd Ind Est
NG34................272 E6
Woodbridge Way 19
LN10.................97 C5
Woodburn Cl LN1........201 E8
Woodburn View 13
LN1..................201 E8
Woodbyth Rd PE1.......226 A6
Wood Carr La DN9........16 C2
Wood Cl DN33...........194 F7
Woodclose Rd DN17.....184 D6
Woodcock La LN1........200 C8
Woodcock St HU3........180 A4
Woodcote Cl PE1........226 A7
Woodcroft Cl 9 PE6....217 A5
Woodcroft Rd
Marholm PE6...........220 A3
4 Saxilby LN1...........66 C2
Wood Dr 4 HU14..........3 A4
Wooden Beck Hill DN10...39 E2
Wood End NG33.........131 A1
WOOD ENDERBY PE22.....98 F6
Woodfield 7 PE9........171 B1
Woodfield Ave LN6......200 C1
Woodfield Cl
1 Birchwood LN6.......200 C1
16 Humberston DN36....36 D8
Spalding PE1...........214 F2
Woodfield La HU13......178 C1
Woodfield Rd
Gainsborough DN21.....197 F5
Peterborough PE2.......225 D3
Woodgarr Ave 4 DN17...17 D6
Woodgate PE6...........173 C4
Woodgate La
Beckingham LN5........105 C4
Kingston upon Hull HU5...179 F8
Maxey PE6.............217 A1
Woodgate Rd
Kingston upon Hull
HU5.................179 F7
Leverington PE13.......170 A2
7 Moulton PE12........157 E1
Woodgates Cl 18 HU14....3 A5
Woodgates La HU14.......3 A6
Woodgates Mount 3
HU14..................3 A5
Woodhall Cl PE11......208 C5
Woodhall Cres 9 LN1....66 C2
Woodhall Dr
Lincoln LN2............201 F8
Waltham DN37..........194 C4
Woodhall Rd
Horncastle LN9.........199 A3
Roughton LN9...........85 C3
Woodhall Rise PE4......220 F6
WOODHALL SPA LN10......97 E5
Woodhall Spa Cottage Mus* LN10.............97 D6
Woodhead Cl 4 PE9.....219 D7
Woodhill Ave DN21......197 E6
Woodhill Cl 2 HU10....178 E7
Wood Hill Rd DN33......29 B3
Woodhill Rise HU13.....178 C2
WOODHOUSE DN9..........16 E3
Woodhouse Gn Rd DN7...14 B8
Woodhouse La
2 Belton DN9...........16 C3
Hatfield DN7............14 D2
Holbeach PE12.........159 A8
Moulton PE12..........146 E1
Woodhouse Rd DN16.....185 E8
Woodhouse St HU9......181 D7
Woodhurst Rd PE21.....231 D6
Wood La
Bardney LN3............83 B4
Beckingham DN10........52 A8
Croxton Kerrial NG32...138 A6
Gringley on the Hill DN10..39 C2
1 Lincoln LN6..........19 A2
Lincoln LN6............204 A1
Little Cawthorpe LN11...61 F2
Louth LN11.............198 D4
Moulton PE12..........158 A7
Norton Disney LN6.......92 B3
Quadring PE11..........135 C1
South Kyme LN4........109 F1
South Kyme LN4........123 B8
South Scarle NG23......91 F7
Sturton le Steeple DN22..52 A3

Thurlby PE10...........213 C1
Woodland Ave
1 Bourne PE10.........213 B5
22 Brough HU15..........2 C6
18 Crowle DN17.........16 D8
Gainsborough DN21.....197 B7
Skellingthorpe LN6.....200 B2
Woodland Dr
8 Broughton DN20.......19 D4
1 Elsham DN20..........20 F7
Grantham NG31.........211 F7
Kingston upon Hull
HU10.................178 C6
6 Woodhall Spa LN10....97 E6
Woodland End HU4......179 C5
Woodland Lea 2 PE6....173 B4
Woodland Rise LN11....198 A6
Woodlands
Langford NG24..........104 B8
Long Sutton PE12......216 D4
5 Louth LN11..........198 C6
Woodlands Ave
Immingham DN40........186 C5
18 Keelby DN41..........23 A4
6 Spilsby PE23..........87 D7
Woodlands Cl 5 DN19...11 C7
Woodlands Dr
1 Colsterworth NG33...151 E7
Grantham NG31.........211 C4
Woodlands La 14 HU15....2 C6
Woodlands Prim Sch
DN33..................191 A2
Woodlands Rd HU5......179 B7
Woodlands Rise HU14....3 A5
Woodlands The
3 Market Deeping
PE6.................217 B5
Peterborough PE1......226 E5
1 Stallingborough DN41..23 D6
Woodland View
2 Barnetby le Wold
DN38................21 B4
Lincoln LN2...........234 C3
Scunthorpe DN15......182 C3
Woodland Way 18 DN9...27 E6
Woodland Wlk 3
DN35.................192 E1
Woodman's Ct 4 PE22...98 F4
Woodmill Bank PE12....159 F2
WOODNOOK NG33........140 C7
Woodpecker Cl LN6.....200 A3
Woodpecker Ct PE4.....221 E2
Woodpecker Way PE21...42 E8
Wood Rd 24 LN13........75 F2
Woodrow Pk DN19.......191 D1
Woodrush Rd 6 LN2....202 C8
Woods Cl 14 NG23......117 D3
Woodside
Boston PE21...........208 E1
Branston & Mere LN4....81 D2
Kingston upon Hull
HU13.................178 D1
WOODSIDE DN9...........26 D6
Woodside Ave NG34.....212 D6
Woodside Cl 1 DN16....164 C8
Woodside Ct DN34......212 D7
Woodside E PE10.......164 D8
Woodside Falconry & Conservation Ctr*
LN3...................69 D3
Woodside La DN9........26 D6
Woodside Rd PE20......136 B5
Woods La 2 DN40........12 F2
Wood's La
Kingston upon Hull
HU1.................180 E5
3 Pinchbeck PE11......145 D2
Woodsley Ave DN35.....192 E5
Woods Mdw 1 DN20......36 F6
Wood St 3 DN32........191 F8
Woods Terr DN21........197 C7
Woodstock Rd DN16.....183 D1
Woodstock St 4 LN1....201 D4
WOODSTON PE2..........230 E6
Woodston Ind Est PE2...230 E6
Woodston Prim Sch
PE2...................230 E7
WOODTHORPE LN13.......77 D7
Woodthorpe Ave PE21...209 C4
Woodvale Cl 4 LN6.....204 C6
Woodvale Cl 14 LN6.....204 C6
Wood View
Bourne PE10...........213 C5
1 Messingham DN17......29 D7
3 Swanland HU14.........3 B7
Woodville Gdns E 3
PE21.................208 D3
Woodville Gdns W 2
PE21.................208 D3
Woodville Rd PE21.....208 D4
Woodward's La
Little Sutton PE12.....160 B3
Long Sutton PE12......216 F1

Wood Way LN11.........198 E5
Woodyard The 4
DN21.................119 B7
Woolcott Ct 2 PE13....170 A1
Woolfellhill Rd PE6....174 F1
Woolgard PE3...........225 A3
Woolley's La
Castle Bytham NG33....152 A4
North Witham NG33.....151 F4
Woollin Ave DN17......185 A6
Woolram Wygate PE11...214 C5
WOOLSTHORPE BY BELVOIR NG32..........128 D1
WOOLSTHORPE-BY-COLSTERWORTH
NG33..................151 D7
Woolsthorpe La
Belvoir NG32..........138 D7
Bottesford NG13.......128 C4
Woolsthorpe Manor*
NG33..................151 D7
Woolsthorpe Rd 3
NG33..................151 D7
Woolwich Dr 2 HU4....179 B2
WOOTTON DN39...........11 F3
Wootton Ave PE2.......231 A6
Wootton Ct DN17.......184 C8
Wootton Dr PE2........230 F6
Wootton Rd
Grantham NG31.........191 A3
Wootton DN39...........11 F2
Wootton St Andrews CE Prim Sch DN39..........11 E3
Worcester Ave DN34....191 A4
Worcester Cl
1 Birchwood LN6.......204 D7
7 Bracebridge Heath
LN4..................81 A2
6 Louth LN11..........198 C5
Scunthorpe DN16.......185 A2
Worcester Cres 4
PE9...................219 B6
Worcester Rd
Grantham NG31.........210 D4
4 Wisbech PE13........170 D1
Wordsworth Cl
6 Grantham NG31......211 E6
Peterborough PE4......225 E8
Wordsworth Ct
5 Grimsby DN32........189 C1
13 Sleaford NG34......212 F4
Wordsworth Gr PE10....213 D3
Wordsworth Rd
North Greetwell LN3...203 C6
Scunthorpe DN17......184 D6
Wordsworth St 6 LN2...234 B3
Workhouse La
Algarkirk PE20.........136 B1
Hogsthorpe PE24........90 C7
Workington Ave 8
HU4..................179 B6
WORLABY
Maidenwell LN11........74 A4
Worlaby DN20...........20 D8
Worlaby Prim Sch
DN20.................20 D8
Worlaby Rd DN33.......191 B1
World's End Rd PE13...160 A1
Worldwide Way DN41...187 C2
Wormgate PE11.........208 F5
Worship St HU2........180 F7
Worsley PE2...........230 A4
Worsley Cl
1 Holton le Clay
DN36.................195 C2
Immingham DN40.......186 D4
Worsley Rd DN40.......186 D4
Worthington La NG32...128 D1
Wortley's La PE21......208 A2
Wortley St DN16.......183 A2
WORTHORPE PE9.........219 B2
Wothorpe Mews 3
PE9.................219 B4
Wothorpe Rd PE9......219 B4
WRAGBY LN8.............70 E5
Wragby Prim Sch LN8....70 D5
Wragby Rd
Bardney LN3............83 C4
Holton cum Beckering
LN8...................70 C7
Lincoln LN2...........234 C3
Lissington LN3..........57 E2
Reepham LN3............68 F1
Scunthorpe DN17.......184 D5
Wragby Rd E
Greetwell LN2.........203 A8
Reepham LN3............68 E1
Wragby St 3 DN32......191 F7
WRAGHOLME LN11.........50 A8
Wragholme La LN11......50 A8
Wragholme Rd LN11.....50 A8
WRANGLE PE22..........114 C1
Wrangle Bank PE22.....114 B4

WRANGLE BANK PE22....114 C4
WRANGLE LOWGATE
PE22.................114 D2
WRANGLE LOW GROUND
PE22.................114 D4
Wrangle Prim Sch
PE22.................114 D2
WRAWBY DN20............20 E4
Wrawby CE Prim Sch
DN20.................20 E4
Wrawby Rd
Brigg DN20............196 D4
Scunthorpe DN17......184 E5
Wrawby St DN20........196 C3
Wray Cl 9 DN37........194 C5
Wray St DN21..........30 B1
Wren Cl
Deeping St Nicholas
PE11.................166 B6
1 Healing DN41.........23 F5
15 Market Deeping PE6..217 C5
Scunthorpe DN16......185 B2
4 Sleaford NG34......212 B3
Wren Cres DN33........191 B2
WRESSLE DN20...........19 F4
Wressle Rd DN20........19 E3
Wright Ave PE2........231 D5
Wright's Dro PE6......175 B7
Wrights Gdns DN10......40 A3
Wrights La 5 LE14.....150 C1
Wright's La
Friskney PE22.........115 A5
Sutton Bridge PE12....160 E4
Wright St HU2..........180 E7
Wrightsway LN2........202 D5
WROOT DN9.............26 C6
Wroot Rd DN9...........26 A3
Wroot Travis Charity Prim Sch DN9..............26 D5
Wroxall Dr NG31.......210 E4
Wroxham Ave DN34.....190 E5
Wroxham Cl 7 LN6.....205 A2
Wrygarth Ave 7 HU15....2 C5
Wulfram Dr NG31.......211 E2
Wulfric Sq PE3.........225 C8
Wulfric Way 4 DN20....19 D3
Wyatt Cl LN4...........96 B2
Wyatt Rd LN5..........205 D4
Wybeck Rd DN15.......183 A6
Wybers Way DN37.......190 D7
WYBERS WOOD DN37.....190 C6
Wybers Wood Jun & Inf Sch DN37..............190 C8
Wybert Cl PE21........136 D8
Wybert La PE21........136 D8
WYBERTON PE21.........136 D8
Wyberton Low Rd 1
PE21.................208 F2
Wyberton Prim Sch
PE21.................136 E7
Wyberton Roads PE20...137 A7
Wyberton W Rd PE21...208 C2
Wyche Ave 6 DN16.....166 F1
Wycliffe Gr PE4.......225 F8
Wydham Pk PE2.........229 D6
Wye Pl PE4............222 C1
Wygate Mdws PE11.....214 B5
Wygate Pk PE11........214 C5
Wygate Rd PE11........214 B4
Wyggeston Ave 22
NG13.................128 A6
Wyggeston Rd 21
NG13.................128 A5
WYKEHAM PE12..........145 F1
Wykeham La
Burgh on Bain LN8......59 C5
Weston PE12...........145 A2
Wykes La PE11.........135 A2
Wykes Rd
Donington PE11........135 B1
Yaxley PE7............233 D4
Wyke St HU9...........181 D7
Wyke The 8 PE11.......214 A3
Wylson Cl 5 NG34.....120 F8
Wyman Way PE2........229 F5
Wymark View DN33.....191 A4
Wymersley Rd HU5......179 A8
WYMONDHAM LE14.......150 C1
Wyndham La LN11......211 C5
Wyndham Rd 8
DN36.................195 C6
Wyndham St HU3.......180 C7
Wynmoor Rd DN17......184 F7
Wyredale Rd DN16......185 D5
Wythes La PE21........126 C2
Wyton Cl 8 LN6.......204 B6
WYVILLE NG32..........139 C4
Wyville Rd
Grantham NG31.........210 E1
Little Ponton & Stroxton
NG31.................139 E8
Wyville Wlk LN6.......204 F7

Y

YADDLETHORPE DN17.....184 E3
Yale Cl LN4...........203 D3
YARBOROUGH DN34......191 A2
Yarborough Cl 3
DN36.................195 C2
Yarborough Cres
1 Broughton DN20......19 E6
Lincoln LN1...........201 E6
Yarborough Ct DN15....182 B2
Yarborough Dr 3
DN31.................191 D8
Yarborough Leisure Ctr
LN1..................201 F6
Yarborough Prim Sch
DN34.................190 F1
Yarborough Rd
Boston PE21...........136 E6
Brigg DN20............196 D3
Grimsby DN34.........190 F6
Keelby DN41............23 A5
1 Lincoln LN1.........234 A4
Scunthorpe DN16.......19 A4
9 Skegness PE25.......206 A4
Yarborough Terr LN1...201 C4
YARBURGH LN11.........49 E6
Yarburgh La LN11.......49 E6
Yarde The 2 PE10......213 C2
Yardley Way 2 DN34...190 D6
Yarmouth Ave
Grantham NG31.........210 D4
3 Kingston upon Hull
HU4.................179 A3
Yarra Rd DN35.........192 F6
Yarrow Rd DN34........190 F2
Yarwell Cl PE2........230 D2
Yarwell Rd PE8........222 A3
Yawling Gate Rd PE22..114 F7
YAWTHORPE DN21.........42 A2
Yaxley Ave PE7........233 E6
Yaxley Jun Sch PE7....233 E5
Yew Tree Ave DN20.....19 B5
Yews La 83 DN40........23 E
Yew Tree Cl 1 PE10....213 C4
Yewtree Dr HU5........179 B
Yew Tree Gr 1 PE21....209 C
Yew Tree Way 1
NG24.................104 C
Yew Tree Wlk PE3......225 A
York Ave
Lincoln LN1...........201 D
Scunthorpe DN16......185 B
York Cl LN4...........203 D
York Gdns
2 Gosberton PE11......145 B
30 Wisbech PE13.......170 D
York House Rd 6
NG34.................120 C
York Rd
5 Binbrook Tech Pk
LN8...................47 B
Brigg DN20............196 D
Hatfield DN7...........14 D
Kirton in Lindsey DN21...30 C
Mablethorpe/Sutton on Sea
LN12..................64 D
Peterborough PE1......225 F
Sleaford NG34.........212 C
8 Stamford PE9........219 B
Wisbech PE13..........170 D
York Ride 4 PE12......216 B
York St (Boston United FC)
PE21.................209 A
Yorkshireside DN17......7 A
York St
Boston PE21...........209 A
Grimsby DN31..........191 C
York Terr 3 DN10.......40 A
York Way
5 Bracebridge Heath
LN4..................81 A
Grantham NG31.........210 C
Youlgrave Ave 6 LN4....77 A
Younger's La PE24.....103 A
Young Pl DN35.........192 B
Youngs Ave 9 NG24....104 C

Z

Zara Cl PE21..........209 C
Zetland St HU3........180 A